Library of M. C. Beasley,
C. P. P.
411 East Broad Street
Falls Church, VA 22046

P9-DUC-135

Library of M. C. Beasley,
C. P. P.
411 East Broad Street
Falls Church, VA 22046

THE SECRET DIARY
OF
HAROLD L. ICKES

THE FIRST
THOUSAND DAYS
1933-1936

SIMON AND SCHUSTER • NEW YORK

ALL RIGHTS RESERVED
INCLUDING THE RIGHT OF REPRODUCTION
IN WHOLE OR IN PART IN ANY FORM
COPYRIGHT, 1953, BY SIMON AND SCHUSTER, INC.
PUBLISHED BY SIMON AND SCHUSTER, INC.
ROCKEFELLER CENTER, 630 FIFTH AVENUE
NEW YORK 20, N. Y.

THIRD PRINTING

LIBRARY OF CONGRESS CATALOG
CARD NUMBER: 53–9701
DEWEY DECIMAL CLASSIFICATION
NUMBER: 92

MANUFACTURED IN THE UNITED STATES OF AMERICA
BY H. WOLFF BOOK MFG. CO., INC., NEW YORK

PREFACE

HAROLD ICKES' *diary is the record of his official and personal life in Washington during the nineteen years between 1933 and 1952. This volume covers only the first Roosevelt administration, from 1933 through 1936. In its complete form, the diary fills nearly a hundred volumes of closely-typed copy—approximately 6,000,000 words. It now seems fair to say that no other document is likely to be discovered which gives such an inclusive and detailed record of the New Deal and the Fair Deal.*

It was a truly secret journal. Few knew of its existence; fewer still saw it and then only selected passages. His secretaries kept accurate notes of whom he saw and talked to, his meetings and his official acts. He often dictated digests of important conferences, especially those with the President, or other meetings of which he wanted a careful record. Then, every Saturday or Sunday, he dictated the full text of his diary for the week, using the digests for reference. It was his invariable habit to destroy the secretaries' shorthand notes and all preliminary drafts, usually burning them himself in the fireplace.

This volume and those to follow do not represent the journals in their entirety. Parts of them are too detailed to interest anyone but historians. Other parts will have to wait until the death of many living persons. Except for these omissions, there have been no changes in the original text, and the complete manuscript will be given to the Library of Congress.

Even these published portions may cause distress to some with whom Harold worked or fought. I have discussed this with friends, including some who may themselves be embarrassed by passages in it. The final decision to publish is, of course, my own. It has been based upon two principal considerations which are relevant to any effort to understand the frankness of the diary.

The first is that the persons mentioned are all public figures, men and women who consciously accepted the risks of being public figures. Through a long life, Harold learned by direct experience that a public career exposes a man's personality, his record, and even his personal habits to public inquiry. He was the object of frequent investigations and attacks, many of them malicious and cruel in the extreme. He fought back, and he accepted this as a part of American public life.

The second consideration bears directly on the spirit of truculent candor with which he always wrote. It is no secret that he did not like to pull his punches and that he did like a fight. He once wrote: "If, in these pages, I have hurled an insult at anyone, let it be known that such was my deliberate intent, and I may as well state flatly now that it will be useless and a waste of time to ask me to say that I am sorry." During his service with President Roosevelt, he came to be known as a man who gave all he had to the job he loved, who loved the din and dust of battle, who could trade blows with the best, and whose razor-edged tongue and ready wit made him loved and hated—but always respected.

So frequently has he been referred to as the "curmudgeon" that few remember this was his own idea of the perfect description of Harold Ickes. He was born in Blair County, Pennsylvania. His preoccupation with politics was apparent almost at once. At the age of nine, he interrupted a heated controversy over the merits of Blaine vs. Cleveland with the remark, "Cleveland is no good anyhow; he can take off his collar without unbuttoning it." Seven years later when he moved to Chicago, he was still a "black Republican," by inheritance and environment. But in 1896 he pushed off into the troubled waters of independent politics by voting for Republican President Mc-

Kinley and for Democratic Governor John P. Altgeld. Before very long, he was managing the mayoralty campaign of independent Republican John M. Harlan, whose name caused the regulars to break out in a sweat. Next and equally unsuccessfully, he espoused the cause of another fine aspirant to the same office, Charles E. Merriam. Chicago was groggy before this campaign was finished. This was the closest Harold was ever to come to electing a reform-Chicago candidate, although of course he never stopped trying.

Early in 1912 he was up to his ears in the fight between Theodore Roosevelt and Taft for the Republican nomination for President. The Bull Moose party was born in Chicago at midnight on June 23, 1912, when Roosevelt's supporters, refusing to take Taft, marched out to hold a rump convention down the street. Harold was an enthusiastic member of this crusading liberal movement which he called the "New Deal" of 1912. With Wilson's victory, the Bull Moosers began to fall apart. However, Hughes considered them enough of a force to appoint six (Harold was one) to sit with nine regulars on his campaign committee in 1916.

A few weeks after Wilson entered upon his second administration, we were at war with Germany. Harold, who had long felt that Germany was menacing the world, was anxious to go abroad. A deaf ear kept him from active service, and a desk job didn't appeal to him. After a brief period with the Illinois State Council of Defense and a national Committee of Public Information, he got a job with the YMCA and went to France.

He returned in 1919 to a vastly changed America. Roosevelt was dying; Wilson was ailing; Harding was about to take over. Disgusted and disillusioned, Harold resumed the practice of law, thinking that he was through with politics. But as the lines began to form in 1920, the old fire horse began to paw his stall. Hiram W. Johnson, progressive Republican from California and Harold's friend from Bull Moose days, was making a bid for the presidential nomination. Harold has written of this convention: "The miserable machinations that went on were stomach-turning. They were poison ivy even to a curmudgeon. A conspiracy was being brewed in the 'small, smoke-filled room' where an evil candidate was to emerge from the witch's cauldron. And so Harding was nominated with his Ohio gang hanging on to his shirttails. But not with my help. The Lord forbid! If a curmudgeon is not true to himself, to whom can he be loyal? A voice vote was called for. And on that vote, a contumelious curmudgeon by the name of Ickes who had not been on a winner for President since 1904 and was beginning not to care if he never was again—yelled 'No' at the top of his lungs. Much good it did him."

Instead of remaining in the Republican fold as did most of his Progressive friends, Harold surveyed the Democratic possibilities. Thinking of the thousands of Bull Moosers to whom the Roosevelt name was magic, he suggested to a Chicago leader that young Franklin D. Roosevelt would pull votes. Franklin Roosevelt was nominated for Vice President, with Cox of Ohio heading the ticket. Although Harold knew in his heart that the Democrats would be engulfed by the "back to normalcy" groundswell, he nevertheless supported the Democrats, as he did again in 1928 when Al Smith opposed Herbert Hoover.

When 1932 rolled around, Harold thought that he had seen everything worth seeing in the way of politics. It turned out that it had been only trial heats for a balky horse. He organized the western independent Republicans for Roosevelt and took an active part in the campaign, managing two local campaigns in his spare time. When he awoke to find himself a winner for the first time in twenty-five years, it occurred to him that he would like to go to Washington. At first he toyed with the idea of becoming Commissioner of Indian Affairs. But why not shoot for the stars? It would be no more fatal to be hanged as a Cabinet Member than as a Commissioner. He set off for Washington to find someone who would present his name to the President-elect whom he had never met. There he received warm assurances of support from Senators Johnson and Bronson Cutting, but only on an "if asked" basis. Ironically, each of these men was himself offered the coveted post of Secretary of the Interior, each refused, and neither was asked for advice regarding anyone else. So when Harold set off for New York where he had been summoned, as a member of an advisory council, to meet with Roosevelt, there was little hope in his heart. At the close of a meeting in Roosevelt's 65th Street house, FDR called Harold aside and said: "Mr. Ickes, you and I have been speaking the same language for the past twenty years. I am having difficulty finding a Secretary of the Interior. I want a man who can stand on his own feet. Above all things, I want a man who is honest, and I have about come to the conclusion that the man I want is Harold L. Ickes, of Chicago."

Later that day they met again. Frances Perkins was there, and the President introduced them: "I would like to have the Secretary of the Interior meet the Secretary of Labor."

Thus it was that Harold went to Washington. For the next thirteen years, the longest tenure of office of any Secretary of the Interior, he directed the activities of this department.

He looked out upon a nation rich but prodigal in the exploitation of its natural resources, knew that wasteful, competitive practices were diminishing its irreplaceable supplies of oil and gas, saw its hills exposed to the erosion of the rains by ruthless lumbering, saw rich farm soil washing into the sea with every flood, envisioned vast potential water power, waiting to be harnessed to lighten the toil of men and women. He was the most fanatical conservationist of his generation, and coming generations may call him blessed.

In the years of the depression, he saw the greatest resource of the nation—its men, women, and maturing youth—demoralized by idleness and hopelessness as the nation's economic processes seemed stalled. He threw himself passionately into the vast program of public works. To keep it free of red tape, delay, parasitic politics, and scandal were to him not merely a duty but a religion.

He saw, long before most, a menace in the growing power and ambition of Adolf Hitler. That little man, whom many Americans thought merely a joke while others deplored his methods but admired his "efficiency," was never a joke or a commonplace to Harold. He opposed totalitarianism from the beginning, whether it was a totalitarianism of the left or of the right. From the outbreak of the European war, which he had seen coming, he never doubted that American interests were on the side of the free peoples, and he lost no opportunity to make American force felt against the enslaving regimes. An America strong, bold and forthright was his ideal.

Harold knew how perishable is the freedom we cherish, how easily liberty can be confused with license. He was impatient of intolerance and discrimination. He fought fear and hate and greed wherever he encountered them and watched jealously over the interests of all the people. Under his leadership, the Department of the Interior, once tainted by the sordid tradition of Albert Fall and the scandals of Teapot Dome, became a great department and a staunch guardian of the nation's natural wealth.

This is not a balanced or a reflective study. It is the intimate history of two of the most fateful decades in American history, written in heat and under pressure by a turbulently active man who changed his mind many times both as to men and affairs and who never hesitated to express himself fully and pungently. It is also the personal history of Harold Ickes. Here is a man who was passionately alive and earthy, yet remote and essentially detached. He had few intimates, but to those whom he called friend he gave himself warmly and generously. He may have seemed forbidding to some, and yet no one in distress was too obscure to claim his attention and his help. One knew where Harold Ickes stood. There was no deviousness in him. He believed profoundly in the constant upward progress of the human race, and it was for this ultimate conviction that he battled to the end of his life. Under the burden of his massive responsibilities, he grew in strength and understanding until, as the years passed, he came to be regarded as the catalytic agent of the New Deal: the point of fusion of the boldness, the vigor, the passion of its early years.

Harold Ickes is no longer here. But the issues he fought for are alive and real; the dangers he helped to avert still threaten. This is why I publish today his private diary.

JANE D. ICKES

Headwaters Farm
Olney, Maryland
May 24, 1953

PUBLISHERS' NOTE

The sections of Harold L. Ickes' diary published here are exactly as they were written by him, with no changes or editing. The complete manuscript will be deposited by Simon and Schuster in the Library of Congress.

A few explanatory notes have been added by the publishers in the text, set off by brackets from the diary itself. The index contains biographical information, for identification purposes, of the principal persons mentioned in the diary.

SIMON AND SCHUSTER

THE SECRET DIARY OF
HAROLD L. ICKES

THE FIRST THOUSAND DAYS
1933-1936

Sunday, March 5, 1933

President Roosevelt called the members of the Cabinet, Vice President Garner, and Speaker-elect Rainey to meet him at the White House at two-thirty to discuss the acute banking situation and agree on a policy. We considered, and the President decided to issue, the Executive Order which will appear in tomorrow morning's papers, the effect of which will be to close every bank in the United States for a bank holiday of three days, to stop the exportation of gold, and to put into effect other emergency regulations designed to stop the run on the banks and to prevent the hoarding of gold or gold certificates.

In the late afternoon I went to the Hiram Johnsons' for supper and then back to the Mayflower, where I arrived, dog tired, about seven-thirty. I told the telephone operator not to put through any calls unless one should come from the White House, and tumbled into bed. Just before midnight, Secretary of the Treasury Woodin called to ask authority to sign my name to cablegrams to the Governors of Alaska, Hawaii, and the Virgin Islands, with reference to the banking situation in those Territories which are under the jurisdiction of the Department of the Interior.

Monday, March 6, 1933

The President and his Cabinet attended the funeral services of the late Senator Thomas J. Walsh, of Montana, who would have been a member of the Cabinet as Attorney General if he had lived.

Following the services, I went to the White House, at the suggestion of President Roosevelt, who desired the Secretaries of Labor, Commerce, War, and Interior to sit in at a conference of governors which he had called together.

I got to my office in the Interior Building about twelve-thirty. At two-thirty I met the heads of the various bureaus and departments and during the afternoon I attended to routine matters until four o'clock, when all of the employees in the building were asked to come up to be introduced to me. They filed past me about twenty-five hundred strong.

[The Department of the Interior, which was incorporated in the Cabinet in 1849, is chiefly responsible for the care of the nation's resources. Its activities, originally concerned with the exploitation of the public domain, have now become its conservation.

[The General Land Office has charge of the public lands of the United States and the minerals therein, involving the survey and management of some 165,000,000 acres. The Geological Survey, the Bureau of Fisheries, the Bureau of Biological Survey, the Bureau of Reclamation, the Bureau of Mines, the National Park Service and the Office of Indian Affairs are some of the Department's chief divisions. Under the New Deal, the department added divisions operating certain controls over coal and petroleum, as well as grazing, and all Federal activities involving United States islands and territories were grouped in 1934 in a Division of Territories and Island Possessions. Mr. Ickes' various assignments to public works and relief projects, however, were independent of the Department of the Interior.

[In 1933, the Department also maintained various assorted institutions, such as Howard University for the education of Negro youth in the liberal arts and sciences, the Freedmen's Hospital, and St. Elizabeth's Hospital, and the Columbia Institution for the Deaf. When Mr. Ickes became Secretary of the Interior, the office was already referred to as the "Department of Things in General."–ED.]

Tuesday, March 7, 1933

I got to the office at nine o'clock but I was kept pretty much on the jump all day. I had appointments until shortly before eleven, when I went over to the War Department to sit in with Secretary of War Dern and Secretary of Agriculture Wallace. The President had requested that the three of us take up with Governor Sholtz, of Florida, a tentative plan the President had in mind for taking over some vacant Florida agricultural lands with the co-operation of the state government of Florida, and settling them with families of unemployed from other parts of the country. We discussed this proposition in detail for an hour, after which I listened to a band of Sioux Indians that had been here to attend the Inauguration, was decorated with a war bonnet, and then went to lunch with Senator Edward P. Costigan, of Colorado.

Senator McAdoo called me up about appointments in my department.

At two o'clock I attended the first formal Cabinet meeting in the Cabinet room in the White House offices. Present were the President, the Vice President, and all members of the Cabinet. The main topic for discussion was again the acute banking and financial situation, after which each of the Cabinet officers was given an opportunity to present any problems that had come up.

Friday, March 10, 1933

The regular Cabinet meeting was held at two o'clock and lasted until after four. Most of our time was spent discussing the banking situation and the international situation, particularly the attitude this country should adopt with reference to being represented at the coming conference in Geneva. There was also some discussion of our relations with Japan.

After coming back from the Cabinet meeting, I found that Dr. Felix Frankfurter, of the Harvard Law School, was in the city. I reached him at the Cosmos Club and went over later for a few minutes' talk about the legal setup of the Department. He agreed to make an appointment with me to discuss matters with Mr. Justice Brandeis.

I was at the White House at nine o'clock with the Secretary of War and the Secretary of Agriculture, to discuss with the President a bill which is being considered to enlist 500,000 of the unemployed for work on Government projects.

Saturday, March 11, 1933

Mrs. Ruth Bryan Owen called me by telephone and wanted to come over to discuss the Assistant Secretaryship which she is a candidate for, but I put her off until Monday.

A delegation from Alaska came in, headed by the Delegate to Congress from that Territory, in the interest of Mr. Troy, who wants to be appointed Governor of Alaska.

Chief Marcellus Hawk (all Indians are chiefs unless they are females, and then they are princesses) wanted to sketch me, and I allowed him to do so while I was signing letters. It is doubtful if this man is even an Indian.

Sunday, March 12, 1933

I called, by appointment, at the home of Mr. Justice Brandeis at six o'clock and had a most delightful talk with him on Government policies, particularly with relation to my own Department. I had never met Mr. Justice Brandeis, although I have been a tremendous admirer of him for years. He is really an inspiration to me, and I felt as if I were sitting at the feet of one of the fine old prophets. Except for this, my day was one of great activity, devoted to relatively unimportant matters.

Monday, March 13, 1933

Mrs. Ruth Bryan Owen came in for a long interview to urge her qualifications as Assistant Secretary of the Interior. I was not predisposed to her favor for this position, although she is a very charming woman, but she surely talked herself out of court with me after telling me what her particular qualifications were. She related in great detail the tremendous sentiment throughout the country for her as Secretary of the Interior, and she concluded by impressing upon me that she wanted an early decision (of course a favorable one) because it was important for her to make plans for her future. I told her that she ought to look out for her own interest but that I intended to move slowly and carefully in such an important matter. Later I had an interview with the President, who told me that Mrs. Owen had been in to see him after her talk with me and had told him that she believed she had sold herself to me.

Tuesday, March 14, 1933

At the Cabinet meeting this afternoon, the question came up of curtailing the overproduction of oil, and the President asked me to call by telephone Governor Ferguson, of Texas, Governor Murray, of Oklahoma, and Governor Rolph, of California, to ask them whether they would either come or send representatives to a meeting here about ten days hence, to consider whether it would be possible to agree on a policy that would limit the production of oil. Governor Murray and Governor Rolph agreed readily, but Governor Ferguson wanted to take it under consideration.

There was a little discussion about appointments for Comptroller of the Currency and Federal Reserve Board at the Cabinet meeting. The President remarked that one man he had in mind was from Chicago and perhaps I might know him. He then turned to me and asked whether I knew Donald Richberg. I said that I had known him for a great many years and that he was a brilliant lawyer. The President asked whether he had had any banking experience. I replied that he had never had any actual banking experience but that he had an economic mind, and that both he and his father before him had represented for many years county appraisers, boards of assessors, boards of review, etc. I added that he had formerly been my law partner, and the President said: "That ought to be enough recommendation for him."

Wednesday, March 15, 1933

I attended a meeting in the office of the Secretary of War this morning, together with the Secretary of Labor and the Secretary of Agriculture, to consider further the bill that the President and the Cabinet have had under consideration to take unemployed men out of the crowded areas and put them to work in the national forests, etc. The bill is to be redrafted in one or two important particulars so as to make it clear that it is to apply only to such public works as would not be otherwise undertaken at this time of financial stringency.

I am fifty-nine years old today.

Wednesday, March 22, 1933

I lunched today with Mr. Justice Hitz, of the Court of Appeals of the District of Columbia. He is a liberal and we had a very interesting talk about Washington and official life. He remarked that there was an old saying in Washington that Cabinet members "dug their own graves with their teeth," by which he meant that the social activities, if too freely indulged in, break a man down in the end. From my brief experience with this, I thoroughly agreed.

I attended a conference at nine o'clock at the White House last night, called by the President. The Secretaries of Labor, War, and Agriculture were there also. It was really a joint hearing by the Senate and House committees particularly interested in the Administration bill introduced on Monday providing for the enrollment of a civil conservation corps to help relieve the unemployment situation. The President presented his views, and answered all questions. We were in session until shortly after eleven o'clock, when I went back to the hotel.

Thursday, March 23, 1933

I went to a luncheon at the Pan American Union in honor of the Mexican Ambassador, Señor Dr. Don Fernando Gonzalez Roa.

Other members of the Cabinet present were the Secretary of State, the Secretary of Commerce, and the Postmaster General. There were only about twenty present. Dr. L. S. Rowe, the Director of the Union, was host. Mexican food was served. It seemed to me such a waste of time, especially since we were asked to be there at one o'clock and didn't sit down to luncheon for almost three quarters of an hour. After the luncheon we solemnly arose, each with a glass of iced tea clasped firmly in his right hand. The ceremonies proceeded as follows:

Dr. Rowe: "I propose a toast to the United States of America." A sip of iced tea. *Dr. Rowe:* "I propose a toast to the Republic of Mexico." A sip of iced tea. *Dr. Rowe:* "I propose a toast to His Excellency, the Mexican Ambassador." A sip of iced tea. *Dr. Rowe:* "I propose a toast to the Honorable, the Secretary of State of the United States." A sip of iced tea. *Dr. Rowe:* "I propose a toast to his Excellency"—somebody or other from the Argentine Republic. A sip of iced tea.

After which solemn performance, we retired in an adjoining room to add a few sips of hot coffee to the prior sips of iced tea, and then we broke away as fast as we could to get back to some honest-to-God work.

Nathan R. Margold, whom I have selected for Solicitor for this Department, after advising with Dr. Felix Frankfurter and Mr. Justice Brandeis, was sworn in after I got back from the ponderous function above referred to. Margold is only thirty-three years old. According to Dr. Frankfurter, he is one of the most brilliant men ever turned out by the Harvard Law School.

Friday, March 24, 1933

Governor Horner, of Illinois, Pat Nash, the new national committeeman elected to fill the vacancy caused by the death of Mayor Cermak, Nash's son, and Cornelius Lynds, special assistant attorney general for Illinois, came to my office at eleven o'clock. Their principal interest here is in the pending St. Lawrence Treaty which will seriously affect the availability of the upper Mississippi River as a ship canal.

The regular Cabinet meeting at two o'clock was shorter than usual on account of other engagements of the President. The President had just had called to his attention a newspaper interview with the Japanese Ambassador, who had retired from the Assembly of the League of Nations at Geneva a couple of weeks ago, and he wasn't at all pleased with that interview.

I had arranged for an interview for Governor Horner and his associates with the President, and Governor Horner was very anxious to have me go with them. While waiting for this appointment, I attended one of the regular press conferences held biweekly by the President. It was very interesting. He sat in the big circular office in the office wing of the White House, with rows and rows of keen-minded newspaper correspondents grouped about him. He met and answered every question, although in some instances his answers were off the record. When I say he answered every question, I mean that he answered every question that he could answer, and when he didn't know the answer, he frankly said so. There was no subterfuge, no beating around the bush. All was frank, open, and aboveboard. It isn't any wonder that the newspaper correspondents like him and his methods, especially as compared with his predecessor.

Saturday, March 25, 1933

I was under very great pressure this morning interviewing people, so that when one o'clock came I was thoroughly tired out. I seem to have an unusual proportion of job hunters. This is the most difficult aspect of this office, as it is of any public office where there is patronage to distribute. Of course, the people who come in to see me about it are nothing as compared to those who write me. Hundreds and hundreds of letters, bespeaking jobs either for the writers or for someone else, have to be answered day after day.

[During this period, neither Harold Ickes nor the Cabinet itself played a major role in the initial legislation of the New Deal. Lewis Douglas, Raymond Moley, Rexford Guy Tugwell, Dean Acheson, Adolf Berle and Charles W. Taussig were closer to the White House during this period than the heads of the departments in which they worked. Mr. Ickes, who was so little known to the public that a *New York Times* dispatch from Washington explained to readers how the name was pronounced, was chiefly busy with mastering the details of the organization of the Department of the Interior.–ED.]

Monday, March 27, 1933

There are a number of representatives of the oil industry in Washington. They had a session at the Mayflower Hotel yesterday that broke up in a row. This afternoon at two o'clock, the representatives of the governors met in an office on the sixth floor of the Interior Building, and I made a statement to them followed by a suggestion that they appoint a committee of five to meet with similar committees representing the big oil interests and the independents. I then called Governor Landon, of Kansas, to the chair, and went down to the auditorium on the first floor, where the representatives of the oil industry were in session. I repeated my statement to them and at its conclusion suggested that they separate into two groups, representing the big interests and the independents, each group to select a committee of five, and both committees to sit down with the committee representing the governors' conference and try to work out a program. Unfortunately, there is only one governor here, Landon, of Kansas, who has come to me highly vouched for by William Allen White.

After talking to the second meeting, I went with Miss Perkins, who at my invitation had gone to both meetings with me, to attend a conference in the President's office on the coal situation. Present at this conference were John L. Lewis, of the United Mine Workers, with several of his officials, Senator Carl Hayden, of Arizona, and Congressman Lewis, of Maryland. The discussion was with reference to possible legislation to cure some of the outstanding evils of the coal industry. After a prolonged discussion the President suggested that Miss Perkins and I hold further conferences, and we agreed to meet in my office next Wednesday afternoon at two o'clock.

Tuesday, March 28, 1933

The oil conference is in full swing. By appointment, I met a group of independents, mainly from southern California and headed by John B. Elliott, who were certainly all hot and bothered. They did a lot of haranguing and speech making. They really had a chip on their shoulders. In the end, I managed to find out that they don't want anything at all done to curtail oil production, but they do want action to break up the big oil combinations, on the theory that they are in restraint of trade. After listening to them for an hour, Elliott asked to have a private word with me, but Margold was with me when we had our talk. What he wanted to tell me about privately was that he had managed the Roosevelt-McAdoo campaign in California, and that he had an "in" with the Administration. On two or three occasions he threatened me rather crudely. He assured me that he was an old newspaper man; that I was being imposed upon, of course without my knowledge; and that he knew how to take his case to the newspapers.

After finishing with him, I sat in with the committee of fifteen, named yesterday to draft a proposal. On this committee, headed by Governor Landon, of Kansas, were representatives of some of the biggest oil industries in the country, such as Teagle, president of Standard of New Jersey; Holmes, president of the Texas Company; and Kingsbury, president of Standard of California. There were five men representing the big industries, and five representing the so-called independents, but just how independent the independents are, God alone knows. Elliott and his crowd insist that they are not independent at all, but really are under inescapable obligations to the big fellows. Anyhow, they presented a draft of a program which on its face looked pretty fair, and at least gave us a working basis. After going over this draft and discussing it, I suggested that they appoint a subcommittee of six to restudy the matter and present concrete proposals.

I have been running from one conference to another all day, except for the Cabinet meeting, which I attended at two o'clock, as usual. It was the saddest Cabinet meeting yet. Mr. Douglas, Director of the Budget, had his figures showing how much each department was expected to cut in order to contribute its share toward balancing the budget to help the President make good on his campaign pledges of a reduction in expenses. This Department is expected for the fiscal year 1934, which begins July 1, 1933, to save over $5 million out of its appropriation. All other departments are cut in greater or less degree. This is certainly going to be a hard nut to crack. I reported progress in the oil situation at the Cabinet meeting.

Wednesday, March 29, 1933

This morning I got to the office at eight-thirty, as I have been doing recently, and after some incidental interviews I gave another hour to Mr. Elliott and his group. Our discussion today, while along the same general lines of yesterday, was much calmer and more sensible. The only concrete suggestion they had to make to meet the present emergency was that nothing at all be done. They think that everybody ought to be permitted to produce as much oil as possible, without restraint or reference. Then I went into session with the representatives of the governors. I found that they were beginning to feel neglected and that they were not being treated with sufficient consideration. I smoothed down their ruffled feathers and we discussed the revised draft of the committee report as prepared by Mr. Margold. After an hour more of this, I went into session with the committee of fifteen. We went over the Margold draft and agreed without much difficulty upon a final draft. Following this, I went back to the representatives of the governors, where we pulled and hauled, and after a number of absolutely unnecessary and lengthy speeches had been delivered, the draft was finally approved on my plea that we conclude the matter and reach an agreement, if possible. Then we went down to the auditorium, where we had a meeting of the committee of fifteen, the representatives of the governors, and others interested. Here, once more, the Margold draft was read and approved.

I called Mr. Early, the publicity secretary of the President, to suggest that, in my judgment, we ought to give out the statement agreed upon by the oil conference, and give the President twenty-four hours to get the reaction from the country before he should be called upon to act under the resolution. I told Mr. Early that even if I had burned my fingers in this oil conference unwittingly, I didn't want the President to become involved and, therefore, I recommended this procedure. After conferring with the President, he approved my plan. So we admitted the newspaper correspondents to our final meeting and gave them drafts of what we had agreed upon.

I have handled this conference so that the Administration is not involved in any way. The findings enunciate general principles and make certain recommendations to the President for specific actions. These recommendations he can follow or not, just as he pleases, or he may modify them at his own will. In this way, the Administration is not involved. No statement has been given out of the Administration's attitude, and no one knows whether the President will act on the suggestions made or not. In the meantime, he will have a chance to find out what the country thinks about it all and then he can do what he thinks wisest in the circumstances.

The last two or three days have been as strenuous as any I have ever gone through in a political campaign. I am thoroughly tired, but have a sense of relief that the oil men have finally departed to their respective hearths. Whether or not we accomplished anything for the betterment of the oil industry and the good of the country as a result of the conference remains to be shown. At any rate, we worked hard at it and tried to keep as sane an outlook as possible on an intricate and difficult situation.

[The oil industry was among the first to press for Government controls in 1933, although there were wide differences of opinion within the industry as to the desirable extent of these controls. The minimum on which both major companies and the larger so-called independent producers agreed was Federal prohibition of interstate commerce in what was called "hot oil"—oil produced in violation of quotas or other laws enacted by the states. This was written into the NRA petroleum code and, after the Supreme Court had declared the NRA unconstitutional, into the Connally Act, in 1936, under which the Department of the Interior set up a permanent Petroleum Conservation Division. This division, under Ickes, also did pioneer work in cooperation with the oil- and gas-producing states in preventing avoidable waste and in working toward uniform oil and gas conservation laws.—ED.]

Thursday, March 30, 1933

I attended the twenty-fifth anniversary of the National Press Club last night. The President was the guest of honor and most of the Cabinet members were present. All of us became new members of the club. It was one of the most pleasant occasions I have ever attended. With only one exception, all the speeches were sparkling and witty, and the President held his own with the best of them. Today I cleared up an accumulation of matters which had piled up on my desk during the three days of the oil conference. The general feeling seems to be that the oil conference went off pretty well, and I have been congratulated by several people on the way I handled it. These congratulations don't mean very much to me, except when they come from newspapermen, but I was gratified to be praised by a group of the correspondents that came to my office late this afternoon. They thought the thing had been very well handled. They told me I had made more progress in three days than Dr. Wilbur had in as many months on a prior occasion in connection with the same matter, and they especially thanked me for my courteous treatment. Of course, the comparison with Wilbur isn't at all a fair one, since he was undoubtedly handling an entirely different situation.

I spent an hour with Colonel Howe, the President's secretary, at the White House this morning, considering the matter of a Governor of Hawaii. Neither of us was satisfied with any of the applicants or endorsements in my file, and so we are going to try to inform ourselves in the matter and try to find a good man for what is a delicate situation.

At two o'clock I had the heads of all the different bureaus of the Department in to break the sad news to them that there had to be radical cuts in their expenditures in order to keep within the limits set by the Director of the Budget. This will mean that a number of people will have to be dismissed from the service and that our activities will be seriously curtailed.

Friday, March 31, 1933

After an unusually crowded morning, I went to the Department of Agriculture for lunch with the Secretary of Agriculture. We went directly from this meeting to the Cabinet meeting, where we had a long and very serious session. We put in a good deal of time discussing the economic situation and what the Administration could do in the nature of a public works bill to relieve unemployment and set money again in circulation. We are seriously concerned with the problem of creating buying power, which in turn, will have the effect of opening factories and stimulating business generally.

I had mimeographed copies of the results of the oil conference to lay before the President and the members of the Cabinet, and we discussed the whole situation quite fully. It was the opinion of the President, in which we all concurred, that he could not go the full length asked by the committee of fifteen, which drafted the majority report. He is willing to act upon certain recommendations for legislation by Congress, but he doesn't want to go the whole length of urging the governors of the states where there is flush production to declare a moratorium until April 15. He asked me to draft a letter to be sent out tomorrow to the governors.

Saturday, April 1, 1933

I came back to the office and worked last night after dinner at the Johnsons'. I wanted a chance to talk with Hiram about the oil situation in which he is interested, and which worries me very much. He had a copy of a letter written by a subordinate, who has been acting as Secretary of the Oil Conservation Board, of which the Secretary of the Interior is Chairman. This letter was written to a close personal friend in strict confidence, but somehow a group of independent oil men from southern California got a copy of it which they gave to Senator Johnson.

This letter was a complete exposé of himself by this man, who boasts of writing speeches for Cabinet members and Senators, running their offices, determining their policies, etc. He boasts about his connection with big oil interests and tells how, year in and year out, regardless of what Administration was in power, he was able to hold his own and affect Government policies. At intervals through the letter ran this phrase: "and I never slipped a cog." This expression must have appeared five or six times. It is one of the most arrogantly boastful, and yet revealing, documents I have ever read or listened to. At its conclusion, I made the remark: "Well, this is one time that he won't be able to say—'and I never slipped a cog.'"

One of the first things I did this morning was to sign an order summarily dismissing this official from the service. I have had two communications from him since. Apparently he doesn't realize that he has the great fault of saying too much on paper.

At half past ten I was at the White House, according to prearrangement, and as soon as we could get in, Secretary Wallace, Senator Norris, and two Southern Congressmen went over with the President at great length a bill drafted by Senator Norris for the development of the President's projects with reference to the Tennessee Valley. We were closeted with him for almost two hours. Then we had to give way for other appointments that were being held up. The Secretary of State was next, and then Secretary Wallace and I went back again.

I had two important matters I wanted to discuss with the President: first, the Indian Commissionership and the other, the oil situation. As the result of a suggestion he made at the Cabinet meeting yesterday, I had drafted and was prepared to submit to him a letter to be mailed by him to the seventeen governors of the oil-producing states who had sent representatives to the oil conference held here the first of the week. My draft with only a very slight change, which was nothing but a transition of two phrases, was entirely satisfactory to him, and the letters will go out today.

The letters did not go to the full extent suggested in the program submitted by the committee of fifteen which drafted the report of the oil conference. The matter of a moratorium on the production of flush pools, the President put back to the governors of the states, where it properly belongs. He took the position that this was not a Federal matter but a state matter. He sent drafts of the recommendations to the governors, with the suggestion that they study them and take whatever action seemed appropriate to them. He did, however, commit himself to the policy of suggesting to Congress the passage of a law preventing the transportation in interstate commerce of any oil illegally produced according to the law of the state of its origin. He agreed also with the suggestion in the major report that a strict account be kept of all gasoline sent into interstate commerce so that the tax payable to the Federal Government and to the various states could be checked. Then, turning to the minority report, he approved the idea of Federal legislation separating the pipe line companies from the manufacture and processing of oil.

While I was with him, I handed him, "as one philatelist to another," a full sheet of one hundred, old three-cent Department of the Interior stamps, and a similar sheet of six-cent stamps. These have been obsolete for very many years, but I had a tip that there were some in existence in the Office of the Chief Clerk and I was lucky enough to get several sheets of each, all that were left. He was delighted and said that he would frame them. These stamps in sheets are very rare indeed, and I am sure he was as pleased to get them as I was.

Tuesday, April 4, 1933

We spent a good deal of time at the Cabinet meeting today discussing the cuts required of us by the Director of the Budget. I think there was a feeling that this Department was entitled to some consideration when I showed what the cuts would mean, as far as the Indian Office and the National Parks and various Negro activities are concerned. I was especially gratified when Vice President Garner spoke up frankly to say that he thought it would be a mistake to cut down on the Negro activities, and one or two others agreed with him.

Wednesday, April 5, 1933

I am moving into my new house today. It is at 1327 33 Street, Georgetown. Most of my clothes have been packed in boxes or hanging in closets here at the Department since I came from Chicago some three weeks ago. I sent everything out to the house this afternoon and gave up my rooms at the Mayflower. I have taken a six-month lease. It has been occupied by Hubert de Wichfeld, Counselor of the Danish Legation, and his wife. It is really quite a charming little place.

Tonight I had dinner with Fred Essary and I had a very pleasant time. Senator Wagner, of New York, was a guest, and so was the commandant of Fort Meyer, who generously offered to provide me with mounts if I wanted to ride horseback. I got home at half past eleven, pretty tired.

Thursday, April 6, 1933

I worked today under a good deal of strain. The weather is hot and muggy, just the kind that goes hardest with me. I received the usual grist of callers, and right at the end of my receiving hour, Governor Pinchot came in. I took him off into the private office and sat down and had a good talk with him. He really acts delighted at my being here in this job and constantly refers to it when I see him. This is the first chance I have had to talk with him since I came to Washington. On the other two or three occasions when he had been here, we had not been able to get together. There were several office policies that I was glad to have an opportunity to discuss with him.

This afternoon I got weary of my task and drove down to the Senate. I had been wanting to speak to Senator Cutting, who came back to Washington last week. He was looking very fit indeed. I had a little time with him in the Republican cloak room and then drove up to the White House to get the ideas of the President about the sale of beer in Boulder City and in the national parks.

Friday, April 7, 1933

A week ago I sent an investigator down to the power plant at Muscle Shoals to look into a report that came to the President, and by him was transmitted to me, that there was some overreaching of the Government there by the power companies which are taking part of the current generated at the dam. This investigator, Louis Glavis, sent me a very interesting telegram today, which I read at the Cabinet meeting. Apparently he has struck one or two very good leads and he will be back in Washington Monday night.

I ran into Governor Frank O. Lowden after the Cabinet meeting and had a pleasant chat with him. He was waiting with the Secretary of Agriculture, George Peek, and Bernard Baruch to talk with the President.

Sunday, April 9, 1933

I went with President and Mrs. Roosevelt down to the Hoover Camp on the Rapidan today. We left the White House shortly after ten, five cars of us. The first car carried the Secret Service men; then came President and Mrs. Roosevelt and their young son, John, in a runabout, with Mrs. Roosevelt driving. Henry Morgenthau was in the party, and Colonel Louis McHenry Howe, the President's secretary. I had Director Albright with me and we went in my car, the last in line.

We were very fortunate as to the weather. It was warm, and, except for a brief period when we were up on the mountains on the way home, clear. Lunch was taken along from the White House. The marines had everything open and in order, with fires burning in fireplaces and ramps in appropriate places to make it easy for the President to get about. We drove the President's car as near to the Hoover cabin as we could, and he started to walk to the cabin but gave up about half way there and was carried the rest of the way. We lunched on porch overlooking the two branches of the Rapidan which join just in front of the cabin. It was a lovely sight and we had a very pleasant time.

This is the first time I have ever had real contact with Mrs. Roosevelt or a chance to talk to her. She is really a very charming woman, natural, simple, and friendly. She doesn't have any more airs than he does. She was a perfect hostess, seeing that everyone was served, helping in that matter herself, and not having her own lunch until she was sure that all her guests, and they included Secret Service men and marines, were served. We left about three o'clock and came back to Washington over the Skyline Drive which lies in the upper reaches of the Blue Ridge Mountains. The President wanted Mr. Albright to drive back with him so that he could discuss various matters with him, and I was glad to have him do it because Mr. Albright not only knows the local history but of course is fully conversant with what is being done and can be done in the national parks. We got back to Washington shortly after six.

Tuesday, April 11, 1933

We had a long and interesting Cabinet meeting. The main subjects of discussion were the banking and currency situation, a proposed popular bond issue in small denominations in order to bring money out of hoarding, and a major program of public works to relieve unemployment and try to restore purchasing power.

At five-thirty I went to the President's study in the White House, by arrangement, to discuss the matter of the Commissioner of Indian Affairs. Senator Joe T. Robinson, the Majority Leader, was also there at the suggestion of the President. We had tea and a long talk, the first part of which was tactfully devoted by the President to a discussion of Government policies and pending legislation at the Capitol. When everyone was feeling very well, the President brought up the question of the Commissionership by saying that he had received many, many protests against appointing Edgar B. Meritt, who is being strongly backed by Senator Robinson, and on whose behalf an intensive campaign has been waged for some time. Senator Robinson then made a short statement about Meritt, and the President indicated that he wanted me to say what I had to say. I went prepared with documentary proofs tending to show the total disqualification of Meritt for this job. I made my points, telling the President and Senator Robinson that every statement I was making was one of fact which I could substantiate by documentary evidence, mostly in the handwriting of Meritt himself. Then the President turned the subject back again to where we had started, namely, general policies, particularly the pending banking bill. When his Secretary came in at six-forty-five to say that dinner would be served in fifteen minutes, he brought us back to the Indian Commissionership, with the remark: "Well, Joe, you see what I am up against. Every highbrow organization in the country is opposed to Meritt, and Secretary Ickes, under whom he would have to work, doesn't want him." He said this in that light friendly way of his, but no one could doubt what he meant. Senator Robinson replied that there wasn't anything else he could say, and I then took my leave, Senator Robinson staying on but I think only for a minute or two, in view of the announcement of dinner.

[The Office of Indian Affairs, originally established in 1832, holds jurisdiction over more than 50,000,000 acres of Indian lands. It handles all relations between the Federal Government and more than 300,000 Indians, acting as a sort of trustee for them. It is concerned with their health, their education, their tribal resources, and the preservation of Indian cultural values as well as the development of their economic self-sufficiency.—ED.]

Wednesday, April 12, 1933

Early in the afternoon I ran down to the Senate Chamber to have a word with Hiram Johnson. I wanted to tell him that Postmaster General Farley had told me yesterday that it was his intention to call on him. I had told Farley that it seemed to me that Senator Johnson ought to have some consideration in the way of patronage and Farley agreed with me. He then told me what his plans were, and he volunteered the statement that he didn't think the Democratic party ought to run a candidate for the Senate against Johnson next year.

On the way back, I stopped at the White House to find out from Colonel McIntyre what the prospects were of the President sending in quickly the nomination of John Collier for the Commissioner of Indian Affairs. McIntyre brought out word from the President that he wanted to let twenty-four hours lapse since the talk last night with Senator Robinson but that he would send in the nomination tomorrow. I then came back to my office and sent in a recommendation for the nomination so that the President will have it to act on in the morning.

The baseball season opens this afternoon and I suspect that most of official Washington are out at the field, including the President and many of the members of the Cabinet.

Thursday, April 13, 1933

I went to dinner last night at the home of Richard W. Hogue, Director of the Independent Legislative Bureau. The other guests at the dinner were Senator Bronson Cutting, Senator Burton K. Wheeler, and Senator Elbert D. Thomas, of Utah, the man who defeated Senator Reed Smoot last November. Following dinner, a group of others came in, one or two newspapermen, Senator Pat McCarran, of Nevada, Congressman Hoidale, of Minnesota, and several past or present representatives in various Government departments. An earnest discussion of the costs of government, of unemployment, and the waste in business was had until half past ten.

I was struck with the pessimism of Senator Wheeler and Senator Thomas. They both think the economic situation is getting worse rapidly and they look for a very serious situation unless something is done speedily. In this connection, a very large and comprehensive public works program was suggested, and the immediate embarking on such a program was urged as of vital necessity. Senator Thomas made the statement that the concentration camps now being set up for the men engaged in reforestation under the act recently passed might be found to have served as concentration camps for men marching against the Government, unless the situation improved rapidly. He also made the statement that in case of any serious outbreaks, those marching against the Government would not be headed by rioters but by Ph.D.'s and the educated classes. He pointed out that a great proportion of the educated classes were out of jobs at this time, more so than on any other occasion.

Some fifteen coal operators from different coal fields in the country met in my office at two o'clock to discuss their business situation. They were plainly opposed to any legislation at this time. They seemed to think that the Supreme Court decision in the Appalachian Coals Case pointed the way to recovery in their business, to a better market at higher prices, and to better wages for the coal miners. I questioned them closely about the situation among the miners and they all painted as good a picture as possible, although even at that, they couldn't paint a very pretty one.

Tuesday, April 18, 1933

I got into Washington from Chicago at nine this morning. Secretary Wallace came up to discuss with me the proposition of putting the Forest Service and the National Parks in the same department, but I thought that department was Interior and not Agriculture. I argued that it was time that the stigma under which this Department has been resting ever since the Ballinger days and down through Fall should be removed and the Department given a chance to function so as to merit a return of public confidence. I added that National Parks were particularly interesting to me and that fifty per cent of my interest in this Department would be gone if they were taken away. The National Forests used to be in the Interior Department but were removed to Agriculture when Hitchcock was Secretary of the Interior.

Following this talk I went over to the Treasury Department, at the suggestion of the White House, to confer with Secretary of the Treasury Woodin and Jesse Jones, Chairman of the Reconstruction Finance Corporation, about the teachers' pay situation in Chicago. A delegation of eight or ten teachers is here, and after they had been brought in and we had had a brief discussion, Secretary Woodin asked them to retire with Mr. Jones and Walter Cummings, his Executive Assistant, also a Chicago man, to discuss the situation.

[In the summer of 1909, Gifford Pinchot, then head of the Division of Forestry, accused his chief, Secretary of the Interior Richard A. Ballinger, of injuring the conservation program in order to aid corporation interests. At issue were certain water power sites in Wyoming and Montana, as well as certain coal lands, and Pinchot publicly accused his chief of helping those who sought to plunder the public domain. A chief witness on Pinchot's side was Louis R. Glavis, a special agent of the Field Division of the Department of the Interior. President William H. Taft ordered Pinchot's removal from office on January 7, 1910, on grounds of insubordination, and a joint Congressional committee, inquiring into the Department of the Interior, sided with Ballinger by a majority vote. A bitter controversy took place in the newspapers and in the end Ballinger resigned, on March 6, 1911, to save the administration further embarrassment. The controversy played an important part in the conservation movement in the United States, as well as in the growing breach between Taft and the insurgent Republicans led by Theodore Roosevelt, who was a close friend of Pinchot.–ED.]

[Albert B. Fall served as Secretary of the Interior from 1921 to 1923 under President Warren G. Harding. In 1924, a Senate investigating committee headed by Senator Thomas J. Walsh of Montana revealed that Fall had engineered the leasing of two great oil reserves to Harry F. Sinclair and Edward L. Doheny. It was also revealed that Fall had suddenly grown affluent, and that he had personally re-

ceived money from both of these men. The Government secured cancellation of the oil leases in 1927. Fall was indicted for bribery and
conspiracy, and convicted of bribery. He was sentenced to one year
in prison and a fine of $100,000. Fall's defense was that the cash
transactions had been for an interest in his ranch properties, and a
jury acquitted him, in April, 1928, on the charge of conspiring to
defraud the government. The scandal took the name of Teapot
Dome, the location in Wyoming of one of the two oil reserves in
question.–ED.]

The Cabinet meeting this afternoon was given over entirely to
a discussion of the economic situation. The President told of the
drive that has been made on the dollar in Amsterdam, Paris, and
London during the last few days. At first he decided to throw
enough gold in to maintain the dollar but finally concluded not to
do so. This is to be the national policy from this time on unless
changed. This may mean that the dollar will go down to ninety
cents or thereabouts. It may also mean a fluctuating dollar for
some time, but in the end it is thought that we will be better off,
and the world will be better off, if the dollar is not artificially
maintained at a value disproportionate to the rest of the principal
currencies of the world. It is likely also that the French franc will
have to come down. The United States, in effect, went off the gold
standard March 4, at the time of the banking crisis, except for
the last two or three days when the dollar was being supported in
the world market. We have been off the gold standard since then.
There can be no doubt that with the Administration failing to
support the dollar further, we are definitely off the gold standard
and that it will be so recognized. I realize that I don't have an
economic mind myself, so in matters of this sort I simply listen
carefully and go along with what those who are better qualified
than I decide should be our policy.

Wednesday, April 19, 1933

A disturbing rumor came to me late this afternoon to the effect
that instead of the National Forests coming over here from the
Department of Agriculture, the latest plan contemplates the transfer to Agriculture of the National Parks from this Department. As
I am particularly interested in the National Parks, this is a matter
of real concern to me and I hope it isn't true.

Thursday, April 20, 1933

I received a letter today from Gifford Pinchot enclosing a copy of a letter that he had already written the President protesting in the strongest terms against bringing the National Forest Service over here. I at once wrote a long letter to Gifford presenting my point of view and the point of view of this Department. I think the National Forests ought to be here but I have not raised my hand to bring that about. I have not made a fight for it, and I shall be content if the National Forests stay in Agriculture and the National Parks are permitted to stay here.

On the understanding that Secretary of Commerce Roper has been having a hand in working out the reorganization plans, I went to see him this afternoon. He, however, disclaimed any responsibility in the matter, but he expressed himself as sympathetic with my point of view. This is the first time I have been in the Commerce Building. It is a magnificent affair, and the private office of the Secretary is a beautiful thing. I thought we had quite a building here where the Interior Department is, but after leaving the Commerce Building, I felt as though I were coming to a humble mud hut. Herbert Hoover certainly was liberal with the taxpayers' money when he brought about the expenditure of the $17 million that went into his pet Commerce Building.

Friday, April 21, 1933

I had two interesting visits from representatives of the coal industry today. First, three men, concerning whose coming Governor Pinchot called me up by telephone yesterday, called on me. They are operators from western Pennsylvania. They are asking for a bill setting up what amounts to a Federal coal dictator. They want the Federal Government to take over the industry, establish minimum wages, regulate output, and set a minimum price. Involved also would be a more equitable setup of coal rates. Shortly after this committee left, F. E. Taplin, president of the North American Coal Company, who operates in three states, and who is the president of a railroad, came up with Margold, the Solicitor. He advanced exactly the same proposition. Margold is looking up the points of law involved to determine just how far the Federal Government might go along the lines suggested by these men.

[The coal industry was in bad shape in 1933, and both owners and miners were turning to the Government for help. The first informal arrangements worked out by Ickes were later written into an NRA code for the industry. In August, 1935, in its attempt to salvage something from the Supreme Court ruling on the NRA, Congress passed the Guffey-Snyder Coal Act, which provided for cooperative and mutual aid in an effort to stabilize the bituminous coal industry. This act was in turn declared unconstitutional by the Supreme Court on May 18, 1936, by a vote of six to three in the Carter Coal Company case, and the Guffey-Vinson Bill was passed in 1937 under which the present Bituminous Coal Division of the Department of the Interior operates. This body superseded the Bituminous Coal Commission, set up by Ickes, and is charged with the same responsibility for stabilizing coal markets, conserving bituminous coal resources, and establishing minimum price and marketing rules and regulations. The Supreme Court decision of 1936, against the Guffey-Snyder Coal Act, led to the gift of $469,870 by John L. Lewis of the United Mine Workers to the campaign fund to re-elect President Roosevelt in the 1936 campaign.–ED.]

We had our usual Cabinet meeting at two o'clock. Most of our discussion was on the coming of Prime Minister MacDonald, the tariff situation, and the result of the new policy of inflation.

Monday, April 24, 1933

Yesterday, with the exception of a drive to Great Falls, up the Potomac River, I spent at home. I went to bed for a couple of hours in the afternoon, and did some work on my stamp collection.

Saturday night I was guest at a state dinner at the White House in honor of Ramsay MacDonald and his daughter Ishbel. According to the newspapers, there were sixty-one guests present, but according to my count, there were about eighty. In any event, it was a big affair. The table was arranged in the shape of a horseshoe and the beautiful old-fashioned gold service, that I understand is reserved for state occasions, was used. I took Mrs. Henry Wallace, wife of the Secretary of Agriculture, in to dinner. She is a very charming, delightful, and personable individual. I liked her a lot. After the dinner we all went into the East Room where comfortable chairs were arranged for all the guests and for some additional guests who were invited to come in after dinner. There was a little professional dancing and an Indian woman gave some songs and told some stories most charmingly. We made our adieux about eleven o'clock.

Of course, it was a very formal affair, but the President's friendly, informal manner robbed it of any austerity. He certainly is a delightful person.

Tuesday, April 25, 1933

There was no Cabinet meeting today because the President is so busily engaged in discussions with the foreign representatives who are rapidly converging on Washington.

In the morning M. L. Benedum, an oil man of Pittsburgh, who is one of the Democratic leaders in his state, called on me to say that unless something along the lines of the Capper bill now pending in the Senate is adopted at this session of Congress, the oil industry will be in as bad a position in a short time as the banking situation was at the time of the inauguration of President Roosevelt. He urged me very strongly to present his views to the President and I shall do so at the first opportunity.

Four high school youths came in to see me about paying the Chicago schoolteachers. They were here to interview everyone they could, from the President down, having some adolescent notion that they might by their pleas succeed in loosening the strings of the Federal Treasury where others had failed. I think it was a fool movement myself and an imposition on all of us who had to submit to prolonged interviews. I gave them a lot of time but no encouragement. When they indicated that they would like to see the President and that my good offices in arranging an appointment might be in order, I told them I would not attempt to make an appointment and that it was unpatriotic on their part to try to add to the burdens of a very overburdened man, especially at this time when he has so many representatives of foreign governments on his hands.

I picked Merriam up at the Hotel Washington at three-thirty and took him around to see the cherry blossoms on his way to the train. The rich, double pinks are now in bloom and they are the most glorious sight I have ever seen. They were at their very best today.

I left the office early in order to go to the tea given by the French Ambassador and Madame de Laboulaye at the French Embassy in honor of Premier Herriot.

Wednesday, April 26, 1933

Senator Bronson Cutting came in to see me this morning about one or two patronage matters. He is a very reserved person, but I have come to like him very much. I do not intend to make any appointments in New Mexico that won't help him. He is very modest about patronage and has never asked me for anything. When I found there was a register of the U.S. Land Office in Santa Fe who was antagonistic to him, I discharged him without Senator Cutting saying anything about it, and then I offered Cutting a chance to fill the job.

Mrs. Henry Wallace called. At the White House dinner Saturday night, in talking about her oldest son, I said we might be able to find a place for him this summer in one of the national parks. She was delighted with the idea and after talking it over with Secretary Wallace, she came in to see me about it. Later in the day I took it up with Director Albright and called back Secretary Wallace to tell him that we could arrange it and to let me know what park his son would prefer.

Thursday, April 27, 1933

Yesterday Colonel McIntyre notified me that the President wanted me to act as chairman of a Cabinet committee, consisting of the Secretaries of War, Agriculture, and Labor, in addition to myself, to consider a public works program. The four of us met in my office this afternoon at two o'clock and went carefully over a draft of a bill presented by Miss Perkins. A number of changes and amendments were suggested, and we left it to our solicitors to prepare a draft over night in the hope that we may be in a position to present it at the Cabinet meeting tomorrow.

Late in the afternoon I went to a reception at the Canadian Embassy given in honor of Prime Minister Bennett who is here conferring with the President on international matters.

At eight o'clock I went to the White House to a state dinner given in honor of Prime Minister Bennett. I took Mrs. Swanson in and Mrs. Hiram Johnson was on my left. As on Saturday evening, we went into the East Room after dinner and Mrs. Roosevelt introduced a woman who related four of the Boccaccio tales, slightly amended to make them possible in mixed company. She also sang three old English ballads, and all that she did, she did charmingly.

Saturday, April 29, 1933

This afternoon at two o'clock we went into a long session with the President in the White House on the proposed public works bill. Present were the Secretaries of Labor, War, and Agriculture, the Solicitor of the Department of Labor, and the Director of the Budget, in addition to myself. After going over the draft of the bill which called for an appropriation of $5 billion, the President asked what public works there were that would call for the expenditure of such a large sum. Miss Perkins then produced a list prepared by some association of contractors and architects covering the entire country. The President at once turned to the proposals for the State of New York.

I had never before seen the President critical in perhaps a captious way, but he proceeded to rip that list to pieces and Miss Perkins was, in effect, put on trial, although she was not responsible for the list but simply presented it as a suggestion brought in by others. The President was perfectly nice about it all, but I got the impression that he had begun to feel the nervous strain resulting from the extra pressure he has been under as the result of the foreign representatives being here during the last ten days. There was no opportunity to go to Miss Perkins' rescue, much as I wanted to once or twice, not that she needed it, as she was perfectly able to handle it herself, but once or twice I did feel a bit sorry for her. I felt, however, that it would be better all around if the President got out of his system whatever he had in it. In the end we got around to a discussion of the subject matter of the bill and made considerable progress. It is hoped to have the bill perfected and introduced in Congress within ten days.

[From the very beginning of the New Deal an effort was made to distinguish between public works and relief projects, although the line between them was constantly fudged by the continuing pressures of the depression and of growing unemployment. Also from the beginning, Ickes became steadily more and more identified with the public-works phase of the New Deal, and Hopkins with its relief program. Public confusion over these two aspects of the New Deal campaign against the depression was compounded by the alphabetical contractions of the names of the new organizations.

[Relief was first organized under the FERA (Federal Emergency Relief Administration) which was started on May 12, 1933. It first gave funds through the states, but by November, 1933, it had also started the CWA (Civil Works Administration) which provided work relief for the unemployed under direct Federal control. By the end of 1935, more than $3 billion had been spent through the FERA.

[Public-works projects were launched under the National Industrial Recovery Act, the bill actually referred to in this entry in the diary. This set up PWA (Public Works Administration). Ickes became its first Administrator and by June 16, 1934, a year after the bill was passed, he had allotted its entire fund of $3.3 billion to 13,266 Federal projects and 2,407 non-Federal projects. Only $1.2 billion had actually been disbursed. The projects included the TVA (Tennessee Valley Authority); 99 per cent of all the counties in the United States had at least one project. Most of them involved heavy construction, and PWA was not required to hire labor from the relief rolls.–ED.]

I waited until after the others had gone and took up with the President the question of selling beer on the Indian agencies. I told him I was opposed to any sale of beer on the agencies and he agreed with me.

I also discussed with him briefly the very critical oil situation and told him about the bill that had been brought in to me drawn by the oil interests, which would have the effect of making the Secretary of the Interior an Oil Dictator for two years with the broadest kind of powers. He asked me to submit this matter to him in a letter.

Tuesday, May 2, 1933

At the Cabinet meeting this afternoon, I brought up again the question of the oil situation and urged the enactment of some sort of legislation before the present Congress adjourns. The President and the other members of the Cabinet seemed to agree that something should be done and the President indicated that he would transmit to the Senate and the House of Representatives the letter I wrote to him yesterday, in which I went into the situation and suggested that some legislation should be passed. Generally speaking, the oil interests are in favor of a bill that I have already referred to, making the Secretary of the Interior a virtual dictator for two years with very broad powers.

The Attorney General said at the Cabinet meeting today that he was informed that a strict espionage was being maintained of Cabinet members and other officials high in the Government Service. This work is under the charge of Lawrence Richey, one of the secretaries to former President Hoover, and is supposed to be in the interest of Hoover particularly, and of the Republican party in general. Richey is maintaining elaborate offices in the Shoreham Building. He warned all of us to be on our guard against people who might thrust themselves upon our notice and he said that the same precaution should be taken by our wives and members of our families. His information is that some women are being employed to worm themselves into the confidence of our wives.

Thursday, May 4, 1933

This afternoon I had a conference with a group of coal operators from Indiana and Illinois. These operators called to suggest that a bill be passed appointing a Federal dictator for their business. They lay most of their ills to differentials in wages as between their fields and other fields. In Illinois and Indiana the basic wage is $5 a day, while in other competitive fields as low as $1 a day is paid, with the result that outside coal can undersell Illinois coal even in the Chicago market, in spite of the advantage Illinois has in freight rates. I remarked to these operators that there seemed to be a wide difference of opinion among coal operators generally with reference to Federal control, and asked them whether they would be satisfied with any bill that the Government would propose and they said that they would be satisfied. They want the Government to set a minimum wage, fix minimum and maximum prices for the coal, and, if necessary, limit the production of coal and prorate such production among the different states and coal fields.

There was an amusing incident the other day that I would like to record. Mrs. Ruth Bryan Owen called me by telephone to urge the appointment as Assistant Commissioner of Education of a lady who used to be a Representative in Congress from one of the southern states. I asked her what the lady's qualifications were and she said: "The qualification that any mother of children has." Then she added: "Of course, she has the additional qualification acquired as a member of Congress."

I am still hearing from oil representatives of various sorts from all parts of the country. Some of the big old oil moguls have the habit of writing to me saying that if I want to see them, they will be glad to call. In my answers I tell them very politely that I have no desire to see them, but if they want to see me they may come in. As a result of this process, my office today made an appointment with H. L. Doherty for one-forty-five today. The coal conference was at two and some of the men came in early. A dapper little gentleman with a closely trimmed beard appeared at the outside door to my main office shortly before two and I invited him to come in and sit down. This he did, only to discover that he was sitting in at a coal conference. Finally he got up and went into the Administrative Assistant's office to explain the apparent misunderstanding. I found out later that this was Mr. Doherty, who left word that he would be in Washington next week and would call to see me then.

I went to the annual dinner of the Chamber of Commerce of the United States tonight. It was a very large affair and the President and most of the Cabinet were there. The President did not come until after the dinner was over and he made a short speech, after which he left, and I took advantage of the situation and slipped out myself. So I got home at a reasonable time. I sat between Julius H. Barnes and Fred H. Clauson, president of the Board of Regents of the University of Wisconsin. Mr. Barnes is the man who was in charge of the grain administration during the war under President Wilson's administration. The great and the mighty in the business world were there in force, and I couldn't help thinking how so many of these great and mighty were crawling to Washington on their hands and knees these days to beg the Government to run their businesses for them.

Friday, May 5, 1933

Just before I went to the Cabinet meeting I was handed a telegram to the effect that oil had actually been sold as low as four cents a barrel in East Texas today. I took with me a revised draft of the bill presented here some time ago. I brought up the matter at the Cabinet meeting and the President said he was preparing a letter to send to Congress on the subject. I left with him the revised draft of the bill and urged again the importance of drastic action. Vice President Garner, himself a Texas man, told me after the Cabinet meeting that it was his opinion that some legislation along the lines suggested should be adopted. What Congress will do is another matter. I am being bombarded with long telegrams and even longer letters, many of them urging the appointment of a Federal dictator, and others objecting to such an appointment. Late this afternoon a telegram came in from Governor Ferguson, of Texas, admitting that the situation is beyond the control of the state authorities, and joining in the plea for stringent Federal legislation.

Monday, May 8, 1933

Professor Paul Douglas called to talk about public utilities. He told me of a bill passed by the Illinois Senate last Thursday providing for the taxing of privately endowed educational institutions where seditious statements were made or permitted. This, of course, is aimed at the University of Chicago and is a most atrocious proposition.

I am receiving many telegrams and letters from manufacturers of cement uttering loud wails and protesting their high virtues, all as a result of the newspaper article that was running last Saturday in which I commented on the fact that we had to reject bids for 400,000 barrels of cement for the Boulder Dam project because, except for a variation due to different freight rates, all the bids were identical. This story was carried pretty generally throughout the country and was given a big display. For instance, it was on the first page of *The New York Times*. Interestingly enough, I am also receiving propositions by telegraph, by mail, and by personal calls from persons willing to manufacture cement for the Government if we will guarantee to buy a quantity sufficient to justify the investment that will be involved.

Judson King came in excitedly to tell me that Senator Norris believes that it is the purpose of the power interests to emasculate his Tennessee Development Bill in conference, denying to the corporation to be set up in the bill the right to build transmission lines without first negotiating with the local power companies. King told me that if this provision stayed in the bill, Norris would fight his own bill when it went back to the floor of the Senate. I had already made an appointment to see the President at half past twelve. I told him about the Norris situation and he was apparently disposed to interest himself in it.

I then talked to him about the report that Senator Borah was to be on the American delegation to the International Economic Conference, and he told me that he had no thought of Borah in that connection but that he did hope that Hiram Johnson would go. He named the list of men he proposed to send. I told him how delighted I was with the suggestion he had made with reference to Johnson.

[A world economic conference had been called by the League of Nations in 1932. Secretary of State Cordell Hull was the leader of the United States delegation when the conference finally assembled in June, 1933. The conference opened in an atmosphere emphasizing the interdependence of nations and the agenda featured measures designed to support a program to stabilize currencies on a gold basis. War debts, import duties, and the growing impact of the world depression were all obstacles to any solution of the problem based on the interrelations of world trade. On July 2, 1933, President Roosevelt rebuked the American delegates, in a radio message, for concentrating on currency stabilization, and the conference broke up in failure. From this point on, American economic policy was aimed at achieving a sound internal economic system, as more important than any international monetary devices, and the New Deal drifted significantly toward a policy of economic isolationism.–ED.]

Tuesday, May 9, 1933

About noon a delegation came in representing the United Mine Workers of America, the Coal Operators of Indiana, and the Coal Operators of Illinois, with a draft of a coal bill which they said had the unanimous support of all these groups. Thurlow Essington, who was here at the conference with the Indiana and Illinois operators last Thursday afternoon as their counsel, was here again today and spoke for the committee.

At the Cabinet meeting the President indicated that matters were not working out as satisfactorily as had been expected in Great Britain, France, and Germany. The latest information is that Prime Minister MacDonald's Cabinet has turned on him and refused to approve the tentative suggestions he took back after talking with President Roosevelt here. It is intimated also that the German government is about to issue an order forbidding the payment of interest on its foreign obligations. There are about $5 billions of German bonds held in this country, all of them dollar bonds and the interest on all of them payable in New York.

Wednesday, May 10, 1933

At two o'clock I was called into conference with a group in the President's office to discuss the Public Works Bill. The Bureau of the Budget now thinks that for a two-year period we can use and probably manage to finance an appropriation of $3 billion, 300 million. I am in favor of $5 billion being set up in the bill, but $3 billion, 300 million is better than the $1 billion to $1.5 billion suggested by the President the last time we discussed this bill at the White House. Present at this conference were quite a group, including the Secretary of Labor, the Secretary of War, Assistant Secretary of Agriculture Tugwell, Assistant Secretary of Commerce Dickinson, Senator Wagner, of New York, Donald R. Richberg, General Johnson, Speaker of the House Byrns, Senator Walsh, of Massachusetts, and Assistant Secretary Moley. Apparently there will be conjoined with this bill a bill providing for the regulation and stimulation of industry, for which Senator Wagner and others have been working.

Today I also appointed Harry Slattery as personal assistant to the Secretary. He will work with me on policy and general administrative matters. Mr. Burlew, who has been First Administrative Assistant, will continue on with that title but with slightly different duties. He will have nothing to do with policy except when and if called in, but he will take care of the budget and attend also to many routine and detail matters, as he has been doing since I came here, for all of which duties he is admirably fitted.

Thursday, May 11, 1933

There were several groups of delegations in today advocating specific public works. I have to tell them all that the only assignment I have had has been to help work on a bill which will provide for a Public Works Administrator, who, in his turn, will consider and pass upon specific projects. This explanation ought to satisfy most delegations, and it does, but this does not mean that they want to leave without getting off their chests all the arguments they had fortified themselves with.

A. Mitchell Palmer, who was Attorney General in the Wilson administration, came in on behalf of clients who are coal operators, protesting against any special legislation dealing with the coal industry. He plainly represents that group from West Virginia and one or two southern states that are reputed to be paying their labor a dollar a day.

Shortly after twelve, I went back to the house to change into my morning coat and silk hat to attend a luncheon at the White House at one o'clock in honor of the Secretary of the Treasury from Mexico, who is the current foreign potentate here discussing the international economic situation with the President. Señor Dr. Don Fernando Gonzalez Roa, the Mexican Ambassador, sat on the President's left and I sat on the left of the Ambassador. His English was good enough so that I was able to have a very interesting conversation with him about social and racial conditions in Mexico, with especial reference to their Indian population. The other two members of the Cabinet present were the Secretary of State and the Secretary of the Treasury. There are so many of these official functions that the President is dividing his Cabinet among them. Mrs. Roosevelt received the guests and then retired, as it was a stag affair, with about twenty to twenty-five people present.

After the luncheon I took Senator McAdoo, who was also dressed in a morning coat and silk hat, and three Democratic representatives, down to the Capitol. Then I went home and got into my working clothes and came back to the office.

While we were waiting in the Oval Room in the White House just before luncheon, Senator McAdoo told the Secretary of the Treasury and me that it was in that room he had married President Wilson's daughter. He said that in the evening while the family was sitting upstairs, Wilson turned to him and said: "Now Mac, since you are a member of our family, perhaps I ought to call you Will." According to McAdoo, he rejoined: "If you do that, I will call you Papa."

This afternoon late I went back to the White House offices to talk with Colonel McIntyre. I told him it didn't seem wise to me to be creating these new special offices, as for instance, the Administrator of Public Works. It seems to me that the thing to do is to appoint a Special Assistant Secretary in some department instead.

This would make for better and more economical administration, in my judgment, and toward the end, when things begin to peter out, a whole new organization would not have to be maintained, but the functions could be turned over to the Department to which the special assistant was attached. McIntyre agreed with me and said he would take it up with the President.

President Robert Maynard Hutchins, of the University of Chicago, called me up about noon. He is very much concerned over the bill which passed the State Senate of Illinois providing that if sedition is taught in any private institution, the property of that institution shall be placed on the tax rolls, and that if this should happen in a state-supported institution, further support would not be granted. This fool bill went through the State Senate with a whoop last Thursday and is now before the Judiciary Committee of the House. President Hutchins wanted me to get in touch with Pat Nash and see if he would help kill it in the Judiciary Committee. Later I got Nash on the telephone, told him how much interested I was and how concerned lest the bill pass. I expressed the hope that he would see that it was killed in the Judiciary Committee and he promised me he would talk the matter over with Chairman Adamowski tomorrow.

Friday, May 12, 1933

At half past ten I attended a meeting of the National Forest Reservation Commission in the Department of Agriculture. The chairman of this Commission is the Secretary of War, and other members are the Secretary of Agriculture, the Secretary of the Interior and two or three Senators and Congressmen. We decided to recommend to the President that he set aside $25 million out of the fund appropriated for the Civilian Conservation Corps, to buy land to round out the various units in the eastern, southern, and central states that the Government has been buying during the past few years for national forest purposes.

The usual Cabinet meeting was held at two o'clock, with a good deal of discussion devoted to the Public Works and Business Control Bill which is apparently nearly in final form and ready to be introduced.

The President said that he was working on the matter of the oil bill last night and would prepare a letter on the subject at once.

After the Cabinet meeting, I dropped into Colonel Howe's office and talked with him about the oil situation, leaving with him two drafts of the final oil bill prepared by Margold. I also had a brief discussion with reference to the Governorship of Hawaii, and I have undertaken to have drafted an amendment to the fundamental law of Hawaii permitting the President to appoint a Governor from outside of Hawaii. The present law requires the appointment of a man who has lived at least two years in Hawaii. We have not found it possible so far to find anyone who seems to measure up to the requirements of that office.

Tuesday, May 16, 1933

At the Cabinet meeting this afternoon, I again urged consideration of the oil situation, and the President said that he hoped to get his letter on the subject up to Congress tomorrow. I asked him whether it would be all right for me, when his letter was sent, to have the oil bill that we have drafted here offered in the House of Representatives by Congressman Marland, and in the Senate by Senator Capper. He said it would be, and I shall proceed accordingly. The plan is to have these bills presented in Congress when the Public Works and Industrial Control Bill is offered, with the idea that in some way they may be capable of being amalgamated in a satisfactory manner.

After Cabinet meeting, Secretaries Perkins, Roper, and myself went to the President's office with him, at his suggestion, to consider the final draft of the Public Works and Industrial Control Bill which the Director of the Budget had. I made two suggestions as to this bill which met with the approval of the President. The first was that there be a definite revision made to include conservation of natural resources among the objects of the bill; and the other was that instead of appointing an independent Public Works Administrator, the new official be assigned to some department. I pointed out what seemed to me to be the obvious advantages of that kind of an organization instead of an independent administrator, and I think the bill will be changed accordingly.

Wednesday, May 17, 1933

A number of insulting letters, some of them anonymous, have been coming in attacking me for changing the name of Hoover Dam to Boulder Dam. Some time ago Dr. Mead, Commissioner of Reclamation, asked me how I wanted this project designated, and I said that I wanted it called Boulder Dam. On Saturday when I went out of Washington somebody apparently gave a story to the Associated Press that I had issued an order changing the name. The story carried a quotation from me which I never gave and which was very unconvincing. This is what started the criticism. As a matter of fact, I never issued any formal order. I have always called this Boulder Dam myself, as do many people, and I have continued that usage since I came to Washington. I consider it very unfair to call it Hoover Dam. Hoover had very little to do with the dam and in fact was supposed to be opposed to it. To call it Hoover Dam is to give him credit for something for which he is not entitled to credit, and ignore those who dreamed of this proposition and brought it to a successful conclusion after years of effort. The dam never was officially named Hoover. My predecessor ordered it named Hoover Dam, but my understanding is that when a bill was introduced in Congress to name it Hoover Dam, the bill could not pass and the proposition was dropped until Wilbur, an appointee of Hoover's, named it after Hoover.

I had an oil hearing this afternoon. It involved oil leases in the Maverick Springs District of Wyoming. This is an Indian reservation. The leases were granted some seventeen years ago and nothing has been done to produce oil except to drill a few wells and then shut them in. Meanwhile, the Indians have been getting a dollar an acre a year out of this land. Secretary Wilbur, a short time ago, issued an order that a move would be made to cancel the leases unless the wells were brought into production at some date next September. The oil companies moved to set aside this order. In their argument this afternoon these attorneys, of course, relied upon the fact that there is now no market for oil. After listening to both sides I held that I would not set aside the order, not because there was a market now for oil, but because the oil companies had not come into court with clean hands. I said that during the years of prosperity, before the present economic situation arose, they had done nothing to produce oil so as to pay a royalty to the Indians. I told them they had taken unfair advantage and for this reason I would not vacate the order. I advised them, however, that if they came in within a week with a modified proposition of some sort which would give the Indians more benefit from their own land, I would consider such a proposition. I added in this connection that they ought to keep in mind that I am half Scotch.

Last night I had dinner with Justice and Mrs. Brandeis. Norman Hapgood was there. The Brandeises live very simply, but I considered it a privilege to dine with one of the greatest men of his generation.

Thursday, May 18, 1933

Bruce Johnstone came in to see me about the oil bill. He is an old friend of mine from Chicago, a director of Standard Oil Company of Indiana, and he had just been in conference with Walter C. Teagle in New York, president of Standard of New Jersey. Curiously enough, so many of these oil people who were in favor of stringent Federal regulation are now opposed to any bill along this line. They think that with the bars let down with respect to the Sherman anti-trust laws, as they will be if the Wagner bill passes the House, they will be in a position to gobble up all their rivals. Meanwhile, pressure for Federal legislation by public officers in the oil states, from independents, landowners, leaseholders, bankers, and local businessmen, continues. My apprehension over this oil situation has not abated one particle.

Jim Farley came in early this afternoon to talk over some patronage matters. I have always found him very considerate. He has never shown any disposition to press for the appointment of anyone not fit. He always says that he doesn't want anyone employed who isn't qualified.

I had an appointment with the President at four o'clock. When I got there I found former Governor Woodring, of Kansas, now Assistant Secretary of War, and another man whose name I can't recall, waiting to see the President to urge him to support the oil legislation that I have been in favor of. There also came in Senators Kendrick, Joseph T. Robinson, and McNary to talk with the President about a reclamation project in Wyoming that Senator Kendrick is particularly interested in. Senator Kendrick had asked me to be present at this conference. The idea was that I was to take up my departmental matters with the President before the Kendrick project was discussed, but we were all ushered in at once. The two oil men had a word with the President, telling him that they were for my bill, as they called it, and then we discussed reclamation. The President asked me what I thought about it, and I told him it was the one reclamation plan that I might consider favorably. The President indicated that it could be built under the Public Works Bill. He asked me to send him a memorandum on it.

Then the Senators left and I had time to take up with the President several matters in which I was interested. First of all, however, he asked me to send reports to him with reference to proposed developments in Oregon and Washington in the Columbia River Basin. I discussed several patronage matters with him.

During our talk the question of changing the name of Hoover Dam to Boulder Dam came up. The President chuckled and told me he was glad I had done this but that he was also glad I had done it without consulting him. I told him that the matter had gotten out inadvertently and there wasn't any occasion for involving him in it anyhow.

The President said he would send his oil letter to Congress tomorrow. The White House correspondents all gathered around me as usual when I came out of the President's office, and I told them that the oil letter would be sent up tomorrow and thereafter the bill for Federal control, drafted by Solicitor Margold, would be introduced.

Friday, May 19, 1933

I got authority from the President today to permit the introduction of the bill giving the Secretary of the Interior wide regulatory powers with respect to the oil industry. The bill was introduced in the House by Representative Marland, and in the Senate by Senator Capper. There seems to be a growing sentiment for legislation along the lines of this bill. Vice President Garner told me after Cabinet meeting he thought the bill would pass if it were attached to some other bill as an amendment.

The Cabinet meeting was very short, as the President had an engagement with representatives of the Veterans' Expeditionary Force. When we left the Cabinet room, Secretary Wallace suggested that since the meeting was short it might be an appropriate time to play hooky. He wanted to come over to my building, get Commissioner Collier, and go for a short ride. This we did in my car. Down by the river we actually got out of the car and sat on the grass. It would probably have been a great shock to the social lights of Washington if they had seen two members of the Cabinet lolling on the grass like any other two human beings. We were out only about a half hour, and then I came back to work later than usual and tried to get my desk reasonably cleared.

Tuesday, May 23, 1933

I attended a meeting in the Department of Agriculture of the Migratory Bird Conservation Commission this morning. It was proposed to ask the President to authorize the expenditure of almost $3 million to acquire additional migratory bird refuges in different parts of the country in order to round out the program of the Commission. It was suggested that this money might come out of the funds appropriated for the Civilian Conservation Corps work, as under that bill the President has the right to buy lands. I raised the point that, much as I was interested in the establishment of bird refuges, this would not be a proper expenditure, since so little of the money to be spent would be used for labor, and the whole concept back of the bill was to give employment in reforestation, soil erosion, etc., to unemployed men and thus relieve the strains on relief funds. Congressman McReynolds agreed with me, but Secretary Wallace and Secretary of Commerce Roper took the other view, as did also Congressman W. Frank Jones, of Michigan. It was finally decided that Secretary Wallace, who is Chairman of the Commission, report the matter to the Cabinet meeting this afternoon. He did so, stating that we took different views, and the President quickly decided that the money was not to be spent for this purpose.

At the Cabinet meeting I told the President that we had come within $2.25 million of meeting the requirements of the Director of the Budget. I explained that it would be difficult to cut any more because so much of our money went out for hospitalization, Indian welfare work, etc. He said we had done very well and indicated that we would not be required to cut any further.

The President is very much disturbed over the status of the banking situation now pending before Congress. He thinks the Glass bill, which is in the Senate, and the Steagall bill, in the House, are both very bad bills in many particulars, and he is distinctly worried. He may be able to bring about their defeat by clever parliamentary tactics. He is especially opposed in their present form to the deposit guarantee features of these two bills.

The oil situation is still very badly muddled. Congressman Marland, who introduced our oil bill in the House, doesn't seem to be able to get forward with it. He called to see the President this morning, and later I talked with Colonel McIntyre, the President's secretary, who, after talking with the President, suggested that I go up to the Capitol and talk with Congressman Doughton, Chairman of the Ways and Means Committee. I did this but I got nowhere with him. He stated very frankly that he wouldn't take any step except on express directions from the President, and I will now have to see the President and see how far he wants to go.

At the conclusion of the Cabinet meeting, the President remarked that he had an appointment with Hiram Johnson to try to persuade him to go to London as a member of the United States delegation at the Economic Conference. Turning to me, he asked me whether I would go into his office with him and help persuade Hiram to go. When Hiram was ushered in, he proceeded to give his reasons to the President why he could not go and why he ought not to go. His position was that no Senator ought to take part in such negotiations because in the end the Senate might be called upon to pass upon the negotiations if they were embodied in a treaty and he would not then be a free agent. He also emphasized to the President his long-standing and well-known views on the international situation, spoke of his independent stand on matters of Government policy, told how he couldn't yield his independence, and yet, if he should go as a member of the delegation, he would not want to support the President at all points. He made a good argument, but the President outtalked him. He told Johnson he didn't expect him to be in accord with any policies that didn't commend themselves to his own judgment; that he would have no objection if Johnson refused to go along with what the conference decided upon. He said he wanted a man of independent judgment who would be able to come back and report to the Senate just what actually had occurred. There could be no doubt that he sincerely wants Johnson to go. At the end Hiram said that he had come with the distinct purpose of declining to go, but that he would give a final answer in the morning, after consulting his "Boss." At this point I intervened to tell the President he oughtn't to let him get away without giving a final answer; that I knew the position his "Boss" would take. The President agreed, however, to wait until tomorrow morning.

Wednesday, May 24, 1933

Mrs. Hiram Johnson called me by telephone while I was at break-fast this morning to ask me to call Colonel McIntyre when I got to the office and ask him to get Hiram on the telephone and postpone until four o'clock the decision that Hiram was to give to the President by eleven o'clock as to whether or not he would go to London as a member of the commission representing this country in the Economic Conference. The "Boss" wants to have that much additional time to work on Hiram and try to persuade him to accept this invitation to go. I did as she wished me to do, but as it developed later in the day, it served no purpose because in the end Hiram declined to go.

I am sorry for this decision, but I don't criticize him for it. He is one of the most conscientious and high-minded men in public life. His convictions on international questions are profound and sincere, and despite his wish to do what the President wanted him to do, and notwithstanding the pressure that the "Boss" can always exert, he couldn't bring himself to agree to go and thus run the risk of waiving his right to express an independent opinion about any measures growing out of the conference.

Late this afternoon Mrs. Essary called me up to ask me whether I would substitute for Mr. Essary and be her escort to a dinner given by Mrs. Eleanor Patterson at her home in Maryland. I accepted, called for her at six o'clock, and drove with her to the Patterson home in Dupont Circle. The party congregated there and then we went out in three or four cars to Maryland, some twenty or twenty-five miles, I should judge.

Mrs. Patterson, some three years ago, bought a partly burned building on a fine hilltop in Maryland and she has rebuilt it mainly around the chimneys which were not damaged by the fire. The original house was built in 1640. The living room had two big fireplaces, one of which was the biggest I have ever seen. This one is supposed to have been designed by Christopher Wren.

The plan was to have dinner out on the terrace. It was a threatening night, notwithstanding which the two tables were set out there. The dinner wasn't ready until eight-forty-five and I was nearly starved, not having had anything to eat since breakfast at seven-fifteen in the morning. It began to rain gently as we sat down. Mrs. Patterson sat at one end of the table. The roof didn't come out far enough to protect her from the rain but she insisted she didn't mind. I was on her right and half of me was in the rain and half under cover. Finally she got a coat for herself and a coat and hat for me and we got along pretty well until it began to rain rather hard; then she deserted us temporarily to go to the other table, which was more sheltered.

Mrs. Patterson is a very interesting and vivacious hostess. She is brilliant, has lived an interesting life, and has had wide experiences. She is the granddaughter of Joseph Medill, the founder of the *Chicago Tribune*. She married Count Gizycki, of Poland, from whom she was divorced at the time of the war. Subsequently she married Elmer Schlesinger, a Chicago lawyer, and upon his death she resumed her maiden name.

Friday, May 26, 1933

I appeared before the Finance Committee of the Senate at ten o'clock this morning to present my views on the oil bill that was introduced by Senator Capper, but drawn by Margold of this Department. I dictated a statement at home last night, and I read this to the committee, occupying about twenty minutes. Senator McAdoo interrupted to ask several questions, and Senator Connally, of Texas, also queried me.

On my way back I stopped at Senator Johnson's office in the Capitol. I haven't seen him since he declined to go to London as a member of the delegation representing this country in the International Economic Conference. I told him that he had done a fine thing but I was sorry he wasn't going. He confessed to me that he was "in the dumps." He said that he really wanted to go; that the greatest disappointment in connection with the matter was that he couldn't take the "Boss" abroad, as they would never have another opportunity, since he was a poor man. He added that he loved to wear spats, a silk hat, and have his picture taken and printed all over the world, just as much as any one. I told him that I thought he was great, and that I was all for him. But he led me over to a corner of his office and showed me what he called his motto, which was a saying of Abraham Lincoln's to the effect that regardless of everything else, a man must be true to himself.

Hiram Johnson is true to himself. In my judgment there are few, if any, men in public life who have ideals comparable to his. He will suffer for a cause he believes in, and his whole soul is in this international situation. Much as he wanted to go, and as much as he was urged to go by the "Boss" and to a much lesser extent by myself, he couldn't bring himself to go because he was afraid of compromising his principles and foreclosing his right to speak freely on international questions as a member of the United States Senate.

At the Cabinet meeting this afternoon a full hour was taken up in discussing the fact that the name of Secretary of the Treasury Woodin has been brought up during the Morgan hearing as one of the men who was sold stock at a substantial figure under the market price at the time he bought it. Woodin was very much concerned, and told the President he would like to have an expression of opinion from "the members of the family," as he called us. The President took the position that many of us did things prior to 1929 that we wouldn't think of doing now; that our code of ethics had radically changed. Of course, Woodin was suggesting that he ought to resign from the Cabinet. Since the President made this point, I said that there was another point involved which seemed to be quite important, and that was that at the time Mr. Woodin had bought this stock he was not in public life, he had never been in public life, and he never expected to be in public life; that, therefore, there could be no thought of an ulterior motive so far as influencing legislation or administrative acts was concerned. I added that it was perfectly proper for Mr. Woodin to buy this stock, although, in my judgment, it was not proper for all of those men whose names appeared on the Morgan list.

Then Woodin turned to the Vice President and asked him his view. The Vice President spoke very frankly. He expressed his personal like for and confidence in Woodin; he spoke of the impression in the minds of the people who would believe that the Morgan interests were dominating this Administration just as they have believed in the past that these interests were dominating preceding administrations. At the conclusion of the Vice President's remarks, Woodin asked him whether he thought that he ought to resign, and the Vice President said he did think so.

Then the Attorney General gave it as his view that while there was a good deal to what the Vice President said with respect to what people would think, he believed that there was no reason for Woodin resigning. The President discussed the matter again briefly and once again I took the floor. I said that I was satisfied with the conclusion of the Attorney General that Mr. Woodin ought not to resign, but I went on to say that I considered that Norman Davis was a distinct liability to the Administration. I pointed out that Davis had been in public life, was in public life, and expected to be in public life when he was permitting the house of Morgan to sell him stock at a figure substantially under the market price. I pointed out further that as a result of our negotiations abroad this year, the United States Government might be brought so close to the League of Nations that the people would believe that we were actually in the League. Davis is representing this Government as a sort of ambassador at large, as the newspapers put it. He has been accused by the newspapers of a deliberate intention to get us into the League; the house of Morgan has, with other institutions in this country, governmental, financial, or otherwise, from the start, been in favor of a closer alliance with the Government of England. I said that if we should approach close to the League or into it under the auspices of Norman Davis, it would be felt by many people that the house of Morgan, through its close connection with Davis, had had perhaps a predominating hand in getting us into the League.

Thursday, June 1, 1933

I appeared before the Ways and Means Committee of the House this morning on the oil bill. Colonel McIntyre called me up at the house last night, suggesting that he would like to take the matter up with the President this morning on their way to Annapolis. So the first thing I sent him over our oil bill redrafted as an amendment to the General Industries Bill, and a shorter amendment comprising eight lines. Just before leaving for the hearing, Colonel McIntyre called me and told me that the President wanted the short amendment and that I was authorized to tell the committee that he wanted this amendment attached to the General Industries Bill.

I was on my feet for all of two hours before the committee answering questions, repeating the statement that I made a week ago before the Senate Finance Committee, and then answering more questions. I don't think there was a single member of the committee, and it is a large one, who failed to ask me at least one question and many of them went at me pretty hard. I was completely tired out by the hearing, but I was grateful afterward when Nathan Margold told me that it was grand the way I had handled myself. He was genuinely and thoroughly satisfied, and he has a critical mind. So apparently I got by all right and I came away with the impression that the committee, if it had taken a vote at the conclusion of my testimony, would have voted almost unanimously for the amendment.

Friday, June 2, 1933

Dr. Abraham Flexner, chairman of the Board of Trustees of Howard University, came to see me this morning and we had a long talk about the affairs of that university. He told me that he had taken this position at the insistence of Julius Rosenwald. He found that the officers of two local banks constituted a majority of the finance committee of the board and were more or less playing ducks and drakes with the university's finances. He has succeeded in having both these men eliminated from the board and gradually reorganizing it to his satisfaction. The board is constituted half of whites and half of Negroes, and he seems to have a higher opinion of the Negroes than of the whites.

Just about eleven o'clock I was called by Senator Harrison to appear before the Senate Finance Committee in support of the oil amendment to the Industries Control Bill. I made a brief statement on the amendment. The only members of the committee who asked questions, or attempted to argue, were Senator McAdoo, of California, and Senator Connally, of Texas.

We discussed somewhat at Cabinet meeting the matter of departmental reorganization. It is the present intention of the President to sign Executive Orders bringing about departmental changes about which there is no dispute, leaving debatable matters to be considered more carefully later. There was more discussion than usual on the subject matter of patronage. The Vice President is strongly of the opinion that the Democrats ought to get every possible job, but he includes in his definition of Democrats entitled to be considered all those who supported the Democratic national ticket last November.

Tuesday, June 6, 1933

The weather is becoming quite hot and I feel it a good deal. Last night I couldn't sleep well at all. At two o'clock I went up to the third floor where I have my stamp collection, hoping to divert my mind as I have done on so many occasions in the past but, clad as I was for the night, I found it too hot to stay long. Today my office has been like a bake oven, and the only respite I have had was during the Cabinet meeting. Providentially, the White House offices are air-conditioned and it is quite comfortable there on the hottest days.

At Cabinet meeting a good deal of discussion was had with reference to how to work out the organization under the Industries Control Bill. It seems that General Hugh S. Johnson, who is to be in charge of administering this part of the bill when it passes Congress, has already been rounding up personnel, and the President and one or two members of the Cabinet took exception to some of his selections. The President told the Secretary of Commerce to get in touch with General Johnson and tell him not to select anyone without first conferring with himself. The Secretary of Commerce then went on to say that General Johnson's duties would overlap to a considerable extent several of the departments. He mentioned his own, Labor, Agriculture, and Interior. He thought that an interdepartmental committee should be set up which would pass not only upon the work in general but on personnel to be employed by General Johnson.

When it came my turn, I pointed out that I thought that such a setup as had been suggested by Secretary Roper would prove too cumbersome and ineffectual, as a similar setup has been found to be in the administration of the Civilian Conservation Corps Act. I said that I thought that General Johnson ought to be attached to the Department of Commerce in some manner. I pointed out that this would give him a Cabinet officer to represent him at the Cabinet table; that he would have someone to whom he could go when he had decisions to make; that it would make for better cooperation and administration all along the line; and that when the emergency work entrusted to him began to peter out, the Department of Commerce would be there to take it over and liquidate it. The President said he thought that perhaps my suggestion was the right one, and he asked some of the other members how they felt about it. Miss Perkins said that she doubted whether General Johnson, with his temperament, would be able to work under a Secretary, and I asked how he could work for four Secretaries if he could not work with one.

Wednesday, June 7, 1933

I cut out my regular appointments today because I had to attend a hearing with the Public Lands Committee of the House in support of a bill that I had introduced to give this Department power to regulate grazing on the public range. This bill passed the House at the last regular session but didn't get through the Senate. Recently, with the approval of the President, I had it reintroduced. The public range is being overgrazed to an alarming extent. Part of it has already been destroyed and there will be more of this until there is some control. Some of the Western states are opposed to it because their stockmen in their greed want to turn their flocks and herds onto the range without the aye, yes or no of anyone. Secretary of Agriculture Wallace also appeared in behalf of the bill. I haven't much hopes of getting it through this session. Senator Kendrick, of Wyoming, is chairman of the committee in the Senate to which the bill has been referred, and Wyoming has always been particularly opposed to this legislation.

After leaving the House Office Building I went over to the Senate to confer with Senator Harrison and Elmer Thomas, with reference to the oil amendment to the Industries Control Bill. Senator Harrison said that he was in favor of the amendment and he thought the best thing would be for Senator Thomas to introduce it from the floor of the Senate. Meanwhile, Senator Thomas had gone up to see the President about it and had been authorized to present the amendment. The President told him, however, that while he wanted the power conferred by the amendment, he didn't want the amendment pressed unduly if it meant deferring a final vote on the Industries Control Bill. I talked with Senator Thomas after he came back from seeing the President and we agreed on this program. I supplied him with an amendment to offer.

While I was at the Capitol, Senator Connally, of Texas, at whose instance the Finance Committee of the Senate had adopted an oil amendment which gives the President no more power than he has at present to control production, ran across me. He had previously called me up by telephone, urged me to accept his amendment, and not to make any further fight. When he saw me in the Senate cloak room, he asked me if I would wait until he could bring Senator McAdoo out. The two of them went at me pretty hard, protesting against any attempt to change the Connally amendment, and Senator McAdoo threatened to move to strike out the entire oil amendment if any attempt should be made to substitute our program for that which has the support of himself and Connally. He took the attitude that he knew all about the oil business and no one else knew anything about it. Both of them were inclined to be dictatorial. I made no comment, further than to say that it was due the Administration that a public record should be made of what powers we think should be conferred upon the President. I told Senator McAdoo that he and I just differed fundamentally on the oil question; that I did not believe that any man or set of men had a right, for their own purposes, to exploit an irreplaceable national resource; that the interests of the nation were paramount.

After leaving the Capitol I stopped at the White House to see the President. He verified the authority he had given to Senator Thomas. I had one or two appointment matters to discuss with him and, as always, I found him most amenable and agreeable. He had had a very hard morning, he said, but when I went into his office his urbanity and graciousness were unabated. I started to leave after I had concluded my business, which took me only two or three minutes, but he held me for a while longer just talking generally. I asked him what the summer held in store for us and he said it looked like a busy summer. He said it was his idea when the legislation now pending was passed to organize some sort of interdepartmental conference. This would be made up of those in charge of the big new public works and other projects authorized by legislation already passed or pending, together with the Secretaries of Labor, Agriculture, Commerce, and Interior. My purpose was to feel him out on my prospects of getting away for a rather extended trip into the West this summer, but the situation doesn't look any too encouraging. He said that he was hopeful now that Congress might wind up its work on Saturday. He is becoming frankly nervous about Congress staying on much longer. The situation on the Hill is really dangerous, although so far he has kept Congress within reasonable bounds. With the pension and other controversial legislation still pending, he doesn't know what might happen at any time. He is looking forward to getting away on his yacht for a short trip. I told him that I was nervous about these yacht trips and pointed out that he was no longer a free agent. He threw his hands in the air and laughingly said: "But I love it!" Then he went on to explain that it was the only way he could rest. I reminded him again how tremendously important he was to the country and then he told me that he had a destroyer and a tender in close attendance. I said that eased me somewhat because my fear had been that he was so lacking in any regard for his own personal safety that he might take undue risks.

Thursday, June 8, 1933

Senator Thompson, the new Senator from Nebraska, Congressman Howard, and several other representatives from the same state, called on me en masse to urge me to prevent the closing of the Indian Boarding School at Genoa, Nebraska. They made a long and earnest plea, based largely on the facts that the Indian children are tubercular and otherwise badly diseased, are insufficiently clothed and undernourished. It was urged that they would not get along happily with the white children. I told them that I would consider the matter carefully and do the best I could, but that we were confronted with the necessity of a drastic reduction in our expenditures in the Indian Bureau, as elsewhere. I pointed out that we had exploited the Indians from the beginning; that we had taken from them their lands; that we had robbed them right and left; that the diseases they were suffering from were due in a large measure to contacts with the whites and were not unrelated to undernourishment. I said that Congress wouldn't give us money for things needed to be done for the Indians; that Congress had assisted in despoiling them and that the man who was largely responsible for Indian appropriations in the House of Representatives for many years had gone publicly on record to the effect that eleven cents a day was enough to feed an Indian child. I added that this same man, after he had been defeated for Congress, crowded himself into this Department at a fine big salary, and that it gave me great joy, as one of my first official acts after I came to Washington, to fire him.

I talked to both Secretary of Commerce Roper and Postmaster General Farley over the telephone this afternoon, telling them that, in my judgment, the President would be making a terrible mistake if he should appoint General Hugh S. Johnson to have charge of the administration of the Industries Control section of the Public Works-Industrial Control Bill. There was a statement in this morning's paper to the effect that he had already selected Walter C. Teagle, president of the Standard Oil Company of New Jersey, Gerard Swope, president of the General Electric Company, and Henry Ford to assist him in his job of reorganizing and rehabilitating industry. I have felt, and I am more strongly every day of the opinion, that the selection of Johnson may be a major mistake, if not a fatal one. As an old Army man he is especially dictatorial and absolutely beyond control. Before the bill had passed Congress, let alone before he had been given any official position in connection with administration under the bill, he had been making his plans, selecting his personnel, and proceeding in what seems to me to be an altogether highhanded manner.

Tuesday, June 13, 1933

Friday was a terribly hot day—so hot that some of the departments, including this one, sent out orders that they would close at two o'clock. Meantime we worked just as hard as ever.

At ten o'clock I attended a meeting of the National Forest Reservation Commission, and we authorized the purchase of a number of parcels of land in several states aggregating something under $1 million. This land is being bought out of the fund of $20 million set aside by the President out of the money appropriated under the Civilian Conservation Corps Act. We are trying to round out some of the national forests already in existence, but in two instances we bought lands in designated national forests in which, however, no land has been acquired to date.

At two o'clock, when the temperature was reported to be 100 degrees, I went to Cabinet meeting. The cool air in the White House offices was very grateful to me. When we were about halfway through Cabinet meeting, the question was raised by the President of an Executive Order which he was preparing to send to Congress that afternoon, making certain transfers between the departments. I told him that I had understood that there was to be none except intradepartmental changes during this session of Congress. I raised the point at once about any possible transfers as between this Department and that of Agriculture. The Attorney General tried to get a copy of the order from his office but it was late in coming. I told the President that I was vitally interested in the whole subject matter, but that I was planning to take the 4:05 train to Chicago, where I had two important engagements on Saturday. It looked for a while as if I would have to ask the Secretary of Commerce to supply me with an airplane to go to Chicago, especially when I found that I couldn't get a seat in the regular airplane that leaves late in the afternoon. The President finally assured me that no advantage would be taken of my going and no changes made that weren't agreed upon. Thereupon I excused myself about twenty minutes to four and took the train for Chicago.

Friday, June 16, 1933

The Cabinet meeting was short and devoted almost exclusively to a consideration of the administrative setup under the two titles to the Industrial Recovery Act which the President has just signed. The President has decided to appoint General Hugh Johnson as Administrator under Title I, which is the industrial recovery end of the act, but he is to have nothing to do with the public works end of the bill, although Johnson, in his impetuous, highhanded way, has already set up a practically complete organization to administer public works, apparently on the theory that he would have control of this also. The President has appointed a committee under the Chairmanship of the Secretary of Commerce to have charge of the Industries Recovery part of the act. On this committee, in addition to General Johnson, are the Attorney General and the Secretaries of Labor, Agriculture, Commerce, and Interior. The Chairman of the Federal Trade Commission is also a member. The President indicated that no final decisions in important matters were to be made without consultation with him and apparently he has made it clear to General Johnson that he was to work in co-operation with his committee.

[The National Industrial Recovery Act became law on June 16, 1933. It set up "codes" of fair dealing for industries. The blue eagle was its symbol. The codes dealt with maximum hours and minimum wages, abolished sweat-shop working conditions and child labor in many industries, gave labor the right to bargain through representatives of its own choosing, and required businessmen to open their books to Government inspection.

[In two years there were 750 NRA code authorities in operation. They fixed minimum wages at a base varying from $12 to $15 a week. More than half the codes provided for uniform prices, and many of them limited production and assigned quotas to individual producers. On May 27, 1935, in the Schechter case, the Supreme Court unanimously ruled the act to be unconstitutional.—ED.]

With reference to the public works job, he appointed Colonel Donald H. Sawyer as temporary administrator, with a similar committee headed by myself as chairman. This committee will have Colonel Sawyer on it, and the Secretaries of War, Labor, Commerce, and Agriculture, together with Assistant Secretary of the Treasury Robert, who is in charge of the Federal buildings. The President made it clear that he did not want any overlapping as between General Johnson's setup and that for public works. He told me that he hoped we could find space in the Interior Building for Colonel Sawyer and his organization because he didn't want that office to be in the Commerce Building where General Johnson will be.

At the conclusion of the Cabinet meeting, the President called in General Johnson and proceeded to dictate the necessary Executive Orders. It was clear that General Johnson was taken quite aback, since he had been counting upon running both shows and had made commitments to many people. I was told afterward that he said to somebody that he might resign, but apparently he is going on with the work.

I went to the White House at nine o'clock tonight to consider with Colonel Howe, Postmaster General Farley, and Assistant Postmaster General O'Mahoney the men to be appointed as Public Works Administrators in the different states. We canvassed the situation rather hurriedly, state by state, and made up a tentative list of men, except for a few states. It was our understanding that this list was to be checked carefully and added to. We all agreed that it was absolutely necessary, to prevent a major scandal, to put only high-class men in these positions and so safeguard the work done as to prevent any graft or anything of an improper nature. Our conference at the White House lasted until eleven forty-five.

An amusing thing happened today. I received from Mrs. Roosevelt the following letter:

My dear Secretary:

My husband said that I might write and tell you that Captain Haring, who has been in charge of details at the White House, has been entirely satisfactory. He seems to be doing an economical job. I do not know, of course, what you will feel are the necessary changes to make in personnel, but I simply want you to know that it would be acceptable to us should you decide to retain him.

Very sincerely yours,

(signed) ELEANOR ROOSEVELT

The explanation of this letter is that the administration of the public buildings, except post office buildings and those devoted to a special purpose, have been brought into this Department. This charges us with the responsibility for administering the White House, among other buildings. All of the Capital parks and the national cemeteries have also been brought into the Department.

I wrote to Mrs. Roosevelt to assure her that I would make no change in the White House staff without first consulting her, and stating also that any expression of desire for changes on her part would be sympathetically received.

Saturday, June 17, 1933

Colonel Sawyer, the temporary Administrator of Public Works, came in to see me early this morning, and we went over his situation in a preliminary way. I am arranging for space for him in the Interior Building and he will come in and occupy that space on Monday. He showed every indication of a desire to work in close co-operation and harmony with this Department, and I don't think I will have much difficulty in working with him. When I explained the situation as the President had stated it yesterday with reference to possible connection with General Johnson, he seemed very much relieved. I told him I didn't see why he should consult General Johnson at all, and he said he would not do so. From my office he went over to talk to Colonel Howe. Howe called me later on the telephone to tell me that both he and Colonel McIntyre had made it clear to Colonel Sawyer that I was the real head of the public works program and that he was to refer all matters to me. I don't understand that this is the situation, or at any rate it is an exaggerated statement of the situation. I believe the President has not yet made up his mind as to what he wants as a final setup for public works, and may keep Sawyer on or he may substitute for him, or he may substitute for me as chairman of the commission.

Later I went to the White House offices to confer with Howe and McIntyre. I also had a talk with Assistant Secretary of the Treasury

Robert, who has prepared a very comprehensive and, as it seems to me, a highly intelligent plan of organization for public works. While at the White House I was informed of how detailed an organization General Johnson had already authorized for public works in advance of the passage of the bill, or the appointment of anyone to administer public works. He had a complete office personnel selected to occupy space in the Commerce Building. There was a complete list of state administrators with salary schedules attached and a form telegram of several hundred words in extent ready to have the names of the administrators filled in and the telegrams put on the wire as soon as the President authorized them to go ahead. It may be embarrassing now to disregard some people already selected by General Johnson but there seems to be no other recourse open to us.

Wednesday, June 21, 1933

At two o'clock we had a meeting of the Board of Public Works, which lasted through three hot and intensive hours. The subcommittee appointed at our last meeting to draft and submit a statement of general principles brought in what seemed to me to be a very disappointing report. It was long and verbose, discursive and too detailed. I asked the subcommittee to try again and see whether it wouldn't bring in a short declaration of general principles at another meeting to be held tomorrow afternoon.

We spent a great deal of time working over a set of rules and regulations to be promulgated and followed by the Bureau of Public Roads in the work that it is to do under the public works program. This also had to be referred back to the subcommittee. Then we discussed at some length our organization, without taking final action, although as to this we are pretty close to a consensus of opinion. Following this, Colonel Sawyer was authorized, subject to my approval where I am not already satisfied, to engage certain persons as part of his personnel.

I went over to the White House offices to see Colonel McIntyre this morning. I especially wanted to discuss with him the matter of a publicity man for public works. I suggested to him Michael Straus, whom I have known for several years as a Chicago newspaperman, and who is here now representing the Universal News Service. Straus is an able newspaperman, is keen and incorruptible. He and his wife, Nancy Straus, the daughter of the James M.

Porters, of Winnetka, are old friends of ours. After checking up on Straus, McIntyre gave him his cordial approval and I have arranged to interview Straus tomorrow.

Wednesday, June 21, 1933

After the Board of Public Works had adjourned, and before I even had time to begin signing the huge stack of mail that was waiting for me on my desk, a call came from the White House and I had to suspend operations here. We had a meeting in Colonel McIntyre's office, at which were present Senator Byrnes, of South Carolina, Jim Farley, Assistant Secretary of the Treasury Robert, and myself. We spent an hour or more discussing the co-ordination of the new Federal activities that have been set up under recent legislation and the method of selecting state administrators under the Public Works program. It was agreed that I was to call a meeting of the chairmen of the various committees that are active in the administration of these new activities to see whether we can agree upon a plan of co-ordination so that there will be some method and understanding between these various activities. It was also agreed that all names for state administrators under the public works, and advisory committees, are to come to me, I to have full power to make recommendations to the President in order of my preference. We are not only anxious to keep these appointments outside of partisan politics, but we want to avoid the appearance of politics. Considering my political history, I am regarded as the appropriate channel through which to have the suggestions flow to the President.

I got home late for dinner and then returned to the office to sign my mail and do some dictating that I was not able to do earlier in the day.

Tuesday, June 27, 1933

Congressman Howard, of Nebraska, was in. He wants to resign from Congress and go into the Indian Bureau, in spite of the fact that he is unbeatable in his own district and has been in Congress for a good many years. He is a Quaker and from boyhood has been intensely interested in the Indian question. If we can work out a salary that will be mutually satisfactory, we will probably take him on. I spoke to the President about this some time ago.

Senator Wagner came in to talk about the administration of the

Public Works Bill. He sees the danger and the pitfalls just as I do. Just another day of hard, unremitting grind.

Monday, July 3, 1933

I called at the Department of Agriculture at ten o'clock to pick up Secretary Wallace and with him went to Annapolis, where the members of the Cabinet in Washington today were asked to join the President on the *Indianapolis*. When we got to Annapolis, the water was so rough that we were held at the Academy for an hour and a half. We were shown over the Academy, which was very interesting. The officers were quite courteous.

We took another look at the water about half past twelve and with my proneness to seasickness, I definitely decided that I would not go. Secretary Roper and Attorney General Cummings were not any too anxious to go either, but Secretaries Wallace, Dern, and Swanson were prepared to venture so finally we all went.

It was a very rough trip but for a wonder I wasn't seasick. We were on one of the old submarine chasers left over from the world war. It was a fast, light boat, about 125 feet long, and we were slithered around the deck two or three times until our settee was tied down with ropes which prevented us from sliding all over the place. The *Indianapolis* is one of the newest cruisers in the Navy and is beautifully built and equipped. It is a flagship and President Roosevelt was occupying the admiral's quarters. We lunched there with him and the boat was just exactly as steady as dry land. Of course we were anchored but the water was quite rough, in spite of which we felt no motion.

Those that lunched, besides the President and the six members of the Cabinet, including myself, already mentioned, were Assistant Secretary of the Navy Roosevelt, Colonels Howe and McIntyre, two of the President's secretaries, his naval aide, Walter N. Bernou, and another naval officer.

After luncheon all who were not members of the Cabinet retired, except Colonel Howe, and we discussed the international situation for two hours or more. The President has been in constant touch by wireless with the American delegation in London on the Economic Conference. In effect, he has been directing this conference so far as the American policies are concerned, first, from the *Amberjack II*, and then from the *Indianapolis*. He read us dispatches that had been coming in from Secretary of State Hull and

Assistant Secretary of State Moley, and his own replies. It seemed to all of us that he had been handling the matter with admirable skill and foresight. He has established a strictly American position which he has been adhering to firmly, in spite of all the blandishments and threats from the European countries.

The water was rougher than ever coming back. At one stage two or three people were being slithered around the deck, but none of us was hurt. The remarkable thing is that I went out and back without being seasick. This is the first time in my experience that I spent as much time as that on rough water when I wasn't sick as a dog.

Wednesday, July 5, 1933

Secretary Roper and I had lunch with the President in his office at one o'clock today and we spent more than two hours with him discussing, first, the Industrial Recovery Administration, and, second, the public works program. A question came up about the retention of Colonel Sawyer as Administrator for Public Works and it was the consensus of opinion that his lack of administrative ability makes it impossible to continue him. As the Administrator for Public Works, Secretary Roper suggested my own appointment after we had discussed one or two others, and the President fell in with the idea quite readily. Naturally I said nothing until it seemed that the President's mind was coming to that conclusion, when I suggested that if he did give me this added responsibility, I hoped he would give me the same generous support with respect to appointments that he has given me as Secretary of the Interior. He replied at once that of course he would.

During our talk I spoke highly of Colonel Waite as a possible Chief Engineer if I should be made Administrator. We spent a good deal of time discussing state organizations and we soon came to the conclusion not to go ahead with the plan to appoint an administrator in every state. There are so many difficulties in the way of this that we gave up this idea and instead agreed on a plan of dividing the country into regions, probably adopting the regional organization of the Federal Reserve System, appointing an administrator for each region with a committee of three for each state. This latter committee would be an advisory committee, serving without pay, and would have associated with it an engineer. All of the personnel, the Regional Administrator, the State Advisory

Committees, and the engineers, would be appointed by the President.

Saturday, July 8, 1933

I got to my office this morning at nine o'clock and found my desk piled high with letters to sign, letters to answer, and memoranda from various bureaus waiting for attention.

I found that an appointment had been made for me to see the President, with Assistant Secretary of the Treasury Robert, at a quarter before ten. We discussed public works and at the conclusion of our talk he asked me to stop in the outside office and arrange for the drafting of an Executive Order which would make me Administrator of Public Works.

While I was at the White House, Colonel Howe asked me to stop at his office. While there he endorsed over to me a check for $900, representing compensation for the radio talk I gave as a substitute for him last Sunday evening. This talk was about nine minutes in length, so that the compensation was at the rate of $100 a minute, which, without being overmodest, I may say I regard as more than ample.

I went to Mrs. Eleanor Patterson's home, Dower House, out in Maryland for dinner tonight. I took out with me in my car Mr. and Mrs. Essary, Miss Hawes, daughter of former Senator Hawes, of Missouri, and a returned Commerce Department attaché from Brussels, whose name, as usual, has escaped me.

Monday, July 10, 1933

Yesterday morning (Sunday) I came to the office and dictated pretty steadily until about noon. In the afternoon I went for a drive and on my return I found that the White House had been trying to reach me. I hurried over there for a hastily called conference at which were present the Secretary of Commerce, the Director of the Budget, Assistant to the Secretary of Labor Battle, Colonel Howe, and General Johnson. General Johnson presented the code agreed upon for the textile industry which the President read aloud, and which was approved with practically no change. I got back home for a seven thirty dinner.

I had a number of conferences today on public works and other matters. T. Arnold Hill was in to urge the appointment of some

Negroes to Federal offices in the Virgin Islands, and Drew Pearson was in, in the interest of the retention of his father as Governor of the Virgin Islands.

At half past two I attended a meeting of the Special Industrial Recovery Board in the Department of Commerce, and two hours later I was posing before cameras and giving what seemed, to me at any rate, to be a very poor extemporaneous, but fortunately brief, talk on public works for the four newsreel services in one of the courts of this building.

Tuesday, July 11, 1933

I had an appointment with the President at nine thirty this morning. I was shown into his bedroom just as his breakfast tray was being brought out. He was sitting up in bed and received me with his usual charm. His bedroom is just to the right of the Oval Room on the second floor which he makes his White House office. I noticed that he had a telephone right at hand and in a nearby corner stood the apparatus that he has to wear to support his crippled legs. Near his bed stood his wheel chair.

He started to tell me a story about Wilson refusing to permit the American fleet to be brought back from Guatanamo Bay in order to be put in shape for the world war that seemed to be inevitable, and just as he was about concluding this narrative, the Director of the Budget appeared. Then Colonel Howe came in and later Miss LeHand. After a short talk, the President asked the other three to excuse him, as he wanted to discuss some questions with me, but before the Director of the Budget got out, there was quite some talk between him and the President about the international monetary situation. Douglas said that, in his opinion, there was a considerable flight of capital from this country.

After all the others had gone, the President and I discussed public works. I think that we see the situation eye to eye. I told him I would like to appoint Colonel Waite as Deputy Administrator, and he agreed to this. We went over a number of plans and projects in a general way and I also took occasion to discuss several departmental matters with him, among them the situation with reference to the Indian schools. The Bureau of Indian Affairs has been holding up its plans to modify seriously its boarding school policy. The President had asked Mr. Collier to do this at the instance of Senator

McNary. The President understood the situation and told me to write to Senator McNary explaining that it was necessary to go ahead with our program.

I left the White House about a quarter to eleven and hurried back to the Department, where we had a meeting of the Special Board for Public Works. A resolution was adopted creating the office of Deputy Administrator, and Colonel Waite was elected to that office, with a salary of $10,000 net a year. In the meantime, Postmaster General Farley had called me to ask about these appointments.

The board was in session until a quarter of two. We went over a number of projects that had been certified to us with approval by a subcommittee of the board which has been working on the matter for the last week or ten days. Some items were approved and others were deferred for further consideration. The principle we worked on was to give out to the country at this time only such projects as could be justified as legitimate public works projects.

Wednesday, July 12, 1933

I had a long line of callers today, the great majority of them looking for jobs or bringing in proposals for public works.

Raymond Robins called me on the telephone. This is the first time I have heard his voice since many months before his strange disappearance last fall. He has just returned from Russia and wants an opportunity to tell me all about it. God knows when I am going to get time to listen to a long recital on Russia, although I am interested.

At one o'clock, by appointment, I lunched with the President. I found Dr. Arthur Morgan, of the Tennessee Valley Authority, discussing the subsistence farm program. Dr. Morgan was presenting a complete plan to the President, including personnel, and he was somewhat taken aback when the President told him that this would be in my Department. Apparently Dr. Morgan has discussed his plan with nearly everyone except myself.

After lunch the President went over in detail the public works projects which the Special Board for Public Works agreed upon at its meeting yesterday. He approved practically everything, but in many instances cut down the total amounts to be spent for certain classifications. He also approved in principle a small number of municipal projects, most of them for water works but a few for sewers. He authorized me to make public the projects agreed upon. I got back to the office shortly after three o'clock and proceeded at once with a meeting of the Special Board for Public Works. I reported the result of my talk with the President and we discussed a number of other matters. We were in session for all of two hours.

When I got to my desk it almost took all my nerve. It was literally piled high with unopened letters that had come in during the day and stacks of other letters waiting for my signature. I worked busily until a quarter after six, went home for dinner, and was back in less than an hour. It is now nearly ten o'clock and while I have signed all the mail that was waiting for my signature, I still have a good deal of dictating to do if I am to go to bed with a clear conscience and find a reasonably clear desk awaiting me in the morning.

Thursday, July 13, 1933

Raymond Robins came in to see me about noon. This is the first time I have met him face to face since his disappearance last fall. I was terribly shocked at his appearance and his manner. There isn't any doubt that he is a thoroughly licked man. He looked much older, and while he tried to talk with his old-time vigor, it was easy to see that he was putting on a lot of pressure. The old laugh and the old fire were entirely missing. In his customary manner he started to make a speech to me about Russia, but I was more interested in the man than in the subject. After he had been here a while, Gifford Pinchot came in and I called him in to the small private office where I had Raymond. It was the first time Gifford had seen him. Raymond greeted Gifford and shortly he went. Gifford had exactly the same feeling about him that I had—that he was a broken man and that he could not come back. It has lain heavy on my heart ever since he was here. He said that he would be here for a couple of days yet and he indicated that he would like a chance to talk with me at greater length about Russia. But where in the world can I get the time? Yet if I don't see him again, he will feel hurt.

We had a meeting of the Special Board for Public Works at two o'clock, and while we got over a good deal of ground, I believe we could accomplish much more if we didn't have so many sitting around the table when we are discussing matters more or less of detail.

There is a man by the name of Malmin who was Judge of the Virgin Islands during the Wilson administration. He wants to be Governor, and before I came to Washington, called at my office in Chicago to tell me that he was going to be the next Governor. I met him in the White House yesterday trying to see the President but he didn't get in to see the President. He told me then he wanted to talk to me, and I advised him to make an appointment through my secretary. Such an appointment was made, but I told Fred Marx that I really didn't want to waste any time on him, so he didn't get in to see me this morning. He did talk to Harry Slattery.

It seems that he has been in touch with a drunken bum of a lawyer in Chicago, who is trying to blackmail me in connection with the Saunders estate which I handled, and which I closed some two or three years ago. Everything was in regular and in perfect order, but just after the announcement of my appointment to the Cabinet, this lawyer appeared in my office with a petition which he threatened to file in the probate court, making all sorts of charges against me, the charges involving fraud, etc. At that time I called up the State's attorney and asked him to investigate. I told the State's attorney that if I had committed a crime I ought to be indicted and it would be only fair to the President to indict me before I came to Washington to go into the Cabinet. He sent for the lawyer who couldn't make good on any of the charges. Since then I have heard nothing about it until today.

Malmin brought these papers to my office. He was angry when he couldn't get in to see me and he told Slattery, in effect, that I could make him Lieutenant Governor of the Virgin Islands and that if I didn't, the Bar Association of Chicago would be presented with a petition to disbar me and a statement would go to the newspapers in connection with the Saunders estate. We called in Glavis, and after talking it over, we decided to have Malmin come in as he had left word that he was going back to Chicago at eight o'clock and had to see me before then. The reason I had him sent for was because I had hoped he would say something that would give me a good case of attempted blackmail against him. Accordingly, I had arranged for Glavis and Mr. Mack, my stenographer, to stand just inside the door leading into the small private office to listen to what Malmin had to say and take it down in shorthand. Malmin came in but he was all friendliness. I talked to him for some twenty minutes to half an hour and tried to get him to threaten me, but without success. He did tell me that he had the papers and that the lawyer was thinking of filing them. He told me that he could prevent it and that he was going to prevent it. I not only gave him a chance to ask me for some consideration in the way of a political favor for holding back, but in the end, in my desperation, I asked him blankly what he expected me to do if he did have the lawyer drop the matter. He told me that he wouldn't do anything: that the lawyer would follow his advice and that I could be assured that nothing would come of it. I told him that I didn't care what the lawyer did; that he could go and jump in the lake so far as I was concerned. And I made no promises to Malmin. He begged me to arrange for an appointment for him with the President, but I told him that appointments had to be made through Colonel McIntyre and that I couldn't make an appointment for him.

Friday, July 14, 1933

The Cabinet had a meeting today for the first time since the President went on his two weeks' vacation the latter part of June. He signed an Executive Order giving me the power to issue regulations to carry out the Executive Order he issued two or three days ago, at my instance, to stop the carrying into interstate or foreign commerce of any petroleum, or the products thereof, produced in violation of the law of the state of their origin. Under the Executive Order I am given broad powers not only to issue regulations but to enforce these regulations. The Solicitor of the Department is at work on a set of regulations.

I worked at the office tonight until ten o'clock clearing up correspondence and dictating a speech on public works to give over the radio Tuesday night.

Sunday, July 16, 1933

At eight o'clock this morning I met General Johnson at the naval airport at Anacostia where we boarded a Navy hydroplane to go down the bay to the President's boat, the *Sequoia*. The weather was cloudy and heavy with a low ceiling, so that, generally speaking, we flew at about 500 feet. We were flying so low that the pilot didn't want to run the risk of going over the land, so we kept pretty close to the river where we could come down easily, if necessary. It took us fifty minutes to reach the *Sequoia*. We landed nearby and a rowboat was sent for us.

The President had eaten something Saturday that didn't agree with him, so we didn't see him until one o'clock, when he appeared for dinner. After dinner he went to lie down again, but late in the afternoon he was out on deck. At two o'clock we weighed anchor and started up the Pawtuxent River, which is said to be the shortest and deepest river in the world. At the point where it flows into Chesapeake Bay it is 60 feet deep and for miles up the river it is very deep, although naturally it becomes somewhat more shallow.

It was a beautiful ride up the river. The day was warm without being too hot and there was enough breeze to keep away the mosquitoes, and the scenery was certainly worth looking at. We dropped Colonel Howe at Benedict and went on up as far as we could. We had supper on our way down and all of us got off at Benedict where cars met us and brought us back to Washington.

In the party besides those already mentioned were Under Secretary of Agriculture Tugwell, Captain Bernou, the President's naval aide, and his personal secretary, Miss Le Hand. General Johnson and I had a chance to discuss matters with him somewhat briefly, General Johnson on the Industrial Recovery Control Administration, and I on Public Works. He approved some more of our public works projects, but he sent back to me for further study all items covering flood control and rivers and harbors improvements.

He also authorized me, at my request, to take steps to proceed against the cattlemen in Arizona and New Mexico who have had many, many acres of the public domain fenced in for long terms of years with the sanction of the preceding Republican administrations.

I was home shortly after nine o'clock.

Monday, July 17, 1933

We had a meeting of the Special Board for Public Works at eleven o'clock this morning. It was heavy going. There are one or two men on the board, especially Assistant Secretary of the Treasury Robert, who are plainly holding back and trying to sabotage. He is disappointed because he hoped the President would make him Administrator of Public Works, instead of which he named me. Robert had carried on an active campaign for this appointment, whereas I didn't lift a hand and didn't expect to be appointed. Another member of the board who is a terrible burden for us to carry is the Solicitor General. He is one of the dumbest persons I know. He isn't a member of the board in his own right but is the representative of the Attorney General, who seldom comes himself. He can smell Federal pork as far off as anyone I ever knew. He becomes very impatient at any suggestion by Director of the Budget Douglas that we ought to proceed carefully in allocating money for projects. My course is a middle one between the two. I think we ought to go ahead on the theory that Congress expected us to spend this money for public works, but I also believe that every project approved should be a sane one, both from the economic and the social point of view. Robert has put it up to us either to approve a big program of public buildings or to vote against it altogether. I stated that he had no right to bring a proposition in on a take-it-or-leave-it basis; that we ought to consider each project strictly on its merits. The majority of the board agreed with me, and Director of the Budget Douglas is selecting a number of building projects which he believes can properly be approved.

I reported back my talk with the President yesterday on the public works program that I had submitted to him. Of course, everything the President wants is accepted without demur.

Tuesday, July 18, 1933

I am trying hard to complete the setting up of our Public Works organization. It has been a slow process because Farley has wanted to visé all the names. Then he goes out of town with his assistant who is representing him in the Public Works organization, with the result that not a wheel can move until one of them comes back. I have no complaint to make about Farley because in the end I have, as a general thing, been able to appoint the people I have especially wanted. But it requires tact and patience with consequent delay.

Thursday, July 20, 1933

Secretary of War Dern is getting all het up because I told the newspaper correspondents the other day, in answer to an inquiry, that he had withdrawn the proposal submitted by his Department for housing, reconditioning, ammunition making, motorization of the artillery, etc., etc., under the public works act. When the question was asked me, I naturally answered it, and I answered it truthfully. He did withdraw it at one of our meetings, but, as I said to the newspapermen, his plan was to submit it again at a later date. At least I so understood and so stated. To my surprise he promptly sent out a statement to the newspapermen explaining that he had withdrawn it temporarily because he thought the temper of the Special Board for Public Works was antagonistic, and that we would refuse his request. As a matter of fact, what happened at the meeting was this: I asked him if he had anything to present and he presented a big batch for rivers and harbors. After a very brief discussion we adopted that proposal without a dissenting vote. I then asked him whether he had any other proposals to make and he promptly replied that the other one that he had in his hand he would withdraw. He was, of course, permitted to do so. It was on these facts that he got out a statement containing the following language: "I was not satisfied with the action that I anticipated was to be taken by the board and, therefore, asked that further consideration be dropped until a subsequent meeting."

Then he went on with an interview of considerable size, which was at least an implied criticism of the Public Works Board. At the newspaper conference yesterday the correspondents again asked me about this matter and I repeated what I had already said—that he had withdrawn this particular proposal but that my understanding was he would submit it at a later meeting. Today I get a long and indignant telegram from him from Des Moines, Iowa, taking me to task for saying that he had withdrawn the Army public works request.

Some of the newspapers have made out of this a Cabinet breach of major proportions. One or two have said that the President would have to intervene to settle the controversy. On the other hand, some of the other newspapers have poked more or less fun at Dern, intimating that the Chief of Staff, General MacArthur, was at the bottom of the whole thing. One well-known correspondent over his own signature this morning even hinted that Dern didn't know what the whole thing was about.

Friday, July 21, 1933

I had an appointment with the President at noon today. He was still in bed, and for forty minutes I went over public works matters. He brought up the matter of Secretary of War Dern by telling me that Dern had allowed himself to be put in an unfortunate position by the Chief of Staff, General MacArthur. I didn't go into the Dern matter except to say that I thought his interview given to the papers was unfortunate and that it wasn't based upon the record. The President went on to tell me how he had had to sit down on General MacArthur pretty hard himself on one occasion, and he expressed the opinion that MacArthur is running the War Department.

The Cabinet meeting was postponed until three o'clock because of the President's luncheon engagement with the Crown Prince of Ethiopia. We discussed routine matters. The President asked me to wait until after the press conference because Assistant Secretary of War Woodring had put up a matter to him that he wanted to discuss with me, so after the press conference, the three of us met in his office. Woodring wanted him to sign an Executive Order allocating $13 million to the War Department out of the public works fund in order to keep the munitions factories going. He said the factories could not open on Monday unless this allocation was made. I objected on the ground that it would set a bad precedent if the President, without consideration by the Board of Public Works, or recommendation from it, should assign a sum to any Department by Executive Order. I said that while it might be a hardship for the men employed in the munitions factories to be laid off for a week or two, they wouldn't be in as bad case as people who had been unemployed for two years or more. I also said that if this matter had not been passed upon by the Board and submitted to the President, the fault lay with the War Department and not with the Special Board for Public Works. The President felt that he should not sign the Executive Order, but he did agree, after asking me whether it would be all right so far as I was concerned, that the War Department should give out a statement that $6 million had been assured for the continuing of the munitions factories and that they would operate as usual on Monday.

Wednesday, July 26, 1933

I had an appointment with the President today at half past twelve. In his outside office I met a delegation of Senators, headed by King, of Utah. This delegation had wanted to see me in the morning but I was too busy to see them. When I saw them in the President's office, they insisted on my going in with them, their appointment being just ahead of mine, and when we got in, Senator King explained to the President that I refused to see them so they had called on him and had brought me along in. They were interested in a number of reclamation projects which they discussed with the President.

I then took up a number of matters with him. He is anxious to go ahead as soon as possible on some of the big Federal projects, and I promised to bring them before the meeting of the Public Works Board tomorrow.

I got back to the office just before two o'clock, at which time I was due to preside over a meeting called to discuss the subsistence farm program which is provided for in the Industrial Recovery Act, and administration of which the President has delegated to me. There were all of fifty people at the conference and nothing much happened except a lot of talk. However, those who had something on their chests had an opportunity to get it off to their own satisfaction. At five o'clock I was back at the White House again in the Oval Room on the second floor where, after we had had tea, the President discussed several matters, but principally the subsistence farm program, with Dr. Morgan, Secretary of Agriculture Wallace, and Harry L. Hopkins, Administrator of the Federal Emergency Relief Administration.

Dr. Morgan is the Chairman of the Board in charge of the Tennessee Valley Authority. He seems to me to be somewhat of a busybody. Apparently he hasn't enough of a job to keep him busy so he keeps butting in on this subsistence farm matter, and instead of coming to me on that project, he always goes to the President. He pressed me very hard today for a declaration of policy as it affected the Tennessee Valley, but I finally told him as we were leaving the White House that I was going to take time to consider matters and not be rushed off my feet. I don't get an increasingly good impression of him as I see more of him, although he has come to Government service with a fine reputation as an engineer. Prior to this job he was president of Antioch College.

We were held at the White House until five minutes to seven. Then I hurried home and after dinner came back to the office, where I signed letters busily until ten o'clock. I succeeded in clearing my desk, which was one awful sight.

Thursday, July 27, 1933

There was a meeting of the Special Board for Public Works at two o'clock and several of the members were once more highly conversational. I told them at the outset that the President wanted us to pass on two or three of the big Federal projects. The first one was the Coulee Dam on the Columbia River, in the State of Washington. This is a power proposition. Power can be made there more cheaply than any place else in the United States and it is a self-liquidating proposition. With these facts and the added one that the President wanted it done, I put an end to the discussion indulged in by Assistant Secretary of the Treasury Robert, Assistant Secretary of Labor Battle, and, of course, the Solicitor General, ably assisted at times by Assistant Secretary of Commerce Dickinson. In the end we passed it, but there was no disposition to pass anything else, in spite of the President's wishes expressed through myself.

After Robert had spent a good deal of time enlarging upon his responsibility as a member of the Board, I finally remarked that the Board didn't have any legal authority. The law gives all the authority to the President with power to delegate and he has delegated the authority to me. The board is nothing but an advisory body and I am beginning to wish that it had never been created. It takes four or five hours of valuable time every week doing something that the engineer, the attorney for the Board, and myself could dispose of in half an hour.

I had asked Chief of Staff MacArthur to come in on some Army projects. He had presented a very large list running into the hundreds of millions, out of which the President allowed him $6 million for coast defenses in the Canal Zone and Hawaii, in addition to $6 million previously allowed for ammunition. MacArthur is the type of man who thinks that when he gets to heaven, God will step down from the great white throne and bow him into His vacated seat, and it gave me a great kick to have him in and break the news to him. While he was here though, two or three of the members foolishly asked him some questions which gave him a chance to deliver a lecture on the subject of the necessity for the little old peanut Army posts that we have scattered around the country.

Friday, July 28, 1933

It was a hilarious Cabinet meeting today, although it wasn't intended to be. The fun all centered around General Hugh S. Johnson, Administrator of the Federal Industrial Control Board. General Johnson is a very dogmatic, active, forceful character, and he is expected to work more or less in co-operation with Secretary of Commerce Roper. Roper doesn't get along very well with him and doesn't like him any too well, but Roper is a consummate politician, never raises his voice, talks quietly, and today he did more than this. His description of some of the episodes in which Johnson figured was such as to make all of us laugh until our sides shook. Then the President added his bit. He told how Johnson rushed into his office two or three days ago with his coat tails standing out behind him, as the President said, and laid three industrial codes on his desk for signature. He said in a hurried voice that they must all be signed at once in order to be taken back and promulgated. As the President was signing the last one, General Johnson looked at his watch and said he had just five minutes to catch an airplane, and dashed out as rapidly as he had dashed in to take an airplane for some place. As the President said, he took an airplane with the codes in his pocket and he hasn't been seen since.

The President signed an Executive Order for me today covering the military parks, monuments, and cemeteries which, under a prior Executive Order, were to come into this Department on August 10. He modified his previous order, with my entire consent, leaving the cemeteries now in use with the War Department, but transferring all of the parks, monuments, Gettysburg Cemetery, and the Lee House at Arlington to this Department. He also destroyed an Executive Order already signed which would have postponed for sixty days the carrying out of an order transferring here the Office of Public Buildings and Public Parks.

When I told him that the Special Board for Public Works had refused to approve the Upper Mississippi River Nine-foot Channel project and the Casper-Alcova project in Wyoming, he wrote directions to me in his own handwriting instructing me to put these projects through at the next meeting of the board. Later, at his regular press conference, he announced that these projects would be approved at the next meeting of the board. He also announced the Columbia River project as already having been approved, and he approved, without announcing, certain other public works projects desired by the Department of Agriculture, the Department of Commerce, and the Department of the Interior.

At the Cabinet meeting he told Secretary Roper to tell General

Johnson not to approve the oil code which is in process of being worked out until it had been submitted to me, and during the press conference when asked who would administer the oil code, he indicated that this Department would. He confirmed this positively after the press conference when he told me to tell General Johnson that he wanted Interior designated as the department to administer the oil code.

The President is going tonight to his farm at Hyde Park, New York, for two weeks.

Wednesday, August 2, 1933

About half past eleven this morning Governor Ely, of Massachusetts, called on the telephone. He proceeded to say that there was some administrative body in his state which had some sort of control over municipal finances, and he wanted me to say that no public works would be given to any municipality in Massachusetts without first being submitted to this board and getting its approval. I told him that our policy as announced was to consider every proposition on its merits and that if we adopted such a policy with respect to Massachusetts, it would embarrass us in other states. He became quite hardboiled and proceeded to lay down the law to me, and said that the municipalities were the creatures of the states; that they hadn't any right to Federal consideration except with the consent of the state. I could not agree with this view of the matter and said that since we had appointed the State Advisory Committee, we would have to work through our own committee. I pointed out that this was a Federal proposition and not a state proposition and that we could not give veto power to the state. He then went on to say that the Federal Government was a creature of the states, just as the municipalities were creatures of the state. I told him I couldn't subscribe to this theory; that we were spending Federal money and that we would have to take up the matters on their merits. He became pretty angry by this time and told me that he would take a public position against the Federal Government if I insisted in my opposition. I told him to go ahead. He then said that I hadn't shown any consideration to the governors. I told him that we had shown consideration to the governors, and called his attention again to the fact that this was a Federal law. I then added that I didn't like his tone, and he replied that he didn't like the position I had announced. I asked him if he had anything further to say. I don't know just what he said in reply to this, but at that point I hung up.

Thursday, August 3, 1933

We had a meeting of the Special Board for Public Works at two o'clock, but it was shorter than usual. I had a good deal of discussion with Robert about the Government building program. The President told me to tell Jim to make a new study of the buildings that had not yet been approved by the Public Works Board to see whether they could not be built at lower figures which would justify them. I find Robert a very difficult man to deal with. As I have set down before, he has been very much disgruntled ever since the President named me Administrator of Public Works instead of himself, and he has been constantly throwing sand into the machinery. He talks, and talks and talks, saying the same thing over and over again, but his talk is evasive and has no effect on me except to fill me with suspicion that he has no disposition to help out. I have taken the position that I am simply transmitting the message from the President and it is up to him to do what he pleases about it. I was compelled to tell him once this afternoon while we were talking after the board adjourned that it was not necessary to tell me the same thing twenty-five times in order for me to get it. He is one of those persons who goes on the theory that he can make a point, even if it is against all reason, by constant repetition.

Saturday, August 5, 1933

I had hoped to get away about noon today and go with Dr. Rex Tugwell, on his invitation, to spend the week end down in the Shenandoah National Park. However, there was so much work to do that I decided not to attempt it, and here I am at the close of day with my desk not yet cleared.

I had a conference with Colonel Waite this morning about public works organizations in the different states. He thinks we ought to have quite elaborate organizations consisting, in addition to the State Advisory Committees, of a lawyer, an engineer, an accountant, clerks, etc., in every state. His setup shows an estimate of sixteen such employees. I asked Mr. Burlew yesterday to give me a rough estimate of what this type of organization would cost us for the states alone and he told me that it would be not less than $2.5 million a year.

This looks very high, and I have been wanting to keep our overhead down to minimum. Accordingly, I asked Colonel Waite to come in. He seemed quite overwrought this morning and excited, so that we hadn't proceeded very far with the discussion before he was showing irritation and impatience. I kept my temper, but Colonel Waite and Mr. Burlew came to words, and, as it was reported to me afterward, Colonel Waite went down the hall exclaiming loudly that the trouble with the God-damned proposition was that there wasn't anyone around the place who knows a damn thing about what it was all about. I found that Louis Brownlow was still in Washington so I asked him to come over to see me, as I have great confidence in his judgment and experience. We reviewed the whole situation, and it is his opinion that it is necessary to set up some such organization as Colonel Waite proposes. I am fearful of the political pressure that will be brought to bear when it is discovered that there is some patronage that can be distributed in the states, but if we have to go ahead along this line to get the best and the speediest results, we will have to go ahead and I will do what I can to resist political pressure. As a result of my conference with Mr. Brownlow and a later one with Colonel Waite after he had calmed down, I decided that instead of selecting lawyers in the states, we would select lawyers for our staff here and let all the legal work come here, except where we have to send out men to get additional facts. I decided on this policy with respect to the lawyers because the selection of the lawyers would be the weakest link in the chain. There are always a lot of incompetent or crooked lawyers with strong political backing, and we can handle that situation better by building up our staff here than by finding a lawyer in each state. We ought to be able to find engineers, accountants, and that sort of employee who are relatively free from political influence.

Tuesday, August 8, 1933

At five o'clock I went to the home of Secretary of Commerce Roper for some watermelon and it was the best watermelon I have ever eaten—a special variety that is grown in only one county in South Carolina. Secretary of State Hull and Mrs. Hull were there, and Secretary Hull was quite frank in what he said about Dr. Moley at the London Economic Conference. Hull is a quiet-spoken man and he spoke quietly in talking about Moley, but it was easy to see that he was speaking with deep feeling and conviction.

According to Hull, the impression at London was that Moley was going to come over and solve all the international economic difficulties. For several days preceding Moley's arrival he was heralded in all the newspapers and the conference practically ceased to do business in expectation of his arrival. The British sent airplanes out to meet him and hundreds of newspapermen in London flocked down to Liverpool or wherever it was that Moley landed. He was escorted in great state to London with all the Premiers and dignitaries from the attending nations doing him reverence. He went at once to the American Embassy where honors were paid him and the statesmen visited him.

Two prior proposals for a temporary stabilization of the dollar had been rejected by President Roosevelt but notwithstanding this, Moley undertook, at the instance of the gold countries, to negotiate a third settlement. Secretary Hull said that Moley went into conference and proceeded to approve a stabilization plan at the American Embassy with representatives of the foreign nations without consulting with Hull and without knowledge on Hull's part of what he was doing. After it was approved he called Hull and told him that the agreement was ready and for him to come down and sign it as Secretary of State. Hull asked what agreement, and when Moley told him it was a stabilization agreement, Hull replied that that was within the jurisdiction of the Treasury Department and had been from the beginning. Hull refused to go and refused to sign. Hull was then told that on a certain morning Moley would be at 10 Downing Street with the assembled statesmen to receive the approval of President Roosevelt to the stabilization agreement. According to Mr. Hull, 10 Downing Street had a crowd in front of it such as hadn't been seen since the war. The visiting statesmen of the various nations entered at intervals and when they were all there and the stage well set, Moley appeared, the cynosure of all eyes, and entered the residence of the Prime Minister. Hull didn't go, but he said that he was later told what had happened by representatives of the British Government, who he said keep a careful record of every event in international negotiations.

Moley and the other statesmen of the world sat there expectantly while the clock ticked on. After two or three hours had passed, Moley began to have some feeling of uncertainty about the President accepting the agreement. About eleven-thirty the assembly adjourned until late that afternoon and they betook themselves to their respective quarters. Late that afternoon they all reassembled, but no Moley. Instead of attending the conference, Moley telephoned that he had had no approval from the President and that there was no reason for him to go down.

The President subsequently turned down the proposition hard. It was this cablegram that he read to those of us who met him on the *Indianapolis* on July 3. As the President read it to us, it was a cold and hard turndown. Of course, from that time on, Moley's balloon was punctured.

I had dinner with Henry Morgenthau after I left the Ropers', at Olney Inn, a delightful place at Olney, Maryland. Here I heard some more dirt about the London Conference. I was told that a certain prominent United States Senator who was a member of the commission didn't attend a single meeting; that he was drunk practically all of the time he was in London. I was told also that former Governor James Cox, of Ohio, was worse than useless as a member of the conference. Secretary Hull was the outstanding man of the delegation and he came out bigger at the end than anyone would have supposed was possible. Senator Couzens, of Michigan, after not so good a start, showed up very well indeed, but the general impression was that the commission was badly put together and didn't contain elements necessary to represent the United States with dignity or with effect.

Thursday, August 10, 1933

Last night I went to Drew Pearson's for a buffet supper. He lives only four or five short blocks from me in Georgetown. His father, Governor Paul M. Pearson, of the Virgin Islands, was there, and so were Rex Tugwell, Assistant Secretary of Agriculture, and Harry Slattery of this office. All the rest were well-known newspapermen of the left wing. Heywood Broun I met for the first time and I was very much taken by him. He seemed very sane, with a delightful personality. Paul Anderson was there, Paul Mallon, Gardner Jackson, and quite a good many others whose names I do not recall. It was a very pleasant evening, with the rapid-fire give-and-take that brilliant newspapermen are capable of when they are at their best. General Johnson and his secretary came in about half past eleven. I walked home and didn't get home until midnight.

Saturday, August 12, 1933

I got up at five o'clock this morning and was at the White House just before six to pick up Colonel Howe for our trip to Harrisonburg, Virginia, to meet the President, who went there by train from Hyde Park. We had a very nice drive during which we had an opportunity to talk over a number of interesting and important political and governmental matters, many of which were highly confidential. As I have seen more of Colonel Howe lately, I have come to have a very high regard for him, and he has had no hesitation in indicating to me that both he and the President had a very good opinion of me, of which, of course, I am very glad.

The President's train got into Harrisonburg about half past nine, about twenty minutes after we arrived, and we started to inspect some of the CCC camps in the Shenandoah Park and neighborhood. Leaving Harrisonburg, Secretary Wallace and I were in the President's car. He drives in an open car, just as old T. R. used to do, and it is not only good politics but good public policy, because it gives people a chance to have a much more intimate contact with him than if he drove in a closed car. Everyone was out en route, especially at Harrisonburg, which is a fair-sized town of ancient lineage. Everyone seemed cordial and glad to see the President, and he has the happy way of waving and smiling which I think makes people feel that they are in intimate contact with him.

[The Citizens' Civilian Conservation Corps camps, organized under the Unemployment Relief Act of March, 1933, varied in membership from 250,000 to 500,000. They were mostly young, unmarried men, scattered in 2,600 camps. By the middle of 1936, 1,600,000 men had received CCC training. The camps were established for the protection of natural resources, but they also provided some vocational and other schooling. Men admitted to the camps shared their wages with their families. The camps proved to be one of the most popular and least criticized features of the entire New Deal program.–ED.]

The first camp we visited was in course of construction. The second was up in the Blue Ridge Mountains along the new Skyline Drive. This was a well-established camp. In all the camps the men seemed fit, and we were told by the commander of this corps area that the average gain in weight had been fifteen pounds per man. The average age is about nineteen years.

At the third camp, which was still farther up on the Skyline Drive, we stopped for lunch. We had steak, mashed potatoes, green beans, a salad, iced tea, and a so-called apple pie, which, while it was made of dough and apples, was not the conventional apple pie. All of the food was good and it was all that anyone wanted. The general in charge told us that this was a typical meal, and that the food supplied the men cost the Government an average of thirty-five cents a day.

The camps are well set up, sanitary, comfortable, and clean. Army officers are in charge. Of course, it is impossible to say whether there is too much of an Army atmosphere, but I suppose it may be granted that some sort of discipline is necessary. Moving pictures galore and still pictures innumerable were taken from the beginning of the day to the end of the day. I often wonder what becomes of the thousands of feet of film that are used on public men, especially the President, who can't go anywhere without being photographed continuously.

We stopped at two more camps on our way to Washington. Secretary Wallace and I left the President's car at our first stop, but at the last stop, which was just shortly after we left the mountains, the President sent word back to my car that he wanted Colonel Howe, Secretary Wallace, and myself to join him. So we rode all the way into Washington with him and we had a most delightful time.

The President is a fine companion to be out with. He is highly intelligent, quick-witted, and he can both receive and give a good thrust. He has a wide range of interests and is exceedingly human.

We reached the White House shortly after four o'clock and there I transferred to my own car and went home to a bath, to dinner, and to early bed.

There is one incident that I must record because it was so amusing, and the President on the way back, when I brought it up, laughingly said that I ought to include it in my memoirs but he couldn't. The commanding general, while probably a very good officer, is just a little pompous and doesn't want to be left out of any conversation. He hasn't a very wide range of subjects he can talk upon so he keeps repeating the same thing over and over again and he speaks with quite a bit of *empressement*. At the camp where we were having luncheon he began to tell what the Army is going to do in the way of educating the CCC boys while they were in camp. Apparently he didn't know, or chose to ignore the fact, that we are going to assign teachers to these camps, not on invitation of the Army but in spite of the Army. At any rate, he is the type of man that is ready to adopt and claim credit for anything for which credit can be claimed. It gave him great pleasure to assure the President and all within hearing of his voice that any CCC boy could receive instruction on any subject. He told how someone was teaching trigonometry to one of the boys, how another was learning French, and he concluded with this gem: "There won't none of these boys leave these camps illiterate."

Sunday, August 13, 1933

I worked at the office in the morning getting my desk nicely cleared and at one o'clock I went to the White House for luncheon. Those present in addition to the President and Mrs. Roosevelt were Mr. Henry Morgenthau, Jr., Secretary of Labor Perkins, Colonel Howe, and a woman whose name I ought to know but can't remember. We had a very delightful luncheon, talking back and forth with all the freedom of a family circle. Then the President and I went to his study on the second floor, where I went over public works matters with him until four o'clock. After that I went home, worked on my stamps until dinner time, and after dinner I went for a drive to cool off.

At the luncheon the President said that the best story that had come out of Washington since March 4 was the conversation I had over the telephone with Governor Ely, of Massachusetts. He said it was grand.

Tuesday, August 15, 1933

It is now nearly six o'clock and I have about thrown my hands up. I had an unusually bad night last night. I got my dictation fairly well done this morning. Then I had to go to the White House for an appointment at eleven, from which I didn't get back until about twelve, to find the Special Board for Public Works waiting for me. We were in session until after one o'clock. Then there was a Cabinet meeting called for two, but the President was lunching with some foreign potentate so that he didn't get in until nearly three. After the Cabinet meeting there was a meeting of the Executive Council. We were in session until a quarter to five.

The result was that I haven't been able to attend to my customary matters and I will have to let them go until tomorrow.

The Assistant Secretary of the Treasury tried to pull a fast one at the Council meeting. Along toward the end of the session when we thought we were through and hoped we were, he started in with his old rigmarole about public buildings, but the President was prepared for him as a result of our talk on Sunday, and after they were through, Mr. Robert was zigzagging toward the rear to find a safe place to hide. The President made it pretty clear what his policy was with respect to public buildings, something that Mr. Robert and one or two others on the Public Works Board haven't been able to gather from my attempts to state what that position was at meetings of the board.

Saturday, August 19, 1933

I had an appointment with the President this morning, mainly on public works. I told him that Colonel Waite and I were very much concerned about our inability to get more money into employment at once, and I discussed with him especially some method of stimulating the production of producers' goods. He was interested in this and authorized me to take up with Colonel Waite certain matters such as the placing of orders for machinery and tools for navy yards, as well as completion of the electrification project of the Pennsylvania Railroad from Wilmington to Washington, which would be very stimulating to business of this sort, especially in Pennsylvania where there is so much unemployment.

At twelve o'clock Mr. Seubert, president of the Standard Oil Company of Indiana, Mr. Farish, of the Standard Oil of New Jersey, Mr. Skelly, of the Skelly Oil Company, and Mr. J. Howard Pew, of the Sun Oil Company, called on me. Apparently all the oil men believe I am to administer the oil code. They were a sober lot of men. They said they were conservatives who didn't believe in price regulation but that they wanted to co-operate with the Government. They said they wanted us to show whatever consideration we could and have in mind always the real equities in the oil situation. Undoubtedly the reason for their coming was because they feel that I am to have the administration of the oil code and they wanted to establish some sort of a friendly relationship with me. The interview was quite pleasant, seemingly, on both sides.

While they were still here, General Johnson and his assistant, Mr. Simpson, came in with the oil code as finally drafted. I had Fahy, Marshall, and Meyers here waiting for him because I knew he was coming, and we went over his draft and made one or two changes which we thought improved the code. Shortly afterward James A. Moffett came in. He still wants a modification of the price-fixing clause and he makes out a strong case. We will try to get it through if we can but all agree that, after all, we can operate under the code because the President is really given very wide powers with respect not only to the fixing of prices but to regulating production.

Monday, August 21, 1933

There was a short session of the Industrial Recovery Board in the Commerce Building at two-thirty. In the absence from the city of Secretary of Commerce Roper, the Attorney General presided and we got through our business in pretty fast shape.

Harry F. Sinclair was in to see me today with Sheldon Clark, of Chicago. This is the first time I had ever met Sinclair and I kept wondering whether the ghost of Albert B. Fall, carrying a little black satchel, might not emerge from one of the gloomy corners of this office.

Wednesday, August 23, 1933

It has been raining in Washington for the last three days. In fact, we have had a lot of rain, but today and apparently a good deal of last night there has been a regular downpour driven by a strong wind. During the noon hour I went over to call on Colonel Howe, and many branches were strewn over the ground, especially in the White House enclosure. A very large tree across the street from the White House was uprooted. Late this afternoon word came in that a cyclone was headed this way, and later still I learned that the wind along the Coast is blowing at the rate of 75 miles an hour. It is really quite some storm.

I went over to have a very personal and confidential talk with Louis Howe. A heavy barrage is being laid down to break my morale. My wife Anna is receiving a quantity of anonymous letters which naturally worry her. They must be deliberately planned because they are being mailed in such large numbers. Colonel Howe assured me that I was only getting my turn, and that the enemies of the Administration, having had no chance to attack the President himself, make attacks successively on those supposed to be close to him. First they were after himself on the contract for the Army kits bought for the boys in the CCC camps. Then they went after Professor Moley savagely. Now they are spreading rumors of a personal nature about General Johnson and myself.

Tuesday, August 29, 1933

Yesterday morning at nine o'clock I started off for Hyde Park in a big Ford transport belonging to the Navy and took Fred Marx with me. In trying to find the airplane at the naval airport, Fred slipped in some mud and emerged a terrible sight, as he had on a very light suit. However, he pluckily went along.

It was a smooth, easy ride. We made New Hackensack Airport, near Poughkeepsie, in two hours and a quarter. I was at the President's house at Hyde Park just about one o'clock. After lunch he and I went into his study where we worked until about five o'clock on public works projects. We covered a lot of ground and he approved a good many projects, running into quite a large sum of money, probably about $200 million.

Steve Early had telephoned from the temporary Executive Offices in Poughkeepsie that newspaper correspondents wanted me to come over there, so after I was through with the President I drove over. There wasn't any real news I could give them, but it was one of those cases where I had to see them. I then drove back to Hyde Park. Just before I left, Montagu Norman, Governor of the Bank of England, came in for tea and the President said he wanted me to meet him. Norman was still there when I got back, but I didn't go into the living room where they were having tea because I wasn't feeling sociably inclined. Jim Farley had come while I was in Poughkeepsie. After tea I met George Foster Peabody, who talked to me about the Virgin Islands. He seems to think that the President will continue Governor Pearson down there, and that would be satisfactory to me.

A picnic was planned for the evening at the instance of the newspaper correspondents. We all drove about two miles to a cottage where Mrs. Roosevelt and two women friends carry on their furniture-making industry, and where Mrs. Roosevelt has her office when she and the President are at Hyde Park. Here on a flat stretch of ground, well drained, we had a very satisfactory supper, cooked in the open, consisting of steak, roast Virginia ham, golden bantam corn, and a salad, followed by ice cream and chocolate cake. There was an enormous fireplace built at one end, in which a big fire was crackling. The newspaper men put on some stunts, mostly songs, and they called upon Jim Farley and me for brief remarks. Fortunately a threatening rain held off and we had a very enjoyable evening. We got back to the President's home about ten o'clock and then I went into his study with Jim Farley to discuss the makeup of the Oil Committee.

The President accepted my suggestions on the Oil Committee. What we did was to take the executive committee of twelve selected by the larger committee of fifty-four, which in its turn was selected by a big oil convention in Chicago a short time ago, and, as I am informed, is a true cross-section of the oil industry. We made one substitute however. I didn't feel, and the President agreed with me, that we could appoint Harry F. Sinclair as one of the committee, and so we substituted Henry M. Dawes for Sinclair. The committee is to consist of fifteen members, twelve representing the oil industry and three representing the Administration. The three men we decided upon were James A. Moffett, Donald R. Richberg, and M. L. Benedum. While I was in his office on this last stretch, the President signed an Executive Order making me Oil Administrator.

The President has a beautiful location and a lovely house at Hyde Park, long and rambling and apparently containing many rooms, with an enormous living room at one end. It is situated on a high bluff overlooking the Hudson and in all directions could be seen running water and tree-covered heights. It is a perfectly charming place, such a place as I would dearly love to live in myself.

Friday, September 1, 1933

Just before leaving the office shortly after six o'clock yesterday afternoon, Colonel Waite and Assistant General Counsel Foley brought in for my signature the contract for the Midtown-Hudson Tunnel in New York City. They told me they would have the contract for the Triborough Bridge in New York City ready for my signature late in the evening, and I gave them my address so they could bring it to me at my house. There were the usual delays, however, so that they didn't get there until eleven-thirty. It was ten minutes to twelve when I signed this contract. The two contracts obligate the Federal Government to spend something like $70 million from its public works fund. Mr. Foley took a night train to New York in order to have the contracts signed there today, and word has come through that one is signed and that the other will probably be signed before the close of the day. This will be an important step in our public works undertaking because these are big contracts and both will help in the unemployment situation in New York and New Jersey.

Saturday, September 2, 1933

The Oil Committee of fifteen has been in almost continuous session for forty-eight hours. It has agreed upon certain amendments to the code, which were submitted to me today. The first of these amendments would give the Oil Administrator such enlarged powers as to make him absolute dictator. As I remarked to our Solicitors when I read it, if we should adopt this amendment, the effect would be the same as if we abolished all the rest of the code and lodged in the Administrator full power to regulate and control the oil industry. They admitted that this was so and I told them that I didn't believe any such power should be lodged, and that if it were, I wouldn't want to have the responsibility of exercising it. I pointed out that under such a broad grant of power every question would be brought directly to the Administrator and there wouldn't be enough hours of the day for him to consider and decide the questions submitted. This would mean that I couldn't even pretend to function as Administrator of Public Works and as Secretary of the Interior. I said that only carefully circumscribed power should be granted.

Later I called up Don Richberg as the third representative of the Administration on the Oil Committee. Richberg had sent me a letter late Friday afternoon raising serious legal questions bearing on the assumed power of the Administrator, on the advice of the Oil Committee, to adopt amendments to the code. We argued the questions involved at considerable length.

It had been the opinion of the committee that prices for oil should be fixed today by the Administrator, and strong representations in that behalf have been made to me. On full consideration, I decided not to declare any amendments to the code today and not to set a minimum price for oil or gasoline. As I pointed out, the fixing of prices would represent a radical departure for the Government and there were questions involved in the adoption of suggested amendments to the code that might have important and far-reaching political repercussions. I didn't feel that I cared to assume the tremendous responsibility involved, nor did I feel that I had the right, without consulting the President, to take action that would involve the Administration.

The President is off for the week end and Labor Day on Vincent Astor's yacht and is, therefore, inaccessible.

My final decision was to allocate as between oil-producing states the amount of crude oil each state may produce until further orders. Meanwhile, the Oil Committee was in session in the Conference Room on the fourth floor. At three o'clock, I went down and told them what my decision was. There were some questions asked, but on the whole, I think the committee was inclined to accept my decision gracefully. At any rate, they showed no violent dissent. Then I came back to my office and prepared the allocation for the production of oil. Late in the afternoon, I gave a statement to the press carrying this allocation and authorized the sending out of telegrams to the governors of the oil-producing states, advising each one of the allocation for his particular state. The allocation order will become effective at 7 a.m. on September 8. My order on allocation included a clause that no oil should be withdrawn from storage without my permission, and it also limited to 90,000 barrels a day the amount of oil that may be imported.

Tuesday, September 5, 1933

I worked at the office on Sunday morning and got my desk in the best shape it has been in for weeks. In the afternoon I went driving. Monday morning, early, I moved most of my stuff over to the new house that I have leased at 4880 Glenbrook Road, N. W.

At 2:30 P.M. there was a meeting of the Executive Council. The President got back to Washington at noon. After the Council meeting, I went into his office with him and arranged for an appointment for tomorrow to discuss public works. I have never seen him looking so well and I complimented him on his appearance. He said he had had three days of absolute rest where no one could get at him. He said that one night he had sat up until six o'clock in the morning playing poker and drinking beer, and I remarked that if it had the effect on him it appeared to have, he had better make a practice of it.

I said something about my being the only member of the Cabinet who had not had a single day's vacation this summer, and he said that I ought to take some, but he agreed with me that he didn't see how I could do it when I told him what pressure there was for the public works program to go ahead. Then he suggested that I might go down to Rapidan Camp for week ends, but I don't see how I could even do this.

I moved the last of my things out of the Georgetown house today and when I leave the office this afternoon, I will go direct to the new house.

Friday, September 8, 1933

I meant to set down yesterday a brief talk I had with the President referring to Don Richberg. The President mentioned Don's name in a way that gave me a real opportunity to say, "You know, Mr. President, that Richberg feels that I climbed into the Cabinet over his prostrate form." The President asked me what I meant. I said that Richberg thought he was being seriously considered for the Cabinet and might have landed it if I hadn't crowded him out. The President threw back his head and laughingly said that he had never for a moment thought of Richberg in connection with the Cabinet.

We had a Cabinet meeting this afternoon. The Cuban situation is very tense and we spent a good deal of time considering it. On two or three occasions late bulletins with respect to the situation in Cuba were brought in to the President. While I was in the President's office this morning, he gave orders to have messages sent to the captains of all American ships lying off Cuba forbidding them to land marines or sailors for the protection of property alone. He said that only danger to lives would justify anyone's being landed, but that, so far as property alone was concerned, there would be no attempt at protection. The question of intervention was discussed very fully in the Cabinet meeting, but it seemed clear that the decision of everyone, from the President down, was against intervention unless it was actually forced upon us.

Toward the end of the meeting, Secretary Roper remarked that some Chinese emperor back in the eleventh century at a time of depression had adopted the same measures for recovery that this

Administration is now back of. The President laughingly inquired, "What happened to that emperor, was he beheaded?" Roper replied, "No, he wasn't beheaded; he was defeated."

I worked until nearly eleven o'clock tonight and I almost succeeded in clearing my desk of accumulated matters. However, I came back tired after dinner and the strain finally became so great that I went home leaving some matters to wait until tomorrow.

Tuesday, September 12, 1933

Tuesdays are the worst days of the week for me. I began to see people at ten o'clock. Prior to that I had finished revising a draft of a speech that I am to make in Chicago at a meeting of mayors on the twenty-third. I had seen some of my bureau chiefs and had opened my mail, but had done little if any dictating.

At ten minutes past ten, I went over to see Colonel Howe because he telephoned me late yesterday afternoon and indicated he wanted to see me very badly. We discussed subsistence homestead farms and then he talked to me confidentially about General Johnson. He told me that both he and the President had great confidence in me and what he was about to tell me about General Johnson was proof of his confidence. The long and short of it is that General Johnson has felt a little piqued about one or two matters and Colonel Howe thought I might help to keep him smoothed down, all of which I am willing to do.

At eleven o'clock we had a meeting of the Public Works Board and we covered a great deal of ground. We were in session over two hours and passed quite a lot of municipal projects and one or two Federal ones. We are really getting much more work done at these meetings now. Robert hardly ever opens his mouth now and even the Solicitor General is comparatively quiet. After this meeting adjourned, I had my usual press conference and this lasted about half an hour. My press conferences are very well attended now and I get along very well with the correspondents.

I had an interval of ten or fifteen minutes to devote to office matters before going to the Council meeting. At the opening of the Council meeting, the President tossed a note down my way and when I opened it, I found it was a letter to him from Judge Malmin, of Chicago, who has been trying to blackmail me into supporting him for the Governorship of the Virgin Islands. The letter to the President was long and was full of insinuations and veiled charges against me. The purport of it was that it was highly important for Malmin to see the President, if the President was interested in preventing a scandal which might reflect upon a man close to him in his Administration. Malmin did not mention my name in the letter, but his references were clear enough. He wanted to meet the President at Hyde Park and boldly said that a means might be found of preventing unfavorable publicity. Attached to the Malmin letter was a copy of a reply that the President had sent him, in which he said, in effect, that he would not enter into any scheme to cover up anything affecting a member of the Administration, for if any member of the Administration had done what was not right, he should stand the consequences, and if he had not, he would doubtless know how to protect his good name. At the end of the President's letter, I wrote the word "fine, H.L.I." and sent it back to him.

After the Council meeting was over, I watched for a chance to talk to the President and I suggested that, as a matter of self-protection for himself, he ought to ask Homer Cummings, Attorney General, to make an investigation of the charges that Malmin was hinting at. I am glad now that when I was at Hyde Park I told the President briefly what Malmin was up to, so that he was not unprepared when Malmin's letter came in. The President called Homer Cummings into our huddle and read Malmin's letter and his reply, to Homer. He made frequent comments derogatory to Malmin as he read the letter and at one place he said, "That is clear blackmail." The Attorney General also agreed that it looked like blackmail. The President told Homer Cummings that he thought he ought to put a quietus on Malmin. I said that I was not proposing a quietus; that what I wanted was that the President ask the Attorney General to find out whether there was any basis for the charges. I repeated this to Homer afterward but, of course, as did the President, he generously took the position that there couldn't be any basis for such charges. I have told Malmin and I have told everyone to whom I have talked on the subject that they could go ahead and fire both barrels whenever they want to. If I am guilty of any unprofessional conduct or of committing any crime or misdemeanor in handling the Saunders' estate case,

I don't know what it is. The whole thing was as clean as a whistle. Malmin must be off his balance to think that he can get anywhere by trying to blackmail me, especially since I have resisted all his efforts so far and have challenged him to go ahead and do his worst.

Wednesday, September 13, 1933

At one o'clock, I went to the President's office to lunch with him. He has never been so friendly, although I have never had any cause for complaint of any lack of friendliness. I had a number of public works and oil administration questions of importance to discuss with him, but all during the luncheon and for ten or fifteen minutes afterward, he insisted on talking about the general financial and economic situation with me. I felt like a babe in the woods on these questions, but I was immensely flattered that he wanted to consult me. The President feels that it is necessary for the Administration to do something within the next week or ten days to improve the price situation. He discussed several methods. First, buying silver; second, buying gold; and third, issuing currency to pay for public works. I agreed with him that it seemed to me advisable to do something to give another financial fillip, and I expressed my apprehension as to what might happen if the public works program we have been trying to work out should halt perceptibly, or break down.

After luncheon he handed me two more letters from Malmin, one addressed to Mrs. Roosevelt and one to himself, and both along the same lines as the one I have already told about. One of these letters said that unless something were done before next Monday, Malmin would start proceedings against me in Chicago in the Saunders' estate case. Malmin, in fact, takes the position in these letters that, although he has been retained by a client to institute proceedings against me, those proceedings will be abated if the President can make some arrangement satisfactory to him. When I got back to the office, J. Edgar Hoover, head of the Bureau of Investigation in the Department of Justice, who had been sent over by the Attorney General, was waiting to see me to discuss the Malmin matter. I gave him my files, as well as the two letters just referred to that the President handed to me today at luncheon. Hoover said he would get busy right away and look into the whole matter.

Thursday, September 14, 1933

Naturally, I got off to a bad start today because of the overhang of work from yesterday and as Anna is due in Chicago on Saturday, I wanted to write her a very full statement on the Malmin matter so that if there should be any publicity during the next few days she would understand it.

I had a long calling list today beginning with Governor Pinchot and Joe Guffey, of Pennsylvania, who are interested both in coal and in a flood-control proposition for the head waters of the Ohio River. Lieutenant Governor Donovan, of Illinois, was in about a couple of jobs. Senator Tydings, of Maryland, called to complain that Henry Hunt, our Chief Counsel in Public Works, at a club in Baltimore the other day, after he had had three or four drinks and was asked what process to follow in making a recommendation for the appointment of a lawyer, told his interlocutor just to send in a letter but not to have any endorsement from Senator Tydings because such an endorsement would do more harm than good so far as I was concerned. I, of course, disclaimed any such attitude on my part and my disclaimer was given force by the fact that only two days ago I had appointed a man from Baltimore, on Senator Tydings' recommendation, as an attorney in the Virgin Islands.

Friday, September 15, 1933

I went to the White House last night just before nine o'clock at the President's suggestion to sit in as a spectator at the meeting he had called on the coal code. He sat at his desk. On his right was General Johnson, then Don Richberg, and a little to the rear, as an interested auditor, Dr. Felix Frankfurter. On the President's left were the Attorney General, myself, and Secretary Woodin in order. After we were seated the operators came in and it looked as if there were about twenty-five or thirty of them. John L. Lewis, president of the United States Mine Workers, was also present with one of his vice presidents.

The President started out to tell them how disappointed he had been that the code had not been agreed to in spite of an assurance every Thursday for several weeks that a code would certainly be signed up by the following Monday, only to be followed by assurances from day to day that the next day would see the finishing of the work. He said that considering the state of mind of the country it was absolutely essential that a code be agreed upon within twenty-four hours and he indicated pretty clearly that unless they got together within that time, with the possible allowance of a few additional hours, he would impose an involuntary code upon the industry under the National Recovery Act. There were several people who spoke. A large group of the operators are ready to sign the code as it stands, but a man by the name of Francis, who has been the chief obstructionist so far, in a very smooth speech pleaded for thirty-six hours' time. In the end the President told them that twenty-four hours was all he could allow, but he indicated that a few additional hours would be added if necessary. He read a statement that he proposed to give to the press of the country, in effect assuming that the code would be agreed to and signed within twenty-four hours.

After the meeting broke up several operators came up to speak to me. I had met a number of them during the two or three coal conferences that were held here in the Interior Building in the early summer when it was being considered whether the Secretary of the Interior would become dictator of the coal business. Some of the operators hope that I will be made Administrator under the coal code. Naturally, the coal belongs over here since the Bureau of Mines is in this Department. But this will be one tough job and it might prove to be the extra straw that would break the camel's back. Accordingly, while I am flattered to be told that some people would like to have me administer the coal code, I really don't want it to come my way.

My son, Raymond, got in this morning on the Pennsylvania Railroad. It is the first time he has been in Washington since the Inauguration. Nor have I seen him since my last trip to Chicago. I was very glad, indeed, to see him. He looks well and says he feels well. He spent the morning hanging around the office with me and this afternoon I sent him out to the Congressional Country Club where he could swim while I attend the Cabinet meeting.

Secretary Woodin was at the White House last night. He has been away for three or four months on account of a very bad throat, but he looks well now and says he is feeling much better. He also attended the Cabinet meeting this afternoon. This meeting was much longer than usual. The first matter we discussed was Cuba. The President first brought up the question of possible recognition of the existing government there and then he went around the

Cabinet table and asked each of us how he felt about possible intervention under the Platt Amendment. It was interesting that the Assistant Secretary of War, who was acting in the absence of Secretary of War Dern, was the only one who seemed to be at all jingoistic. He thought it would be a salutary thing if we could intervene promptly. One or two of the Cabinet members seemed to feel that intervention might be inevitable, and perhaps it might be said that they were more or less reserving judgment. The majority, however, were against intervention unless forced to do so as a matter of absolute necessity. When my turn came, I said that we ought not to intervene unless it was a matter of real compulsion. I commented on the order issued to the Navy by the President stating that no persons should be landed from American ships in Cuban waters to protect property alone; that only American lives were to be protected. I took the position that even if there should accidentally be a loss of one or two American lives, still we should not intervene. I suggested that if intervention should become necessary, it might be well for us to go in with the active or at least the tacit approval of some of the leading Spanish-American countries of Central and South America.

We spent a good deal of time talking about the monetary system, the possible necessity of inflation, and also the necessity during the next two or three weeks of an appreciation in the price of certain commodities. It is quite clear both from the discussion at the Cabinet and from what the President said to me when I lunched with him the other day that he is turning over in his mind various more or less drastic financial and economic policies.

Saturday, September 16, 1933

Raymond and I went to a movie last night and we saw a most disgusting exhibition put on by a low-class comedian as NRA propaganda. It would hardly appeal to the lowest order of human intelligence and I am wondering if this sort of thing is being put on extensively. If it is, it will do the NRA more harm than good. I happened to mention it to Miss Perkins this afternoon, after we were through with a conference, and she said that she had been told that movie audiences in New York City were booing NRA propaganda that is put on at the movies.

At one-thirty in my car I joined the President and other members of the Cabinet in the White House grounds whence we proceeded to Glenwood Cemetery for the funeral of Ike Hoover, who died suddenly on Thursday and was Chief Usher at the White House for many years. He served in various capacities in the White House under every President beginning with President Harrison.

Monday, September 18, 1933

Pressure continues unabated. I would welcome even a half-hour's letup. I feel like the man who tried to sweep the ocean back. There is a never-ceasing avalanche of mail, communications, memoranda, telephone calls, and visitors. So far I have reasonably well kept my poise, although I am conscious of my nerves getting on edge pretty frequently. I realize that it might be fatal if I should once allow myself to feel overwhelmed.

Wednesday, September 20, 1933

I saw the President in his office at the White House for three-quarters of an hour this afternoon. He approved of the public works projects I submitted to him and we discussed a number of other matters. He authorized me to go ahead and institute prosecutions for violation of regulations issued in relation to the production of hot oil. I told him frankly that I thought it was a tactical mistake for General Johnson and Don Richberg to give such a clear impression that they were apprehensive of the constitutionality of the National Recovery Act. I told him that instead of waiting for the fight to come to us, we ought to select our own issue in our own forum and make them take us on. This is what we are going to do by starting prosecutions for violations not only of the hot oil regulations but of the oil code itself.

Thursday, September 21, 1933

At two o'clock we had our regular public works meeting and it was the shortest on record. We went through everything in a hurry and at half past three I was at the White House to keep an appointment with the President. He is still keeping to his rooms, although he has not any temperature and seems to be quite all right again. I was late in getting in to him because Senator Lewis was ahead of me. After I did get in, he approved the public works projects that the board had just passed, and then we had a general discussion about the business and economic situation. It is clear that the President believes that prices of farm commodities must have a substantial raise, and that if inflation is necessary to accomplish this, I suspect that he will turn to inflation in some form or other.

I am under tremendous pressure from the oil people to put into effect a schedule of prices. The Oil Committee has been wanting to discuss the matter with me nearly all day and I finally met with them at half past five. They are literally obsessed by the idea of the necessity of fixing prices. They say that the oil industry will go to pot if prices are not fixed, and that the industry itself has been led to expect this result and are becoming more and more discouraged and dissatisfied as time goes on without this being done. I told them that it was the President's view, as it is mine, that price fixing should not be resorted to except as to the last measure. I insisted that we try out every other power given us by the oil code before fixing prices. Most of all I told them that it was absolutely necessary for them to get together with our solicitors and agree upon a factual basis for price fixing and which the solicitors felt they could defend in court, because it seems inevitable to me that we will have to maintain our ground in court if and when we fix prices. They finally agreed to my suggestion that our solicitors should go into session with a subcommittee of the Oil Committee and keep at work until they could either agree or come to the conclusion that they could do no better than disagree.

I am working again tonight until rather late. I find that necessary interruptions for important conferences cause work to back up on my desk to an extraordinary degree.

Monday, September 25, 1933

Last Friday I had an appointment with the President on public works. He approved the lists submitted, as usual. In the afternoon we had a Cabinet meeting, and following the Cabinet meeting I took the B.&O. train for Chicago with Raymond.

Anna met us Saturday morning, and there was the usual retinue of newspaper reporters and newspaper photographers. In fact, I was photographed almost continuously all day long, which caused me to wonder again at the wanton waste of valuable film. There was also a delegation of mayors at the station who bade me welcome and told me with what keen anticipation they were looking forward to my speech in the evening. They told me that they had adopted, or were about to adopt, some resolutions on public works and they wanted me to go over to the hotel and receive them. I told them I didn't think it would be proper for me to sit down and discuss resolutions referring to one of my own activities, and that the resolutions could be presented to me before the meeting.

A representative of A Century of Progress insisted that the officials wouldn't die happy unless they had the opportunity to give me the same honors they had given other Cabinet members. Accordingly, I agreed to be at the University Club at quarter after two. There Anna, Raymond, Robert, and I were put in an official car and taken down to A Century of Progress grounds. As we entered the grounds two field pieces started to fire off the nineteen guns, which constitute the salute of honor accorded a Cabinet Minister. A squad of cavalry escorted us into the grounds, where an infantry squad was lined up. They presented arms and did one or two other military stunts appropriate to the occasion, and then I reviewed them fore and aft. I must say they were a fine-looking body of soldiers, which was easy to understand when it was explained that they were regulars. Then we went in to the Administration Building, went around the lagoon in one of the boats, and then started out to Hubbard Woods.

I had run across in the lobby of the Congress Hotel, H. L. Hopkins, the Federal Relief Administrator, who had just spoken to the mayors, and Paul V. Betters, who is secretary of the Mayors' Conference. Betters had in his pocket a copy of the resolutions adopted by the mayors and he gave me this copy. I read them on the way home and as soon as I got home I demanded pen and paper and sat down to write about three hundred words to insert in my speech. These resolutions made me just a little hot under the collar. They recited how the public works program was being retarded in Washington, and in almost every other sentence deplored the red tape with which we are supposed to be enmeshed. I wrote a pretty forthright and convincing reply and marked it for insert in my speech which had already gone out to the newspapers of the country with a release date.

We got to A Century of Progress about seven o'clock, where we had dinner. After dinner Rufus Dawes introduced Mayor Curley of Boston. Mayor Curley read a short speech in which he also referred to red tape in connection with the Public Works Administration. Then he laid down his speech and began to wander all over the map. He refused to stop when signaled to do so, although he was running badly into my radio time. Finally he did bring his remarks to a close and I launched into my speech. I was just mad enough to be spirited without being too mad. Fortunately my prepared speech, in general, fitted the occasion, and with what I wrote at Hubbard Woods, I met the situation head on. I looked those mayors in the eye and I told them what the exact truth was—that the reason the public works program was delayed was because they and others like them, and governors of states, didn't get their projects in to us but were trying to excuse their own delay and ineptitude by blaming us. I called for facts and specifications and told them not to indulge in any more generalities. I deplored their joining in a hue and cry without knowing what the facts were, and finally I challenged them to appoint a subcommittee to send to Washington to find out just what we were doing and if we weren't doing it right, to tell us where we were wrong.

My speech got over in good shape. I could feel that it was going over well, and all the expressions I got afterward were to the same effect. Charles E. Merriam had been rather worried about the situation and he called me by long distance from Chicago on Thursday to caution me not to allow myself to get on the defensive. My speech had already gone out, however. Sunday morning he called me up at the house to say that the speech was fine, that the mayors I had not convinced I had stopped. Betters came to see me out at the train on Sunday to tell me that it had had a very good effect. After I got back to Washington, I heard from a good many sources that my speech was a very good one indeed. Some of my friends here told me it was the best I have made. I received a number of letters and telegrams of congratulation, and when I was with the President today he showed me a very congratulatory telegram that had been sent to him.

Tuesday, September 26, 1933

I led a large delegation to the President's office today to keep an appointment with him at twelve o'clock. The conference was on oil. There were with me Margold, who on Monday returned from his vacation, Fahy, Meyers, Marshall, Kingsbury, president of the Standard Oil of California, Wirt Franklin, Judge Beaty, Moffett, and Benedum. I told the President that in view of his prospective absence from Washington for a week, we wanted to discuss the general policy of price fixing. I then let Wirt Franklin state the case from his point of view and I followed, saying that while I believed that price fixing for oil was inevitable, we were unwilling to fix prices on any basic figures that we didn't thoroughly understand and which our solicitors didn't believe sufficient to sustain a case in court. The President agreed with this point of view, and I told him that I thought we were approaching an understanding on figures and that we ought to be able to get together.

At the end of the discussion I asked the President to tell us what to do if while he was still away a case for price fixing seemed to be made out and if at the same time our solicitors were satisfied that the facts upon which prices were fixed could be sustained in court. The President said to go ahead and fix prices in that event.

Wednesday, September 27, 1933

This takes rank with the worst days I have had since I came to Washington. Almost directly after I came to the office I started in seeing people. Until eleven o'clock I had in rapid succession individuals and delegations from my own Department and from the Public Works Administration. Sandwiched in between I had a long conference on oil, participated in by Messrs. Moffett and Benedum and Margold.

Then at eleven o'clock the callers began to come in. There was a long list of them. Worse than this, they didn't clear rapidly today. Some of them were here for extended interviews, with the result that it was after one o'clock before I finally got through the list. At two o'clock I welcomed representatives of the States of Colorado, Wyoming, and Nebraska who came here at my suggestion to see whether they could reach an understanding with respect to the use as between their three states of the waters of the North Platte River. Then I came to my own office for more interviews with more heads of departments. This kept up until very late in the afternoon, when I finally had an opportunity to do some dictating.

The oil situation has gotten into quite a snarl. Margold was away for three months and returned to the Department only last Monday. He hasn't kept in touch with the oil situation, especially the move toward price fixing. He has attacked it as a new matter and has wanted to traverse all of the ground that we have been over during these past weeks. On the other hand, members of the Oil Committee will not or cannot furnish us with the facts and figures that we think we ought to have in order to feel ourselves in a safe position if we have to go into court, as we will undoubtedly have to do. I asked the oil people to supply the solicitors with necessary facts and figures. They keep promising to do it but according to the solicitors they don't furnish them. The result is that we have been running around in circles. Late this afternoon I had Margold, Meyers, and Marshall in. I told them that the oil people were too practical and that the solicitors were too theoretical. I think there must be some basis for us to get together and I am insisting that this be done. The final understanding was that our solicitors would build up a price structure of their own. I will then consider their price structure, together with the one already prepared by the Oil Committee, and will decide what to do.

All of these negotiations and pulling and hauling are very tiring. I do think it necessary to be ready to fix prices. The oil people have been insisting for days now that the whole bottom is likely to fall out of oil prices, and while they may be acting the role of alarmists in order to get the price fixing that they want, on the other hand we ought to be prepared if an emergency should arise.

Thursday, September 28, 1933

Anna and I went to dinner at the home of Secretary of the Treasury and Mrs. Woodin last evening. Others present were Secretary and Mrs. Hull, Attorney General and Mrs. Cummings, Secretary and Mrs. Roper, Secretary and Mrs. Wallace, Secretary of Labor Perkins, and a married daughter of the Woodins. They live in a very spacious and attractive home which they have rented.

After dinner the men, all of us being members of the Cabinet, went upstairs to smoke and have our coffee. This gave us an opportunity to talk rather confidentially about important national matters. I was very much interested to hear Secretary Woodin talk. He has been ill and away from Washington all summer, but I distinctly remember that at Cabinet meetings that he attended late in the spring or early in the summer he expressed great optimism about the economic situation. I recall that on one occasion he said that we had definitely turned the corner. Last night he was worried and frankly said so. He doesn't like the situation. He thinks the dollar ought to be stabilized and he doesn't care much at what point, provided only that it is stabilized. He said that the big financial men in New York are all down in the mouth and think that the NRA campaign will be a failure. As they look at it, it is going to put the country entirely in the hands of labor.

Secretary Roper brought up the question of the Deputy Administrators selected by General Johnson to administer the various codes remaining within his jurisdiction. He said, and I think that all agreed with him, that these Deputy Administrators ought to be outstanding men whose characters and reputations were generally known and whose prestige would be sufficient assurance to the country that their administration of the codes would be in the public interest and free from any bias or favoritism. He expressed dissatisfaction with the four men designated by Johnson, and I am very strongly inclined to agree with him.

It was a hot night and I was very tired and uncomfortable. I felt like a boiled owl in my formal dress, and it was so hot that when I got home I found that my collar was in process of wilting.

Friday, September 29, 1933

Acting on the suggestion I made in my speech to the mayors at Chicago last Saturday night, a committee has been here for the last two days looking over the public works organization. This morning they presented a number of resolutions, which I objected to in one or two important particulars. They have no chip on their shoulders, but in view of the resolutions they adopted last Saturday morning, accusing us of being involved in yards and yards of red tape, they want to save their faces without at the same time doing us any damage. When they presented their resolutions to me yesterday, I discussed the matter very frankly with them and today they came back with a revised draft which, while mildly critical, was such as we could stand without much concern. Accordingly, these resolutions will go out to the country today by way of a press release.

In the absence of the President at Hyde Park, there was no Cabinet meeting today, so that I was able to put in full time at the office. A great many people have been in to see me the last couple of days and there is absolutely no letup in the pressure upon me. I am very tired this week, more so than usual, but I am trying to hang on. I have one satisfaction and that is that at least I have outlasted General Johnson. He went to the hospital several days ago for a minor operation but apparently he was so run down that he hasn't strength to recuperate as fast as he ought to. While he was going, General Johnson undoubtedly put in longer hours than I did, but when it is considered that I have been working as I have since March 5, I have him beaten by several miles. In fact, I don't think there is any man in the Administration who has done as much work over as long hours day in and day out, week after week, as I have.

Monday, October 2, 1933

At the meeting of the National Industrial Recovery Board this afternoon I urged very strongly that prosecutions for violations of the various codes be instituted. I deprecated the impression that has gone out over the country that General Johnson is so fearful of the unconstitutionality of the act under which the codes have been set up that he is afraid of a test case. I pointed out that sooner or later we were bound to get into court and that it was far better policy to choose our own tribunal and our own case than to be haled into court before an unfriendly judge on a weak case. I said, moreover, that the sentiment among the big businessmen was more unfavorable to the code now than it was two weeks ago, and that two weeks ago it was more unfavorable than it had been prior to that. I pointed out also that there would be more likelihood of getting a favorable opinion from a court while public enthusiasm for the code was running high than after a cold sweat had begun to break out. I made the further point that people who had been for the code are beginning to turn and this might become a very significant movement in reverse. It is my opinion that a court decision upholding the theory of the codes and the constitutionality of the NRA would have a very stimulating effect at this time.

Tuesday, October 3, 1933

A few days ago I received from Assistant Secretary of War Woodring a most astonishing letter in which he expressed strong disapproval of certain acts of mine relating to personnel matters, both in the Public Works and in the Oil Administration. His letter was not even courteous and he lectured me as if I were a school boy. I sent a letter off to him today in which I told him, in effect, it was absolutely no concern of his how I ran my Department and that I didn't propose to be dictated to by him or anyone else. My letter was a pretty strong one.

I have also received a letter from Senator Key Pittman, which is very critical and which also is very far from being courteous. I shall write him a strong letter also on the theory that if I permit some of these politicians to get the idea that they can shove me around, they will not only do it but others will join them in the exercise. After all, so long as I am head of this Department I am going to run it subject only to the President's expressed wishes. I don't propose to take any orders from any Assistant Secretaries or Secretaries, or United States Senators. Pittman is an important man on the Democratic side in the United States Senate and he really is in a position to make some trouble for me, but based on my experience in the past, he will be much less likely to make trouble if he knows that I am not only able but willing to fight back than if I take such a letter as he wrote me lying down. After all, I can't do any better than I am doing. I am putting everything I have into this job.

The Oil Committee is still seething because I haven't fixed oil prices, but I am letting them fight it out with Margold and his assistants. Sooner or later, I will have to get into it, but in the meantime I prefer to move cautiously. The last oil allocation decided upon has improved the price of crude, and I am not yet persuaded that it will be necessary to fix prices if we can balance the consumption and production fairly accurately.

Thursday, October 5, 1933

Our usual Public Works Board meeting was held at eleven o'clock this morning instead of two because some of the members wanted to go to the World Series baseball game between New York and Washington which was played here. I was finally persuaded to go to the ball game myself, although I had very much hesitation on account of many matters pending. When I came back to the office two and a half hours later, I was distinctly sorry that I had gone because I found an enormous lot of work waiting for me. I might as well confess, too, that I didn't enjoy the game very much. In the first place, I am not enthusiastic about baseball, and in the second place, it did lie somewhat on my conscience that I was away from the office when there was so much work to do. Since I haven't had a day's vacation all summer, I shouldn't have felt this way about it but the fact is that I did.

Late this afternoon I had an appointment with the President in his study in the White House. We went over all the public works projects that we have been making allocations for since he left for Hyde Park, and he approved all of them. I brought up again the question of public buildings, and had with me a report prepared by the special committee appointed by the President, consisting of Messrs. Hoopingarner, Rabinowitz, and Dresser. This report was very intelligently prepared and showed just what the actual situation is with respect to post office services in the cities where the Treasury wants to erect new buildings. I told the President that when Congress met again it would raise hell because these post offices hadn't been built. In that cheerful way of his he remarked that he would laugh them out of court. He seems as determined as ever not to authorize the building of post offices that cannot be justified from an economic point of view, and, of course, I am in full accord with him on this policy. Then I suggested that we appoint an independent committee of three, two architects and an engineer, to go over this list and see whether a considerable number cannot be redesigned, thus reducing costs of construction and justifying us in going ahead with them. My theory is that instead of erecting monumental buildings in small towns, more appropriate buildings providing necessary space but conforming architecturally to the towns themselves can be built for much less money. If this can be done it will satisfy the postal needs of the towns, take the pressure off us from the Congressmen, and will provide employment for the building industries. He agreed with this suggestion of mine and told me to go ahead.

We also discussed a proposition brought up from the Post Office for the building of substations in big cities. The point he raised on this matter was that real estate speculators would boost the prices of land. He then suggested to me the name of a real estate man in New York who he said was honest and who could be trusted to help us without pull or graft in buying sites. I shall send for this man and see what he can do in the way of buying sites at a reasonable figure.

After we discussed these matters, the President, as he has done on several occasions lately, began to talk about general matters with me. He is very anxious that a way be found under the law for the Government to buy gold, but no one has yet discovered how it can be done.

I congratulated him most sincerely on the brave stand he took at the American Legion Convention in Chicago on Monday, with re-

spect to the use of Federal funds for veterans of the world war.
Many of his advisers had urged him not to go to Chicago, but, as he
told me a couple of weeks ago, their very urging made him so mad
that he made up his mind to go. Mayor Kelly told me when I was in
Chicago to speak at the mayors' meeting that he didn't want the
President to come because he didn't think he could protect him.
But the President went in spite of everyone and he got a great reception, as a brave, forthright man always will when he frankly
faces a situation.

[President Roosevelt opposed the veterans' bonus from the beginning of his first administration. On May 27, 1935, he appeared before the Congress to read his veto of a bill providing for the immediate payment to veterans of the First World War of their adjusted
compensation certificates which were due in 1945. At that time he
kept the Senate (by a vote of 54 to 40) from overriding his veto. But
on January 9, 1936, Congress passed the bill again over his veto,
obligating the Treasury to pay out to veterans nearly $2 billion.
The payment was made on June 15, 1936.–ED.]

I took occasion to tell the President that if we only had a fair
break of luck so that we didn't hit any more economic bumps and
were able to hold our own and perhaps pull gradually out, his
Administration would go down in history as one of profound and
far-reaching social changes. I told him that there wasn't another
man in the United States who could lead the country at this time
along the paths that it ought to tread. Of course, he demurred to
this, but I profoundly believe it to be true. He said that what we
were doing in this country were some of the things that were being
done in Russia and even some things that were being done under
Hitler in Germany. But we are doing them in an orderly way. I
said to him that I didn't know whether, as a candidate, he realized
that he had the capacity to give the kind of leadership that he is
giving or that, possessing the ability, he would give it, but that I
was sure the country didn't elect him for any such reason but for entirely different ones. He said that, of course, he had been thinking
along these lines for a good many years, but it was evident that he
himself had not anticipated the problems that have arisen, nor am
I sure that he was certain in his own mind when he came into office how he would meet those problems if they did arise.

At one o'clock today I went to the Carlton Hotel as one of the guests invited by the Secretary of State to a luncheon in honor of President Arias of the Republic of Panama. There were twenty at the table including, besides the two mentioned, the Panama Minister, Dr. Ricardo J. Alfaro, the Secretary of War, the Secretary of Commerce, Assistant Secretary of the Navy Roosevelt, Senators Robinson, Pittman, King, and a few others. Amusingly enough, Senator Pittman sat on my right.

Just before leaving the office I made a final revision of a letter that I have written to Senator Pittman in reply to his insulting one to me of about a week ago. My reply, while courteous, gives him blow after blow. Our conversation at the luncheon was pleasant and friendly enough. I signed the letter after I got back to the office and it will go to him by messenger tomorrow morning.

At four o'clock I went to the White House to talk with the President. Secretary Wallace was just ahead of me and we took occasion to discuss with the President the land policy that he announced some time ago. At that time he proposed that whenever new land was brought into cultivation by irrigation or similar methods, the Government would withdraw from cultivation submarginal land of an equivalent productive capacity. Two or three days ago I had an opinion from the Attorney General upholding the right of the Public Works Administration to buy such submarginal land, provided it was part of a general plan of public works. This opinion seems to me to border on the hair-splitting but it will serve our purpose. The President expects to go ahead with this policy, and Wallace and I will arrange to set up the machinery necessary to make a study of the question and decide what land shall be bought back from the Government.

I find myself again working tonight until a late hour.

Thursday, October 12, 1933

At five o'clock I went to the White House for an interview with the President. It was the President's day for officially receiving the members of the Supreme Court. We waited in the parlor until this reception was over. On our way to the second floor the President remarked that whenever he saw a certain member of the Supreme Court he thought of that musical comedy—*Of Thee I Sing*. I told him I had the same feeling; that I didn't see why the member of the court in question hadn't shaved off his whiskers after that play.

A few days ago I submitted to the President a proposition with respect to fixing prices for oil which was worked out and presented to me by Margold. This contemplates the freezing of prices at their present level and simultaneously announcing that on January 1 a complete schedule of prices will be put into effect if it is consid ered that an emergency then exists. In the meantime we will hold hearings so as to hear objections to the prices proposed. The schedule we will suggest in anticipation of its going into effect on January 1 will be the schedule prepared by the Planning and Co-ordination Committee. The President and I have discussed this two or three times and today he told me to go ahead. We know that the whole thing is experimental, but we feel that with these it will be a safer takeoff than to put a full schedule into effect at once.

Friday, October 13, 1933

Most of our discussion at Cabinet this afternoon was on the pending negotiations with Great Britain on its debt to us. Under Secretary Dean G. Acheson, of the Treasury, is representing the United States Government in these negotiations, and I must confess that he didn't give me the impression of being a man who could vigorously represent the views of the Administration. It was perfectly clear from the discussion that he is willing to make the utmost concession to Great Britain. Director of the Budget Lewis Douglas, who has been sitting in at Cabinet meetings this summer during the absence of the Vice President, very vigorously argued for an agreement on such terms as Great Britain might be willing to submit. In fact, I wouldn't be surprised if either one of them would not go all the way in wiping off the debts entirely.

The President said that Great Britain had always been a hard bargainer, and he is holding out for much more favorable terms than the British have so far suggested. He told Acheson to take the position firmly that Great Britain has not yet made a proposition and we are waiting for one. Acheson said that he thought the British delegates might go home, but this did not seem to worry the President.

The thing that surprises me about this whole matter is that the President should have appointed Acheson as the representative of the Government, considering his own view on this matter. Unless a negotiator is a vigorous and conscientious advocate, he can't go very far, especially when he is dealing with such shrewd diplomats as usually represent the British. If, on the other hand, although supposed to oppose such a course, he is willing to go all the way demanded by the parties with whom he is negotiating, he is worse than useless, in my opinion.

Secretary Hull expressed the opinion that these debts should be used as a club to force these nations to give us some reasonable trade concessions. I did not express myself and the other members of the Cabinet were almost equally as silent. The only reason I did not express myself was because the President seemed able to sustain his own views without outside help. Personally, I do not believe the debt should be canceled, although we could consider a reasonable compromise settlement.

The British do not want to default, but I can't see much difference between a voluntary default or a default with our consent, and it is the latter that the British want. In neither event would Great Britain be paying her debts. Moreover, to wipe off these debts actually or in effect would, it seems to me, not go at all well in the country.

Monday, October 16, 1933

Several of the members of the Planning and Co-ordination Committee of the Oil Industry came to my office to discuss the proposed order that I expected to issue today. Our plan was to freeze prices as of 7 A.M. last Saturday and then announce that the price schedule submitted some time ago on behalf of this committee would go into effect on January 1, next, subject to objections and hearings on the objections. This subcommittee stated that this would be a disastrous thing to do because it would freeze prices on an inequitable basis. They pointed out that in a number of places, of which Chicago is an example, gasoline under such an order would be selling at a number of different prices in different parts of the city. I sent for Margold, Marshall, and Meyers to discuss the matter with us. I readily admitted that this would be an undesirable situation and said that the prices ought to be at least uniform for any one community. Margold admitted too the undesirability of such a situation but said that, in the absence of some sort of a hearing, uniform prices could not be fixed. Wirt Franklin, on behalf of the oil men, then said that from their point of view they would rather not have any price fixing at the moment at all, and we finally agreed not to freeze prices at this time but to announce that, as of December 1, the proposed schedule of prices would go into effect subject to hearings. It was understood privately among those of us attending the conference that if, prior to December 1, I should come to the conclusion that enough time had not been given for hearing objections, I would extend the time of the going into effect of the price schedule for a further period, but not later than January 1.

Tuesday, October 17, 1933

We passed our biggest list of non-Federal projects at the Public Works Board meeting this morning in the quickest time on record.

Ray Tucker and Thomas H. Beck, the latter publisher of *Collier's Weekly,* came in at ten-thirty. Mr. Beck had a most interesting suggestion to make with reference to putting people back onto the land in Connecticut. His plan contemplates men past fifty years of age who, even if prosperity should return, could not hope to be reemployed in industry. He wants to buy up a lot of cheap land and inaugurate an extensive campaign of reforestation, including such crops as Christmas trees and laurel, for which there is a big market in New York. He would also restock with game birds and animal life so that the hunting privileges would be worth while. He thinks that the thing could be set up so that these older people could support themselves with the aid of a garden to supply their own immediate needs for food.

The President adjourned the Council meeting about three-fifteen and then asked the members of the Cabinet to remain, together with General Johnson, George Peek, Harry L. Hopkins, and Henry Morgenthau, Jr. The President first touched on the commodity market. Henry Morgenthau, Jr., was instructed to place orders for wheat in the market today and he did buy on behalf of the Federal Government about $11½ million worth, putting prices up three cents over the close last night. This wheat will be turned over to the Federal Surplus Relief Corporation for food for the unemployed. Then he went on to say that the bankers of the country were in a conspiracy to block the Administration program. He said the banks were not lending any money even on good security and that they were seriously hampering the business recovery. Reports have come to him from a number of sources as evidence of the unwillingness of the bankers to help out in this situation. He was quite clear in his own mind that a conspiracy existed, and he spoke of the possibility of extending Federal credit to businessmen who could not secure loans on good security at the banks. He said one thing that was hurting commodity prices was the belief engendered in the minds of the bankers that the dollar is to be stabilized and no further effort made to advance commodity prices. Two or three of those present, especially Lewis Douglas, defended the attitude of the bankers. Morgenthau made a suggestion that some of the big bankers be talked with to see if they would organize a pool of credit out of which loans could be made. The President approved this plan, and it is clear that he has in mind drastic action if the attitude of the bankers continues to be what he thinks it has been in the past. I related that word had come to me on several occasions that the Chicago bankers had made up their minds that Chicago should not apply for money for any municipal projects, and certainly it is a fact that Chicago has not applied for any of the Public Works money. It seemed to be the general opinion that the Chicago banks were tighter on credit than any other banks in the country.

At nine o'clock I went to the Department of Agriculture to discuss with Henry Wallace and Harry Hopkins the purchase of surplus butter for the unemployed. We agreed to buy $10 million worth of butter and to make a bid for the surplus apple crop in the Northwest. It was also agreed to buy about $10 million worth of wheat.

Wednesday, October 18, 1933

One of my callers this morning was Fenner Brockway, M.P., Editor of *The New Leader,* a British Labor paper. He attended my press conference yesterday. I noticed he was standing against the double doors and I wondered who he was. He appeared to be quite interested. He told me today that no member of the Government in Great Britain would hold a conference in such a free and open manner, and he commented also on the fact that I was in my shirt sleeves. He said he liked it.

At one-fifteen Colonel Edward M. House called on me. Earlier Colonel McIntyre had called me by telephone to say that Colonel House was with the President and that the President especially wanted him to meet me. McIntyre remarked that my ears ought to be burning from all the nice things that the President had said to House about me.

I was very much interested to meet Colonel House. He was such an important figure during the Wilson administration and the world war. He was very friendly and cordial and repeated what McIntyre had told me about the President wanting him to meet me. He said that the President had spoken of me in very complimentary terms and had said that he had great plans for the future in which I and one or two other Cabinet members figured. He quoted the President as saying that I was both able and strong and he went on to remark himself that this was a rare combination. He commended me on the work I have been doing and told me that if I ever got to New York, I was to call him up and have lunch with him. Before leaving he asked me how I was working with Secretary Roper and Secretary Hull. I told him I was working very well with Roper and that while I hadn't had so many contacts with Hull, our relations were very pleasant and that I had a very high opinion of him. I gathered that these two men were looming rather large in his mind out of the Cabinet membership. He spoke highly of both of them and indicated that he thought that Hull had come into his own. He told me that he had suggested Hull to the President for Secretary of State. Later in the afternoon when I called up Secretary Roper on another matter, he told me that Colonel House was with him.

Thursday, October 19, 1933

The President said to me this afternoon that there was an agrarian revolt on in the country and that this was our chief concern just now. He said there was one more remedy he proposed to try and that was the purchase of gold. He has made arrangements for this to go forward, and it seems clear to me that if this fails there will be frank inflation. There is a burden of debt weighing down upon everybody, especially the farmer, and while cheap money doesn't buy much in the way of goods, it does pay debts.

The President suggested that we might buy for Government post offices a number of bank buildings throughout the country where the banks themselves have been closed and are in process of liquidation. These buildings can be bought very cheaply, generally far below the cost price. They are fireproof, generally speaking, and contain vaults. This will have the added effect of releasing these frozen assets which will help the credit situation. He has asked me to pursue this matter with Mr. Merriam of the Reconstruction Finance Corporation.

Friday, October 20, 1933

I lunched with the President today to take up a number of matters with him, but he had so many things he wanted to talk about that I didn't really get through. However, he did scrutinize the list of public works that I submitted to him. On the Army list that Secretary Dern got us to adopt yesterday on the theory that it had the prior approval of the President, he did just what he said he would do. He allowed $15 million for aviation for both the Army and the Navy, and $10 million for motorization and mechanization for the Army. This was quite in contrast with the $172 million that Dern had had us put through for the Army alone. He also disapproved a considerable allocation for coast defense purposes.

At luncheon he told me that the Government would begin to buy gold on Monday and would keep on buying it. This will be for the purpose of creating a wider credit basis, pushing up the price of commodities.

He also read to me a letter from himself to President Kalinin, of Russia, and the latter's reply. The President in his letter proposed that Russia send a representative to talk with him and his suggestion was cordially received. This is undoubtedly paving the way to recognition, something that I have been in favor of for several years, and which pleased me very much indeed.

The Cabinet meeting was one of the most interesting we have had. The President repeated to the Cabinet what he had told me just before at luncheon about the Russian situation and what he said was received with varying emotions. Much to my surprise, both Secretary Wallace and Secretary Perkins seemed to doubt the wisdom of the move, the former on the theory that it would raise trade complications to the disadvantage of the farmer. No other member of the Cabinet said anything or indicated any feeling. I know that Secretary Dern is in favor of recognition because he so stated some time ago, but I didn't know how the other members of the Cabinet felt about it.

Miss Perkins told me a long, circumstantial, and lurid story about German propaganda in this country. What she said seemed to be well substantiated by the facts and if what she related was anywhere near the truth, Germany is exceedingly active here building up German sentiment along the line already so well developed in Germany itself. This movement, of course, is anti-Jewish, pro-Nordic, and extremely nationalistic. Germany, according to the story, is sending several hundred big men over here who have systematically joined the German societies, the control of which they are rapidly taking over. Following assumption of control, Jewish members are expelled, even those who have been members for thirty or forty years. A particular appeal is being made to Germans of the younger generations and, according to Miss Perkins, with marked success.

In this connection Judge Harry Fisher, of Chicago, called me up this morning to say that a number of prominent Jews had met last night, the number including General Abel Davis, Max Epstein, Rabbi Mann, and others whose names were mentioned. It is rumored in Germany that the German Ambassador, Hans Luther, is proposing to travel to Chicago with Eckener on his proposed Zeppelin trip. It was urged upon me that an intimation ought to be given to Luther not to make the trip. Fisher seemed to anticipate that there might be riots among the Jewish population, apparently in the form of a demonstration against Luther as the official representative of Germany. I told this at the Cabinet meeting, and the President asked the Secretary of State whether such an intimation could be made to the German Ambassador.

Last night Anna and I dined with the Wallaces. The other guests were the Secretary of Commerce, the Director of the Budget, and Dr. Rex Tugwell. Henry Wallace looked completely fagged out. In fact, he has had this appearance for several days now, and it is little wonder, considering the strain he is under.

Monday, October 23, 1933

At three-fifteen I went over to see the President. Colonel McIntyre had called me to express the President's interest in the All-American Canal project. The President suggested sending a large delegation over to see me, but I told McIntyre that I had been visited by delegations ad lib, for this project; that I knew all that there was to be known; and that the only question to decide was one of policy, which it was up to the President to pass on. Accordingly, the President sent word for me to come over at three-fifteen.

He thinks we ought to go ahead with the All-American Canal

and said to appropriate $6 million to cover what he thought would be required for the first year's work. This we will do at the Public Works Board meeting tomorrow. Then we talked over a number of other things, including the choice of a Republican for membership on the Civil Service Commission. I had taken with me a list of suggested names and the two that he thought the most highly of were former Governor Gardiner, of Maine, and Professor Leonard White, of the University of Chicago.

We got to talking about his speech last night, in which he announced that the Government would begin to buy gold, and that it was the purpose of the Administration to put up commodity prices before stabilizing the dollar. He said that Wall Street did not like his speech and that for the first time in his memory, or mine, Wall Street was not dictating the fiscal policy of the Government. He said that it was the most significant thing that had happened during his Administration.

Then I told him how happy I was over the *rapprochement* between Russia and the United States, and in this connection he told me how the thing was brought about. The old line State Department men fussed over the proposition of how to approach Russia and the way it was worked out was this: Henry Morgenthau, Jr., had been discussing a loan for some weeks with Boris E. Skvirsky, who represents Amtorg in this country. Recently, at the suggestion of the President, he told Skvirsky that there was nothing doing presently on the loan but that some good news might come soon. Then William Bullitt met Skvirsky in Morgenthau's office. Bullitt said: "As you know, I am Assistant Secretary of State, but I am talking to you as private citizen William Bullitt." Bullitt showed him a draft of a letter that the President subsequently signed and asked Skvirsky what would be the reply of President Kalinin, of Russia, if he should receive such a letter. Skvirsky's reply was that he would take it under consideration and give a reply later. A few days later there was another meeting in Morgenthau's office at Skvirsky's request. Skvirsky said that as a private citizen he felt justified in saying that if such a letter as the one referred to should be sent to President Kalinin, the latter would reply in some such manner as appeared in a draft of a letter which Skvirsky then proceeded to show to Bullitt. Bullitt asked him whether he was perfectly sure that such a reply would be received, and Skvirsky assured him that he was not only head of Amtorg but that he represented the Russian Government in the United States. He gave the solemn assurance that the reply would be along those lines. Whereupon Bullitt took from his pocket an official letter signed by the President, this letter being the duplicate of the tentative one he had shown at the previous conference, and said to Skvirsky that in view of his assurances he was authorized to present that letter in behalf of the President of the United States. Then Skvirsky, on his part, produced an official letter signed by President Kalinin, and the deed was done.

Saturday, October 28, 1933

I was overrun with delegations and individuals today pressing for particular public works projects. My first callers were Sir William Beveridge and Sir Arthur Steele-Maitland, the latter of whom was a member of the MacDonald Labor Cabinet in Great Britain. They were interested in public works and in the oil administration, so I sent one of them down to talk to Major Fleming, in the absence of Colonel Waite, and the other I sent to Mr. Margold to discuss oil. When they saw the unusual numbers of people waiting at the other end of my room to interview me, they were very apologetic for coming in at all. I am sorry they felt the pressure of these numbers and told them that if they wanted to see me again, I would be glad to make a special appointment for them.

The largest delegation, consisting of some thirty people, was composed almost entirely of Congressmen who proceeded to bedevil me for post offices. The pressure for post offices has been terrific and is becoming even more insistent, if that is possible. I told them that we had a special committee making a study of this situation with a view to seeing whether many of these post offices could not be built at such reduced figures as would justify us in going ahead with them.

Then a delegation from Utah, headed by Secretary Dern, and including Senator King, Governor Blood, Congressmen Murdock and Robinson, and Mr. Wallace, came in to nag again about some reclamation projects for their state. This group has been hanging around Washington for more than three weeks. At intervals they come in to see me, then they go to see Colonel Waite, and then they go over to the White House. They seem to be proceeding on the theory that they can just wear down our resistance and get what they want. I wonder a little at a fellow member of the Cabinet appearing with such a delegation to harass another Cabinet officer, but such is politics.

Thursday, November 2, 1933

I had a good many callers today, including Senator Capper and a large committee from Kansas who are here on a public works project. Senator Bone, of Washington, was also in and I simply couldn't make him understand why his state, which has already been allotted about fifty per cent more than it is entitled to out of public works funds on the basis of population, should not be given many, many millions more. He acted puzzled and hurt at the very suggestion.

This was a big day in public works. We put through two big propositions, one for the purchase of 100,000 tons of rails for the railroads throughout the country, with some 30,000 tons of fasteners of various sorts. We also voted something over $80 million for the Pennsylvania Railroad to complete electrification of its line from Wilmington to Washington and to buy locomotives, build cars, etc., etc. This money can be put to work at once and its beneficial effects will be felt in many parts of the country. This is the biggest financing of capital goods that we have had an opportunity to make to date, and Colonel Waite and I were both very much pleased.

After the Public Works meeting I went to the President with the projects that we had adopted and he approved all of them.

Friday, November 3, 1933

We had an interesting Cabinet meeting today, a good deal of our discussion being with reference to the economic situation. Director of the Budget Douglas was quite strenuous in expressing his opinion, and it seemed to me that in arguing with the President he went a little far both in the substance of what he said and the manner of its expression. It is clear that he is tremendously worked up over the possibility of using to any further considerable extent the credit of the Government for public works or farm relief, or anything else along those lines.

At six o'clock I took a train to Philadelphia. I had promised to make the principal address at the one hundredth anniversary of the Philadelphia Board of Trade. Since it was to be a prolonged session, I decided to go up late. I was met at the train by a small committee and escorted two or three blocks to the Bellevue-Stratford Hotel by motorcycle men, although why they were considered necessary I cannot explain. Then I dressed and went to the banquet hall. I had known that this was a very conservative group and perhaps there was some malice in the dose that I had prepared for them. The president of the Board of Trade seemed to me to be old almost to the point of senility, and the total age of the banqueters must have run into very high figures indeed. At the speaker's table were General Atterbury, president of the Pennsylvania Railroad; President Charles H. Ewing, of the Philadelphia and Reading Railroad; Samuel Vauclain (who, by the way, was a former resident of Altoona), president of the Baldwin Locomotive Works; and Congressman James M. Beck, Solicitor General under President Taft and one of the outstanding conservatives of the country. These were typical of the audience and I suspect that my speech must have convinced them that I am an extremely dangerous citizen.

In my speech I pointed out how ruthlessly we had exploited the natural resources of the country and then the human resources, including women and children. I went on to say that we were in the midst of a social revolution and that the days of rugged individualism and ruthless power were over forever.

Monday, November 6, 1933

At twelve o'clock Secretaries Wallace and Perkins, and Harry Hopkins, Emergency Relief Administrator, came in for a conversation by direction of the President. Professor Rogers was also here at the suggestion of Secretary Wallace. We discussed a plan of Hopkins to put anywhere from two to four million men back to work for standard wages on a thirty-hour-week basis. He would continue to pay on account of these wages what he is now contributing toward relief, and the balance would be made up out of the public works funds. This would amount to a maximum of $400 million for the next sixty days. This would put a serious crimp in the balance of our public works fund, but we all thought it ought to be done.

There was a general feeling that we really are in a very critical condition and that something drastic and immediate ought to be done to bolster the situation. Secretary Wallace believes that the public works fund ought to be increased to $10 billion.

Tuesday, November 7, 1933

Harry L. Hopkins and I lunched with the President to discuss Hopkins' plan of putting four million of the unemployed to work. In order to do this, he is counting upon a certain contribution by municipalities and states. He will put in, out of his emergency relief funds, what it would cost for relief for these men, and Public Works will appropriate about $400 million. Under this plan he will have two million men now on relief work putting in full time by November 15 on various public works throughout the country, the men to receive the normal wages for the type of work they are doing. He will have another two million men at work by December 1, and the money appropriated will run him until February 15.

Wednesday, November 8, 1933

I was one of the guests at the White House at a luncheon given by the President today in honor of Maxim Litvinov, Commissar of Foreign Affairs of the Soviet Government of Russia. Mr. Litvinov sat on the President's right and I sat on his right. On my own right was Constantin Oumansky, press relations man of the Russian Foreign Office. Both men spoke excellent English so that I had no difficulty in getting along. Mr. Litvinov naturally spent most of his time talking with the President, but I had a very good chance to talk with Mr. Oumansky about Russian affairs.

At the end of the luncheon an interesting thing occurred. Mr. Litvinov put his hand into an inside pocket of his coat and pulled out a couple of booklets of Russian stamps which he proceeded to show to the President. On Mr. Oumansky's right was Henry Morgenthau, Jr., who remarked to Mr. Oumansky that I was a stamp collector too, whereupon he also drew out several booklets of Russian stamps which he handed to me for my inspection, later making me a gift of three of the booklets. They are all new issue stamps, some of which have not yet reached this country. Mr. Litvinov gave the President the stamps he had been showing him and Mr. Oumansky also gave some to Mr. Morgenthau, whose son is a collector.

Mr. Oumansky told me that he collected stamps and he also confided to me that Mr. Litvinov was a secret but passionate collector. According to his story, Mr. Litvinov does not advertise this hobby. On one occasion Mr. Oumansky called at his home and found him behind a closed door. He kept him waiting until he could put all of his stamps away so that he wouldn't be caught at it.

Personally, I have been in favor of the recognition of Russia by the United States for a good many years and so it was a particular pleasure for me to be at this luncheon to meet members of the Litvinov party. I have no doubt that recognition will result from conversation in progress here now, and I sincerely hope so.

Friday, November 10, 1933

We spent an hour at the beginning of the Cabinet today having our pictures taken. It was the first full meeting of the Cabinet for a number of months and it was the first official photograph. I believe I am the only member of the Cabinet who has a perfect record for attendance. I haven't missed a single meeting since the first one in the White House on March 5. Secretary of the Treasury Woodin has probably the worst attendance record, with Farley close second. Woodin has been ill all summer and Farley has been doing politics around the country a good deal of the time. We were, at first, seated around the Cabinet table and then we went into the President's office where we posed before a movie talkie machine, with the President doing what little talking was done.

At Cabinet meeting the President paid a very lovely tribute to Secretary of State Hull, who is about to go to Montevideo as the head of the American delegation that is to meet with other representatives of North and South American countries. The President said that Hull was the one man not only in the United States but in the whole world who could go to Montevideo with any hope of bringing back any tangible results in the way of better understanding among the countries on this hemisphere.

We had some discussion about liquor control. The President seems to be leaning toward a Government monopoly plan. I strongly favor Government monopoly myself.

The President indicated that things hadn't been going quite so smoothly in conversations with the representatives of Soviet Russia, but I think he hopes that an understanding will be reached. Apparently he is finding Litvinov a good trader.

After the Cabinet meeting I went into the President's office. I asked him what he thought of the plan to name the Casper-Alcova Dam in Wyoming after Senator Kendrick, since the Senator died. I suggested this because this matter was nearest to Senator Kendrick's heart of anything of a public nature. The President thought well of the idea and then went on to tell me that, without consulting him at all, Dr. Morgan had proceeded to name the new dam in the Tennessee Valley after Senator Norris, which, as the President said to me, "is against your policy of naming things after living persons." I asked him if he didn't think that was sound policy and he said he did. He went on to say that his son Elliott had called him up from Los Angeles only a few days ago to say that the people out there wanted to name a certain big conduit being constructed there the Franklin D. Roosevelt Conduit. According to the President, he said to Elliott: "I am still alive. I wouldn't think of such a thing."

Saturday, November 11, 1933

There was a meeting in my office at two o'clock this afternoon participated in by Harry L. Hopkins, Federal Relief Administrator, and ten or twelve bureau and division chiefs interested in the civil works program which has been made possible by the allocation of $400 million that we made last week to him for this purpose. We met to discuss the line of demarcation between his work and that of the public works organization and also to discuss in general the type of work that he can undertake. The bureau chiefs were here because they were interested in presenting plans for work to be done within their respective jurisdiction by Hopkins' forces.

In general, we came to the conclusion that all of the work undertaken by the Federal Civil Works Administration would be by force account. This organization will undertake no contract work. It will put up no buildings. It won't build any sewers or water works or incinerators or bridges. But these men will be put to work on projects of a minor character. They will work thirty hours a week and they will be paid the wage scale set up in our public works program. After the meeting the newspaper correspondents were in and I made the statement for publication that any state or municipality withdrawing a project submitted to the Public Works organization for consideration in the hope or expectation that the Civil Works organization would do this work instead, free of cost, would not only not have such work done by the Civil Works organization, but that it might not again resubmit its project to the Public Works organization. I announced, however, that if, as a result of its own conclusions in the matter, the Public Works organization should turn over any project to the Civil Works organization, the latter would be free to go ahead with it.

Monday, November 13, 1933

Last night I dined with Henry Morgenthau, Jr., who was giving a dinner in honor of Maxim Litvinov. There were several members of Mr. Litvinov's staff present, and in addition the Turkish Minister, the Attorney General, Senators Wagner and Pittman, Henry Morgenthau, Sr., William C. Bullitt, Don Richberg, and two or three others. Shortly after dinner the Russians left for a conference at the White House with the President, so that the party broke up early and I was able to get home at a reasonable time.

Tuesday, November 14, 1933

Late yesterday afternoon Colonel McIntyre called me to say that he wanted to have a talk with me on a personal matter. He stated that he would be able to get away late in the day, but he didn't come and I called him and he asked me if I could drop by the White House. Then a funny thing happened. I was very tired all day and I left fifteen minutes earlier than usual intending to drive around by the White House. Instead, I got into the car and before I realized it, not having said anything to Carl, I was pretty nearly home. I called Colonel McIntyre from the house. He asked whether I would be at the office after dinner and when I said I would, he said he would get in touch with me.

He came over about half past ten and what he had to tell me was this: The former Governor of North Carolina, Oliver Max Gardner, had told him during the day that he (Gardner) had been instructed by his clients to start suit against me on my old brokerage account with A. O. Slaughter, Anderson and Fox. His clients told him that if he didn't want to handle the case, they would get someone else to do it. Gardner told McIntyre that he was perfectly willing to decline to go ahead with the case, although that wouldn't stop it. He was willing to do this in order not to embarrass the Administration, but McIntyre told him, and properly so, that the Administration would rather have him handle the case than anyone else. Then McIntyre went in to speak to the President, and the President said to him: "You like Harold and Harold likes you. Suppose you just go and talk it over with him." I told McIntyre just what the situation was with respect to this account; how at a certain stage when I had it well covered, I had told the brokers that I couldn't bring in any more collateral and instructed them to close out the account. But this they didn't do. Like everyone else, they thought the market would come back shortly. I had been one of their very best customers and they didn't want me to be out of the market when it did come back. Finally when I was proceeding on my own account to sell First National Bank stock in order to reduce my debit balance, Kingman Douglas, one of the partners, sent for me voluntarily. He told me he hated to see me sell that stock; that he had made a personal investigation of the condition of the bank; that he thought there wasn't any better security anywhere and that it was bound to come back. He told me not to sell any more and that the firm would carry me until the stock did come back.

Then I went away to New Mexico for the summer. On my return in the fall a suggestion was made that I close out the account, but I reminded Douglas of his voluntary undertaking and the thing rested. It went on for quite a long while. In the meantime First National Bank stock sold off further and further until it wasn't worth anywhere near enough to pay me out on my account. Then various suggestions of settlement were made. The firm wanted me to sign a demand note to cover the balance and I refused to do so. Then after some further negotiations the bank stock was sold, leaving me still with a considerable debit balance.

I had called Fred Marx in to help me out in the negotiations and the firm finally promised to let the matter rest. They did this for two reasons. They knew that I couldn't pay the balance and they also believed that sooner or later I would get back on my feet and would pay. Then came the offer to come to Washington and once again I asked Fred Marx to talk with Douglas and one or two of the other partners because I felt I would have no right to accept President Roosevelt's invitation to go into the Cabinet if there were any danger of a suit being filed against me. Again I was assured through Marx that the thing would be allowed to ride.

Last Saturday I got a letter from Marx telling me that the firm was being reorganized with some of the Chicago partners displaced and with the New York partners in control. He told me that the Chicago people had advised him that they were no longer able to do anything about my account.

This afternoon, after the Council meeting, I had an interview with the President. As I entered the office he greeted me in his usual friendly way and said: "Well, Harold, I see they are after you now." I laid my resignation on his desk. He opened it, read it, handed it back to me and told me to take it away with me and forget it. He said: "I know you." He is clearly of the opinion that big interests somewhere along the line are using this to get at the Administration through me, but that didn't seem to worry him any. He referred to the attack which was made on Woodin when newspapers all over the country demanded his resignation or dismissal because his name had been discovered on some of the Morgan preferred lists. He took the position then that what Woodin had done was a perfectly legitimate thing for Woodin to do as a private citizen. He remarked: "All of us have been in trouble some time or other." His final suggestion was that I try to make a reasonable settlement of this account and if I couldn't make the grade myself, he said he would call in some friends of the Administration and see whether enough couldn't be raised to handle the matter. Naturally I demurred strongly at such a suggestion as this but he said it was nonsense; that it wasn't a personal matter at all but a public matter.

I feel very much relieved at his altogether human and friendly attitude. Whatever may be the outcome, I can never forget his kindness and understanding. I have never been given to hero worship, but I have a feeling of loyalty and real affection for the President that I have never felt for any other man, although I have had very deep attachments for other men.

Wednesday, November 15, 1933

Fred Marx got in from Chicago this morning. I went over the Slaughter, Anderson and Fox matter with him, and later he went over to talk with Governor Gardner. He reported that Governor Gardner is a very nice person. They talked settlement. Gardner said he would call up his clients and later in the afternoon Fred got word by telephone that they would settle at fifty cents on the dollar. This, of course, would be on the basis of what they claim to be due which, according to my view, is way out of line. They claim about $107,000. The last time I looked at the account I think it was about $54,000 and that was only a few months ago. How it could have doubled in a few months just on interest, I don't know.

I told Fred to go back to see Gardner tomorrow and tell him that

I would like to put an accountant on the books to figure the legal interest instead of usurious and compound interest. Fred told Gardner that the President knew all about this matter and was standing back of me, so that if his client is trying to bludgeon me through any idea that I will settle on an unfair basis because I don't want the President to find out, he is barking up the wrong tree.

I saw the President at the noon hour to dispose of a number of matters. He asked me whether I had heard anything more and I told him that Fred Marx was in conference with Gardner. He wanted to know whether they were being decent but I had nothing to report.

Governor Ely, of Massachusetts, was in. It was with him that I had a passage of arms by phone some time ago. He seems like a pretty high-class man and we got along very well.

Thursday, November 16, 1933

Today has been a very heavy day. I started in with my interviews early in the morning. At any rate I made one delegation happy and this was a big one consisting of Senators, governors, Congressmen, and others from Virginia, North Carolina, and Tennessee. I made known to this delegation that the President had approved in principle their plan for a scenic highway connecting the Shenandoah and Smoky Mountains National Parks and that we were ready to proceed with the preliminary survey of the route. The cost of the survey will be borne by the three states and they will also provide a right-of-way 200 feet wide. The driveway is to be well up toward the top of the mountain range all the way. This driveway when completed will become a part of our national park system and for that reason our Bureau of National Parks will be charged with the selection of the route, the surveyors to be furnished by the three states in question. Everyone in the delegation was delighted and said many complimentary things.

Friday, November 17, 1933

The President and Mrs. Roosevelt gave their official dinner to the members of the Cabinet last night. There were fifty who sat down at the table. The only missing member of the Cabinet was the Secretary of State who, with Mrs. Hull, is on his way to Montevideo. After dinner we went into the East Room for some music, and other guests came in—quite a lot of them. Mr. Litvinov, Mr. Oumansky, and one or two others of the Russian delegation came in after the dinner and I had an opportunity to speak briefly to both Litvinov and Oumansky. The President had told me when I saw him at noon that the Russian situation was just about cleared up and these two gentlemen confirmed it. At eleven o'clock the President announced that he was going up to his study with Mr. Litvinov and shortly after, the party broke up and Anna and I went home.

I have had conferences recently with Ross Woodhull, who came here with full power to represent the Sanitary District. I think we have agreed on the terms by which we will consider lending them about $36 million for the sewer works in Chicago made necessary by the Supreme Court decision handed down some time ago. I had a special appointment with Tom Courtney who was here yesterday but stayed over in order to have a chance to talk with me. He would like to have some recognition by the Federal Government, and I told him that there was a very good chance for some person like himself with a decent record to assume leadership of the Democratic party in Cook County on behalf of the national administration. I talked with Jim Farley about him last night and I called up Jim today and arranged for Courtney to see him late this afternoon.

At Cabinet meeting the President told how he and Litvinov had arrived at a meeting of minds last night about midnight. They exchanged letters covering the points in controversy, and friendly relations with Russia have been resumed after all these years. Personally I am very glad that this should be the result. I have been in favor of recognition for a long time and as near as I could make out, the President got everything that he wanted out of these conversations.

Secretary Woodin is going to Arizona on an indefinite leave of absence without salary. He has had a bad throat for months. He has wanted to resign but the President hasn't permitted it. In referring to his early departure today the President said that he believed that Woodin was the best-loved man in the Cabinet. I think everyone does have a feeling of affection for him. I know I like him very much.

After the Cabinet meeting I stayed to take up some public works and other matters with the President. Although he has been planning to leave on a train at six o'clock for Warm Springs, Georgia, he was unruffled and friendly as ever. On three occasions lately he has asked me to come to Warm Springs these next two weeks for three days. He told Anna in the receiving line last night that he was going to order me down there and today he renewed the invitation. Probably I will run down next week end as he suggested this time.

Saturday, November 18, 1933

Mr. Litvinov gave a luncheon in the Chinese Room at the Mayflower Hotel today, to which I was invited. The Turkish Minister sat on my left and Mr. Moore, of the State Department, on my right. Other Cabinet members present were the Attorney General, the Secretary of the Navy, and the Secretary of Commerce. There were also present Under Secretary Henry Morgenthau, Jr., of the Treasury, and Assistant Secretary Phillips, of the State Department. It wasn't a very lively affair and we had altogether too much to eat.

Just to show how work piles up on me: Thursday night I couldn't come to the office because of the official dinner to the Cabinet at the White House. The result was that a lot of work was left on my desk undone that night. I worked all day yesterday and last night until after ten o'clock without clearing my desk. I have worked all day today and until eleven o'clock. I am leaving my desk still uncleared so that I will have to come down tomorrow to finish the job.

Wednesday, November 22, 1933

Last night Anna and I went to dinner at the Turkish Embassy. There were twenty-two guests present. Sir Ronald Lindsay, the British Ambassador, and Lady Lindsay, were guests, as were the German Ambassador, Dr. Hans Luther, the Egyptian Chargé d'Affaires, Nicholas Khalil Bey, Mr. H. Gabreil da Silva, First Secretary of the Portuguese Embassy, and others, whose names, as usual, I did not get. Secretary Wallace was there with Mrs. Wallace but there were no other Cabinet members present.

The house is a large one, richly furnished and beautiful. The appointments were magnificent in every respect, but when I got through dinner I was no longer surprised at what Mrs. Hiram Johnson told me on one occasion. I happened to drop in there about dinner time once and found that she and the Senator were having dinner although they were going out to an official dinner later. She explained that they always did that because at official dinners they gave you very little to eat and if you happened to turn your head to talk to a neighbor, when you looked around again you were likely to find that the butler had grabbed your plate from in front of you. There wasn't much to eat at the Turkish Minister's and it was a race against time to consume what you had before the butler disappeared with your plate. The result was that I actually got up from the table hungry. Despite it all, it was interesting, but I was desperately tired when I got home—so tired that I didn't sleep well. I don't see how I can keep up this sort of thing and do my work too.

I called the heads of the Interior Department bureaus and the chief executives together in the auditorium at four o'clock just to talk to them and explain that in spite of the little attention I had been giving them I was as devoted as ever to my own Department. I explained the necessity for having to move so many of the bureaus out of the building and apologized for the inconvenience and disorganization caused thereby. It was quite a nice friendly meeting and I think it was a good thing to have done.

Thursday, November 23, 1933

Major La Guardia, former Congressman and Mayor-elect of New York City, came in to see me today about public works for his city. I had never met him before and I liked his appearance. He is short and quite stocky and apparently full of vigor. His career in Congress shows that he has real ability and high courage. If he makes as outstanding a record as Mayor as he has made in the House of Representatives, he ought to give New York a great administration.

Wednesday, November 29, 1933

Saturday afternoon at four forty five I took the train for Atlanta, Georgia, arriving there at ten o'clock Sunday morning. Colonel McIntyre and a friend picked me up and drove me over to Warm Springs, where I was the personal guest of the President. He has a small cottage beautifully located on the edge of a well-wooded ravine just a little way out of Warm Springs. He has only three bedrooms but Mrs. Roosevelt was not there and I occupied her room. A common bathroom connected the President's room and mine.

Miss Le Hand, his personal secretary, had the other bedroom. Meals are served in the living room and the President works there.

The President is always charming but he was delightful at Warm Springs. Everyone there loves him, and crowds hang outside the gate, especially on Sundays, just to see him and cheer him as he drives in and out occasionally. They stay there literally all day long, hour after hour. He didn't leave the house on Sunday until about three o'clock in the afternoon and there they still were, men, women, and children. He drives his own car at Warm Springs, an open Plymouth, so arranged with some contraption on the steering wheel that he can operate it without having to use his feet which are helpless.

Warm Springs is at the foot of the last spur of the Appalachian Range. The President's cottage is higher up on the ridge itself. Beyond that he has some 2,000 acres of farm land where he raises some crops and is experimenting with a herd of cattle. He bought some ordinary cows throughout the adjoining country and then two full-blooded bulls, with the result that he is getting pretty good stock for that country. Some of the surrounding country is very lovely, and while I was there he took me driving on two or three occasions. He goes anywhere in his car, right into the woods, taking a real delight in making it difficult for the Secret Service car to follow him. But the Secret Service men love him like everyone else and they get as much fun out of it as he does.

I have never had contact with a man who was loved as he is. To the people at Warm Springs he is just a big jolly brother. They swarm all over him and around him and their genuine affection for him is apparent on all occasions. On our drive Sunday afternoon we went clear out to the end of a knob where we had a wonderful view of the surrounding country. This was on his property and there we ran into a group of people, including Colonel McIntyre, who were having a beefsteak picnic. He couldn't get his car stopped before they all came swarming around it. In fact, he almost ran into one woman. So eager was she to reach him that he scarcely had time to come to a halt. They climbed all over the car. One woman whose legs were badly crippled with infantile paralysis was hoisted onto my side of the car and sat on the edge of it with her feet in my lap while she led in the singing of two or three songs for the President. Then, happy and laughing, they all backed away from the car when he insisted that he had to leave them.

General Hugh S. Johnson was there when I arrived, as was Henry Morgenthau, Jr. Secretary Wallace came down on Monday. I had a chance for two short private sessions with the President. We were able to clear up a lot of matters that I was anxious to talk over with him. He usually goes over to the pool to swim late in the morning just after he gets up, then back for lunch. He works in the afternoon, then dinner and to bed by ten o'clock. He was looking very well and apparently is feeling well.

When I was there the newspapers carried the interview with Al Smith attacking the President on his monetary policy and referring to "baloney dollars." I really believe that the President is glad to have Al Smith frankly in the open now. He has been opposed to the President for several years but has kept up more or less of a pretense of friendliness. Now Al Smith has definitely aligned himself with the bankers and Wall Street and the rest of the predatory interests. The issue is being drawn more clearly every day and the fight is opening up all along the line.

Friday, December 1, 1933

Yesterday was Thanksgiving, but this didn't mean much to me in the way of a rest. I got to the office about nine o'clock, worked through until one, went home for dinner, and returned to the office and worked through until six. At that time I was so nervously exhausted that I went home and after a light supper went to bed at half past seven. I dictated all day long on correspondence and office matters. The only interruption I had was just before noon when Pierce Miller, of the Hearst Service, came in to show me a release from Al Smith savagely attacking the Public Works Administration. I dictated a short statement of two or three hundred words which I gave to Miller. I called Mike Straus, who came down and sent copies of my statement to the other press agencies.

This morning the Washington papers, and I imagine the papers generally throughout the country, carried Smith's statement on the front page. But my statement was also carried on the front page in a parallel column.

During the morning Steve Early, the President's assistant secretary in charge of press relations, called me about my statement. He was very enthusiastic about it. He said it was a complete answer to Smith and that it was a job well done. I had the same comment from others during the day. Late in the afternoon four of the leading correspondents in Washington came in to ask me for a follow-up for Sunday showing affirmatively what Public Works had done in the way of getting men back to work. J. Fred Essary, head of the *Baltimore Sun* bureau here, personally congratulated me on my Smith statement.

I have ground away all day desperately attacking the work on my desk. Tonight at eleven o'clock I am pretty well cleared up. Another hour would do it, but I haven't got another hour's work in me.

At the invitation of Secretary Wallace, I joined him, Dr. Tugwell, Joe O'Mahoney, and Secretary Roper at the Cosmos Club at lunch to discuss lining up the progressive Republicans in the Middle West behind our program and behind the Administration. We all agreed on policy, leaving details to be worked out later.

Saturday, December 2, 1933

I am giving a good deal of thought to strengthening the Public Works organization and making it more directly responsible to me. I have wired to three men in Chicago to come on to see if I can fit them in somewhere along the line. The more I look into it, the less satisfied am I with the situation in Public Works. I have allowed it to get out of hand so that I am in the position of having to assume the responsibility for mistakes without having exercised my powers of control.

We organized the Subsistence Homesteads Corporation today. We made Dr. Wilson, who is in charge of that work, president, with myself as chairman of the board. We approved a number of projects. I am becoming worried about the Reedsville, West Virginia, project. I am afraid that we are due for some criticism for our work there. In the first place, we undertook it too hastily. Colonel Howe, in a rash moment, told the President that we would start work within three weeks. This was too short a time considering that no foundation had been laid. The result has been, in order to make good on this rash boast, that we have rushed ahead pell-mell. I am afraid we are spending more money than we have a right to spend. Another thing that bothers me is that Colonel Howe, with I think the approval of Mrs. Roosevelt, wanted us to enter into a contract for some sixty or seventy-five knockdown houses. I understand these houses are only about 10 feet wide and I am afraid they will look a good deal like a joke. I know that Wilson is not satisfied with the Reedsville project. I haven't been down to see it myself, but I have a disturbed feeling about it.

Monday, December 4, 1933

I worked under a great deal of strain and stress today due to personal matters of a serious nature.

In the afternoon I had Colonel Waite in for a frank talk. I told him that perhaps, without any definite intention so to do on his part, he had in effect built up an organization which looked to him as the Administrator of Public Works. I reminded him that I was the Administrator and told him that I couldn't get along any longer on the present basis. We talked things over in the utmost friendliness, but he said that the best thing for him to do would be to resign. I told him I didn't want him to do that and that he ought not to think of doing it. I assured him that I have every confidence in his character and ability and that I have a feeling of real affection for him, but that since the President had given me instead of him the particular responsibility of Administrator, since the country understood I was Administrator, and since Congress would hold me responsible as Administrator, I would have to exercise the power that went with the responsibility. We talked over the organization from several points of view. He told me that our views on organization were fundamentally different and he believed it should head up to one man and not consist of independent bureaus. I told him I had exactly the same conception as he did about what the organization ought to be and that in my opinion the difference between us wasn't the type of organization but that he wanted the organization to head up to him, the Deputy Administrator, instead of to me, the Administrator. I pointed out that not only he but others in the Public Works Administration had been exercising powers that they didn't have and which I had never delegated to them. Finally I suggested that he think about the matter overnight and take it up again.

Tuesday, December 5, 1933

The Public Works Board meeting went off in good shape today. We passed a number of projects. It is really functioning quite satisfactorily now and all the hard feeling that was so evident at the outset has disappeared. The press conference following the board meeting was interesting and longer than usual. I really enjoy my press conferences and the correspondents seem to like them too.

The President got back to Washington yesterday and so I attended the Council meeting at two o'clock. I have been terribly tired today. I didn't sleep more than three hours all told last night and I found the Council meeting very dull and uninteresting. I stayed after the meeting because I had a lot of public works projects to submit to the President for his approval. The President is looking fine. He has clearly benefited from his two weeks at Warm Springs. He said he regretted the necessity of having to come back and went on to caution all of us to watch our health, reminding us that Congress would shortly be in session, and remarking that he didn't want any of us to break down next winter. I remarked to myself under my breath that I could tell as good a joke as that myself.

Saturday, December 16, 1933

Last Monday morning Carl could not get the car up the incline in front of the house and so I started down to meet him at the garage. Halfway down both feet went out from under me and I came down harder than I ever have done in my life on the ice. I felt stunned and bruised and the breath was practically knocked out of me. After a minute or two I was able to get to my feet and I then proceeded to the garage where I got into the car and then went to the office. All the way I felt very badly with a good deal of pain, but my sensation was mostly shock and breathlessness. I was a good deal the worse for the wear when I got to the office and I wasn't able to seat myself at my desk in my normal manner. I had to have help. The pain began to increase and so I had a doctor brought in. His guess was that I had broken a rib. I then called Anna up to tell her what had happened and to say that I was about to go to the Naval Hospital. Getting to the hospital was an excruciatingly painful operation. By that time the pain had become more intense and I had the greatest difficulty in getting myself into the car and out of it when I reached the hospital. An X ray at the hospital showed that one rib had been broken and almost broken loose as well from the spinal column. Fortunately, the spinal column itself was not injured, as it was feared at first it might be. Accordingly, I was taped and taken upstairs and put to bed, where I have been all week with several more days of the same sort of thing in prospect.

The President sent his personal physician, Dr. McIntire, over to the hospital as soon as he heard of the accident and later in the day he came over again with a lovely personal note from the President written in his own handwriting. On Tuesday afternoon, shortly after five, the President came over to see me. He must have spent some twenty-five minutes in my room chatting about public affairs and other matters in his natural and delightful manner.

I have, of course, had a great many messages and flowers and calls from various people. Secretary of Navy Swanson came to see me Monday afternoon, only himself to be brought low that same night with a very bad attack of high blood pressure. He is now on the same floor of the hospital but is being kept secluded from visitors. Dr. Tugwell has been in to see me and a number of others. My room looks like a florist shop. Fresh flowers keep coming in every day and I keep sending them out at nights to the wards because they are more than I can take care of.

Generally speaking, I have been able to carry on departmental work here. As a matter of fact, I have kept pretty full office hours, although I haven't worked nights and I haven't been able to see as many people or to work as hard as usual. As a matter of fact, I find I tire easily. The pain I suffered took a lot out of me and I have had to lie on my back ever since I came here. Thursday night was one of the worst nights I have ever had. They filled me full of dope but I couldn't sleep and on Friday I was just about ready to give up the ship. I didn't see how I could carry on any further. I don't know just how a man feels if he has what is known as nervous prostration, but I felt that I was on the very edge. However, things took a little turn for the better with me. I had less work and Friday night I managed to put in a pretty good night.

Today is Saturday. I have done quite a lot of work today but on the whole I have taken it easier. The doctors changed the dressing today and that made me more comfortable. The doctors also put down their collective feet about seeing so many people and I find that they have been turning people away without giving me a chance to say whether I wanted to see them or not. This afternoon I kept pretty quiet and managed to get a good nap. I find myself tremendously tired but on the whole the work has gone on quite satisfactorily.

I was scheduled to be on the radio Monday night. I agreed to go on from the hospital here but today when I discovered that I really have been losing ground generally, although my rib has been doing well enough, I decided to give it up.

Tuesday, January 2, 1934

I continued to work hard at the hospital day after day, and I found it very tiring signing contracts and letters in bed, seeing people, and dictating in the intervals. The worst of my trouble was that I couldn't get a normal night's sleep. I would start in with a lot of whisky and end up with some soporific, with the result that the next morning I would feel very badly indeed. Friday morning, the twenty-second, I felt so tired out that I was almost desperate. I decided I didn't care whether school kept or not, and that being so, I felt I might as well go to the Cabinet meeting that afternoon. Over the protests of the doctors I did go. When the President was wheeled into the Cabinet room and saw me, he stopped stark still and stared at me for a long interval and then remarked that it looked very much like insubordination. I had taken some public works projects with me and I had a little talk with him after the Cabinet meeting. He told me I ought to go back to the hospital and stay there and then when the doctors discharged me to go away for a couple of weeks' rest.

I told him that it had been impressed on me while I was at the hospital how badly organized I was for shifting responsibility, due to the fact that I did not have a First Assistant Secretary upon whom I could depend. I asked him whether he couldn't kick my First Assistant upstairs and let me get a good man in. He said he would be willing to do that and would try to figure out what could be done.

The President sent word to the hospital through Dr. McIntire after the Cabinet meeting that he was not at all pleased with them letting me out and that they were to keep me there until I ought to be discharged. All of which didn't make the doctors at the hospital feel very happy about it when it wasn't their fault at all.

Late the afternoon of the twenty-third, the doctors allowed me to go home over Christmas on the explicit promise that I would come back the day after Christmas and become a patient again for a week. I made the trip home comfortably enough, although I had to be exceedingly careful. On Sunday morning Raymond and Robert came on for the Christmas holidays. I spent the day quietly at home and Christmas day itself was also quiet. Only the four of us were there for Christmas dinner. Late that afternoon Anna and I went to a rum party at Mrs. Patterson's, and on Tuesday morning, as I promised, I went back to the hospital.

I took the position flatly, however, that I wasn't going to stay in the hospital. My nerves wouldn't stand much more of it, and I was convinced that I would be better off at the office working under normal conditions than doing the same amount of work under abnormal conditions. I had a tough argument with Captain McDowell, who had me in charge, and with Captain Munger, the head of the hospital. They said I was the worst patient they had ever had. They told me how displeased the President would be and so on, but in the end I prevailed and I came from the hospital to the office.

Saturday afternoon at three o'clock I had over an hour with the President. When I went into his study in the White House, Raymond Moley was there and the President told me some of the arguments he had had with Lewis Douglas over the budget for the coming year. He also showed me in confidence a written memorandum that Douglas had submitted to him on the question of the budget, and he remarked to me afterward that in a case like that he often wondered whether the man writing such a memorandum wasn't trying to make a written record. Apparently the President is going ahead along his own lines, which are the lines he has been adhering to since he took control of the Government on March 4.

Saturday, January 6, 1934

On Friday there was no Cabinet meeting but I postponed to that day the meeting of the Special Board for Public Works, which normally would have been held on Thursday. As I took my seat at the table, my attention was called to copies of two Executive Orders that had been signed by the President. I glanced at these Executive Orders hastily and then passed them over to Henry Hunt, our Chief Counsel. He said that under these Executive Orders the Public Works Administration could no longer function without the approval of the Director of the Budget in major matters and without the approval of the Comptroller General in many other matters. The orders forbade entering into any obligation without the prior consent of the Director of the Budget. This meant that as Administrator I could not even sign contracts for allocations already made and approved by the President. The main Executive

Order, in effect, gave the Director of the Budget a veto power on the acts of the President himself in all emergency Administration matters.

I got very hot under the collar when I read this order and had my own fears as to its scope confirmed by Mr. Hunt. I indulged in some criticism of the attitude of the Director of the Budget that I hoped would get back to him through his representative on the board. One of the points I made was that I had understood it to be the policy of the Administration that no Executive Orders affecting another department were to be presented to the President for signature until they had been submitted to the other departments affected. Another point I made was that the Director of the Budget was a member of the Special Board for Public Works and either sat in at all of our meetings or was represented by a member of his staff. I pointed out that all of our actions had been taken by and with the consent of the Director of the Budget as a voting member of the board, and I expressed doubts as to the propriety of his joining in our decisions and then, without notice to us, presenting to the President for signature an Executive Order which in effect substituted his judgment for that of the board of which he is a member. I announced that since this order prevented us from functioning, the meeting stood adjourned.

Gordon Battle, who represents the Secretary of Labor on our board, went back to the Labor Department and told Miss Perkins what had happened. She at once called Colonel McIntyre and expressed her criticism pretty vigorously. She suggested that a conference be held immediately to straighten the matter out, since the effect of the order was to stop all emergency relief matters, not only PWA but CWA, RFC, and everything else.

McIntyre called me and I was pretty vigorous in what I said. Later he called me again and at his suggestion, before going home, I went around by the White House.

In the meantime McIntyre kept running in to the President about the order and the turmoil it had caused. McIntyre told me confidentially that he thought Douglas had put the thing over on the President, who had signed the order without reading it carefully or suspecting its scope. I told McIntyre that the order in effect gave the Director of the Budget veto power over the acts of the President; that as it stood, although the President had approved all of the projects announced by the Public Works Administration, we could not go forward and give effect to those projects. The President didn't want to call a conference because of Douglas's absence from Washington, but I told McIntyre that what the President ought to do was to sign at once another Executive Order rescinding the ones complained of.

While I was at dinner Saturday evening McIntyre called me and told me that the Attorney General had been working on the Executive Orders and had prepared a new one modifying the ones complained of. He read me the new order over the telephone and as I got it, it merely went to the extent of requiring the various relief emergency administrations to report to the Director of the Budget from week to week what obligations they had made on behalf of the Government and what obligations were in prospect. Of course no one objects to a thing of this sort, because the financial representatives of the Government must be in a position to know what obligations have been entered into or are about to be entered into. Accordingly, I came back to the office Saturday night and signed a number of Public Works contracts that had been on my desk but which I had refrained from signing in view of the former Executive Order.

I had telegraphed to Professor Charles E. Merriam that the President wanted to talk with him and he reached Washington today. At twelve o'clock I took him to the White House for a conference with the President. The President offered him an appointment as the Republican member of the Civil Service Commission. The President wants a man with Merriam's background to sit on this commission in order to make a complete study of the whole civil service system as it applies to the Federal offices. Merriam told the President he thought his membership on the National Planning Commission was more important from the Administration's point of view than his membership on the Civil Service Commission would be, and in this I concurred. Our Planning Board is just beginning a very wide and important work and I particularly want Merriam on that board. Merriam renewed a suggestion which I had already made to the President of Professor Leonard White, of the University of Chicago, for Civil Service Commissioner, and after the President had asked some questions about White, he told Merriam to telegraph him to come on so that he might have a talk with him.

After the interview with Merriam was concluded, the Speaker of the House came in. He had called me up previously to ask me to go with him to the President to press upon him an invitation from the City of Springfield which wants him in that city on Lincoln's Birthday, February 12. The President declined the invitation. While Speaker Rainey was there the President brought up a very interesting matter. He had been told that the greatest private collection of Lincolniana in the country was in the possession of an estate in New York, which was anxious to sell it. Speaker Rainey not only knew about this collection, but he had brought with him to show to the President two exhibits from it. One was a small blank book in which Lincoln had personally kept clippings relating to slavery, and the other was a larger book used by Lincoln in his debates with Douglas. In the latter book he had exact quotations from Douglas' interviews and statements which he quoted at a number of the points in the debates to Douglas's great confusion.

The President and the Speaker discussed the possibility of the purchase by the Government of this collection and it was agreed that the purchase should be made if the material could be bought at a reasonable price. The original value of the collection was something in excess of $1 million, but Speaker Rainey felt it could be bought for $75,000. The Speaker said that some of the material had only recently been examined. He said that letters in the collection proved conclusively that Lincoln was illegitimate and he asked the President whether in the event of purchase by the Government these facts should be suppressed or destroyed. The President said that they should not be; that Lincoln's parents were married before Lincoln himself was born, and I made the remark that even if he were born before the marriage of his parents, Lincoln was Lincoln just the same, and I thought it would be a great mistake to destroy documentary evidence, the destruction of which would be greatly deplored in times to come.

Monday, January 8, 1934

I saw the President at three o'clock this afternoon and told him about the status of my negotiations over the claim of A. O. Slaughter, Anderson and Fox. I said that our own audit disclosed the fact that on the basis of simple interest at five per cent, which is the legal rate in Illinois for unliquidated accounts, my apparent indebtedness is slightly over $11,000. The firm originally claimed something in excess of $113,000. Then it was willing to settle for

$50,000 and now it is asking for $30,000. Yesterday while Fred Marx was still here, he called Governor O. Max Gardner, who is representing the Slaughter firm, and Governor Gardner came to my office. He seemed very frank and well disposed and repeated to me what he had already told Fred Marx, namely, that he didn't want to embarrass either me or the Administration and that if his client insisted that suit be brought he would throw up the case. He added that the New York members of the firm were insisting on suit.

I advised the President that since I owed only $11,000, according to my figures, I had no disposition to pay $30,000 and that besides I didn't have $30,000 and didn't know where to get it. I told him further that which Gardner had told me about the possibility of suit being filed. I assured him that I didn't want to embarrass the Administration in any way and that he was at liberty to accept my resignation at any time. He insisted that he didn't want to accept my resignation and said that he didn't see how it would be any reflection on me or on the Administration if suit were filed. In that event he advised me to do what I had already made up my mind to do, namely, tender the amount I justly owed, a refusal of which tender would put the claimant in the position of having to pay costs in the event of failing to get a verdict for more than the amount of the tender. He also advised me to be ready to go to the country with a newspaper statement giving my side of the case the minute suit was filed. This I had also already decided to do.

The President was exceedingly kind and friendly. He didn't have any great pressure of callers waiting for him so he talked to me for quite some time. I must have been there all of an hour. My experience with the stockbrokers called to mind some experiences of his own. He said he had done his stock speculating when he was a student in law school. He told me a story about a friend of his that is perhaps worth repeating since it came from him.

This friend worked in a brokerage house where the President did his trading. He was an old family friend of the Roosevelts who had been to Groton with Roosevelt but whose family had not been able to afford to send him to college. He got to speculating himself and owed the firm some $2,000. One afternoon he and Roosevelt and another friend, after the market had closed, went to a bar and did some drinking. The young broker drank enough to become very tearful. He cried out over his liquor that if he could only make enough money to clear up that debt, he would go as far west as he could and start life all over again. Upon leaving the bar they went into a nearby gambling joint where there was a roulette wheel, a high-class place, the President said, where one had to be introduced to be admitted. The drunken broker begged his two friends to stake him to $25 apiece to try his luck. They did it and each one played $25 of his own on the wheel until that amount was lost.

The broker continued to play and at the end of a couple of hours had $10 left. He refused to leave when he was urged to do so but drunkenly wanted to play through for the rest of the money he had. He staked his $10 and won. He continued to play and continued to win. He won at the rate of $500 an hour. When he had almost $2,000, Roosevelt and the other friend decided they would try to get him to leave since he had just about made enough money to pay his brokerage debt. He refused to leave, whereupon the third man went to the bar and got him a drink of whisky which he spiked. The broker drank the spiked drink and then Roosevelt got him another similar drink which he in turn consumed. Shortly the broker passed completely out but not before his total winnings reached $2,250. They put him into a cab and went to the Waldorf-Astoria, where they deposited an envelope containing the money, which the keeper of the gambling house had given them in currency, with instructions that it was not to be opened except in the presence of the broker and one of the other two. Then they took the broker home and put him to bed.

The next day they couldn't find him. He had left at one o'clock in the morning and no one knew where he had gone. For three days it was a case of total disappearance and then the broker finally woke up somewhere and came to with a terrific headache. He didn't know where he had been and he never did know. He didn't remember playing the roulette wheel.

Roosevelt and his friend bought a round-trip ticket to Italy on a slow boat and shipped him off. When he returned to New York they had already purchased for him a ticket to San Francisco and they hustled him right to the train. In the meantime his brokerage account had been paid in full. They gave enough money to the conductor of the train to pay for his meals en route to San Francisco and they had written to a bank there in advance to see if they could help get him a job.

The man went to work in San Francisco in a small clerkship position in the bank, and when Roosevelt was there in 1914 he was the cashier of the bank and one of the respected members of his staff. The man had married, had a nice family, and was a leading member of his community. A few years ago he died leaving an estate of $350,000.

Friday, January 12, 1934

At Cabinet meeting this afternoon we disposed of departmental matters quickly and then the President read us the draft of a message that he will probably give out on Monday. It had to do with the taking over by the United States Treasury of all the gold in the reserve banks, with stabilization, and with currency questions in general. A good deal of it was beyond me because, as I have heretofore noted, I don't know much about finance or economics. Moreover, I was so tired that I actually dozed off on three separate occasions, much to my chagrin. I only hope that the President didn't see me.

The day was full of conferences and interviews and at times I wondered whether I was giving the right answer. Tired as I was, my brain felt muddled. I went home for dinner fully determined to go back to work at night, but I didn't have it in me after dinner. I think I was nearer a complete collapse than I have ever been in my life, so I went to bed and tried to forget that my desk was still crying out for someone to clear it.

Tuesday, January 16, 1934

We had the regular meeting of the Public Works Board today. We are still finding it possible to make a few allotments out of money that comes back to us from former allotments that either have been rescinded or cannot be availed of by the allottees for one reason or another.

Just before the press conference Mr. Landau, General Counsel for PWA, came back from a conference with the Comptroller General to report that the latter had taken a position which would make it impossible for the Housing Corporation to function at all. So when a question was asked me about the Housing Corporation, I let go full blast at the Comptroller General, giving the correspondents an earful, which was front-page stuff for them. Then McIntyre called me up from the White House to ask me what it was

all about. Following that, Louis Howe called me up and I dropped
in to see Howe when I went over to the Council meeting.

I found him very much disturbed. Steve Early was with him.
Howe seemed to think that matters were in such a delicate situation
that anything might overturn them, with portentous and unpre-
dictable consequences. I told him that this wasn't a fight between
two members of the Administration, since McCarl was not a member of the Administration, having been appointed by Coolidge.
Early and I thought that Howe's psychology was wrong. It seems to
me that the result will be beneficial for the Administration in the
end if it results in any curtailment of the arbitrary power assumed
by the Comptroller General. I saw Louis Howe again after the
Council meeting and he was more lugubrious than ever. He had
sent two notes in to me at the Council meeting. I don't quite see
why he is worrying so much, but one would think from his attitude
that the Administration is about to crack right in two.

I authorized the filing of a bill for an injunction today against
the Standard Oil Company of New Jersey for alleged violation of
the Petroleum Code.

After the Council meeting I asked the Vice President to auto-
graph some sheets of postage stamps. And as he sat down he told
me that if there was anything he could do for me to come to him.
He said: "I thought a lot of you last summer and of the work you
were doing up here and I want you to know that I think you have
done a wonderful job." This was very pleasing to me because of
his power and influence with the Democrats in Congress, to say
nothing of the fact that it was gratifying to have such an expression
of opinion from a man of his experience and position.

Tuesday, January 23, 1934

Colonel Waite came in this morning after an absence of several
days and handed me his resignation as Deputy Administrator. His
point is that we don't see eye to eye in the matter of organization.
My reply to that is that we do see eye to eye except that he thinks
the organization ought to head up to himself as Deputy Administrator and I think it ought to head up to me as Administrator. I
told him I didn't want him to resign; that I had every confidence
in him and liked him personally. Several things recently have bothered him. I had thought that things were ironed out pretty well
between us. I called in some of my advisers in the Department and

we talked over the situation. We decided that if he was going to resign, this was the best time, but it was the consensus of opinion that he ought to be persuaded to stay if possible.

There was a long-drawn-out and verbose meeting of the National Emergency Council this afternoon at the White House. Toward the end the President and the Vice President came in. I couldn't see that we really got anywhere at all except to talk interminably.

After the Council meeting I took the Vice President aside to tell him that the oil situation in East Texas was again becoming critical. My advice is that hot oil is being produced at the rate of 60,000 barrels a day. I told the Vice President that the Railroad Commission down there is not co-operating with us and that Senator Connally was against us, and said that I would have to put the whole Texas field on a permit basis unless things improved radically. He remarked that the only way to deal with the situation was to take a strong position; that we couldn't appeal to the consciences of those oil people because they didn't have any consciences and he advised me to go after them with a club.

I had a short conference with the President in his office and told him what the Vice President had said.

Wednesday, January 24, 1934

The Secretary of Labor, Harry L. Hopkins, Dr. Zook, Commissioner of Education, and I had a conference with the President at noon about the educational situation. On account of the depression many thousands of children are being denied educational opportunities in the schools. Many schools are running on part time and thousands of teachers are either unemployed or, if employed, work at salaries, which, if paid, are mere pittances. The President authorized Harry Hopkins to do what he could to relieve the unemployed teachers and also to go as far as possible to help keep in college students who must have help in order to get through. He also indicated that as part of our public works program we might work out a plan for helping to build consolidation schools in those parts of the country where school facilities are very poor, if they exist at all.

I stayed for a moment afterward to tell the President that I was very much worried about the $500,000 that Public Works has appropriated for the Aeronautics Branch of the Department of Commerce in order to experiment in the production of cheap airplanes.

Disturbing rumors have come to me indicating collusion between men in the Government and outside interests as a result of which this money will really be expended for the benefit of outside interests. Although the money has been voted, we have not issued warrants for it. The President told me he was worried about it too and authorized me to continue to hold up the warrants.

Thursday, January 25, 1934

Secretary Wallace and I lunched with the President today. We are both supporting a bill introduced in the House by Congressman Taylor, of Colorado, which would give the Secretary of the Interior authority to control grazing on the public range. This bill is a most important one if we are to stop the practices that are rapidly destroying the range in many parts of the West. Our advices are that this bill will not pass, on account of Western opposition, unless the President gets back of it. The President is in sympathy with the bill and told us to talk to the Senate and House leaders. He proposes to write a letter to the appropriate committees in the House and the Senate in support of the bill. Failing the passage of the bill we discussed with him the withdrawing of all public lands from entry. My solicitors advise me that the President has this power of withdrawal and probably, even if the Taylor bill does not pass, I can exercise sufficient control over the public range.

The President told us in confidence that he is having a good deal of trouble in getting Director of the Budget Douglas to line up with him on his relief program. Colonel Waite had a conference with Douglas today and reported back that Douglas is firmly set not to allow more than $500 million for public works.

Friday, January 26, 1934

Most of the Cabinet meeting today was taken up with a discussion of the complaints of the Congressmen covering their treatment in the various departments, especially in the matter of patronage. A committee appointed by the recent Democratic House caucus spent an hour or more with the President just before Cabinet meeting relating the woes of themselves and their colleagues. They complain of harsh treatment at the hands of the executives, of being shoved from pillar to post, of brusque and irresponsive letters, and, of course, of lack of consideration in the matters of appointments. Apparently the President handled the matter with his customary tact, but he did impress us with the advisability of being as considerate and helpful as possible with the members of Congress. I have tried to establish this as a principle in this Department, although I suppose that all of us become overstrained at times and are brusque and lacking in courtesy. In the matter of letters, however, I do think that this Department has a pretty good record. Except for a very few form letters I sign all communications to Senators, Congressmen, and governors, and other important public persons. Moreover, I spend a good deal of time correcting letters presented for my signature to such persons and many letters I send back for correction or rewriting.

The President has been urging me lately to go away for a rest. Yesterday when Henry Wallace and I lunched with him, he told us he wanted both of us to go away and he opened the Cabinet meeting today by recurring to the same subject. He said he didn't want any members of the Cabinet to break down and he especially wanted Henry and me to go away for a week or two. I waited after Cabinet meeting to take some matters up with him and he again brought up the subject. He was quite insistent about it. He told me that it was beginning to worry him just to look at me and that if I didn't go away he would get mad.

Tuesday, January 30, 1934

Last night Anna and I went to the Eugene Meyers' for dinner. It was an uninteresting dinner party but both the food and wine were excellent and the atmosphere hospitable. Among the guests were General Johnson, Mr. and Mrs. Ogden Reid, of New York, and Senator Bulkley, of Ohio. Mr. and Mrs. Forbes Morgan were also there.

General Johnson was almost gushing in his greeting of me. He spoke about the interchange of letters between Don Richberg and me. He told me that he believed I was doing a great job, that he was for me, and that any time he could uphold my hand all I had to do was to let him know. When I bade him good night he "God blessed" me. I don't understand it at all.

I got home after eleven utterly dragged-out and weary. This kind of an affair takes more out of me than it is worth and I wish I didn't have to go to them. I have come to the conclusion that a man can stand the gaff better in Washington if he is a bachelor because then he won't be expected to go to so many parties.

Friday, February 2, 1934

The President was in fine form at Cabinet today. His spirits soared high and he was full of good humor which expressed itself frequently in that infectious laughter of his. He took up practically all of the time of the meeting discussing questions that he himself raised. The first and most serious of these had to do with the independence of the Philippine Islands. It seems that there is a great deal of opposition in the Islands to the terms of the Hawes-Cutting bill. Three modified plans were suggested which we considered.

Another matter he brought up was the pressure from all parts of the country for expenditure of Federal money for flood control. Many bills have been introduced in Congress covering individual flood-control problems, and the President finally suggested to a group of members of Congress that the way to approach it was by means of a general plan covering the whole country. At his suggestion a resolution was passed by the Senate yesterday asking him to prepare and report such a plan. He named a committee to prepare this plan, with me as chairman. The other members are the Secretary of War, the Secretary of Agriculture, and the Secretary of Labor. He suggested that we could organize a number of subcommittees, and what he had in mind apparently was a study to meet the question of the control and use of rivers and of the territory drained by those rivers. He suggested that a subcommittee be appointed for the territory that was drained by the Atlantic Ocean, another for the watershed that drains into the Gulf of Mexico, another for the section of the country that drains into the Mississippi River from the east, another for the west of the Mississippi, and still another one for the Pacific Coast states. We are to consider not only flood control, but navigation, soil erosion, irrigation, reclamation, sewage, power, and reforestation where the latter relates to control and use of water.

It was the idea of the President that after the present emergency has passed, which has resulted in extraordinary expenditures for more or less unrelated public works, a considerable sum of money, say $500,000 a year, should be expended for a term of perhaps twenty-five years in carrying out a broad national plan along the lines to be covered at least in part by this study. To that end he wants each subcommittee to list in order of importance ten projects for each particular region. It will then be the duty of the committee appointed today, out of all of these projects, to submit in order of importance the first ten from a national viewpoint.

Wednesday, February 7, 1934

We had a short meeting of the Public Works Board today. We are now holding only one meeting a week and we can get through that in half an hour. I have decided to send out orders to all the state engineers not to receive applications for any more projects, and in a day or two notice will go out to the State Advisory Boards and the Regional Advisers terminating their services on February 28, next. We already have either here or in the state offices municipal and state projects exceeding $3 billion by a substantial amount. We cannot possibly get any such sum to carry on our program, and it is not good policy to continue to receive and pass on projects in the states only to cause disappointment later.

For the last few days I have been feeling considerably better and so I was very much taken aback when my nerves snapped late this afternoon. I have never so completely lost control of myself, at least in the office. I have been under tremendous pressure all day talking with people and meeting delegations, and this is always a strain on me. I started seeing people this morning at half past nine. At a quarter to ten we had a Public Works staff meeting for three-quarters of an hour. Then Mr. Walter Teagle, president of the Standard Oil Company of New Jersey, came in at my instance by prior appointment. We discussed settlement of the gasoline war that has been raging here in Washington, and he also brought up the subject of the suit we filed against his company here and offered to settle it. We did settle that suit during the day and we are negotiating a settlement of the price war. Then came my reception hour, following which I went over for an appointment with the President, and then I came back and found a number of people waiting to see me, with the result that work began to pile on my desk which I couldn't even undertake to move and along about six o'clock I blew up.

Friday, February 9, 1934

At Cabinet meeting this afternoon we had some interesting matters to discuss. Among others we took up the cancellation of the air mail contracts. After Cabinet meeting the President announced at his press conference that these contracts had been canceled on account of collusion and fraud and that the Army planes would carry the mails for the time being.

Also at Cabinet meeting Secretary Dern read a long prosy defense of the beet sugar interests. This matter has been up for discussion several times. The President is chafing under the present system by which, under the heavy tariff on beet sugar, the whole population is taxed in order to pay a subsidy to the beet sugar growers. This tariff tax adds something like $150 to $200 million to the cost of living while only a relatively small portion of it goes to the beet sugar people. If it were not for the political questions involved, the President would put sugar on the free list and pay a subsidy. On two or three occasions he has discussed the possibility of wiping out the beet sugar industry over a series of twenty years, which would give time to the beet sugar farmers to substitute other crops.

After Cabinet meeting I had a talk with the President. I told him that I thought it would be sound public policy for the Post Office to build its own airplanes and carry its own mail. He was inclined to think that the Army could do it to better advantage, but my objection to this was that the people would not take kindly to the extension of Army activities. I pointed out that the men trained for the Post Office air mail service would be available as pilots in time of war. He thought it might be possible to have the Army Air Corps train the Post Office pilots and perhaps supervise the service but have those pilots wear civilian uniforms.

He also referred to the lengthy exposition by Dern on the sugar question. He seemed to think it just a little absurd. There isn't any doubt that Dern was very earnest about it all and a bit contentious.

Wednesday, February 21, 1934

At eleven-thirty there was a specially called meeting of the Cabinet. We spent most of our time discussing the air mail situation.

General Johnson made a savage attack over the radio last night on the *Washington Post* for publishing in serial form a book about to be issued on the subject of "The New Dealers." The attack was out of all proportion to anything critical that has so far appeared in the *Post,* but he laid about not only upon the unknown author but on the *Post* itself. Secretary Roper brought up the matter for discussion at Cabinet meeting and the President remarked that every Administration had to have a Peck's Bad Boy. He said that

Johnson had called up Barney Baruch and told him tearfully over the telephone that he couldn't stand it much longer and wanted to resign. Thereupon Baruch, who has been a friend of Eugene Meyer, the owner of the *Post,* called up Meyer and gave him hell. Following this, Johnson delivered his attack over the radio. The President laughingly said that he was going to leave the issue to Johnson, Baruch, and Meyer.

This afternoon Harry Hopkins and I had an interview with the President, at which I proposed that, instead of turning certain projects involving doubtful security over to CWA, these projects be undertaken by PWA. My point is that there are a good many projects which properly are PWA projects but which, under the policy heretofore followed of requiring reasonable security, it has not been possible for us to go ahead with because the municipalities involved are in such financial shape that they cannot give reasonable security. It seems to me that rather than have this work done by CWA, without any expectation that any part of it will be repaid by the benefited municipalities, it would be far better to have it done by PWA. We could take the security even if it wasn't so good and we would have at least a moral obligation on the part of the municipalities to pay. This moral obligation would doubtless yield us some returns. The President concurred in this view and said to go ahead with it.

Then Secretary Wallace joined our conference and the President signed a letter expressing his approval of the Taylor Grazing Control Bill which is now pending before Congress. This bill would give the Secretary of the Interior the right to regulate grazing on the public range.

Mayor LaGuardia came in to see me at one o'clock, by appointment, I having sent word to him a week ago that I wanted to see him. The matter I had to discuss was with reference to the naming of Robert Moses as a member of the Triborough Bridge Authority. Moses is a bitter personal enemy of the President's. The President and such friends as Jim Farley and Louis Howe think that Moses would leave nothing undone to hurt the President and we don't want to do any business with Moses. He is a very close friend of Al Smith's. LaGuardia regretted the situation and said that if he had known it existed he wouldn't have thought for a minute of putting Moses on the board. He expressed the highest possible regard for the President and asked me to give him a few days to see what he might work out. I told him he could lay the responsibility on my shoulders that the change was necessary.

Wednesday, February 28, 1934

I left Washington the afternoon of February 23 for Chicago, where I was scheduled to make two speeches.

My first speech was Saturday night at Orchestra Hall, under the auspices of the League of Women Voters. It was a very cold night. I have always regarded this as the hardest hall in Chicago to fill for a political meeting, and I didn't expect much in the way of a crowd. I was agreeably surprised. Except for the top gallery, the theater was very well filled, and the woman at the University Club who handles theater tickets told me that she had had inquiries for tickets Saturday afternoon that she couldn't fill at a premium.

It was a pay meeting, the best seats selling for $1.65. All the boxes were filled. I didn't know it was to be a pay meeting or I would not have accepted because I don't approve of admission being charged to hear a public official. It must have yielded quite a profit to the League of Women Voters.

My speech in many respects I consider the best I have prepared. Generally speaking, my audience was a very conservative one. I was gratified to see so many people from the North Shore as far north as Lake Forest, including numbers of my neighbors and friends. I was cordially received and the applause at the end of my speech was very gratifying indeed. Professor Merriam presided.

In the audience was Frank Knox, publisher and editor of the *Chicago Daily News*. I didn't see him until toward the end of my speech, when I paid my compliments to certain gentlemen who had made speeches on Lincoln's Birthday quoting Lincoln in the criticisms they made of the Administration. This part of my speech had been inspired by a speech Frank Knox had made on Lincoln's Birthday. I called on him Monday afternoon at his office. He said my speech was damned well done and remarked that anyone who wanted to justify the policies of the Administration had only to marshal, as I had done, facts prior to last March 4. He also said that the audience was a great tribute to me; that he didn't believe any other man in politics would have had such a turnout.

On Sunday, by appointment, I met Phil LaFollette, former Governor of Wisconsin, at the University Club. This meeting had been arranged by Senator LaFollette at his own suggestion. We talked over the situation in Wisconsin, the Progressive situation generally, and as a result of our talk that afternoon I suggested to the President over the telephone that he call in Senator LaFollette and have a talk with him before Thursday, when Senator La-Follette was going to Wisconsin to attend a conference of his followers. Phil LaFollette thinks that the President has overlooked an opportunity in handling the Progressive Republicans of the West. He believes that Farley has not understood the situation in the Middle West and that his appointments have caused real damage to the Progressive cause and to Roosevelt's best interests.

On Monday night I spoke on conservation at the seventieth convention of the Chicago Dental Society in the Stevens Hotel. The weather was still very cold. I didn't have a particularly good audience but I was on a national radio hookup and that gave me a chance to get out over the country my views on conservation.

I had to see a good many people on Monday, and on Tuesday until the time I took my train for Washington at two o'clock. In fact, I was hounded and besieged. Even some of my friends showed me absolutely no consideration. People of slight acquaintance with me insisted on appointments in furtherance of some private or professional interest, so that when I got on the train I was thoroughly tired out. My nerves were all gone, just about ready to crack. These trips to Chicago are the hardest possible things for me because I know so many people and they won't let me alone. One man who had tried in vain to reach me by telephone and whom I had not called up actually had the nerve to break in on me at luncheon at the University Club to ask me whether I wouldn't do something to make the railroads hurry up in buying supplies. I nearly bit his head off. It passes all belief how utterly selfish and inconsiderate people will be when a public man is concerned. Each one thinks that his own matter is of paramount importance and that a public official ought to be willing to forgo any personal matter or convenience of his own in order to give an audience.

Friday, March 2, 1934

I took Richard J. Finnegan, editor and publisher of the *Chicago Daily Times*, to see the President today. Mr. Finnegan is trying to get from the transcript of the Moe Rosenberg testimony the names of the aldermen who were given Insull money at the time of the traction fight in 1930 and the amount paid to each. The President was sympathetic but was confronted with the inadvisability of giving an exclusive story to a particular newspaper. In the end he called in Stephen Early, and Early and Finnegan took the matter up with the Department of Justice.

I had a number of important matters to hurry through with the President at our meeting this morning. Secretary Swanson came to Cabinet meeting today, the first he had attended for ten or twelve weeks. He looks very bad and I notice that he has difficulty in managing his cigarette.

Wednesday, March 7, 1934

I lunched with the President today and had a particularly interesting time. After we had disposed of Public Works matters, he told me in confidence that it is his plan next summer to transfer Puerto Rico to this Department. It is now under the War Department. A few days ago we appointed an Advisory Committee for the Virgin Islands. It is his idea to have similar committees set up for Alaska, Hawaii, and Puerto Rico. From these Advisory Committees there will be a Central Council under the Chairmanship of the Bureau Chief in charge of these outlying possessions. I think this is a capital idea and told him that the advisory commissions for Alaska and Hawaii ought to be set up at once so that they could visit those possessions next summer. He agreed to this and said that he would have the War Department also appoint one for Puerto Rico. He suggested that the Hawaiian committee might be in Hawaii at the time he expects to be there next summer.

It is his plan to have a warship take him to Puerto Rico, the Virgin Islands, then through the Panama Canal to Hawaii. He suggested that he would like me to go with him as far as Puerto Rico and the Virgin Islands, whence I could fly back.

Then I took up with him the question of transferring the National Forest Service to the Interior Department. At first he seemed to doubt the advisability of doing this on account of the opposition that would come up through the National Forest Organization, but I told him that I believed the Senators and Congressmen are distinctly in favor of the move and pointed out to him the obvious advantages of such a transfer. He went into the matter in question in some detail and admitted that Forestry should be in this Department. In the end he said that if I could bring it about, it would be quite all right so far as he was concerned.

Saturday, March 10, 1934

At noon I went to the White House where the President wanted to look at some exhibits of the Reedsville, West Virginia, Subsistence Homestead project. Director Wilson, of the Division of Subsistence Homesteads, was there as were Mr. Grimes of the same Division and the architect selected by Mrs. Roosevelt to do the work, Eric Gugler. The sketches and pictures were very attractive indeed but the cost of the thing is shocking to me. The President said that we could justify the cost, which will run in excess of $10,000 per family, by the fact that it is a model for other homestead projects. My reply to that was to ask what it was a model of, since obviously it wasn't a model of low-cost housing for people on the very lowest rung of the economic order. After the President left, I expressed myself pretty forcefully to the others and later I sent for Director Wilson to tell him that I was really concerned about the whole thing. I don't see how we can possibly defend ourselves on this project. It worries me more than anything else in my whole Department. The theory was that we would be able to set up families on subsistence homesteads at a family cost of from $2,000 to $3,000 and here we have already run above $10,000 per family. I am afraid we are going to come in for a lot of justifiable criticism.

Thursday, March 15, 1934

I am sixty years old today. There was a time when that seemed to be very old indeed and there is no blinking the fact that it isn't the same as being thirty or forty or even fifty. I might even add, or being fifty-nine. Somehow fifty-nine seems much younger than sixty. I think we realize our age by decades and not by years and I have just lived through another decade. I am glad that at sixty I am still able to do a full day's work and that there is interesting and important work for me to do.

Monday, March 19, 1934

On Friday, the sixteenth, I had an appointment with the President and attended the regular Cabinet meeting at two o'clock. Usually the President starts with the Secretary of State and then goes down in order of precedence, giving each member a chance to present any questions that he has. On Friday he started with the Secretary of Labor. She must have taken up a good forty minutes, although the Cabinet meetings usually are held within two hours. The next one was the Secretary of Commerce, but Mr. Roper was not there. Assistant Secretary Dickinson substituted for him and he had no matter to bring up. The Secretary of Agriculture followed, but to him Miss Perkins had passed one or two moot questions which she urged him to discuss. The result was that when it came time to leave to catch my train for Chicago I had not yet been reached, although it was then later than half past three. So I excused myself and took the Pennsylvania for Chicago.

Within an hour or two after I arrived in Chicago I learned from a very authentic source that the *Chicago American* was preparing a vicious attack on me which would be printed after they got through with the Moe Rosenberg exposé. I had received an intimation to this effect in a letter from Leo J. Hassenaur, First Assistant U. S. Attorney, just before leaving Washington but I had paid little attention to it. However, when Tom Courtney sent Jim Denvir to me with a rather detailed story, I began to sit up and take notice.

The result was that in the afternoon I tried to reach Homer Guck, publisher of the *Herald-Examiner,* the Hearst morning paper. When I found he was in Florida I called on Victor Watson, the managing editor, by appointment. Both Guck and Watson have been very friendly. I went into the matter fully with Watson and he advised me to call William Randolph Hearst by telephone. I was reluctant to do this because I have never tried to influence any newspaper as to what it might say about me, but Watson said it was the thing to do and so I set about it.

I wasn't able to connect with Mr. Hearst until after ten fifteen Chicago time when I got him at Santa Monica. I told him of the report I had heard and went on to say that I would not even suggest to him what any of his papers should print or refrain from printing with respect to anyone, that if either of his papers had a legitimate story against me based on facts the story ought to be printed. I made it clear that all I wanted was a day in court. I told him I would like, before any story was printed, to discuss it either with his attorneys or with his editors. He said: "I suppose the story is political." I told him that I understood it was personal. He said my suggestion was entirely fair and that he would instruct his Chicago editors to talk with me if they proposed to print any story.

I had put it up to Mr. Hearst in this way at Mr. Watson's suggestion. I did not concentrate on the *American,* although that was the paper in question. I know that Mr. Hearst immediately called Mr. Watson back and gave him his instructions because when I reached him five or six minutes later, Mr. Hearst had already talked to him. He told Watson that he would also reach the *American* and I have no doubt he did.

Tuesday, March 20, 1934

I ran across Colonel McIntyre in Colonel Howe's office this afternoon and I am more than ever certain that something is the matter with him so far as I am concerned. His manner was different from anything it has been at any time in the past. He was distinctly reserved.

This morning I called in Dr. Wilson, head of the Division of Subsistence Homesteads, Gugler, the architect at the Reedsville project, and Pickett, assistant to Dr. Wilson. I expressed myself in no uncertain terms about the way this project has been managed. Gugler was greatly offended at first. He said that more money had been spent than he had been in favor of spending but that the committee had insisted on his doing what he had done. By the committee he really meant Mrs. Roosevelt. He criticized the purchase of the fifty houses that Colonel Howe had bought. He said they were a joke and that he had had to go to great trouble and expense to make them at all presentable or habitable. He said this was one of the main reasons for the large amount of money spent.

Late this afternoon Colonel Howe called me to ask if I could come to his office. He said that Mrs. Roosevelt was hitting the ceiling about my criticism of Reedsville. When I got over there, I found out from Howe that she had the idea that I was criticizing her activities. As a matter of fact, her name didn't come up in our talk this morning and I didn't criticize anything particularly but only the general proposition. I found out from a call by Wilson that he and his two colleagues went back to Wilson's office where they sat down with Miss Cook, Mrs. Roosevelt's friend, who has been working on the Reedsville project, and reiterated to her my general criticisms. Miss Cook ran right over to Mrs. Roosevelt so that she must have gotten a highly distorted report. All in all it has not been what I would call a successful day.

Wednesday, March 21, 1934

I lunched with the President today. I told him that once again I was bothering him with a personal situation and he said: "Why not?" I replied that he had enough troubles of his own without having to help to carry mine. He told me to go ahead, that he was glad to hear from me.

I then went on to tell him that in my judgment a well-conceived conspiracy was in process of being carried out to make my position in the Cabinet untenable. I told him about my letter last week from Hassenaur, the information that was sent to me by Tom Courtney in Chicago on Saturday, my interview with Watson of the *Herald-Examiner,* and my telephone conversation with Hearst. I told him about Malmin's activities in Washington and showed him the blackmailing letter from Malmin to Jim Farley. The President remarked that this was clearly blackmail. I had dictated last night and handed to him a statement covering all of my dealings in Skokie Valley property. He certainly could see nothing to criticize in that.

The President said that what I was being subjected to was in line with some other things that were going on. He told me about anonymous letters attacking a member of his own household which he had been unable to trace. The President sent for Chief Moran, of the Secret Service, told him what I had brought in in the way of information, and told him that he believed that someone was financing this whole attempt to make it difficult for the Administration.

One thing I have omitted to say and that is with reference to McIntyre. I told the President that it had been represented to me in Chicago that McIntyre was unfriendly to me and the President at once emphatically said: "I don't believe it." I, of course, assured him that I didn't either but that I wanted to tell him everything that had been said to me and that I had also told McIntyre because I thought he was entitled to know.

I am relieved to have had this talk with the President. He took the whole thing just as I thought he would. He was friendly and understanding and human, as always.

I am keeping pretty close touch on Malmin. Today I sent over to Chief Moran, of the Secret Service, my file in this matter, including the report of the investigation conducted by the Department of Justice several months ago. Later today I talked with Chief Moran and he agrees with me that I ought to break this matter first by filing with the Chicago Bar Association a petition looking to the disbarment of Malmin. Homer Cummings agrees, subject, of course, to the approval of the President. Tonight I dictated a petition to the Grievance Committee of the Bar Association which I hope to have ready for transmittal tomorrow after a final approval by the President.

Friday, March 23, 1934

Jesse Jones, Harry L. Hopkins, and I had an appointment with the President at noon today to discuss a plan for helping to finance public works in municipalities that are able to furnish sound bonds. According to this plan the RFC would buy bonds representing seventy per cent of the cost of a proposed public works project after certification by the Public Works Administration that the project was a sound one and was approved. The Public Works Administration would then contribute the remaining thirty per cent. By this method we could make our public works fund go much further since we would be furnishing only thirty per cent for a given project instead of as at present, in so many instances, contributing thirty per cent and then lending seventy per cent. The President approved the proposal and authorized Jesse Jones to attempt to secure the necessary legislation.

The President was in highly good humor at the Cabinet meeting this afternoon. We discussed the labor difficulty that is cropping out in the automobile industry and in other states. His plan is to leave Washington next Tuesday night for a ten days' vacation, provided by that time he can settle several pressing matters. It is wonderful how he keeps his poise and good cheer. His ability to laugh and relax is priceless to him and means a great deal to those who work with him. We didn't have any very important discussions nor did we reach any momentous decisions at the Cabinet meeting, although we did cover a good deal of ground in our general discussion.

Monday, March 26, 1934

I wrote to Mrs. Roosevelt a day or two ago asking her if she would write me her impressions of the situation in the Virgin Islands which she visited recently. She called me Saturday morning and said she would rather talk to me than write and asked Anna and me for lunch. From our talk at lunch it developed that she felt rather encouraged about the situation in the Virgin Islands and she seemed to approve of what Governor Pearson is trying to do there. She said that she wasn't sure that he had always been the right kind of a Governor but she does believe he is trying now. She thinks a business manager is needed to run the rum factory and of course that is what I have had in mind right along. She spoke of the hotel that we are building and said it was beautifully located, that the Virgin Islands could be made a winter resort rivaling the Bahamas but attracting people of more moderate means.

The President told me recently that it was his intention to transfer Puerto Rico to the Interior Department and he brought up the subject again today. It seems that the Governor there, Blanton Winship, would rather be under the Interior Department. The President said that Lew Douglas would be back in Washington within a day or two and that he would then talk to him about an Executive Order necessary to effect the transfer.

Saturday, March 31, 1934

I have not written a memorandum for several days because with the going away of the President Tuesday night there has seemed to be little of interest of an official nature to set down. I wasn't able to have any talks with the President this week, although I was anxious for him to give an interview to men representing the oil interests of California.

The President attended the Executive Council meeting briefly Tuesday afternoon and there was little opportunity to discuss the oil situation in California. He said that he thought the Attorney General and I ought to be locked together in a room until we could iron the matter out. The Attorney General responded that he and I had agreed to disagree. The President remarked that we oughtn't to do that. I stated that the situation was a very serious one, explaining that the oil indictments brought there by the United States District Attorney were ill-advised and were throwing the oil industry into the same state of chaos it was in last summer. The Attorney General observed that the indictments did not have to be brought to trial for some time, but the President expressed the view that he thought there ought to be a speedy trial, especially after the Attorney General had said that the defendants could demur and a quick decision consequently had. I agreed with the President that the proceedings ought to be speeded up in order to resolve the uncertainty of the situation. The President told the Attorney General to send orders to California to hurry up the hearings as much as possible.

The President suffered his first serious political setback when both branches of Congress this week overrode his veto of the Independent Offices Appropriation Bill. What he especially objected to in that bill was a large appropriation for former servicemen, the passage of which is a serious blow to his economy program. The bill was first overridden by the House of Representatives, when man after man, like so many scared rabbits, ran to cover out of fear of the soldier vote. It was a closer fight in the Senate but the President lost there too with every Republican voting to override the veto.

In the meantime, the President, at Miami, Florida, embarked on Vincent Astor's yacht for a fishing trip off the Bahama Islands.

Continued reports are coming to me, some of them with great circumstantiality, of an insistent pursuit, on the part of the *Chicago American,* to find something which will blow me out of the water. I have information today that the managing editor of that paper told some of his staff the other day that he would have me out of the Cabinet in thirty days.

Tuesday, April 3, 1934

Men representing eighty per cent of the oil industry, as measured by capital invested, called on me at two o'clock yesterday to discuss what should be included in the new oil bill that we have been working on. Representing the Oil Administration were Messrs. Margold, Swanson, and Fahy. These oil men are willing to back a bill giving the Oil Administrator the fullest possible power to regulate the production of crude oil. We want to go further and give the Oil Administrator the right to regulate refinery runs of gasoline. The oil people say that they can manage that by voluntary agreement, but I am skeptical of that and asked them what they could do if their attempted voluntary agreement should break down. I took the view that whether the power would ever have to be exercised or not, it ought to exist and that without some such ultimate power in the Government no voluntary agreement could be relied upon to effect the result. The discussion was entirely friendly and at its conclusion Judge Ames, president of the Texas Company, expressed himself in complimentary terms of the results achieved to date by the Oil Administration.

Today Walter C. Teagle, president of the Standard Oil Company of New Jersey, came to see me by appointment. He was present at the oil conference yesterday, at which time he asked me if he could see me today. His proposal is that the Government make an oil reserve out of the East Texas oil field. He said this is the way, and the only way, to control the production of hot oil. His company is the largest producing company in the oil field, but he seemed to think that not only his company but other large producers would readily fall in with the plan, which contemplates the issuance by the Government of bonds for the value of the properties taken over, such bonds to bear interest at 3½ per cent. The Government would then put someone in charge of this whole field and would produce whatever oil it wanted to produce, such oil as produced to be allocated among the refiners in the proportion represented by the respective ownerships of the properties at the time they were taken over. After all, it seemed rather a startling proposition to come from the president of the Standard Oil Company of New Jersey.

Raymond, who had been here spending a week with me on his spring vacation, flew back yesterday afternoon. Ann and Jane Dahlman were with us for several days last week. Raymond and I drove them over to Baltimore on Sunday.

Friday, April 6, 1934

Two or three days ago Arthur Mullen came over to tell me, confidentially, that he had heard from a most reliable source that Hearst was after me to strip from me the title that had been given to me on many occasions in the newspapers—"Honest Harold." This title has always made me squirm anyhow. I simply hate it. Besides, it makes me a target for sharpshooters, and God knows I have never claimed any credit for my honesty.

Saturday, April 14, 1934

I had an appointment with Louis Howe yesterday. His health has been such that he has been spending most of his time in bed and I saw him in his bedroom in the White House. We discussed subsistence homestead matters and he agreed with my proposal to change our method of organization. Instead of having a parent corporation with a separate local corporation for each project, we will operate under the one general corporation and send out project managers for each project who will be directly responsible to Washington. With each project we will also set up a local advisory committee. This system seems more simple and efficient for the long run. If we should try to operate each project by a local corporation, it would mean that we would be operating under boards of directors that had no financial interest in the enterprises and we might have difficulty in having proper control. The revised plan fits in with the theory I have always strongly stood out for, namely, that of insisting on having authority if there is to be responsibility.

Before I got through with Howe the President came wheeling his way into his room. He had just returned from Miami, Florida. He was in fine spirits and looked the picture of health. His son Elliott was with him and so was Colonel McIntyre. His other secretary, Steve Early, had come in just before the President. We had fifteen or twenty minutes' lively conversation with the President leading at all times, and we celebrated his return by a very slight indulgence in some extraordinarily fine brandy that Louis Howe had.

The Cabinet meeting this afternoon was extended for all of the regular two hours. There were a number of matters discussed. I had an opportunity when in Howe's room in the morning to tell the President that, in my judgment, he ought to resist any weakening of the Securities Act which is now pending before Congress. I told him that I felt he ought to make a stand on this bill and go over the heads of Congress to the country, if necessary. At Cabinet meeting the Vice President was very strongly of the opinion that a real securities bill ought to be enacted. There was some discussion also of the revenue bill which passed the Senate yesterday. There was particular reference to the Senate amendment which forbade consolidated returns. The President said that he was in favor of this amendment.

I had learned yesterday that when a newspaper reporter called recently to interview Dr. William Wirt at his camp in Gary, Indiana, he asked Wirt if he could use his telephone. Assent being given, he was shown into a closet and when he turned the light on in there, he saw a pile of silver shirts, the uniform of a Fascist order that is attempted to be built up in the country at this time. I suggested to the President that it might be well to have an investigation made of this matter.

Two days ago Mrs. Gifford Pinchot drove down from Harrisburg, Pennsylvania, to ask me whether I would make a speech for Gifford in his primary campaign for United States Senator. I spoke to the President about this this morning but as I anticipated, he did not approve of it.

Tuesday, April 17, 1934

I went to the Gridiron Club dinner Saturday night. It seems to me that there is a good deal of chaff for the very small amount of wheat at most of these dinners. Many of the stunts are forced. What particularly struck me Saturday night was the persistent attack on the Administration program. The shafts were rather barbed and the whole effect on me was one of rather sharp criticism rather than of indulging in good-natured pleasantries. It is the custom at these dinners to have only two speakers, the President, who concludes the dinner, and a member of the opposition, who precedes him. Senator David A. Reed, of Pennsylvania, was the other speaker Saturday night and his remarks were certainly highly critical. There was nothing pleasant about his manner or courteous in his tone. The remarkable thing about the whole evening was the way the President handled himself when he was called upon. Without taking issue sharply with any of the stunts or with Senator Reed, he certainly disposed of the latter in an expert way and yet in the most courteous possible manner. He was clearly the star of the occasion.

Today I went to the White House for luncheon. The guest of honor was President Vincent of Haiti. I sat on the right of the Minister of Finance, an intelligent-looking Negro who spoke quite good English. President Vincent responded to the President's toast in French. The three or four Haitians who were present at the luncheon were fine-looking men.

Wednesday, April 18, 1934

Henry Wallace and I had lunch with the President in his office today. We discussed with him the proposed interchange of some bureaus in our two departments and he seemed to be very much taken with the proposal, although he does not want to do anything about it during this session of Congress. This is a sound position for him to take. He did say, however, that he would transfer the Bureau of Fisheries from the Department of Commerce to Interior at once. Fisheries formerly belonged here and I will be glad to have it back.

Friday, April 20, 1934

Anna and I went to the Frederic A. Delanos' for dinner last night.

At Cabinet meeting today, Vice President Garner said that the House of Representatives had never been in such turmoil for thirty years as it is at this time. It was the consensus of opinion that the Democratic leadership in that branch of Congress is woefully weak. The Speaker and the Majority Leader seem to have no control over the situation and apparently little disposition to get strongly behind the legislation desired by the Administration.

Monday, April 23, 1934

We were guests at the British Embassy at dinner last Saturday and I had the honor of taking Lady Lindsay in. This Embassy is the biggest and most elaborate of any in Washington, and the entertaining is on a scale commensurate with the establishment.

On Sunday at one o'clock Anna and I went to the White House for dinner. We were invited because Mrs. Roosevelt wanted to discuss the subsistence homestead program with me. She asked me to come half an hour earlier and we had a chance for a talk which showed that we were in substantial agreement on the principle involved in this Government enterprise. There had been what appeared to be some difference of opinion with respect to the Reedsville project and from this Mrs. Roosevelt had apparently drawn the conclusion that we didn't see the whole proposition from the same point of view. As a matter of fact, we do, except possibly as to slight details. I do think, however, and I so expressed myself, that we must keep our costs down or we will lose the popular support that is absolutely essential if we are to carry through the program at all.

After dinner the President and Mrs. Roosevelt asked us to go over to the Corcoran Galleries to look at some paintings by artists under the CWA allocation. I will say that most of these paintings were terrible from my point of view and I left wondering why men who turned out that kind of stuff should be supported as artists.

Tuesday, April 24, 1934

I am working pretty steadily evenings again, although I am not under such a driving compulsion as I was for so many months. I am really working evenings because I find it necessary to keep my mind occupied. I am thoroughly tired out these days, my nerves are badly on edge, and I am not getting anywhere near enough sleep. Last night I went to bed about ten and read for fifteen or twenty minutes, turned out my light and was awake again at one. I didn't sleep the rest of the night.

There was an exhibit this afternoon by the Subsistence Homestead Division, principally relating to the project at Reedsville, West Virginia. The President made a speech and so did Harry Hopkins and myself. The program was to have begun with the introduction of Harry Hopkins by Dr. Wilson, Director of Subsistence Homesteads. I was then to be introduced, make my speech, and end by introducing the President. However, the plans went awry. When the President arrived on the platform he kept on his feet, supported by the back of his chair. Wilson started to introduce Hopkins but just as he announced Hopkins' name, I whispered to him to introduce the President instead. Accordingly, he switched so that the President spoke first. After his speech half the audience left. Of course, it was difficult to follow the President but my speech was only ten or eleven minutes long and Hopkins' was even shorter.

Tonight we are going to the White House at ten o'clock to one of those tiresome musicales which customarily follow one of the formal dinners at the White House. The chairs provided for guests in the East Room are as uncomfortable as any I have ever sat in. The backs are concave so that the top catches one just at the lower portion of the shoulder blades.

Friday, April 27, 1934

The President closed the Cabinet meeting today by giving us his views on what he has in mind with respect to social insurance. It is evident that he has thought very deeply on the subject. He is looking forward to a time in the near future when the Government will put into operation a system of old-age, unemployment, maternity, and other forms of social insurance.

Friday, May 4, 1934

Gifford Pinchot spent the night at the White House last Friday. The President, in speaking of me, as the story came back to me, said that I was the greatest executive he had ever known. He told Gifford that during the war he had seen high-powered executives in Great Britain and elsewhere but that none of them compared with me. All I can say is that I hope he never wakes up if this is what he really thinks. I know that I am a hard worker, capable of rapid and sustained work covering long hours. I wish I could believe that I deserved the high praise of the President but I think his estimate of me is very, very much too high.

William H. Woodin, who was President Roosevelt's first Secretary of the Treasury, died yesterday and I feel as though I have lost an old and dear friend. I had never met him until we met here in Washington when we both came to be sworn in as members of the Cabinet, but I have liked him from the beginning. He was a lovely, gentle soul and yet a man of great capacity and courage.

Friday, May 11, 1934

Recently the President said at Cabinet meeting that he had traded Rex Tugwell for the favorite murderer of Senator Smith, of South Carolina. A short time ago he sent in the name of Dr. Tugwell for Under Secretary of Agriculture. The nomination was referred to Senator Smith's committee. But Senator Smith proceeded to pigeonhole it and let word go out to the wide world that he wouldn't report it favorably. It happens that Senator Smith has wanted a certain man appointed United States Marshal. This man is said to have a homicide record, but aside from that seems to have a very good reputation. So the President sent for Smith and told him he would give him his United States Marshal if he would report Tugwell's name favorably.

An oil bill drafted by the solicitors of the Interior Department has been introduced in the Senate by Senator Thomas, of Oklahoma, and in the House by Congressman Disney, of the same state. This bill will give more effective powers to the Administrator to control the output of crude oil. Since the courts have badly crippled our administration by injunctions, this bill is considered necessary. We believe that if it is passed it will give us powers that the courts cannot interfere with. The overwhelming mass of the industry, so far as we can ascertain, is in favor of this bill and is getting behind it. The hot oil people are, of course, opposed to it, just as they have opposed every bit of regulation. Our feeling is that unless the bill passes, the oil industry may take a nose dive this next summer after Congress has adjourned, in which event we will be likely to find ourselves in as bad a condition with respect to oil as we were in a year ago.

Tuesday, May 16, 1934

Monday afternoon I talked with Colonel McIntyre and he told me that the President was sending me over a personal message. A little later it came in a White House envelope addressed to "Secretary Ickes—Personal and Official." The envelope contained the following:

Dear Harold:

I want a report on the Indian country and land purchases. Please join Henry Wallace at Santa Fe evening of May 20, then to Winslow evening of May 24. I really want your opinion with that of Henry in these proposed purchases.

Yours—F. D. R.

The continued concern for my well-being really touched me greatly. This President of ours is a really remarkable human being. To think of him bothering about whether I am taking proper care of myself and taking a vacation when I need one!

Today I had an appointment with the President. I told him that I couldn't possibly get away now on account of important legislation pending on the Hill that my Department is especially interested in. I told him about the speech that I have promised to make at Tulsa and the later one before the Presbyterian General Assembly at Cleveland. He told me that I might tell the Presbyterians he had ordered me away. I countered with the suggestion that that might lose him the Presbyterian vote, and his retort was that I might lose that vote for him if I made the speech. I promised to be good after I get through with my commencement addresses, and we let it go at that.

Monday, May 28, 1934

We had an interesting Cabinet meeting on Friday. A number of questions were discussed that were of pressing concern. I was particularly interested in the discussion of the drought conditions in the Middle West. The situation is extremely serious there. The President remarked that a Harvard geologist has advanced the idea that we were in a geological cycle of a hundred years, during which the western part of the country would become a desert waste. Rex Tugwell, who was substituting for Henry Wallace, said that Department of Agriculture experts thought that we were about half through a fifteen-year cycle. In any event, the people in the drought country are apparently facing a terrible situation next winter, during which relief will have to be extended on a broad scale. The President announced, without even Lewis Douglas dissenting, that estimates for relief would have to be considerably enlarged.

Sunday I spent at home working on a statement covering the first year's administration of Public Works which had been prepared for me by Mike Straus. Mike is a very valuable man to me because he is highly intelligent and has fertile ideas but, generally speaking, I can't use anything he writes. His writing does not read like me and I don't think his English is good. The result was that instead of having a day to myself I spent some three to three and a half hours revising this draft. Then I went over my commencement address again.

Today I had a short time with the President. He read to me a message which he dictated last night, or rather two of them, on the subjects of water flow and of national planning generally. I liked both of the messages and told him so. What I like particularly about the President is that he has imagination and is always looking into the future. I consider him in a very real sense a far-seeing statesman.

I took occasion to discuss the PWA appropriation with him. He realizes that as the bill now pending in Congress stands practically nothing will be left for public works. He told me to get in touch with Buchanan and find out whether PWA could draw on the unobligated balances of RFC. Later I found out that the language of the bill would not permit this and so told the President over the telephone, whereupon he told me to get in touch with Buchanan again and tell him that he, the President, would like him to change the language so that PWA could draw on these balances. This I did.

Saturday, June 9, 1934

Sunday night I left for Berea, Kentucky, where I delivered the commencement address at Berea College, Monday morning, June 4, and had conferred upon me the degree of LL.D. I discussed the subject of the brain trust. I had some trouble in whipping this address into shape but it seemed to go pretty well. The president of this college is Dr. William J. Hutchins, father of Robert Maynard Hutchins, president of the University of Chicago, for whom I have a very high regard. I saw something of Berea College and I came away very enthusiastic over the work that is being done there. Over ninety per cent of the students come from the mountain areas of Kentucky, North Carolina, South Carolina, Alabama, and Virginia. This is the purest and oldest Anglo-Saxon stock in America, but their living conditions have been most primitive, and there is a high percentage of illiteracy among these people. The students seem to respond to the education that is offered them and they were on the average as fine and sturdy a looking group of students as I have ever seen. They all live simply at the college. I believe the average expenses are about $250 and the students are of all ages. One man of thirty-five was among the graduating class from the ninth grade this year, so I was told. It is remarkable and worthwhile work that is being carried on. It ought to yield rich returns to those who are engaged in it.

I took the night train Monday from Berea to Chicago, arriving there early Tuesday morning. The disbarment proceedings that I had instituted against Lucius J. M. Malmin and C. W. Larson had been set for hearing and that was the occasion for my trip to Chicago. The hearing was held in the Appellate Court room and was before seven Commissioners appointed by the Supreme Court under the new procedure which is in effect in Illinois in disbarment proceedings. I was on the stand for about three hours, most of the time under cross-examination by Malmin. We made out a very strong case, especially against Malmin, of an attempt to blackmail me into supporting him for Governor of the Virgin Islands, and I think he made a very bad impression himself. He tried to pull some dirty work by asking me highly improper questions of a more or less personal nature. These questions were objected to and the objections were sustained in every instance, notwithstanding which he continued to pump them at me until at one stage I turned and looked at him squarely in the face and said in a distinct voice: "Counsel, in addition to proving that he is a blackmailer, is proving that he is a blackguard." He shut up after that, but of course an opportunity was furnished to the rotten *Chicago Tribune* to try to spread around a little dirt. The day was very hot and trying.

At night, as I sat down to dinner at the University Club, William Allen White happened to come in and we dined together. Then I drove out to the home of Mayor Kelly, who wanted to discuss with me the city airport which certain interests want the Federal

Government to build as a municipal project in Lake Michigan. Merrill C. Meigs, publisher of the *Chicago American,* who is president of the Air Club of Chicago, was at the mayor's home. I told him very frankly that I thought it would be a great mistake to build the airport in the lake, which ought to be preserved at all times for the benefit of the people.

The disbarment proceedings lasted for three days but I left Chicago by airplane at eleven-fifteen on Wednesday and reached Washington at seven o'clock that night. The ship I took out of Chicago was one of the new Douglas planes which holds the time record on the transcontinental trip from New York to Los Angeles. We made Pittsburgh without a stop in a little over four hours.

On Thursday morning at ten-thirty I appeared before the Appropriations Committee of the Senate in connection with the Deficiency Appropriation Bill. The committee wanted to hear from me on the matter of public works and I went over some of the same ground I did before the House Committee on Appropriations. I received very good treatment at the hands of the members, although Senator Dickinson, of Iowa, asked me a great many questions. He, of course, is opposed to the Administration and was looking for a chance to criticize on the floor of the Senate. I had no complaint of his manner or anything of that sort. He was courteous and well within his rights in asking me the questions he did. I urged that the limitations of $500 million for public works set up in the House bill be removed and that the President be permitted to draw on the unobligated balance of RFC for PWA for an unlimited amount. I think that the matter should be left to the discretion of the President so that he will have considerable leeway if an emergency should arise. The House bill appropriates $65 million for the construction of buildings outside of the District of Columbia, to be expended by the Post Office Department and the Treasury Department. I urged that this money be appropriated to the Public Works Administration, pointing out the danger of a recurrence to the old park-barrel system if jurisdiction in this matter were taken away from Public Works.

On Friday I had a talk with the President after Cabinet meeting. Before I went to Berea I had from him a memorandum that he wanted to discuss with me the airport site in Chicago. I told him very frankly how I felt about the matter. He said to me jokingly that complaint had been made that I was too aesthetic, but after I got through talking to him I felt that he was not unsympathetic with my point of view.

The oil bill that I had been hoping would pass this session of Congress is in bad shape. Congressman Rayburn, Chairman of the House Committee on Interstate Commerce, is plainly stopping the bill. I firmly believe it would pass both Houses of Congress if it were brought up for a vote. Unfortunately, the President is anxious for an early adjournment and some of the Congressional leaders have more or less persuaded him that the session would be prolonged by as much as two weeks if he should insist upon the passage of the oil bill, which he in reality strongly favors. I have urged him very strongly indeed to get behind the bill and insist that Congressman Rayburn report it from his committee. The matter does not look encouraging now, and I think a serious mistake will be made if Congress is permitted to adjourn without the enactment of this bill. I am also concerned about the Wheeler-Howard Indian Rights Bill, and the Taylor Grazing Control Bill, although both of them have a chance to pass and I believe will pass if they are put to a vote.

I have had a severe struggle the last three days trying to catch up with the work that piled up on me during my absence from Washington. Today, which is Saturday, signature mail was brought in to my desk by the armfuls, just as it was last Saturday, with the result that I didn't get around to my dictation until well along in the afternoon. However, I have succeeded tolerably well in clearing my desk, but the unfortunate thing is that I have three commencements ahead of me in the next ten days and I am not in shape for any of them.

Monday, June 25, 1934

Last Wednesday I had a conference in my office on the Taylor Grazing Bill which passed the House and which the President has not yet acted upon. Secretary Wallace, Under Secretary Tugwell, Chief Forester Silcox, and two members of their legal staff were here, and on my side I had Solicitor Margold, First Assistant Solicitor Fahy, Poole, and one or two other solicitors. The attitude of the Department of Agriculture has been that this is an anticonservation bill and should be vetoed. In coming to this view, however, it seems to us that they have overlooked entirely certain vital amend-ments to the bill which were adopted at the last minute. As we pursued the matter my conclusion was that the legal points raised by the Department of Agriculture were not well taken and that the bill, if signed, will neither alienate from the Government any rights we now have in the domain, nor confirm in the Western public land states any rights which they may claim that are adverse to the Government.

At the end of the conference I called the Attorney General, told him that there was a difference of opinion, and asked him whether he would arbitrate the legal questions involved. He agreed to and I have sent him briefs of this Department and of the Department of Agriculture.

[Under the Taylor Grazing Act, the Department of the Interior set up a Division of Grazing which was empowered to work out a program of conservation covering those public lands, roughly 140,000,000 acres, on which cattle and sheep are allowed to graze. The program was intended to conserve forage resources, soil and wild life by controlling the grazing use of the lands.–ED.]

Saturday morning I had all of the members of the Oil Adminis-tration in except the very lowest grades. I had read in the society columns of the papers yesterday that certain members of the Oil Administration had been entertained at dinner the night before by the president of one of the large oil companies. At the meet-ing I dwelt on the danger of the social lobby here in Washington. I said that any member of the staff who accepted social favors from men in the oil industry was not only subjecting the Oil Ad-ministration itself to criticism, but laying himself open along the same line. I said that it wasn't a question of the personal integrity of any member of the Oil Administration, because I believed in their integrity, but I pointed out the danger of laying themselves open to attack that was sure to follow. It seems to me inevitable that the small minority of especially crooked oil interests that have been fighting the Oil Administration will not overlook any oppor-tunity to charge that we are hand in glove with the big oil interests if they can cite as evidence of their charges close social contacts be-tween the members of the Oil Administration, and in my judg-ment, there should be no further social contacts of this sort.

Thursday, June 28, 1934

On Wednesday I had luncheon with the President in his office. I have been trying to get an appointment with him for several days because I have a number of important matters to discuss with him before he goes away on his trip. I learned by a long-distance telephone talk with Mr. Delano that the President had decided to reestablish the National Planning Board, which was set up some time ago by the Public Works Administration, as an independent agency. The plan as outlined would have made this Planning Board, consisting of Mr. Delano, Charles E. Merriam, and Wesley C. Mitchell, supreme in its own field, without any Cabinet responsibility, although the proposal named several Cabinet officers, myself included, in a consultative capacity. Charles Eliot, 2d, would be the Executive Secretary, and, of course, considering all the circumstances, he would really run the whole show. I hit the ceiling when I learned of this plan. In the first place, I don't believe in establishing any more independent agencies; in the second place, I think planning should be attached to the Interior Department; and in the third place, I think Eliot would just run amuck if he were given such power and authority as is contemplated.

Thursday, June 28, 1934

There was a meeting of the Cabinet Committee appointed by the President at the last Cabinet meeting to formulate a plan for Land Use Planning. This meeting was held in the office of the Secretary of Agriculture and was attended by Henry Wallace, Miss Perkins, Harry Hopkins, and myself. Eliot had come down from Newburgh with a draft of an Executive Order. He presented a draft to me and then had taken one over to Wallace. Before I got to this committee meeting, Wallace, Miss Perkins, and Hopkins had been discussing the matter and they were as strongly opposed to the proposed plan as I was. After Council meeting Tuesday afternoon, I discussed it with the President. I had gone, but in talking with Henry Wallace over the telephone later, he admitted that they made no impression on the President and that he seemed bent on putting the new plan through.

The whole thing worried me very much. I thought it was poor politics and bad administrative policy. So at luncheon, at the first opportunity, I went after him hammer and tongs on this proposal.

It was plain to see that he was pretty deeply committed to it in his own mind but I had him pretty well around my way before I left.

At four o'clock I was back at the White House again to attend a meeting that the President had called and at which were present Miss Perkins and Messrs. Hopkins, Eliot, and myself. At the very outset it was clear from the President's remarks that he had changed his position. Sensing this change, Eliot laid on his desk the Executive Order which he had drafted, which would have exalted him and made an independent commission out of the National Planning Board. We discussed the thing pretty frankly. The President outlined his ideas, which were along the lines I had suggested, and in the end instructed me to draft an Executive Order setting up a Cabinet Committee, with myself as Chairman, and containing in addition, the Secretary of War, the Secretary of Agriculture, the Secretary of Labor, the Administrator of Emergency Relief, and Messrs. Delano, Merriam, and Mitchell. Under this would be an Advisory Committee, with Delano as Chairman, and consisting of Merriam and Mitchell; and there would also be a technical board, varying in personnel, to be called upon for advice and counsel from time to time. It was plain to see that this new setup did not please Eliot at all, but he couldn't break through the line and he left the White House a wiser but sadder man.

Today I took over to the President the Executive Order setting up in place of the National Planning Board, a National Resources Board, in accordance with his instructions to me the previous afternoon. The Executive Order had the approval of Hopkins and the Attorney General, but I didn't submit it to Eliot for his opinion or approval.

There has been quite a difference of opinion between the Department of Agriculture and this Department over the merits of the Taylor Grazing Bill, which would give the Secretary of the Interior the right to regulate and control grazing on 90,000,000 acres of the public range. Agriculture is opposed to this bill but we favor it and the Attorney General, when called upon to act as an umpire on the legal points involved, sided with Interior. Today while I was in the President's office, he signed this bill and gave out a statement which had been drafted for him, at my request, by Margold, our Solicitor, and approved by the Attorney General. It has been a long, hard fight to get this bill passed and if it gives the powers that I believe it does give to the Secretary of the Interior, we can at least make a start toward preserving and redeeming the range which is rapidly being destroyed as a result of overgrazing, with resulting erosion.

Saturday, June 30, 1934

At Cabinet meeting yesterday afternoon the President talked over the appointments he had in mind on the new commissions that have been created by act of Congress. I am afraid I do not agree with him as to the chairman he is going to name for the Securities Commission. He has named Joseph P. Kennedy for that place, a former stockmarket plunger. The President has great confidence in him because he has made his pile, has invested all his money in Government securities, and knows all the tricks of the trade. Apparently he is going on the assumption that Kennedy would now like to make a name for himself for the sake of his family, but I have never known many of these cases to work out as expected.

The President said that he hoped that Bernard Baruch would persuade General Johnson to go to Europe with him for a month. Baruch is hard at work on the General, who, however, is proving to be balky. The President is really anxious to have him out of Washington for a month, and said that he might have to order him to go if he didn't consent to go willingly. Johnson has been in bad health lately and his nerves are more or less cracked. If Johnson does go abroad, the President will name a committee to be supreme in NRA matters during Johnson's absence. The members of this committee, among others, would be the Secretary of Agriculture, the Secretary of Labor, Donald R. Richberg, and myself. I have forgotten whom he mentioned as the fifth member. If this happens it will throw an additional burden on me but one that I cannot very well decline to carry.

After Cabinet meeting, and after the President's press conference, which is held regularly at four o'clock every Friday afternoon, I had a further conference with the President. We had taken up at the Cabinet meeting the question of the PWA allotment out of the last Emergency Appropriation Bill. I told the President that Douglas was insisting that a number of items, including $48 million for TVA, were to come out of the $500 million designated for public works. Douglas wants the President to hold us down to $350 million. After some figuring the President decided that he could make it $450 million. When I sat down at his desk, however, he found figures from Douglas which disturbed him very much. From these figures it would appear that there isn't going to be anywhere nearly enough money available for the President to run relief and public works. As a result of these figures, the President began to cut all along the line and ended with allocating $400 million to PWA, and he remarked that that might be all that we would get. Since we have already allocated or earmarked in excess of this amount, it is going to leave us in quite a bad situation and I don't quite see how we are going to work matters out.

As I was talking to the President, his son, Franklin, Jr., was sitting at the other end of the desk—an interested observer and listener. While we were discussing Douglas and his attitude toward Public Works, the President looked up and said: "There is something I want to say here in the family in case I should die: After I fired Dean Acheson as Under Secretary of the Treasury, Lew Douglas set out to make a written record. He makes a written record of everything. If things go wrong he wants to be in a position so he can show that on such and such a date he advised the President not to do thus and so. Of course, he makes a very good watchdog of the Treasury but I don't like it."

As I was leaving, the President again urged me to plan for a real vacation. He was most friendly and touching about it. Here is a man who is probably carrying greater burdens than any other man in the world and yet he charges himself with the responsibility for seeing to it that a recalcitrant Cabinet member takes a vacation. I told him that I would go away and he remarked that I had made such promises to him before. He said: "Go away and take your stamps with you. I am going to take mine with me." He was really most friendly and considerate and I came away deeply touched.

Thursday, July 19, 1934

On Wednesday we had a Public Works Board meeting at which we approved a large number of projects, totaling about $25 million. Following the Public Works Board meeting, we had the first meeting of the newly created National Power Policy Committee, of which I am Chairman, and the following members: Frank R. Mc-Ninch, Chairman, Federal Power Commission; Robert E. Healy, Member, Federal Stock Exchange Commission; T. W. Norcross, Assistant Forester, Forest Service; David E. Lilienthal, Tennessee Valley Authority; Morris L. Cooke, Mississippi Valley Committee,

PWA; Major General Edward M. Markham, Chief of Engineers, War Department; and Dr. Elwood Mead, Commissioner of Reclamation. This committee was appointed by the President at my suggestion and we are to report directly to him. It will be our duty to consider power questions in a very broad way and recommend legislation, if we feel that legislation is called for on particular phases of this question.

Thursday, July 26, 1934

With Mr. Lee, one of my secretaries, I left Washington on the Pennsylvania last Friday at four-ten P.M. I got into Chicago at eight-thirty-five Saturday morning and ran into the hottest day I think I can ever remember in that city. I had a few personal matters to attend to in the morning. Fred Marx lunched with me at the University Club and then I drove out home where I took a cold shower and rested for a bit. The house was delightfully cool and quiet and I fell in love with it all over again. It is the loveliest house I have ever known anywhere.

We pulled out of the Northwestern station for Sacramento, California, at nine-thirty-five Saturday night. It was very hot all the way across country until we struck the Rockies. Iowa and Nebraska seemed to be burning up. The corn looked dried out and the tassels were a bad color and seemed to lack vitality. I have never seen the country so dry. Fortunately, I was in an air-cooled car. Those that were not air-cooled were so hot that they were scarcely endurable. As we crossed southern Wyoming the second day out, I fell in love all over again with that country. It has been a good many years since I have crossed Wyoming, but I found that it had the appeal for me that it has had since I first went there many years ago.

In the afternoon, we drove around the Yosemite National Park. Next to Yellowstone, this is the most popular national park in the system, but as compared with the wide open spaces of Yellowstone, the area available for camping is restricted.

There are several thousand people camped here most of the time during the season, but the camps are well distributed under the trees and well kept. The park itself seems to be well set up and well taken care of. It has its own electric light plant and its own sewage system.

On Wednesday we drove up to Glacier Point where we had a fine view of magnificent mountain scenery. After lunch we drove to Mariposa Grove. I had wanted for years not only to see Yosemite but to see the sequoias and yesterday I certainly saw many most magnificent specimens. The biggest of the trees in Mariposa is the "Grizzly Giant," which is the third biggest *Sequoia gigantea* in existence. It is estimated to be thirty-six hundred years old. There were other wonderful trees too—many of them, throughout the grove—and they made a great impression on my imagination with their strength and endurance and majesty. Apparently they are absolutely immune to any enemies except man—insects, water, or even fire. Some of these trees show that they have been badly burned on several occasions, but each time the tree grows on, covering the old wounds and making new growth. They appear to be as irresistible as time.

We had dinner at an inn in the grove and then waited until the moon rose. We drove back to the valley by full moon and it was one of those drives that will live long in the memory.

Mrs. Roosevelt has been in this part of the country for some time. She was at Lake Tahoe to see her daughter, Mrs. Dall. She is now camping on a lake about a day's trip from the valley, but is expected down tonight.

I have already begun to feel the benefit of my trip. There isn't any doubt that one should get away once in a while as far as possible from human contacts. To contemplate nature, magnificently garbed as it is in this country, is to restore peace to the mind, even if it does make one realize how small and petty and futile the human individual really is.

Tuesday, July 31, 1934

Thursday we drove out to the sugar pine grove. I had never seen sugar pines before. I found them to be truly magnificent trees, second only to the sequoias. They are very valuable for lumbering purposes and this particular grove was saved from the woodman's ax only through the generosity of John D. Rockefeller, Jr., who, a few years ago when it was threatened with destruction, bought it and gave it to the Government as an addition to Yosemite. These trees grow to a great height and are symmetrical in shape. There is a beetle that is very destructive of them, but which the Park Service is doing its best to check. Unfortunately, the presence of this beetle cannot be discovered until it is too late to save the tree. Then the tree has to be cut down and burned to destroy the larvae. The branches of the tree are irregular, thus giving it a different appearance than any other pine. The cones are of large size and hang pendant, giving the crown of the tree a very attractive appearance. We ate our lunch in this grove and after lunch drove on to the Hetch Hetchy Valley.

It was a very hot day. We had received word that Mrs. Roosevelt was coming down on this day from the mountain camp where she had been staying. When she found that we were going to Hetch Hetchy, she said she would like to see that too. We got to the dam at Hetch Hetchy a little ahead of her, but we waited and soon she drove up. It was interesting to meet her in that remote nook, especially since she and I had had a tentative engagement to go together to the Reedsville, West Virginia, Subsistence Homestead project the week end of August 5. She was very tanned and was enthusiastic about the park. That evening we had dinner at the Rangers' Club at Yosemite, and Mrs. Roosevelt asked me to dine with her. Later she went on a moonlight trip through the valley with Colonel Thompson, but I went to bed early.

On Friday I took it easy in the morning. I lunched at noon as a guest of Mrs. Curry, head of the Curry Camp in the park. Immediately after lunch we started off with Dr. Tresidder in his car for Merced. Dr. Tresidder is president of the consolidated company that operates all of the concessions in Yosemite. He was educated to be a doctor, but he married Mrs. Curry's daughter and had to assume management on Mr. Curry's death and when matters were not going so well. He is a very fine person. The trip to Merced was one of the hottest I have ever had. In fact, I think it was the hottest. The heat was terrific. I am sure it must have been all of 120 degrees.

We made Merced in less than two hours. Dr. Tresidder has an airplane of his own which he keeps at Merced and he volunteered to take us to San Francisco. We made San Francisco in just about an hour. I had been given permission to land at the Army airport, which is right in the city, and this saved a long trip from the public airport at Oakland. As we stepped out of the airplane at San Francisco we found the temperature cool, so cool in fact that I found myself buttoning my coat.

The Park Service had a very good Packard car, which Colonel Thompson offered to let me have to drive up to Crater National

Park in Oregon. This car had gone ahead to San Francisco and was ready, with all baggage aboard. I had accepted an invitation to spend Saturday night at Bohemian Grove about seventy-five miles north of San Francisco. Mayor Rossi had been at the Grove and was returning, having come down just for luncheon. He asked me to drive up with him and I accepted the invitation. Mr. Lee and Dr. Tresidder, who is a member of the Bohemian Club, drove up in the Packard.

I had heard of the Bohemian Club, but knew little about it. I was invited to the Grove last year, but, of course, could not accept. Apparently it has quite a large membership. The club owns some 1,500 acres of redwood forest beautifully located. The members go to the Grove for three weeks every summer. The encampment closes on a Saturday night and that night they have what is called their "High Jinx." This silly name led me to believe it was a roisterous, drinking occasion. I will not deny that I found a good deal of drinking; in fact, there was a lot of it, but there was much more besides.

There are a number of small camps in the Grove, but they are well hidden and well managed. The members live in cabins, but there is sanitary sewage, hot and cold running water and gas for both light and cooking. The food was excellent. There is a general bar for the camp and each particular subcamp has a bar of its own.

The camp grounds have been laid out beautifully. There is one pond at the end of which is a big stone impressionist figure of an owl before which the light always burns. But the thing that made the greatest impression on me was the play that night. The theater is an open-air one in a natural opening, surrounded by towering sequoias. The stage is at the foot of a sharp hill. The hill is covered with trees and undergrowth and the proscenium arch of the stage consists of two giant sequoias with intermingled tops. It was one of the most impressive and magnificent settings I have ever seen. The play that night was a serious one, the theme being the conversion of the old Irish Druids by St. Patrick. It had been written by the late Professor James Stephens, an Englishman, who had been a member of the English faculty at the University of California. All the parts were taken by the members of the Bohemian Club and the acting could not have been better if it had been done by professionals; in fact, I doubt whether it would have been so well done. It was very impressive to see the actors carrying torches and following the trails down the hillside. The costuming and the lighting were very well done. I was told that the lighting for that one play cost $25,000, and certainly it would have been difficult to improve upon it.

After the play there was a very good time had throughout the camp. Members visited various camps and everyone was expected to drink long and often. I met Eugene Meyer, Chairman of the Federal Reserve Board under President Hoover, and now publisher of the *Washington Post*. Mr. Hoover himself had been there the day before. Amon Carter, of Fort Worth, Texas, was there, as was Assistant Secretary of the Treasury Robert. Jim Farley had been there the week before. I also met Mr. Giannini, president of the Bank of America, and Arthur Reynolds, former president of the Continental-Illinois National Bank of Chicago, who is now working for Giannini. There were many other well-known men there, some of whom I met and some of whom I did not meet.

Those in charge of me started to visit the various camps, but I soon begged off and went back to Woof Camp where I was quartered. I explained that I was leaving early in the morning, and about twelve-thirty I went to bed. I got very little sleep because the festivities continued practically all night. I know that at four o'clock they were still singing in our camp. At half past five I got up. Mr. Lee and I had an early breakfast and at six-thirty we were on our way to Crater Lake National Park.

We reached Crescent City about half past six and decided to stay there for the night. We found a tolerable hotel on the ocean. Monday morning we left Crescent City about seven o'clock. We were striking northeast on this part of the drive and that meant that we were not going through the mountains with their twists and turns and grades. We made very good time and arrived at Crater Lake National Park Monday about noon.

I had never seen Crater Lake before, but its charm and beauty made a great impression upon me. As its name implies, the lake occupies the crater of an extinct volcano. The lake lies well within the crater. At some points the crater walls tower 1,500 feet above the surface of the lake and at no point is the rim of the crater less than several hundred feet above the lake. The lake itself is about six miles long and four miles wide. The water is 2,000 feet deep and is absolutely pure, being fed as it is from underground streams.

But it is the color of the lake that gives it its particular charm. When I first saw it, the shade was a deep, indigo blue, but the color varies with the intensity of the wind and with the shifting of the lights and shadows. I think the blue, when it is blue, is more intense than that of any lake I have ever seen, including the lakes at Glacier Park. Practically all shades of blue can be seen from different situations or at different times. In the afternoon we took the rim drive which enabled us to see the lake at intervals from different points.

Monday night I had dinner with Acting Superintendent Canfield and Mrs. Canfield. Tuesday morning the proprietor of the hotel, Richard Price, drove Mr. Lee, Mr. Canfield, and me over to Diamond Lake to fish. Diamond Lake is in the national forest and the general testimony is that it is a great place for fishing. However, our fishing party was badly managed. We set out in a decrepit old car of Mr. Price's which had to make much of the distance, going and coming, in second speed. Moreover, we did not arrive at the lake until nine o'clock. We tried a little casting and more trolling for two or three hours with a total lack of success. Then we drove back to Crater Lake for lunch. Immediately after lunch we started down to the Klamath Indian Agency.

I felt that I could not be so near this Agency without stopping. The superintendent of the agency, Wade Crawford, is a Klamath Indian; I believe he is a half-breed. He is well educated, able, and I think, sincerely interested in the welfare of his people. Robert Marshall, Chief Forester of the Indian Service, was at Klamath and Crawford took him, Mr. Lee, and myself to have a look at the reservation. We drove many miles through a forest containing very valuable yellow pine trees available for lumber. He took us to a fire lookout station located about the middle of the reservation and from here we could see valuable timber for miles in every direction. This Indian tribe, consisting of some fifteen hundred or sixteen hundred Indians, has the greatest wealth per capita of any tribe in the country. It owns over a million acres of land, a great portion of which consists of valuable yellow pine timber. The lumber companies, of course, have made great inroads on these forests and are busy trying to acquire additional rights. In order to do this they are paying money under one pretext or another to members of the Indian Council. It is Crawford's policy, as it is that of the Indian Bureau, to preserve all of these rights for the benefit of the

Indians themselves. We hope in time to have timber manufactured in small sawmill units by the Indians themselves and solely for the benefit of the Indians.

It was after five o'clock when we got back to the agency. The soil through this reservation is volcanic ash. It is the lightest and most friable soil I have ever walked upon. One's feet actually sink into the soil. In trying to make a curve in the road in the woods, Crawford momentarily lost control of the car because he was driving fast and we shot off the road into a deep pile of this volcanic ash before he could stop. The car became deeply imbedded and it was only after a good deal of trouble by the others in the party that we were able to get it out. The harder we tried, the deeper the car sank. Finally, by scraping away the soil from under the rear wheels and piling twigs and small branches under the wheels, we were able to get out.

The Park car had brought me down to the agency and was waiting to take us into Klamath Falls. We made fast time into Klamath Falls and there I was met by Mr. Hayden, manager of one of our reclamation projects located down the valley. He wanted to take me down to look at the project, but it was so late that even he saw it was impossible. I declined an invitation to go to his home for dinner and I did it with some compunction. I felt sorry that he and Mrs. Hayden had gone to the trouble of preparing dinner, but after all, I had not accepted for dinner and I was so tired that I couldn't stand the thought of going into a private house and trying to keep up my end of a conversation about indifferent subjects with people I did not know. I bolstered my resolution by the reflection that people will exploit a public official for their own self-glorification, and while it was hard on the Haydens to have me decline, nevertheless I felt that I was well within my rights in doing so. After dinner at the Elk Hotel, Mr. Lee and I killed time in this most uninteresting frontier town until train time at half past nine when we boarded the Southern Pacific for Tacoma, Washington.

Monday, August 6, 1934

We arrived at Tacoma shortly after one o'clock the afternoon of August 1 and were met there by Superintendent Tomlinson, of Mount Rainier National Park, who drove us up to Mount Rainier, a distance of about sixty miles. I found that I was pretty tired when

I reached the park. Tomlinson was one of those poky drivers who make me nervous. He drove us about a little in the park on the way to Paradise Inn, and I told him finally I wanted to drive directly to the inn.

As it happened, this afternoon was the only glimpse I was to have of the park because a rain set in that night and the next day was rainy and very misty. I saw enough of the park, however, to give me a realization of its charm and beauty. I took a little walk after I had settled myself at Paradise Inn and saw some beautiful landscape. I was particularly taken with the wild flowers which grew in colorful profusion in the open spaces. There was a great deal of closed gentian. I had never seen it in such masses. It is a lovely flower, although it does not rank in my opinion with the fringed gentian. There was beautiful lupine too, and the Indian paint brush was doing itself proud. There were other varieties of flowers, some of which I recognized and some of which I did not know.

We reached Portland, Oregon, at half past six, Friday morning, the third. Photographers and newspaper reporters met me at the train and then we drove to the Portland Hotel for breakfast. We had reserved rooms there. This hotel was the headquarters of the President's party. Mrs. Roosevelt was already there and James came up just after I had registered, he having driven all night from Seattle. He had started out by airplane, but the bad weather forced him down and in order to make connections, he had to drive in an automobile.

Shortly after eleven o'clock we left with General Martin, who has just finished a term in the House and is the Democratic candidate for governor, for the dock where the *Houston* was tied up. Secretary Dern's car preceded us, he being the only other Cabinet member in Portland. There was a great crowd at the dock, but Secretary Dern and I were ushered on board ahead of the other dignitaries and were given the customary honors by the officers of the ship when we reached the deck. The President looked fine and he was especially cordial in his greeting of me. We had a buffet luncheon on board ship and then we boarded automobiles and formed a procession which toured several miles of the streets of Portland. There was a great crowd out. It looked as if everyone in Portland was lined up along the right of way, and many besides.

After traversing the city, we headed toward the Bonneville dam-site, a couple of hours away by motor. The weather was not at all good. The day, generally speaking, was cloudy and there were in-termittent showers, but the weather did not seem to have the effect of keeping people away. There were many signs of activity at Bonneville. The Army engineers are in charge of this work and they have already made considerable progress. The dam that is to be built here is for power and navigation. The Columbia River at this point is considerable of a stream and the dam will be a very large one. The salmon go up this river in order to spawn and the dam will be provided with fish runways so that this habit will not be interfered with. At Bonneville the President made a speech to a very large crowd which was waiting for him and after the speech we boarded a special train which was standing on the track nearby. We pulled out of Bonneville late in the afternoon and woke up on a siding at Ephrata, Washington. We had gone through Spo-kane in the night and then turned west again to Ephrata.

This was the morning of August 4. After breakfast we again took automobiles, which were waiting for us, and drove to the Grand Coulee damsite, which is also on the Columbia River. Here the Reclamation Service is erecting a low dam for power purposes, but ultimately the project will be a very high dam for both power and irrigation. There are at least a million acres of extremely fertile land which will be able to produce abundant crops if and when they get water from this project. At present the plan is merely to build a low dam at something in excess of $30 million. The final project, when completed, will run into $200 or $300 million. There was a large crowd at Ephrata and at intervals along the road. Where all the people came from, I can't imagine. But the greatest surprise of all was when we got to the damsite itself. Here there was a very large concourse of people, some said more than 20,000. It was perfectly astounding to see so many people in a desert coun-try. Some of them must have driven two or three hundred miles to see and hear the President.

The Reclamation engineer in charge of this project, Mr. Banks, explained what had been done and what was to be done. The dam to be built here will take six times as much concrete as will be required at Boulder Dam. It is a very important project. The topog-raphy of the region calls for a dam. The chief engineering diffi-culty during construction will be to divert and manage the strong and heavy current of the Columbia River which passes at this point. The river is not so wide here, but it is deep and swift. Salmon come up the river as high as this but not in such large numbers as at Bonneville. The Bureau of Fisheries has decided to take the salmon out of the river at this point, take the eggs from them, and hatch them. This will make it unnecessary to provide a fish runway, even if such a thing could be done with a dam of the height that this one will be ultimately.

After driving back to Ephrata, we boarded our train again on Saturday night. We had a late lunch on the train and, consequently, a late dinner. The President sent word back, asking me to dine with him. He and his family and Louis Howe had occupied a private car on the rear of the train. The rest of the five or six sleepers attached to the special train were filled with governors, Senators, members of Congress, newspaper correspondents, etc., etc.

At the dinner there were, besides the President and Mrs. Roosevelt, James Roosevelt, Franklin, Jr., and John Roosevelt, Senator Burton K. Wheeler, of Montana, Secretary of War Dern, Louis Howe, a friend of the younger Roosevelt boy, and myself.

This was a most interesting dinner. It resolved itself into a debate between the members of the Roosevelt family, with all of them frequently talking at one and the same time. Mrs. Roosevelt precipitated the discussion by raising some social question and her three sons at once began to wave their arms in the air and take violent issue with her. She expressed belief in a strict limitation of income, whether earned or not, and the boys insisted that every man ought to have a right to earn as much as he could. The President joined in at intervals, but he wasn't President of the United States on that occasion—he was merely the father of three sons who had opinions of their own. They interrupted him when they felt like it and all talked at him at the same time. It was really most amusing. At one stage when they were all going on at once, I raised my voice and observed to the President that I now understood how he was able to manage Congress. Senator Wheeler followed my remark with the observation that Congress was never as bad as that. That was about the sum and substance of outside contribution to the dinner talk that night, but it was all very interesting and very amusing.

After dinner Mrs. Roosevelt and the President retired and the rest of us had a little talk about general political affairs. We pulled out fairly early because the President had to prepare the speech that he was to broadcast from Glacier Park Sunday night. Sunday morning found us alighting at Belton, Montana, the western entrance to Glacier Park. After breakfast we all boarded seven-passenger touring cars with the tops let down. We started up the west side of the park along the shore of Lake MacDonald. The roads traversed have been put in since I visited Glacier Park in 1916, with Ernest Hiler. We saw magnificent scenery—high mountains, glaciers, deep valleys and wooded plateaus, and there were beautiful lakes and waterfalls, and water trickling over sharp precipices from glaciers. Few in the party had ever before seen Glacier Park and all of them seemed to be very much impressed. We climbed mountains by excellently graded roads until at times we were above the tree line and above some of the glaciers. We lunched at Many Glaciers Hotel and after lunch we proceeded on our way to Two Medicine Chalet, which had been prepared for the President's broadcast and where it was expected he and Mrs. Roosevelt would spend the night. He had decided against spending the night there, however, because his train was pulling out at eight o'clock in the morning and he thought he would rather go back to the train that night and so avoid having to get up so early Monday morning.

A group of Blackfeet Indians was waiting for us on the edge of Two Medicine Lake. They were a fine-looking bunch of Indians and they had on ceremonial habiliments. They chanted and some of the children danced and then they proceeded to make the President and Mrs. Roosevelt and myself members of the tribe. They did this by a ceremony which, of course, meant much to them and the spirit of which we respected. They gave the name "Lone Chief" to the President and the name "Big Bear" to me. In Blackfeet my Indian name is "Omuc Ki Yo." They gave to the President a war bonnet, two peace pipes, one of them an historic one of the tribe descended from an old chief fifty years ago, and one or two other presents. To me they gave a very beautiful war bonnet, a bow and arrows of the kind that they formerly used to kill buffalo; also a beautifully beaded belt for Mrs. Ickes. Some of the boys from the CCC camps were present and sang songs. One of these groups was composed of Negroes. It was really a very well-staged and very well-managed exhibition. After the President had gone in for a bath, the Indians asked me to make a talk to them. I did so through an interpreter. What I said they seemed to like very much and I was glad to have this opportunity to talk to representatives of the Blackfeet Indians who constitute one of our very best tribes.

About nine-thirty Steve Early called me into where the President was. George Dern also came in and we had a little talk. I told the President that I was going to stay over at Glacier for a couple of days, but that I would join his train at Chicago. He said that this was fine and that we would have a chance to talk some matters over on the trip from Chicago to Washington. Then he and his party left for their train at Glacier Park station, and I stayed on in the chalet where the President would have spent the night if original plans had been carried out.

This morning I spent signing mail and revising the manuscript of the speech I am to make at Titusville, Penna., on the twenty-seventh. At lunch time Superintendent Scoyen of the park came up with Mr. Hays, who runs the transportation company here. I had planned to go on a fishing trip but decided against it because it seemed so complicated and there were other things I ought to be doing. Instead of going fishing, I went over to the Blackfeet Agency, which is some twenty miles from Two Medicine Lake.

At the agency I had a very interesting talk with Superintendent Stone. I discussed agency matters with him. Affairs at this agency are in pretty good condition although great improvements could, of course, be made. The Indians here number about four thousand and they still have about 1,200,000 acres, most of it grazing land. They are expecting the Government to turn over to them a large bunch of cattle purchased by relief funds in drought areas that will not support cattle the coming winter. The Blackfeet understand the care of cattle. As I have already said, they are one of our best tribes. Many of them have their own little farms on which they manage to make a living, although not a good one. Mr. Stone wanted me to see one of the new community houses that had recently been built and I drove some ten miles with him for that purpose. The community house was a very creditable affair indeed. The architecture seemed characteristic and the hall was entirely built by the Indians. It was a piece of real work. Then we drove back to Two Medicine Lake through a very heavy wind storm which raised a most annoying dust since none of the roads that we traveled outside of the park were oiled.

Another matter of particular interest in connection with the agency is the house-building campaign that Stone has been carrying on. Last winter Glacier Park sent down to the reservation a number of carloads of good timber which had been killed by fire a number of years ago, but was still usable as timber. On the agency the Indians out of this timber have been building homes for themselves. They are substantial homes and are far superior to anything they have heretofore occupied. Stone told me that the Indians liked these homes and kept them clean and sanitary, although they have no running water in any of them. He said that with $10,000 more they could build enough homes to take care of the Indian families who needed them, some two hundred in number. I told him I would try to get this money for him, and what I have in mind is to make an allocation of $10,000 out of public works funds.

Monday, August 13, 1934

The return trip to Chicago was much more comfortable than I had any reason to anticipate, in view of the fact that the Great Northern does not run any air-cooled cars. In the middle of the second night out, the weather turned hot, but except for that it was quite agreeable. I got into Chicago on Thursday morning, August 9, and was met at the train by Anna, who had gotten in fifteen or twenty minutes earlier from Washington, D. C. She is on her way to New Mexico, but will be in Chicago for several days.

That night just after I had finished my dinner in the diner, the President's secretary, Dorothy Jones, came through the car looking for me. She told me that the President had expected me to have dinner with him and that he and his party were waiting for me. She asked me to hurry up and not to say anything about having already had my dinner. Sure enough, when I got into the President's private car I found that he and his other guests were waiting. He remarked that he suspected that I had not been told that he wanted me to dine with him and I confirmed his suspicion. I sat on his right and Miss Jones was on his left. I put up a very good bluff at eating a second dinner. Miss Jones was so highly amused with the performance that she finally told the President that I had already had one dinner.

The train was scheduled to make a stop at Garrett, Indiana, because Congressman Farley, from Indiana, was aboard. However, the President had taken the braces off his legs and so could not appear on the rear platform. We got into Garrett about ten and the President asked me to make his excuses to the crowd. There must have been all of 15,000 people pressed around the rear end of the train —an eager, expectant crowd—who wanted to see the President. When I was introduced by Congressman Farley, I received a most cordial reception indeed, but when I told them that I was pinch-hitting for the President, a roar of disappointment went up. I remarked that this expression of theirs was highly complimentary to the President and that I realized it was like going to a wedding at which the bride was missing. I didn't attempt to make a speech and I could not have done so anyhow. That crowd wanted to see President Roosevelt and no one else. It was not a cheerful occasion so far as I was concerned, but fortunately the train resumed shortly its trip toward Washington.

I had hoped that I would have a chance to talk over various matters with the President on this trip, but that was not to be. We got into Washington about noon on Friday, and we found the weather hot here too. I came direct to the office, where I put in the balance of the day that day, all of Saturday, and Sunday morning until one o'clock. Everything seems to have gone smoothly during my absence, but there were a number of tedious and knotty questions waiting to be solved.

There isn't any doubt that my trip, notwithstanding everything, did me good. But I was delighted to get back to Washington and I feel more energy and more desire to work than I have felt for some time.

Thursday, August 16, 1934

Wednesday morning we had a Public Works staff meeting and at two o'clock a meeting of the board at which we voted over 250 projects totaling about $30 million. At three o'clock I was again at the White House sitting in at a conference called by the President to consider the relief program. It is clear that there will hardly be enough money to carry on the Government relief program and the other emergency work until the first of March. The President does not want to have to ask for money from Congress before that date. It is perfectly clear that we won't get any more money out of the last appropriation for Public Works. As a matter of fact, the President told me that if we could find any way of paring down, he would like to have some of the money already allocated to us. How we can do this, I do not know, but, of course, I will make the effort.

I told the President early last summer on two or three occasions that in my judgment he would be making a great mistake if he permitted Congress to adjourn without giving him almost plenary powers to meet any emergency. I pointed out to him that no one knew what would happen, and unless he had wide direction to use money for relief and public works, it might be necessary to call Congress together in extra session before January. I made substantially the same statement before the Appropriation Committees of both the House and the Senate. Instead of giving the President the broad powers that should have been granted him, Congress held him down, with the result that the Administration is now being pinched. The drought relief will cost a great deal more money than Congress had any reason to anticipate. The funds voted for that purpose will be totally inadequate and I cannot see, on the basis of the figures that were discussed at the conference on Wednesday, how the situation can be carried over until March 4 without having new funds.

Wednesday, August 22, 1934

I had a very busy morning on Friday, the seventeenth, because I was taking a train at noon for Maine. In the end I wasn't able to sign all the stuff that was on my desk but I did pretty well.

I took Raymond with me to Maine, and Major Fleming, of the Engineering Division of the Public Works Administration, also went along. The occasion of my going was to look at the Passamaquoddy power project. This project has been pressed upon us vigorously by many and the whole State of Maine is very much interested. The plan was developed by Dexter Cooper, an engineer, and it involves the use of the tides, which run very high in the Bay of Fundy and in Passamaquoddy Bay, to generate electric power. The scheme is to build a low dam and a high dam, the larger to be filled by tidal waters, the low dam to be used to stabilize the water in the high dam. There is also projected a reservoir of very large size into which water is to be pumped by the surplus power and the water itself is to be used to generate power when there is not enough water in the high dam for that purpose. The whole plan seems rather fantastic to a man who is not an engineer, but engineers say that the proposition is sound from an engineering point of view.

The plan to go up at this time was set out by Colonel Louis

Howe, who is anxious about the result of the election in Maine on September 12. The Public Works Administration does not have the money necessary to finance this project, even if we should approve it, but Louis thought that at least a graceful gesture could be made with beneficial results on election day. So he asked me to go up and look at the thing, and the President was also in favor of my going.

It is possible to get a through train to northeastern Maine only on certain days of the week. At this time of the year such a train runs on Friday and that is the reason we left on that day. We arrived at Ellsworth, which is the railroad station for Acadia Park, early Saturday morning. We did not have to be at Eastport in connection with the Quoddy project until late Monday and we thought that we might as well spend a couple of days at the park.

On Monday a Mr. Cram, treasurer of the Bangor and Aroostock Railroad, came over from Bangor at the instance of Governor Brann, of Maine, to take us up to the Quoddy project. We arrived at Lubec where we were to be parceled out among the different members of the Trout family as guests. The Trouts, by the way, are a prominent family in those parts and they are very delightful people and hospitable. However, before we got settled in, Dexter Cooper came over and asked Major Fleming and me to be his guests. He has a home on Campobello Island and not far from the President's summer home. This island is in the Province of New Brunswick, just a stone's throw from the Maine coast. Raymond stayed with one of the Trout families and Mike also.

Early Tuesday morning two of the Trout men brought in a motorboat, with them Mike Straus and Raymond, and took Mr. Cooper, Major Fleming, and myself aboard and started to cruise the bays so that Mr. Cooper could give us an idea of the project he has been working on for the last fifteen years. This part of Maine, like the Bar Harbor section, is very beautiful. It is wilder than the Bar Harbor section but not so picturesque. We cruised the waters for a couple of hours and then went into Eastport, where Governor Brann and a commission recently appointed by him were waiting for us. The chairman of this commission is President Sills of Bowdoin College. Another member is President French of the Boston and Maine Railroad; a third member is Mr. Cram, already referred to, and the other members are Mr. Campbell, who is head of the biggest textile concern in Maine and apparently a very rich man because he boasts of three airplanes, and I was told afterward that two or three years ago he had ordered seven Rolls-Royce cars at one time. The fifth member of the commission is the Master of the Maine Grange.

We went to the East Hotel, where I had a chance to discuss the project with the members of the commission. I found them very keen men who will investigate the facts and make their own report on the basis of the facts. I was especially taken with President Sills of Bowdoin. He and I had a chance for quite a long talk on general matters before the commission and I went into session. I promised the commission to send them at a meeting to be held in Augusta next Wednesday two or three experts from our Public Works staff.

Shortly after one o'clock we went down to the hotel for lunch and the dining room was full of men from that part of Maine. It was a very substantial-looking crowd. Immediately after lunch we adjourned to the bandstand in the middle of the town. There were some two thousand people assembled, which I was told was the biggest audience ever congregated in those parts. There is no doubt of the interest in this project in that section of Maine. They think that their economic life depends upon it. Certainly, unless something happens, Eastport and other communities like it will die a death of slow economic strangulation.

The mayor of the town made a speech and then the Governor made a speech introducing me. I found myself in a very difficult position but managed to carry off the situation in good shape. I couldn't promise the people that we would finance this project, because even if the Government should be able to do that eventually, it hasn't the money to do it at this time. I praised the project as a project which I could do with propriety. Then I told them that their likelihood of being able to finance it at any time in the future depended upon their ability to develop a market for the power that could be generated. I discussed several methods by which a market might be developed, but I made it clear that this was an essential prerequisite to any financing by the Government. I told of President Roosevelt's interest in the project and the willingness of the Public Works Administration to co-operate with the Governor's commission. What I said seemed to be very well received.

Sunday, August 26, 1934

On Thursday, August 23, I had a very interesting conference with Sir Henri W. Deterding, Director General of the Royal Dutch Petroleum Company, Walter C. Teagle, president of the Standard Oil of New Jersey, and Dr. Hornbeck, of the State Department. They came to discuss the Japanese oil situation. Japan imports practically all of its oil products. It has two or three small refineries of no consequence so that it has to depend on the foreign market for fuel oil for the navy and for gasoline and lubricating oils. Under the Japanese law the prices of all oil products can be fixed by the state. During recent months Japan has been buying fuel oil for the navy in very large quantities, which is a significant fact of itself. Lately it has issued an order that the companies supplying gasoline shall keep a six months' supply. This process could be repeated indefinitely.

The principal, and in fact the almost exclusive, sellers of refined petroleum products to Japan are the Dutch Shell and the Standard of New Jersey, with their affiliated companies. Mr. Teagle and Sir Henri frankly said that they could not stand this sort of pressure because it would mean great losses to their companies. Their proposal is that the United States join with Great Britain and Holland in protesting against this demand for a six months' supply to be held in reserve for Japan, the protest to be backed by a threat of a boycott which would cut off Japan from all oil supplies from the outside world. The reason for coming to me was because as Oil Administrator I would have to issue the boycott order.

I told them that it seemed to me that it was largely a matter of international policy, to be determined by the State Department. I indicated that I would be very glad to issue the necessary boycott order if in the judgment of the State Department I should do so. Dr. Hornbeck indicated a responsive state of mind but took the position that he thought the first move should come from Great Britain and Holland. Sir Henri Deterding, who is sailing for Europe in a few days, will undertake to sound out the governments of these two countries, with which he has very close connections. The plan is to have these two countries ask our Government if we will join with them in the necessary representations, and from what Dr. Hornbeck said, our Government is willing to do that.

We had a Cabinet meeting Friday afternoon. I went back to the White House about half past five. I had had an appointment with the President at twelve-thirty to take up Departmental matters, but he was behind in his appointments and McIntyre suggested the tea hour. We adjourned upstairs for our tea, which consisted of a very delicious rum highball concocted of Haitian rum and ginger ale, which I had never before tasted, and fresh caviar, of which I am very fond. In addition to myself, there were present Mrs. Dall, Miss Le Hand, and another woman of the President's secretarial staff. We had a very pleasant time and I was able to dispose of all the matters I wanted to discuss with the President. We had such a good time in fact that I didn't get home for dinner until after half past seven.

Wednesday, September 5, 1934

It seems rather quiet in Washington with the President away, although there is no lack of things to do. Mr. Burlew tells me that our mail is increasing very much. The incoming mail for the Interior Department now amounts to approximately 3,000 pieces daily and Public Works accounts for approximately 4,000 additional pieces. The task of handling this mail is in itself a mighty one.

Friday night, the thirty-first, I gave a farewell dinner at the Congressional Country Club for Colonel Waite, who has resigned as Deputy Administrator of Public Works. I invited the members of the board and the heads of the various divisions in Public Works. Twenty of us sat down to dinner and we had a very pleasant time. Secretaries Dern and Roper attended as members of the board, but the other Cabinet members who were invited were out of town. We had a little speaking after the dinner in a light vein but the speeches were few, short, and well put. The affair was over at ten o'clock.

I am sorry to see Colonel Waite go. My association with him has been very cordial and pleasant on the whole. Even when we differed on matters of policy, my liking for him did not abate. He has a very kindly, friendly disposition. He has imagination and character, and he comes of a distinguished family, being the grandson of the late Chief Justice Waite of the United States. At the beginning of the Public Works Administration I had to make it clear that I was Administrator, since he showed a disposition to build up an organization that looked to him and was responsible to him. He spoke of resigning on a couple of occasions but I dissuaded him, and while in the end I had my own way with respect to the reorganization heading up to me, our personal relations continued friendly and close until he resigned to accept a position in Cincinnati which will pay him more than he received here.

Harry Hopkins came over to have lunch with me today. He had spent the week end with the President. He urged upon the President a public works program beginning next year, involving the expenditure of $5 billion a year for five years. He thinks the Relief Administration ought to be abolished next year. He doesn't believe in unemployment insurance. He wants the public works program to take up any slack in employment, and there is much to be said for his plan. He thinks the relief situation is going to be very serious next winter.

Lewis W. Douglas resigned as Director of the Budget two or three days ago. He has been out of sympathy all along with the fiscal policy of the President. He is, of course, a conservative, and while he is an attractive young fellow and has a good deal of ability, he was not in step with the Administration. His loyalty to the President kept him on until lately, but the President remarked to me several months ago that one thing he didn't like about Lew Douglas was that he was making a written record of his position in opposition to the Administration. Whenever he disagreed with the President on a question of important policy, he would go to his office and write the President a memorandum confirming his position. Harry Hopkins told me that Douglas wrote an unpleasant letter of resignation to the President. Hopkins thinks the lines are forming for a test of strength between the conservatives and radicals, and he remarked plaintively that, outside of two or three of us, all of the men prominent in the Administration are conservatives. Hopkins also said that there has been a falling out between Henry Wallace and Rex Tugwell. For this I am sorry. I had supposed that they were still as close and devoted friends as they had been. Rex Tugwell is going abroad for a while. Hopkins is of the opinion that Wallace is becoming more conservative. He says that Wallace has the Presidential bee in his bonnet and that that is driving him to the right. In commenting on the addresses made on Labor Day by Secretaries Roper and Perkins, he remarked that the speeches sounded exactly like speeches that were made twenty years ago. He regards Secretary Perkins also as a conservative. According to this record, I am the only progressive-minded member of the Cabinet left.

Friday, September 7, 1934

We had a meeting of the Board of Directors of the Federal Housing Corporation yesterday afternoon. We elected Colonel Hackett to fill the vacancy caused by the resignation of Robert Kohn, and Harry L. Hopkins to fill the Colonel Waite vacancy. After the meeting Rex Tugwell said he wanted to talk with Secretary Perkins, Harry Hopkins, and myself. What he had in mind was the General Johnson situation, which has become acute and is scheduled to reach a final crisis, after a long succession of minor ones, at Hyde Park next Monday evening when he goes to see the President. We, as well as practically everyone else in the Administration, believe that General Johnson is so serious a load to the Administration that the President ought to get rid of him at once. It seems that the President has been trying to lose him, but he is so tenderhearted that he has not been able to say the final word. Johnson persists in staying. He becomes highly emotional and goes through all sorts of theatricals with the President in order to hold on. The President simply hasn't been able to tell him point blank that he has to go. It was this that Tugwell wanted to discuss with us. Don Richberg came in for an hour this afternoon on the same subject. Everybody is very anxious about the situation. We all feel that if Johnson is permitted to hang on any longer, it will be almost disastrous to the Administration, and yet we are afraid that the President, out of his goodness of heart, will not be able to do what seems to us necessary and essential.

Saturday, September 15, 1934

Thursday night I went to 15 Dupont Circle to dine with Mrs. Patterson. John Lambert, one of the leading writers for the Hearst Service, and Mrs. Lambert, were other guests, along with Mr. Whyte, who is general manager of all of the Hearst publications. We talked quite a lot about the recent elections. I pointed out that the trend was distinctly radical. I expressed the opinion that the country is much more radical than the Administration and that it was my judgment that the President would have to move further to the left in order to hold the country. I said, as I have said on a number of occasions, that if Roosevelt can't hold the country within reasonable safe limit, no one else can possibly hope to do so, and that a breakdown on the part of the Administration would result in an extreme radical movement, the extent of which no one could foresee. I pointed out that I thought a lot of the newspapers that are now so busy attacking the Administration, if they had any regard for their own interests, would be supporting it because a wide swing to the left would engulf all of us in an extreme situation that might readily get beyond control. I said that I would a whole lot rather give up fifty per cent of whatever property I might possess than be forced to give up all of it, and that the latter was a distinct possibility if affairs were permitted to get out of hand.

Tuesday, September 25, 1934

Last Sunday I finished revising the draft of the Foreword for my book and in the afternoon the entire manuscript was mailed to the publisher. Some time ago I sent this manuscript by Mike Straus to Steve Early with the suggestion that he look it over and see whether, in his judgment, it should not be printed. Early waved it aside and suggested that I write a letter to the President. I did this immediately and in a couple of days McIntyre called me from Hyde Park to indicate that the President was a little worried about anyone publishing a book during the campaign, and suggesting that I send the manuscript up to him. I sent it at once.

I heard nothing on Sunday, and on Monday morning I called McIntyre. He told me that the President had read only part of the manuscript but that he liked it. The President said for me to let my conscience be my guide, but McIntyre did intimate something about the risk of printing the book before election. I told McIntyre I didn't want to take the responsibility and he said I oughtn't to have to. He volunteered to speak to the President again after he went up to Hyde Park.

In the afternoon I got a telegram from the President, as follows: HAVE READ IT AND LIKE IT. WILL BE BACK WEDNESDAY. I still didn't know whether to go ahead with the publication and so I called McIntyre back. He said the President liked the book but that he didn't want to give me written authority to print it. He told me "unofficially" to go ahead with it. Later in the afternoon I called the President on another matter and he asked me if I had received his telegram. I told him I had and expressed my gratification. He said the book was fine and that he had thought of writing at the end of his telegram: HIT THEM AGAIN. So word has gone to the publisher through Dr. Foreman to go ahead.

The title of the book will be *The New Democracy,* and the publisher expects to have it out the latter part of October. I have a feeling that it was rather sketchily done, although I worked tremendously hard on it. But it certainly was a hurry-up job. While Dr. Clark Foreman prepared most of the manuscript for me, a good deal of it was a reassortment of passages from my various speeches. There were two chapters that were statistical and factual which Foreman himself wrote. But all the manuscript I had to go over painstakingly in order to make the language mine. I practically re-wrote all of it except the quotations from my own speeches. In addition, I wrote an entirely new chapter dealing with Individualism, Liberty, and Constitutionalism. The Foreword I dictated Saturday afternoon and I think it was the best part of the book.

Thursday, September 27, 1934

All my plans were made to go to the second of the United States Army–Mexican Army polo games Wednesday afternoon, when I got a summons from the White House to attend a meeting of the National Emergency Council at half past four. This was a secret meeting called by the President to consider the reorganization of NRA; the resignation of General Hugh S. Johnson as Administrator was accepted yesterday by the President, effective on October 15.

I have been hoping for some time that General Johnson would resign or be forced out. I think he has been a heavy load for the Administration to carry. The first part of his job he did well. I don't know anyone who could have done nearly so well as he did. He aroused enthusiasm throughout the country, he was a past master at carrying on the type of ballyhoo campaign that was necessary to put NRA across, but when it came to settling down to administrative work, he seemed to be a total loss. He never appeared to be able to get out of his head that it wasn't all to be ballyhoo. He was so used to streaming headlines on the front pages of the papers that he had to keep reaching for these headlines, with the result that he said and did many reckless things.

Then his relationship with his administrative assistant, and secretary, has been distinctly detrimental. She went with him everywhere, sat in all conferences, and was as obtrusive as a certain type of wife is in the private affairs of her husband. Then, according to the reports, he took more and more to drink. He would go on regular drunks, during which for a day or two at a time he was incapacitated for public business. His temper became worse and worse; he became suspicious of everyone, believing the hand of every man was turned against him. Meanwhile, NRA became more and more disorganized and sentiment in the country more and more adverse.

It was decided at our meeting Wednesday afternoon that the National Emergency Council would be charged with responsibility for determining the policies for NRA. The National Emergency Council consists of Donald R. Richberg, as Chairman, the Secretary of Labor, Harry L. Hopkins, Chester Davis, and myself. Johnson was on it originally but, of course, there is a vacancy now.

I made two or three suggestions, about the setup and about the Executive Order that will issue shortly, that were accepted and which I believe will improve the situation. I insisted very strongly that the five executives suggested to do the actual administrative work would be a failure unless they had at their head a man of outstanding executive ability. I pointed out that with NRA under fire as it has been, the Administration could not afford to risk a failure. I was just about to suggest to the President that we try to get President Robert Maynard Hutchins, of the University of Chicago, to add to this Council, with a view to making him the actual head of it in effect if not in name, when the same suggestion was made by Charles Wyzanski, Solicitor for the Department of Labor, who attended the meeting in place of Miss Perkins, who was out of the city. The President thought well of the suggestion and asked me to get in touch with President Hutchins. Accordingly, later in the afternoon I called him by telephone and arranged for him to come to Washington on Monday morning to talk with the President. I am afraid we can't get him but he would be an excellent man. I suggested that the President ask him to secure a leave of absence for a year. I don't believe he would give up the presidency at Chicago, and he really ought not to be asked to do so, since that is, in effect, a life job.

I thought the President looked tired and I have really felt some concern about it since. He appeared to me more tired than at any time except at the end of a long winter. Now we are just entering the winter. He looks far differently than he did when I met him at Portland on his return from Hawaii. I am wondering too whether he showed the same carefree spirit that has been so characteristic of him. When I entered the Oval Room in the White House, where he is still having his temporary office while the new office wing is being rebuilt, I shook hands with him and he greeted me with: "Hello, Harold. I liked your book; it was grand."

Tuesday, October 2, 1934

Last Friday, September 28, the first Cabinet meeting in a long time was held. While we were waiting to go into the Oval Room, where the Cabinet meetings are being held while the new office wing is under construction, Morgenthau asked me whether Public Works had made a certain allotment that he recently requested. I told him we hadn't but that I was willing to consider it on its merits. He had asked that we give this money out of an allocation that was rescinded because the Post Office Department has not gone ahead with the construction of a number of postal substations. I told him that that appropriation originally had been for the Post Office Department, although, technically, it went to the Treasury Department, which is in charge of building construction for the Government. He became highly peeved and acted exactly like a spoiled child. He said I hadn't given him any allotment that he had asked for except a very minor one and that he wasn't going to ask for any more. I told him that he was the only member of the Cabinet who went direct, in the first instance, to the President for public works allotments, and he replied that that was the only way he could get anything. He said again in a highly excited voice that he would not ask for anything more. All during Cabinet meeting he pouted.

Saturday morning we arrived at Atlanta at eight thirty-five to start the demolition for the first slum clearance program ever undertaken by the Federal Government. There are two slum clearance projects projected for Atlanta, one for Negroes and one for whites. A delegation of citizens met us at the train and took us to a hotel, where, after a press conference, I was hustled out to the site of the Negro project, which is near Atlanta University. This is the outstanding Negro university in the world, I am told, and the university itself made a very good impression with its fine buildings on a good campus. A temporary platform had been built, and before it were congregated a large number of students and others. The students did a little singing in those wonderful Negro voices of theirs.

They were really a fine-looking lot. Then I spoke extemporaneously for ten or fifteen minutes, following which I set off a charge of black powder which blew up an old shack one hundred yards or more away on the site of the Negro housing project.

We then drove to Georgia Tech, where Dr. Brittain, president of that institution, met us. Here Governor Talmadge, of Georgia, caught up with us also. There was a meeting in the chapel of the college, where I went on the air for thirty-two minutes over both the big national broadcasting companies. The audience was a small one but I didn't mind that because I had written my speech from the point of view of reaching a national audience. At the conclusion of these exercises we went to the site of the white project, which is near Georgia Tech. There I made another extemporaneous speech from a temporary platform, spoke for a couple of minutes before the newsreel machines, and then blew up another house.

Hutchins had an appointment with the President at eleven o'clock and later came over to see me. It seems that the President didn't definitely tell him what kind of a job he was being considered for. He told Hutchins that he wanted him to come down here three or four times a week for a couple of months just to give aid and advice to the NRA bunch and help draft legislation. Hutchins told me he was not interested in this kind of a proposition and he was rather puzzled about it all. I told him that I didn't understand why the President hadn't gone through on the original suggestion but that there undoubtedly was some reason.

I was scheduled to speak Monday night before the Recreational Congress but late in the morning word came from the White House that the President wanted me to join a conference at eight-thirty there that night so that I had to cancel my speaking engagement. I took Dr. Hutchins home to dinner with me and then went to the White House. Those present besides the President were the Secretary of the Treasury, Harry Hopkins, Dr. Jacob Viner, Under Secretary of the Treasury Coolidge, Acting Director of the Budget Bell, and another man from the Treasury whose name I have forgotten. The subject for discussion was how much money we might need during the next two or three years for relief or for public works. It seemed clear from the President's attitude that he proposes to continue the public works program in some form. Harry Hopkins wants to discontinue relief next spring and have Public Works supply every man out of work with a job. There were various sums of money discussed, ranging from $5 billion for the fiscal year beginning July 1, 1935, to smaller amounts. There was also a general discussion of present and possible future fiscal policies for the Government. It was put up to Hopkins and me to get together and see what sort of an outline of a program we could agree upon.

At the conclusion of the conference I asked the President if I could speak to him for a few minutes and upon his consenting to do so, I asked Hopkins to stay. I discussed the Hutchins situation with him, telling him that Hutchins was in a distinctly receptive state of mind. I emphasized again the importance of having a strong executive if NRA was to get anywhere at all. I strongly urged Hutchins upon him. He said he wanted Hutchins but he was afraid to go too far at first. His idea was that if he could get Hutchins down here on some temporary basis, he could work him in from that point. I told him that it seemed to me the thing to do was to put all the cards on the table and tell Hutchins frankly that he wanted him to be the executive and directing force of NRA. He told me to have Hutchins come to see him at a quarter to eleven this morning.

One interesting remark made by the President when he and Hopkins and I were alone was that the way the Government is being run now there is an inner Cabinet. He said the members of this inner Cabinet were Morgenthau, Cummings, myself, Miss Perkins, Wallace, Hopkins, Davis of the AAA and the man who would head up NRA.

Morgenthau was unusually cordial to me last night. Probably he felt ashamed of himself for his juvenile behavior last Friday.

Hutchins saw the President this morning and called me up later. The President did come all the way across and Hutchins is going back to try to get a leave of absence from his Board of Trustees. The plan is for him to come down as soon as possible and in effect take charge of the administration of NRA.

This afternoon there was a meeting of the Executive Council, after which the President asked the members of the National Industrial Council to wait for a few minutes. We discussed procedure and the relationship between the National Emergency Council and the NRA Board that has taken over the powers formerly exercised by General Johnson.

Mrs. Roosevelt wanted to talk to me about the Reedsville, West

Virginia, Subsistence Homestead project and asked me to the White House at a quarter to six. I ran into a tea. The President was there and so was Mrs. Dall, in addition to Sir Ronald Lindsay, Mrs. Ruth Bryan Owen, who is home from Denmark on a vacation, Bernard Baruch, a British admiral and his wife, and an American admiral. Baruch took occasion to say some complimentary things to me about my work here.

After the others had gone, Mrs. Roosevelt and I had a talk. She asked for the report that Glavis's men made down there and I promised to send it to her. She also wanted to see the report made by the Division of Investigations in the Virgin Islands, and I shall send her that.

Friday, October 5, 1934

Joseph Guffey, Democratic candidate for United States Senator in Pennsylvania, came in to see me the other day. He wants me to make a speech for him. I told him I was willing to, but that I would not go into any state and make a campaign speech except on orders from the President. I have not yet received any such orders and my impression is that the President does not want members of the Cabinet to get into the campaign. The particular reason Guffey wants me is because Gifford Pinchot is going to come out for Senator Reed. I cannot understand such a decision on Gifford's part. He has always bitterly opposed Reed and his reactionary affiliations in Pennsylvania. They have fought each other like two tomcats on a back fence, and I never before have known Gifford to eat crow. It is suggested that he has made a deal with Reed as a result of which Reed will support him for Senator to succeed Davis in two years. I hope not, but I do find it difficult to explain Gifford's reported decision.

Sunday, October 7, 1934

At Cabinet meeting Friday, Homer Cummings raised the question with the President whether members of the Cabinet should go into any of the states to make campaign speeches. The President said No, except as to any man's own state, in which case he said it would be perfectly proper to go in. This ruling does not apply to the Postmaster General, who, as the political representative of the Administration, is expected to range far and near during the campaign.

Farley discussed the political situation somewhat. He seems quite optimistic. He thinks the Democratic party will undoubtedly gain six or seven Senators and he doubts whether they will lose any Representatives in the total.

Gifford Pinchot made a speech at Wilkes-Barre, Pennsylvania, Thursday night, violently attacking the Democratic candidates for Governor and United States Senator in his state. While he blasted Guffey, he didn't go so far as to come out for Reed. He also praised the national Administration. His failure to endorse Reed openly does not mean that he is not supporting Reed if he is opposed to Guffey, since they are the only two candidates to choose from. I think this is an extraordinary proceeding on Gifford's part, in view of the bitter attacks that he has made on Senator Reed and the Republican machine for over twenty years.

Thursday, October 11, 1934

Last night I attended another conference at the White House at which were present Harry Hopkins, the Secretary of the Treasury, the Under Secretary of the Treasury, and other members of that Department. Also present was Joseph Kennedy, Chairman of the Securities Exchange Commission. We had up for discussion again the question of relief and/or public works for the fiscal year beginning July 1, 1935, and thereafter.

It is clear that the President is thinking very favorably of a public works program for the fiscal year 1935 and 1936 of $5 billion, with perhaps $3 billion for the next year and $1 billion for the following year. He wants to do away with direct relief altogether and embark on a public works program that will give employment to all who are able and willing to work. Kennedy and Under Secretary Coolidge did not warm up to this proposition at all. They both expressed the confident belief that we were on the very edge of a business revival, but it was remarked by others in the conference that that has been held out now from 1929 on. The President instructed me to set the PWA engineers to work to see what kind of a program they could recommend. I am then to discuss it with Harry Hopkins and report back to the White House at another conference next Tuesday night.

Today I was the guest at a luncheon of the National Press Club. I spoke informally on free press, free speech, and free assemblage. It was announced that my talk was "off the record." I received some very high compliments afterward on what I said, and a number of the newspaper correspondents expressed regret that they could not print anything about it. Mike Straus, who is one of my severest critics, was especially eulogistic.

Following my press conference this afternoon, John Boettiger, of the *Chicago Tribune*, came up to me in a very shamefaced manner. He apologized for the questions that he had orders from his office to ask me. He had told Mike Straus in advance that he felt badly about having to discuss the matter with me at all. He showed me a dispatch from the *Tribune* telling him to ask me about my brokerage account with A. O. Slaughter, Anderson and Fox. According to the dispatch, I owed the firm $90,000 which I settled at forty cents on the dollar; that this money was raised for me by the Democratic National Committee; that payment was not with my own check but with a Democratic National Committee check; that on two previous occasions I had gotten into financial difficulties from which Anna had pulled me out, to the serious hurt of her private fortune. I told Boettiger that this statement was ninety-nine per cent lie. Mike Straus was present at the interview and advised me against denying any of the allegations. He made the point that my very denials would make it possible for the *Tribune* to print a story on the basis of them. I followed his advice and contented myself with telling Boettiger that for my part I hoped the *Tribune* would print the story exactly as it stood, as it would then give me excellent grounds for a suit for libel. Later in the afternoon I called Fred Marx at Chicago and asked him to get in touch with the members of the firm of A. O. Slaughter, Anderson and Fox and tell them to refuse to say anything at all in the event an attempt should be made by anyone on the *Tribune* to interview them.

Friday, October 12, 1934

I didn't get to sleep last night until about half past one, and then only after taking a pretty stiff drink of whisky. The result has been that all day I have been tired and sleepy, and yet I know that if I should go to bed I couldn't sleep.

I lunched with the President today. I told him about the latest from the *Chicago Tribune,* and he agreed with me that it was the rottenest newspaper in the whole United States.

I had planned to meet Mrs. Roosevelt at the Reedsville Subsistence Homestead project over the week end, but on account of pressure to get out my speeches, I had to change my plans at the last minute. She went down, however, and came in to see me at twelve o'clock. After I got through with my interview with her, I was glad I hadn't gone to Reedsville. Apparently things down there have been going very badly. Along about last May I authorized the immediate building of some seventy-five additional houses and not a lick has been done on any of them. There are thirty barns waiting to be built and nothing has been done on them. Meanwhile the cows get along as best they can while the weather is getting colder every night. The management down there has been simply terrible. Mrs. Roosevelt was very ladylike about it all, but she certainly wasn't pleased. Nor was I. We have transferred the project manager from Reedsville but have not yet put anyone else in charge. After Mrs. Roosevelt left, I called Pynchon and told him to bring Mac Flynn down from Reedsville. He has been in charge of purchasing there since the beginning, and while there is nothing brilliant about him he seems to have people's confidence. Today Pynchon and Flynn came in. I started in innocently enough to ask Pynchon certain questions about who was in charge of construction at Reedsville and to my astonishment I found he didn't know anything about it. First he said that one man was in charge of construction. I sent for that man and he proved he wasn't responsible. Then Pynchon named a second man and I repeated the operation. Exactly the same thing happened with respect to the third man. The sum and substance of it seems to be that no one is much in charge of anything at Reedsville.

I have been becoming more and more dissatisfied with Pynchon, and we have definitely decided to send somebody over there as an executive, to take over the management of the project. He means well, he is hard working, and he is loyal, but he simply can't get anything done. Burlew and Slattery tell me that one trouble is that his wife has social ambitions and keeps the poor man running hither and yon every night, with the result that he is worn out and has no real pep to put into his work. I feel sorry for him.

Last night was the opening night of *Jayhawker*, written by Sinclair Lewis. Fred Stone was the star. I had some qualms about going, but I finally decided that I would take a night off. Anna, Assistant Secretary Chapman, and Bill McCrillis went with me on four tickets secured by Dr. Gruening. About half of the play was very funny indeed. The other half was peace propaganda. It was all worth while and interesting, but it seemed to me that it wasn't well put together.

Saturday, October 20, 1934

Tuesday night there was another of the conferences at the White House where we have been considering a public works program for next year. It seems quite clear that the President is more and more firmly coming to the opinion that we ought to undertake a public works program of approximately $5 billion the next fiscal year, followed in the next two fiscal years by $3 billion and $1 billion, respectively. Harry Hopkins prepared a plan in general outline and we discussed it fully. I am glad that the President is in favor of a big slum clearance and housing program. We discussed the possibility of $2 billion for these purposes alone. For some time I have been advocating a great highway from the Atlantic to the Pacific, and he thinks well of that also. He has great imagination and I told him the other day when I was lunching with him that if he had been President at the time when the Treasury was overflowing, he would have gone down in history as the greatest builder since the world began. He probably will anyhow if we go ahead with such a program as we are discussing. At our last meeting, Joe Kennedy, Chairman of the Securities Commission, was quite cold on the matter of a big public works program. He had the distinctly conservative point of view. Tuesday night he had swung clear over and favored such a program. Under Secretary Coolidge of the Treasury was not at the Tuesday night meeting. He has been opposed to such a program from the beginning. I think Morgenthau would be too, but he follows the President.

I have come to the conclusion that we must have a different executive in the Subsistence Homesteads Division. Pynchon, whom I started in the Housing Division and later transferred to Subsistence Homesteads to put the project in good shape. He seems to be in a maze. He doesn't appear to know what is going on in his organization and can't give me information when I ask for it. He has made the mistake on several occasions of guessing at answers that he ought to know and then having to correct his mistakes. He is loyal and hard working, but lacks the drive to put a proposition across. Accordingly, I am looking for a real executive to try to save that situation. Of course, the Reedsville project is just one big headache and has been from the beginning. Colonel Howe made the initial mistake there by insisting on rushing ahead with some flimsy knockdown houses from a manufacturer, ready to set up, and then these had to be redesigned and reconstructed and finally made over. And then Mrs. Roosevelt took the Reedsville project under her protecting wing with the result that we have been spending money down there like drunken sailors—money that we can never hope to get out of the project. This project has been attacked in a number of articles and magazines and newspapers, and we are distinctly on the defensive with respect to it.

On Wednesday, Mrs. Pinchot called Harry Slattery to say that she had heard that I was going into Pennsylvania to make a speech Friday night. She asked him what I was going to say and Harry told her that that put him in a very embarrassing position. She then said that she would call me and ask me. She did call me Thursday morning to tell me that Gifford was going to let loose a blast Friday morning against Guffey. I never thought Guffey was fit to be United States Senator, but in Pennsylvania the choice is between him and Reed. Reed is a bitter opponent of the Administration and its policies, and an able one. Guffey would go along like a lead lamb. Accordingly, I prefer to see Guffey elected. Two great trends of political and economic thought are in conflict at this time and we have to take help wherever we can get it, provided that in the taking there are no improper commitments made or questionable acts committed.

At Pittsburgh last night I spoke before the Hungry Club at the Chamber of Commerce Auditorium on "Pennsylvania and the New Deal." It was really a political speech in which I paid my respects to the Pennsylvania oligarchy headed by Mellon and Atterbury and Grundy. I opposed the re-election of Senator Reed. I did not mention Guffey by name although, of course, my purpose in coming into Pennsylvania and the object of the speech was to help him. For reasons already explained, however, I did not have much stomach for Guffey personally. I certainly couldn't permit myself to indulge in any panegyrics in his behalf. His running for Senator in this state when there is a real chance to carry it is nothing short of an imposition upon the President. I wish the President had made him get off the ticket. As a matter of fact that is what Pinchot wanted. After he was defeated as a candidate for the Senate in the primary, he wanted a rearrangement, the setting up of a new ticket, which would be a combination of his followers and the Democrats in the state and on which ticket Earle, the Democratic candidate for Governor, would be the candidate, and he, Pinchot, the candidate for Senator. He put this suggestion up to me on two or three occasions, one of them when I was at Titusville making my oil speech, and Mrs. Pinchot has put it up to me not only by letter, but by personal interview and by telephone. I referred to Pinchot last night in my speech, but in no unfriendly vein. If I had wanted to, I could pretty nearly have blown him out of the water by mere recital of his disappointed political ambitions, but I am too fond of him and he really is too fine a man to be attacked except as a matter of ultimate necessity.

Tuesday, October 23, 1934

I reached Toledo about six o'clock Saturday evening and was met at the train by President Nash of the University of Toledo. The Forum meeting was held by the Toledo Forums Association and I was the only speaker. It was a good-sized audience—about twelve hundred people. The subject for my Toledo, Chicago, and Detroit addresses is "America Faces a Changing World." I had not been any too well pleased with this speech. For some reason, it seemed a difficult one for me to write and I never had a chance to work at it, except between times. I started it at Cincinnati and ended it after I got back to Washington. I was not pleased with the way it went over at Toledo, but I thought afterward it was more my fault than the fault of the speech. I simply felt dead and I had no life or punch. There was a session of questions and answers following the speech, and I did very well in that, so that, on the whole, I think the evening was worth while.

I went back to the hotel to change my clothes and took the New York Central to Chicago, where I arrived Sunday morning at half past six. Eric met us and after breakfast at the University Club, we went out to Hubbard Woods. It was a very lovely day; in fact, I have had fine weather ever since leaving Washington. Raymond drove me out to see President Hutchins, who has the summer home once occupied by Samuel Insull, Jr. It is west of Mundelein and is built on an artificial island in an artificial lake. The house is simple enough. The only way to get on the island is by a boat, but it is only a short stone's throw from the nearest point of the mainland.

I wanted to discuss with President Hutchins the Richberg–NRA situation in Washington. What I had to tell Hutchins was a conversation I had with the President at luncheon last Thursday. Here was the situation as told to me by the President, and, with his permission, related by me on Sunday to Hutchins.

On the occasion of Hutchins' last visit to Washington, it was agreed between him and the President that he was to go to Washington as soon as possible and be made Vice Chairman of the Administrative Board of NRA and Vice Administrator. The understanding was that Clay Williams, the Chairman and Administrator, would be retiring very shortly and that Hutchins would then succeed him. Hutchins agreed to this proposition and left Washington. The President sent for Clay Williams and told him the arrangement. Williams appeared to be perfectly satisfied and said he would discuss it with his board. Later the same day, but after Hutchins left for Chicago, Williams rushed into the President's office to say that his board was very unhappy about the proposal. There followed a session with the board, at which strong objections were made to having Hutchins brought to Washington. Two of the members of the board said that they had worked with Hutchins on other occasions and that he was impossible to work with because he was arrogant and dictatorial. Another objection was that the balance of the board would be disturbed since there were already two college professors on it and Hutchins would make a third.

The President told the board that he was committed and that he would go through with his commitment. The members of the board offered each one of them to resign to make place for Hutchins, and the President told them that they were acting like a bunch of children and to go back and think it over. Then the President had Steve Early telegraph to Hutchins that he (the President) would wire him on Monday.

It also developed from my talk with the President that when Don Richberg had heard of the arrangement about Hutchins, he had gone to the President to object. He told the President also that the balance of the board would be disturbed. The President remarked to him that the commitment to Hutchins had been made and that he was going through with it. Then Richberg suggested that Hutchins take the Chairmanship of the National Compliance Board, and asked the President if he had any objection to his (Richberg's) calling up Hutchins. The President said he hadn't, but he did not want Hutchins to be told that Richberg was calling him up at his instance. Apparently it was following this that Richberg called up Hutchins for the first time and had a long talk during which he openly assured Hutchins that he had not talked with the President and that he was calling him without the knowledge or consent of the President.

Hutchins told me of an interesting incident that happened two or three days ago. One of the Swopes was at Hull House and asked Miss Addams if she would not ask Dr. and Mrs. Hutchins to dinner. During the conversation Swope said something about how fine it was that Hutchins was going to Washington. Hutchins supposed that Swope knew in what capacity it was proposed that he go to Washington, and inadvertently told what that was. It appeared that Swope thought he was going down as a member of the National Compliance Board, and he was aghast when he found out what the President had really arranged with Hutchins. The question of Richberg came up and Swope spoke of Richberg in very warm terms. Hutchins asked him what he knew about Richberg. Swope said that when he first went to Washington, business was very much disturbed because of Richberg's connection with labor. Then he went on to say that Richberg was coming more and more into favor with the business interests; that he was swinging further to the right all the time and that business was strong for him. He said that the position of General Counsel of the Iron and Steel Institute had been offered to Richberg.

I am thoroughly convinced that Richberg's connection with NRA can only result in harm to that organization. I believe that he is out to make a place for himself at whatever cost. I do not believe he can be trusted. I am convinced that it was he who inspired the opposition expressed by the NRA Board to Hutchins. In my judgment he will leave no stone unturned to prevent Hutchins from going to Washington. As matters stand, he has a board that has been carefully hand-picked by himself and through which he can control in his devious, indirect way since there is not a strong or outstanding man on it. As I remarked to Steve Early, Richberg was entirely agreeable to the suggestion that Hutchins be asked to come to Washington until he found out Hutchins was willing to come, and then he began to see grave reasons why he should not come. I recall that when Hutchins' name was first proposed, Richberg remarked that he did not believe Hutchins would think of giving up a life job for the uncertainties of an official appointment.

While in Chicago I had an opportunity to talk this matter over with Merriam. Merriam knows Richberg almost as well as I do and he has almost the same opinion of him that I have. He distinctly does not trust him. He told me of the talk he had with Dr. Preston Kies, who was a classmate of Richberg's. Dr. Kies told Merriam that he had known Richberg all these days and he knew that he was utterly untrustworthy. Incidentally, he also told Merriam that he hated me, and that I was a S.O.B., but that one always knew where to find me.

Friday, October 26, 1934

I authorized the filing of suit at the opening of court Thursday morning to condemn land on the South Side, in Chicago, for a Negro slum clearance project. In ordinary course I would have had this suit filed so that it would break in the morning papers, but the *Tribune* has been such a rotter and it was so thoroughly angry when we broke the big West Side project for the afternoon papers that I decided to repeat. However, the papers got wind of something doing and when I got to the train I found John W. Dienhart, city editor of the *Herald-Examiner,* who wanted a break on the story. He promised not to print it before the late morning edition. I didn't give him the story, but I gave him enough so he could break it in general terms and thus make the *Tribune* madder than ever. There was a *Tribune* reporter on hand also who was nosing about for this story, but I told him I would not be interviewed by his paper. He followed me about for some ten or fifteen minutes and I repeated my statement in no uncertain terms, but telling him at the same time that there was nothing personal so far as I was concerned. He then betook himself off. When I reached Chicago in the morning, I refused to pose for a *Tribune* photographer and refused to answer any of his questions.

I reached the office about the middle of the afternoon with Raymond. As we stepped out of the car to go into De Lang's, we ran into Homer Guck, publisher of the *Herald-Examiner.* We had quite a long talk with him, standing on the curb. He told me several amusing incidents about the newspaper situation in Chicago and especially about Colonel McCormick. He said that, at his instance, there had been, a short time ago, a meeting of the Publisher's Association. His description of it was quite funny. He said that at the end of the meeting, he turned solemnly to Frank Knox of the *News* and told him that what he ought to do was to print a signed front-page editorial declaring for Colonel McCormick as the Republican candidate for President in 1936. He said that if he would do that, he, Guck, would get in touch with Mr. Hearst and urge him to agree that the *Herald-Examiner* should also come out in support of McCormick. He told them he thought Hearst would consent to this. He said that during it all McCormick sat there looking somewhat puzzled, but Guck believes the bait was a tempting one and that McCormick is a candidate, all of which amuses Guck very much as he was only spoofing the Colonel. He said as soon as he had made this proposition, Knox declared the meeting adjourned and they all left.

It is surprising with what unanimity everyone, inside the newspaper profession and outside, says that the *Tribune* is the rottenest newspaper in the United States. Colonel Knox actually thinks that its violent and unreasoning opposition to the Administration is such as to gain sentiment for the Administration. Knox came over to see me at my temporary office and we had a long and friendly chat, which was interspersed with some chafing back and forth, he poking fun at me on account of the New Deal, and I twitting him about his lineup with the reactionaries and the Republican party. Knox is becoming more and more partisan in the *Daily News,* but he and I are still good personal friends and he doesn't overstep all the bounds of decency as does the *Tribune.*

I drove home with Raymond, stopping at Mrs. Bowen's home on the way to call on Miss Addams. I had not seen her for some time and I wanted to pay my respects. She seemed quite well and she was keenly interested in what is going on in Washington. She is particularly keen about the slum clearance program and offered to do anything she could in connection with our Chicago projects. Raymond and I had dinner at the Shawnee Country Club and then I drove back to the University Club to pick up Mr. Lee and the baggage and then took the Northwestern Overland Limited at 9:35 P.M. for San Francisco.

Tuesday, October 30, 1934

Early last Friday morning while I was stretching my legs on the platform at Ogden, Utah, where we were scheduled to stop a half an hour, the superintendent of schools bore down on me and before I realized it, he, a member of the Board of Education, a representative of the Chamber of Commerce, and a couple of newspaper men had enticed me into an automobile and whisked me off to look at the high school building. The superintendent plaintively told me that Ogden badly needed a new building, and I agreed with him. Unfortunately, Ogden is just about up to its debt limit and cannot issue bonds as security for seventy per cent of the cost of a new building. Like lots of other people, he seemed to think that we ought to let Ogden have the money anyhow. He was quite persistent about it, and I became quite abrupt and specific in my rejoinder that Ogden was not entitled to any more consideration than other municipalities similarly situated. I pointed out that in the National Industrial Recovery Act it was specifically set out that the money was to be loaned on reasonable security; that no one could regard no security at all as reasonable security. He argued that money for public works came from taxes and that taxes were paid by the people. I replied that while this was true, these taxes were not paid by the City of Ogden exclusively and that I could not do for Ogden what I could not do for any other community. It really peeved me quite a lot to be subjected to this pressure. It does not seem to me fair to drag a man off the train merely because he is a public official and harass him with importunities that he cannot satisfy.

At Oakland we were met by a number of newspaper reporters and by Franck Havenner and one or two other members of the citizens' committee. Crossing the bay on the ferry, I had a chance to see the progress that is being made in the construction of the great bridge that is being built to connect San Francisco with Oakland. When we disembarked at San Francisco we were met by a larger committee, headed by Mayor Rossi and Senator Johnson. We went to the Mark Hopkins Hotel where there was more interviewing and picture taking by newspaper representatives. After an early lunch with Senator Johnson and the "Boss" in their apartment at the Mark Hopkins, we drove to Palo Alto with Mayor Rossi to see the football game between Stanford and the University of Southern California. It was just a fair football game, which was won by Stanford.

Then we drove back to San Francisco where a dinner was given in my honor at the Bohemian Club. This is a new club building— quite a pretentious one. There were some fifty or sixty covers and the dinner was a very good one indeed. Fortunately, there was not much oratory. Mayor Rossi announced at the outset that there would not be any speeches, but at the conclusion he called upon Senator Johnson, who introduced me, for a "good night." In his introduction Senator Johnson was very kind in his references to me and our long continued friendship over many years.

I spoke extemporaneously and briefly. Chester Rowell, who used to be an old Johnson Progressive, and whom I have known for a good many years, was one of the guests. He is now editor of the *San Francisco Chronicle,* and several years ago he went decidedly reactionary. There is nothing in common now between him and Senator Johnson. Hiram refers to him in private conversation as "an intellectual prostitute." I have not seen Rowell for a number of years and in my speech I good-naturedly poked fun at him. I recalled our old friendship and remarked that those who knew him as the editor of the *Chronicle* and me as an adherent of the New Deal would have difficulty in believing that when we were both members of the Hughes Campaign Committee, I had held Rowell's general and unrestricted proxy. I said that either Rowell or I had gone wrong in the interval. I said some other things along the same line and the crowd liked it a lot, especially Hiram Johnson. Rowell took it all good-naturedly, but I think he was considerably fussed. He came up afterward and said that it seemed like old times, just as if we were back in the old days, and that nothing had ever happened since. He even said something of like tenor to Hiram.

Sunday about noon we drove down to Crystal Lake where the first water from the Hetch Hetchy Dam was to be turned into the San Francisco reservoirs. I was the principal speaker on a nationwide hookup. My talk was on the general subject of conservation with, of course, appropriate references to the occasion that we were celebrating. It has taken twenty years to build Hetch Hetchy Dam and the conduits that extend some 155 miles from the dam to the reservoirs. The project has cost pretty close to $1 billion but a bountiful supply of pure water is assured to San Francisco for the next sixty or seventy-five years. San Francisco also develops power from this water, and will increase this development in later years. Unfortunately, the private utilities have such a grip on San Francisco that it cannot actually sell its own power to users in San Francisco, but I am undertaking to see if I cannot help to remedy the situation so that San Francisco can sell its own power. In that event it would be able to make a very substantial profit in addition to what it makes from the distribution of water.

Sunday, November 4, 1934

I reached Chicago the morning of the thirty-first and spent several busy hours at the Housing Administration office. Mayor Kelly came in to see me by appointment to discuss the unpaid bills of the city to the Sanitary District for electric current. There is one bill amounting to $3½ million that has been reduced to judgment, and, according to a law passed at our instance at a recent session of the Legislature, this judgment will have to be paid when it is reached in its turn. There are unpaid bills amounting to an equal sum which could be reduced to judgment at any time. Of course the city has been in grave financial difficulties. I told the mayor that I would not insist upon the open account being reduced to judgment, provided the city settled with the Sanitary District for current sold to it during this year and would pay the Sanitary District bills hereafter as they came in from month to month. The mayor brought Comptroller Upham with him and I had some of my staff in. The city can pay in tax warrants, but we have to look into the marketability of these tax warrants before authorizing the District to accept them.

Privately, I told the mayor later that when the Sanitary District Board was reorganized I hoped very much he would see to it that Ross Woodhull be made president of the Board of Trustees and be permitted to retain his chairmanship of the Finance Committee. The mayor consented to this and I so advised Woodhull by telephone later.

I left Chicago at two o'clock and arrived in Washington the morning of November 1. I was plunged, as usual, into a mass of work. There was a greater volume held up for me for personal action than I had found on my desk when I got back from my summer trip. The first thing I had to tackle was the report that had been prepared on a public works program for next year, at the request of the President. This report had been worked out under the direction of Burlew and Slattery, in co-operation with engineers from PWA. Harry Hopkins and members of his staff had also collaborated but the heavy oar was pulled by members of my own staff.

At half past eight in the evening Secretary Morgenthau, Harry Hopkins, and I went to the White House to consider this program with the President. At prior conferences there were members of Morgenthau's staff present with him but the President wanted to restrict this conference to the ones mentioned. We worked over matters until a quarter after twelve.

It becomes clearer at every conference that the President is more and more of the mind to go ahead with a substantial public works program in the hope of being able to do away with Federal relief altogether. We are discussing $5 billion for the first year, with decreasing amounts for the following two or three years, in order to assure the country of a continuing program that will be an encouragement to manufacturers and contractors to restock with machinery and retool, which will have a revivifying effect on the heavy industries. What we are working on is a program which will commend itself to Congress and to public opinion. The program, of course, is one in broad outline and does not set up specific projects.

Since the first of these conferences, at the President's instance, we have been working on the theory that only self-liquidating projects would be entertained. I have felt in my heart from the beginning that we would have to do a great deal in the way of non-self-liquidating projects if we were to carry out a program of any scope. Toward the end of this last conference the President came to that same conclusion after consideration of the facts. He said that we would have to make allowance for $500 million to make a start on the program that it is expected the Planning Board will submit, and before he got through, he roughly calculated that we would have to put in a billion dollars altogether for Federal projects. Then the question was raised about the Army and the Navy. It was estimated that something in the neighborhood of a billion dollars for rehabilitation, replacements, etc., for these two branches of the Government would be necessary. We discussed whether this would be included in the $5 billion or be additional thereto. I made the remark that there was no use going ahead with a seventy-five per cent program; that the money for the Army and the Navy would not give work to the unemployed but would merely keep those now employed at work. The President seemed to be inclined to the view that expenditures for the Army and Navy should be in addition to the $5 billion which would bring the total public works fund up to about $6 billion for the next fiscal year.

Before we started to consider the public works program, the President discussed certain unfortunate publicity which has been appearing in the newspapers lately with reference to that program. There have been serious leaks and I think they have come through Hopkins' organization. In fact, too many people have been brought into this discussion. Members of my staff tell me that last Monday Hopkins held what they referred to as a town meeting. Some sixty or sixty-five men, many of whom are not connected with the Government at all, were called into a meeting by Hopkins to discuss the public works program.

From discussing leaks of this sort, which the President does not like, he went on to talk about the crosscurrents of gossip that are existent in Washington at this time. He seems to feel, as a result of information that has come to him, that big business is out on a deliberate policy of sabotaging the Administration. There is an impression in some quarters that big business is carefully planting its own people wherever it can in various Government agencies and these people not only keep big business advised of what is going on but block the program whenever they can. He has some very definite information along this line.

The President asked me what I had to report from my Western trip and I told him what I knew about the political situations I had come in contact with. He was particularly interested in the California situation, and it seemed clear that he had swung clear over from his earlier attitude of tolerance of the Sinclair candidacy for governor. I took an opportunity to tell him that the opposition of the Administration to Senator Cutting, of New Mexico, had created a bad feeling among the Progressives in the West. Senator Johnson was very much worked up over this and I too am very unhappy over it. I think that the Administration should have given the same measure of support to Cutting in New Mexico that it has given to Bob La Follette in Wisconsin.

The oil situation, which was in such a critical state when I left

Washington on my trip, is in much better shape. The threatened cutting of prices, although a start had actually been made in that direction by one or two small concerns, has been averted, or at least postponed. The Tender Board, set up in Texas under a recent executive order from me, has worked excellently. No oil can be shipped out of Texas without a clearance from this board, and the board works quickly so as to avoid any criticism that it is hampering the free movement of oil in commerce. No hot oil is now moving out of Texas; at any rate, no hot oil of any consequence is moving out. A number of refineries, twenty-seven I believe to be exact, that formerly processed hot oil into gasoline, have been closed. The attitude of the courts is more favorable and altogether the situation is better than it has ever been.

On Friday I had luncheon with the President. I gave him an autographed copy of my book, which reached the bookstores last Monday. He told me that my book and Henry Wallace's complemented each other perfectly. He said he had told Henry Wallace that his was a scholarly treatise, looking at the New Deal from several points of view critically and dispassionately. On the other hand, he added, my book looks at it from only one point of view and is full of punch.

I told the President about the improved situation in the Oil Administration and then remarked that I had a different report to make with reference to Subsistence Homesteads. This Administration has been in a bad way. The original Director was Dr. M. L. Wilson, now an Assistant Secretary in the Department of Agriculture. Wilson is not a good executive and under him Subsistence Homesteads got off to a very bad start. He not only was not a good executive, but he did not know how to pick the right kind of personnel. Then, too, Mrs. Roosevelt and Colonel Howe have interfered altogether too much with its administration. The result has been a project at Reedsville that really cannot be effectively defended. Work down there has been extravagant and wasteful to a degree. Mrs. Roosevelt, especially, has interfered all along the line, of course with the best intentions. As the President remarked to me: "My Missus, unlike most women, hasn't any sense about money at all." He added with respect to Louie Howe that Louie didn't know anything about money, being as he is an old newspaper man, although he did pay a tribute to Louie's political sagacity.

Before Wilson left I had sent Pynchon over there as Assistant

Manager. I thought he was the executive I was looking for. Despite the fact that Pynchon has been manager ever since Wilson went back to Agriculture, which was several months ago, things seemed to be getting more and more into a hole. Pynchon has been a distinct disappointment as an executive. I had high hopes for his success. He is a good man working under someone's direction, but he lacks the final punch to put over a proposition on his own account. About a week or ten days ago I drew on Hackett for two good men from the Housing Administration and I have sent them over to Subsistence Homesteads. I told the President that this was the only phase of my administration that I felt apologetic for. I assured him that I was taking the matter in hand myself and that I could and would bring it out, but I did have to apologize for the situation in which it was at the moment. Naturally I couldn't criticize Louie Howe, much less Mrs. Roosevelt, but I believe he realizes the situation.

I also discussed the Hutchins situation with him. I told him that Hutchins had called me when I was in Chicago and wanted to know just what was doing. The President said he wished he knew and then we discussed the whole matter very frankly. He told me that he had sent for Hutchins in good faith and that the whole thing was understood but that the members of the NRA Board had expressed great opposition to Hutchins. He said that he didn't want the board to resign as a body and that is what actually has been threatened. It is argued against Hutchins that he is dictatorial and hard to get along with. A further argument is that NRA has just been rescued from the one-man control of General Johnson and that it would be a mistake to go back to a one-man control. I said that, in my judgment, there would be a one-man control in the end anyhow, repeating my argument that there cannot be successful administration by a board. I remarked that if there wasn't a strong man on the board who in the end would dominate it, then a very weak board had been appointed.

At the beginning of our luncheon the President referred again to the matter of sabotage which he had discussed the night before. I asked him frankly if there wasn't some sabotaging going on in the Hutchins matter. He said he didn't believe so. I then said: "Mr. President, I am going to say something that perhaps I oughtn't to say, but my suspicion is that Richberg is sabotaging." The President listened carefully but remarked that Richberg had been in favor of getting Hutchins down here. In reply to that I said: "He was in favor of Hutchins coming until he found out that there was a real chance of getting him. Don't you remember that when Hutchins' name was first suggested, Richberg said that there would be no chance of getting him because it would be asking him to give up a life job?" I went on to say that Hutchins was in a very embarrassing position, since, at the request of the Administration, he had asked for and obtained a leave of absence from his Board of Trustees. The President then tentatively suggested appointing Miss Perkins and me as a subcommittee to look into the matter and later he also suggested the possibility of asking the NRA Policy Committee to advise him with respect to it.

The matter was left in that nebulous shape. The President is plainly embarrassed and, of course, so is Hutchins. I am firmly convinced that as soon as Richberg found out that Hutchins would come, he started a backfire among the members of the NRA Committee. Of course, it is known that he went to the President himself to try to sidetrack Hutchins. As the matter now stands, Richberg, through his self-appointed NRA Committee, is in pretty firm control of the situation and he will fight any man who threatens to jeopardize that control. I think he is more dangerous in this situation than Johnson ever was, and in this view Merriam agrees.

I neglected to say that during my talk with the President about NRA I asked him when Clay Williams was going to resign as Chairman of the Committee. He said that was a puzzling situation; that he had had to use all his powers of persuasion to get Williams to consent to accept for a short period. Williams was expected to leave on November 1, but he continues to hold on and the President hasn't the least idea whether he is going to resign, and if so, when. I told the President that my information was that big business was perfectly satisfied with Williams, and for the purpose of blocking Hutchins, had been sending emissaries to tell him that it was more important for him to stay on as chairman of the NRA Board than it was to go back to his tobacco business.

At Cabinet meeting the President referred to the stories that have appeared in the newspapers during the last few days, especially the one in *The New York Times* which, in a sensational manner, announced that Richberg is a sort of an Assistant President and outranks the whole Cabinet. These stories annoy the President very much indeed. He spoke of this matter Thursday night during the

White House conference and he dwelt on it again at the Cabinet meeting. To listen to the President, one would never think that Richberg was more than an exalted messenger boy, but to read the newspapers, one would think that the President really shares his power with him. A good many people think that these news items exalting Richberg are being fed out by his own staff. There seems to be little doubt that Richberg is reaching out in every direction for all the power he can possibly gather unto himself. He is even talking about suggesting to the President a reorganization of the Departments. He is as busy as a bull pup in fly time. I discovered last night that Morgenthau does not like him and certainly Harry Hopkins feels about him as I do. Morgenthau's nose is out of joint because Richberg made a speech recently on the budget and fiscal policies that the Treasury was not consulted about in advance. Morgenthau took Richberg to task for it.

My own feeling is that Richberg is a dangerous man for the Administration. He is utterly selfish, and undoubtedly his great ability is being used to build himself up. On the other hand, he is highly temperamental and nervous and likely to go off at half cock. Merriam thinks he will blow up before a great length of time and he regards him as highly dangerous, just as I do. One thing I do feel certain of and that is that if I find him trespassing on my preserves, I won't lose any time in calling him to sharp account. Hopkins told me when I drove him home from the White House conference Thursday night that his belief is that Richberg is trying to reach out and get Public Works and the Oil Administration back under the general NRA administration, just as Johnson planned it originally. The idea of Richberg as an executive is ridiculous. I asked Merriam the other day if he could possibly think of anyone less qualified to suggest a reorganization or act as an administrator than Richberg and he said he couldn't.

Thursday, November 15, 1934

I have been having some difficulty in arranging with Secretary Morgenthau about building the new Interior Building. Originally it was understood between the President and me that my own department would build this building, but later Morgenthau lodged a protest. He wanted his Procurement Division, which has been in charge of public buildings generally, to do this one. The President told me to talk it over with Morgenthau and see what arrangement

I could make. I did so, and Morgenthau said that anything I wanted would be all right with him. This was some time ago. I went ahead on this assurance only to run into an objection from the Comptroller General, who is a specialist at making objections. I talked to Morgenthau again and he said that if I could iron it out with the Comptroller General, it would be all right with him. He repeated that he wanted to do whatever I wanted to do. Then Burlew took it up with the Comptroller General and he did succeed in ironing out the difficulties. Then, to my surprise, Morgenthau backed out. He would not come to grips with me, but kept running to the President. Somehow or other, he succeeded in persuading the President that the Comptroller General would not yield. But apparently Morgenthau had won the President over to his point of view. I think the explanation is that the latter did not want any row. Then the President suggested that I let the Treasury put up the building under an agreement by which the Treasury would name the Interior Department as its agent in the matter. I discussed this with Morgenthau and once again he said it would be satisfactory. I wrote him a letter to this effect just before I went on my trip to San Francisco.

Once again Morgenthau refused to come to grips, but went to the President direct. While I was away, the President sent duplicate memoranda to Morgenthau and to me which did not carry out the understanding at all. When I came back and read this memorandum, I became pretty hot under the collar. Finally I decided to go to Morgenthau and talk this matter over in a friendly way.

Last Thursday, after a meeting that we had on public works in his office, I did talk it over with him. I told him that I was asking a personal favor, that it would not mean anything to him personally whether he built this building or not, but that it did mean a good deal to me. He said he was willing to do everything he could and I told him I would be satisfied if he would agree to employ whomever I might designate, the building meanwhile technically to be built by the Treasury Department. He said this was satisfactory and I asked him if he would give me a memorandum in writing. He called in his Executive Assistant and dictated a memorandum covering the points at issue, but reserving the right to negotiate with Waddy Wood, the architect with whom I had made a contract after discussing the matter with the President and after obtaining his permission. He said he was willing to pay Wood for what he had done, with a fair profit, and engage him as a consulting architect. I told him that Wood had a valid contract, which I had been authorized to execute, but that it was up to him to see what he could do if he was not satisfied with that contract. This was not all I wanted in the way of an understanding, but I pretended to be satisfied with it and we parted on friendly terms.

Friday night, while we were waiting for the President to see us at the White House, Morgenthau told me that he had not signed this memorandum because his counsel had objected. He said that his counsel had made the point that if he signed that memorandum, he would be ratifying my contract with Waddy Wood. I became angry and told him that I was tired of fussing with the thing and that we could just forget all about the Interior Building. I proposed that we build an Army or Navy building instead and let the Interior Building go by the boards. I told him further that I did not know who his lawyer was, but if that was the advice he had given him, he was not very much of a lawyer, because he could not so obligate himself under a contract made by me with someone else. I regarded the thing as a mean renege on his part and strongly indicated my views on the subject. He began to show the yellow feather. He protested that he would work something out and said that his lawyer was willing to have him sign a modified memorandum. He had kept urging that he was willing to go ahead on the arrangement, but did not want to sign anything. I told him I wanted something in writing. He finally suggested that he would send me a modified memorandum, which, if satisfactory to me, I could adopt, and which, otherwise, I could throw into the wastepaper basket. I told him in no very courteous tones that he could do what he pleased about it. Then he tried to be very pleasant indeed, seeking to mollify me.

We had another conference at the White House with the President at which were present Morgenthau, Hopkins, and myself. We had a further discussion of public works. Morgenthau's position apparently is that he would like to defeat the proposal for public works, but that he doesn't want to oppose the President. He presented a financial statement covering the financing of a $5 billion program for public works next year. The President looked at it and remarked, "This isn't so hot." Then Morgenthau drew another paper from his pocket and asked the President whether he wanted to hear the worst. He indicated that what he was prepared to offer would cut all the ground out from under the proposed public works program for the next few years. The President said he wanted to know the worst, that he was willing to take poison, although he would like to know what the ingredients were. With great unction Morgenthau then started to read a statement prepared by Jacob Viner, one of his experts and a former professor of economics at Chicago. He had not gotten very far before the President began to laugh and I could not help joining him. I don't pretend to be an economist, but the argument presented was so ridiculous as to be absurd. The President so viewed it, and at this stage Louis Howe came in and the President greeted him with a hilarious statement, referring to the Viner document in highly jocular tones. Morgenthau was willing to desist, but the President told him to go ahead as he wanted to hear what Viner had written. But Morgenthau's attitude perceptibly changed and by the time that he was through reading the Viner statement, his tone was almost apologetic. It was clear that the Viner argument had made no impression at all on the President. In fact, it hadn't on any of us, although undoubtedly Morgenthau had thought it was perfectly devastating. After he had concluded, Morgenthau swung clear around. He was strongly in favor of the public works program and was willing to do anything he could to put it into effect. Turning to Harry Hopkins, he said he would be willing to put in half a day for the next week with Hopkins trying to work out a program and he suggested that I might sit in too. I remarked that I was leaving for Texas the next day and could not participate for that reason.

I left the conference with a low opinion of Morgenthau. He showed clearly that he was willing to waive his own opinions and fall in with the President's suggestions even, although he did not agree with them. He had already demonstrated to me that his word is not good. I had started with a very friendly feeling toward Morgenthau, but I must confess that that feeling has changed drastically.

Monday, November 19, 1934

I boarded the train shortly after six o'clock Friday morning at Cincinnati after spending the night at the Netherland Plaza. City Manager Dykstra supplied me with a police car and a motorcycle escort in anticipation of there being a crowd which it would be difficult to get through. However, it was so early in the morning that there were few people at the station.

From Cincinnati the train went to Harrodsburg, Kentucky, where the President was to dedicate a monument in honor of John Rogers Clark and the early pioneers who made that the first settlement in the Middle West. There was an enormous crowd at Harrodsburg. Governor Lafoon, of Kentucky, presided. After Harrodsburg we headed for Coal Creek, Tennessee, to inspect the Tennessee Valley Authority projects.

Secretary Hull was the only other member of the Cabinet on the train and he left the train at Knoxville. He had been suffering from laryngitis and did not want to have to use his voice any more than necessary. Senator Barkley, of Kentucky, was on the train as far as Muscle Shoals and Senator Bachmann and Governor McAlister, of Tennessee, joined us en route for the trip through that state. We did not go directly to Knoxville by train. We got off at Coal Creek, Tennessee, where we were met by members of the Tennessee Valley Authority, and motored to Norris Dam. They are making very fast progress on this dam and the dam, when completed, will have enormous capacity, with a shore line greater than that of Lake Superior.

From Norris Dam we drove through the town of Norris. This has been built by the Tennessee Valley Authority to house members of its personnel. It is very attractively laid out and the houses created a good impression. They are small, but attractively built, the object being to furnish adequate housing at as low a rate as possible. Then we drove to Knoxville where another great crowd lined the streets.

We arrived at Nashville, Saturday morning, the seventeenth, at eight o'clock. There was a tremendous crowd here not only at the station but lining all the streets and we traversed several miles of streets. We drove out to the Hermitage where Andrew Jackson lived and where he is buried. Here we had a very bountiful breakfast served in the Jackson dining room. I was told that no meals were ever served here except on the occasion of a visit from the President. The Hermitage is in charge of a women's organization and is full of original furniture, as well as many of Jackson's books and manuscripts, some of which have never been published. The association wants an additional 250 acres of land to protect the Hermitage grounds. The President at breakfast suggested to the president of the association that the property be deeded to the Federal Government upon which the Federal Government would turn its management back to the association which is now in charge. When I was asked whether there was any way to buy the additional land, I said I knew of no way unless the property belonged to the Federal Government. There is said to be a good deal of sentiment for such a transfer and we may be able to bring it about.

There was so much to do in Nashville that we were an hour late in leaving that city, with the result that we arrived at Town Creek, Alabama, at 3:15 P.M. instead of 2:15. Here we detrained again and motored to Wheeler Dam, another of the TVA projects. Here also the Tennessee Valley Authority is making great progress and apparently is doing a very fine job. From the Wheeler Dam we drove to the Wilson Dam at Muscle Shoals. We did not leave the cars at Muscle Shoals, but merely inspected the project from the road. From Muscle Shoals we took the train at Sheffield. We pulled out of Sheffield just a few miles and spent the night on a siding.

We arrived at Tupelo, Mississippi, at eight o'clock Sunday morning and drove a few miles outside of Tupelo to inspect a subsistence homestead project. The project is well situated and the houses seemed very well built and attractive. With two or three acres of land to a homestead, the cost to the homesteaders will be from $2,500 to $2,800, amortized over a period of thirty years with interest at three per cent. We drove back to Tupelo where another great crowd was gathered in a natural amphitheater to hear the President make a short extemporaneous speech. This speech was very significant in that it served notice on the power companies that have been obstructing the TVA program and upon the country at large that the Government is not only going ahead to carry out its TVA program but will undertake similar enterprises in different parts of the country. The President is a great believer in cheap power and rural electrification and he went all the way for cheap power at Tupelo.

Leaving Tupelo we headed for Birmingham, Ala., making two or three very short stops en route during which the President appeared on the rear platform and said a few words to the people. He did this throughout the trip at the larger places, and it was a matter of astonishment to see how many people came to greet him. I do not believe that any President has ever had such enormous

turnouts or that any has ever been held in such affection and regard by people generally as President Roosevelt. Even where we
did not stop along the route, whether it was early or late, there
would be people gathered and the President would wave to them
from the chair that he occupied in the rear end of the observation
section of his private car.

Sunday morning the President told me that he was considering
turning over to Harry Hopkins the Subsistence Homesteads Division and rural housing. Of course, there is no rural housing yet, but
we plan an extensive program of rural housing if we go ahead next
year with the public works program that we have been discussing.
As a matter of fact, I have been turning over in my own mind some
sort of a tie-up with Hopkins along these same lines. I won't be at
all put out if I lose Subsistence Homesteads. It has been nothing but
a headache from the beginning.

Months ago I went to the President and told him that the only
thing in my whole administration that had me worried was Subsistence Homesteads, particularly Reedsville. I predicted then that
at the rate we were going, each homestead would cost $10,000 on
the average. I pointed out that while this was a demonstration of
what could be done in the way of an interesting development for
people with considerable incomes, it was not a demonstration of
what could be done for people in the lowest income classes, and the
latter were supposed to be what we were striving for.

We never have gotten Reedsville straightened out. Mrs. Roosevelt
finally became dissatisfied with the second manager we have sent
down and dissatisfied also with some of the people she had sent
down. I also was dissatisfied. I recalled the manager and made Mac
Flynn, whom I have known all his life and who had gone down
originally as purchasing agent, manager. At one stage the *Saturday Evening Post* carried a long article attacking Reedsville and
pointing out the weakness in the project.

Sunday on the train Mrs. Roosevelt said she would like to visit
all of the subsistence homestead projects there were anywhere
near completion and asked me whether I would like her to do so.
Of course I said Yes, but this was after the President had said that
he was thinking of turning the management of these projects
over to Hopkins. I am very fond of Mrs. Roosevelt. She has a fine
social sense and is utterly unselfish, but as the President has said

to me on one or two occasions, she wants to build these homesteads on a scale that we can't afford because the people for whom they are intended cannot afford such houses. The President's idea is to build an adequate house and not even put in plumbing fixtures, leaving that sort of thing to be done later by the homesteader as he can afford them. He remarked yesterday that he had not yet dared say this to the people (undoubtedly meaning Mrs. Roosevelt) who wanted to build houses with all modern improvements.

I suggested to the President that he tie Hopkins in with the Public Works Administration as Deputy Administrator or Associate Administrator in charge of rural housing and subsistence homesteads. I told the President that I liked Hopkins and that we got along very well together, but I pointed out that many of the people relied upon by Hopkins were purely relief workers, used to handing out money, who have no idea of economy or close management. I said that there had never been a breath of scandal in connection with the Public Works Administration and that he would not want any scandal in connection with rural housing. He said, "That's right." Just what he will determine upon in the end, I do not know, but I gave him something to think about.

I have been thinking for some time of some such sort of tie-up with Hopkins. I suggested, in addition, that Hopkins ought to have the responsibility for seeing that persons now unemployed be put to work under the new Public Works, and such an arrangement would not be distasteful to me at all. I am willing to run the risk of getting along with Hopkins. On the other hand, I have the feeling that if he is made an independent administrator, there will be a good deal of criticism before he is through. He and his organization are used to spreading money with a lavish hand. They want to get money out, but it is an entirely different proposition to expend money on housing or any other permanent improvements. People will overlook waste and extravagance and even a certain amount of graft in handling charity funds. There is no doubt in my mind that an investigation of CWA would disclose many situations that would have ruined PWA over and over again. My contacts with Hopkins' organization have not impressed me as to his personnel. I don't think he is equipped to do a housing job such as is contemplated, and so far as Subsistence Homesteads is concerned, he won't have any easier task there than I have had.

Friday, November 23, 1934

On Wednesday we had a staff meeting of PWA, followed by a meeting of the board at two o'clock. On the list of projects to be submitted for approval were several for New York City, aggregating a considerable sum. All of these I struck off the list before the meeting. I have been insisting for some time that Mayor La Guardia get rid of Robert Moses as a member of his Triborough Bridge Commission. This has been at the instance of the President. It seems that Moses is a bitterly persistent enemy of the President's, and the President has a feeling of dislike of him that I haven't seen him express with respect to any other person. La Guardia has been putting me off for months. Then came the campaign in New York with Moses as the Republican candidate for Governor. Naturally I had to declare a truce during that period in order to avoid a charge that I was playing politics. Since the election I have called La Guardia twice. The last time he told me he could not get rid of Moses, unless he was willing to resign, without preferring charges. I told him that that was his funeral and not mine and that I did not see any reason why we should be expected to go in on a Federal project with a man who criticized the Federal Administration as bitterly as Moses has. Accordingly, I have decided not to make allocations for any more projects in New York City until this matter has been adjusted, and I am considering refusing to honor requisitions for funds on pending projects.

On Thursday I held a conference in my office to consider the policies to be adopted by the new Grazing Division. Some time ago I appointed F. R. Carpenter as Director of this Division and I have been very well satisfied with his work. Carpenter is a stockman in Colorado. He has the third largest pure Hereford herd in the United States and specializes in pedigreed bulls. He was born and raised in Evanston, Ill., and is a graduate of Harvard and Harvard Law School, but he looks like a typical cow man. At the conclusion of my press conference on Thursday I learned that Carpenter had given out news covering our grazing conference to the United Press correspondent. We had decided at this conference that I should recommend to the President that he withdraw temporarily all public lands now in the hands of the Government in order to give us an opportunity to work out our grazing districts. There have been an unusual number of entries filed on public lands recently and we want to stop that for the time being. This important information was given out by Carpenter before I had a chance to discuss the matter with the President and before the Executive Order had been drafted for consideration.

I tried to find Carpenter and learned that he was taking the 4:10 train on the Pennsylvania to Chicago. Burlew got hold of someone connected with the Pennsylvania Railroad and told Carpenter to report to me. Late in the afternoon he came to my office and when I asked him what he had given to the newspapers, he made a statement to me which I later discovered was far from being frank and complete. Mr. Deeds, of the Geological Survey, who had also sat in at the grazing conference, was in Carpenter's office with him while he was being interviewed by the UP man, and, as it developed, also by an AP correspondent. I asked Deeds what had happened and from him learned to my surprise that Carpenter had showed these correspondents a copy of the agenda containing all the subjects we had discussed at our grazing conference. Carpenter naïvely said that he had told the newspaper correspondents that he was giving them this information in confidence.

I raised particular hell. I wouldn't have been surprised if Carpenter had resigned and I confess I wouldn't have cared much. However, he assured me that he realized his mistake and that a similar one would not occur again.

Saturday, November 24, 1934

At my press conference Thursday afternoon, correspondents for the *Washington Herald* and *The New York Times* questioned me closely about a housing program next year in connection with public works. I expressed myself as being in favor of such a program, but made it clear that we wanted private capital to put over the program if it would, leaving it to the Federal Government to do it if private capital continued to hold back the traces. Recently, Moffett, of the Housing Administration, went on record publicly against a Federal housing program, and an effort was made at the conference to have me take issue with Moffett or say something critical of his announcement. This I avoided doing, although I did make it clear that I was personally in favor of a housing program and considered it one of the most socially desirable undertakings that we could engage in.

Friday morning the *Washington Herald* led the front page with

a great story to the effect that Moffett and I were in distinct disagreement on housing. The story was sensational. *The New York
Times,* while less sensational in its handling of the news, also tried
to make it appear that Moffett and I were at swords' points.
Generally speaking, the other newspaper correspondents, including
those representing the news agencies, handled my interview conservatively and justly.

From what I gathered later, Moffett, or Mrs. Moffett, called
Colonel McIntyre at Warm Springs and stirred him up about this
story. The result was a call to Steve Early, but whether from Mc-
Intyre or the President, I do not know. At any rate, Steve got me
on the wire and I told him that I had not criticized Moffett or cast
any reflections on the Housing Administration. I told him further
that I would issue a statement later in the day clarifying the situation and denying some of the statements that had been made. I
proposed also to call up Moffett and explain things to him.

Mike Straus was set to work to draft a statement for me and I
called Moffett early in the afternoon after I had come back from a
meeting of the National Forest Reservation Commission. I had a
very pleasant talk with Moffett. He tried to make me believe that
he had not been at all disturbed about this story; that he took it
for granted that I had been misquoted; and that everything was all
right. I told him that I was going to issue a statement and asked
him whether he wanted me to send a copy over to him. He said he
would like to have a copy and I did send one to him. In the meantime Moffett had called a press conference for two o'clock. When he
found out that I was to give out a statement, he postponed the
conference until four o'clock. At his press conference he was asked
numerous questions based upon my supposed criticism of his housing program and he met every one of those questions head on. He
didn't try at any point to evade the issue with the result that he
added fuel to the fire and gave a distinct impression that there was
a wide-open breach between himself and myself.

I had the President on the telephone a little before eight on two
matters I had to take up with him and he referred to the housing
story. I explained the situation to him, telling him what I had
done to try to smooth matters out, and of my talk with Moffett. It
was clearly the President's wish that nothing further be said to give
the appearance of dissension in the Administration ranks. I told
him about Moffett's press conference and what had transpired there.

As I expressed it, Moffett had permitted himself to be tied up in a double bow knot. I also said to the President that I didn't understand that Moffett had anything to do with housing, and he said, "You're right."

The President suggested that Moffett and I issue a joint statement and he said I should call Moffett up right away. I told the President that I would be at the office and would be there if Moffett wanted to talk with me. I was at the office until well after eleven o'clock. About a quarter to eleven, McIntyre called me to ask whether I had called Moffett and I told him that I was expecting to hear from Moffett. He said that he had talked with Moffett and that he had said that he had tried to reach me. When I got home Anna told me that Moffett had called the house and she had told him that I was at the office. I learned the next day that Moffett had tried to reach me at the Department, but the switchboard girl, not realizing that he was entitled to get through to me, had told him that I didn't answer my telephone. In any event, Moffett and I did not talk last night.

This morning there was a real story in the newspapers. Moffett had gone all the way in criticizing what I had said on the housing program and in telling what a disaster to the country and recovery such a program would be. He went on record in favor of a coordination of all housing activities. In general his remarks were uncalled for and highly critical.

I called Steve Early, after I got to the office, and told him I wanted to go over and see him. His reply was, "I don't blame you." I took Mike Straus with me and we talked the situation over very frankly. Early agreed with me that Moffett's attack was deliberate. Of course, he was very much disturbed about it. He told me that he had talked to Moffett on the telephone yesterday. Moffett said to him that he was going to have a press conference, and Early said he would not ask him to call off his press conference since it had already been arranged for, but he asked him not to say anything critical. He wanted to help to smooth things over. Moffett said that he would not say anything that anyone could object to and with that assurance Steve went to the races. Steve said that this was the first instance of any member of the Administration breaking faith with him. His theory is that the new Mrs. Moffett has stirred Moffett up to do what he did. There is a general impression in Washington that Mrs. Moffett is intent upon making a big man out of Moffett. As Steve remarked: "She is more likely to end up by making a martyr out of him." Of course, Steve was mad this morning, and he clearly indicated that he did not see how Moffett could last in the Administration. Finally he called Moffett by telephone and suggested that if Moffett would come over to the White House, he (Steve) would get hold of me and we would talk things over.

Moffett came to Steve's office while Steve was upstairs talking to Louis Howe. He looked like a scared schoolboy. I made it pretty clear what I thought of the way in which he had handled matters. He was frightened, but stubborn. Mike Straus got in some good licks. Then Steve came down with word that Howe had talked to the President and that the President had suggested again a joint statement by Moffett and me. We discussed what type of statement we could make. Moffett could not keep on the subject. He constantly recurred to his puerile economic views and at one point said he had to defend himself. I said to him very sharply that it wasn't necessary for him to defend himself any more than it was for me to defend myself and that as members of the Administration we had to defend and protect the Administration. He still thought he had to defend himself. Under my prods he finally lost his temper and turned on me with the accusation that I had put him in a bad spot in the Oil Administration. I asked him what he meant and then to my astonishment he said that I had told him that I was going to make him Oil Administrator. I told him that was not true. Then he said that I had told him that in the Oil Administration I wanted his advice and that I wanted to keep him at my side. I told him that this was true: I had hoped that I could count on his help in the Oil Administration, but all the help he ever offered was to insist upon my putting into effect a schedule of price fixing based on figures furnished by him that would not stand up. I told him that when it came to a matter of that sort, I had to use my own judgment. I remarked that he did not know me if he thought for a minute that I ever had any intention of making him Oil Administrator.

When Moffett got through I said to him that it was clear that he had an animus. Once more we tried to agree on a statement. I outlined one that struck Steve as being quite all right and he called in a stenographer, to whom I dictated it. Moffett did not like this statement, but he did not know what to do about it. He wanted a statement to contain his highly controversial language and, of course, I would not agree to that. While we were still milling about, a telegram came through from Warm Springs that the President would have a suggested statement on the wire in a few minutes. In ten or fifteen minutes it did come through and it was a perfect statement. We changed only one word. To the President's statement we added two paragraphs from mine. These two paragraphs were submitted to the President and he approved them. As the statement finally appeared, the main part of it was from the pen of the President and the last two paragraphs were mine. In his part of the statement the President said in principle what I had said in the first part of my statement, but much more clearly. I did not think that it would be possible to concoct a statement that we could both agree to. As a matter of fact, holding the position that he did, I don't see how Moffett could bring himself to subscribe to the President's statement, but I suspect he felt that it was in the nature of an order. Anyhow, he is a stupid person and probably did not understand the implications in the President's statement.

The statement said in effect that our jurisdictions were entirely separate and distinct: that it was Moffett's job to stimulate the lending of money to people who were in a position to borrow money; that it was my job to help with the housing program those who needed houses and who could not borrow money. Of course, Moffett is against a housing program of any sort. He does not want to interfere with private capital. He belongs to the capitalistic class. He is very rich. His father, during his lifetime, was president of the Standard Oil Company of New Jersey, and I understand that Moffett inherited a large fortune from him, to which he probably had added materially himself. In addition, the wife that he recently married is also very rich in her own right.

I called Steve up late in the day and he told me that he was glad that Moffett had made the charges against me that he had because that clearly showed his animus. The whole thing has been unpleasant and highly distasteful. Of course, the thing to have done was for both Moffett and me to refuse to say anything when we found out that the newspapers were trying to breach the wall of the Administration. I did take this position. I haven't said anything to a single correspondent since the Thursday press conference on this subject and I said nothing at my conference which justified such a story as appeared yesterday morning in the *Washington Herald*.

Even if I had deliberately attacked Moffett, out of regard for the Administration he should not have come back at me, but should have left the matter for the President to handle. I haven't the slightest doubt that, harboring the resentment he disclosed against me today, he has been waiting for a chance to attack me. Neither do I have any doubt that he has been encouraged in this attitude by Mrs. Moffett through a mistaken notion that she was helping him to stand out as a big man in the country. Perhaps others, too, encouraged him in his attack. I have wondered why everyone I have fired for incompetency over here should at once get a job at an increased salary under Moffett, but I begin to understand now.

Steve Early thinks Moffett's attack was deliberate and so does Mike Straus. Moffett is a very close buddy of McIntyre's and I haven't any doubt that McIntyre will try to put the best face possible on things for Moffett to the President. Unfortunately, Early is not at the President's elbow to tell him what he knows and thinks about the situation.

It all goes to show that with the utmost caution, and I do try to be careful in my press conferences to maintain the integrity of the Administration, a reckless or unscrupulous newspaper correspondent can make up a story almost out of the whole cloth and precipitate what seems to be a serious row between two members of the Administration. If this can be done with all persons on their guard, how much more easily can it be brought about if one person is looking for a chance to make a frontal attack and has malice in his heart!

Tuesday, November 27, 1934

I had a telegram from Hutchins today, telling me that he wanted me to let him wire the President calling off all negotiations looking to his coming down here to tie up with NRA. He had called me on Saturday to the same general effect, but I told him then that Rex Tugwell was at Warm Springs, that he intended to talk to the President about NRA, and that I hoped Hutchins would wait until Tugwell came back. Tugwell got into Washington today. Charles E. Merriam was also here and all of them came in my office late this afternoon. Tugwell reported that the President very much wants Hutchins in Washington and he wants him to head up the NRA. As the members of the present board threatened to resign if Hutchins is put in a position of power over it, the President is hesitating because he doesn't want any blowup on the eve of the next Congressional session. He wants to get legislation through making the NRA a permanent institution. He suggested to Tugwell that Hutchins come down and accept membership on the board, which would give him time to learn the ropes, help with the legislative program, and then later step into command.

I called Hutchins on the telephone and Merriam also talked with him. Hutchins agreed to hold off until next week. I am expecting to be called to Warm Springs and I told him that I would get in touch with him as soon as I got back. As a result of my talk with Hutchins I think he will be willing to come down here on a temporary basis as an adviser on NRA matters. This would give him a chance to get in touch with the situation and prepare himself for taking hold when the time is ripe.

Sunday, December 2, 1934

On November 24, while the Moffett row was raging, I wrote a letter to the President giving him a chronological statement of the facts covering the whole matter. I didn't expect him to answer my letter, but last Friday a reply came in as follows:

Warm Springs, Georgia,
November 30, 1934.

Dear Harold:

Thanks for your nice note of Saturday, and also your letter of Friday explaining the situation in regard to Moffett. When I get back I will have a talk with him and make it quite clear that there are four or five million families in the United States who are so poor that they could not possibly come under his home-building plan, which calls for private investment backed by a small Federal guarantee. You are right that the two fields are entirely separate. It would have been so easy for Jim Moffett to have gone to see you and talk the whole thing over without talking to the press at all. He will learn—I hope! I think you handled the situation excellently.

I do hope you can come down here the first or second of December, returning with me the fifth and arriving in Washington about noon on the sixth.

As ever yours,
(Signed) FRANKLIN D. ROOSEVELT

This letter made me very happy, not only on account of its friendly tone, but because it endorses my position on the housing controversy. This letter was written while Moffett was en route to Warm Springs. The newspaper dispatches from Warm Springs indicate that the President set him right on the housing question and that Moffett left there a sadder and wiser man.

Mrs. Roosevelt came in to see me yesterday morning by appointment. There have been two mixups with respect to men appointed at her instance and she has been led to believe that Burlew has been blocking the transfer of one to Washington, and the promotion of the other. The men involved are Osthagen, an old family friend, who is at present in Denver, and Larry Waterbury, a third or fourth cousin of Mrs. Roosevelt's, who is in the Oil Inspection in East Texas.

I think I straightened Mrs. Roosevelt out on both matters. I had on my desk a letter sent to the Department by Waterbury asking for a sixty-day leave of absence, without pay, in order to look after some oil interests of his father in Tulsa, Oklahoma. I also had a letter from a bank in Texas, from which Waterbury had apparently borrowed money, dunning him and referring in the body of the letter to the fact that Waterbury was related to Mrs. Roosevelt.

I don't think Mrs. Roosevelt liked the way her name is being used by Waterbury. I told her that it was quite out of order for any employee of the Oil Administration to have any interest in the oil business. She told me I should write and tell Waterbury this and insist on his severing all connections with his oil interests if he wanted to stay in our employ. She also suggested that I write him that he would not be of much use to the Department if he took a sixty-day leave of absence when we needed him. She said she would write him a sharp letter herself and I understand that she did so later in the day.

As to Osthagen, a man on the staff here led Osthagen to believe that there was a position for him in Washington and that someone, probably Burlew, was blocking his transfer here. I gave Mrs. Roosevelt the history of this case and told her that the matter had never been put up either to Burlew or to me; that the talk about a place here for him was entirely unauthorized, since there was no place and he had never been considered for a place here. I have had the man who made this statement to Osthagen on the carpet. It is just one of those cases where a talkative, officious individual can make a lot of trouble and create a misunderstanding that leads to bad feeling. It is apparent that Mrs. Roosevelt wants Osthagen brought to Washington and I will find a place for him here. I don't mind that so much but I do not like the unjustified criticism leveled against Burlew, who has been under almost constant fire ever since I came here.

I went to the White House Friday to show Steve Early the letter from the President that I have just incorporated in this memorandum. I had a nice, long talk with Steve. I like him very much. He seems to me absolutely sincere and sounds true all through. He told me some things that are worrying him in connection with White House affairs.

My talk with Mrs. Roosevelt was very friendly too. She told me how the President shrank from saying anything to anybody of an unpleasant nature. He does not like to hurt people's feelings. In family matters she has to assume the unpleasant duties because of his tender-heartedness. I am told that while he practically never loses his temper, he makes a very good job of it when he does. For my part, I have never seen him angry. His patience and understanding are really remarkable.

Friday, December 7, 1934

I arrived at Atlanta, Monday morning, at eight-thirty-five, and was met at the station by Colonel Starling, of the Secret Service. We picked up Henry Morgenthau, who had arrived two or three hours earlier. With Henry driving, we started for Warm Springs where we arrived about noon. We went down to the swimming pool where we met the President and afterward we had lunch with him in the Little White House. In the afternoon he drove us out in his own car to the airfield to watch a stunt flier perform in a monoplane. It was raining steadily and the clouds were quite low. That night we went to supper at the house of a man whose name I don't remember. There was a large crowd present and we went back to the hotel, where we were stopping, and played poker until about midnight. Mrs. James Roosevelt was in the game and was the heavy winner. Others who played were Harry Hopkins, Rex Tugwell, Henry Morgenthau, and Frank Walker.

On Tuesday Jim Farley, who had stopped off at Gainesville to dedicate a post office, came over to Warm Springs. Several of us had lunch with the President, including Farley, Morgenthau, Hopkins and Mrs. Hopkins, Tugwell, James and Mrs. Roosevelt, Miss Le Hand, and myself. After luncheon the President excused himself to all except Morgenthau, Tugwell, Hopkins, and myself and we discussed the public works program for next year.

We did make very fast progress with this program because it is clear that the President has made up his mind to expend about $5 billion but Henry Morgenthau is always raising some childish objections. I have been puzzled to decide whether he is being obstructive or is trying to impress us with the profundity of his wisdom. I have really come to the conclusion that he is somewhat stupid. When everything is sailing along nicely, he will come in with some childish objection. Just now he wants to see the plans and specifications in our Housing Division and the Hopkins Administration for slum clearance and low-cost housing, although what bearing the cost of such projects will have upon whether or not we should go in for a public works program is more than I can understand.

Tuesday night there were a couple more parties, chiefly a farewell party given by the newspaper correspondents who have been following the President about. I attended both briefly and then went back to the hotel again where once more we played poker. I had my usual luck. Until I played on this occasion at Warm Springs, I don't think that I have played poker for twenty-five or thirty years. The game has never appealed to me. There may be some skill in it that is beyond me, but if there is skill, I don't grasp it and certainly I have never had any luck in the game. However, at Warm Springs it furnished occasion for some social times. None of us lost enough money to hurt and it was good fun.

We left Warm Springs at noon on Wednesday by special train. I was disappointed that I had not had a chance to take up a number of matters with the President that I have been waiting to discuss with him, but by the time I got to Warm Springs there were so many people there that the President did not seem to have any time except for the brief discussions that we had on public works. The result was that we had a good deal of time on our hands for cocktails and parties and poker.

Just after we had pulled out of Warm Springs, the President sent back for Hopkins, Morgenthau, and me, and we went to the observation end of his car where we once again took up the question of public works. And also once again Henry Morgenthau raised the same childish objections. He had the effrontery to say that he had been trying for several weeks to get from Hopkins and me plans and specifications and costs on slum clearance and housing. I told him that he was mistaken as he had asked for these data for the first time the night before at Warm Springs. He started to turn on me quite indignantly, but the President interposed and said that I was right, that all that we had been discussing were general plans. I said that I did not see what bearing on the general program detailed plans on housing would have, but I said my files were open to Morgenthau if he wanted to inspect them. The President suggested that the three of us have another discussion prior to Sunday afternoon when we would meet again at the White House.

I find it difficult holding my temper with Morgenthau. When I told Tugwell the difficulty we were having in getting anywhere with Morgenthau sitting in at the conferences, Tugwell said: "That's Henry." I don't want to lose my temper with Morgenthau, but it is all I can do not to bring him up with a short turn.

After we got through discussing public works, the others came into the observation section and we had some old-fashioned cocktails. James Roosevelt and his wife, Jim Farley, Miss Le Hand, and Miss Tully joined the party. It is delightful to see how the President can enter in at a party. He had as good a time as anyone there, laughing and talking and joking. Anyone not knowing him would not for a moment have thought that he was the President of the United States. Yet, in spite of all his fun-making, no one ever presumes to treat him with familiarity, although everyone knowing how friendly and approachable he is looks on him as a real friend and most desirable companion.

That night after dinner we had another round of poker in the dining section of the President's private car after the President himself had gone to bed. Those in the party were Mrs. James Roosevelt, Harry Hopkins and wife, Jim Farley, Frank Walker, Rex Tugwell, Henry Morgenthau, and myself. We played until midnight and I lost as usual.

I had a good talk with Rex Tugwell on the train. It seems that it was he, at President Roosevelt's New York house, who stopped me at the head of the stairs, after I had left the conference I had been invited to, and told me that Governor Roosevelt wanted to see me. This was the occasion when he offered me the position of Secretary of the Interior. I had never met Tugwell before that occasion and I had not known until he told me that it was he who was the Governor's messenger. I had always thought it was one of the secretaries, although I could not place him.

Tugwell told me that I had been the surprise of the Cabinet and that I would go down in history as the man who had made over the Department of the Interior. We got to talking about conservation, in which both of us are very much interested, and I told him again how much I would like him for Under Secretary of the Interior in charge of all the activities of this Department having to do with conservation. On two previous occasions I have mentioned this to him, both times in the presence of his chief, the Secretary of Agriculture. This time, however, he seemed to take to the idea and I would not be surprised if he should accept such a position here if I can have it created, as I am planning to do, and if we could arrange an attractive setup. Tugwell is an able man and if I had him as next in line in the Department, it would ease my burdens considerably. I wouldn't have any hesitation in delegating powers to him or in permitting him to act during my absences.

I gather that Tugwell is not quite so happy in Agriculture as he was. I have had a feeling for some time that Agriculture is badly administered and I am more than ever certain of that since my talk with Tugwell. Henry Wallace is not a good administrator, in addition to which he is a good deal of a religious mystic. The other Assistant Secretary, Dr. M. L. Wilson, is as bad as, or worse than, Henry Wallace when it comes to executive work. The result is that Tugwell has a lot of responsibility without the necessary power. This is especially true since Wallace insists on keeping men in important posts in Agriculture whom Tugwell regards as untrustworthy and lacking in ability.

Today we had a Cabinet meeting and every member was there. The Vice President was also present. The meeting was held in the new Cabinet room in the rebuilt office wing of the White House. The Cabinet room is larger and pleasanter than the old one and there is much more room in the rebuilt wing than in the old one. The old one was not large enough by a good deal to take care of the President's staff, but now his staff ought to be comfortably housed.

The Vice President today made one or two statements that met with my cordial approval, as I told him afterward. He took the position that fifty or sixty men in the United States, through interlocking directorates and holding companies, should not be permitted to control the economic life of the nation. He expressed the utmost distrust of these men and told the President that, as he had urged on one or two other occasions, this was the time to put them in their place and keep them there. The Vice President realizes that there are reactionaries in both parties and that when money and financial power are concerned, these men will show no consideration to anyone. He even doubts their patriotism when money is concerned.

The President suggested the possibility of one or two members of the Cabinet visiting Canada during the next year, or even going as far as Australia and New Zealand next summer. He is anxious to keep on friendly terms with the British Dominions. It seems to be his opinion that Great Britain itself is headed for a decline, that the old days of her trade and financial supremacy are gone.

Tuesday, December 11, 1934

The Gridiron Club dinner was along conventional lines. At dinner I sat between the Ambassador of Turkey and the Minister of Greece. Some of the stunts were clever and funny but others were rather forced. I suppose on the whole it was rather a fifty-fifty proposition. I got the same impression I did at the last such dinner that I attended—that the gibes at the New Deal were somewhat acidulous. Practically every stunt centered on the New Deal. It is customary at these dinners to have a speaker of the opposition party, with the President making the closing speech. This year, instead of a Republican leader, the speaker was Henry L. Mencken, of the *Baltimore Sun*. His remarks were cleverly cynical, as usual, but he wasn't particularly ill-natured. When the President followed him, however, he simply smeared him all over. The President, knowing that Mencken was to be the speaker, had had someone look up some of his writings and he quoted Mencken against himself in the most devastating fashion. I looked over at Mencken two or three times while the President was speaking and it was clear to see that he didn't like it at all. He seemed to me to be distinctly put out.

The National Emergency Council held a meeting at two o'clock and it was evident that Richberg has been getting in some fine work. He is steadily building up his own power, and he acted today like the fair-haired boy of the Administration. He looked like the cat that had swallowed the canary. He is gathering under his control all of the various interdepartmental committees, although why the Director of an Emergency Council should have anything to do with committees that attach to the permanent branches of the Government is more than I can understand. He also suggested the possibility of eliminating all, or a large number, of the various legal staffs of the Departments, and a committee was appointed, under the chairmanship of the Department of Justice, to canvass this situation. If an attempt is made to abolish the Solicitor's office in this Department, I shall certainly put up a stiff fight. I could not function without my legal staff. I lean a great deal on my staff and I have a fine one, made up of able, young, straight-thinking lawyers. I would be helpless if I had to wait for an opinion from the Department of Justice in the many matters on which I want legal opinions before making decisions. Moreover, I would not have any confidence in decisions from the Department of Justice. That Department is simply loaded with political appointees and hardly anyone has any respect for the standing and ability of the lawyers over there. Cummings himself is a man of considerable ability, but he is easygoing and apparently has deliberately delivered himself entirely into the hands of the place hunters.

Thursday, December 13, 1934

At the Emergency Council meeting on Tuesday the President was especially vigorous in his remarks about the necessity of every member of the Administration minding his own business. It seemed to me that he was directing these remarks particularly at Moffett, because he went on to explain the housing policy of the Administration, and the housing policy as he expounded it was exactly in line with what I have been saying about a low-cost housing program. He said that very few members of the Administration knew how to protect themselves from newspaper correspondents; he told us that no one was to criticize any other member of the Administration and that what went on in a department was the affair only of that department.

Yesterday I had an appointment with the President, during which he grinned at me and asked me whether I thought that what he had said for Moffett's benefit at the Council meeting on Tuesday had registered. I replied by asking him whether he had read Moffett's interview in the *Post* that very morning, in which interview, Moffett, in answer to a question, had said that I had driven the pigeons away from his pasture but that they would come back. The President looked quite taken aback. He hadn't seen the interview. He asked me whether I really meant that Moffett had gone straight from the Council meeting and given out such a statement. I told him I didn't know whether he had done that, but that the interview had appeared in the *Washington Post* the morning following the Council meeting. The fact is that Moffett doesn't know how to handle himself with newspapermen and if he isn't careful, he will talk himself out of Washington.

I went over to the White House this afternoon at two-thirty to a conference called by the President on the proposed transcontinental highway. Present also were Secretary Morgenthau, Harry Hopkins, Thomas H. MacDonald, Chief of the Bureau of Public Roads, and Admiral Peoples. At intervals during the last year I have suggested the possibility of such a highway to the President. He has always been rather taken with the idea, but it has now really struck his imagination and he is giving very serious thought to it. Recently at one of our conferences to consider a program of public works for next year, the President outlined a route for a transcontinental highway from east to west and routes for two or three north and south highways. The meeting today was to consider these routes as outlined on a map of the United States and to consider costs, etc.

Monday, December 17, 1934

At the Cabinet meeting on Friday, when it was Secretary Roper's turn, he started in his unctuous way to tell the President that he believed he was in a position to assure him that business in general was prepared to go along with him and work for the economic recovery of the country. He was very fulsome about it and I could see one of those mischievous expressions come over the President's face. Finally he said: "Well, Dan, all I can say is that business will have only until January 3 to make up its mind whether it is going to co-operate or not." Roper was quite dashed. Then the President went on to say: "I believe it is the custom in hospitals, when a patient is to be operated on, to try to build him up, and we ought to build up our patient as much as we can before January 3." Developing this thought further, he remarked that two or three years ago James Gerard, of New York, had named a list of eighty men who, he said, controlled the business and finances of the United States. The President said that not one of these eighty men was connected with the United States Government, and that he was tired of eighty men controlling the destinies of one hundred and twenty million people. He said that in his opinion the only way to curb this control was to do away with holding companies.

I had a short session with the President at the White House proper on Saturday at noon. While I was waiting in the corridor on the second floor, I was talking with Miss Le Hand. I noticed a portrait of the President hanging in the corridor and asked Miss Le Hand whether that was the one which was being painted by a woman artist when I was in Hyde Park in the summer of 1933. She said it was. I told her I didn't like it at all and she expressed the same feeling. I then said that I wished the President would let Mr. Hubbell, who has just finished me, paint the President, and she said that Mrs. Ruth Bryan Owen had shown her a photograph of my portrait and that she thought it was fine. She suggested that if I got her a photograph, she would show it to the President.

While we were talking she told me the following amusing story: she and Marvin McIntyre were in the President's office and he was talking about how he wanted his marine pictures hung. He said that, after all, he thought he ought to have the pictures hung the way he wanted them since it was his office. McIntyre solemnly said: "You are right, Mr. President, you ought to have them hung to suit yourself. After all, you are in this office more than anyone else except Henry Morgenthau." This story led to a discussion of Henry Morgenthau, and it was apparent from what Miss Le Hand told me that he is breaking in on the President on all occasions. I gathered from her that at least some members of the President's staff are quite fed up with Henry and believe that he will wear out his welcome at the rate he is going.

During my interview with the President I expressed concern over Richberg's proposal to consolidate all of the law staffs of the various departments with the Department of Justice. I told him that I simply could not operate without my own legal staff, that I had a group of fine, devoted and very able young lawyers. The President said of course I couldn't and that some of the other departments and offices were in the same situation. He remarked that this was just one of those periodic reviews, and I gathered the impression that he was not seriously considering any such consolidation as I have been afraid of.

On Saturday Frank Knox called me up from Chicago to say that his advices were that William Hale Thompson would be a candidate for the Republican nomination for mayor and that he had already lined up a majority of the Republican county committeemen. He had tried to see Merriam but Merriam had left for Washington. He told me that I could tell Merriam that if he wanted to run for mayor, the *Daily News* would support him with all of its strength either as a candidate for the Republican nomination or as a fusion candidate at the general election. He said, however, that it would be difficult to beat Thompson in the Republican primaries if the organization was back of Thompson and that to run as a fusion candidate with both Thompson and Kelly in the field would be a setup for Kelly. During my talk with the President on Saturday I told him what Knox had said to me about Thompson being a candidate and the President said: "That would be a fine choice, wouldn't it, Thompson or Kelly?" I urged him again to do what he could to get Kelly out of the race, and he said that Farley had the matter in hand and would try to do something over the week end.

On Sunday morning I had Merriam come to my office and I told him what Knox had said. Merriam doesn't want to run but I think he would be willing to run if, by doing so, he could save the situation for Chicago, provided, of course, that there were a chance of making a real race. I told him that the President had assured me that if Kelly were the Democratic candidate and Merriam should run against him, no aid or comfort could be given to Kelly, and no disclaimer of Merriam would come from Administration sources if it should be claimed during the campaign that Merriam, as a member of the National Resources Board, and as my close personal and political friend, really had the blessing of the Administration.

Victor Watson, of the *Herald-Examiner,* came in to see me last Thursday or Friday. He is very pessimistic over the Chicago situation and seemed thoroughly discouraged. He said that he would never get over the fact that Farley, apparently with the knowledge and consent of the President, had gone into Illinois during the last campaign and cordially endorsed Kelly, Nash, *et al.* The previous time that Watson had been in to see me he wanted me to get out word to the oil interests that I would be gratified if they would advertise in his paper. I told him at once that I couldn't do that sort of a thing, that I wouldn't ask the oil people for a stick of chewing gum.

Harry Slattery had dinner Saturday evening with the Brandeises and brought me word today that Justice Brandeis had told him that I was doing the best job in Washington. He also talked to the Justice about Richberg and found him very much disturbed in his own mind on the subject. Harry has also had a talk with Senator Norris. Norris is worried about the way in which Public Works has been handling municipal power projects, and he also is puzzled about the apparent change in Richberg. Several months ago I set up a special committee in Public Works, under the chairmanship of Henry T. Hunt, just to make sure that power projects would be given a square deal, but I have begun to hear lately that this program is being sabotaged. So I have decided to appoint three persons from the staff, of whose sympathetic point of view in such matters I feel sure, to go into the whole subject matter and find out whether the Hunt committee is functioning properly or not. I am afraid also that Hunt has gotten me in bad with respect to the Colorado River project in Texas. I have had submitted to me recently some letters written by Hunt on his own authority, without referring them to me, which I would not have permitted to go out if I had known of them.

Late this morning, Felix Frankfurter came in by appointment. I had sent him word through Ben Cohen some time ago that the next time he was in Washington I would like to see him. In great confidence he told me that he had had a talk Sunday night with the President about the Department of Justice, and that the President now thoroughly understands the weakness of that Department. It is indeed weak. It is full of political appointees. It has some hard-working, earnest lawyers, but no outstanding ones. It makes me sick when I think of the way Special Assistant Attorney General Stevens handled our oil case before the Supreme Court last week, and yet men on my legal staff think he was the best man in the whole Department to argue it.

Frankfurter and I also talked about Richberg. Frankfurter has known him for a long time. Like the rest of us, he can't understand what has happened inside of Richberg, but he feels that something has gone wrong and that he is a real danger to the Administration. He remarked that nobody knew what Richberg was saying at his private conferences with the big businessmen that he has been holding from time to time. Frankfurter thinks that Richberg now represents exactly the opposite point of view from that which was supposed to be the one of this Administration, particularly so far as the President is concerned. He told me that in a recent talk with Senator La Follette, the latter had expressed himself as being heartbroken over Richberg and as having lost all faith in him. La Follette and Richberg used to be particularly close, their friendship going back to the days of the elder La Follette. In fact, it was Richberg who brought young Bob La Follette and Basil Manly to my house in Hubbard Woods at the time the elder La Follette was a candidate for President to urge me to take an active managerial part in that campaign. According to Frankfurter, La Follette told him that Richberg had said that he regarded the speech the President had made at Tupelo, Mississippi, as a great mistake. It was in this speech during the President's tour of the Tennessee Valley that he went definitely on record on the power question.

Wednesday, December 19, 1934

There was a short Cabinet meeting Tuesday afternoon, followed by a Public Works conference attended, as usual, by the President, Secretary Morgenthau, Harry Hopkins, and myself, and in addition this time, Secretary Perkins and Assistant Secretary of the Treasury Josephine Roche. The President seems thoroughly committed now to a $5 billion program for next year. This was the first time he had discussed it with Miss Perkins and she seemed to be in grave doubts as to the wisdom of the wage scale that we have been considering. We have been going on the theory of declining to pay the union wage rates. As a matter of fact, we do not refer to the proposed remuneration as "wages" but as "security income." The theory is that the purpose of this money is to take men off the relief rolls and that if we can assure them an annual income of about $600, they will be getting much more than they are getting on relief. Another thought is that with a low rate of pay men will be very glad to accept employment from private industry at higher wages. We want to get the men off relief, but at the same time we don't want to have the burden of carrying them on the Federal payroll indefinitely. Hopkins has worked out a schedule which, if it will work, will mean that all employables will be off the relief rolls by October or November of next year.

The President and Mrs. Roosevelt gave their annual official dinner to the Cabinet last night. There were about eighty at table. I am bound to confess that the White House dinners are neither inspiring nor do they stand out as Lucullan repasts. I am not very fussy about my food and I suppose one ought to be satisfied with dining on and with a solid-gold service, but it does seem a little out of proportion to use a solid-gold knife and fork on ordinary roast mutton. Besides which, I never did like carrots.

Wine was served officially at dinner for the first time since prohibition went into effect back in President Wilson's administration. Mrs. Roosevelt had announced that she would serve one glass each of two domestic wines and she kept her word. The sherry was passable, but the champagne was undrinkable. I hopefully took one drink and then set my glass down with a final gesture. Mrs. Farley almost made a face when she tasted the champagne. She was quite indignant but consoled herself with the reflection that she had had some real champagne before she went to the White House and that more would be awaiting her on her return to the Mayflower. She seems to be quite fussy about the quality and quantity of her wines, although Jim never touches a drop. I am bound to say, however, that probably on only one other occasion have I ever tasted worse champagne, and it does seem to me that if decent champagne can't be made in the United States, it ought to be permissible, even for the White House, to serve imported champagne. There are some good domestic still wines made, and it would be better to serve one of those than such champagne as we were given Tuesday night.

The dinner was followed by a musicale in the East Room. It wasn't a particularly good one and I found my chair as uncomfortable as I did last season. Mrs. Francis Biddle sat on my left and introduced herself to me. She seemed very nice indeed.

Saturday, December 22, 1934

There was a meeting Thursday afternoon of the National Emergency Council but I did not go. I felt out of sorts all day. Several things have annoyed me lately. I have resented keenly the effort of the Division of Procurement to break the contract that I had made with Waddy Wood as architect for the new Interior Building. I made this contract with the full knowledge and consent of the President, and I resent the suggestion that a contract so made in good faith is not a valid one. Procurement takes this position with Wood. It is in effect standing him up against a wall and telling him to take what it offers or nothing at all. I will stand behind

Wood. I have carried the matter to the President on several occasions and have made my views very clear. He has not stood up as I feel I have a right to expect that he should.

Another matter that has disappointed me is the change in the attitude of Henry Wallace with respect to a certain reorganization as between our Departments which would bring over here Forestry, the Bureau of Roads and Biological Survey, and take from here to Agriculture, Reclamation, Lands, Subsistence Homesteads, and Erosion Control. I am firmly of the opinion that, in the interest of a broad policy of conservation, all of the conservation activities ought to be grouped in the Interior Department, which now has the major portion of them, and which is the natural home for such activities. I don't see how we can go forward with a broad and intelligent policy of conservation unless all of these activities are grouped under the jurisdiction of an able and sincere conservationist. With the approval of the President, I have asked for the setting up of an Under Secretaryship and my hope has been that I can persuade Rex Tugwell to come over from Agriculture as Under Secretary to have jurisdiction over all the conservation bureaus.

On Thursday, at six-thirty, I dropped in on a cocktail party at the Willard Hotel, given by Miss Le Hand and Miss Grace Tully, the President's personal secretaries. The occasion was the announcement of the engagement of Grace Tully's sister to a lawyer in Public Works by the name of Larrabee, a friend of Wilmarth's from Chicago. We had a jolly time and I didn't get home for dinner until nearly eight o'clock. My hostesses wanted me to stay at the Willard for dinner but I thought I ought to go home. However, I promised to go back after dinner and that I did, intending after a brief stay to come back to the office to work. I found that Miss Le Hand, the Tully girls, and Larrabee were going to the White House and they insisted on my going with them. We got up to the President's study in the Oval Room just as he and Dr. Moley were finishing some work on his message to Congress. Two bottles of champagne were brought up and we had a jolly time until close to midnight. The President was at his best, laughing and joking, telling stories and relating incidents.

The President joked about the champagne that had been served at the Cabinet dinner on Tuesday night. He asked me whether I had ever tasted worse champagne and I frankly told him that I never had. He said that about fifteen minutes before dinner he had asked Mrs. Roosevelt about the wine and she said she was going to serve domestic champagne from New York State, recommended by Rex Tugwell. The President told her that she ought not to serve domestic champagne, but she replied that it had been on the ice and that it was too late to change. The President said that he has been apologizing ever since to dinner guests for this champagne.

The President had noticed that I was not at the Council meeting, and I told him that I had not gone because I was in bad humor. I jokingly remarked that he had spanked us all at the previous Council meeting and that I didn't want to be spanked again. He said that he didn't see that I had much to complain of, that the spanking was really administered to Moffett. He added that he understood that Moffett had regarded what he had said as a great vindication of his position on housing.

I had an appointment with the President at noon on Friday and we came to grips on the Division of Procurement. We were both somewhat spunky. I told him that Procurement is assuming unwarranted power under a certain Executive Order. It is asserting the right to dictate to the other departments, which have always done their own building, as to whether or not they should carry on their building. The President said he had to have somebody to decide such matters for him, and I insisted that when PWA made an allocation and he had approved it, that settled the matter, without reference to the Division of Procurement. I told him further that if it was his decision that all of the other departments were to discontinue building, it was a matter of such grave policy that they should be called together for a conference and not be deprived of powers that they have always exercised by a strained construction of the word "structure" in an Executive Order. He admitted that there ought to be a conference and made a note of it. The Quartermaster Corps of the War Department has always done the building at Army posts. In the Interior Department, the National Park Service, the Indian Office, and the Reclamation Service have been engaged in building and are thoroughly equipped in that regard. Also, since taking over the management of the buildings here in Washington, the Park Service has done local building. We built the new office wing of the White House and we are now putting on the extra story to this building. I think we are equipped to do better work and quicker work than the Office of Supervising Architect under Procurement.

Today Henry Morgenthau, Harry Hopkins, the Director of the Budget, and I had a conference with the President on the public works program for next year. He is definitely committed to the proposition of asking Congress for $5 billion. He wanted to make sure that we could spend this amount of money in approximately a year from November 1, next, and that it would take care of the employables now on the relief rolls. Hopkins thinks this amount of money will put about three and a half million men to work directly on the projects and of course there will be that much or more indirect labor. Some statisticians figure that the men back of the lines working indirectly on a project are two or even three to one to those directly employed. The plan is to ask that this money be granted to the President, leaving him to make it available for different classes of projects in his own sound judgment.

I am thoroughly persuaded that there is an active cabal working against me, probably with the idea either of having the President curtail my powers or at least not grant me any extension of them. There has been a great deal of underground criticism going on and a lot of it has reached the White House. A good deal of this criticism is aimed at Burlew directly but really is meant for me, or at least I so believe. Glavis is also being criticized. The sum and substance of this criticism is that I am not really running the Interior Department but that Burlew is doing it, and he is being described as a standpat Republican who is out of harmony with this Administration. I have defended Burlew on two occasions to the President and on one to Mrs. Roosevelt. The latter is the most outspoken critic so far as I know. She has even gone so far, on at least two occasions at her own dinner table in the presence of Interior Department officials, to criticize the Interior Department, particularly Burlew. I think such criticism in such circumstances is in extremely bad taste, but I am at a distinct disadvantage in a matter of this kind with the wife of the President.

Last week Burlew told me that he had in mind writing Mrs. Roosevelt a letter asking for an interview. I told him to go ahead and he did draft a letter which I redrafted. She told him she would see him at the White House last Sunday afternoon at four and he spent almost an hour with her. He reported that she was very cold and that he had difficulty in making any headway. He came away satisfied, however, that he had done some good. He met the charges that are being bandied about with respect to him, explained the working of the Department and his own place and functions in the organization.

I have never objected to meeting an enemy in the open, but I am restless under an attack by innuendo. So I came to the conclusion that I would try to force the issue into the open. Accordingly I have written a letter to the President, which I sent to Miss Le Hand late this afternoon, to deliver to him personally. In this letter I referred to the various charges that are being made, defended both Burlew and Glavis, explained what I have tried to do myself as Secretary of the Interior, and suggested that the President cause an investigation to be made by some fair-minded man of the Administration, such as Frank C. Walker of New York. I asked that since the President himself on previous occasions had expressed some concern about rumor-mongering that had been going on with respect to certain members of the Administration, it would be well to dig into this one situation and try to clear it up. Of course, I didn't say anything about Mrs. Roosevelt, but the President must know himself that she has been saying what she has been saying.

I think it is too bad that Mrs. Roosevelt has been doing this. She can't make such statements as she has been making at her own dinner table without the thing spreading all through the official life of Washington and finally seeping into the newspapers. Moreover, a constant repetition of these groundless charges on her part is bound to have an effect sooner or later on the President. I want the thing out in the open, and I think it is a good time now to bring it out before we get started on our new public works program and a possible reorganization of the Departments. I am entirely willing to have a showdown. I have worked hard and faithfully putting everything into my job that is in me and if I am not serving the President satisfactorily, I want him to have the opportunity to find someone who will. Moreover, it rather dashes the spirit to be criticized when there is no occasion for it.

I think what got Mrs. Roosevelt off on this line was the subsistence homestead program, especially Reedsville. That has been one part of my administration that I feel apologetic about. I told the President this a good many months ago. But when all is said and done, the falldown in the subsistence homestead program is largely

due to Mrs. Roosevelt herself. She practically took hold of Reedsville herself, where most of our mistakes and our greatest extrava-
gances have occurred. Louie Howe mixed in there too, to our sorrow. Mrs. Roosevelt took to Reedsville a temperamental architect
from New York who spent money lavishly and just about broke
down the morale of the staff. Finally I had to ride over him and
one or two other members of the Reedsville staff roughshod and I
know they carried their tales of woe straight to Mrs. Roosevelt.

I don't know what reaction the President will have to my letter,
but I want the situation cleared up or else I want to get out. I
have no stomach for working like a dog if I have to carry the additional load of the insinuating disapproval of Mrs. Roosevelt and
perhaps of the President himself. I don't want to be unjust to him.
As a matter of fact, I think he is all right in his attitude. At any rate,
I have no evidence to the contrary, but neither have I any assurance
that he won't believe, at least to some degree, the slanders that are
current.

I know some of the people in Washington who have it in for me
and would like to see me come a cropper and I suspect others. I
think Richberg is one of those who would spread poison if he could
and I rather suspect that he has found a means of doing so. As a
matter of fact, he has been quoted to me as saying that he understood that Burlew ran the Department of the Interior. Moffett and
his crowd are unfriendly. So is Farley. The Forest Service believes
that I am trying to get that service for the Interior Department
and it is knocking. The Bureau of Fisheries is in the same state of
mind. Harry Hopkins himself, I am sure, is quite all right, but
people on his staff want him to have a goodly share of the next
public works program in order to assure themselves of their own
places in the sun. I have been told that the Attorney General was
not friendly, but on the surface he seems to be quite all right. However, I think there are people on his staff who are critical. Then
the whole Procurement Division under Admiral Peoples, and including the Supervising Architect's Office, are jealous as can be and
undoubtedly are doing all the knocking possible.

Assistant Secretary Chapman came in to see me this morning.
He told me he had had a feeling lately that I didn't have the confidence and trust in him that I formerly had, and he expressed the
fear that in some way I connected him with all of these stories that
are going the rounds about me. I told him very frankly that while

I thought he was loyal, I believed that he was not discreet. He admitted a tendency to indiscretion. I also told him that he liked people and he wanted people to like him, with the result that he was more or less all things to all people. He admitted the truth of this allegation also. We discussed the stories that are going about with reference to me and the manner in which I am running the Department, and Chapman expressed the feeling that I have had, namely, that there is an active, underground campaign going on with particular bitterness against me at this time. He knows what Mrs. Roosevelt has been saying because she has been saying some of it to him, and he was a guest at a White House dinner when she openly criticized Burlew, with an inference about me.

Hopkins has only enough money left to carry on his relief work until the middle of February and the President has sent out orders impounding all unexpended and unobligated balances. This will probably mean an abrupt stop for the time being of our public works program, although it is the intention to repay practically all of these impounded funds out of the new appropriation.

Saturday, December 29, 1934

Late the afternoon of the twenty-seventh I called Miss Le Hand to tell her I was sending to her a personal letter that I would like to have her give the President when she thought he would have time to read it. The letter referred to was the one I had written to ask the President to have an investigation made of my Department.

On Friday I went over shortly after one o'clock to the Mayflower Hotel to talk informally to a group of editors of college newspapers, who are in Washington for a convention. I talked about the rights of a free press, free speech, and free assemblage, making the point that all were equally vital if we were to retain our liberties, and remarking also that while the newspapers are pretty jealous of the rights of a free press, they do not so much concern themselves about the equally important rights of free speech and free assemblage. I also said that constitutional guarantees were to protect the rights of minorities, since majorities could always take care of themselves, and that the smaller the minority, the more vital to them were these guarantees. I told them that while newspaper writers ought to write freely and fearlessly, they ought to be good sportsmen and not twist a phrase or change a word in order to create a wrong impression.

From there I went to the Cabinet meeting. Before the President came in, Kannee, who is assistant to Colonel McIntyre, came in to say that Frank Walker wanted to see me and asked me whether I would be willing to go into McIntyre's room as Walker did not want to go into the Cabinet room. Walker told me that he had just lunched with the President and that he wanted to see me before he went back to New York. He didn't say what he wanted to see me about, but I assumed it was with reference to the letter that I had sent the President the evening before. I made an appointment for my office at ten o'clock Saturday morning.

At Cabinet meeting, after we had had our usual round table, at which each member of the Cabinet was given the opportunity to bring up questions of mutual interest or concern, the President gave an outline of his public works and relief program for next year. It was probably my imagination, but up to that point I had a feeling that his manner was a little aloof so far as I was concerned. But in discussing public works, he said, referring to our program: "When Harold took hold of public works, he had to start cold. He had no program and he had no organization. It was necessary to develop both. A lot of people thought that all he would have to do would be to shovel money out of the window. There have been a good many complaints about the slowness of the public works program and Harold's caution. There hasn't been even a minor scandal in public works and that is some record." This statement by the President made me feel very happy and indicated also that he had read my letter and that some of it at least had stuck in his mind.

The President also discussed the CWA program last year. He said that we could not undertake such a program as that again because the country was not satisfied with it, that it had made a bad impression on taxpayers to see men raking leaves or mowing grass along the roadside. He was for a program of real public works, which, at the same time, would give work to practically all idle employables on socially useful structures. The plan is to let the states and local communities take care of their own unemployables as they did before the Federal Government assumed the responsibility. The plan also contemplates wages considerably below the prevailing daily wage, but while the wages are to be lower, there is to be an assurance of continuous employment so that the yearly income will not vary so radically from the one earned under the present prevailing daily rate of wage. I noticed that the President did not divulge to the whole Cabinet the amount that he has in mind to ask Congress for carrying out this program, although I believe the amount is firmly fixed in his own mind and is the same as that which we have been discussing in smaller conferences that we have been holding. He doesn't want any authoritative leak to the newspapers, and he was probably particularly cautious because Harry Hopkins more or less discounted what he was going to say in his annual message by a statement that he made at his press conference Thursday when he said that the plan would be to put the employables to work and let the unemployables be taken care of by the states and local communities as formerly. The President referred to this statement by Hopkins very critically.

After Cabinet meeting I waited because I had to discuss with the President an important change in public works policy due to the fact that our unappropriated and unexpended balances have been impounded in order to finance Harry Hopkins' relief work. They have taken about $280 million away from Public Works and Interior. As I stepped up to the President's chair I remarked, "Mr. President, it looks as if I am out of luck again." What I meant was that his press conference was waiting for him so that I wouldn't have a chance to talk with him. Apparently misunderstanding me, he turned toward me, put his hand on my shoulder, and said, "Harold, I wouldn't worry about the matter that you wrote me about if I were you; that matter is straightening itself out." I went on to explain that I was referring to an opportunity to talk public works, and he asked me to wait until after his press conference.

I had a number of projects to present to him for approval, totaling about $20 million. He approved them all in principle, after some discussion, on the understanding that I would not go forward with any of them until we had the money. There were several other matters that I took up with him while I had the chance and our conference was entirely satisfactory and pleasant.

Saturday morning Frank Walker came in at ten. He didn't tell me outright that the President had showed him my letter, but I think the President had either done so or had told him in general what the letter contained. Frank told me that he appreciated my confidence in him and I replied that I thought he was a square shooter and that I was perfectly willing to have him look into matters. He said that there was no reason for an investigation, that the President was entirely satisfied with the way I was doing my job, and that there was no question about who was running the Department of the Interior.

Walker went on to say that the only thing that bothered him was the breach between Jim Farley and me. Walker is very close to Farley, and this confirmed the suspicion that I have had for some time that Farley does not look upon me with favor. Walker said that the trouble with Farley went back to the appointment of Dr. Finch as the Director of the Bureau of Mines; that Farley thought I had put him on the spot on that occasion. I asked Frank if Farley held me responsible for publication of the story that the Finch appointment had been held up because Farley had objected to it, and Walker said that was the trouble. I then told him that I had had absolutely nothing to do with that; that the information that the appointment had been held up, apparently at Farley's instance, came to me through the newspapers; that I had never made any comment on it. I told him that my personal feeling toward Farley had been very friendly and that I had never criticized him, even privately, to anyone at any time.

Walker said that what he was afraid of was that the breach would widen unless it was closed, that the President needed both of us, and that we ought to get together. He said that he had told the President on the return trip from Warm Springs that he ought to knock our heads together. I told him that I had nothing in the world against Farley; that I was willing to discuss matters with him at any time. I agreed with him that the breach would widen if things were allowed to go along as they were and that if the newspapers, many of which are unfriendly to Farley, once got an inkling of the situation, they would magnify every incident and create a breach even if none in fact existed. Frank said he was going to New York and would talk with Jim and try to arrange for us to get together next week. I told him this would be satisfactory to me. Frank seemed satisfied with our interview and said he was going back to report to the President the result of it. He again expressed pleasure at the confidence that I had shown in suggesting that I would like him to investigate the Department, but he insisted again that there was nothing to investigate. This undoubtedly expressed his own views as well as the President's.

It begins to look as if the Department of Agriculture is opening a campaign on this Department. The Forest Service has become a law unto itself. It is a tight little organization which does a lot of lobbying. Some time ago a sudden barrage was laid down against me on the theory that I was trying to get Forestry over here. I do want it, but I have never raised my hand to get it, except to talk in a friendly way with Henry Wallace and Rex Tugwell, and jointly with them, with the President. As a matter of fact, there was a movement in Congress at the last session to transfer Forestry over here, but I discouraged it and succeeded in stopping it. Recently Henry Wallace took up with me the question of transferring to Agriculture the Erosion Control Service. I am half inclined to agree with him that it properly belongs in Agriculture, but the other day the President brought up the subject and I found him inclined to believe it belonged here. Anyhow, Henry has been pushing the matter. Today I got a letter from him enclosing copy of a letter to Don Richberg in which he invited Richberg's consideration of the question whether or not certain land purchase and land policy programs should not be administered by the Department of Agriculture instead of by us. Congressman Taylor, of Colorado, was in to see me today too, and from him I learned that members of the Forest Service in the West are opening an active campaign to have the Grazing Control Service sent to Agriculture to be administered.

So on Saturday I wrote a letter to Henry Wallace telling him that while nothing had been done here to disturb the friendly *status quo* between our Departments, it was apparent that the Department of Agriculture was opening a fight on a broad front and that if I found it necessary to defend this Department, I would do so although with great reluctance. I concluded by saying that while I was perfectly willing to discuss with him and the President matters of organization as between our Departments, I was not willing to refer the matter to Richberg since, so far as I was aware, he had neither the experience nor the special attainments that qualified him to pass judgment upon such a matter.

Henry Morgenthau called me up voluntarily Saturday night to thank me for the fine co-operation that this Department had given the Treasury in working out the problem of impounding all unobligated and unexpended balances to finish the relief program for this fiscal year. He spoke with special consideration of what Burlew had done and told me that he had spoken to the President about it. I told him that I was very glad indeed that he had done that, and he said that he remembered that recently there was some criticism of Burlew. This was a very decent thing for Henry to do and it may help to clear the air so far as Burlew is concerned.

Saturday, January 5, 1935

Monday, the last day of the old year, was a quiet day. I cleaned up everything at my office before going home for dinner. I had declined all New Year's Eve invitations and I went to bed at nine o'clock. On New Year's Day I was at home all day and Raymond was with me practically all the time.

On Wednesday hell began to pop and it has been popping ever since. The *New York Herald Tribune* carried a front-page story by Lindley to the effect that the President had practically ordered me to discharge Glavis and Burlew. The story was a highly sensational one. It charged Glavis with wire tapping, with espionage of high Government officials, both inside and outside of the Department, and Burlew with disloyalty to the New Deal, with terrorizing employees in the Department, and with building up a machine of his own within the Department. There were other charges made against Burlew, having to do with the Reedsville Subsistence Homestead project and other matters.

At his conference later in the day the President denied this story. He said it had been made out of whole cloth. Then I saw a group of correspondents and denied it categorically. I also answered the charges against Burlew and Glavis, pointing out that they were two of the best men on my staff and saying that I did not have the slightest intention of dismissing them. I left no doubt in the mind of anyone that I intended to stand behind both men. Late in the afternoon of Wednesday, Lindley came in to see me and he must have been in my office for about two hours. He told me that notwithstanding the denials of the President and myself, he was going to write another story. He started to ask me questions and I talked to him very confidentially, but off the record. I explained the duties of Burlew, told what an efficient and able man he is, and went the limit in his defense. I did likewise for Glavis, although it so happens that Burlew is under heavier fire than Glavis.

It was difficult making an impression on Lindley. Finally, toward the end, I called Burlew in. Lindley had never met him. Lindley continued to ask about certain matters over here in connection with which he evidently felt that some blame attached to Burlew, but I was able to show in every instance that this was not the case. There was one patronage matter in which Mrs. Roosevelt has been perniciously active and on which Lindley had entirely the wrong slant. I explained that to Lindley and I could see that my explanation made a very deep impression on him. Before we were through, Lindley had been considerably shaken in his point of view, and after Burlew left my office, Lindley told me that Burlew had impressed him with his ability.

Lindley had a full column in the *New York Herald Tribune* on Thursday. It was inevitable that he would have a follow-up story of some sort, but the Thursday morning story did not do any particular damage. It was plain to see that at his interview in my office we had taken a good deal of the wind out of his sails. Both the Wednesday and the Thursday morning stories were sold to a good many newspapers throughout the country so that the story had pretty wide circulation.

Thursday morning, Kluckhohn of *The New York Times* came over to my press bureau and said that Steve Early had called in the White House correspondents and told them that while the denial of the President still stood on the Glavis-Burlew story, they could say that a White House aide had suggested to me the dismissal of these two men. This report was a great shock to me because, if true, it indicated that the President was willing to have these men dismissed, but that he didn't want to appear to be asking for it directly. I decided to call Steve Early and did so. When I told him what had been reported to me, he replied vigorously that it was a "damned lie." We had quite a talk over the telephone from which it was clear to me that Steve sympathized with the position that I was in and was doing everything he could to protect me. It was also clear, because he practically said so, that he believed Mrs. Roosevelt was responsible for the story. This places all of us, the President included, in a very embarrassing position. As Steve explained to me over the telephone, it could be said that neither the President nor any one on his staff was responsible for this story, but it could not be said that no one in the White House had had anything to do with it. He said that if such a statement as that should go out, Mrs. Roosevelt might, in answer to a question at her press conference, divulge that she had been responsible for the story. I remarked to Steve that this put me on a very hot spot indeed, and he agreed that it did.

I refused to see Kluckhohn alone, but he was present at my press conference in the afternoon, at which I was bombarded with questions about the Glavis-Burlew incident. I repeated my statement that no one in the White House had indicated to me that I should dismiss either man, and in reply to a question whether I was contemplating dismissing either, I said No in a decided manner.

This episode has had a very bad effect on my staff. Both Burlew and Glavis are very much cut up and Harry Slattery is disturbed over it too. It has worried me a good deal, although I do not believe that anything will come of it. But whether it does or not, I resent having these two men, who have worked loyally and diligently for the Government, made the object of such an attack. Of course, my feeling is that the attack is intended for me. My enemies can't make a frontal attack. They can't charge me with graft or inefficiency or inattention to duty, and so they are attacking me through these two valued aides of mine. I resent particularly the loose talking that Mrs. Roosevelt has indulged in, even at her own dinner table when guests were present, particularly about Burlew. I have known that it was only a matter of time until these stories would break into the public print. In addition to what she has been saying about Burlew, there has been an accumulation of petty gossip here and there which in sum total makes a formidable bundle. Lindley has been gathering all this stuff apparently and has woven it into a sensational story.

I have sent Burlew and Glavis out of town for a few days. None of us has been able to do very effective work and I thought that a spell away from Washington would do them a lot of good. They left tonight for Pinehurst, but before going, they both declared that they intended to start a number of libel suits when they come back. I wouldn't much care if they did. It might have a very salutary effect.

On Friday Congressman Sirovich, of New York, came in to see me. I have never met him but once or twice. He is a Harvard man, a physician and surgeon, and also a Tammany man, who has been in Congress for about ten years. I don't know how influential he is, but he is very active and he thinks he is influential, whether he is or not. It happens that he was in Harvard with President Roosevelt, and, I think, knows him quite well. He is progressive, too, in his outlook.

Sirovich said that he had been intending to come down for some time to see me and when he saw the story in the Thursday morning papers about Glavis and Burlew, he made up his mind he wouldn't put it off any longer. He said that he considered me the outstanding man in the Administration, next to the President, and that he had told the President so. Then came the really amusing part of the interview. In the recent Speakership fight, Sirovich supported Congressman Byrns, of Tennessee, because he regarded him as more progressive than his principal opponent, Congressman Rayburn, of Texas. He regarded Rayburn as Vice President Garner's candidate, and in order to start a backfire on Garner, Sirovich and Byrns began to discuss me as the candidate for Vice President with President Roosevelt two years from now. Congressman Blanton, of Texas, also a supporter of Congressman Byrns, was in conference with Byrns and Sirovich and they told him of the Vice Presidential plan. Blanton then went to see the Vice President and told him what was in the air. According to Sirovich, this scared him off Rayburn.

Sirovich went on to assure me that he and his friends were for me for Vice President and that I could be nominated. He told me that if I began to hear of this movement from unexpected sources, I was to pay no attention to it. According to Sirovich, I am to be nominated and elected Vice President two years from now, and in six years I am to be the candidate for President. I told him that I would be too old, but he assured me that I would only be in my prime. He said that he and Jim Farley were friends and that Farley had been vice president of a bank of which he, Sirovich, was president. He is willing to support Jim in his political ambition to be Governor of New York. He said that Farley wanted to be governor and then be the first Catholic President of the United States, but he didn't believe he could be elected because he is a Catholic. But he might be available for Vice President, and that Ickes and Farley would make a good ticket in 1940. He even assured me that the Tammany delegation would be for me, that what I had just done to force Robert Moses out as a member of the Triborough Bridge Authority in New York would endear me to that organization. I listened to all of this with a straight face because Sirovich was undoubtedly quite in earnest. If anyone can think of me as Vice President two years from now and candidate for President four years from now, he ought to be allowed to dream on without being awakened rudely. Anyway, he undoubtedly meant well.

Anna and I went to the diplomatic reception at the White House Thursday night. There was the usual array of gold braid, feathered hats, etc. Both of us were tired and we didn't stay long. Hiram and Mrs. Johnson were there. It was the first time I had seen them since their return to Washington. I didn't think Hiram looked so very well. He seems to me to be thinning in the face and looking older. Anna and I left at ten o'clock.

On Friday the President delivered his annual message to Congress and all the members of the Cabinet were present in the House of Representatives where the Senate and the House of Representatives were assembled in joint session. The message was, I think, one of the finest things he has ever done. It was a real social charter and was very well received by those who heard it.

Wednesday, January 9, 1935

The Glavis-Burlew incident has quieted down but I still feel uneasy over the general situation.

In his message to Congress, the President had a short paragraph preceding his general discussion of public works in which he announced the policy of a co-ordinated control, as I understood it, of public works and Federal relief. This has bothered me a good deal and I have been speculating about it without having any known facts to go on. The President has intimated no such thing in any of his conferences on public works and I am at a loss to understand what he has in mind.

My first fear was that he proposes to set up a small commission with Admiral Peoples, Director of Procurement, in charge, with me handling public works under him, and Hopkins handling relief and rural housing. The very thought of this made me uneasy. Then my mind began to revolve around the idea of Richberg being made co-ordinator of our public works program, including Hopkins. The thought really upset me. It is clear to me that if the President asks me to go ahead with any part of the public works program under either Richberg or Peoples, I will have to decline. I could not work under either one of them, or even on a parity with them. I have no respect at all for Richberg's organizing ability. He would be swimming in waters that for him were unplumbed. Hopkins and

I would do the work and he would get the credit. He is good at that sort of thing. As for Peoples, he is a dull, old ex-admiral, who went from civilian life into the Navy and out again via the Paymaster's Office. He has neither imagination nor force of character.

The more I thought of it, the less inclined I was to adjust my mind to the idea of being made secondary to anyone in public works. For the President to ask this of me would be to indicate a lack of confidence in me. He would, in effect, be saying to the country that I had not made good as Public Works Administrator. He has never intimated this to me; on the contrary, I have always had every reason to believe that he has felt that I was doing a good job. I have already set down in these memoranda what he said at a Cabinet meeting about ten days ago, when he spoke in high terms of what I had done as Public Works Administrator.

Harry Hopkins has been laid up at home with a touch of the flu that is so widespread in Washington and I drove out to see him Monday afternoon, after calling him up and making an appointment. I find that he does not know what is in the President's mind, but he feels as I do both about Peoples and about Richberg. He said he wouldn't work under either, and if he and I will only stick together on this, I feel confident that no attempt will be made to force us to work under either.

I went into matters very fully with Hopkins. I told him that what I would like to see was the establishment of a new department with himself heading it as Secretary. Into this department ought to be assembled all of the social service activities of the Government. Interior would contribute the Office of Education, Howard University, St. Elizabeths Hospital, Freedmen's Hospital, and Subsistence Homesteads. The new department would also, as I see it, have transferred to it the Children's Bureau and the Women's Bureau, from Labor, and the Public Health Service, from the Treasury. It would have charge of Federal relief and of all of the social insurance activities that are now being mooted. With Hopkins in charge of such a department, he could also administer the subsistence homestead program. As an alternative, I suggested that he be made Deputy Administrator of Public Works with a definite assignment of duties, that assignment to include subsistence homesteads and the supplying of labor for the public works projects from the relief rolls. It seemed clear to me that Hopkins took very much to the first suggestion and I think he would not be averse to the second one.

I have not been able to see the President for about ten days, first, because he has been working on his message to Congress, following which he was laid up with a cold. Naturally I am most anxious to see him. What is running in my mind is that if I am not to be permitted to go ahead with any part of the new public works program except under a cloud, I will decline to do it, although I will be willing to go ahead and concentrate on the Department of the Interior if that be the wish of the President.

Some months ago there was assigned as project manager to the Reedsville Subsistence Homestead project a man on the staff of Howard A. Gray by the name of O. B. Smart. Mrs. Roosevelt took a great dislike to him and she practically insisted not only that we recall him but that we discharge him from Government service. She told me frankly at an interview we had some time ago that he shouldn't be in Government service anywhere. I haven't wanted to fire Smart because Gray is thoroughly satisfied with him and because it seemed to me highly unfair and unjust. However, when the Burlew-Glavis controversy began to rage around my head, I came to the conclusion that perhaps after all we had better let Smart go. I thought that even if it was a sacrifice that would go distinctly against my grain, it might be a justifiable sacrifice in that it would save more important people to my organization. Then I devised a plan. I told Gray on Saturday to send for Smart and ask for his resignation. I figured that Smart would be clever enough to know what was the occasion for this demand, and if necessary Gray could stimulate his imagination on the subject. Gray did this on Monday. I don't know how much he played his hand but I do know that Smart made an appointment with Mrs. Roosevelt to see her Tuesday at eleven o'clock. This was what I wanted. I felt that if Smart would throw himself on the mercy of the court, so to speak, I would not be under the unwelcome necessity of having to let him go. I did not believe that Mrs. Roosevelt would want to take the responsibility for having a man turned out of a job that he was doing to the satisfaction of his immediate superiors in times such as these.

Apparently the plan worked perfectly. Smart told Mrs. Roosevelt when he saw her that his resignation had been asked for and that he knew it wasn't because his work was not satisfactory. His conclusion was that it was because he was displeasing to her and that her displeasure related to his services at Reedsville. He showed her carbons of two letters tending to prove that the delay at Reedsville was not due to him as project manager but due to the architects for that project who had been selected by Mrs. Roosevelt herself. It was reported back to me that Mrs. Roosevelt told Smart it was silly of me to dismiss him and that she would talk to me. I haven't yet heard from her, although she was coming over to see me this afternoon, an engagement that she broke later through her secretary on account of a cold. I have heard since, however, that she still has some resentment against Smart and I don't know just how it is going to work out.

I am being subjected to very heavy fire by every newspaper in New York, so far as I know, except one. The occasion of these attacks grew out of my effort to terminate the services of Robert Moses, who was appointed by Mayor La Guardia as a member of the Triborough Bridge Authority. I have done this at the President's specific request. I don't know Moses. From all accounts he is a highly disagreeable and unpleasant person, who is also tremendously efficient. He has done great things for Greater New York and for the state in developing a wonderful park system. He has served as both county and state park commissioner without pay, and last fall he was the Republican candidate for governor against the incumbent, Governor Lehman.

I have been after Mayor La Guardia for some time on this matter. I started in several months ago. He would make promises and then he would break his promises. He did this both to me and to the President. Finally, I began to lose my patience and, with the President's consent, I served notice that I would honor no more requisitions for funds for PWA projects in New York until the Moses case had been disposed of. I suggested to Mayor La Guardia that I would be satisfied to go along if he would write me a letter that upon the expiration of Moses' term the latter part of June he would not reappoint him. Instead of doing that, La Guardia wrote me that he would reappoint him, after leading me to believe that he had agreed to my suggestion. Then I drafted what I called a general order but which in effect was aimed specifically and solely at La Guardia. This order announced that as Public Works Administrator I would honor no more requisitions for a project where the supervising authority also held a state or local office. The President helped me draft this order and he discussed it personally with La Guardia so that La Guardia knows that it is the President who is interested in Moses' removal. I advised him that if he would write me a letter that he would not reappoint Moses, I would be satisfied with that and it would not be necessary to force Moses out at this time. He said he would write such a letter. I asked him to mail it to me. This was over the long-distance telephone some time ago. He said he was coming to Washington and he would bring it to me. He came in last Saturday and I again asked him for the letter. He said he would write it when he got back to New York and mail it to me. It has not come, nor will it.

Meanwhile the New York papers began to roar in their wrath and I don't much blame them. They have a legitimate cause, and I am left holding the bag. But La Guardia has followed a crooked course in the whole proceeding. He let Moses see the letter that I had written him, in which was incorporated my order. Moses gave out this order to the newspapers, together with a long statement. La Guardia tried to deny to me that the story had leaked in New York, but I told him that I knew it had and finally he admitted that Moses had seen the order. I called La Guardia on the telephone on Monday and before I got through with him I told him very clearly and distinctly just how accomplished a double-crosser he in fact is. He equivocated and evaded, but I know that I had him dead to rights. This was a great disappointment to me. I had felt that La Guardia was a man of real courage and substance, but in this matter he has acted like the cheapest kind of a double-crossing politician. Meanwhile the storm continues to rage. At my press conference on Thursday I was asked whether Farley had ever spoken to me about Moses. To that question I could honestly say No. Then I was asked whether the President had ever done so. There I had to lie, but again I said No. I never had any interest in this enterprise. I think it is a great mistake on the President's part. Moses' defeat for governor eliminated him completely as a political figure of any prominence in New York State. By making a martyr of him we are only serving to build him up. But I have to take it on the chin and act as if I liked it.

Morris L. Ernst, a fine young liberal lawyer from New York, came in to see me today very much worried over the situation and its effect on my reputation. He justly pointed out the fact that my action in the Moses case is at utter variance with any other act of mine. He says I am being bitterly criticized by all the liberals of New York. He told me frankly that everyone realized that I was acting for the President but apparently that isn't saving my face or helping my reputation. He suggested a formula by which the Administration could retreat from what really seems to be an indefensible position with some show of grace, but I can't make a move without consultation with the President.

Friday, January 11, 1935

I finally succeeded in getting an appointment with the President yesterday at half past two, and I was with him for better than half an hour. He seemed to have recovered entirely from his recent cold and he remarked as I sat down by his desk that he had recovered his sense of humor. He seemed entirely friendly and cordial.

The first subject I took up with him was the Robert Moses matter in New York. He knew that the newspapers up there have been raising all kinds of hell with me and he remarked that I was the whipping post. I told him that I didn't mind that, but that I did want to know whether he wanted me to go through along the lines of the order that I have issued, which has been the occasion for all the turmoil. He told me very firmly that he did want me to go through. I said that I did not mind the hammering, that I was able to take it on the chin, but that a good many people believed the order originated with him and not with me. I told him that I had been asked point blank at my last press conference whether he had ever discussed the matter with me and that I had said No. He replied that at any time I could give it out that he was responsible for the order. This, of course, I do not intend to do, but it is only inevitable that the thing will leak out. As a matter of fact, in the "Merry-Go-Round" column this morning it was stated definitely that the order had emanated from the President.

The plan is for me to honor requisitions for other Federal projects in New York, but to advance no new money for the Triborough Bridge. There is still enough up there in the general fund to pay the labor for a few weeks and transfers will be made to do that. But I shall approve no new requisitions unless instructed to do so by the President or unless the Moses matter is settled to the President's satisfaction.

I asked the President whether he had any idea where Lindley

of the *Herald Tribune* found out that I had written to him (the President) about Burlew and Glavis. He said he didn't know. He said my letter had been brought in to him by "Missy," meaning Miss Le Hand, who, of course, had not read it, and that it was in his own correspondence basket. I told him that I felt confident that there had been no leak in my Department. I am still sure that that particular part of the leak came through the White House.

The President brought up the question of Glavis. He said he had asked Jim Farley whether he was responsible for any of the criticisms of Glavis and had told him that if he was, he might just as well forget it. As he expressed it to me, he said to Farley: "If, in the course of his investigation, Glavis runs across your brother or my son, that will be just too bad, but it will be in the line of his duty." The President remarked a little later that, of course, Glavis ought not to go on the proposition that everyone he investigated was guilty, and I told him that I was trying to hold Glavis down as much as possible because I realized that he was somewhat of a man-eater.

As an illustration of how stories start and spread, the President told me that the other evening at the White House he had himself heard Henry Morgenthau asking "The Mrs.," as he generally refers to Mrs. Roosevelt, whether she had heard the latest story about the Department of the Interior. Upon being answered in the negative, Morgenthau proceeded to tell Mrs. Roosevelt that when a girl employee went to the toilet in this building, there was always a man on guard with a watch in his hand and when she had been in the toilet for five minutes, he would knock on the door and call "Time's up." The President said he told Morgenthau that that was undoubtedly a funny story, but that he ought not to tell things like that since it created a bad impression and was a story such as would be carried. I remarked that probably that story would, in course of time, get all over the country and would be believed by a good many people.

As I was leaving, I told the President again that he need have no question in his own mind about Burlew's loyalty and he said very sincerely that he knew that that was right. He said, "It's just as you put it in your letter to me. If he weren't all right and weren't loyal, he would be running the risk of losing his job." The President then suggested that some time after this whole thing had blown over, and when it would excite no comment on the part of the newspaper correspondents, I should bring Glavis and Burlew over to see him on the pretense of having some business to discuss. I was entirely and thoroughly satisfied with the President's attitude.

Mrs. Roosevelt found out I was with the President and sent word that she would like me to come over to see her, so I went over to the White House. She seemed to be very friendly. She wanted to talk about the Smart matter. She told me about Smart's having called upon her. She assured me that she did not want Smart fired and that she never had suggested that he be fired. In this she is clearly mistaken because she told me on at least two occasions late last summer that Smart should not be kept in the Federal service in any capacity. However, I let her down easy. She told me that she had felt that Smart should have been disciplined by a reduction in grade. She said to me that she had gathered from Smart that there was a feeling in the Department that she had given out the Burlew-Glavis stories. I told her I didn't think that at all and I didn't think there was any such feeling. She assured me that such was not the case. What I do think is that the story was based on the indiscreet statements that Mrs. Roosevelt had been making. When I found out that she was criticizing these men so strongly, I felt that it would be only a question of time before the newspapers would get hold of it.

After my interview with Mrs. Roosevelt I hurried back to my office and my press conference which was then an hour overdue. After the press conference, I called in Glavis and Burlew to tell them what the President had said. They were, of course, very much pleased, as I am, because I think this particular incident now is a closed one.

Then I went back to the White House to see Louis Howe, with whom I have wanted to have a talk for some time. He stays in his room most of the time. He looks very frail to me. Instead of sitting in a chair, he stays on his bed on his knees, bending forward. He talks and dictates in that position. I should think the mere physical strain of such an unnatural position would of itself be more than he could stand up against.

Louis told me that if I had any idea that he had had anything to do with the criticisms of my Department, I should forget it. He assured me that if he ever had any criticism, he would give it to me himself. I believe this is true and I never did think Howe had been responsible for the Burlew-Glavis story.

Then we talked about the Democratic setup in some of the Western states and about Jim Farley. On the subject of Chicago, Louis told me that as soon as I had talked to him about it, he had gone to the President and they had sent for Farley. Farley had asked them to keep hands off until he had had a chance to talk with me. This they said they would do, and he was to report back as soon as he had talked with me. That was over a week ago. I told Louis that I hadn't heard a word from Farley about Chicago. He then called up Farley and asked him what the result was of his talk with me. After a little sparring, Jim told him over the telephone that he had talked with me about Chicago but that he had not been able to change my point of view. This was a definite and distinct lie because the subject of the Chicago mayoralty situation has never been mentioned between Farley and me. This incident satisfied me that Farley has been double-crossing the President on the Chicago situation. There is no doubt in my own mind that he is for Kelly and that instead of trying to get Kelly out of the race, he has encouraged him to stay in.

Louis Howe is not at all satisfied with some of the political moves that have been made by Farley in the West.

Then Louis got to talking about Burlew, but really not in an unfriendly manner. He spoke of the tendency here in Washington for competent, efficient people like Burlew to become dominant in a department merely because they last on from one administration to another. I told him that I was perfectly aware of this tendency and that I tried to guard myself against it in every way possible.

Then he went on to discuss the Subsistence Homesteads Division and it was clear that he felt that Burlew was responsible for our lack of success in that division. I told him that this was the one part of my administration that I felt apologetic for, and that I realized it had not been a success. I know why it has not been and I explained those reasons to Louis Howe. He agreed with me, at least in the most part. But I made it clear that Burlew had never had any administrative responsibility for Subsistence Homesteads, that Wilson, who had made a mess of it to start with, had been succeeded by Pynchon, and that immediately over Pynchon was

Chapman. Louis was gracious enough to say that evidently he had been mistaken and I think I met successfully the general criticism that he had of Burlew.

I went to a stag dinner last night at the home of the Danish Minister. The Danish Embassy is the house that formerly was occupied by Vice President Dawes. There were twenty at table, the food was good, the wine was good, and the atmosphere was cordial and pleasant. Mr. Justice Stone and Mr. Justice Roberts, of the Supreme Court, were there. I like both of these men very much. They are friendly and human, and, especially with Mr. Justice Roberts, there was a little joshing back and forth about the decision in the oil case. He assured me that he is entirely sympathetic with what we are trying to do in the oil matter and that he hoped we would pass a statute that would enable us to carry out our policy. The reason for the dinner was because we are negotiating now to buy out the Danish Bank that has continued to operate in the Virgin Islands since it came into our possession. From Copenhagen has come what is known as a Supreme Court lawyer and from the Virgin Islands has come the managing director of the Danish Bank. Both were at the dinner.

At Cabinet meeting this afternoon the Attorney General, who had just finished arguing the gold cases before the Supreme Court, gave us a report on the matter, which was very interesting. He thinks that the Government will probably win by a divided opinion. It looks as if the decision might lie in the hands of Justice Roberts and Stone. The Administration is very much interested in this case because if it is decided against the Government, we may have economic chaos and heavens knows what might happen. The Attorney General said that if the Court should decide against the Government in the gold certificate and Liberty Bond cases, the situation could be saved by Congress hurrying through a statute taking away from the citizens the right to sue the Government for the damages that they might claim by reason of having accepted payment in currency on bonds that, by their terms, were stated to be payable in gold. A dollar's worth of gold is now worth $1.69. A good many Government securities, payable in gold, have been paid, and an adverse decision from the Supreme Court would result in every one of those former bondholders coming in and claiming from the Government an extra sixty-nine cents on the dollar. A number of railroad bonds are involved also. If the decision goes against the Government, a number of big railroads of the country will be thrown into bankruptcy without more ado.

The Attorney General went so far as to say that if the Court went against the Government, the number of justices should be increased at once so as to give a favorable majority. As a matter of fact, the President suggested this possibility to me during our interview on Thursday, and I told him that that is precisely what ought to be done. It wouldn't be the first time that the Supreme Court had been increased in size to meet a temporary emergency and it certainly would be justified in this case. I told the President yesterday that only a few years ago I had predicted that sooner or later the Supreme Court would become a political issue as the result of its continued blocking of the popular will through declaring acts of Congress unconstitutional. During the discussion today the Vice President said that he had read a pamphlet which had been written about a hundred years ago in which the author advanced the theory that sooner or later, through the aggrandizement of power by the Supreme Court, a political crisis of major magnitude would be precipitated in this country.

[In his inaugural address of March 4, 1933, President Roosevelt had challenged the nation to meet and solve the depression in accordance with the terms of the Constitution which, he said, "is so simple and practical that it is possible always to meet extraordinary needs by changes in emphasis and arrangement without loss of essential form." He warned the nation at the same time, however, that the "unprecedented demand and need for undelayed action may call for temporary departure from that normal balance of public procedure."

[By 1936, the Supreme Court had declared unconstitutional nine major New Deal measures. President Roosevelt had not had a single chance to make a new appointment to the court. The decision to press for new legislation on the Supreme Court was not a campaign issue in 1936, but by February 5, 1937, President Roosevelt was ready with his plan for a reform of the judiciary, centering on the Supreme Court, which was finally defeated in the Senate on July 22, 1937.—ED.]

Sunday, January 20, 1935

Last Tuesday I had a talk with Jim Farley. Frank Walker had suggested that Farley and I talk matters over since it was apparent to him that Farley was holding something against me. We tried to get together on two or three occasions but didn't succeed until Tuesday. We had quite a frank discussion. He had taken exception to the manner in which Finch was appointed Director of the Bureau of Mines, although I cannot see that that was not handled properly. I spoke to the President about Finch and then one day at Cabinet meeting I told Farley that I had discussed Finch with the President and that the President was agreeable to the appointment. However, just before the nomination was to go to the Senate, Farley put in a stop order on it. The newspapers learned of it and were critical of Farley. The whole matter was held up until the President came back from his trip to Hawaii, when he went through with the appointment, and then the newspapers wrote the incident up as a victory for me over Farley. Naturally, this didn't set very well with him.

We talked over appointment matters and politics. There is no real disagreement between us but we don't see eye to eye. The Chicago mayoralty situation came up, as to which I am firmly convinced he put a fast one over on the President. I believe that Kelly could have been pulled out of the race without any difficulty at all and the President wanted this done. Farley pretended to be going along with the President but he was not in fact, as I am thoroughly persuaded. I told Farley that the Chicago Democratic crowd was the rottenest crowd in any section of the United States today and that the danger was that there would be a blowup there before 1936 that would damage the Administration considerably.

I am having difficulty these days in seeing the President enough to keep current with departmental business. I had lunch with him on Friday. We covered a good deal of ground but I wasn't able to take up with him half the things that I needed to discuss with him. His daughter, Anna Dall, was married to John Boettiger, formerly of the *Tribune,* Friday morning in New York and the President referred to it. I am frank to say that I think he had some reservations about the marriage, but it has been rumored for some time and appeared to be one of those inevitable affairs. I have always liked Mrs. Dall. She seems like a very fine person.

The President's attitude during this interview with me seemed to be all that anyone could ask for, but developments since Friday indicate to me that his purpose is to go along with the new public works program without consulting me and with a new setup. It is significant that the new public works bill has been drafted without either myself or anyone on my staff being consulted. Jerome Frank, chief counsel of AAA, and Harry Hopkins seem to have been charged with responsibility for it. The newspapers this morning indicate that Hopkins is to be in charge of the new program. It appears that he was with the President for four hours yesterday and while they were together, others went in and out, including Richberg, Moffett, and Langdon Post, chairman of the New York Housing Authority.

Of course, the President is well within his rights in setting up his Administration to suit himself. I would be the last one to dispute that right. I am not only reconciled to the possibility of losing Public Works, aside from the pangs a man naturally suffers at the severance of a well-established connection, but from my own point of view I would welcome it. I believe whoever administers the new program is going to have a terrific and difficult job. There will be, naturally, conflicts with labor over wages; there will be interminable fights with politicians in all parts of the country; I think it will be practically impossible to restrict the labor to be employed on the new works to those now on relief rolls; I am persuaded that the chances of corruption and graft will increase with the continuance of the public works program and with the magnitude of it; I have grave doubts of the success of the new program in any such degree as Hopkins predicts and as the President doubtless hopes for. I am perfectly satisfied with the record I have made as Public Works Administrator and someone else can have the job so far as I am concerned, but I don't like being eased out. I don't like to get my information through rumor or from the newspapers. I think I am at least entitled to being called in and told frankly by the President what he wants to do with respect to Public Works and why he wants someone other than myself to administer it, if that is in his mind, as appears to me to be the case.

I hear all sorts of rumors from the Hill. Burlew brought word in the other day that a member of the Appropriations Committee, Congressman Scrugham, had told him that a majority of that committee, including Chairman Buchanan, wanted to write in the bill that I was to administer the new PWA fund. He said that the sentiment was distinctly against Hopkins. On the other hand, Jim Farley assured me that I am very unpopular on the Hill. There are rumors, too, that Senator Borah is going to insist on an investigation of Hopkins' administration of relief. If there is a *bona fide* investigation, some unpleasant facts will be brought to light, in my judgment. I don't blame Hopkins for certain situations that developed in connection with the relief program, especially the CWA phase of it, because he was called upon to do an impossible job without time to organize the plan for that job. Necessarily there were waste and graft and corruption which no man could have prevented under the circumstances. On the other hand, it is only fair to say that the type of administration to be expected from Hopkins and his associates, especially the latter, is of the sketchy kind.

I discussed with the President on Friday the desire of Burlew and Glavis to file libel suits as a result of the stories that appeared to the effect that he or someone in the White House had indicated to me that these men should be discharged from the service. He didn't express a definite opinion on the matter. Later, at Cabinet meeting, Miss Perkins, I think it was, brought up the question of attacks that are being made upon members of the Administration from time to time in various newspapers. It is evident that a number of members of the Administration, including several members of the Cabinet, are beginning to be restive under libelous statements that are made about them in various newspapers at frequent intervals.

At our interview, the President referred again to the Moses incident in New York. He said that I was taking it on the chin. He said that in a situation of that kind, the thing to do was just to go along, say as little as possible, and let it work out. On this point he is entirely sound. He seems quite satisfied with the way I have handled it.

Saturday, January 26, 1935

Tuesday noon I was the guest of the Dutch Treat Club at the Hotel McAlpin in New York. I had been invited to speak before this club by William Chenery, the editor of *Collier's*. This club is limited to a membership of three hundred and is composed of high-up newspapermen, editors, publishers, etc. I spoke extemporaneously but I seemed to get away with it all right. With the burning Moses issue in mind, concerning which the New York newspapers still continue to expatiate at length, when I rose to my feet I remarked that the chairman had introduced me as Secretary of the Interior, whereas, to judge from the newspapers, I should have been introduced as Pharaoh's daughter. This remark brought down the house and got me off to a good start.

At four o'clock John D. Rockefeller, Jr., called on me by pre-arrangement. I had never met him before. He is shorter than I by about half a head and he seems quiet and friendly and intelligent. We had a good deal to talk about on the one topic that interests both of us, namely, national parks. He has been very generous to the national parks, more so than any other individual has ever been. I think his contributions to various parks so far total something like $12 or $15 million. He is interested in Indians, too. He told me that he had planned to ask me to lunch or dinner with him but that he understood I had speaking engagements for both occasions.

Julian Mason came in at half past six, I having asked him to have dinner with me, and said that he would like to take me over to the Brook, which he described as a club to which the richest men in New York belonged. He wanted some of the members to meet me. He said that he had been trying to persuade them that I was not a dangerous citizen and withal a pretty decent sort of fellow. I went with him and met six or eight of the members while we drank cocktails.

Julian and I rode back to the Roosevelt, where I ordered dinner to be served in my sitting room. While the dinner was being brought up I changed my clothes and packed. Immediately after dinner I went to the Pennsylvania Hotel, where I was scheduled to speak on conservation at ten o'clock before the American Game Conference. I had been asked for dinner but I declined that, preferring not to appear until just before the time for me to speak.

On Friday at Cabinet meeting I referred to an article by Paul Mallon that appeared in the *Washington Star* last Friday, which, in effect, charged Glavis with tapping Farley's telephone wires at my instance. I explained that Glavis had never tapped anyone's telephone wires and that he certainly would not have done so with my permission or knowledge. I said also that we have never investigated any member of the Administration, reports to the contrary notwithstanding, and that his activities were strictly confined to my own Department and the interests of my Department. I suggested that it was time to do something to put a stop to the libelous attacks that are becoming more and more frequent against members of the Administration. I said that people were not able to attack the President directly, with the result that they were attacking members of the Administration and trying to drive wedges in between us. Henry Morgenthau took occasion to remark that Glavis in his investigations went far beyond anything that investigators of the Treasury or, as he believed, of the Department of Justice, were accustomed to do. It seemed to me that Morgenthau deliberately took advantage of this situation to knock Glavis and, indirectly, myself. He was quite profound in his remarks and extremely serious. After he had concluded his open statement, he and Homer Cummings put their heads together as if in a common cause, and it was clear to me that they were discussing Glavis and this Department.

The President referred to the libel suits that Glavis and Burlew are anxious to file, and which are all ready to be filed. He said that Lindley, of the *Herald Tribune,* had heard about these suits and had come in to say to him that if suits were started against a number of newspapers and correspondents, they would all make common cause. He frankly intimated that they would make it as hot as possible, which was, in effect, serving notice that if these two men dared defend their reputations, these newspapers would go after them hammer and tongs, both directly and indirectly, even if it hurt the Administration. The President said he thought it would be better not to start any libel suits for a while, when perhaps more members of the Administration would have suits that they could file. He thought it would be more effective if a number of people sued at once. My own view is that he doesn't want these suits filed at all and that he is merely seeking to postpone them in the hope that the desire to start them will die.

On Thursday I announced my decision in the Elk Hills oil case involving damages for oil and gas already sold and for oil and gas still in the ground of an aggregate value of $25 million to $30 million. Mike Straus strongly urged that I advise with the President before giving this decision out, but my own judgment was just as strong the other way, and Burlew, Slattery, and Glavis agreed with me. I didn't want to run any risk of a leak, and it is difficult to say anything at the White House without the newspaper correspondents finding out about it. Moreover, I didn't want to run any risk of the President suggesting that I discuss the matter with the Attorney General or that I withhold my decision for a while longer. After all, the statute charges me with responsibility for passing upon the facts in a case of this sort and I couldn't make my views subservient to those of anyone else, even of the President himself. At Cabinet meeting I referred to the fact that I had announced this decision and the President said it was all to the good.

After the Cabinet meeting the Vice President came around his end of the table to me. He told me that I ought to suggest to some writer the following story: that there was a Secretary of the Interior who was found to be dishonest and who was forced out of the Cabinet; that then Secretary Fall came along and during his term was found to be dishonest and was forced out of the Cabinet; that now we had an honest Secretary of the Interior and some people were trying to force him out because he wasn't a good enough politician. He was, of course, referring to recent criticisms that I have above referred to. I noticed that the Vice President stopped at the President's chair and from a word or two that I overheard I believe he repeated what he had told me about the honest Secretary of the Interior.

Some of the newspapers lately have had perfectly fine editorials about me. The *Evening Star* has had two and this morning the *Washington Post* had one. I haven't checked up much on out-of-town newspapers lately but one came to my desk the other day from the *Cleveland Plain Dealer* that was very flattering.

I am still in utter ignorance as to what the new PWA setup is to be. On Wednesday afternoon I went over to see Louie Howe. I told him that if the President wanted someone else to administer PWA that would be all right with me, but that I didn't want to get up some morning and get my information from the newspapers. I told him that if there was to be a new setup I ought to know it in advance and it ought to be worked out in a way that wouldn't reflect on me. After all, I did not have that coming to me. Then I went on to say that I would be very much pleased indeed if the President would give me all the conservation activities and let someone else have public works; that my real interest was in conservation and I would like a chance to build up a strong conservation department and develop a strong public opinion for conservation. Louie told me that Harry Hopkins had been coming to see him to find out what his place in the new scheme was to be. He said he hadn't talked much with Hopkins but that he would talk more frankly with me. It seems that he has made a certain recommendation to the President, but whether the President will act on it or not, or whether he has made up his mind what he is going to do, Howe does not know.

It developed from my talk with Howe that apparently he is in favor of a different setup for public works. I would not be surprised if he wants Hopkins to administer public works, but he also is in favor of certain other activities being transferred to the Interior Department. He specifically named Forests, the Supervising Architect's Office, the Bureau of Public Roads, and the building activities that are now carried on by the Army engineers. I don't know whether he was speaking for himself or whether the President has been considering this realignment. If the President should send these activities here where they properly belong, and should add to them Fisheries and the Biological Survey, which logic would also make a part of the Interior Department, I would be quite happy and satisfied. As I was leaving, Louie Howe told me not to worry, that he believed everything would come out all right.

Mr. Delano and I had an appointment with the President today but it was just before lunch and we had only a few minutes with him. I didn't even get started to take up with him a number of things that are really pressing for attention. He told us that Senator Byrnes, of South Carolina, had come down from the Hill to say that the Republicans on the Appropriations Committee were insisting on summoning a number of us, including Mr. Delano and myself, for a hearing in connection with the Public Works Bill. He outlined to us the attitude that he thought we ought to adopt if we were summoned.

Mr. Delano came in to see me the other day. He, Merriam, and Mitchell had been having a meeting in New York over the week end and he and Merriam had an argument as to which one should come in to tell me that I oughtn't to work so hard. Mr. Delano told me that at the New York meeting he had told his associates that the proposed National Planning Board should be attached to the Interior Department instead of being made an independent agency. His colleagues agreed with him so far as I was concerned but remarked that they didn't know who the next Secretary of the Interior might be.

Mr. Delano then went on to talk about the new PWA program. He said that he had always scrupulously kept away from the President with his advice and that the President might not accept his advice on any point anyhow. He expressed himself as being willing to go to the President at any time on any matter in which I was personally interested. I told him what I had told Louie Howe and which I have already set forth herein in considerable detail. Mr. Delano said he didn't believe the President would ignore me in the new public works setup. And then he said that he had never discussed me with the President but once. About three months ago the President told him that he thought I was perhaps the strongest man in his Cabinet and Mr. Delano replied that he was sure I was. This expression on Mr. Delano's part meant a great deal to me. I have found him a fine man to work with down here and we have seen eye to eye on practically every matter. He has spoken several times of the fine support I have given his Planning Board, and it has pleased him that I have given this Board the public credit that I have for the work that it has done.

Senator McNary, of Oregon, the Republican leader of the Senate, told me a day or two ago that he couldn't believe the President would scrap the fine Public Works organization that I had built up.

Wednesday, January 30, 1935

Monday morning at nine-thirty I was at the railroad station where the first official electric train on the Pennsylvania Railroad was ready to make a trial run to Philadelphia and back. On New Year's Eve, 1933, I signed a contract allocating about $70 million to the Pennsylvania Railroad Company to finish its electrification from Washington to Wilmington, Delaware, to finish the Thirtieth Street Station in Philadelphia, to build some electric locomotives and other rolling stock, and to purchase a lot of rails. In one month the Pennsylvania Railroad was at work on this project and last Monday it was ready to operate its electric service all the way from Washington to New York. The ranking vice president of the railroad, who is in charge of operations, was aboard, and also Mr. County, the vice president in charge of finance, with whom I had negotiated the allocation and the contract. Other officials were there too and some representatives of PWA, including Frank Wright, who has been in charge of our railroad loans, and whom I have found to be most able and helpful.

I took the trip as far as Baltimore because I had other engagements that made it impossible for me to go all the way to Philadelphia. We hit a speed at one time of eighty-five miles an hour and on the return trip I am told the high speed was a hundred and two miles. It was a quick, easy, pleasant run. Mike Straus, who was with me, and I got off at Baltimore and came back on the private car of the division superintendent, who was coming to Washington from Baltimore. We got back to the office at twelve o'clock.

At two o'clock I had a meeting in my office, attended by the road commissioners of the States of Massachusetts, Connecticut, Vermont, and New York. I had written to the governors of these states inviting them to come or send representatives to consider a scenic highway from a point well within the northern part of Vermont, running down along the Green Mountains, then over the Berkshires, across the corner of Connecticut, west into New York, to the Bear Mountain country, crossing a bridge near West Point and connecting with an existing road. I told these state representatives that the Government would consider building such a highway, provided the states that it would cross would give us a right of way of one thousand feet, we to own the road, maintain it, and operate it under the Park Service. They were interested and thought their states would be equally interested.

Tuesday afternoon Mr. Delano and I had a long talk with the President. For the first time for quite a period I was able to discuss a number of matters with him. We were together for over an hour. We first took up several matters in which both Mr. Delano and I were interested, local District of Columbia matters, one of which was a proposal to purchase the Chesapeake and Ohio Canal from the Baltimore and Ohio Railroad. We also discussed enlarging the boundaries of the District of Columbia, and in connection with that proposal Mr. Delano made the unique suggestion that those residents of the District on the Maryland side of the Potomac River be permitted to vote as citizens of Maryland, while those on the other side vote as citizens of Virginia. The President thought this was a very good suggestion and said he would give it consideration. We also discussed an airport at Gravelly Point, a civic stadium, the building of the Apex Building, a memorial to Thomas Jefferson, and the building of the new Pan American Building in such a way as not to obstruct the view from the new Interior Building.

I told the President that I was not disposed any longer to sit quiet under the charges that have been printed all over the United States that I had tapped, or caused to be tapped, the wires of other Government officials, especially those of Jim Farley. I pointed out that this was criminal libel and that I especially object to being charged with a crime of such a sneaking and despicable sort as that of tapping wires. I told him I was no keyhole peeper. I pointed out that people came to believe stories, especially if no denials appeared, and that I thought the least I should be permitted to do was to deny this vigorously. He told me to send him a letter setting forth the facts which he would bring up himself at his own press conference. I don't think this will quite cover the matter, but it would help some to have the President vouch for my integrity of character in this matter. I have accordingly written him such a letter containing quotations from newspapers in New York, Philadelphia, Washington, and Missouri, showing a wide dissemination of this brutal libel.

The proposal to take the United States into the World Court was defeated last night by the Senate. Seven votes were lacking to confirm the treaty. I regard this as a decisive defeat of the Administration. I have been surprised all along that the President should make this such an issue as he has made it. I am confident that the sentiment of the country is overwhelmingly opposed to going into the League Court. Friday, before Cabinet meeting and before the President came into the Cabinet room, Vice President Garner said that if this proposition were put to a vote of the people, it would be defeated two to one. Jim Farley thought it was a political mistake to urge adherence to the World Court, and I think Roper was of the same opinion. Others did not express themselves on the subject.

[Rejecting a plea by President Roosevelt to "throw its weight into the scale in favor of peace," the Senate had refused to join the permanent Court of International Justice at The Hague (popularly known as the World Court). The opposition was led by Senator Huey P. Long, of Louisiana. The vote of 52 to 35 failed by seven votes to achieve the two-thirds majority required to ratify a treaty. American adherence to the World Court had been pledged on repeated occasions by both Democrats and Republicans, and press opinion favored the court by three to one, but the opposition was strong in the Hearst newspapers, the radio speeches of Father Charles E. Coughlin, and the deep-rooted isolationism of the "irreconcilable" Republicans of the Middle West.–ED.]

When the matter was discussed at Cabinet, it seemed to be the general consensus that the proposal might win by one or two votes, although the contest was regarded as being exceedingly close. The lack of seven votes was a great surprise. I regard this as a particular victory for Senator Johnson, although Senator Borah also has been an outspoken opponent of adherence to the World Court from the beginning. But it was Johnson who made the real fight. I called him up by telephone last night to congratulate him and he was as happy as a boy. Mrs. Roosevelt went on the air the other night in behalf of the Court, and Father Coughlin, of Detroit, was on the air the same night strenuously opposing it. Telegrams have been pouring in on the Senators from all parts of the country. Hiram Johnson told me last night that some Senators had been receiving as high as seventy to eighty telegrams a day, and that a great many of them were bitter in their criticism of Mrs. Roosevelt for mixing up in this fight. It does seem to me that she is not doing the President any good. She is becoming altogether too active in public affairs and I think that she is harmful rather than helpful. After all, the people did not elect her President, and I don't think the country likes the thought of the wife of the President engaging prominently in public affairs to the extent that she does. The President is such an able politician himself that I cannot understand how he allowed himself to become entangled as deeply as he was in this issue. He might have let the Senate pass on it without showing his own hand. In my own judgment he would have lost politically in the country even if he had won this fight in the Senate.

Saturday, February 2, 1935

On Friday at eleven o'clock I appeared before the Appropriations Committee of the Senate at a hearing on the $4 billion Work Relief Bill that is pending before that body. Senator Carter Glass is chairman of the committee. There was quite a big attendance, some fifteen or sixteen senators, I should say. Senator Glass opened the proceedings by remarking that a number of people seemed to be of the opinion that I ought not to administer this new fund but that he felt that I should. During the proceedings, Senator Hale, of Maine, asked me several questions to develop whether or not I was offered or accepted political advice in administering the PWA. I told him that I had received political advice but that I didn't follow it. Senator Townsend, of Delaware, a Republican like Senator Hale, remarked that I didn't play politics, and Senator Glass interjected that it was not only my theory but it was my practice to keep free from political influence. The last question asked was one by Senator Glass, who asked me whether, in my modesty, I would object to the Senate writing in the bill that the fund was to be administered by me. To this I replied that that would flatter me but that I preferred to have the bill passed in the shape in which the President wanted it.

I was before the committee for a full hour but the attitude throughout toward me was most friendly. This was true not only of the Democrats but of the Republicans. In fact, I am not sure but that the Republicans' attitude was more cordial than that of the Democrats. I have never had a more favorable hearing, and I left with the feeling that I stood very well indeed with the committee. I had taken with me Burlew, Schnepfe, Chambers, and Mike Straus. Burlew and Straus were especially enthusiastic over my reception, and the showing I made. It was very encouraging to me to have had a session where such good feeling toward me was evident on all hands. Senator Byrnes, of South Carolina, the Administration's spokesman, came up to me afterward and remarked that I had no need for an attorney for the defense. Senator O'Mahoney called me up afterward by telephone to say that I had made a fine impression and that he had heard remarks to this effect from men whose names would surprise me. Altogether, I feel that my time before this committee was well spent.

So far as I am concerned, I am more than willing now that the Public Works Administration should be sent to someone else. I know it is going to be full of pitfalls as compared with the administration that I have been responsible for. If someone else gets it now other than myself, he will certainly have troubles ahead of him and he will be appointed Administrator despite the very widespread opinion throughout the country that I have been honest in my administration and on the whole careful and efficient. Of course, I don't want someone else to be appointed Administrator because I have a sneaking opinion that he will suffer by comparison at the hands of the critics. I want someone else appointed because I am really beginning to feel the weight of the burdens that I have been carrying. I don't know how much longer I could continue to carry such a load. My nerves are all shot and I am sleeping badly.

Moreover, there will be grave difficulties to overcome. Labor will be very much dissatisfied, and I look for all kinds of labor troubles if an attempt is made to pay the scale that is in contemplation, namely, $12.50 to $15 a week for skilled labor. Moreover, with such a big program it will be increasingly difficult to check corruption and graft. I am entirely willing to stand on the record I have already made without running the risk of spoiling that record, despite the best that I might be able to do. And over and above it all, I am really tired, worn out, and willing to go at a slower pace.

[In this month, strengthened by the increased Democratic vote in the November, 1934, Congressional elections, President Roosevelt announced to Congress a broader scheme of action on both relief and social security. He asked for, and obtained in April, an appropriation of $4,880,000,000, to be spent virtually at his own discretion, but it was clear that he intended to stop direct relief as quickly as possible, to concentrate on socially valuable projects, and to try to return to the states responsibility for relief of unemployables.

[As the program slowly evolved, it resulted in the liquidation of the FERA and its replacement by the WPA (Works Progress Administration), also under Hopkins. The PWA (Public Works Administration) continued, under Ickes, but it was no longer financed by independent appropriations.–ED.]

At Cabinet meeting on Friday I thought the President distinctly showed that the defeat of the World Court protocol had cut pretty deeply. At times there seemed to be a bitter tinge to his laughter and good humor and perhaps a little showing of willingness to hurt those who brought about his defeat. At one point he said that whenever he looked at me he thought of the newspapers. He remarked on the battering that I have been receiving lately and said that Hugh Johnson had been in to see him the other day and had referred to the fact that I was now the Presidential whipping post instead of himself.

There isn't any doubt that the pace I have been keeping up for a year and eleven months now is beginning to tell. Or perhaps it is the variety of the attacks that have been made upon me from so many directions during the last two or three weeks. At any rate, my nerves are in the worst shape I have ever known them to be in. Physically, I am all right, and yet I am so tired that I am utterly without energy. For several days now I have had a very severe nervous headache, without cessation. I am not sleeping well, I am irritable, and I tire more easily than I did even a short time ago.

I saw the President today. I reminded him that a year ago I had told him that Subsistence Homesteads was one administrative unit for which I felt apologetic. I told him that I was going along with it not knowing what he proposed to do with it in the end. He said that he had been talking with some English people lately and that their experience, both as to public works and subsistence homesteads, had been somewhat along the same line as ours. He felt that we were still in an experimental stage with respect to subsistence homesteads and he showed no disposition to criticize me for what I regard as a very bad administrative endeavor. He said that Hopkins was doing something in the way of subsistence homesteads and that Agriculture was doing a little. He said Hopkins did not want subsistence homesteads and that he had in mind to put them all together into a new independent unit. I asked him whether he wanted me to limp along with my division until he could bring this about and he said to do that.

The discussion of subsistence homesteads led him to say something about his proposed setup for public works. Apparently he has in mind to set up quite a large Works Board along the English plan. On that board he would have representatives of the Army Engineers, the Forest Service, the Park Service, the Indian Service, the Reclamation Service, and other various services having to do with construction. This board would have submitted to it all applications for projects and would allocate funds as between the classes of projects and the localities. He said that then there would be one man in charge of procurement (evidently having in mind Admiral Peoples), one man in charge of labor, and one man to keep track of the progress of the projects on a schedule basis. Over the whole setup he would be in charge. He said that in England the Prime Minister was Chairman of the Works Board.

I told him that it all sounded very well but that I didn't see how he could do that and do anything else. He said that, after all, it was his baby. I told him that I recognized that he was a great executive but I still didn't see how he could manage it.

Nor do I believe he can work it out along any such line. In the first place, his idea of a board is nothing new because we have been operating our public works under a board which, however, I have dominated. We, too, have checked on the progress of the projects but not as minutely as apparently he has it in mind to do. We have never attempted, through a procurement division, to do the buying for all the projects.

I believe his plan is unworkable. I don't believe that there can be a successful administration through a board, especially a large board such as he proposes. Here is the biggest program on record in the history of the world in peace times, and, in my judgment, the administration will break down or else it will find itself in the hands of one man, just as I took over the control of the Public Works Administration that he set up in 1933. It seems to me that the President is either fooling himself or has hit upon this device as a means of setting up an entirely new Public Works Administration without unduly jarring me.

I have in mind that last summer he told me that he was going to run NRA. Then he set up two NRA boards, one under Williams, as an administrative board, and the other as a policy board, under Richberg. On the latter with Richberg he named Miss Perkins, Hopkins, Williams, and myself. Yet this board has not even pretended to meet for months. The result is that the President isn't running NRA but Richberg is, and he isn't even calling meetings of his board. The same thing will happen with his public works setup. He will not be able to run it and in the end Peoples or someone like that will be found to be in charge.

Burlew estimates that I have been putting in on Public Works alone the equivalent of a full working day every day. That is probably true. Public works probably takes three-fourths of my time and my normal working hours are from eight to eight-fifteen in the morning until six-fifteen at night. Then I go home to dinner and come back to the office at eight o'clock, from which hour I work on through until about ten-fifteen or ten-thirty. It will be seen that if I put in three-fourths of my actual working hours on PWA, I am doing what Burlew says I am doing, namely, devoting to it at least a normal working day every day. And I work hard and fast. It is obvious that with all the President already has on his hands, he can't devote one normal office day every day to public works, and he can't administer it in any shorter time than that.

Since it is my belief that the new setup will not have the effect of making the President Administrator, but of disposing of me as Administrator, I propose to devise some method of retiring from public works while the retiring is good. Probably I can't make any move until he indicates what disposition he has in mind for me, but I shall move then, and I shall endeavor to move out. I think also that the President has in mind to keep the present PWA going, probably under my administration, to handle non-Federal projects. He as much as said this today. However, I prefer to get out altogether.

Sunday, February 10, 1935

The President's public works-relief bill is having hard sledding in the Senate. It is still before the Appropriations Committee, but there it has been amended by a vote of twelve to eight to provide for the payment of the prevailing rate of wages instead of the security wage of $50 a month that the President has in mind. Interestingly enough, the real fight on the bill is being led by a group of Democratic Senators, with Glass, of Virginia, and Adams, of Colorado, taking the lead. A motion in the committee to restrict the bill entirely to relief received a tie vote and lost only for that reason.

There is no doubt that the President is finding much greater opposition than he has had heretofore. I suspect that his defeat on the World Court treaty has stiffened the backbones of those who otherwise might reluctantly have gone along with his program. I still think that his strong advocacy of the World Court was a major political blunder.

It is clearer to my mind every day that I don't want to administer the public works program, but I am tremendously gratified at the feeling of confidence in me that prevails in many quarters. Editorials in papers from all parts of the country that have come to my desk recently comment favorably upon what I have done as

Public Works Administrator. Almost without exception they refer to my honesty and ability. The only criticism that appears is that I have been too slow and too meticulous. There have been a number of favorable cartoons also in various papers. It is noteworthy also that there is no public sentiment for anyone for Public Works Administrator, except such sentiment as there is for me.

The one thing that has hurt me in public estimation recently has been the Moses incident. I would not have supposed that the country outside of New York would be very much interested in this matter, but the newspapers have made it almost a national issue. They have cited it as an example of PWA being used for political purposes. I regret this incident very much. My action in the case was entirely out of keeping with my whole record and with my political philosophy. I asked the President the other day if he had noticed how the editorial comment was running and he said he had. The President, I know, would welcome a way out of this cul-de-sac, but no way offers itself. He has sent for Mayor La Guardia, who is coming to Washington next Tuesday, and if he can, he is going to get an assurance from La Guardia that he will not reappoint Moses as a member of the Triborough Bridge Commission when his term expires on June 30. If La Guardia will do this, the President will probably order me to retreat, but I don't see how that could be done now with any degree of grace.

I have continued to carry this load without wincing, and I hope the President appreciates what a load it has been. Without the Moses incident I would have ridden through the political storm that beset me so violently during those two or three weeks with high credit. Even as it is, I have weathered the storm. I think the President does appreciate the criticism I have uncomplainingly endured, and yet one never knows. At the Cabinet meeting again last Friday, he said that everyone had to have a whipping post and that I had been his since Hugh Johnson resigned.

At the first opportunity I shall tell the President that I would like to be relieved of any responsibility for the new works program. I can't very well do this unless he indicates that he wants me to have some part in that program, although I think he has in mind now that I am to run the non-Federal projects part of the program. I doubt very much whether there will be any non-Federal projects program to speak of unless the President greatly modifies the terms that he has in mind for such projects. But I want to get out of the whole thing because I can see very heavy breakers ahead. I have made my record on public works and I am content to stand on that record.

The new program is likely to make or break the President. This is not only my opinion but the opinion of some very keen political minds, some of them Democratic members of the United States Senate. I don't believe I want to carry that responsibility, especially since I have the feeling that the program will be very difficult indeed to put over to the satisfaction of the country. The more I think of Admiral Peoples as the possible responsible executive for the works program, the less am I convinced that he has the ability to carry it through successfully. I have no doubt that Peoples made an ideal Paymaster of the Navy, but I think that anything beyond that would find him way beyond his depth. He lacks force and aggressiveness, and I doubt very much whether he could withstand the criticism that would inevitably be his if he took this job over. Like a good many men of small caliber, he is smug and self-satisfied. He attended the meeting of the Public Works Board on Wednesday, the first time he has appeared for some time, and he looked like the cat that had swallowed the canary. I suspect that he thinks he made a very good showing before the House and Senate committees. As a matter of fact, Assistant Secretary Chapman brought back word to me to this effect yesterday. He had been talking with Josephine Roche, Assistant Secretary of the Treasury, and she told him that Peoples felt that he had made a great showing, while members of the Treasury staff were distinctly of the contrary opinion.

There is trouble in the Department of Agriculture. Chester Davis, Administrator of AAA, has forced out Jerome Frank and other liberals in that administration, and Henry Wallace supported him. Rex Tugwell, whose friend Jerome Frank is, went to Palm Beach last Saturday and these men were forced out Monday without Tugwell knowing anything about it. He hurried back to Washington, but the thing was done. He told Harry Hopkins he didn't know himself whether he was in or out and he went to see the President and apparently got some reassurance. I called Tugwell yesterday afternoon to tell him that if he wanted any shoulder to weep on, mine was a broad one. I didn't want to leave town without some word of encouragement to him. He told me that matters were not in very good shape but that all there was to do for the time being was to sit tight. I counseled him that this was sound policy indeed in most of the situations in life. He said he would talk with me when I got back to Washington.

Harry Hopkins is distinctly unhappy. There was a meeting in my office on Friday to consider what has been done under the sub-marginal land-purchase program and Harry stayed for a little while to talk with me. It was plain to see that he was way up in the air about his own future in the Administration. He feels as I do about Peoples and is also full of criticism of Don Richberg. He told me that he felt that Richberg had double-crossed Frances Perkins in not telling her in advance that it was proposed to extend the automobile code. At the Cabinet meeting Friday, a week ago, Miss Perkins said that she had not known that this code was to be extended until she saw it in the newspapers. From her point of view, this created a serious situation because of the labor factors involved. Harry Hopkins also indicated how much he was hurt at the President's reference in his message to Congress to the CWA program as having been one of raking leaves and mowing grass. I think that cut Hopkins very deeply indeed. He hasn't the slightest idea where, if at all, he is to fit into the new works program.

The result of the whole situation is that there is a feeling of distinct uneasiness in Washington. No one knows what the Senate is going to do with the works bill, although the Vice President said at the Cabinet meeting on Friday that it would go through substantially as the President wanted it. The Vice President admitted, however, that he was having lots of trouble, that he no sooner had put out a fire in one spot than another one broke out somewhere else. He said he had never had so much trouble since he had been in Congress. After all, this doesn't augur well for the Administration. Here is a Congress that is overwhelmingly Democratic in both branches, but which is showing, at least on the Senate side, distinct indications of getting out of hand.

Several days ago I told Glavis to try to find out just what was back of the recent bitter attack on me. He brought word to me the other day that one of his men, who was close to Senator Walsh, of Massachusetts, gathered from Senator Walsh's office that the opposition to me was largely based on fear of me. Some clever minds have evolved the theory that if I am continued in charge of the public works program and continue to administer it with success, I may be a formidable candidate for President next year on the Republican ticket. I could base my campaign on what I had done, leaving it to the Democrats to say what they would do. Of course, this is thoroughly absurd, but I can understand how this thought might occur to some anxious political minds in view of the lack of strong candidates in the Republican party for next year. I can conceive of no circumstances that would make me a candidate against the man in whose Cabinet I am serving. Neither can I conceive of any circumstances that would induce the Republican party to nominate me as its candidate. I may be unduly modest, but I just can't think of myself as a candidate on any ticket. I don't think I would be a popular candidate and I am older than a candidate for that office ought to be.

The Administration is somewhat jittery about the gold decision, the rendering of which is being constantly postponed. Chief Justice Hughes announced again yesterday that no decision would be handed down on Monday, the usual decision day. It looks like a tug of war on the gold case.

Sunday, February 17, 1935

On Thursday I found that the President had tried to get me by telephone and I at once called him back. It seemed that Senator Huey Long had introduced a resolution calling upon me to lay before the Senate any reports of any investigation that Glavis or anyone in the Department had made into the building materials activities of Jim Farley and his connection, if any, with the contract for the New York post office annex. The President wanted to know whether we had made such an investigation. I told him that we had looked into the circumstances surrounding the granting of the contract in question to James Stewart & Company. Senator Joe Robinson had been in touch with the President, and the President was trying to make up his mind whether the resolution ought to be defeated or permitted to go through. Unless there was something in our files seriously reflecting upon Farley, he thought it would be good tactics to let the resolution go through. I assured him that there was nothing in Glavis' report reflecting on Jim. I reiterated again what I have told him on former occasions, that we have never made an investigation of Farley, but I said I would talk to Glavis.

This I did and then I called up the President again. I told him in general what we had, and then I sent Glavis over to the White House with the complete file in the New York post office investigation. When Glavis came back he said the President seemed to be entirely satisfied with the state of the record. There was only one portion of the record which might reflect in any way on the Post Office Department, and that does not connect up directly with Farley. It appears that at a hearing on this post office question called some time ago by Morgenthau, it was brought out that a letter from the Post Office Department referring to the project had been written to the Treasury Department, Division of Procurement. This original letter was destroyed by Assistant Secretary Robert, of the Treasury, and the carbon copy was destroyed by the then Assistant Postmaster General Silliman Evans. The record that we have shows this destruction of official documents, and, of course, this highly improper act on the part of these two officials can give Long an occasion for quite a beating of the tom-toms. As a matter of fact, it is a criminal offense to destroy a public record.

On Thursday Long's resolution went through by unanimous vote. Morgenthau at once called me up to say he would like to see the file regarding this investigation. I told him that he could have free access to it if he wanted to send someone over. Later he sent Admiral Peoples, his Administrative Assistant, McReynolds, and two other men. I sent them down to Glavis, who already had instructions to let them look at anything he had bearing on this subject. A little later, Assistant Postmaster General Howes called me up, in the absence of Jim Farley in Florida, to say that he wanted to look at the file.

At Cabinet meeting Morgenthau came in mad and I could see that he was very angry, and apparently at me. This was evident from the way he glared at me from the time he took his seat. When the President asked him if he had any matter to bring up for discussion, he brought up a routine matter and then in a very angry tone, the while glaring at me, he proceeded to demand an explanation of me as to why there was a certain letter in the file from Glavis to one of his subordinates as late as last December ordering that it be ascertained why there were so many cancellations of bids and rebidding on this project. His tone and manner were quite belligerent.

I took exception both to his tone and to his implications. Looking him straight in the eye, I said that I took exception both to what he had just said and to the tone in which he had said it. But he was mad clear through. He went on to say that I had assured the Cabinet that I had never caused an investigation to be made of any of them. I then said that this was the fact and that I reaffirmed that fact. Meanwhile the President was trying to calm him down. The President had remarked that the letter that had caused so much disturbance with Morgenthau did not amount to anything, that it was only a letter from one subordinate to another. I said that I had never seen the letter.

Morgenthau remarked that I had said on previous occasions that Glavis worked directly under my orders and that his reports came to my desk. I said this was true, and that so far as this report is concerned, some time ago I considered that the matter had been washed up and thereafter paid no further attention to it. I said further to Morgenthau that, strange as it might appear to him, I do not read every letter written by every member of my staff, and that I had never seen the letter in question. He was still going on at a high rate when the President raised his voice in order to make himself heard and said angrily that he wanted co-operation between the members of the Cabinet, that he wanted the Treasury and the Post Office Departments to search their files and produce everything they had on this New York post office matter and voluntarily send it in so that the Senate might have everything before it.

The President succeeded in stopping Morgenthau, but he did not improve his disposition any. For the balance of the Cabinet meeting, which ran its full time, until four o'clock, he sat in his seat like a sulking child, glowering at me at intervals. I did not lose my temper, and the madder he got, the calmer I became. I met every glower of his with a calm look that made him lower his eyes. It was clear to me that he thought he could rely upon his personal relationship with the President to put me in a very embarrassing position, but the President plainly indicated that he had no patience with Morgenthau's attitude.

Friday night at ten o'clock, the President called me up. I was still at the office. He said that he hadn't had a chance to talk with me after the Cabinet meeting. He wanted to talk over the Morgenthau affair and he was plainly trying to apologize for Morgenthau. He deprecated Morgenthau's attitude at the Cabinet meeting and hoped I hadn't minded. I told him I hadn't at all. He said that what was bothering Morgenthau was that certain letter which Morgenthau thought indicated that Glavis was investigating him and his Department. I told the President that I had never seen that letter and that it appeared to be only a routine letter between Glavis and one of Morgenthau's own subordinates. I assured him again that I had never investigated Morgenthau or any other member of the Cabinet. He replied that Morgenthau seemed to think that I had, and I said that there was nothing to that at all. The President said that Morgenthau had written me a letter and asked whether I had received it. I thought he meant a personal letter and I told the President that I had not had a letter. As a matter of fact, I had received a curt, formal letter, asking me to come to a meeting in his office at ten-thirty Monday morning, to which Jim Farley is also being invited, at the instance of the President, to discuss this post office matter. Apparently Morgenthau tried to give the impression to the President that he had written me a personal letter out of a desire to smooth matters over between us. I told the President that Morgenthau was young and he agreed with me. It was very clear that the President thought that Morgenthau was the aggressor and had assumed an unwarranted attitude toward me.

We had gone through our files very thoroughly, and I do not see that there is anything in them that reflects in the slightest degree upon Jim Farley. Of course, we have never tried to investigate him. I do not mean to imply that we would have found anything wrong if we had investigated. As a matter of fact, I have a feeling that Jim is pretty scrupulous in his dealings with the Government. He did want Stewart to have this post office contract and there were some suspicious circumstances in connection with its repeated letting and the reletting. However, that was in the hands of Procurement. The file that we have reflects much more seriously upon Morgenthau than it does upon Farley. It appears that Morgenthau himself presided at the conference at which it was shown that these two official documents had been destroyed and yet he had done nothing about it. It is true also that Stewart & Company have been buying their building supplies for this building from the Materials General Builders Supply Corporation, of which Farley was president before he became a member of the Cabinet, and of which his brother-in-law is now president, while Jim himself holds stock control. However, there is nothing wrong, per se, in this, if Farley sells supplies at the going market price and if there is no grafting or bribery or overreaching in connection with the undestanding by which he furnishes the supplies. Farley has never in the slightest degree sought to influence my action as Public Works Administrator with respect to any project or any contract. His record here is absolutely clean and I think that he rather leans backward so far as his company is concerned when it comes to furnishing supplies on Government contracts.

Saturday morning Chapman, Dr. Gruening, and I had a session with the President. Chapman and Gruening had been down to Puerto Rico and the Virgin Islands and we wanted to discuss matters pertaining to these two dependencies. Both men feel more strongly than ever that Judge Wilson is a thoroughly bad actor in the Virgin Islands and both are convinced that he ought to be removed at as early a date as possible. I share this belief. Gruening made a strong plea for Pearson. He told the President that if he would remove Wilson, he would guarantee a highly satisfactory situation in the Virgin Islands at the end of six months. I told the President that if in his judgment he thought Pearson ought to be removed, that would be satisfactory to me but that Wilson certainly ought to be removed first. I believe that with Wilson out of the way, the situation could be worked out satisfactorily and perhaps the President, with peace in the Islands, would decide to let Pearson stay on. I think on the whole Pearson is doing a satisfactory job. His attitude toward the natives is sympathetic, and that is the kind of a man we want in the Virgin Islands.

Wednesday, February 20, 1935

Last Monday morning at ten o'clock, Henry Morgenthau, Jim Farley, and I went to the White House to see the President before he went to his office. I took Glavis along because I thought something might come up that would require information that he might have in his possession, but I left him downstairs and he was not called upon. We kept this meeting very secret. Mr. Muir, Chief Usher, sent my car around to the east entrance and Morgenthau and Farley dismissed theirs so that none was standing in the front of the White House where an alert correspondent might see them.

We discussed the situation with reference to the Huey Long resolution. Morgenthau's manner to me was entirely different from the bitter anger that he had displayed at the Cabinet meeting on Friday. He was inclined to be a bit obsequious and I disliked him more for that than for his ill-natured outburst on Friday. I told Jim Farley that there was nothing in our records that reflected on him in the slightest degree. There are one or two references, one in a memorandum from Dresser and another in a letter from Green, a special agent of Glavis' in New York, that Morgenthau thought reflected on Procurement. Both were capable of an explanation that was not so unfavorable to Procurement and I volunteered to have Dresser come from Chicago and Green from New York to sign statements. These statements I subsequently drafted on Tuesday and I had them signed after I submitted them to the President, and he said they were satisfactory.

But to return to the conference on Monday. The President said that Senator Robinson had advised him that we would be in plenty of time if the reports asked for in the Long resolution should go up next week. The President wanted us to be very careful to go into matters thoroughly and send the reports up in proper form. He did not seem to be unduly anxious about the result, although he realizes that Huey Long may be able to make a Roman holiday out of one or two statements in the report that I will send up. However, it is perfectly clear that Procurement was interested in James Stewart & Company getting the New York post office contract and that they obstructed our investigation all along the line.

Morgenthau referred to an investigation that Glavis' division had made of the court house in New York. He said that this was not a PWA project and that Glavis should not have been investigating it. I did not have the record fresh in my mind, but I agreed with him as a general principle and I said I did not know why we should be investigating any project not financed by PWA money. The President said that Glavis was a grand person, but he ought not to do any investigating outside of his own department. Later I found that I had suggested this investigation to Glavis because a letter had come in hinting that there was some scandal there. Investigation was hardly undertaken before it was abandoned because we realized it was not a PWA project. Later this project seemed to hook up with the post office contract as both were being built under contract with James Stewart & Company. When this was pointed out by Glavis to Admiral Peoples, the latter suggested that Public Works and Procurement co-operate in an investigation of the court house. We proceeded under this arrangement for some time until Glavis felt that the obstructive tactics pursued by Procurement made it inadvisable to go along any further with Procurement, whereupon we abandoned the investigation altogether. I laid these facts before the President in a memorandum from Glavis on Wednesday and he was entirely satisfied with the explanation.

On Tuesday I had an appointment with the President. I had a number of matters to take up with him and toward the end of the session I told him that it would make me very happy if all the conservation activities of the Government could be transferred to Interior and I be given an opportunity to work on a real conservation program. He said that would be all right, but it was hard in some instances to distinguish between conservation activities and agricultural activities. I didn't press the matter then, but I am going to bring it up again at an appropriate time. I still feel that I would like to devote my major effort to conservation during the remainder of my service with the Government.

Harry Slattery went to a stag dinner at Senator Shipstead's on Tuesday night. There were a number of members of Congress there, and he said that Senator Bone, of Washington, was especially bitter in his expressions about the President. Senator Bone said that he could not get in to see the President any more, whereas the President used to send for him to confer with him. He told Slattery that on one occasion he had gone to the White House to see the President and had waited an hour and a half without getting in. In the meantime, McIntyre strung him along. There is a good deal of feeling against McIntyre in certain quarters. Many believe that he is keeping important progressives away from the President, while he permits any kind of nondescript conservative to get the President's ear. Senator Bone said he would be "God-damned" if he would dangle his heels any more even in the office of the President. He is a high-tempered person and he feels things very deeply.

I suspect that there is a good deal to the feeling about McIntyre. I know that ever since I have come back from Warm Springs I have had difficulty in securing appointments with the President, whereas formerly I could get in to see him practically any day that I called up. Lately it takes me generally a week or ten days to get an appointment with the President and on one occasion it took me all of two weeks. Even then McIntyre generally puts me in at the twelve-thirty hour, which is the worst period of all. By twelve-thirty the President is way behind on his schedule and he has the lunch brought in on a tray at one o'clock. On two occasions I have sat in McIntyre's office until five or ten minutes before one and then have told him that there was no use of my going in to see the President for the short period that was left because I couldn't get anywhere in that time.

I went up to the Capitol Tuesday afternoon to talk with Pat Harrison. He had written to the President a letter on the Virgin Islands, containing some very bitter expressions about me, and following my usual custom, I thought I would have it out with him face to face. However, I didn't get anywhere and I came back with a very low opinion of Harrison. He doesn't fight things man-fashion. He was like an old, complaining woman and, also, like a woman, he keeps running around in circles and coming back to the point of departure. He could not be made to face the issue. On the contrary, he kept whining about his grievances. He pretends to think that he has had no consideration at all at the hands of this Department and little courtesy, when, after all, the only thing that is bothering him is my outspoken opposition to Judge Wilson of the Virgin Islands, who was recommended for that post by Senator Harrison.

I can usually sit down with a man, even if he feels pretty bitter about me, and arrive at some sort of an understanding, but I couldn't get anywhere with whiny Pat. The result was that on two or three occasions I told him pretty categorically what I thought about certain matters. Nor did I concede anything so far as Wilson is concerned. I told Harrison that nothing would please me better than a Senatorial investigation of the Virgin Islands. So, instead of coming to any kind of an understanding with him, we really quarreled for over an hour. On the question of the consideration shown him by this Department, I told him that he had over sixty jobs and if he had that many from the other departments, that would make a total of over six hundred, without counting appointments from the independent agencies and emergency organizations.

Anna, Julia, and I went to the White House reception Thursday night. The President and Mrs. Roosevelt were receiving some of the Departments, including my own, and so I felt that I had to go. When I went into the breakfast room where the Cabinet assembles to meet the President before these receptions are formally launched, I went up and shook hands with Morgenthau in a perfectly normal manner, not because I wanted to, but because it is necessary for Cabinet members to preserve the amenities in public. I left the reception shortly after ten o'clock.

Friday was Washington's Birthday but I was at the office all day, or rather I was at work all day. At ten o'clock I appeared before the special Senate committee that is investigating the munitions question. I was questioned for better than an hour on allocations to the Army and Navy out of public works funds. The committee was particularly interested in the $238 million set aside for the Navy by the Executive Order of the President the day that the Public Works Bill was signed. I confined my replies to statements of fact. When my opinion was asked in order, if possible, to reflect upon the President, I declined to answer. While I was still "witnessing," Senator Pittman sent a note to me asking me to stop in at his office after I was through. This I did.

I found Senator Pittman very much concerned over the political situation. He told me, as he had sent word to me several days previously, that the President was losing a good deal of ground. He said that the President is consulting only three Senators, Harrison, Robinson, and Byrnes and that new Senators haven't been able to get in to see him, with resultant loss of dignity and hard feelings. The McCarran amendment to the Public Works Bill providing for the payment of the prevailing rate of wage passed the Senate yesterday by one vote. Senator Pittman said that if the matter had been properly handled, the President would not have lost this fight in the Senate. When I got back to the office, the President called me to ask me to be at the White House at half past five with the draft of the report that I propose to send up in response to the Long resolution. I went to the White House at that hour, taking with me Foley, chief counsel of PWA. Present also were Morgenthau and Senators Robinson, Connally, O'Mahoney, Bailey, Byrnes, and McCarran. The President went rather carefully over the situation for the information of these Senators. Once again it was clear that, so far as Farley is concerned, there is nothing in the record for him to worry about, but it seems equally clear to me that Procurement may come in for some rough sledding. Morgenthau, who sat next to Foley, seemed quite unhappy, and he told Foley he wanted something put into the record to cure it as to a certain matter. He laid a document before the President but the President ignored it.

This afternoon Rex Tugwell came in to see me. He told me that he was definitely through in the Department of Agriculture. He criticized the recent dismissal and resignation of certain liberals in the AAA as a sellout. After the first of these dismissals Tugwell hurried back from Florida and promptly resigned to the President, but the President asked him to stay at least for the time being. Tugwell told him that he would be willing to come over here or take some other place where he could do some work for the Administration. The President asked him how he would get along with me, saying that some people found me difficult. Tugwell told him that he and I might have some real rows but that he would rather be over here than with Secretary Wallace, who was preparing, as he put it, to take a broad jump from a bowl of jelly. The President told him to talk things over with Henry Wallace. Tugwell did this. Wallace assured him of his continued esteem and said he wanted him to stay on in Agriculture but with the understanding that he would have nothing to do with AAA. Tugwell said that he was the superior officer of Chester Davis, Administrator of AAA, and he wouldn't stay on any such terms. There the matter rests for the time being. Tugwell seemed determined to get out of Agriculture and says that he would rather go back to Columbia but that he does not want to let the President down. I told him that I felt confident I was going to get the Under Secretaryship that I have asked for and that if I could get the conservation activities over here, I would still be willing to have Tugwell come here as Under Secretary.

Tugwell is of the opinion that this Administration has done all that it can be expected to do in the way of social advance. He thinks too that the President is slipping and that the big business interests have him stopped.

Monday, February 25, 1935

I have been wanting for a week or more to have a real talk with Steve Early and at noon today I went over to see him. Unless I am greatly mistaken, Early is an absolutely sincere, straightforward man. I have come to like him very much indeed. He seems to me always to play with his cards face up on the table. I wanted to tell him about what I have been hearing about the President losing his strength and to report to him the feeling that has come to me from the Senators and Congressmen about the inability of the new men to get in to see the President. I found that Steve already knew a good deal about the situation and that he agreed with me in general. I told Steve about my recent set-to with Morgenthau, about which he had heard nothing. I told him that my purpose was to preserve all the amenities with Morgenthau on public occasions,

but that as a private individual I was through with him. He said
that while it was not in order for him to say so, he agreed with me
fully. I think Steve is somewhat worried not only about the general
political situation but also about the attitude that is developing
on the Hill with respect to the President. I told him that on only
one or two occasions did I offer political advice to the President. As
a matter of fact, I don't feel like volunteering advice when I am in
doubt as to whether it will be welcome or not. As I told Steve, I
think I know something about broad political movements, and
even about politics as a practical art. I said to him that I was so
much concerned about the situation, involving, as it does, the possible future political welfare of the President, that I wanted to talk
with somebody who might get it over to the President. Steve assured me that he would do this and I hope he will.

Thursday, February 28, 1935

I spent some time writing a letter to Secretary Morgenthau sum-
ming up his unwarranted and unpardonable actions with respect to
myself, and telling him that while officially I wanted to preserve the
amenities that should exist between fellow Cabinet members, my
desire was that our relationship in the future should be strictly official. I called in Burlew, Slattery, Straus, and Glavis to consider the
policy of sending this letter. We had several long and argumenta-
tive sessions. Burlew and Glavis were in favor of it and the other two
were opposed. Harry Slattery, who has unusually sound judgment
in such matters, was very firm in his disapproval. I would not have
paid so much attention to Mike Straus because Mike is inclined
to give this kind of advice, but I did not feel like going so dia-
metrically counter to Harry Slattery. So in the end, with much
reluctance, I decided not to send the letter. My own judgment
is strongly in favor of it. I feel that there is a much better chance
of our getting along on a tolerable basis if I send the letter than
if I don't.

Last Saturday Dr. Gruening, Director of the Division of Islands
and Territories, came in to tell me how greatly disturbed he is over
the political situation and the apparent decline in the popularity
of the President. I asked him whether he knew Colonel House and
when he said he did, I suggested that he run up to see him on his
own authority. He went up to New York over the week end and
reported back to me on Tuesday. He had had a long talk with

House during which he learned that Secretaries Hull and Roper and Attorney General Cummings had all been to see him, and all expressed their concern over the present situation. The consensus of their opinion was that the Administration was drifting and was losing popular strength. I did not understand that these three men visited Colonel House at the same time, but they all did have the same point of view. Secretary Hull complained that he could not get in to see the President. Colonel House told Gruening that he thought the situation was not a healthy one. He thought he might do something about it if his health permitted his coming to Washington and staying here for a while, and he suggested to Gruening that some of us progressives here in Washington ought to get together and see if we cannot agree upon a program that we could put up to the President. Gruening told me he thought the whole thing was up to me. I replied that I did not feel like taking the lead, that my political advice had never been asked, and that I was loath to volunteer it where it might not be welcome. Gruening said that he had also seen Felix Frankfurter, who was coming to Washington and who said he would look me up.

Chapman came in to see me late Wednesday afternoon. He had been up to Atlantic City to make a speech before the National Education Association and he found a very strong current running against Roosevelt. He said that in his speech he had quoted Roosevelt on the Security Act and only that. After his speech three people went up to him to protest against any mention of the President. Chapman was very much worried. He said the tide was running strongly against the President, as he found it, and that unless the President did something to change the current during the next thirty days, he did not believe he could be re-elected next year. Mrs. Roosevelt had telephoned to Chapman at Atlantic City to have dinner with her informally at the White House Wednesday night. He told me afterward that what Mrs. Roosevelt wanted to talk to him about were reports that had come to her of a critical attitude toward the President.

Wednesday night Anna and I went to the Swiss Legation for dinner. Madame Peter, the wife of the Minister from Switzerland, is one of the most charming women in Washington. I have met her on several occasions and like her very much indeed. The Minister himself is a very nice man. Madame Peter told me last night at dinner that the Minister is a stamp collector and that he also collects books and paintings. The Morgenthaus were at the dinner also and butter would hardly melt in Morgenthau's mouth. I was courteous but not gushing. I am determined not to display any great enthusiasm for him because I cannot overlook his recent actions. The Swedish Minister and his wife were guests as were the Chinese Ambassador and Madame Sze.

I was called to the White House for a conference this afternoon at which were present, in addition to the President who had returned to Washington in the morning, Robert Fechner, Harry Hopkins, and Acting Director of the Budget Bell. The President had up for discussion the need of Harry Hopkins for more money. He wondered whether it would be well to permit Congress to pass a bill giving Hopkins the necessary relief money and another bill to provide for the continuance of Fechner's CCC camps. In the end the decision was to stand by the original bill appropriating $4,880,-000,000 for work relief. I must say that the President seemed to me to be distinctly dispirited. I have never seen him in quite such a state of mind. He looked tired and he seemed to lack fighting vigor or the buoyancy that has always characterized him. I came away not at all reassured as to his ability to fight his program through.

I stayed, after the others had left, to talk with the President about an Executive Order that I had already sent over to him to make it possible for us to carry on under the new hot oil bill that has just become a law. Cummings had suggested a proviso to this Executive Order which would reserve in the President the right to issue regulations giving effect to the order. I strongly protested that this merely meant that regulations would have to be submitted to the Attorney General and that would mean inevitable delay in the future as it had in the past. The President was inclined to agree with the Attorney General on the theory that in the end he would have to represent the Government in litigation growing out of the regulations. I told him that it had been very difficult in the past to co-operate with the Attorney General in oil matters. I pointed out that the Attorney General did not personally pass upon these matters, but referred them to some subordinate. I suggested that I had an exceedingly able legal staff that I would not trade man for man with members of the Attorney General's staff. As I pointed out, we have several lawyers who don't do anything except handle oil matters. They know more about the subject than anyone else in the Government. We take a matter over to the Attorney General's office and he passes it to some subordinate who doesn't know anything about oil and who has to be educated on the subject. I told the President that I had been criticized for certain failures which were not the failures of the Oil Administration but of the Attorney General's office, that I had taken all of this on the chin, and that the administration either ought to be here or with the Attorney General. I said that only one oil case had been lost and that had been lost by the Attorney General. I pointed out that while he had designated his best man, Judge Stephens, to the trial of that case, Stephens hadn't even gone to the precaution to have with him in court a member of the legal staff of the Oil Administration, who could very readily have answered some of the questions that Stephens fumbled, much to the embarrassment of the Government in the trial of the case. The President didn't think that matters would be delayed, as I insisted they would be, and he finally said that if I would send the regulations over to him by four o'clock, he would have them back to me by six. I got them to him shortly after four and it is now almost half past nine and they have not come back yet.

I didn't overlook the opportunity to remind the President that Pierson Hall, United States Attorney for the Southern District of California, over my protest, had indicted, many months ago, several oil men in California. These indictments had been kept hanging over their heads for months and then finally he had to go into court and move to dismiss them because there were no legal grounds to sustain them. I warned him that every minute counted and that unless we issued the regulations and set up our Federal Tender Board in East Texas, temporary injunctions granted in Texas by the state courts would probably be dissolved and hot oil would again begin to flow across the borders of that state.

Felix Frankfurter had had a conference with the President just before we went in. I am hoping that I may have a talk with him while he is in Washington.

Sunday, March 3, 1935

Last Friday morning, February 28, I was able to take up some departmental matters with the President. The Moses affair has broken out again rather virulently, although there has never been a complete letup in that counterattack since my Order No. 129 was issued. I discussed this with the President today because Mayor La

Guardia, at the President's instance, had boarded the President's train at Philadelphia on the recent trip to Cambridge and Hyde Park so that the President might discuss Moses again with La Guardia. The President had a draft of a letter from La Guardia, which he produced. This letter called attention to the fact that Langdon Post's term of office as chairman of the Municipal Housing Authority of New York had expired, and since Post occupied a city office, the same situation existed here as with respect to Moses. Al Smith issued a violent statement attacking me directly, and the Administration indirectly, on account of the Moses episode, and the President and I came to the conclusion that a retreat on our part was in order.

The President called in Miss Grace Tully and dictated a draft of a letter to La Guardia, in reply to La Guardia's proposed letter to me. I didn't think this was a particularly strong letter. The President said I might edit it and he handed me the rough draft later at Cabinet meeting.

The first hour of the Cabinet session was taken up with a discussion of the situation in the Senate with respect to the relief bill. The Vice President did most of the talking. It was clear that he didn't like the situation, and he was somewhat critical of the way the matter had been handled and of the attitude of some Administration Senators toward the bill. Aside from this, only the barest routine matters were discussed. All of which leads me to set down what has been running in my mind for a long time and that is just what use the Cabinet is under this Administration. The cold fact is that on important matters we are seldom called upon for advice. We never discuss exhaustively any policy of Government or question of political strategy. The President makes all of his own decisions and, so far at least as the Cabinet is concerned, without taking counsel with a group of advisers. On particular questions he will call into his office persons directly interested, but it is fair to say that the Cabinet is not a general council upon whose advice the President relies or the opinions of which, on important matters, he calls for. Our Cabinet meetings are pleasant affairs, but we only skim the surface of things on routine matters. As a matter of fact, I never think of bringing up even a serious departmental issue at Cabinet meeting, and apparently the other members follow the same policy, at least to a considerable extent.

Saturday morning I redrafted the President's suggested letter to

Mayor La Guardia. I lengthened it considerably because of certain matters that seemed to me to put us in a stronger position. The last portion of the letter drafted by the President criticized Moses sharply for the attacks he made, as the Republican candidate for governor of New York, during the last campaign against Governor Lehman while holding two separate positions by favor of the Governor of New York. During this same campaign he attacked public works while holding a position on the public works Triborough Bridge project. I put a lot more teeth in this portion of the President's letter in my redraft. In fact, I made it quite savage. However, I am doubtful whether the letter should take up any political issue at all since that would have the effect of admitting what has been charged since Order No. 129 has been issued, which is that the reason underlying that order was politics. In the afternoon I sent over to the President his draft and mine, with an accompanying letter in which I raised the question of policy whether the letter to La Guardia should include the criticism of Moses along political lines.

Tuesday, March 5, 1935

I had luncheon today with the President and it was the most satisfactory time I have had with him for several months. He was his old friendly self again. First, I discussed oil legislation with him. I told him that two or three bills were being mooted up on the Hill, in all of which an oil board of five members is set up, to be appointed by the President, and none of them providing for an administrator. I told him that I thought our present setup was as good an organization as could be devised, but that it would, of course, be quite proper for him to name the Petroleum Administrative Board which I now name. I suggested that it was necessary to have an administrator who would have the right to veto or approve the decisions of the PAB. He agreed with me and said that he wanted the Oil Administration to stay in the Interior Department. He authorized me to send word up to the Hill to that effect.

We got off to such a good start that I then took up again the question of subsistence homesteads. I reminded him that at our last session I had suggested that all of the subsistence homestead activities be grouped together and placed in charge of Assistant Secretary Chapman. He said that, much to his surprise, Rex Tugwell wanted to run subsistence homesteads, that Rex felt he had reached the end of his usefulness in the Department of Agriculture (something that Rex had already told me), and that he wanted to come to the Interior Department. I told him that, as he knew, I would be very glad indeed to have Rex over here and that I thought the plan proposed would be admirable. I went on to say that subsistence homesteads ought to be in Interior and in this he concurred.

This led us to a discussion of the pending Under Secretaryship. I explained that this was thrown out of the appropriation bill in the House of Representatives on a point of order, but that Senator Hayden had assured me he would get it back in the Senate. The President told me I could tell Senator Hayden that he wanted this to go through and that I could also tell Senator Hayden, in confidence, what the plans were with respect to Tugwell. I replied that I thought that this would be inadvisable, since it would almost inevitably leak out. I went on to say that if we couldn't get the Under Secretaryship through in the appropriation bill, I believed we could pass a special bill. At this point I said that there had been a complete reversal in the feeling of antagonism toward me on the Hill and the President said that he knew that this was so.

Then the President started to discuss public works. He spoke of a setup consisting of three committees. One committee would receive projects, and former Congressman West, of Ohio, whom he has in mind as the head of that committee, would spend all of his time interviewing Senators, Congressmen, mayors, etc., about projects. After these projects are submitted to this committee, they would be checked by the legal and financial departments and then forwarded to what the President said would be the main committee. On this committee he said that he and I would be members and that he had no one else in mind so far for membership; that would be discussed later. He said that I would be chairman of that committee.

At this point I interrupted to say that I had a deal to propose to him. He looked somewhat taken aback and asked me what it was. I explained that I had in mind to retire gracefully from public works if he would turn over all the conservation activities to the Interior Department. I told him that I was more interested in conservation than in any other phase of Government and that I wanted his Administration to stand out as having done more for conservation than had been done in the last fifty years. He said: "You know,

Harold, that I want to do that, but how can I?" I then asked him whether he would let nature take its course if anything should happen up on the Hill. He said he would, which I regard as giving me carte blanche to try to put some legislation through bringing certain bureaus over here, such as Forestry, that I really want very much.

The President went on to say that this would fit in perfectly with his Public Works organization. I said, of course, that I was a good soldier and would do anything he wanted me to do. He went on to explain his plan further. His third committee would be in charge of Harry Hopkins, who would be called "progress" man. It would be his task to check up on all public works projects after they had been passed upon and assigned by the main committee and see to it that the work was done according to schedule. He also had lines radiating from the central committee, such as Army engineers, Bureau of Reclamation, Housing, etc., to which would be allocated money for specific projects. Then down as more or less detached bodies he designated a group on Procurement and another to carry on Harry Hopkins' relief work.

It was evident that the President has in mind for me to have the principal place in the new public works setup next to himself. Probably I would be called chairman instead of administrator, but as I see it the new setup wouldn't work out very differently from the present one. It was most gratifying to me to know that apparently he hasn't lost confidence in me and that he wants me to fit into the new organization in a very real way. I haven't changed my mind, though, that I would like to get out of public works altogether but, of course, if the President wants me to go ahead I haven't much option, especially since there was no indication, today at any rate, that he proposes to place anyone over me. As he outlined his plan today, Admiral Peoples would have a place in the setup that would be far from prominent. His name was not mentioned, but I take it for granted that he would run the Procurement Division.

I went into several other matters with the President. He brought up the question of certain wild life reserves which "Ding" Darling wants, and I told him that I would look out for them in the setup of the Grazing Districts. What pleased me especially was that he was his old friendly self and he seemed to have his former buoyancy back.

Monday, March 11, 1935

On Friday Anna and I went to the funeral services of former Justice Oliver Wendell Holmes, which were held at All Souls Unitarian Church. I practically never go to a funeral but here was a really great man who had died, one of the greatest of his generation. I had always regretted that he had not been made Chief Justice of the Supreme Court. The President who would have done this would greatly have honored himself. Yet it is heartening to realize that this Associate Justice has been able to make the impress that he has upon his generation. The people had come to appreciate his real worth, to sense his nobility of character and his extraordinary ability. I could not forego the opportunity of attending these services to testify to my own very deep esteem of him.

At Cabinet meeting Friday afternoon the President read a letter from Breckinridge Long, the Ambassador to Italy, in which the Ambassador frankly proclaimed his belief that there would be a general European war, probably in 1936. He expressed the fervent hope that the United States would not permit itself to be drawn into what he regarded as an impending conflict of direful portent. I believe that every member of the Cabinet felt just as strongly as did Long that it would be a dreadful thing if we should again be dragged into a war which, if it comes, may be the final blow to our present civilization.

The Work Relief Bill has again been reported to the Senate and the feeling is that this time it will pass. However, it is still in bad shape and as the bill stands there will be no continuance of PWA beyond June 16, next, when it will expire by limitation of law. There are many reasons why it would be a serious thing if the life of PWA should not be extended. We would not even have the time to liquidate in orderly fashion by June 16. A great deal of our work would be left unfinished, contracts would still be in course of being carried out, some projects would not be started, we would have no further right to supervise construction, there would be no method of handling the bonds that we have taken as security, etc. As a matter of fact, a chaotic condition would result. I have talked to one or two Senators about this matter, and Foley, our chief counsel of PWA, has drafted an amendment which I sent him up to present to Senator Costigan, of Colorado. Senator Costigan had said that he would introduce this amendment and I have also talked with other Senators.

On Wednesday night Anna and I were guests at dinner at the home of Senator and Mrs. Burton K. Wheeler, of Montana. Senator and Mrs. Costigan, Senator and Mrs. McCarran, and Sir Charles Ross, correspondent of the *London Times,* were also guests. There was a good deal of discussion of Senator Long, of whom both Senator and Mrs. Wheeler seem to be fond. I kept a quiet tongue in my head, although I cannot see how anyone with decent instincts can feel anything except a sense of repulsion for this man.

Wednesday afternoon I went up to the Senate to see Hiram Johnson. Felix Frankfurter had told me that Senator Johnson would be the best possible man to talk to the President about the political situation in the West, and I went up to discuss it with him. He listened to what I had to say and said that if he had an opportunity, he would talk to the President.

Late Saturday I sent the President a letter accompanied by a proposed amendment to the Work Relief Bill which would prolong the life of PWA for two years. This was substantially the same amendment which has been handed to Senator Costigan. Ordinarily I would not have encouraged Senator Costigan to introduce this amendment; rather I would have asked the President to sponsor it, but time was getting short and the situation almost desperate. It seemed to me best not to take any chances.

Late on Monday the President sent this amendment with a letter advocating it to Senator Glass, Senator Byrnes, and I presume to Senator Robinson. During the debate on the bill Senator Glass took the floor to say that in order to allay the fears of those Senators who thought that if PWA should expire in June it would leave many projects unfinished, he would assure the Senate that the Appropriations Committee would present an amendment to cover the matter. Later he and Senator Byrnes agreed to the amendment that Foley had drawn and sent to the President, so that we ought to be all right so far as PWA is concerned in the new bill.

It seems to be pretty generally agreed that Richberg is facing the setting sun, so far as this Administration is concerned. General Johnson is insisting, and continues to insist in his writings, that Richberg betrayed him, and labor is vociferous in its charge that he has sold it out. The other day he made a speech in which he said that there would be no inflation during the next six years, and that has made the inflationists in Congress angry. His influence certainly seems to be on the wane. My information is that he is playing very close to McIntyre, but there is a growing feeling that McIntyre is using his position improperly. It has been notorious from the beginning that his friends are among the reactionaries. He loves to drink and go to parties. He is on the go all the time, drinking until all hours of the night, and his bosom companions are the rich and the conservative. Richberg seems to be playing up very strongly to McIntyre, and as Don likes social affairs and likes to drink and talk, they ought to get along very well together. Harry Slattery tells me that "Chip" Robert gave a party the other night at which Moffett, McIntyre, Richberg, Senator Byrnes, and others were present, during which a good many derogatory things were said about me.

Tuesday, March 12, 1935

Last night I thought that everything was in the clear with respect to the Work Relief Bill. Senator Glass, Senator Byrnes, and Senator Robinson all expressed their approval of it and indicated that it would be reported to the Senate today as an amendment of the Appropriations Committee of the Senate. This morning word came to me that overnight Senator Glass had changed his mind. He called up the President this morning and told him that it would endanger the passage of the bill to introduce this resolution. As he is the chairman of the committee in charge of that bill, the President had no option except to tell him to follow his own judgment. He authorized him either to use the letter that he had sent to him advocating the amendment or to destroy that letter.

Foley suggested that I personally talk with Senator Glass about the PWA amendment, so about one o'clock I went down to the Capitol. I went to the office of Colonel Halsey, Secretary of the Senate, and he brought in Senator Glass. The Senator looked as angry as a wet hen. He has the reputation of being very testy, but it really surprised me that a man of his age and experience in public affairs could be so downright mad. I suspected that the reason he had turned his back on this amendment was not because it would jeopardize the main bill, but because he was piqued, and I think my surmise was correct.

I told him that it had never been our intention to undermine him or to go around him, that there was a good deal of concern entertained by a number of Senators with respect to the fate of PWA, and that, following my policy, I furnished information and help to all Members of Congress who asked for it. He said something about this amendment having been put in the hands of a man who was against the Work Relief Bill. As a matter of fact, Senator Costigan is in favor of the bill, although he also favors the McCarran wage amendment. I told him that I furnished information to any Senator whether he was friendly or not, and Glass grudgingly admitted that that was the thing to do. I explained to him that I held him in very high regard and that I wouldn't want to do anything to offend him but that I did feel very anxious about the fate of PWA. He said that under the bill as it stood, PWA could continue to function and I told him that my lawyers advised me that it could not do so. He said that he had always spoken of me in the highest terms. I replied that I knew that and that I didn't want to do anything to change his good opinion. He said that there was nothing in the situation to impair the personal relationship between us. I didn't have much chance to talk with him because some amendments were being voted upon and he had to hurry back to the Senate Chamber.

Then I called Hiram Johnson out. I wanted to advise with him about the permit that has been asked for to raise the height of the Hetch Hetchy Dam in Yosemite Park. I told him that Solicitor Margold had advised me that, in his opinion, the Raker Act was being violated, and I suggested to Hiram that I issue a permit which would negative any intention to waive any right to claim for breach of the Raker Act and at the same time set a hearing in my office on the question whether that act is being violated or not. He thought this was a good plan and I shall proceed accordingly.

As I was leaving I ran into the Vice President and he took me into his office. He locked the door and we had the most confidential talk that we have ever had. He feels as I do, that our Cabinet meetings are of little value. He is as surprised as I have been that the President does not bring into the Cabinet questions of broad general policy for discussion. I told the Vice President very frankly that if it were not for the questions that he raised, our Cabinet meetings would be very barren indeed. He said he felt the same way about it but that he was hesitant at times of butting in too much because he was after all only a guest.

Then we got to discussing the political situation and I found that he is even more anxious than I am about it. He told me very frankly that he was afraid. This was his exact expression and he used it several times. He said that last night he lay awake in bed listening to the clock strike two, and then three, and then four, and then five. He was worrying about the political situation and the state of the country. He knows that the President has been losing ground very rapidly and he believes, with me, that Jim Farley hasn't the slightest idea of what the state of mind of the country is.

The Vice President on several occasions has shown to me a vein of liberalism which I had not expected to find in him. Today he said that if the Democrats failed to carry the election next year, it would be many, many years before the country would again vote for a liberal Administration. He remarked that he didn't pretend to be any more patriotic than anyone else, but that he did love his country and he wanted it to be a country of a happy, contented, and prosperous people. He said that if Roosevelt is not re-elected, a reactionary Republican will succeed him and that then will follow either a fascist government or a communist one. He could actually foresee a revolution in certain circumstances. He spoke with deep feeling and with sadness. After all, he is a pretty substantial and sturdy character. I have come to feel a growing regard and respect for him. There isn't any doubt that he has the real welfare of the country at heart.

He feels that this Administration has done little to satisfy the expectations of the people for a liberalized Government. He said we had done practically nothing along liberal lines, although he referred to the slight changes in the banking laws, the Securities Commission, and one or two other matters. I urged him to go to the President and tell him frankly how he felt, but he said that he couldn't do this very well unless the President should invite his opinions. He doesn't like to thrust his advice upon anyone. I told him that this wasn't a question of pride; that the whole future of the country might be at stake.

One thing he said interested me very much. It appears that the President, before he had selected his Cabinet, told the Vice President that he would not appoint anybody with whom he had not talked and from whom he had not obtained assurances that he would go along with him, the intimation being that the President wanted a docile Cabinet. I told him that the President had never asked me a single question and he said he was glad to know that.

Thursday, March 14, 1935

We have had to back down on the Moses case as I have known for a long time would be necessary. The whole thing was a mistake from the start and our position became more untenable as time went on. It became a national issue. I think it was pretty well understood that the President was responsible for the policy adopted, but I have stood the attack and I have had it from all quarters ever since my famous Order 129 was issued. I have regretted this instance all the more because I have never been in a position to defend it, and the whole thing was inconsistent not only with my principles but with my present record as a public official.

The way the thing worked out finally was this: by prearrangement, Mayor La Guardia wrote me a letter, calling my attention to the fact that the order would prevent the reappointment of Langdon Post as chairman of the Housing Commission since he, too, was involved in the same kind of a situation. The whole letter was written around Post and then, as a postscript, the Mayor called attention to the fact that the issue also involved Moses. The letter was dated back to the latter part of February. By a predated letter of my own, so as to antedate by one day the blast let out the latter part of February by Al Smith, I advised La Guardia that I would interpret Order 129 so that it would not be retroactive. This would permit both Moses and Post to continue in their dual capacities in New York, the understanding being, however, that the order would be effective as to future projects.

The newspapers have made a great play of my defeat by Moses, and that, too, I have had to take with a smile. However, the incident is a closed one now and I hope there will be no similar one.

I have been trying to get out a book on public works. Several people have been gathering the material for me and writing draft chapters on various phases of the subject. I was able to work over the first two of these chapters on my trip to Denver. The original drafts of these chapters, fortunately, were in quite satisfactory shape, but, as always, I was not satisfied to use someone else's writing as my own, with the result that I worked at it hard, rephrasing, rewriting, adding and subtracting.

It seems that there will be a good prospect, after all, of amending the Work Relief Bill so as to continue the life of PWA for another two years. Apparently my trip to the Senate on Tuesday, trying to smooth Senator Glass's ruffled feathers, had a better result than I thought at the time. He has modified his views considerably. Besides, other Senators have been talking to him, some of them at our instigation, and he now expresses a willingness to accept a PWA amendment. Foley went up to the Senate today to work out an acceptable amendment with Senator O'Mahoney. After they had agreed on a draft, O'Mahoney took the matter up with Senator Glass and, much to his surprise, found that Senator Glass proposed to sponsor the amendment originally sent to him by the President, which amendment was drafted by Foley.

Late this afternoon Senator Glass called me up. He told me that he was afraid he had hardly been intelligible during our interview the other day. It seems that he was very much put out because ten days had elapsed during which the Administration had had plenty of time to submit amendments to the bill during which time nothing was said about this amendment until the time he was trying to pass the bill through the Senate. He said it made him look like a fool and he objected to being made to look like a fool. I told him I recognized his position thoroughly and sympathized with him. He said he would offer a PWA amendment and he wanted me to know that he had never criticized me. I told him he had always been very courteous and considerate to me and I wanted to negative any idea that he might have that I was lacking in consideration of him. He said that I had always been nice to him and he appreciated it. His changed attitude really pleases me very much because, by common consent, he is the crustiest man in the Senate and he has no hesitation at all about expressing his feelings very frankly.

Foley brought word back that he found Senator O'Mahoney very strong indeed for me. O'Mahoney hopes I will administer the work-relief fund, and he told Foley that unless it was administered as well as I have administered the PWA fund to date, the Administration would be defeated next year. He said that the fate of the President in next year's election will depend upon the way this money is handled. I realize this very keenly and that is one reason why I don't want to have any such responsibility as will be involved in trying to spend this tremendous sum of money in a way that will meet with the approval of the country. I feel that it would be tempting fate, but, of course, I will have to do it if that is the wish of the President. I think I can say in all modesty that the country has confidence in me as Public Works Administrator.

Harry Slattery had lunch today with some New York friends, who, he said, know what is happening on the inside. These men reported to him that the President had come to terms with some of the big interests and that they are now satisfied with the Administration. They told him that there was no occasion for being afraid of Long or of Father Coughlin and that the man to be feared was Ickes, who had built himself up in the confidence of the people. I remarked to Harry that if this was so, the interests undoubtedly would demand my head on a platter at the hands of the President. They probably wouldn't dare ask for it during this present term, but they might very well make it a condition of their support of the President that I be not reappointed in the event of his re-election.

Sunday, March 17, 1935

Last Wednesday night I went to the Willard Hotel to a dinner given by Assistant Secretary Chapman to members of the faculty of Howard University. They were really a very fine group of people, and I was glad of an opportunity to meet them and talk to them informally.

At Cabinet meeting on Friday the President said that after Father Coughlin's recent speech over the radio replying to General Hugh Johnson's attack, the first man to call him on the telephone and congratulate him was Henry Ford.

Louie Howe is very ill indeed and there is a feeling in some quarters that he won't get well. This would be a serious loss to the President. Louie Howe has very keen judgment of men and of political trends. He is absolutely devoted to the President and he is the one man who is in a position to tell the President what the facts are, no matter how unpleasant they appear. Moreover, he can talk straight out to Farley and to all others. His loss would be irreparable, especially at a time when the political situation is shifting to the extent that it seems to be. At that, I don't see how he has kept going as long as he has. For months now he has been a very sick man. He has been going on his nerve, but he has had fine nerve. I haven't seen much of him lately, but when I have, it has been in his bedroom in the White House where, on his elbows and knees on his bed, he carries on conferences and such business as he is able to attend to.

Yesterday Senator Glass introduced his promised amendment continuing the existence of PWA until June 30, 1937. On motion of Senator McNary, the Republican leader, the matter went over as a special order for Monday. Senator McNary is not opposed to this amendment, as he told me last night when I met him at dinner at the Japanese Embassy. He expects the amendment to carry without any difficulty and that is my own belief. He wanted it put over merely because it was the expectation that no controversial amendments would be introduced on Saturday, as a result of which a good many Senators were absent.

After dinner last night when I was in the smoking room, Senator McNary, a member of the Japanese Embassy, and I happened to fall together in a group. Senator McNary, addressing himself to the Japanese, said that he was an old-timer in Washington and that in all his experience here there had never been such an able administrator as myself. He repeated this statement with variations and commented on my honesty and sincerity. He was so generous in his praise that I really felt embarrassed. Senator McNary had taken Anna in to dinner and on the way home she told me that he had been most fulsome and continuous in his praise of me during dinner.

I asked Senator McNary what would be the fate of the resolution calling for an investigation of the Virgin Islands and he said there wasn't anything to worry about at all, that I had many friends in the Senate, and that everything was all right.

The Japanese Embassy is a very beautiful and attractive home. I have never seen such lovely Japanese paintings. The china was unusual too. Some of the best art objects were Chinese, as was to be expected, but the whole thing was very charming and delightful. It was a large affair, many of the guests being members of the diplomatic corps, and the dinner was good. I took out Madame Sze, wife of the Chinese Minister, and on my left was Madame Munir, wife of the Turkish Ambassador. The Japanese Ambassador, Mr. Hirosi Saito, made a very gracious host. His wife was dressed in her native costume, as was Madame Sze, who had on a most beautiful blue gown.

I met at the Embassy for the first time the Peruvian Ambassador. He was born in this country during the time when his father was

Peruvian Minister here, and he has spent most of his life here and in Great Britain. He spoke absolutely perfect English without the slightest accent. He was very charming and I had an unusually good time talking with him. He was poking fun at precedents and all that sort of thing. He said that as a diplomat he had to carry some pretty heavy social loads at times, but that occasionally he got up a party with just the people whom he wanted to have. He said he would like to have such a party for me and he told me that if I got an invitation from him with a star in the corner I was to be sure to accept. I promised that I would.

My job really got me Saturday afternoon. From about half past eight in the morning I had been signing mail and documents all day long except when I was interviewing people. The stuff kept piling up on the right of my desk. About the middle of the afternoon Rawls, my messenger, told me that there was no more signature mail to come in. When he brought some more in just before six, before I had my desk cleared, it was almost more than I could stand. As a matter of fact, I became so tired and nervous that I literally couldn't sign my name any more. My arm had a numb ache and finally I had to give it all up as a bad job and go home leaving mail both unsigned and undictated. I was very tired all last night and I didn't have a good night. This morning I am still under par, but I have managed to clear my desk by noon.

Saturday, March 23, 1935

On Sunday, March 17, Anna, Raymond, and I took the Atlantic Coast Line bound for West Palm Beach, Florida. John Collier, Commissioner of Indian Affairs, accompanied us, and so did Mr. Lee, my secretary. I had been insistently urged to make this trip with expenses to be paid for myself and party. Assuming that the so-called Seminole Sun Dance, to which I was invited, might be largely an advertising stunt, in an effort to protect myself against gross exploitation I had sent Mr. Fairman on ahead to get the lay of the land. He reported that the plans were legitimate and urged my going.

Tuesday noon I attended a luncheon of the West Palm Beach Rotary Club and gave a short speech of fifteen minutes. Then four carloads of us, with one extra car carrying our baggage, started south toward the Everglades. We first went to Lake Okeechobee to see the work that the Army engineers are doing there to prevent a repetition of the disaster that visited the surrounding country in 1928 when a terrific hurricane blew the water out of the lake and drowned, according to reports, some two thousand persons, in addition to killing not only all of the livestock in the fields but the alligators and the fish in the lake as well. This project is costing the people of the United States $17 million. Lake Okeechobee is over seven hundred square miles in extent, much larger than I had any idea of. The Army is building a dike around the lake more than 30 feet in height and it hopes to have the project completed by 1937.

Lieutenant Colonel Dunn, United States Engineer in charge of that area, met us at West Palm Beach and drove us to Lake Okeechobee. Here two large Army engineer launches were waiting for us and we went out on the lake for several miles. We saw a great deal of bird life. I was particularly interested in a number of egrets that we saw. I had always imagined them to be rather small birds, but on the contrary they are big. Thanks to the Federal law passed years ago prohibiting the sale of egret feathers in interstate commerce, these birds have been increasing quite rapidly after they had become almost extinct.

Leaving Lake Okeechobee, we drove down into the Everglades. At one point we left our cars and followed a trail into the swamplands to visit a Seminole Indian camp. We had seen some Seminoles the night before at West Palm Beach but here we saw them in their natural living conditions. They are the wildest Indians I have ever seen, but they are a fine type, self-respecting and independent. They live in these isolated camps, some of them way inside the swamps where whites never come in contact with them. They don't live in huts or cabins or even tepees. Their dwellings consist of thatched roofs sustained on piles with platforms about a foot from the ground, on which men, women, and children seem to sleep indiscriminately. Except in the rainy season they sleep on these outdoor platforms. They cook over open fires and their cooking looked pretty messy. Apparently they seldom, if ever, wash their cooking utensils. They are far from being sanitary, and they don't regard the white man in any too friendly a spirit.

At this camp there was a Creek Indian woman, young, good looking, and attractive. She spoke perfect English and had perfect self-possession. Someone told us that she had a bachelor's degree from some college. She just recently married a member of her own tribe who had been brought on from Oklahoma by Commissioner Col-

lier to do some ECW camp work. The two were living with the
Seminoles quite unself-consciously and apparently quite happily.
The photographer with us wanted to take a group picture of the
village, but the Seminoles demurred and I upheld their right to refuse being photographed.

From there we went to Everglades where we stayed at a fishing
and hunting club for the night. The following morning we left
Raymond and Fairman to fish, unsuccessfully, for tarpon while the
rest of us went on to Miami via the Tamiami trail. Raymond's
zest for fishing had been fired by the sight of two huge tarpons that
had been caught the day of our arrival, one of which weighed 143
pounds and the other something over 120 pounds, both having
been caught by women.

En route to Miami we detoured at one point in order to go down
a back road across the Everglades which, however, paralleled Tamiami trail. This land is technically swamp, but it happened to be the
dry season and it didn't look at all like a swamp. A good deal of
drainage work has been undertaken and there throughout the area
we came across large tomato fields. A more or less persistent attempt
is being made to farm some of these lands, but in my opinion it
ought to be returned to swampland and kept as such. Down this
road we saw a great many birds but Mr. Wright, who is in charge of
the Wild Life Division of the National Park Service, told us that it
was the mating time and that most of the birds had retired to the
rookeries deep in the swamp. He said there were literally thousands of birds in the swamp and that ordinarily they were very
plentiful along the roads.

We passed right through Miami and on to the Boca Raton Club
which is situated between Miami and Palm Beach but nearer the
latter than the former. This is the most luxurious club I have ever
seen in my life. The claim is made for it that no club in the world
equals it for luxurious appointments, beautiful architecture, and
rich furnishings, and I can well believe that. I have never seen anything like it. The report was to the effect that the initiation fee
was $5,000 but someone else said it was $10,000. We were also told
that the cover charge for dinner at the club was $10. The club has
over seven hundred sleeping rooms. The lounge and the dining
rooms have beautiful vaulted ceilings. I shall not attempt to describe it because I could not do so adequately.

Luncheon was served for over twenty people and it was one of the best lunches I have ever sat down to, as well as the most elaborate. We started off with cocktails and during the luncheon we were served a sauterne and a champagne, with liqueurs to follow afterward. The luncheon was ostentatious but I must confess that the food was exceptional.

Then we went back to West Palm Beach where we were due at the Indian celebration that was the occasion for my going to Florida. On a wooden platform under a blazing sun and in an arena surrounded on three sides by bleachers with open water on the fourth side, John Collier and I squatted on the bare boards with a group of Seminole medicine men who proceeded to tell me through an interpreter what they wanted from the Government. Principally what they wanted were large additional holdings of land so that they might have their hunting restored to them. They also wanted $15 a month from the Government as compensation for past losses and injuries. They presented me with a written petition and in my response I told them that I was sympathetic so far as additional lands were concerned. I said nothing about the $15 a month.

As a matter of fact, I think the Seminoles ought to have more land and I shall do what I can to bring that about. I may say that we are planning a great national park to take in practically all of the Everglades, and I can see no reason why the Indians should not have hunting privileges in the park when it is established, with considerable lands of their own outside of park boundaries. There are only about six hundred to six hundred and fifty Seminoles living in southern Florida. One hundred years ago when the United States tried to remove to Oklahoma all of the Seminoles then living, a band of them turned back and fought the United States under Osceola, their chief. A thousand Indians stood off an army of the United States regulars and militia that at its height numbered forty thousand soldiers. They killed about twenty-five hundred regular officers and men in this fight, and the United States Government and the states supplying the militia piled up a total cost of $40 million. Even so, the Seminoles were never conquered. Finally, President Tyler put an end to the war, although a treaty of peace has never been proposed or entered into. This brief recital gives some idea of the quality of these Indians. They are still savage, they still distrust the white man, and they still live in primitive conditions.

On Thursday Anna and I went over to Miami in a Coast Guard

aquaplane, one of the new ones recently bought with PWA funds. We went to the home of Dr. Fairchild to discuss with a group of local men the proposed national park. I told them that I was very much interested in the park and that I hoped during my tenure of office to receive the deeds to it. This local group is tracing titles to lands and doing all it can to get the thing under way. Then we went back to West Palm Beach. We left there Friday at twelve thirty-five and got into Washington today at eleven o'clock, just an hour late.

One thing happened while I was away that has distressed me very much. A couple of weeks ago at Cabinet meeting the President brought up the question of transferring the Division of Soil Erosion Control to the Department of Agriculture. I objected at the time and asked for a hearing. The President told me he would give me one. About ten days ago he sent for H. H. Bennett, Director of that Division, to discuss the matter with him but without saying anything to me. He has never suggested a hearing since that Cabinet meeting. At an interview in the interval I had told him of my great desire to have all the conservation activities concentrated in this Department. He had expressed sympathy with that desire and told me that I must realize his difficulties in the matter. I then asked him whether, if anything happened up on the Hill, he would "let nature take its course" and he said he would. Whereupon I instigated the filing of several bills in both the Senate and House of Representatives, setting up in this Department on a permanent basis a Division of Erosion Control.

On Thursday I learned from Slattery over the telephone that word had come from the White House that the President wanted this division transferred at once. He was reminded that I was away. The present Division of Erosion Control is a creature of PWA, and it required a resolution of the PWA Board to transfer it to Agriculture. The President said he wanted such a resolution adopted. I at once sent him a long telegram reminding him of his promise to give me a hearing and protesting the removal of this division in the circumstances. Friday morning Burlew talked with me and made it clear to me, as it had not been before, that the President wanted a special meeting of the board called, even during my absence, to pass this resolution. I told Burlew to have Slattery or someone else get in touch with the White House and ask that the matter be delayed as requested in my telegram until my return. I was at the station at West Palm Beach waiting for my train when Chapman got me on the telephone to say that McIntyre had called him and insisted, in the name of the President, that a meeting of the board be called yesterday afternoon. Chapman wanted instructions from me and I told him that, of course, he would have to do what the President wanted done. The meeting was held yesterday afternoon and the resolution adopted.

This meeting was held at four o'clock yesterday afternoon and I reached Washington at eleven this morning. It seems very strange to me that the President could not have waited these extra few hours. I found on my desk a letter from the President, in response to my telegram, saying that he felt it was necessary to take action at the time because of the situation on the Hill, referring, I suppose, to the bills pending up there, one of which was on the verge of being reported by the House Committee on Public Lands with a recommendation that it pass. I really think that this bill would have gone through both branches of Congress with very little difficulty.

I am not at all pleased with this situation. In the first place, the President owed it to me to give me a hearing, and, in the second place, there was no reason to call a meeting of the board at four o'clock yesterday afternoon when I was to be back in Washington this morning.

Another thing happened, too, that I didn't like. McIntyre caused Chapman to be called by telephone and told him to attend the Cabinet meeting yesterday in my absence. There certainly was no justification for this, since First Assistant Walters was here and it was his privilege to attend the Cabinet meeting if there was occasion for anyone doing so on account of my being away. I told Chapman that he shouldn't have attended and that hereafter if I happened to be out of town on Cabinet day and it is felt necessary for someone to be present in my stead, Walters is to have that privilege.

Just what I shall do in this situation I have not yet made up my mind. I want to be perfectly sure that I am doing the wise thing, but I have no disposition to submit to many incidents of this sort. At the very least I shall feel obliged to speak quite frankly to the President. He had no right to go over my head in my absence. It looks like disciplinary action. Neither do I think he has the right to do what he does so frequently, namely, calling in members of my staff for consultation on Department matters, without consulting me or advising with me.

Monday, March 25, 1935

I fully made up my mind this morning to have a frank talk with the President about the removal of the Division of Soil Erosion, the manner thereof, and the instructions that came from McIntyre to Chapman to attend the Cabinet meeting last Friday, as well as other matters affecting me intimately in the Administration. I called McIntyre to ask for an appointment and he said he would get me in tomorrow. Late this afternoon the President called me to say that he was leaving tonight for Florida on his fishing trip. He informed me that the doctors had said that Louie Howe would live for two weeks and probably longer and that he thought it would be a good time to get away for ten days, although he would hold himself ready to return at once if Howe's condition required it.

What he called me about was to discuss the Work Relief Bill. By way of preface, I may say that Congressman Buchanan, chairman of the House Committee on Appropriations, called a meeting in his office at three o'clock yesterday afternoon. I had talked with him over the telephone on Saturday telling him that I would send Foley as my representative. Foley reported to me today that Admiral Peoples was there representing the Treasury, with Acting Director of the Budget Bell. Present also were Gill, of Hopkins' organization, and one or two others. According to Foley, there was a concerted drive on the part of these men against PWA. They did not like the PWA amendment that went through as part of the Senate bill and seemed generally put out. Foley maintained his ground and fortunately Congressman Buchanan was with him all along the line so that he lost nothing. This is really the first time that these various interests have appeared in the open against me with respect to this legislation, although I have had no doubt for some time, and neither have those who have been following the matter closely, that there has been a persistent effort to torpedo me. Fortunately, this hasn't disturbed me any because I really have been wanting to get rid of PWA anyhow.

What the President wanted to discuss with me was the proposed setup under the new bill. He went over the ground that he had covered when we last discussed it one day recently at luncheon in his office. He spoke again of a committee that would receive "the visiting firemen," as he put it, so as to relieve the real administrators of the burden and duty of a lot of personal interviews. Then he referred again to the Progress Committee, on which he said Hopkins will be placed, and Procurement. He said there would be a main committee which would make the allocations of the money but which would not do any of the building. He said that I would be the senior member of this committee, and I suppose that what he has in mind is to be the chairman himself, at least in title. He said that the money when allocated would be spent through the regular agencies, which I suppose will include PWA.

He asked me what I thought of this setup and I told him it seemed reasonable to me but that I was still up in the air personally. He asked me, with a note of anxiety in his voice, as I thought, what I meant. I told him that my position was what it had been when I discussed the matter with him last, namely, that I would like to be relieved of any responsibility with respect to the works program and that I would like to have all the conservation activities in this Department. He told me that this would require legislation and that he had been thinking of setting up a Conservation Department or one on social activities. I said that if a new Conservation Department should be set up, it would take over practically all of our activities and leave us nothing to do. I urged that the conservation activities ought to come to Interior. This was the natural place for them. He said that I was right and he suggested that I canvass the situation up on the Hill to see whether we could get the necessary legislation. I said to him that I felt that the Interior Department was stronger on the Hill than it ever had been, and he said he thought that was so. I then asked him whether I had his authority to go into this matter on the Hill and see what could be done, and he told me to go ahead. He then came back briefly to his Public Works proposal again, leaving me with the impression that he wanted to go ahead along the lines suggested. He said that a rough draft of an Executive Order had already been prepared, that Harry Hopkins had to go down to Savannah, Georgia, on some errand, that he would go as far as that on the President's train tonight. They will work over the Executive Order and then Harry Hopkins will see me when he comes back to Washington.

Wednesday, March 27, 1935

The papers this morning announced that Hopkins was to head up the new work relief program. I went over to see Steve Early this morning and found him in a terrible state of mind. He had already heard from Congressman Buchanan, chairman of the Appropriations Committee of the House, and from other members of Congress. The Hopkins' story actually puts the bill in jeopardy again. According to Steve, the story was given out last night by McIntyre at Jacksonville and was rewritten here in Washington. Steve said that the basis of the story was probably the fact that Hopkins went South on the train with the President. He regarded that as a mistake and said that he hadn't known about it.

Steve said that what the President had told me about the setup was what he understood it was to be, and he verified the fact that the President was to be the chairman of the main committee, of which, according to the President, I am to be the senior member. Steve also told me that there was to be an advisory committee, of which General Robert Wood, president of Sears, Roebuck and Company, is to be the chairman, but his idea is that this committee is for window dressing. I told him I regarded this setup as a mistake and that General Wood would object to being window dressing. Colonel Waite came in to see me yesterday and told me that General Wood had asked him to be a member of this committee. The Colonel said he was willing to do it if the committee wasn't to be window dressing, and General Wood assured him that there wouldn't be any window dressing so far as he was concerned.

I told Steve that I felt he ought to know, since the story was breaking the way it was, my own attitude on the whole matter. I revealed to him that I had told the President that I wanted to be relieved entirely of public works. I said that if the President wanted me to go along on a committee of which the President himself was to be the chairman and I was to be the ranking member, I would do that, but that I would not serve under Hopkins, or Peoples, or General Wood, or anyone else. Steve said that I was right about it. As a matter of fact, he said he felt about ready to quit. I have never seen him in such a state of mind.

It was clear, too, that he was worried about the President having gone south with Louie Howe in the condition that he is in. Howe has been under an oxygen tent for twelve or fourteen days and is now in a coma. They have to keep him alive on oxygen. Steve told the doctors that since they had guaranteed to the President that he would live for two weeks longer, it was up to them to keep him alive, and even made the statement, although he didn't mean it, that if Howe died before the President returned, he wouldn't allow it to be announced. What is in his mind is, of course, the effect on the public of the President's closest friend dying in the White House while the President is off on a vacation trip on the Astor yacht. He told me that McIntyre had said that if Howe should die while the President is out at sea no one would think anything of it if they went ahead with the funeral during the President's absence. Steve told Mac that he would care a hell of a lot and that if Howe should die, the President would have to come back for the funeral.

This afternoon I went up to the Capitol. I wanted to see the Vice President and I had a long talk with him. I told him what my ambition was about making this a Conservation Department and what the President had said in that regard. On this the Vice President said the only thing to do was to draw a model bill, bring it up, have it referred to a committee, and see what we could do. He expressed sympathy with the idea of the bill.

Then we discussed the Work Relief Bill. I found him very bitter against Hopkins, and he said it would be absolutely suicidal if Hopkins should have the administration of this bill. He also said that Tugwell should not be put in charge of the land program that the President seems to have in mind for him. He said that Hopkins had done more harm to the country than any man in history. He regards him purely as a spendthrift and he said he thought this morning when he got up and saw the newspapers that it might be his duty to see to it that the conference committee hold this bill until the President should return and give some assurance as to Hopkins. He spoke very cordially about my administration of Public Works. He said I had done a good job and that what he liked about it was that I was trying to benefit the entire country, and had built up an organization not only of honest men but of competent men. He said that if there should be an investigation of the Public Works Administration, he didn't think that any preventable graft would be found and that there wouldn't be more than one or two rotten apples in the whole barrel. Contrasted with this, he said that Hopkins' administration of FERA was almost an open scandal and that if there should be an investigation, they would hardly find a sound apple in the barrel.

I told the Vice President that, in my opinion, the President would be making a great mistake if he himself assured the chairmanship of the new Work Relief Board. If he does that he will have to accept full responsibility for any failures. He can't blame them on anyone else. The Vice President fully agreed with me. I told him also that the way this money was administered might mean the defeat of the Administration next year, and for that and other reasons I honestly wanted to be relieved of any responsibility in connection with the whole matter. I told him also that while I would serve under the President, I wouldn't serve under anyone else and he said he didn't blame me.

The Vice President thinks the Treasury Department is the most important in the Government. He does not believe Morgenthau has any sympathy with progressive ideas. He believes that in his heart he is against the bill to abolish the holding companies, and that in general his sympathies are with the big interests of Wall Street. He told how Morgenthau comes up to hearings with a retinue of experts from his Department and that when he is asked the simplest kind of a question, he turns to one or another of his experts for an answer before he vouchsafes it himself. He spoke of one Senator, whose name he said he wouldn't give me, who had had a few drinks, who told the Vice President that he was going to ask Morgenthau what day of the week it was, declaring that if he did so he didn't think Morgenthau would be able to answer the question without reference to an expert. He said that Morgenthau is the weakest Secretary of the Treasury who has ever held that office and that he is regarded as a joke on the Hill.

We went somewhat over the ground we had both covered the last time I talked with him in his office. He thinks the President is in very bad shape politically and that he is losing steadily. He says that no one can talk to the President and that the President changes his mind easily. He especially criticized him for not taking the advice of his Cabinet or apparently of anyone else. Yet he is very fond of the President, just as we all are. His criticism was not in a captious or bitter vein. It was just a man speaking in great sorrow of the difficulties into which another man of whom he is fond has gotten himself.

The Vice President wants the Government itself to control the issuance of currency and he says now that it is too late under this Administration, although the President could have done it at the outset. He deplores the control of our Government by the big-moneyed interests. He says that the one thing that we ought to teach our people is that money is not all there is to life. For the last fifty years, he declared, money has run this Government.

He said that so long as a Republican was President, he didn't care what Republican it was because they were all controlled by Wall Street, but he did regret the opportunity that this Democratic Administration is losing to do something real for the country. He talked again of the very distinct possibility of the reactionary Republicans naming the next President of the United States.

I met a number of Senators in the cloak room, all of whom were quite friendly. I was struck by one thing that Senator White, of Maine, said, which was that he had voted for war once but that it would be a long time before he would vote for it again. Senator Vandenberg, who is on the committee investigating munitions, said that John T. Flynn had made a suggestion about preventing war which struck him as being both simple and effective, and that is not to borrow money with which to wage war but to pay for it out of revenues as we go along. He believes that there will be little inducement for anyone to force us into war if the profits that are made out of war are immediately taken back in taxes in order to keep the war going.

The Vice President came out of the Chamber to tell me that the resolution for an investigation of the Virgin Islands would go through. The Committee on Contingent Expenses had voted $12,000, with $13,000 more in prospect if needed. He said Senator Tydings would be the chairman of the committee but that the committee would be a fair one. Senator Tydings' idea, according to the Vice President, is to send a first-class investigator to the Virgin Islands. If he brings back a report that there is nothing to all the hullabaloo down there, then the investigation would be dropped; otherwise it would go ahead. I told the Vice President that I was ready to go on the stand any day and that I had my statement all prepared.

Friday, March 29, 1935

Anna and I went to the Russian Embassy for dinner last night. The Embassy occupies the old Pullman house, which is large and magnificent, although it is not one of the new houses of Washington. There were fifty-two at dinner. I sat on Madame Troyanovsky's left. After dinner there was singing. A large number of additional guests came in after dinner and there was a supper served after the concert but we went home as soon as the concert was over, as it was then about half past eleven. I was pretty well tired. In the music room were those same back-breaking chairs that the White House uses in the East Room for entertainments there after state dinners.

This was my second night out in succession. On Wednesday night members of the PWA staff gave a dinner at the Racquet Club for Major Philip Fleming, who has been acting as Deputy Administrator since Colonel Waite resigned. He is an Army engineer who has been recalled to the Army for detail on the Passamaquoddy Power project. We had a very good party.

Late yesterday afternoon Foley came in to tell me that the Senate conferees on the Work Relief Bill were insisting on amending the PWA clause to prohibit the lending of money on a non-Federal project unless it could be shown that fifty-one per cent of the money was to go to labor employed directly on the project. As soon as Congressman Buchanan, who headed the House conferees, told him about this, Foley pointed out that it would kill PWA entirely, since on practically no non-Federal project is there such a heavy proportion of direct labor at the site. Finally, the House conferees fought the percentage down to thirty-three and one third per cent. I told Foley to go over and talk to Steve Early about it. When I got to the Russian Embassy I found a call from the White House. Steve Early wanted to discuss the matter with me. He was on one wire and Tom Corcoran on another, so that we had a three-way conversation. I told Early how serious the situation was. He had already sent a long telegram to the President apprising him of what was happening.

This morning as soon as I got to the office I called Steve Early. He arranged for a conference in Senator Robinson's office at which were present Senator Robinson, Senator Byrnes, Speaker Byrns and Congressman Buchanan, E. H. Foley, Jr., and Benjamin V. Cohen, who went with me. Later Senator Robinson called in the Parliamentary Clerk of the Senate.

We had up for discussion the effect of this amendment. It seems to me to be quite devastating. Under this amendment we cannot lend money for any rural electrification, slum clearance, or grade elimination projects and for few, if any, general non-Federal projects. It simply puts us out of business. Foley made the point that this amendment could be knocked out on a point of order because it is really new legislation. The House bill as passed gave the President unlimited authority to lend money up to the full amount of the appropriation. The Senate bill gave him unlimited authority to lend money up to $900 million for public works. The amendment limits this authority by reciting that no loan can be made unless it can be shown that thirty-three and one third per cent of the money will go for labor employed at the site. If such a limitation is valid, then ninety-nine per cent could just as well have been put in as thirty-three and one third per cent. In other words, if a high enough percentage were put in, it would effectively take away from the President all the power given to him by Congress to make loans. Thus it is new legislation and, therefore, in the opinion of Foley, subject to a point of order. In this view, after consideration, the Parliamentary Clerk of the Senate concurred.

We pointed out to the Senators and Congressmen the devastating effect of this amendment. If this amendment stays in, I do not see how there could be any new public works program. The President can give away money but he can't lend money. It came out that this amendment was sponsored originally by Senator Copeland. He frankly stated during the conference that he did not propose to make it possible for the Administration to lend money to New York to build a power plant. Obviously the amendment is in the interest of the power companies, since no public power project can be financed by a loan under this amendment. It developed today that Comptroller General McCarl had been called in to the conference and that he had drafted the original fifty-one per cent amendment. He made the point that without some such limitation, money could be spent to acquire power plants and other properties instead of going for the employment of men.

Saturday, March 30, 1935

The work-relief pot still boils. I went up this morning to see the Vice President with Foley and Cohen. I found him very much alert to the situation. It is his opinion, too, that the heart has been cut out of the Work Relief Bill by the thirty-three and one third per cent direct labor amendment. He says that in their hearts, the majority of the Senate are opposed to the whole Work Relief Bill, and he is afraid that if a point of order should be raised, even if he should sustain it, he might be overruled. I gathered from what he said that he thought a point of order ought to be well taken. He suggested that the best way out of the mess was for the House conferees to call up the conference report on Monday, frankly state that they had misconceived the effect of this amendment, and ask that the House reject the report. Then it could go again to conference. In that event he thought that Senator Glass and his fellow conferees would yield on this point, or it might even be possible to appoint new conferees.

When I got back, I called up Steve Early. He had been talking with the Vice President and others and had sent a radiogram to the President advising him to wire Speaker Byrns and Congressman Buchanan to reject the conference report and recommit. I drafted a long radiogram of several hundred words to the President, telling him just what this amendment, in our judgment, would do to the work-relief program and urging him strongly to wire Speaker Byrns to reject and recommit. I certainly hope that he will do this, although I admit that I am somewhat worried and fear that he will take a compromising position, not realizing the full implications of this amendment.

Then I addressed myself to the task of writing a friendly and yet firm letter to Senator Glass telling him just what I thought the effect of this amendment would be. This letter, to which I attached a memorandum from Mr. Foley on the same subject, I sent late this afternoon to Senator Glass at his hotel. It was delivered to him personally and I hope that it may have good results, although he is a difficult man to deal with.

The irony in this whole situation is that Glass and others regard Hopkins as a spendthrift and don't want him to have anything to do with this program. Yet, as a result of this amendment, nobody but a Hopkins ought to be put in charge of the program. The effect of this amendment is that the President can give away all the money that is being appropriated, but can't lend money because the terms on which the money may be loaned are impossible of fulfillment.

Another interesting phase of the matter is that the Comptroller General, who really drew this amendment, should be permitted to enhance his own powers to a degree passing anything in history. It happens that McCarl, the Comptroller General, is not only a Republican, he is a reactionary Republican. It may very well be that he sees an opportunity to build himself up and make a great national figure out of himself. Certain it is that under the bill as it stands, he would in effect be Public Works Administrator no mat-

ter who else might hold that title. I have been telling people today, with whom I have discussed the matter intimately, that I
did not want to have anything to do with the Public Works Administration under the limited powers given to it by this bill.

Monday, April 1, 1935

In reply to the letter I wrote to Senator Glass on Saturday, I received a reply from him at home last night. This morning, as
soon as I got to the office, I dictated a further letter to him to meet
certain statements in his letter to me and I think I answered them
very effectively. This letter I sent up to him by hand late in the
morning. Yesterday morning, while I was at the office, the White
House sent to me a radiogram from the President and also a copy
of a radiogram from him to the Vice President and the Speaker of
the House. In this latter radiogram, he raised the point that the
two Senate amendments constituted new legislation, and he suggested that the conference report ought to be rejected either by
the House or by the Senate or by both.

The House this morning did reject the report and recommit it
to conference. The vote was overwhelmingly for the motion to recommit, although it was, strictly speaking, a party vote. While the
House was considering the matter, Senator Robinson brought up
the matter in the Senate. Senator Glass argued for the report and
during the course of his argument he had the Reading Clerk read
his letter to me of yesterday. Then my letter to him of today was
read. I must confess that when I wrote my letter of today, as well
as the one of Saturday, I had no idea that they would be made public. There were one or two expressions in those letters, referring
to raking leaves and cutting grass and thus constituting a reflection
on CWA, that as a matter of policy I would not have made if I
had thought for a moment that I was writing for the public. However, I have no regrets. As a matter of fact, I am rather glad that
my letter of today went into the record. I don't know whether my
earlier letter was also read in the Senate today or not, but that
would be all right too. I understand that my letter was well received and made a good impression. There was a good deal of
laughter at my reference to the leaves and grass.

As the matter now stands, the bill has been recommitted to conference. Congressman Buchanan, the chairman of the House Com-

mittee on Appropriations and head of the House conferees, called me up late this afternoon to tell me that now that the bill had been recommitted, he wanted to put in whatever language I might desire, if he could. I told him that I wanted the thirty-three and one third per cent limitation cut out and general power given to the President to make loans.

Harry Hopkins has come back to Washington. He called up and asked if he might come over and lunch with me at one o'clock. He brought with him a rough draft of an Executive Order that the President has been considering in connection with setting up an administration under the Work Relief Bill when it should pass. The President has put himself down as chairman of the committee to allocate the funds and next in line appears my name. However, this is a big committee, with practically everyone on it, including Henry Wallace, Rex Tugwell, Harry Hopkins, Admiral Peoples, General Markham, Dr. Mead, and two or three others. Then there is the committee the President has discussed with me, which is to receive applications and interview those presenting them. The other committee, of which Hopkins is to be chairman, has, it seems to me, been given the real power. While on the face of it, it is not given final authority or even complete executive authority, the setup is such that I haven't the slightest doubt that before long Hopkins would emerge as cock of the walk. After reading this, I haven't the slightest doubt that Hopkins or McIntyre gave out the story that came from Miami last week to the effect that Hopkins was to be the big man in the new work-relief organization.

Hopkins said that the President wanted this redrafted and then sent down to him so that after he has signed the bill, he can announce the setup from Miami. I told Harry Hopkins that I preferred not to be in the organization at all and that I hoped the President would not make any announcement from Florida. Hopkins said that I had better write to the President telling him how I felt. I noted that he did not even intimate that he hoped that I would go along as part of this organization. It is clear as day to me, both from what he said and from what he didn't say, that he is not averse to looming large and with as few rivals as possible in the new setup.

This afternoon I went over to see Steve Early. I was much more outspoken with him. I told him very flatly that I would not go along on this organization. I said that two or three months ago I had talked with Louie Howe about the matter, telling him that I was perfectly willing to step aside as Public Works Administrator, that I didn't relish the thought of reading one day in the newspapers that I had been set aside. I remarked to Early that this was just what had happened, in view of the story that came out of Miami last week. I assured Early, as I had assured Louie Howe, that I really wanted to step aside, but I added that there was nothing in the situation that justified my getting a slap in the face. Early understood my point of view and sympathized with it. He asked me whether the Interior Department might become involved and I told him very frankly that, if necessary, that would have to go too, but that I would not take a window-dressing position in the new organization. Then he remarked: "You're Public Works Administrator, you're Secretary of the Interior, and Oil Administrator. I believe the President will work it out."

Early thought it would be all right for me to write to the President telling him frankly how I feel. He said that Hopkins had just been in to see him but that he had not shown him (Early) the draft of the Executive Order. Hopkins told him that he was under instructions from the President to draft this order in final shape and then submit it to me. Early strongly urged me, when the order is presented to me, if I do not approve of it, to draft one of my own and send it on to the President with a letter explaining the state of my feelings. I told him that I felt reluctant about making any countersuggestion to the President involving myself, but I promised to take the matter under consideration.

So here the matter rests for the time being. If there is to be any change in my position, I want it to take place now because I am in the strongest position I have ever been as far as both the Congress and the public are concerned. I gather this from so many sources and from so wide an area that even allowing for the discounting that a man in my position must allow for, on account of the disposition of people to say pleasant things to him, I feel reasonably confident that there is some basis for these reports. I am more than ever certain that the administration of the Work Relief Bill will be pretty messy. I wouldn't want to have anything to do with it even if I had absolute power, but I certainly don't want to touch it where I might seem to have a semblance of power but be totally lacking in authority. I really feel quite easy in my mind and at peace with the world. I am as well prepared as any man can be for whatever may happen.

When Harry Hopkins was here he spoke of the amendment to the Work Relief Bill which would require confirmation of the leading executives. He said: "Why, that would mean that you and I would have to be confirmed," to which I replied: "I don't care so far as I am concerned." A little later he said: "I am told that Jack Garner is in favor of this amendment." I made no comment, but I could not help but think of the opinion of Hopkins that the Vice President frankly expressed to me. In fact, I have heard within the last day or so that Garner has said that Hopkins could not possibly be confirmed by the Senate. Governor Earle, of Pennsylvania, attacked Hopkins and his Relief Administration in that state in a statement that he gave out yesterday.

Chapman came in to see me on Saturday. He told me that he hadn't realized for a long time that people had been using him, but that he had come to realize it a short time ago. He said he thought that I had had a rotten deal; that he didn't know what I had in mind to do, but that if I came to the decision at any time to resign, he hoped that I would tell him so that his resignation could go in with mine.

Tuesday, April 2, 1935

I wrote a letter to the President on the transfer of the Soil Erosion Service from this Department to Agriculture in which I set forth the complete record and commented pretty vigorously, not only on the manner in which the transfer was effected, but on the question whether it should have been made at all. I submitted the letter to Slattery and Burlew for their comments and both were strongly of the opinion that it should not be sent. I suspect that they are right. It was a pretty savage letter to write to the President of the United States who at the same time happens to be my boss, but it was justified by the facts. However, I reluctantly filed it away with other similar letters that have had no effect except somewhat to relieve my feelings. In this particular case my feelings have not been relieved. I resent very much indeed the way the President treated me in this instance and I am not likely to forget it.

Word has come to me that Harry Hopkins and members of his staff have been announcing pretty generally all over Washington that Hopkins is to be the big man in the work-relief organization.

I told Senator Adams, Senator O'Mahoney, and one or two other men on the Hill, that this was the setup and they didn't seem to be very happy over it.

I have discussed with Slattery, Burlew, and Glavis what the attitude of the President would likely be if, due to the situation that may be created when I decline to go along on the work-relief program, I should find it necessary to resign as Secretary of the Interior. They all thought that the President would want to accept my resignation but at the same time wouldn't want to. They think that with his campaign for re-election coming on next year, he wouldn't want to run the risk that he might be running in letting me go. They all think that I am very strong in the country and that people are more and more coming to resent a wasteful and extravagant use of public funds. The opinion they expressed to me is about as I feel about it. I don't think the President would want me to get clear out, and it may be that he won't want me to sever all connections even after refusing to have anything to do with the work-relief program.

Wednesday, April 3, 1935

The conference committee is still deadlocked and the Senate conferees show no disposition to compromise. Late this afternoon Foley came to me with word that Senator Glass had told Senator Byrnes that his group would be willing to cut the direct labor requirement on the project from thirty-three and one third to twenty-five per cent and leave it to the President to determine whether the condition of twenty-five per cent was complied with. I regard this as rather a hollow victory. It would represent no change in principle, but we could operate under this language and I came to the conclusion that I would not be justified in opposing such a compromise. If I should do that and something worse should happen to the bill, the President might think that I had exceeded my powers. So I determined to tell Senator Byrnes that while I did not approve of this compromise, I would not oppose it.

Monday, April 8, 1935

This afternoon Harry Hopkins sent over to me a draft of an Executive Order which he had prepared to submit to the President for a setup of an organization to administer the Work Relief Bill. He gives himself absolutely all the power there is. It seems to me that he even arrogates to himself things that normally would belong to the President. This is the most sweeping and arrogant thing I have seen here. I asked him to send over to me a copy of the preliminary draft which had been prepared by the President and which he brought back with him from Florida. There is no comparison at all between these two drafts. The President's draft was along the line of his discussion with me, and there is no indication in it that he intends not only to abdicate himself in favor of Hopkins but to subordinate everyone else to Hopkins. I called in Burlew, Slattery, and Foley, and after discussing the matter I asked Foley and Burlew to prepare a draft along the lines of the President's original suggestion. At ten o'clock tonight Foley and Ben Cohen came in to discuss the draft with me, they having been working on it during the evening.

Wednesday, April 10, 1935

Yesterday I sent over to Steve Early to be handed to the President a draft of a suggested Executive Order for an organization setup under the new Work Relief Bill. I also sent a memorandum pointing out some of the particularly objectionable provisions in Harry Hopkins' draft. Both of these were prepared by Foley and Ben Cohen, but I worked in close touch with them and had both drafts rewritten two or three times.

My draft of the Executive Order was an attempt to carry out the ideas that I have had from the President on the two occasions that he has talked to me on the subject and as expressed in the rough draft that he handed to Hopkins on the Florida trip and which Hopkins brought in to me on his return. The only new matter in my order was that I set up a Planning Board, consisting of Messrs. Delano, Merriam, and Mitchell, in an important capacity in the new scheme of things, and I also tied in the State Planning Boards. In other respects I dealt with the same subject matter treated by Hopkins but in quite a different manner. Instead of giving Hopkins all the power, I cut him down very sharply in my draft and I made each of the new agencies self-sufficient— that is, I gave them power to select their own personnel, issue their own rules and regulations, and generally conduct themselves as independent agencies instead of as agencies subordinate to Hopkins.

In the afternoon Tom Corcoran came in to see me. Corcoran is a young lawyer whom I met the first summer after I came to Washington. He is on the legal staff of RFC. He is a Harvard Law School man, was formerly private secretary to Justice Holmes, and is close to Justice Brandeis and Felix Frankfurter. Recently, since Louis Howe has been put out of business by his illness, Corcoran has been called in to help out in the White House offices, and the liberals are certainly hoping that he will become a permanent fixture there because he is not only a liberal, he is a very able lawyer with general all-round ability and, I believe, a keen political sense.

Corcoran had heard rumors of the way I have been feeling about the proposed setup under the new Work Relief Bill. He came over to tell me that he hoped I would not do anything that would lead to my resignation. He said that I was the last hope of the progressives in the Administration and that if I would only manage to hang on for three or four weeks, he felt that everything would work out all right, with the President seeing the situation more clearly from the liberal standpoint. He thinks there are going to be some changes that will improve the situation materially from our point of view. He says that if they don't improve he will have no more interest in staying here than I would have, and he will have to reconcile himself to the thought of waiting for ten or twelve years for Bob La Follette to come along. He believes in Steve Early and in Miss Le'Hand.

While he doesn't want me to get out of the Government, he does think that I ought to take a very firm stand with the President. He advised me to talk straight out to him and not let him put me off with his pleasant ways. He doesn't think the President would let me go unless I made no other course possible. He said the President realizes that I am the spearhead of the progressives and that the progressives on the Hill are interested in me. He thinks further that the President knows that he must have me in the new works administration as an assurance to the country that it will be honestly administered, and that he will want my help in the campaign next year.

This morning I had an appointment with the President at eleven-thirty. I found him looking well and in good spirits. His manner to me was most friendly. I had gone over with the full intention of discussing matters frankly with him. He told me some stories about his fishing trip and then I broke in to say that Harry Hopkins had sent me a copy of his proposed Executive Order. Then the President interrupted to say that it was on his desk but that he hadn't read it. He told me that at his press conference this morning he had said to the correspondents that they had gotten way out on a limb on the new organization and that he was going to leave them there. He told them, and he emphasized to me, that he hadn't come to any definite conclusion in his own mind; that his intention was to use existing agencies, so far as possible; that he was going to consult with a number of people before coming to any conclusion. He said to me that some other drafts of Executive Orders were on his desk but that he hadn't had time to go into any of them. I asked whether, having made up his mind on the new setup, he would give me an opportunity to have a private talk with him before he had made the announcement. He said that he would.

It was Steve Early's intention, as soon as he could get to the President after his return, to intimate to him that I was pretty restive. This morning's papers carried the story that I was dissatisfied with the proposed Hopkins setup. It looks to me as if Hopkins has overreached himself. Apparently the President hasn't taken kindly to newspaper announcements that Hopkins was to run the whole show, and I suspect that when he reads Hopkins' draft of an Executive Order, especially if he goes over it with Corcoran, he won't be any too much pleased. Psychologically, I think the situation has somewhat changed, and my impression is that Hopkins will never again be as close to the clouds as he was in his own imagination when he drafted that Executive Order.

This matter disposed of, I asked the President whether he was trying to discipline me in transferring Soil Erosion to Agriculture. He said, "Certainly not," and wanted to know why I felt that way. I told him that he had promised me a hearing and that the transfer was made late of a Friday afternoon and I was due back in Washington the following morning. He said that he had found a bad legislative situation and had to take quick action. I told him I knew all about the legislative situation and that if it had been let alone, Congress would have passed a bill making Soil Erosion a permanent function of this Department. The President said that he thought it belonged to Agriculture and I told him that, in my opinion, I believed that it was a matter of conservation. He went on to explain that a great deal of soil erosion work is necessary in the national forests and that the national forests are in Agriculture. I interjected that they are but that they belong to Interior. He agreed with this and I then asked him whether he was still of the mind that I could go ahead with my bill. He queried me—"Your Conservation Department Bill?"—and I answered in the affirmative. He said, "All right, go ahead," and then I asked him whether he would make it an Administration measure. He hesitated and then said that perhaps he might. I told him that I was having the bill drafted.

At this point I remarked that I didn't find it easy to get into an argument with him this morning and he laughed. Then I went over some Public Works and Interior Department matters. I was allowed all of half an hour with him today, which must have been Steve Early's work.

Friday, April 13, 1935

Yesterday I signed a contract with Macmillan for the publication of my book on public works. Dr. Foreman promised the manuscript by Monday and I don't see how I can possibly finish it by then. The trouble is that I have a lot of speeches on my hands. I keep refusing invitations to speak, then I accept one, and before I know it I have a lot to deliver. I have had to give the right of way to my speech next Monday at the Wharton School of Finance and Commerce, University of Pennsylvania.

It is extraordinary the amount of time that I put on these speeches. They look fairly easy when I start them, but they are indeed a chore before I work out the final draft. I finished this speech in final draft yesterday and I also revised the draft of one of the chapters of the book. In the meantime, I am working hard on my speech for the Associated Press on the twenty-second. I came back from Chicago with this speech dictated and the first draft revised. This has been passing through the hands of the men here whom I ask to look over my manuscripts, and last night Ben Cohen brought me in an entirely new speech which he and Tom Corcoran had drafted.

Today I worked on a manuscript on housing that will appear under my name in the May issue of *The Journal of Land and Public Utility Economics*. This was written by Onslow and he did a very good job indeed.

Wednesday, April 17, 1935

Yesterday afternoon I had almost an hour with the President and I found him in a very good state of mind. He told me to go ahead with my book.

At my morning press conference I had paid my respects to Senator Long and the President said he liked what I had said. He also spoke approvingly of my speech at the University of Pennsylvania in which I had taken issue with Lewis W. Douglas's views on the duties of the Government with respect to the present economic situation.

I told the President that I felt that we ought to have the right to cross-examine witnesses in the Virgin Islands investigation and that it was my belief that Senator Tydings was intending to go down to the Virgin Islands to open the investigation so that he could smear the Administration before giving us any chance to reply. The President called Senator Tydings by telephone and said that he thought that the whole truth ought to be brought out and that the way to do that was by proper cross-examination. He intimated that if he had reason to believe that the truth was not being adduced from the witnesses, he might feel like calling them before himself personally and questioning them. He also told Tydings that he did not think that five Senators ought to go to the Virgin Islands until after the adjournment of Congress. He asked Tydings whether charges had been filed against Judge Wilson, and when Tydings replied in the negative, the President remarked that charges ought to be filed. He went on to say that Wilson had the southern Mississippi point of view toward the Negroes in the Virgin Islands and that there wouldn't be any difficulty down there if he hadn't stirred it up.

The President brought up once more his plan of organization under the Work Relief Bill. It is about as he has discussed it with me heretofore. Apparently he had read the draft of the Executive Order that I submitted to him. He said he agreed in general with my point of view about a big committee to make the allocations but that he wanted a big committee in this instance consisting of perhaps twenty-one or twenty-two people. He wants to put on General Robert E. Wood, president of Sears, Roebuck and Company, representing business, a representative of labor, and a representative of the farm organizations. He said he would then have an executive committee of not to exceed five, of which I would be the chairman. He told me that Comptroller General McCarl had ruled that lump sums could not be allocated out of this fund but that specific projects would have to be submitted and acted upon. I remarked that that was similar to our PWA procedure and he said that it was. This, of course, will throw a tremendous administrative burden upon the new organization. I told the President that I hoped that he would not have a larger executive committee than five. I said that he was a great executive but that if he had to call in a group of men before he made a decision on any matter, he would never be able to get anything done. He agreed. His manner was most friendly throughout.

Friday, April 19, 1935

I finally got the speech that I am to deliver at the annual luncheon of the Associated Press in New York next Monday whipped into shape. Considering the occasion and the fact that most of my remarks are devoted to free press, free speech, and free assemblage, I wanted Steve Early to pass on the manuscript and so Mike Straus took it over to him. He said it was fine and clicked in every sentence. He had no criticism to make of my text but suggested that I add one sentence, which I was glad to do. As I dictate tonight, the speech has gone through final revision and is being mimeographed to send out to the newspapers.

Senator Huey Long and I have been having a passage at arms during the last two or three days and so far I haven't had the worst of it. At my press conference yesterday I remarked that the trouble with him was that he had halitosis of the intellect. This made a great hit with the correspondents. I have never seen them so interested and amused. The papers this morning carried this remark pretty generally, together with others, and this afternoon at Cabinet meeting the President commented on it. He said it was fine and the best thing that has been said about Huey Long. He really seemed quite pleased with it.

At Cabinet meeting Vice President Garner said that he wanted to make a political prediction. It was this: that Senator Long would come to the next Democratic national convention at the head of the Louisiana delegation but that there would be a contesting delegation and that the Long delegates would be unseated; that Senator Long would be renominated to the Senate next year but that there would be an independent candidate and that Long would be unseated.

Saturday afternoon Miss Le Hand called me and asked me if I could go over to see the President at half past three. I found him in the Oval Room on the second floor of the White House proper, which he uses as his study, and I spent over an hour with him. He was again in a fine state of mind.

First I took up with him the bill to change the name of this Department from Interior to Conservation and Works. I suggested that a matter affecting the Cabinet was one of concern to him and that the bill ought to go up to the Hill in his name. He said the difficulty with that was that he had told the Congressional leaders that aside from certain enumerated bills he would not have anything to urge on Congress. He suggested that I cause the bill to be introduced and tell the chairmen of the committees to which it is referred that they can consult him about it. He will then tell them that the bill is all right. I will try to have these bills introduced next week when I get back from New York.

The President himself brought up the work-relief organization. His setup is the same that he has been discussing with me recently, except that today he said I would be chairman of the allocation committee. He started out with himself as chairman and with me as ranking member. Then his idea was to have an executive committee, of which I would be chairman, with him still retaining the chairmanship of the general committee. This last shift is significant and means to me that he has finally come to the sensible conclusion that he ought not to put himself in a position where he would be criticized for everything that goes wrong in the administration of this program, as he would be if he were chairman of the committee. Under this plan his relationship to the new program will be exactly what it has been to public works. He will have the final say, but he won't have to take part in the actual administration. This plan will also protect him from criticism.

The plan contemplates a large committee of over twenty, with every interest represented that ought to be represented. This committee will discuss the projects submitted to it, but the actual allocations will be made by a subcommittee, of which I also will be chairman. The other members of this subcommittee so far decided upon are Harry Hopkins, Acting Director of the Budget Bell, and Frank Walker.

I don't like the idea of this big committee. It will mean a lot of time wasted in useless debate, with no power to take final action. I just can't bear to take all the time that will be necessary as chairman of this committee and I can't very well delegate the duty of presiding to a vice chairman. However, perhaps I can handle it in the way I did the Public Works Board. At the outset we took a good deal of time to consider projects but before long it was running very smoothly, which means that I was running it practically to suit myself. There is likely to be some trouble at the outset, especially with the executive committee.

The committee that will receive the projects and handle the information will have Frank Walker as chairman. The President told me today that he had agreed to come back. He will reinstate him as Director of the Emergency Council, dispossessing Richberg in that job. I didn't ask him what would happen to Richberg, who is now chairman of NRA, but it looks to me as if this will mean a distinct change in his status. Certainly he won't be entitled any longer to the characterization of "Number One Man" or "Assistant President." It looks to me as if his usefulness in the Administration is practically at an end.

If this administration plan of the President goes through, it will mean that instead of having less power, I will have greater power and will really outrank all the other men in the work-relief organization. This will be a surprise to a good many people who have been proclaiming that I was to have a back seat and an inconspicuous part in the new program. It is a surprise to me, too, because only a few weeks ago there was every indication of a disposition to sidetrack me and to make Harry Hopkins the top man in the organization. However, it has also become clear lately that Harry Hopkins has been losing in favor, due largely to the fact, in my opinion, that he took too much for granted, creating the impression that he was to be the top man and thus overshooting himself.

Senator Long, according to the newspapers, has put through his new legislative program in Louisiana and is on his way back to Washington. He has threatened to go after me on the floor of the Senate on Monday and I suppose he will. However, I won't be here, since I am leaving for New York this afternoon. Tomorrow is the occasion of my speech at the annual luncheon of the Associated Press.

Charles Merriam spent some time with me this morning. He thinks there is a deliberate and well-planned campaign throughout the country on the part of the conservative interests to attack liberals all along the line, especially in colleges and universities. The Illinois State Senate has appointed a committee to investigate communistic and subversive activities in the Illinois colleges. This is the outgrowth of the absurd charges of Charles Walgreen, the chain store druggist, who has withdrawn his niece from the University of Chicago because, he said, she was being subjected to communistic influences.

According to Merriam, an acute situation may arise between the faculty and the Board of Trustees of the university. One of Merriam's assistant professors, Schuman by name, is up for reappointment and the trustees apparently are considering very seriously whether they should keep him on. Merriam wanted my advice as to what he should do in such a situation. He is ready to resign and he seemed inclined to think that he would do that if Schuman should be turned down. I told him I thought he ought to make a stinging statement and stay on and then see what the trustees would do. He seemed to think well of this idea. He said that it wouldn't take much to cause President Hutchins to resign on this issue and that if he did, probably some twenty or twenty-five professors would follow him.

Tuesday, April 23, 1935

I went to New York with Anna on the two o'clock train Sunday afternoon. Paul Moss, New York Commissioner of Licenses, met us at the train at the instance of Mayor La Guardia, who was in Arizona. He took us to the Folies Bergère where we had dinner and saw a very artistic but a very naked performance.

Monday morning Commissioner Moss gathered in one of the officials of the park system and an engineer of the Triborough Bridge, and we drove up to see the bridge, which is in course of construction. Not only the bridge but the approaches and the connecting roads are well under way.

Just before one o'clock I went to the Waldorf-Astoria where I met Mr. Noyes and other members of the Associated Press. It was the annual meeting of the organization and I was the guest speaker at the luncheon in the ballroom. There was a large attendance. Someone said there were over a thousand people present, but I would guess that the number was fewer. At any rate, the ballroom was filled. I talked for thirty minutes over both national hookups. The main part of my theme dealt with the necessity of safeguarding the rights of free press, free speech, and free assemblage as guaranteed in the Bill of Rights. My speech seemed to be well received and a number of men came up later to congratulate me. John W. Davis, who was the Democratic candidate for President against Coolidge, was present and was one of those who congratulated me, whether merely as a formal matter or not I do not know.

Thursday, April 25, 1935

Yesterday Senator Lewis came down to the Department in response to a telephone call from me. I gave him a draft of a bill changing the name of this department to Department of Conservation and Works and giving the President the power for two years, subject to review by Congress, to take bureaus out of this Department and bring other bureaus in. Senator Lewis said that he would be glad to introduce the bill and that he would carry it through.

Congressman Cochran, of St. Louis, was also in. I gave him a draft of the bill which he promised to introduce in the House. I don't know whether he has done so or not, but Senator Lewis introduced his bill yesterday afternoon and the newspaper correspondents saw in it a conflict between Agriculture and Interior for control of the National Forest Service. They are not far wrong at that.

I have had some very fine editorials, letters, and telephone calls on the speech I made Monday before the Associated Press. Roger Baldwin, of the Civil Liberties Union, told Harry Slattery that it was a much better speech than Borah had made on civil liberties just a few days earlier. It is very gratifying that there should have been such a response to this type of speech. A feeling of intolerance has been growing in this country, and I had a good deal of doubt as to the expediency of my talking as I did. However, it would appear that there is a large section of sentiment in the country ready to respond to political fundamentals. It is significant when such newspapers as *The New York Times,* the *Wall Street Journal,* and the *Washington* Post should write so cordially and appreciatively of a speech devoted to free press, free speech, and free assembly.

Saturday, April 27, 1935

Yesterday afternoon the President announced Harry Hopkins' place in the new work-relief setup. The newspaper correspondents have been a good deal puzzled by the whole situation. For weeks they have been proclaiming that Hopkins was to be the real administrator next to the President, and they haven't known what to make of it all. As was natural, some of the newspapers that have been most insistent upon Hopkins' prominence have seized upon his appointment as justification for their predictions, although their protestations sound just a little hollow. They say that while I am Chairman of the Allotment Committee, I will have merely one vote, ignoring the fact that that has been true of me as a member of the Public Works Committee. They also say that the President will have the final decision on allotments, again ignoring the fact that that has been true in the Public Works setup. Of course, in the end, Hopkins may appear as the outstanding man in the new organization. No one can predict one way or the other, but I am still Administrator of Public Works and in addition I am chairman of the committee to make the allotments. It will be Hopkins' duty to see that the labor is provided from the relief rolls and to keep track of the progress of the work on the projects.

The Cabinet meeting yesterday afternoon was devoted to more serious discussions than any I can remember. It really was like what one would expect a Cabinet meeting to be. The President asked our advice, one by one, as to what should be done with the NRA bill that is pending in the Senate, and we discussed other matters of moment seriously.

Last night at half past eight a group of us met with the President in the White House to discuss informally the new Work Relief Administration. All of those present, aside from Steve Early and Secretary Morgenthau, were men who were to be connected with the new administration. No explanation was necessary as to why Steve Early was there because he handles press releases at the White House, but I could not see why Secretary Morgenthau was there because he is not on the new organization, and the Acting Director of the Budget and Admiral Peoples were both there.

Others there were Frank Walker, Harry Hopkins, Rex Tugwell, and Joe Kennedy. Kennedy, by the way, was also an outsider so far as the new setup is concerned. The President was quite serious when he said that the administration of the Work Relief Bill might affect the election next year and might mean a change in administration during the next term. He said that he expected everything to go like clock work and that he would accept no excuses. I think he realizes the grave responsibilities that he has assumed, but I don't think he has any real conception of the difficulties that lie ahead. Rex Tugwell on the way home remarked that he didn't think the President had any notion what the Public Works Administration had really done and the difficulties it had overcome. I agreed, and I think also that Hopkins will find the new Administration an entirely different proposition from giving out money without regard as to whether or not it is being invested in permanent projects.

It seemed to me last night that Hopkins was playing up to Walker and, if so, it was to try to keep me within what he might regard as the proper bounds. He suggested that all publicity should go through Walker and that Walker should sift out our personnel for us. I made no comments on the first suggestion but I intend to continue to select my own personnel and I shall go along with my press conferences, although naturally Walker ought to hand out a good deal of the canned information. I do not believe that Walker can handle press conferences very successfully. He confided to me the other day that one thing he couldn't stand was criticism by the newspapers. However, there isn't any doubt Walker's selection for the particular place that he holds was the best possible choice. He is sincerely interested in the success of the Administration and I don't think that he will try to aggrandize power to himself at the expense of anyone else. He will try to maintain harmonious relationships and do everything in his power to make the program run smoothly and successfully. Hopkins will fly off on tangents unless he is watched, and I am quite likely to be bulldoggish and want to have my own way. The conference lasted a long time. I didn't get home until after midnight.

Last night at six-fifteen I spoke for five minutes over the radio, Columbia network, in connection with the brief memorial for Justice Holmes that was held under the auspices of the Civil Liberties Union.

Letters continue to come in to me on my speech before the Associated Press. This was my first opportunity to gauge sentiment in the country on Senator Long, Dr. Townsend, and Father Coughlin. I have been getting a good many letters professing warm adherence to the doctrines and purposes of these three men, but I am also getting many other letters complimenting me on my speech and backing me up in the set-to I had recently with Senator Long.

Monday, April 29, 1935

Congressman Sirovich came in to see me Saturday morning to talk to me about certain interesting facts that have been developed in an investigation by a committee of which he is chairman. The field for investigation is "pooling of patents." He has been giving a good deal of time to an investigation of the airplane situation and what he has developed so far is little short of scandalous. According to Sirovich, the United States Government was about to buy the patents of the Wright brothers and the Curtis people, about the time of the world war, because both of these outfits were bankrupt. The war came along and a group financed by Wall Street money bought the patents and made the "flaming coffins" that we sent abroad for our aviators. I have forgotten the sum of money that these flaming coffins cost us in royalties to the patentees but it was an enormous sum, in addition to which the American airplanes during the war were not only useless but were really death traps.

As a result of a prior investigation by Congress some of these men were indicted and convicted but not one has served a single day of his sentence. They still control the airplane industry in the country according to Sirovich. He says that Japan has bombing planes of much greater speed than anything we have and capable of sailing so much higher that our defense planes could never even get up to them. They also have a flying radius of five thousand miles, about twice as far as any American Army or Navy plane. They can carry much heavier loads. They can sail above the clouds, drop their bombs and get away without anyone knowing whence they came or whither they went, or what nation they belonged to.

Tuesday, April 30, 1935

Anna and I went to the German Embassy to dinner last evening. Mrs. Justice Stone sat on my left and Mrs. MacWhite, wife of the Irish Minister, on my right. It is really extraordinary how these formal dinners tire me. I was nearly dead when I got home. I had a bad night, and I have been very tired all day today, not only tired but nervous.

Mr. Delano and Charles Eliot went with me to an appointment with the President at two o'clock. I had an hour and a half with him and covered a good deal of ground. The reason I took Mr. Delano and Mr. Eliot was because I wanted a definite understanding with reference to the continuation of the National Resources Board and the Advisory Committee with the new work-relief setup. The President will continue the National Resources Board by Executive Order and we will tie it in with the work-relief organization.

After Messrs. Delano and Eliot left, I stayed on for quite a long conference with the President. I told him of Congressman Sirovich's call on me Saturday afternoon. He made a note of it and said that he would send for Sirovich. He has changed his mind about having an executive committee of the Allotment Committee, which bores me very much indeed because it will take a tremendous amount of time for the big committee that has been organized to consider and pass upon all of the allotments. I have less stomach for this new plan the more I think of it. We planned for the first meeting to be held in the office of the President Monday afternoon at two o'clock, but when I got back to the office I recalled that I was having a hearing that afternoon on the Raker Act so I will have to call the President and suggest another time.

I brought up again the question of Walter T. Fisher for Under Secretary. I had forgotten to tell the President when I first mentioned Fisher that he had acted as attorney for John Strachey when the latter was arrested in Glencoe, Illinois, some time ago, to face deportation charges on the ground that he was a communist and had entered this country under false representations. The President was disturbed at this suggestion. He is anxious just now not to do anything to stir up William Randolph Hearst. He told me that he had had a talk with Arthur Brisbane, who had assured him that, regardless of Hearst's attitude, he (Brisbane) was with the President and would be with him. Brisbane told him that Hearst was pretty erratic these days but that he believed that if he kept sending him friendly messages and didn't do anything to disturb him unduly, Hearst would support him next year in the campaign. The President remarked that, outside of Hearst and one or two other strings of newspapers, all the balance of the press of the country would be against him and naturally he wants all the support he can get. Therefore, he wants to watch his step on the Hearst matter.

I told him very frankly that Victor Watson had been back of the Strachey arrest. The way we left it was that I was to call Charles Merriam and ask him to go to see Watson, but not as coming from me, to say that he had reason to believe that I was considering Fisher for Under Secretary and thus feel Watson out. When I came back I did call Merriam but he said he hadn't been able to see Watson lately. Then I suggested that Merriam go to see Homer Guck, the publisher of the *Herald-Examiner*, and he said he would try to see him in the morning.

Wednesday, May 1, 1935

I was deluged today with callers and delegations. In spite of the fact that the President has announced that projects under the new Work Relief Bill are to be filed with Frank Walker, people come in to see me. I haven't seen all of them because Harry Slattery has managed to divert some before they got into my office. Unfortunately, a couple of delegations that I sent to Walker's office were sent back and they were highly indignant. I don't blame them very much for this and I can't understand why Walker doesn't have someone to talk to them.

There was a meeting in the President's office at three-thirty this afternoon. Those present were substantially the same men who attended the conference last Friday night at the White House. We spent an hour and a half in order to do exactly nothing at all. The only things brought up were purely administrative matters that could have been settled in five minutes' time. As usual, Morgenthau was there and also as usual, he was very impressive and interruptive. Harry Hopkins told me that the President had not wanted to call this meeting, but Morgenthau has instigated it. As it was, it wasted a lot of valuable time for all of us.

Friday, May 3, 1935

Yesterday Frank Walker, Harry Hopkins, and I were called to the White House for a meeting with the President at three o'clock. Governor La Follette and Senator La Follette were present, the former with a work-relief plan covering the entire state. Governor La Follette assured us that if we would give the necessary sum of money to a finance corporation to be set up in the state under legislative act, the state would see to it that every employable now on the relief rolls will be put to work for a period of a year or eighteen months and that a considerable portion of the money advanced would be repaid to the Federal Government. It looks like a well-thought-out and intelligent plan and we were all favorably disposed toward it. Governor La Follette said he was going to stay in Washington until he got favorable action. He sent me the plan today so that I could have it photostated and distributed among the agencies that ought to study it.

Last night a dinner was given in honor of Jane Addams of Hull House in the Willard Hotel. It was her seventy-fifth birthday and the twentieth anniversary of the founding of the Women's Inter-National League for Peace and Freedom, an organization that was founded at The Hague under the leadership of Miss Addams during the war. The hotel management said this was the biggest dinner ever given at the hotel. Five hundred people who wanted reservations were turned away and after dinner a good many people stood at the entrances to hear the speeches.

The toastmistress was Mrs. Caroline O'Day, Representative-at-large from the State of New York. Mrs. Roosevelt was the first speaker and I was the second. Both of us were on the air. Gerard Swope, of the General Electric Company, followed me; then came Oswald Garrison Villard, publisher of *The Nation;* Sidney Hillman, of the Amalgamated Clothing Workers of America; and Dr. Alice Hamilton, formerly of Hull House but more lately of the Harvard Medical School.

At Cabinet meeting this afternoon the Vice President said that the best thing that could happen on the pending bonus legislation would be for the Patman bill to go through, the President to veto that bill, and then to have the bill passed over the President's veto. He said that practically all of the Republicans in the House had voted for the Patman bill and that the Republicans in the Senate would do likewise. They would vote to pass it over the President's veto so that the President would have no responsibility for the legislation. The Patman bill provides for the printing of enough money to pay the bonus. If this should happen, the bonus would be taken out of next year's campaign and the Republicans, having been responsible for the legislation, would be in no position to attack the bill and the resultant issue of money in order to pay the bonus.

Wednesday, May 8, 1935

Monday afternoon I held a hearing on the question of whether the Raker Act, under which San Francisco was given the right to build a dam in Hetch Hetchy Valley in Yosemite Park for water storage and power purposes, was being violated. This act strictly prohibits San Francisco from selling or reselling power, except directly to consumers. Under a so-called "consignment contract," its power is distributed in San Francisco through the Pacific Gas & Electric Company, apparently at a very large profit. Representatives of the city and county of San Francisco were present, and also a lawyer representing the Chamber of Commerce and allied organizations of that city. I was not impressed with the soundness of their legal views or the ability with which they were presented. It seemed to me to be the old question of trying to do indirectly what may not be done directly and then attempting to justify it. An effort was made to have it appear that the Pacific Gas & Electric Company was performing this service for San Francisco at a distinct sacrifice, and the question was also raised about the amount of taxes paid into the city treasury by this power concern. As nearly as I could see it, San Francisco's position was: "We have made it impossible for ourselves to build a transmission system of our own and therefore an emergency exists which justifies the present arrangement with the Pacific Gas & Electric Company." Franck Havenner, formerly secretary to Senator Johnson, and one of the commissioners of San Francisco, attacked the position of the other official representatives from that city, as did also the president of the Board of Commissioners, who attended with Havenner.

Tuesday afternoon we held the first meeting of the Allotment Advisory Committee of the work-relief setup in the Cabinet room at the White House. There were twenty members of the committee present and the President was also there. I presided as chairman and I felt somewhat embarrassed about occupying the President's official Cabinet chair while he sat in a low easy chair at my right. We spent about two and one-half hours covering ground that should have been covered in twenty to thirty minutes, but the President was highly pleased with the meeting and afterward complimented me on it two or three times. I hadn't thought myself that it was much of a meeting or that I had particularly distinguished myself as chairman, although I did try to keep proceedings moving at a tolerable pace.

After the meeting the President wanted to talk with Frank Walker, Harry Hopkins, and me, so we went into his office. Harry Hopkins has a scheme of getting all the men off the relief rolls by the first of July. He and the President discussed it for quite some time and then the President turned to me and asked me what I thought of it. I told him that my psychology was somewhat different and that I was always rather slow about claiming in advance what I was going to do. I remarked that it would be better to let results speak for themselves. I suggested that Hopkins be authorized to go ahead without any advance claims of future results, do what he thought he could do, and then announce the whole thing as a *fait accompli* if he had been able to put the thing over. I said this would make a great impression on the country, but that, on the contrary, if it was announced that this was going to be done and it should fail to be accomplished, it would subject the Administration to a lot of criticism. I also said that a good deal would depend on the type of project to be undertaken; that the country was reconciled to pay relief for those out of work and that it would approve of well-built, worth-while public works; that if, however, the work was just make-believe, it would do more harm than good on public sentiment.

I didn't want to say this before Hopkins and I wouldn't have said it if the President hadn't asked me for my views. Since he did, I did not have much option except to speak frankly. The President agreed entirely with me and so did Walker. Perforce Harry Hopkins did also, and that ended the discussion.

Friday, May 10, 1935

I have felt very keenly the death of Senator Bronson Cutting in an airplane accident near Kansas City, Missouri. I liked him personally and he was undoubtedly one of the strong men of the Senate. He had a fine family and cultural background and with it all, he was forceful, independent, and progressive. It is really rare for a man of his wealth and social position to have the force of character and the independence that he undoubtedly had. Suffering with tuberculosis, as a young man he went to New Mexico. He did a good deal of his college work lying on a cot, notwithstanding which he was able to graduate with honors from Harvard where he was a member of Phi Beta Kappa. President Roosevelt offered him the position in the Cabinet that he later offered to me after Senator Cutting and Senator Johnson had refused it, but when Senator Cutting ran for re-election, the Administration opposed him, much to the disgust of myself and the other progressives.

I was at the President's office when Steve Early brought in word of Senator Cutting's death. The President spoke regretfully of the occurrence and said that he had known Cutting since he was a boy. He referred to the fact that he had opposed him for re-election and then said that while he liked Cutting, he could not stand for the crowd that he traveled with in New Mexico, whereupon I remarked, "Mr. President, no one can come out of New Mexico into political life who doesn't have a bad crowd somewhere in the background, and his crowd was not a bit worse than the Democrat crowd in that state." The President admitted that this was true. It will be a long time before New Mexico has such another Senator as Cutting.

I lunched with the President on Thursday and James Roosevelt was also there. We lunched on the porch, just outside the President's office and it was very pleasant in the open air with the White House grounds looking their best. The President said that he had understood that Senator Norris felt very bitter about Cutting's death and was inclined to blame him (the President) because Cutting had gone to New Mexico to get some affidavits in connection with his election contest, which was pending in the Senate. I told the President that I was afraid that there might be some feeling of that sort. I think the President felt a little conscience-stricken about the whole thing. He said that he had told Cutting that he was willing to give Chavez, the contestant, a job and have him drop the contest, but that Cutting had told him he didn't want him to do that because it would have the appearance of being what in fact it would be, and Cutting felt that there was no basis for the contest. I asked the President if he would have any objection if I offered Puryear, Cutting's secretary, a job in my organization, and he said he didn't object. I told him I thought it would be a nice thing to do, considering all the circumstances.

I discussed with the President that part of his Executive Order setting up the work-relief organization which apparently gives Hopkins the right to supervise all investigation and inspection. He said that that did not apply to me and that I could go on with my own inspection and investigation as I had been doing. I think this will be a shock and a surprise to Hopkins, but I could not have consented to go along on this program without authority to see that the work done under me was done honestly and according to contract.

We had a more than interesting Cabinet meeting today. There was quite some discussion about George Peek and his place in the Administration. Everyone seems to want to get rid of him, but the President is afraid that if he eases him out, Peek, who has a good deal of strength with certain farming elements, might proceed to organize against the Administration. Secretary Hull is particularly antagonistic toward Peek because Peek is stepping on his toes right along. Recently Peek gave out a news release on our foreign trade and the President said he had gotten himself pretty well out on a limb because of the figures which he incorporated in his release.

Then Farley spoke for the first time about the political situation in the country. He was plainly worried. He said there had been a decided shift and that it behooved everyone to see that only loyal Administration men were in the service. No one urged the appointment of party Democrats, but it was quite properly the general feeling that appointments should be made only of men and women who are loyal to the New Deal. With this I heartily concur. I don't want to appoint people for political reasons, that is, as to whether they are Republicans or Democrats, but by the same token I can't see the sense in putting in charge of New Deal activities people who don't believe in the New Deal. That just isn't common sense.

The Vice President remarked that the success or the failure of the Administration next year would depend upon the manner in which work relief was administered. In this the President concurred and I think all the rest of us did too. In view of this fact, it seems to me altogether too bad that such a cumbersome and unwieldy organization should have been set up, but so far as I know, the President has only himself to blame for this, although it was Hopkins who sold him the idea that with this sum of money all the employables now on relief could be taken off the relief rolls and put to work.

I took occasion to say to Harry Hopkins the other day in the presence of Frank Walker that I did not believe the program would work out. I said that as fast as men were taken off relief rolls, others would go on. People who have been able to keep off relief to date are gradually exhausting all their resources and sooner or later will have to turn to the Government for support. Moreover, the plan contemplates that only those on the relief rolls will be given employment under the new program and that will mean that if a man wants a job, he will have to go on relief rolls. I think this is bad psychology and bad politics. Self-respecting, independent people who have been able to keep going will resent it exceedingly to be denied an opportunity to work, while the less provident and the less independent, and even the less fortunate, will be given preference at the jobs that we expect to create.

An amusing, but irritating, incident occurred today. The Reverend Christian F. Reisner was on my list of callers. It happened that I was unusually tired because I had been out to dinner twice this week and I have not been sleeping well. The reverend gentleman sat composedly by my desk when his turn was reached and proceeded to tell me that his principal object in coming to see me was to bring some joy into my life and cheer me up. I remarked sarcastically that I needed time more than I needed to have joy brought into my life. He remarked that he had been in to see me a year ago with Mayor La Guardia, of New York, and after he had rambled on for a while I brusquely asked him what he wanted of me.

He said his principal object was to talk with me as he had talked at various times with other public men. He said he and I had a hero in common in Theodore Roosevelt. He has, it appeared, written a history of the religious life of Roosevelt and he told me how truly religious "TR" was and how he had never failed to go to church each Sunday. I knew the contrary to be the fact, but I didn't contradict the gentleman because I was too anxious to speed him on his way. Then he came around to a housing project that he wants to finance and I told him that we couldn't do anything for him. I did, however, refer him to Colonel Hackett. It was a case of anything to get rid of him. Even then he was slow to move, although I was becoming more and more nervous. Finally he told me that in God's eyes I was doing just as important work as he himself was doing. This really did cheer me a lot. It was pleasant to have such an authoritative message from the Most High, lacking which I never would have ventured to consider myself as useful a citizen as the reverend doctor. Along about this stage

I surreptitiously pushed Fred Marx' button and he dashed in to the rescue. Between us we got the cheer dispenser out. He delivered the balance of his godly message to Fred Marx out in the hall, but at any rate I was rid of him.

Tuesday, May 14, 1935

I saw the President this afternoon. I took word to him that Senator Reynolds, with the consent of Senator Tydings, had continued the Virgin Islands investigation until next fall. I half suspect that Senator Tydings has found this to be rather a hot potato. Margold has been bulldogging his investigators and some of the local malcontents in the Virgin Islands, while I have been nipping at the calves of Senator Tydings up here. I doubt whether the investigation will ever be resumed now. I told the President that Judge Wilson's term expired in August and that if the President refused to reappoint him, the whole matter would quiet down. I think he will do this.

Oscar Chapman told me today that Harry Hopkins told him last night that my engineering staff was the best in Washington and was much superior to his. He wants to strengthen his and told Chapman he was going to try to get Colonel Waite to head it up for him. He also told Chapman that Waite had suggested Dykstra, the City Manager of Cincinnati, for the job. I am wondering whether Waite would be willing to come back to Washington, having resigned from here only last September. Waite is a fine person and a good engineer, but he never was in sympathy with the care that we exercised in carrying through our PWA program. Dykstra is a much stronger character and I doubt whether he and Hopkins would get along very well together.

Chapman also told me that last Friday night Ernest K. Lindley, Washington correspondent for the *New York Herald Tribune*, told him that during the past two days there were indications that the President was going to lean more heavily on me in this new work-relief program. Lindley is close to the White House. There is a feeling of great uncertainty and unsettlement with respect to this program. The machinery that the President has set up is just as unwieldy as I thought it would be. There is no snap or efficiency to the organization, and I am wondering how long it will take for the President to realize that a reorganization under one responsible man will be in order. Heaven knows I do not want that job myself, but I do believe implicitly in an executive job being done by one competent executive at the head of the organization.

Wednesday, May 15, 1935

Anna and I went to the Belgian Embassy for dinner last night. Immediately after dinner, I excused myself and hurried over to the White House. The President had in Senators Johnson, Norris, La Follette, Wheeler, Costigan, Dr. Felix Frankfurter, Niles, a progressive from Boston, Secretary Wallace, and myself. Wallace had also been attending a dinner and arrived shortly after I did. Apparently before I got there the President had asked for a very frank discussion of the legislative and political situation and his request for frankness was being taken at its face value.

Senators La Follette and Wheeler did most of the talking, but they did a pretty good job of it, especially La Follette. Niles also had a good deal to say, but I thought he was just a little brusque in his manner. However, it was made clear to the President that in the opinion of those present the time had come for him to assert the leadership that the country is demanding. Professor Frankfurter told him that Justice Brandeis had sent him word that it was "the eleventh hour."

La Follette said that the attack on the President by the United States Chamber of Commerce was a most fortunate happening. It was the opinion of all that big business in no circumstances will support the President, and I made the observation that this opposition should be capitalized. La Follette also said that the President has a fine legislative program pending before Congress and that the best answer to Huey Long and Father Coughlin would be the enactment into law of the Administration bills now pending there. Senator Wheeler said that it was all right for the President to get all that he could out of Senators Robinson and Harrison, but he made it clear that neither man has any sympathy with the President's program, although he admitted that the President has gotten a great deal out of Robinson. La Follette reminded the President that Theodore Roosevelt did not hesitate on occasion to take open issue with members of his own party, and suggested that it might be necessary for the President to do the same thing.

We talked until nearly twelve o'clock and I left with a distinct impression that it is the President's intention to take a firm stand on his progressive policies and force the fighting along that line.

At one point the President asked Senator Wheeler why he hadn't come in to give him an opinion that he had just expressed. Senator Wheeler said that he was never able to see the President; that McIntyre always reported that he was bogged down and wouldn't give him an appointment. The President said that he could get in to see him any time within twenty-four hours, but Wheeler insisted that he couldn't get in at all. Then the President told him the next time he should call up Miss Le Hand.

I sincerely hope it is the intention of the President to go ahead along progressive lines. There isn't any doubt at all that something ought to be done to arrest the trend away from the Administration. The President should, as La Follette urged him, reaffirm the position of vigorous leadership that he occupied during the first year or more of his Administration.

Friday, May 17, 1935

Thursday morning the Senate Committee on Expenditures in the Executive Departments had a hearing on my bill to change the name of this Department to that of Department of Conservation and Works. Senator Lewis, of Illinois, is chairman of this committee and he introduced the bill at my request. I had sent a fine statement, drafted by Mr. Burlew, to the members of the committee explaining what was involved in the change and I made no formal statement before the committee, although I discussed the matter informally and answered a number of questions that were put to me.

To my surprise, Chief Forester Silcox, Sherman, and one or two other members of the Forest Service, appeared to oppose this change. Their opposition consisted of a metaphysical discussion of what conservation might mean. What they had in the back of their minds, of course, was the fear that the change of name might be influential in causing the taking of the Forest Service away from Agriculture and bringing it to my Department. However, they were afraid to raise this question frankly because no such change is proposed in the bill. It simply gives power to the President for a period of two years to make changes respecting my Department.

I became impatient with the character of the opposition and expressed myself quite frankly on the subject. I resented the fact that Henry Wallace should permit members of his Department to oppose me on a matter that was not the slightest concern of his Department. Of course, if and when it is proposed to transfer Forestry to this Department, then it will be well within the rights of Agriculture to object, but it did seem to me to be highly improper for his Department to object to a change in the name of this Department. A name after all is a matter of choice and taste. I didn't mince matters very much in my answer to the arguments that they made. Moreover, I think that if Wallace had wanted to oppose this bill, he should have appeared personally and not permitted subordinates to appear and catechize me.

Yesterday afternoon we had a two-hour session of the Allotment Advisory Committee, during which we approved allotments aggregating more than $1 billion. As usual, Morgenthau was there and he actually had the nerve to ask if he might say something when a certain matter was before us for consideration. I could not very well refuse, since he was sitting with the President just back of me. He said what he had to say and then, without any comment of any sort, I passed on to the next order of business, completely ignoring him. It was noticeable also that Admiral Peoples was on his toes ready to take part in the discussion on the slightest excuse. On a tip from Morgenthau he offered a resolution, but as another one was already pending I ruled him out of order. He did not bring it up subsequently.

I am becoming more and more sick of this whole setup and wish that I could find a way to get out of it. The thing is clumsy and cumbersome. It takes altogether too much time conferring with Hopkins and Walker and then with the President and then presiding over this town meeting that we call an Advisory Allotment Board. What this organization needs is an Administrator and I wish the President would see that. The publicity is handled clumsily and badly. Mike Straus tells me the newspaper correspondents are commenting upon that fact.

Fritz Wiener, whom I sent to the Virgin Islands with Margold, got back today. He thinks that rapine and murder are likely to break out there at any time. He was plainly scared within an inch of his life while he was there, and he says that a cruiser ought to be ordered at once to Culebra, which would be within three hours' steaming distance of St. Thomas. He reported that Senator Reynolds was utterly disgusted with the situation on the islands and declared he would not go back for any further hearings. Morris Davis, the local demagogue who has been fighting the Governor right along, addressed a mass meeting in the market place last Sunday, at which he made attacks upon Reynolds' sobriety and virtue. He says that Senator Reynolds is coming back thoroughly wise to the situation and he doubts whether any further attempt will be made to carry on the investigation. When Judge Wilson returned to the Islands last week, he was greeted at the wharf by a large crowd and escorted by a parade headed by Morris Davis to his residence. Reynolds saw this and was disgusted by it.

Tuesday, May 21, 1935

On Monday I had an appointment with the President and today I was called to the White House, with Hopkins and Walker, to listen to work-relief plans presented by Hopkins' directors from Alabama and Indiana. They both seemed to be very good men and they had good plans, but I continue to live in a maze so far as general work relief is concerned. It seemed to me today that Hopkins is undoubtedly hedging on the proposal that he made so blithely a couple of weeks ago that he would have all of the employables off the relief rolls by July 1. He is now in favor of holding back until November 1. Walker justly pointed out that we couldn't start a works program on November 1 with so many cities winter-bound as there would be in the North. But we seem to be working out this program by charts and not on the basis of experience and realities. It also begins to look as though we would shortly abandon altogether any hope of getting any of our money back. The President has told me to negotiate separately with each application with a view to getting as much money back as possible, but I just can't quite envisage one city being satisfied with a thirty or forty per cent grant, while a neighboring city is getting perhaps a one hundred per cent grant. It just isn't human nature, much less political human nature.

Tuesday, May 28, 1935

I left Washington at ten-thirty-five the night of May 21, on the Chesapeake and Ohio for Cincinnati, where I arrived the next day early in the afternoon. Mr. Dykstra met me at the train and took me to the Netherlands Plaza. Mr. Delano and Charles E. Merriam came to my rooms during the afternoon. At dinner the night of May 22, at which Mr. Delano presided and at which Governor McNutt, of Indiana, and Merriam also spoke, I talked on housing.

I plainly advocated a Government subsidy in order to provide decent housing for those in the lowest income groups.

I took the Pennsylvania shortly before midnight for Chicago, where I arrived the following morning at seven-thirty, an hour late. At eleven o'clock the morning of the twenty-third, I spoke before the student assembly at the junior high school at Sixty-eighth Street and Stewart Avenue. There were about fifteen hundred present, and Superintendent of Schools Bogan introduced me. Raymond, who had met me, went out with me. I talked extemporaneously for forty-five or fifty minutes on social and political matters, and I made a great hit with the audience, if genuine and prolonged applause is any indication. After the meeting, Raymond and I met Merriam at the University Club where we had lunch, and then the three of us went to Jane Addams' funeral. The funeral was held in the court of Hull House. The court was crowded and so were the surrounding streets.

One thing that touched me particularly was the display of crude strips of purple cloth on the stores of the Greek merchants, restaurants, etc., along Halsted Street in the vicinity of Hull House. The services themselves were simple, as Miss Addams doubtless would have had them. There was a little music, a talk by Dean Gilkey of the University of Chicago, and a benediction by Dr. Graham Taylor, who is well over eighty, and is showing his age. Dean Gilkey gave a good talk, but it didn't seem to me that he quite rose to the occasion. However, I doubt whether anyone could have done so. There were a number of old friends and admirers of Miss Addams there, and all of us felt the occasion very deeply. She was a great spirit, gentle and simple, and yet able and with rare vision. I have never known anyone like her, nor shall I ever. Hers is really an irreparable loss, not only to Chicago and the United States but to civilization.

After the funeral, I drove out to Hubbard Woods with Raymond. The mertensia and the daffodils, that years ago I massed along to the west and the south of the house, were at their best. It was a glorious sight. I had not seen this display since the spring of 1932. While nothing has been done to it since, it is still doing wonderfully well, although the daffodils are dying out. On the other hand, the mertensia are increasing. The lilacs were not yet in bloom, but altogether the place looked very lovely. It is easy to understand Raymond's attachment to it.

Friday noon I went to the Union League Club at their invitation with some twenty members of the PWA staff in Chicago. Friday night I attended a dinner of the Teachers Welfare Associations in the Grand Ballroom of the Stevens Hotel. This was the real occasion of my being in Chicago. The ballroom was crowded, and it is the biggest place of its sort in Chicago. I was told that there had been over two thousand reservations for the dinner, and afterward the balcony filled up so that I should judge there were about twenty-five hundred people there. Merriam introduced me, and I had a national hookup.

I talked about academic freedom with especial reference to the charges of Walgreen, the druggist, that in some of the classes at the University of Chicago subversive political theories are taught. I took several humorous but savage digs at Walgreen to the delight of my audience. In fact, they were interrupting me so much with applause that I had to caution them that I was on the air and that, therefore, my time was limited. My speech made a great hit, and I received many compliments on it afterward.

It happened that the committee of the Illinois State Senate that is investigating the so-called teaching of communism in the colleges had been having a hearing on Friday. Senator Barbour, who was on that committee, was at the Friday night meeting. He came up afterward to tell me that he agreed with me all along the line, and he told another man that my speech was very timely. On Saturday morning the *Tribune* and the *Herald-Examiner* gave columns, beginning with headlined stories on their front pages, to the investigation, but neither of them gave my speech, which related to the same subject matter, more than a stick apiece. Here is another example of how fair newspapers are when they are on a man hunt.

I reached Birmingham, Alabama, at half past seven Monday morning the twenty-seventh. A reception committee representing the Chamber of Commerce met me with a band and a police escort, and took me to the Tutwiler Hotel for breakfast. It was some breakfast. There were eggs, fried, scrambled, poached; French fried potatoes; boiled Tennessee ham; sausages and bacon; and two or three kinds of rolls; all of this after strawberries and cereal. Coffee as a matter of course. There were some twenty or twenty-five of the leading businessmen at breakfast.

After breakfast I begged off to go to my room, because I had had two or three bad nights, and was very tired indeed. When I got to my room, I read the draft of the speech that I had prepared to deliver to the Chamber of Commerce at noon. I had not read it for several days, and I confess that it sent cold chills down my spinal column. It was a ferocious attack on the United States Chamber of Commerce based on the resolutions adopted by the chamber attacking the policies of the Administration at the conclusion of its annual meeting three weeks ago. I had, of course, intended to attack the chamber, but when I read the speech in cold blood and realized that I would be standing before a local chamber of commerce to deliver the speech, I felt somewhat abashed. I called Washington, and Harry Slattery and Mike Straus and I had a three-way conversation about the thing. They said that the speech had already been sent out, and that I couldn't make any changes. Harry Slattery told me that he had heard that the United States Chamber of Commerce was preparing a reply to the speech. It was also reported that an attempt would be made to induce me to soften my attack on Silas Strawn. They justly remarked that any change now would look as if I had yielded to outside pressure.

I went back at my speech again, and a rereading of it did not make me feel any better. I did proceed to cut out a section here and there with the idea of softening the attack somewhat. Heavens knows that even with these elisions, it was a smash between the eyes. Once again I called Slattery and Straus, and indicated to them the changes I had made. After all, these changes were more a tribute to my belated sensibilities than they were the pulling of a punch.

I wasn't at all comfortable in my mind when I went down to the big dining room of the Tutwiler for the luncheon. It wasn't a particularly large dining room, but it was crowded. James G. Smith, president of the Chamber of Commerce, presided, and Governor Graves introduced me. I told both of these men that my speech was a criticism of the United States Chamber of Commerce. Mr. Smith looked a little surprised, but said he believed in free discussion, and Governor Graves said he would throw in a sentence or two in his introduction to pave the way for me.

Taking my courage in both hands, I delivered the speech, and I delivered it as if I meant it, which indeed was the fact. It was something that needed to be said, but whether I should have said it on that occasion in the manner and form in which I said it, I am not at all sure. My audience was courteous, but very far from enthusiastic, although a few people came up afterward to commend me, as might have been expected. However, it was only fair to say that the speech did not make a hit.

I forgot to say that at eleven o'clock three or four members of the reception committee came to drive me in and around Birmingham. The surrounding country is very lovely. I had no idea that Birmingham was such an attractive city, or so beautifully set in the valley between graciously wooded mountains. My hosts were certainly very considerate throughout, although I didn't see many of them after my noonday speech.

Saturday, June 1, 1935

I got back to Washington early Wednesday morning.

The people in Public Works are not at all happy over the way things have been going under the new work-relief program. Frank Walker is building up a good deal of an organization after all. I doubted whether the pressure from members of his staff or even his own inclination in the end would make it possible for him to stick to his original intention of not building up a staff. Members of my staff think that Walker and Hopkins, between them, have Public Works pretty well stymied and they may be right.

Another interesting thing happened while I was away. After the President had decided on a grant of forty-five per cent and a loan of fifty-five per cent on non-Federal projects, he was influenced by Morgenthau to declare that fifty-five per cent had to be borrowed from the Federal Government and the interest was fixed so low as practically to insure this. The object is to make the municipalities borrow so that they will have to pay back their loans, and the Federal Government will then be in a position to say that so much of the money was paid back. I think this is looking at the program from the wrong point of view. Our object ought to be to get as much money into use as possible, and it stands to reason that if the municipalities, in consequence of grants of forty-five per cent from us, go into the market and borrow fifty-five per cent, there will be that much more money put to work.

But the real joke lies in the fact that Hopkins withholds his approval of PWA projects unless the fifty-five per cent is obtained outside of Government sources. And, according to his theory, he is correct. Our plan is to put three and a half million employable unemployed to work with the $4 billion that Congress has voted. To do this means an average expenditure of just so much per man.

The average cost of employment per man on public works projects is relatively high. If Hopkins can figure this on the basis of the grant of forty-five per cent instead of a total loan and grant of one hundred per cent, it stands to reason that he can figure the wages per man much lower.

The result is that under the Morgenthau plan we can't build any non-Federal public works unless the municipalities borrow the fifty-five per cent from us over and above the grant. According to Hopkins, we can't undertake the projects if we do loan the fifty-five per cent. The result is a stalemate so far as public works are concerned. The further result is that instead of getting money back into the Treasury, as Morgenthau thinks he is doing under his plan, we won't be getting any money back into the Treasury because we won't be lending any money to do public works if Hopkins insists on his position. The whole thing is absurd and inconsistent and I shall try to convince the President, when I see him, that it is wrong.

Anna got pretty well through with moving while I was away. We spent Wednesday night at the old house in Spring Valley and had dinner there Thursday night. Then we moved over to the new house, into which we have moved the balance of our belongings since then. It is really lovely there on the top of the hill with trees and garden and more birds than one can imagine. There is a charm about the old house, too, although it does need redecorating. But with a good deal of our old furniture in, it is comfortable and homelike.

When I came back to Washington, I had just a little hoarseness, but nothing to bother me. After dictating all day Thursday, being Decoration Day and therefore a holiday, which gave me plenty of chance to dictate, I discovered late in the afternoon that my voice had gone out on me entirely. All that night and on Friday I could not talk above a whisper. On Friday morning I went to see Dr. Ross McIntire, the ear, nose, and throat specialist who takes care of the President. He has a fine setup in the way of offices in the basement of the White House. He told me that my vocal cords were all right, but that the soft tissues in my larynx were badly congested. I kept as quiet as possible all day Friday, and today I am able to talk again, although my voice is somewhat husky.

Yesterday's Cabinet meeting was one of the most interesting we have had. Friday morning before Cabinet meeting the President had a press conference and he talked for two hours to the correspondents discussing the decision of the Supreme Court on NRA. He characterized that decision as an effort to put us back to the horse-and-buggy age and pointed out that national progress along economic and social lines would be impossible in the light of that decision and that it would be necessary to rely on the states for whatever advances along those lines might be hoped for.

We spent practically all of the time at Cabinet meeting discussing the new issue that the President has raised. I think the issue is a sound one and one that would have to be raised sooner or later in any event. In fact, some years ago in a speech that I made before the City Club of Chicago, I predicted that sooner or later the Supreme Court would become a political issue. Apparently that time has come and I, for one, am ready to meet it. Apparently the President is too. As a matter of fact, we have to meet this issue or abandon any effort to better the social and economic conditions of the people. The fight ought to be clean cut, but it is bound to be strenuous. I shall welcome an opportunity to write and speak on this issue and since I shall probably do so, I won't take the time to set down, even in brief, my views here.

Tuesday, June 4, 1935

As indicated in my memorandum on the Cabinet meeting last Friday, the President took pretty advanced ground on this court decision. Harry Slattery, who went to see Justice Brandeis yesterday at the request of the Justice, brought word to me this morning that Justice Brandeis thinks the President is making a great mistake in taking the position that he has on this decision. I do not agree with this point of view, but, after all, its wisdom or unwisdom will be proved by the event. If business holds or takes an upturn, then the Court will be vindicated along with those conservative gentlemen who have been saying that the NRA has retarded business. If, on the other hand, business takes another nose dive, in my judgment the Supreme Court will be placed distinctly on the defensive and will be made a political issue. The people will demand the right to determine for themselves whether the nation is to have a clear road to economic and social development, just as other civilized countries have that right, without the insistence of any court that we return to the strait jacket of fifty years ago.

I had a conference with the President yesterday morning and he told me that Morgenthau had reported to him that the Treasury experts saw distinct indications of a falling off in business in the late summer and fall. These indications are not at all reassuring. There isn't any doubt that there is a feeling of uncertainty and unrest as the result of the NRA decision.

At my conference with the President, I told him that I was very much worried about the way the work-relief program was operating and he told me that Harry Hopkins was worried too. He took pencil and paper and proceeded to do some figuring, but his figures only demonstrated to me that there is cause for worry. I told the President very frankly that I didn't think the program would work on the basis of Hopkins' plan and that I never had thought it would work out. The President said that it must work out, with emphasis on the "must," but that isn't going to make it work out. I particularly urged him not to get out on a limb himself.

I brought up Morgenthau's plan of a fifty-five per cent loan on PWA non-Federal projects at three per cent interest in order to make the borrowers take their money from the Federal Treasury so that they can repay it later. I told the President that when this news came to me while I was away, it had shocked me. I pointed out that this plan would mean that there would be no non-Federal projects at all and that instead of getting money back into the Treasury, it would assure that all projects would be on the basis of one hundred per cent grants of Federal money. The President said that I was right and asked me to return at ten minutes to two before the meeting of the Allotment Advisory Committee. I did so. Morgenthau, Hopkins, and Walker were also there. The President brought up the point that I had made at our morning conference. Morgenthau tried to explain and defend, but the President agreed, as did the other three of us, that the interest rate should be raised to approximately four per cent in order to make it possible for borrowers to go into the money market when they can borrow at a lower rate, thus saving to us for other projects money that otherwise we would be lending at three per cent.

The President called a special Cabinet meeting at eleven-thirty and it was one of the most satisfactory Cabinet meetings I have attended. The whole discussion was on our present policy and our future program. The President still thinks that he cannot permit the people, in justice to himself or to the country, to believe that he is a magician who can pull rabbit after rabbit out of the hat. His theory is that we ought to accept the opinion of the Supreme Court, letting credit or blame rest where it belongs in that respect and salvage what we can out of the program that was wrecked by this decision, without going beyond legitimate bounds or putting ourselves in a position where the Supreme Court can overturn the apple cart again.

The President has made up a list of bills that he wants to have passed and on this he has put an oil bill, much to my delight. I think he has a sound program, considering all the circumstances, and that this program represents an equally sound political point of view.

The Vice President made another of those propositions of his that I find myself so much in accord with. Referring to the Humphreys decision, in which the Court denied the right of the President to dismiss a man appointed to the Federal Trade Commission prior to the expiration of the term for which he was appointed, the Vice President said that our method of appointing members to such commissions was altogether too slipshod. He said that confirmation by the Senate is a mere formality if the Senators from the state of the suggested appointee are favorable to the appointment. He thinks there ought to be a rigid examination of a man's qualifications. He goes so far as to suggest that notice of a nomination should be widely published and an open hearing held on the man's qualifications before confirmation by the Senate. He pointed out that not only many incompetent men find lodgement on important Government commissions from which they cannot be removed by the President, except for good cause proved, but that improper appointments are made. He cited Humphreys as such an improper appointment, saying that he should never have been named on the Federal Trade Commission. The President said that he had made a mistake in not preferring charges. He had actual proof of malfeasance in office, but he didn't want to file such charges against Humphreys, believing as he did that he could get rid of him by milder methods.

Thursday, June 6, 1935

The President told me today that Richberg was very much excited yesterday. He went into the President's office waving his arms and declaring that he couldn't stay another twenty-four hours. It seems that the President had given out an interview about the continuance of NRA that Richberg didn't like and Richberg was very much excited about it. The President said he succeeded in calming him down. Today Harry Slattery told me that Smith, Chief Counsel of NRA, had told him over the telephone that he was hunting an outside business connection because Don was going to quit NRA. I wonder if Richberg doesn't rather wish now that he hadn't blocked the appointment of President Hutchins, of Chicago, as NRA Administrator. Here he is holding the bag. He has alienated labor, the unions no longer trust him, and, as I see it, he is of no use now to the conservative business element because of the knockout of NRA by the unanimous decision of the Supreme Court. Don was the main draftsman of the NRA bill. He prepared the case that was tried before the Supreme Court and argued it.

Saturday, June 8, 1935

Don Richberg resigned yesterday and the President accepted his resignation to take effect on the sixteenth. He goes out almost in total eclipse. At one time probably the outstanding labor lawyer in the country, he has been suspect of labor for some time. The liberals do not believe in him any more and since NRA has come such a cropper, I cannot see that he is of any particular use to big business. It is like a house falling down on a man. He says he is going back to private practice.

In my judgment, Don could have held on and gone much further in the end if he had only kept himself in hand. When luck did break his way and he flashed across the sky as a new star of great magnitude, he permitted himself to be carried away. I believed that in the long run the talk of him as "Assistant President" and as "Number One Man" would prove fatal, but this would not necessarily have been true if he hadn't taken these designations too seriously himself. He was conscious that he was Assistant President and that is indeed a dangerous role. With his temperament it wasn't possible for him to go along steadily every day, doing his job the best he knew how and leaving events to take care of themselves. It is the greatest downfall to date in this Administration. When Johnson went out, he went out with a blare of trumpets while NRA was still at its strongest. Lewis W. Douglas resigned as a matter of principle and Moley left to go back to Columbia University and to become editor, at a large salary, of *Today*. Don was simply swept out of office.

I know Don must be feeling badly and I wish, for old times' sake, that I could at least extend him a word of sympathy. But I can't without being hypocritical. He certainly was very jealous of me, and I have reason to believe that he had a good deal to do with the fight that was waged on me a few months ago.

Charles E. Merriam is in Washington again and came in to see me this afternoon. He thinks the investigation of the University of Chicago that was instigated by Walgreen's charges of subversive teaching has about flattened out. At a continuance of the investigation yesterday neither Walgreen nor his attorney showed up. Walgreen has been making distinct overtures to Merriam and Merriam thinks he is pretty sick of the whole business. The latter thinks my speech in Chicago had a very good effect and he is certain that Walgreen either heard my speech or was told about it.

Saturday, June 15, 1935

I was called over to the White House Thursday at eleven forty-five with "Ding" Darling and Dr. Mead, of the Reclamation Service, to discuss wild life refuges in connection with our reclamation projects. Darling is one of the greatest enthusiasts I have ever known. Of course I am in sympathy with what he is trying to do and I am willing to help him out wherever I can. I couldn't stay until the end of the conference because I had planned to leave in my car for Altoona at twelve o'clock. So I pulled away at twelve-fifteen.

I drove directly home, where I stopped for a sandwich and a glass of milk, breaking my rule not to eat lunch because of the long automobile trip that was ahead of me. Anna was ready and we got away a little before one. The day was hot. We were due to meet a reception committee from Altoona at Bedford, Pennsylvania, but Carl made such good time that we actually had to slow down after we had passed Hagerstown. The ride over the mountains was very lovely. When we reached Bedford, the committee was there ahead of us. One of the members was Dan Slep, publisher of the *Altoona Mirror,* who used to go to the same Sunday school class that I attended when I was a boy. I don't think I have seen him since I left Altoona in 1890.

Preceded by two state motorcycle policemen, we proceeded into Altoona in two cars. We went through Newry, where as a boy I used to visit frequently at the home of my great-uncle and aunt, Alexander and Elizabeth Knox. The large spreading house where they used to live, an extension of which was a big general country store, had only a portion of the house remaining, but the old pump that I used to operate was still in front of what was left of the house. The great barn was also gone and it was with difficulty that I recognized the place.

There are really few people that I now know in Altoona. Two or three older men were introduced to me as men who had known my father. There were a few relatives on hand, like May Knox Hillis, Daisy Ickes, whose married name I do not know, and George and Nellie Smith, although George had to leave the meeting before I spoke since his health is not at all robust. Nell Moser Bloomhardt and Walter Moser were also there, and of course Clinton and Julia. The Congressman from the district, Don Gingery, of Clearfield, had come on from Washington for the affair, and the Democratic State Chairman, David L. Lawrence, was also there, as was the Attorney General. The town really was most friendly and did the best it knew how to show that it was interested in and proud of me. They were very sincere, worth-while people and I was glad that I had accepted the invitation, although I wished very much indeed that my voice had been in good shape.

As for Altoona, it looked as dingy and forlorn as ever. It really is one of the ugliest and most unattractive cities that I have ever seen. The buildings are all packed together on small lots. Most of the houses look as if they had never been painted. There is said to be something in the locomotive smoke which eats the paint off the buildings. Whether this is true or not, it is evident that paint does not stand up. It becomes dingy and dirty so that the whole town looks unkempt and down at the heels.

This morning we got away early. Miss Margaret Ross, one of my old school and Sunday school teachers, wanted to see me. She had said that she would die happy if she could only take my hand. She had intended to go to the meeting last night, but when she didn't show up, I decided to hunt her up this morning. I found her on Twelfth Street above Sixteenth Avenue, a little old dried-up wisp of a woman who stood just as straight as I remember her as a young boy. She was always a peppery little thing and I have no reason to be grateful to her because she actually set me back a whole year in school once because I laughed out loud in class one day. However, she had forgotten that episode years ago and I have forgiven her even if I haven't forgotten. I was glad to see her and delighted if that simple act on my part would give her any pleasure during her remaining years. She must be well over eighty and I think that all of her family have died except herself.

Tom Corcoran came in to see me this afternoon. I told him some time ago that I wanted to have a talk with him. He told me that the break between the President and Richberg is absolute and complete. The newspapers the last day or two seemed to confirm the view that Richberg is through here. Apparently he is going to close things up here and then leave Washington for good, but where he is going has not yet been announced, although the *Chicago Tribune* had a story a couple of days ago to the effect that he might resume the practice of law there.

His has been the greatest fall of the Administration. There isn't any doubt that Don led himself up on the mountain and pointed out to himself the whole world and all the treasures thereof. The publicity that he got as "Assistant President" and "Number One Man," etc., etc., was more than he could stand with his temperament. The result is a complete blowup. He has declined to have a farewell meeting of his staff, and Harry Slattery tells me that a movement to collect some money from the staff to give him a farewell gift, such as was done for General Johnson, fell flat because the employees would not contribute. Tom Corcoran tells me that when Blackwell Smith, who succeeded Don as chief counsel of NRA when Don moved on to become "Assistant President," and who is a real liberal, went up to Boston one week end to talk to Felix Frankfurter about his troubles over NRA affairs, Don refused to have anything further to do with him. He has shut him completely out for the last two months. Corcoran says also that Smith at times had great difficulty trying to decide how he could agree to some of the compromises proposed by Don without violating his own conscience.

Tuesday, June 18, 1935

On Monday afternoon we had the regular meeting of the Allotment Advisory Committee of the work-relief program. It is becoming ever clearer that Hopkins is dominating this program and this domination will mean thousands of inconsequential make-believe projects in all parts of the country. It is also becoming increasingly clear that opposition to the expenditure of vast sums of money on a glorified CWA program is growing daily, especially among Congressmen and Senators. This may become very formidable and the Administration is likely to suffer from it, especially if it proceeds with the Hopkins program.

The meeting Monday afternoon ran true to form. The President was back and, of course, so was satellite Henry Morgenthau, who had the presumption to ask for the floor toward the end of the meeting. Harry Hopkins was present, perched on the small of his back, as usual, and Frank Walker must still be ill, because he wasn't there. We passed a number of projects, with Colonel Robert E. Elbert, vice president of the Singer Sewing Machine Company, who has been attending meetings lately as the representative of General Robert E. Wood, objecting to everything that was proposed "on principle." He is so anxious that every project voted shall be well within the stated objectives of the President. He doesn't seem to think that the President can take care of his own objectives. I suspect that he thinks he has to make some kind of a record. At one stage on Monday I remarked, in reply to an observation of his, that I didn't know of any private business concern that could make absolutely accurate estimates of building costs, that all of them had to revise their estimates and that the Government was just as accurate as private business. This seemed to take him aback somewhat.

This afternoon I went up to the Senate. First I dropped in for a talk with the Vice President, who usually turns over his job as Presiding Officer of the Senate to someone else when a debate is in progress. He always goes back to preside when votes are being taken. What took me to the Senate was my concern over the prospects of my Departmental bill which seeks to change the name of this Department and make it in name as well as in fact the Conservation Department of the Government. The Vice President said that he was for the bill. I talked with Senators Wagner, Bone, King, O'Mahoney, Clark, and Byrnes.

After the Senate adjourned, a group of us gathered in the Vice President's office and partook of his whisky. It was the consensus of opinion of those particularly interested that I ought to ask Senator Lewis to bring back this bill which is pending before his Committee on Expenditures in the Executive Departments and have it recommitted to the Committee on Lands. Senator Wagner admitted that his committee, and even himself, had felt a bit slighted when this bill was referred to Senator Lewis's committee. In fact, word had come to me from two or three sources that the members of this committee will oppose the bill even if it is reported out favorably by Senator Lewis's committee. Accordingly, I shall see Senator Lewis in a day or two and see whether I can get him to consent to the switch.

There was a good deal of talk about Burlew. Senators Byrnes and Clark said that he was more damned than anyone else in the Administration by Democratic Senators as they met in the cloak room. Senator O'Mahoney came to the defense of Burlew and the Department. He told his colleagues that I was the cleverest man in the Government because I had built up a public opinion to the effect that I paid no attention at all to politics in making appointments, whereas I paid a good deal of attention and went as far as anyone in making such appointments. As a matter of fact, this is true. I have never objected to political appointments and I make them right along, but I do insist on fitness and ability.

O'Mahoney put up a very convincing argument for Burlew, in which I joined vigorously. We almost persuaded Byrnes and Clark that they didn't know what they were talking about. Byrnes remarked that he didn't know Burlew himself, but he did know what the talk was, and he suggested to O'Mahoney that he state his case before Burlew's critics among the Democratic Senators. O'Mahoney said he would be very glad to do so. Clark had never been friendly to me or to the Department, but he mellowed up quite a bit. He remarked that the man we had appointed as state engineer for Missouri was not a man to his liking, and I reminded him that I had withdrawn this man. I then reminded him also that I had appointed this man at the instance of the White House. He said he had never asked for any appointments so he didn't know how those matters worked out. I ventured the guess that we had made appointments for him and promised to supply him with a list tomorrow. He said two or three times that he was very glad that he had had the chance to talk with me and indicated that our talk had resulted in a better feeling on his part. When we left I drove Senator O'Mahoney over to the Senate Office Building and he said that my coming to the Senate had been a very good thing and had done a lot of good.

Tonight I told Burlew about this encounter on the Hill. He looked up his records and found that we have made twenty-six appointments on the recommendation of Senator Clark. Burlew will take the record up with him personally tomorrow.

Raymond Robins was in to see me today about money to finish certain Department of Agriculture projects that have been partially finished on his estate in Florida, Chinsegut Hill, which he deeded to the Government several years ago, reserving life estates for himself and Margaret. Since these buildings are partly completed, I told him that I would see what I could do to get money to finish them. Raymond looked and talked quite like his old self. He told me that he had been refusing invitations to make Republican speeches. I may be unjust, but I suspect that he is keeping footloose so that he can jump either way next year.

Wednesday, June 19, 1935

Almost without exception, Members of Congress, public men, and students of public affairs with whom I have talked recently deplore the program to which the President has committed himself. They all think it is a mistake and that he cannot realize his objectives. So worried have I become over the situation that I decided to go over to talk to Steve Early about it. As I was due for an appointment with the President at three-twenty, I went over at three o'clock, having first called Steve to ask him whether I could weep on his shoulder.

I told Steve how I viewed the situation. I explained to him my embarrassment because I am associated in the mind of the public with a program that would restrict the expenditure of money to useful and socially desirable public works as opposed to Hopkins' program, which contemplates the expenditure of money on practically anything that it can be spent on, without hope of any return to the Federal treasury. I told him by book and chapter what certain Congressmen and Senators have been saying to me, and he asked me whether I had read the President's statement to Harry Hopkins' state directors. I told him I had and his comment was that he believed that that statement justified the interpretation that the plan was for something along the line of CWA. I told Steve that I was deeply concerned about the effect of this program on the President's political fortunes next year. I made it clear that I didn't think the program could be successfully carried out.

Steve asked me to go in and talk to the President just as frankly as I had talked to him. I told him that I did not think the President would find it pleasant listening and that I was doubly embarrassed to carry my apprehensions to him, first, because I didn't think the

President would like my point of view, and, second, because I was fully aware that there had been a great deal of knocking of me at the White House. I told Steve that I thought I knew who was doing most of this knocking and Steve said that no one knocked me in his office, implying that he wouldn't permit it. In this connection, Steve inadvertently made a statement the significance of which I saw at once. When I said that I knew certain of the people who had been knocking, Steve said that Henry had been around a good deal. I asked him whether he meant Henry Morgenthau and he said Yes. I said I knew what Morgenthau's attitude was, and Steve said that it was perfectly surprising to him the "in" that Morgenthau had made for himself with the President, not only with respect to his own department but generally. I told Steve I couldn't understand this because in my opinion Morgenthau had nothing that he could really contribute. Steve said that was so but that the President was greatly impressed with his loyalty. I remarked that other people were just as loyal and that some had more ability. Steve thinks that Henry Morgenthau's loyalty and industry have put him in high favor with the President.

I told Steve I would talk frankly with the President and when I got in to him, I asked him whether I might speak frankly. He said I might and I proceeded to tell him in general what I had said to Steve. Steve had said that if I wanted to do so, I could tell the President that he (Steve) had suggested that I talk to him, but I told him that I always stood on my own feet and would do so in this instance. The President said that others had come to him with the same statements, but that we were in for it and he didn't see what we could do except to go through with it. He asked me what suggestions I had to make and I told him I didn't have any. He wanted to know if he should ask for more money and I told him no, that I didn't think he could get it. He agreed. Once again I begged him not to involve himself too intimately with a program that, as I told him, I didn't believe could succeed. He said he was already in volved, but I urged him to let some of the rest of us take the blame if blame was to be our due.

It seemed to me that the President was less sure of the Hopkins program than he has been at any time in the past that I have talked with him. I told him that I was very fearful of the effect next year. I pointed out that under the Hopkins program we wouldn't have anything substantial to show the people for the expenditure of their money, and I urged him for this reason to let us go ahead with our slum clearance program and do what we could with the limited PWA program that it is possible for us to embark upon. He referred again to the $250 million that would be available if RFC took the bonds that we hold in the PWA treasury as security for the various non-Federal projects that we have financed. He asked me if I had talked to Jesse Jones about it, and I said that there was only one man living who could talk to Jesse Jones about it with any result and that was himself. He said that he would talk to Jones and I remarked that unless we knew what we had to go ahead on, we would get started too late to accomplish anything. He said we could go ahead in the expectation of getting this $250 million which we can use as loans on non-Federal projects in conjunction with the forty-five per cent grants which will be allowed out of the work-relief appropriation.

The President also said that last Monday he had signed the order segregating $249 million for slum clearance projects. I told him that this had not yet been reported to me and that if we did not get this release pretty soon, we would not be able to undertake any program at all.

I pointed out also that it would be helpful if Harry Hopkins were required to confine his program strictly to those enterprises where there was no chance of a contribution by the municipality. I said that any project where the municipality could make some contribution should come over to us as a PWA project. The President concurred. I told him that, with all due respect to Harry Hopkins, in his eagerness to get results he would finance as Federal projects undertakings that could be financed jointly by the local municipality and the Federal Government. I told him that Hopkins had done this under the old program, proof of which I had submitted to the President. The President concurred in this point of view also, and I urged him to make it clear to Hopkins that all projects that could be partially financed by the municipalities were to be turned over to PWA.

The President promised to send word to the War Department to withdraw its opposition to my Department bill and he also expressed his willingness to send a message to the Senate in support of the oil bill. While I was with him, word came that the Security Bill had passed the Senate and that his message on taxation was being read. The President read this message to me. He told me that he thought it was the best thing he had done as President. It was a fine message and I think it will go well with the country. He boldly demands a graduated increase in estate and gift taxes, an increase in taxes levied against incomes in the higher brackets, and a graduated income tax levied against corporations. He also suggests a constitutional amendment providing for the taxation of interest on national, state, or municipal bonds to be issued in the future. Altogether the President takes an advanced stand on the question of taxation. At one place in the message he looked up at me with a smile and said, "That is for Hearst." I can imagine the clamor that will go up from Hearst and the big-moneyed groups generally. But I believe that the position he has taken on this question will go far to strengthen his position with the average man and woman.

Friday, June 21, 1935

This afternoon I was served with a subpoena to appear before Senator Tydings' committee investigating the Virgin Islands at ten-thirty on July 2. I found out afterward that Governor Pearson had been subpoenaed as well as some six or seven men in the Virgin Islands. I at once called in certain members of my staff and instructed them to get ready for this investigation. Since the right granted originally to cross-examine witnesses has not been withdrawn, I am going to assume that we will still be accorded this right and I am going to ask the President if he has any objection to my doing the cross-examining myself. I don't see why there should be any objection, although it would be a very unusual proceeding.

Wednesday, June 26, 1935

I had a session with the President today. I brought up again my Department bill and from all I can see, he is in favor of the bill and is willing to help me with it. Curiously enough, however, representatives of other departments continue to appear to oppose it. There will be another hearing tomorrow before the House committee and I am advised that Secretary Wallace will once more appear in opposition. The President told me he had stopped the Army, but I replied that General Markham, Chief of Engineers, had been at the last hearing before the House committee and had opposed it. He said the opposition would be carried no further. I told him that if he would get word to the War Department to notify the committee that it had withdrawn its opposition, it would mean one or two favorable votes on the committee and would help assure an affirmative report by the committee. He said he would do so. He promised also to talk to Henry Wallace. I told him that it would be a simple matter to pass this bill if he would only crook his little finger.

One matter I discussed with him was the historic monuments bill in which he is very much interested, as I am also. This bill has passed the Senate and has been reported favorably by the House committee. It is on the House calendar, but Bertrand Snell, Republican leader, said he would oppose the bill because I had rescinded an allocation for a bridge at Ogdenburg, New York. The President called Snell and told him he understood that he had both his big feet on the bill and Snell admitted the soft impeachment. He also confirmed the reason for his opposition. The President told him that the reason we hadn't gone ahead with the Ogdenburg Bridge was because Canada hadn't passed certain necessary legislation. He assured him that he (the President) was in favor of the bridge and that as soon as Canada passed the necessary legislation, money would be forthcoming. Snell then assured the President that he would not oppose the historic buildings bill.

I took occasion to tell the President that in my judgment the position he announced last week on increased taxation for income in the higher brackets, for a greater tax on large incomes, for greater taxes on gifts and inheritances, and for a graduated tax on the incomes of corporations was the best thing he had done since he became President. I think that as a result of what the President has advocated at this session of Congress, he is now definitely committed to the progressive side and for that, of course, I am very glad.

I suggested to the President the other day that we name the proposed international park that, if it goes through, will lie on both sides of the Rio Grande River in the Big Bend area of Texas, the Jane Addams International Park. He was enthusiastically in favor of the proposition and told me to discuss it with the Vice President. That I did and, to my pleasure, I found Mr. Garner also in favor of the name. Since Congress recently passed a bill setting up a national park on our side of the boundary and named that park the Big Bend National Park, I am having drafted and will cause to be introduced a bill changing this name to Jane Addams National Park. I have also written a letter to the Secretary of State, expressing the hope that he will be able to interest the Mexican Government in this international park. If Mexico does undertake the matter, then I hope that we can name the whole thing after Jane Addams, which will be a deserved tribute to her memory.

Thursday, June 27, 1935

There was another hearing on my Department bill before the House Committee on Expenditures in the Executive Departments. Once again, Henry Wallace appeared but this time he read a prepared statement. Notwithstanding this, he didn't make a good impression, in my judgment. He read rapidly and in a voice that was far from clear and the burden of his statement had to do with the Forest Service, its happy situation in the Department of Agriculture, and the calamity that would befall it if it should be transferred to Interior. As a member of the committee aptly remarked at the conclusion of his remarks, that question was not up for consideration. Following Henry I was given an opportunity to reply. He had left me some beautiful openings which I took advantage of in a manner that was not too serious. I kept the committee amused as I dissected and answered Henry's arguments and even Henry himself had to laugh on one or two occasions. The committee had to adjourn before I was through on account of a call for a quorum from the House, but I came away feeling that our position had been strengthened not only by what I said but by what Henry had said. There will probably be at least one more hearing at which I will finish what I had to say.

In response to a summons from the White House, Hopkins, Walker, and I met the President at two-fifteen for a session of over an hour. It was clear from the questioning that the President had read the memorandum on public works and work relief that I had left with him yesterday and had been impressed by it. He started in by discussing the relationship of PWA to the new program and said that something must be done to segregate PWA projects from work-relief projects. He frankly recognized the impossibility of PWA bidding for projects against WPA. Frank Walker insisted that there was a great deal of confusion in the minds of the public, that they didn't know with whom to file their applications. Harry Hopkins scoffed at this suggestion but I came to the support of Walker, insisting that there was not only confusion throughout the states but even here in Washington.

I made the statement that we could not hope for PWA applications with the municipalities holding out in the hope that they would be able to get grants of one hundred per cent from Hopkins' organization. I said that the only thing that would clarify the situation would be a clear statement from the President delimiting PWA, WPA, and announcing unequivocally that no municipality that could qualify under PWA would receive any consideration at the hands of WPA. It was plain to see that Harry Hopkins was growing more and more unhappy as the discussion proceeded. Apparently he wants no rules that will prevent his organization from grabbing everything in sight. Finally it was agreed that in each state a board of three would be set up, one representative of PWA, one of WPA, and a third representing Walker's organization, the third, at my suggestion, to be chairman in each instance. These boards will determine in what classification projects shall be listed and in case of great doubt an appeal can be taken to Washington, where Walker and I will decide the matter.

Walker and I both strongly feel that we do not care to vote affirmatively on Harry Hopkins' projects. They are small, scattered, and diversified and we will have neither time nor the opportunity, nor the people for that matter, to pass upon them. He has a list of five hundred to submit at the meeting next Monday of the Allotment Committee. Both of us are agreed that we are willing to vote lump sums to be expended by Hopkins in his own discretion and on his own responsibility, but we do not care to assume responsibility in any way for his program as to detail. We explained this position to Harry in McIntyre's office after we left the President and he said he didn't blame us.

During this same interview, Hopkins showed plainly that he was far from pleased at what had transpired in the President's office. He said that the whole setup had been a mistake from the beginning. I agreed with him that there should have been one Administrator here, with an Administrator in each state. He insists that the President has committed himself to such an extent that we cannot now turn back. I put this case to him:

The President's program contemplates the taking of three and a half million men off relief rolls and putting them to work. Suppose that this can be done but that the event demonstrates that a new three and one-half million men, or even a lesser number, are on the relief rolls. How then can it be demonstrated to the satisfaction of the country that the President has accomplished his object, which is really to take all employables off relief rolls?

Harry Hopkins had no answer to this question, nor do I believe that there is any answer. I am afraid that this is precisely the possibility in the situation. Harry Hopkins admitted to us before we went into the President's office that the employment situation was getting worse.

As I say, Harry was in a sad state of mind. He said that the only thing to do was for the whole program to be turned over to me and leave him free to go back to New York and find a job. Neither Walker nor I made any comment on this petulant statement. During the conference with the President I insisted that what we ought to do was to define what are public works. The President agreed and at our subsequent conference in McIntyre's office, I arranged for a meeting of representatives of our organizations to try to agree upon a draft covering this matter.

Just before leaving the President's office I told the President that there was one other thing I would like to bring up. I then said that on several occasions Executive Orders had been issued affecting, among other things, the work in my administration and that I had gotten my first information with respect to these orders from the newspapers. He expressed surprise at this, but I told him it was a fact and that I felt I ought to be consulted on matters affecting my Department. He asked me for examples and I said I would send him some.

Tuesday, July 2, 1935

Late Saturday morning I had a session with the President in his study at the White House. When I told him that there had been another hearing before the House Committee on Expenditures in the Executive Departments on my Department bill at which Henry Wallace had appeared, he said: "Why, I told him not to do that." I confess that I don't quite know what is happening with respect to that bill. It is difficult for me to believe that Henry Wallace and other members of that Department would oppose it actively if the President had told him not to, and yet the President professes interest in the bill and keeps asking me how it is getting along. Perhaps he just hasn't gone quite to the length of saying specifically to leave the bill alone. At any rate, Secretary Wallace continues to oppose it.

I also spoke to the President about the pending Virgin Islands investigation. He said he would send for Tydings and have a talk with him on Monday. He had previously told me he would have a talk with him on Saturday. On Monday when I saw the President for a few minutes before the meeting of the Allotment Advisory Committee, just before two o'clock, I asked him whether he had seen Tydings and he acted surprised. I was persistent and reminded him that he had said he would see him and he made a note on a pad of paper, telling me that he would talk with him. When I got back from the committee meeting later in the afternoon, I called Miss Le Hand to tell her that the President had promised to talk with Tydings and to ask her to try to see that he did, telephoning me the result. Later she called me to say that the President had not seen him but was going to talk with him by telephone Monday night.

This morning just before the hearing was called to order in the caucus room of the Senate Office Building, the President called me on the telephone. He told me that he had just had a long talk with Tydings. Tydings assured him that the investigation would be fair and impartial. He said to the President that I never talked things over with him and that things would go easier if I would show more consideration. He discussed with the President the possibility of my making an opening statement and said he would be willing for me to do that if I made it short. The President told him he understood that I had a rather long statement prepared and Tydings suggested that I be allowed ten minutes. The President told me he didn't know whether Tydings meant what he said when he assured him he wasn't out after anyone and would give everyone a square deal, but that he thought we ought to give him the benefit of the doubt. He suggested that at the outset I go easy as possible and give Tydings a chance to make good on his word.

I told the President that the difficulty with Tydings' assurances was that his investigators in the Virgin Islands in no single instance had tried to get any evidence except such as would support the ridiculous charges made by Yates, *et al.* However, I told him that I would go easy.

As I left the telephone, I met Tydings who had just come into the hearing room and we went off into a corner to have a talk. He told me in substance what he had said to the President. I told him that I would want to make a preliminary statement for the record, and I also told him that his investigators had given no indications of an intention on their part to have a fair investigation. He assured me that the witnesses would be kept to a recital of the facts and that he would not permit any hearsay or anything of the sort.

Senator Tydings called the committee to order shortly after ten o'clock with a very brief statement and then he called on counsel for the committee to open proceedings. At this point I arose to my feet. I said that I was there in answer to a subpoena and that I had appeared in the expectation that I would be permitted to make the opening statement. I said I believed I should be permitted to make the opening statement. I then referred to the great assortment of wild charges and suggested that a rule should issue requiring him to file a verified bill of particulars. I then said that I took it for granted that we would be accorded the right to cross-examine, referred to the expense that we had been put to to prepare photostatic copies of the documents demanded under the subpoenas, suggesting in that behalf that the committee might properly reimburse us for that expense, which already amounted to some $1,500, and closed with the remark that we wanted a fair and impartial investigation and would co-operate with the committee to that end. I said also that the actions of the committee's investigators in the Virgin Islands did not indicate that it was in their minds to give us an impartial investigation.

Tydings more or less passed over my demands, but he made it clear that I would not be permitted to make the opening statement and would not be accorded the right to cross-examine. I, of course, knew this from my preliminary talk with him.

Counsel then called the first witness, George H. Gibson, Government Attorney of the Virgin Islands for some six or seven years until I discharged him shortly after I came to Washington. He made one of the worst witnesses I have ever seen. He had nothing to say worth while and he couldn't say crisply and intelligently what he thought he was saying.

Senators Bone and Clark, who are members of the Committee on Insular Affairs, of which the investigating committee is a subcommittee, came into the session. Bone was very helpful to our side in the questions he asked. Clark asked only two or three, but they were helpful, too, as he wanted them to be. Senator King did some questioning and he was helpful. Senator Tydings didn't seem to me to be very happy. His questions were neutral.

The reason Gibson was put on as the first witness is an interesting story. Paul C. Yates, the man who presented the charges that resulted in the investigation, was to be the first witness. Yates is a former newspaperman. He had been recommended for the place by Robert S. Allen, collaborator with Drew Pearson, son of Governor Pearson of the Virgin Islands, in the "Merry-Go-Round" column which serves some three hundred newspapers in the United States. I had appointed Yates at the insistence of Governor Pearson, although he never made a good impression on me.

Yates and Allen ran across each other in the Senate Office Building prior to the hearing. As I got the story, Allen called Yates a double-crosser and Yates called Allen a son of a bitch, whereupon Allen, who is a little fellow but husky, proceeded to beat Yates up. He knocked him down once or twice, closing one eye and cutting his lip. The Senate Office Building police intervened and separated them. But Yates had to be carted off to a hospital for temporary repairs and wasn't available to go on as the first witness as had been intended. That was the reason the bovine Mr. Gibson was put on, much to the satisfaction of myself and those members of my staff who were there to hear him.

I did not stay throughout the whole session of the investigating committee. If it hadn't been for the fist fight, the newspapers would have paid little attention to the investigation as it progressed today because it had no news value. It would not have appeared in any more favorable position than the third or fourth page.

Wednesday, July 10, 1935

On Monday the committee investigating the Virgin Islands resumed its sessions, holding one both in the morning and in the afternoon. Judge Wilson was put on in the morning and, according to reports that were brought to me, he was very suave and unctuous, just overflowing with the milk of human kindness. Tydings helped him to get over the story of his self-admitted fine services as a judge, and he also helped him to smear everyone possible connected with the Virgin Islands administration belonging to the so-called Pearson faction. Wilson was allowed to tell half-truths without any attempt to bring out the real facts. A great deal of his evidence was hearsay and opinion evidence, and while he was on the stand, Tydings took occasion to say that there wasn't anything in the situation to reflect upon Judge Wilson but that there were matters that reflected upon other members of the Virgin Islands administration.

In the afternoon Yates went on but did not make much of an impression. It has become abundantly clear that Tydings has no intention of giving a fair hearing, while, on the other hand, he has every intention of bringing out everything possible that will reflect upon the Department or the administration of the islands. He and his lawyers, who are men of very mediocre ability, work together with the witnesses to weave a story which they try to make as impressive as possible, although it is composed almost entirely of hearsay and opinion evidence. Senator King asks searching questions on occasions, but he is not familiar with the situation and hasn't the necessary background to do the damage that a clever cross-examiner could do.

I have given Tydings a week now to make good on his promise to the President and to me that all he was interested in was the facts and that the hearing would be an impartial one. In view of the gratuitous coat of whitewash that he gave Judge Wilson even before the case has been concluded and before a single witness has gone on the stand for the defense, I dictated a letter Monday night to Tydings in which I told him he had not kept his promise to adhere to the facts or to conduct a fair and impartial investigation. I charged him with whitewashing Wilson even before one side of the case is in and without permitting his evidence to be tested by cross-examination. I incorporated in the letter Tydings' letter to me of some time ago in which he said we could cross-examine witnesses and I demanded that we be granted this right.

Tuesday morning I got the letter to Tydings in final shape and then had a conference on it with some of the members of my staff. Mike Straus was against sending the letter at all, but the general consensus was that it should be sent. Accordingly, I sent it up by special messenger and it reached Tydings just after he had opened the morning session of the investigation. From all the reports that came to me, it had a very decided effect on Tydings. They say that his face turned white and that the perpetual smile that is on his face vanished entirely. Moreover, his attitude toward the Department during the morning session was decidedly less hostile. He gave out word to the newspaper correspondents that I had written a letter and they asked Tydings to release it, but he declined saying that I could do so if I wanted to. It was my intention to release it for this morning's papers, but on further consideration I decided to hold it over. One reason I held it over was because Mike Straus arranged to have some questions asked of me at my press conference Tuesday morning relating to the Virgin Islands investigation. These questions gave me a chance to say some things I wanted to say of publicity value.

At my press conference I commented rather freely on Judge Wilson. I also made some unflattering comments about the manner in which Tydings was conducting the investigation. The result was that I took the headlines away from Tydings and his investigating committee in both the afternoon papers of Tuesday and the morning papers today. When Tydings was told about the comments I had made about Wilson, he was very angry and made a statement to the effect that I was giving out statements to the press that did not comport with the facts that were adduced by his committee.

The committee went into executive session yesterday, at the conclusion of which Tydings made the statement that it had been brought to the attention of the committee that some of the witnesses were being intimidated, and he implied strongly that this Department was responsible for such intimidation. This was published in the papers this morning and I promptly wrote another letter to the Senator telling him that I knew he would not thoughtlessly cast an aspersion upon the Department and that I hoped he would give me the names of any persons in this Department who were intimidating persons so that I could take appropriate action, since the idea of intimidating witnesses was as abhorrent to me just as it seemed to be to him. Burlew saw that this letter reached him during the hearing. When he saw who the letter was from, he threw it indignantly aside but later he opened it, and read it.

Meanwhile, this morning I did give out to representatives of the press a copy of my letter of yesterday to Senator Tydings. I don't know what play it will have in the newspapers, but it was a pretty hot letter. I will probably give out tomorrow morning a copy of the letter I sent to Tydings today on the question of intimidating witnesses.

My theory is that since we are denied the right of cross-examination and since Tydings seems bent on smearing us all he can, we ought to fight back day by day through the newspapers, which is the only means available to us to meet the vague charges that are being produced before the investigating committee.

Thursday, July 11, 1935

Senator Tydings became berserk when I gave out to the newspapers a copy of my letter to him in which I accused him of gross partiality, whitewashing Judge Wilson and failure to keep his promise that we could cross-examine witnesses. Late in the afternoon he wrote a letter to me that was a perfect tirade. He scolded like a fish wife and made wild charges that cannot be sustained by the facts.

Tydings gave his letter to the newspapers before I received a copy and it was through them that I first heard of it. When I got back to the office a little after eight o'clock, my copy had come in. I at once dictated a reply which, if he had received it, would have made him madder than ever. In my letter I took advantage of the fact that he had lost his temper and I played with him while at the same time categorically denying his misstatements.

Just as I was finishing this letter, the President called me. He said that the Vice President had called him to say that members of the Senate were feeling that I was infringing on their prerogatives and that his legislative program was threatened. He did not seem unduly alarmed about it, but he did ask me to go over to the White House at nine o'clock this morning with letters and documents bearing upon my controversy with Tydings. There were several members of my staff available last night so I started at once to get the material that the President asked for and such additional material as I thought would throw light on the subject.

At nine o'clock this morning I was ushered into the President's bedroom. He seemed cheerful enough, and, as a matter of fact, he was cheerful all during our interview. He proceeded without loss of time to go into the case with me. He made copious notes and I put into his hands certain pertinent documents. He was very much interested and impressed with what I told him of the situation. The reason he wanted to see me so early was because he had a later appointment with Senators Tydings, Robinson, and Harrison.

I was with the President about three-fourths of an hour and, as usual, with his keen mind he grasped the situation and seemed to understand my point of view. I told him very frankly that I had given Tydings every opportunity to make good on his promise that the hearing was to be conducted fairly and impartially, but that when, on top of his refusal to permit us to cross-examine, he had proceeded day after day to bespatter the Department with mud and to build up a case on hearsay and opinion evidence, on innu-endoes and insinuations, punctured at intervals with highly preju-dicial remarks by himself, I decided that my only recourse was to carry the thing to the newspapers. I told the President I had done that deliberately and that I was able to lick Tydings' pants off him in that kind of a battle because I had the facts. The President said, "I know you can."

This interview gave me an opportunity to talk very frankly to the President and I did so. I told him that there was no excuse in the world for this investigation. I pointed out that when an investiga-tion of Jim Farley was threatened, although there was consider-able demand for such an investigation, the Democratic Senators as one man rallied to his defense and prevented an investigation. I said that so far as the Virgin Islands were concerned, there wasn't, so far as I knew, a demand in a single newspaper in the United States for an investigation and that no Senators outside of Tydings and Harrison wanted an investigation.

I told the President also that there had been no breath of scandal with respect to PWA and that the McIntosh case revolved around $47 worth of PWA materials that, according to an admittedly loose custom in the Virgin Islands, had been given to McIntosh in ex-change for certain articles that PWA needed and which he hap-pened to own. I told him that I had said both to Tydings and to Harrison, as well as to the Vice President, that an investigation would do no one any good but that, on the contrary, several people would be smeared.

At the end of our interview he said that he was going to tell the Senators that he had instructed me not to give out any more state-ments on the Virgin Islands. I said I hoped that would not mean that I could not defend myself if Tydings continued his present course.

The three Senators mentioned had a long session with the Pres-ident beginning at ten-thirty. When I lunched with the President at one o'clock, he told me in high good humor and with much self-satisfaction of the fun he had had with Tydings. According to his report, he went after Tydings very directly. He told him that he (Tydings) couldn't get away with the kind of an investigation that he had been running, that at the rate he was going he would soon constitute a Trinity since he was already judge and prosecutor.

He reminded Tydings that he himself, as Governor of New York, had made quite a reputation out of the fair and judicial manner in which he had conducted a hearing on the charges against Jimmy Walker, Mayor of New York. At this point I interrupted to say to the President that one reason he was sitting where he was was because of the fair manner in which he had conducted that hearing.

When Tydings protested that he had been conducting a fair hearing, the President read two or three of his highly prejudicial statements during the hearing and then asked him whether he considered those fair and judicial. Apparently he also read, for the edification of the Senators, Tydings' statement exonerating Judge Wilson from all blame, and in connection with that incident he remarked to the Senators that it was an extraordinary proceeding for a judge hearing a case, before the evidence was all in, before a single witness had appeared for the defense and with cross-examination denied, to give a verdict of "not guilty."

On two or three occasions he turned to Joe Robinson remarking that he was an innocent bystander and asking him on the basis of a quoted statement from Tydings whether he thought Tydings could claim that he had been an impartial investigator. Robinson had to admit that Tydings had not been impartial.

The President was particularly impressed with an affidavit read into the record on Wednesday. This affidavit was subscribed and sworn to by an Episcopal clergyman and in it he had referred to Governor Pearson as "a thief and a liar." The President asked whether any court in the land that pretended to be giving a fair hearing would permit an unsupported affidavit like that to be read into the record. Robinson had to agree with the President and so did Tydings.

The President then suggested that something be done to control the situation. He pointed out that the investigation be suspended for a week, and when the question came up whether it should be discontinued altogether, he said that the Interior Department, since it had been attacked, ought to be given the right to defend itself. He told Tydings that he had asked me not to give out any statements to the newspapers and not to write any letters on the subject of the Virgin Islands provided Tydings did not give me occasion to do so, adding that he had instructed me to report the facts to him every day and that if any situation developed that seemed to warrant it, he would issue statements himself.

In the absence of Senator Tydings, Senator King presided over the hearing this morning and according to several reports that reached me, an entirely different atmosphere pervaded the hearing. It was orderly and well conducted, with extraneous matter, generally speaking, kept out. The other members of the investigating committee became interested, asked questions, and acted much more comfortably than they had under the chairmanship of Tydings. Shortly before twelve o'clock Tydings appeared and after a brief consultation with his colleagues, he announced that the hearing would be recessed subject to the call of the chairman. In the meantime, Yates had finished his testimony and Baer was preparing to take the stand.

The newspaper correspondents are, of course, hot on the scent of what has actually transpired. Some have set forth that I have been rebuked by the President. I should think the fact that Tydings for some reason had seen fit to postpone further hearings indefinitely would speak for itself. I have refused to comment upon the situation in any manner.

Two or three days ago Harry Slattery came to see me to say that he had had some talks with one or two of his friends among the White House correspondents. They told him definitely and in some detail about McIntyre's feelings toward me and his activities based upon those feelings.

As they see it, McIntyre dislikes me intensely and is doing everything he can to undermine me. They say that he overlooks no opportunity to knock me, especially to the President, but that he is very clever about it. They think the President has confidence in my ability to do things when he assigns me work, but McIntyre is likely to meet any suggestion that a matter be sent to me with the remark that I already have too much to do and that it isn't fair to load anything more onto me. In many ways he knocks me, but he conceals his real feelings as much as possible, for reasons of policy.

I made up my mind to have a talk with Miss Le Hand and I did so the day following my talk with Harry. We went into the Cabinet room, which is just off her office, so that we could be undisturbed. I told her that I was fully aware of Mac's attitude toward me and the extent that he went to to undermine me. I told her also that I knew that Mrs. Roosevelt did not regard him with any favor. Miss Le Hand is a very discreet person, but there is no doubt at all what was running in her mind with respect to McIntyre. When I told her the difficulty I had in getting appointments with the President and that Mac's disposition always put me in at twelve-thirty, which is a period that is badly telescoped between the President's luncheon hour at one o'clock and preceding appointments that are behind schedule, she intimated that other people had difficulty in getting appointments through Mac. She also remarked upon Mac's fondness for rich people. She said that he would go out to parties and come back and tell her whom he had been with and would then relate how many millions the person was worth.

I told her also that I believed Mac had been largely responsible for the taking away from Interior Department of the Soil Erosion Service when I was in Florida last spring and that I believed he was encouraging Tydings in his investigation of the Virgin Islands. I pointed out his close personal relationship both to "Chip" Roberts, who was jealous of me when I was appointed Public Works Administrator and to James A. Moffett, who entertained the same sort of feeling toward me when I was appointed Oil Administrator. I told her that I wasn't the sort of a man who would keep running to the White House to tell the President how hard I was working and how busy I was; that I transacted my business as speedily as possible with him and was a poor hand at currying favors.

That same night, as it developed later, Miss Le Hand told the President what I had said to her. He expressed regret for the situation and said he realized how difficult it made my work. When I was with him Thursday morning, about halfway through our interview, he unexpectedly said: "You are lunching with me today, aren't you?" When I replied that I had had no word that he expected me to lunch with him, he said rather impatiently: "Why, I sent a written memorandum to Mac two days ago telling him that I wanted you to lunch with me today." I then said: "Well, perhaps Mac doesn't think that you ought to have me to lunch."

The President smiled at that and made some remark indicating that all had not been going well so far as Mac was concerned. Just as I was leaving the President's bedroom about a quarter of ten, Mac came in and at once the President pounced on him with, "Mac, I sent you a memorandum two days ago that I wanted Harold to lunch with me today." Mac replied that that was so but that he had not notified me yet.

This incident pleased me very much indeed because it gave such strong point to what I had told "Missy" and what she had related to the President. Here was evidence right out of McIntyre's mouth that for two days he had neglected to pass on to me an invitation from the President to lunch with him, which certainly didn't indicate any enthusiasm on his part to make the engagement.

Friday, July 12, 1935

At Cabinet meeting today the President told about his interview with Senator Tydings yesterday. With great gusto he said that at the very beginning he said to Tydings: "Millard, if I had been the Secretary of the Interior, I wouldn't have written you that letter." According to the President, Tydings quite expanded on that suggestion. The President went on, "Neither would I have given out a statement to the press," whereupon Tydings could be seen to unfold like a flower. Just as he was thinking as well as possible of himself, the President added: "No, I would have gone to your office and punched you in the nose."

Tuesday, July 16, 1935

I went down to Jefferson Island in Chesapeake Bay on Sunday as a guest of the Jefferson Club, which is almost exclusively a Democratic Club. The officers and directors, almost without exception, are Democratic members of the Senate. I left the house at seven-thirty, picked up Secretary Dern, and arrived at the pier in Annapolis about nine o'clock. Senator Tydings was there to receive the guests and we shook hands as if nothing had ever happened between us. Boarding the *Du Pont,* a sizable and substantial yacht, we went down the bay to the island. The trip took almost two hours. We arrived at the island about eleven o'clock.

The President, with a party, of which the Vice President was a member, had gone down on Saturday. His party was just getting up when we arrived, as the result of a poker game the night before which had lasted until four o'clock Sunday morning. The Vice President is supposed to be the best poker player in Washington, but the President took him into camp. He told me with great delight later how on one hand, when there was a big jackpot, he had outbluffed the Vice President, inducing him to lay down two pairs topped by kings, whereas the President had only 7's and 4's. According to reports, this just about broke the heart of the Vice President. During the game Senator Pittman remarked of the Vice President that when he bet ten cents, it wasn't merely ten cents but the interest on $2 for a year. The Vice President was chaffed a good deal during the day on his playing, particularly by Congressman Rayburn, of Texas, but it didn't ruffle his feathers any.

There was a plentiful cold lunch and abundant liquid refreshments. There was a little card playing, some clay pigeon shooting, and some crabbing, but generally people just sat around and talked and had a good time. Senator Joe Robinson was there as well as Senators Guffey, of Pennsylvania, Ryan Duffy, of Wisconsin, Dieterich, of Illinois, Radcliffe, of Maryland, Speaker Byrns and others. Of the members of the Cabinet, in addition to Dern and myself, there were present Cummings, Farley, and Roper. There was a good deal of chaffing about the Virgin Islands for the benefit of Tydings and myself, but it was all in good nature.

We boarded our yacht for the return trip about four o'clock and reached Annapolis shortly before seven. We got into the worst traffic jam I have ever seen in this part of the country on our way back to Washington so that I did not get back until nine o'clock. This was a long session for a little fun, but I really had to go because I am more or less suspect as a non-Democrat and for the further reason that my set-to with Tydings last week made it more than ever advisable.

Three representatives of Senator Huey Long came in to see me yesterday about Louisiana projects. One of the three was President Smith, of the State College of Louisiana. I told them that we would not be disposed to do anything for them in the way of projects so long as there remained on the statute books laws which made it necessary to take into consideration any state body other than the one applying for the project. They were particularly interested in two projects, one of them a hospital. They assured me that there would be no interference by any state board with these two projects. I told them that it wouldn't make any difference so long as the state assumed the right to exercise any measure of control over any project. I explained that we would not allow ourselves to be put in the position of being permitted to go ahead with a project in Louisiana merely by grace of one of Huey Long's boards.

They told me how badly the projects were needed and that the people needed work as well. In reply to this I remarked that they were committing *lèse-majesté*, since Senator Long had assured the country that Louisiana was all right economically and didn't need any help from the Federal Government. President Smith then asked me why there had been so much delay in passing upon applications for projects from State College. I told him that some people believed that this wasn't so much an educational institution as it was a political institution. He announced that he took great exception to that statement and I told him that was his privilege.

I pointed out to them that the rule that we were laying down for Louisiana was no different from the rule that I had laid down for Massachusetts in the summer of 1933. I said that so long as this was Federal money, we would exercise the right to allot and supervise its expenditures without any interference from any outside authority. They were quite discomfited, but they went away without any comfort from me.

I sent for Governor Pearson this morning to tell him that the President wanted him to write him a letter asking that he (Pearson) be transferred to some other Government agency. He strongly rebelled at this idea. He said that it would mean that his name would be under a cloud and that he would rather be fired, which would at least give him an opportunity to clear himself.

I told him that I realized that he had been jobbed and that the whole situation was terribly unfair. I pointed out to him, however, the difficult situation in which he found himself. If Tydings goes along with his investigation, denying an opportunity to be heard, until the people have lost interest in the investigation, it will do him no good. Even if Tydings should put him and his witnesses on the stand, by refusing them the right to be interrogated by their own counsel, while subjecting them to cross-examination at the hands of himself and his counsel, it would be difficult, if not impossible, for Pearson to clear himself. I advised him that the President's plan contemplated a statement by me before the committee, meeting all of the accusations that had been made against the administration of the Virgin Islands and this Department.

Pearson was satisfied to leave his defense to me, but he still objected to writing such a letter as I told him the President had suggested. Finally he asked me if I had any objection to his asking for an interview with the President. He thinks it would be more satisfactory if the President would write him a letter offering him a position commensurate in dignity with that of Governor of the Virgin Islands. I told him I would be very glad to have him see the President.

My respect for Pearson went way up as a result of this interview. He is a mild-mannered man, even to the point of gentleness, but his Quaker stability of character showed when the test came. Quakers have real moral courage, and that is the highest form of courage. He is not willing to retire under a cloud and for that I respect him.

Late in the afternoon Pearson came back after having seen the President. He told the President that while his exterior was calm, he was bleeding inwardly. He put the situation up to him in much the same manner as he had to me, and the President agreed that he would write Pearson a letter instead of asking him to write one. It was also understood that Tydings' investigation would be tapered off and an opportunity given to put in an answer to the charges that have been so recklessly made.

I had an interesting talk on Sunday with Secretary Dern as we drove down to Annapolis on our way to Jefferson Island. I have grown to like Dern a good deal and to respect his point of view. He is really a Progressive, but he is the quiet, self-contained sort that does not express himself very much. But he has principles and stands by them. He feels about Red hunting just as I do and thinks it is absurd to deny communists an opportunity to express themselves or to have a ticket on the ballot. I believe he would be as unhappy in a communistic state as I would be. He feels, as I do, that it is better to bend somewhat to the wind than to be torn from the trunk of the tree and dashed to the ground.

We discussed the political situation. He thinks the President is not nearly as strong as he was, and he deprecates as much as I do the fact that the Cabinet meetings are such a waste of time. We both agreed that members of the Cabinet should be used for real counsel and advice on important questions. He thinks that the President's family handicaps him politically, especially Mrs. Roosevelt. He has the same opinion of the Secretary of the Treasury that I have and we agreed also on the Vice President. He thinks the Hopkins plan of work relief is a bad thing which may have serious repercussions next year. He is in favor of a public works program such as we carried out under the first appropriation.

Saturday, July 20, 1935

Thursday afternoon Dr. Felix Frankfurter came in to see me. I had called Tom Corcoran and told him I hoped that Frankfurter could come over. Frankfurter is delighted with the way the President is fighting and remarked that he is at his best when he is in a fight. He believes that the utilities probably spent as much as $10 million in their fight against the utilities bill and if this, or anything like it, is the truth, some people have lined their pockets pretty well. The investigation of lobbying activities is bringing many interesting facts to light.

At luncheon yesterday I asked the President if he would send word to Joe Robinson that he wanted my Department bill passed and he said he would. It is apparent, however, that the President has given up any idea of getting an oil bill through at this session. He talked about a draft of a bill to be introduced at the next session. I think this is a great mistake. I have urged the importance of this legislation right along and I thought the President was convinced. I don't know what it is that has sidetracked his interest, but I suspect that influences from the State of Texas have had a lot to do with it. It is altogether too bad because I believe a good bill could be passed if the President would get behind it.

Friday night I undertook to dictate a statement to be made before the Tydings committee. In view of the changed situation, I cannot make the attack that the statement I prepared two or three weeks ago would have constituted. I am simply meeting the charges made by the witnesses so far before the committee. In working on this statement Friday night and this morning, when I completed my dictation of it, I was more than ever struck with the total lack of factual evidence reflecting in any degree upon Pearson or any of the other members of his administration. It has been a veritable tempest in a teapot. That it was a deliberate plot to discredit Pearson I haven't the slightest doubt. It has been a thoroughly discreditable piece of work, and I hate to think of Wilson merely being transferred to another job and of Pearson being required to accept a transfer.

While I have tried to limit myself in my reply to the unsupported and largely false statements made by the witnesses, my statement is far from being meek. I suspect that Tydings will not care particularly for it.

Monday, July 22, 1935

I had an exceptionally bad night last night. I hardly slept at all, in spite of liberal libations of whisky, which usually puts me to sleep.

I suppose I was overtired but undoubtedly the Virgin Islands situation was working on my subconsciousness.

I called the President early this morning to find out what the program was with respect to the Virgin Islands matter. He had been down the river over the week end, but he called Tydings and then called me back to say that it would be all right for me to appear before the committee at ten o'clock with my statement. However, I became acutely worried about certain parts of my statement and I decided that I wanted Steve Early to look over the draft, with particular reference to those passages in which I discussed the evidence offered by Judge Wilson at the hearings. Accordingly, I called Senator Tydings just before ten o'clock. I told him that I wasn't any too sure that my statement as prepared would not raise new controversies, although it reflected in no degree upon himself or any other member of the investigating committee. I said that I would like to have another day to consider it, and he said it would be all right for me to come up at ten o'clock tomorrow. As a matter of fact, he indicated that he would prefer that I send my statement by somebody else and that I offer it for the record without its being read, although he left it to me whether to appear personally or by representative. Later I took the statement over to Steve Early.

It seems to me that if I refrain from making any statement at all, Tydings will have some difficulty in extricating himself from an embarrassing situation. Here he is with no more fireworks to shoot off and his investigation petering out. It will grow duller and duller if I don't furnish any fireworks and I don't think I ought to furnish any unless I give a real display.

I had a chance for a little chat with Steve Early today. He dislikes Morgenthau intensely and he says that Morgenthau knows it. He said he could hand Morgenthau credit for just one thing and that was for his loyalty. He hastened to add, however, that that was all Morgenthau had. He told me that on one occasion he was in the President's office when Morgenthau and his chief counsel, Herman Oliphant, were there discussing some question with the President. The President asked a question and Oliphant answered it, whereupon Morgenthau turned on him and said: "Mr. Oliphant, you are not to answer any questions. That is for me to do." Steve remarked to me that he wondered why Morgenthau had Oliphant there if it was not to answer questions, and I said that

Morgenthau, generally speaking, would be at a loss if he didn't have experts to answer the numerous questions that he was not able to answer himself.

Steve also told me that Louie Howe was really a great care. They have to have someone at the telephone exchange checking on his messages because Louie will call up someone and order something done. Then a countermand has to be put in before any damage results. Howe is gradually sinking and Steve thinks that he will just snuff out suddenly one of these days. Steve says that after the President is re-elected and re-inaugurated, he is going to resign because he has to make money to educate his children and pay the mortgage on his house.

Thursday, July 25, 1935

The newspapers haven't taken kindly to the manner in which the casualties in the Virgin Islands war have been redistributed. There has not been any particular criticism of my giving Governor Pearson a job as Assistant Director of Housing, but there has been a lot of adverse comment respecting the appointment of Judge Wilson as a member of the Parole Board. It seems that, in order to create a vacancy, Attorney General Cummings had to ask boldly for the resignation of Dr. Amy Stannard, a woman psychiatrist with Civil Service status, who has served on that board, with credit, for a number of years. The reason Cummings gave was that he wanted to create a vacancy and in his press release he said he didn't think it was any job for a woman.

Even newspapers friendly to the President have been rather caustic in their criticisms. It does look rather raw. I note also that practically all of the newspaper comment is to the effect that Wilson had not made much of a success as judge in the Virgin Islands. Apparently confirmation by the Senate was not necessary so that he slipped right into the job before public opinion could be brought to bear. My guess is that this episode will not do the Administration much good, and I am afraid that I am Indian enough to get some comfort out of the animadversions that are being made with respect to Judge Wilson's record in the Virgin Islands.

At four o'clock yesterday Senator Tydings led his investigating committee up to see the President. The President told me about it today when I saw him. He said he had a great time. The question of Cramer as successor to Pearson came up, and the President asked what objection they had to Cramer. Someone said he had been identified with the Pearson faction. The President told them that Cramer had been over on another island and never saw the Governor more than once a month and then he asked again what the objection was.

Senator Tydings then said that he had been told during the investigation in the Virgin Islands that after a certain witness had testified favorably to Pearson, Cramer went up, when he left the stand, patted him on the back and told him, "Good work." Then the President said, "Someone told me that an investigating committee of the Senate was holding a hearing on the Virgin Islands. A witness by the name of Yates or Baer, or something of the sort, testified and when he left the stand, the chairman of the committee who was a Senator by the name of Tydings, patted him on the back and said: 'Good work.'" I had told the President this incident and he had kept it stored away in that retentive memory of his.

The President said Senator Tydings' face turned crimson. He said that perhaps he had been a little excited on that occasion, and the President remarked that perhaps Cramer had been a little excited on the occasion in the Virgin Islands. The President then told the committee that he hoped it would not receive any more such evidence as it has been receiving. He said, "For instance, you actually admitted into evidence an affidavit signed by a minister down on the Virgin Islands who called Governor Pearson a liar, a thief, a crook, a bastard, and a son of a bitch. You allowed this affidavit to be offered in evidence and I hope you won't permit any other evidence of that sort to go into the record." The President told me that all the members of the committee were very much embarrassed at this point.

I saw the President today but only for a short time. As usual, McIntyre put me down for the twelve-thirty hour although originally I was down for ten-thirty. The result was I didn't get in until a quarter of one and Senator Norris came in promptly at one to keep a luncheon engagement with the President. I have about made up my mind that the next time McIntyre puts me in at twelve-thirty, I won't even attempt to keep it.

Former Congressman Charles West, of Ohio, came in by appointment to see me this morning. I talked with him briefly and I am satisfied that he is a good choice for Under Secretary. I believe he will be loyal and I am certain that he can be quite useful. He seems to be a man of character, not the sort, I think, who would try to undercut me or build himself up at my expense. Immediately following my talk with him, I sent his nomination papers over to the White House and later they were signed and sent to the Senate by the President. There ought to be no difficulty at all about his confirmation.

Saturday, August 3, 1935

Anna left Thursday afternoon for New Mexico, via Chicago. She planned to be in Chicago for a few hours on Friday and then go on by airplane to Albuquerque. Thursday was a terrifically hot day here. I took her to the train and it was like going into a bake oven from my air-cooled office.

Cabinet meeting as usual Friday afternoon. And, also as usual, nothing of moment occurred. I continued to be astonished at Miss Perkins' lack of sense of proportion. Fortunately, she is the last member of the Cabinet to be reached, but when she is reached, if there is any time left, she is extremely voluble. She goes into the minutest details with respect to routine matters in her own Department and she repeats herself persistently. She talks in a perfect torrent, almost without pausing to take breath, as if she feared that any little pause would be seized upon by someone to break in on her. Yesterday I noticed that the Vice President and one or two members of the Cabinet looked distinctly bored and amused while she pursued her subject into the smallest and most obscure corners. Then, as usual, at the end of the Cabinet meeting, she rushed up to the President, although two or three of us had indicated that we had matters to take up with him. She pushed in ahead of everybody else and continued to talk and talk and talk, regardless of the fact that some of us were waiting for promised brief moments. I didn't get a chance to talk to the President at all, although at Cabinet when my turn was reached I had only taken enough time to say that I had some matters to take up afterward. Before the adjournment of the Cabinet I could see that the President was simply not listening to her at all, and he took advantage of the first opportunity to bring the session to a close.

Tuesday, August 6, 1935

At noon yesterday I went up to the Capitol to see Senator Tydings. He made it so clear that he wanted to see me and arrive at an understanding that I was persuaded it was the thing for me to do. He treated me in the friendliest possible manner and we had a talk for half an hour. I don't trust him at all with respect to the Virgin Islands investigation. We skirted that controversial subject, although I did tell him that I had no use for Yates. He indicated that Yates meant nothing to him either. He disclaimed any intention of trying to get Governor Pearson's job and he made it very clear that he hoped that Drew Pearson would lay off of him in his "Merry-Go-Round" column. I really believe that he is a little nervous about what Drew Pearson may write about him, although he pretended not to be worried.

I told him I had had a talk with Drew Pearson in which I had tried to convince him that he ought to let bygones be bygones. As a matter of fact, I did urge this upon Drew Pearson, pointing out to him that, after all, his father had not been hurt and that it is always better to drop a controversy while there is an opportunity to do so. Tydings and I both agreed that there wasn't any sense in our fighting, and I told him that so far as I was concerned all that water had gone over the dam. He said the same was true with respect to himself.

Of course, I don't really trust Tydings. He is not a fair fighter. I happen to know that while the investigation was in progress, he did me all the personal damage he possibly could by circulating stories about me that had no remote resemblance to the facts. He did this while professing to Burlew that while certain stories had come to him, he had buried them and would not use them in any way.

However, there isn't any use in carrying on this particular fight and I do believe in burying the hatchet whenever that is possible. Life simply can't go on on the basis of continued and implacable resentments. I still think that it was necessary for me to do what I did when I wrote Tydings and gave copies to the newspapers. That really put an end to his investigation. If I hadn't done that, it would have continued indefinitely with a lot of mud being thrown on both sides. I think Tydings wants peace with me. He has had enough of fighting and I am willing to accommodate him.

I had a conference with the President at twelve-thirty today. He approved an additional allocation of $1,640,000 for the new Interior Building, which will bring the total estimated cost to $12,-750,000. He wasn't any too eager to do this.

I told him that I was fearful of the effect on the teachers throughout the country of the administration of the youth movement as it has been projected. It seems that the Catholic hierarchy has opposed the administration of the youth movement by the Office of Education. I told the President that I thought the teachers composed the most active political force in the country; that when they were really interested, they could do more than the professional politicians because they were zealous and devoted and had no personal ax to grind. He finally worked out, tentatively, a modified plan which will throw a good deal of responsibility upon Commissioner of Education Studebaker. I hope it will work out.

At two o'clock we had our regular meeting of the Allotment Advisory Committee. Everything went along smoothly until Hopkins threw in a lot of his projects. I objected to approving them in blanket form without even giving us an opportunity to find out whether his list contained projects that ought to belong to PWA. We had a long and tense discussion. The President sat quietly by without interrupting once. Hopkins took the position that we ought to endorse his projects without even looking at them, since there were so many and they were so varied that we couldn't hope to go over them carefully. I urged that it was bad practice to come in with a lot of projects at the meeting that even our Executive Secretary hadn't had a chance to see and prepare formal resolutions on. I said it was all right in an emergency matter to put through an allocation without formal study or preparation but that it was becoming a habit. Hopkins plainly resented any suggestion of interference with, or even scrutiny of, his projects. I also asked that where a city, as is the case with Atlanta, Georgia, is in a position to finance its projects on a 45-55 basis, it ought not be given any more favorable terms. What I had in mind was a sewage system that Hopkins is financing on the basis of a seventeen per cent contribution by Atlanta, although Atlanta has ample bonding power and is able to sell its bonds in the open market on a basis of less than three per cent.

Hopkins insisted that it would hold up his program if we even looked for PWA projects on his lists. He said that what was or wasn't a PWA project was a matter of opinion, whereas I said it was a question of fact. I urged that to hold up a few projects for further consideration could not possibly delay his general program. Frank Walker agreed with me and expressed the opinion that I ought to have an opportunity to look for PWA projects. Tugwell, in his supercilious way, supported Hopkins, and Mayor La Guardia also supported him for reasons that are plain to understand when it is remembered that Hopkins is pouring millions into New York and into other cities. Little Admiral Peoples also piped up on two or three occasions, parrotlike echoing Hopkins' argument that it was necessary to get people to work. In the end the motion to allocate the money asked for by Hopkins was carried, although not a member there knew what states were covered or how much money was to go into each state. Then, just to show the committee my contempt for it as a careful and deliberative body, I rushed through some other projects without any discussion or any information being furnished except the amounts of the projects. And all during my colloquy with Hopkins the President said never a word.

I came away thoroughly disheartened and just about convinced that I ought to go to the President and tell him that he must relieve me from all responsibility in connection with the Allotment Advisory Committee. I can see all kinds of possible scandals ahead and I don't care to become involved. Moreover it doesn't set well with me that Hopkins has a veto power on PWA projects, while we have to vote him immense sums of money without even knowing what we are voting. All PWA projects go to Hopkins so that he can pass upon whether there is enough unemployed labor in the communities where the projects are to be built as well as upon the man-year compensation to be paid. Hopkins holds up our projects for an indefinite period. Some he approves and some he doesn't approve. He pretends to exercise judgment, but I suspect it is largely a matter of whim. Schnepfe said afterward in my office that he gives us just enough PWA projects to bait the hook for us and make us feel that we are getting something.

My own feeling is that Hopkins is playing the game of a desperate gambler. I really feel that he knows in his heart that he can't put over his program and he is becoming more and more reckless and desperate. If I am right in this surmise, great trouble is ahead of the Administration, and the President cannot escape involvement. Hopkins is intolerant and impetuous. I never knew anyone more sure of his own judgment. In effect, he said today that we must take at their face value all projects brought in by his organization. Yet it must be manifestly impossible for his organization to scrutinize with any degree of care all the many projects that they bring in, since they run literally into the thousands. And the pity of it is that the President cannot escape personal responsibility. He has fathered this program of Hopkins. He has stood up for it from the start and he insists upon attending all meetings of the Allotment Advisory Committee and of supervising all details up to the time that the money is actually granted.

When I got back to the office I was feeling pretty down in the mouth, so I called Dr. Frankfurter and asked him if he would come over. When he came I called Harry Slattery in and then I told Frankfurter just what I thought about the whole situation. I said that I had about come to the conclusion that I must ask the President to relieve me of further responsibility with respect to this program. He heard me very carefully and then suggested that I ask the President during the next day or two to give me a quiet hour in the morning when I could really talk to him. He thinks I ought to talk perfectly frankly to the President from the point of view of my concern for his political future and for the welfare of the social program in which we are both interested.

Frankfurter told me that he was with the President when the storm broke over the Tydings' letter. He was with him that night, at dinner, late that night, and the following morning. He said this was a real political crisis, a matter of major concern, and yet the President never by word, expression, or tone indicated impatience or displeasure with me for having stirred up the hornet's nest.

Judge Pecora was there too. According to Frankfurter, the President said some nice things about me, and he particularly quoted a remark of the President that "Ickes would be a tower of strength in any Administration." Frankfurter thinks that the President has confidence in me and real affection for me. I pointed out to Frankfurter that it was absolutely necessary for me to go after Tydings the way I did and that the result proved the soundness of my judgment because I had brought the investigation to a close. Frankfurter also said that Steve Early this morning in talking about me remarked that the Interior Department had been a Department of all kinds of scandals but that under my administration not only had all scandals been stopped but that I actually had built up a good reputation for the Department.

I shall follow Frankfurter's advice.

Saturday, August 10, 1935

Wednesday night I went to a stag dinner given by Senator Burke. There were about fifty there, I should judge, including from fifteen to twenty Senators and the Vice President. The Senator served a good sirloin steak from a Nebraska steer. After dinner he called on four or five of the guests to speak but none of them talked over five minutes. I was the last one he introduced and I don't think I talked over three minutes. What I said, however, made a tremendous hit and I have heard about it quite a bit since, both directly and indirectly. Two or three men seemed to be surprised that I had it in me and said that I ought to do more of it because it gave an entirely different impression of me. The President told Felix Frankfurter that he had heard that I had made a very witty and helpful speech.

I saw the President at nine-fifteen Thursday morning, before he got up. This was following the advice that Frankfurter had given me. At first he seemed inclined to wave aside my objections but after I had presented him with certain facts and figures, he modified his views. He said that I was entitled to look over Hopkins' projects to see whether any of them were properly PWA. His idea is that, with respect to such projects, if Hopkins and I can't agree, either Walker or he, himself, should act as umpire. I told him this was perfectly satisfactory to me. I also presented figures showing that there has been an average delay of approximately fifteen days from the time a PWA project leaves us to go its rounds through Walker and Hopkins until it reaches the Advisory Committee on Allotments. Practically all of this delay is with Hopkins, since Walker clears in about two days.

I went over some of the old arguments with the President about the advisability of as comprehensive a program for PWA as possible. I remarked that if Hopkins has any PWA projects on his list, there isn't any reason why we shouldn't do that as well as he. I pointed out that we were better equipped to do projects of a permanent character than is Hopkins, and with this he agreed. He said at one point that some people objected to PWA because of our slowness. It should be remembered that the President wanted us to go slow at the beginning of the PWA program so as to stretch out that program as long as possible. I told the President that PWA had made greater progress at the beginning than Hopkins was now making and that we could make just as good speed as Hopkins.

I left with the President a statement of my views on the proposed Cole oil bill. It is perfectly clear to me that the purpose back of this legislation is to take the administration of oil away from this Department. The bill really gives no power or supervision or control over the oil industry, but it does set up a separate commission and provides that the President may transfer to that commission any oil activity from any other department of the Government. If the bill should pass, pressure would at once be exercised to transfer to the commission the fact-finding and scientific functions now performed by the Bureau of Mines and the Geological Survey, and later would come pressure to transfer our jurisdiction over oil on the public domain and the Indian reservations.

I told the President that, in my opinion, this was a bad bill and that we would be better off without any legislation. I remarked that if I had been a lawyer retained by the oil interests to make control and supervision of oil ineffective, I couldn't do better than draft some such bill as this. In my opinion Federal oil control is bound to come and the big oil interests will be well served when that day comes if they should have an ineffective commission of five already in existence. It is notorious that a commission cannot function as an executive, and of course there would always be the chance that the oil and allied interests would be able to name, if not a majority, at least a strong minority of any such commission as is proposed.

The President proposed a conference at noon Wednesday to be attended by Hopkins, Walker, and myself, to discuss the respective fields of PWA and WPA. We didn't get in to see the President until nearly one o'clock. While we were waiting in McIntyre's office, Walker had a chance to tell me that Hopkins had called him up to ask him if he knew what the conference was about. Walker told him what he thought it was for. Hopkins said that he wouldn't stand for any disturbance of his plans. However, when we got into the President's office, he was quite meek and mild. The President repeated in effect what he had said to me, and it was agreed that I am to have the right to search out such PWA projects as may be included in Hopkins' submissions. If he and I then can't agree whether such projects are his or mine, Walker is to act as umpire.

The President also brought up the question of the delay in passing on PWA projects. On the whole, the conference was friendly and satisfactory, that is, as satisfactory as any conference with Hopkins can be because while he may agree to keep in his own back yard today, he is pretty sure to be found climbing the fence into my back yard tomorrow.

On Friday morning when I came to the office, I found a memorandum from the President on the oil bill in reply to the statement that I had left for him. He told me very categorically that the Interior Department was not to fight this bill but leave it to Congress. This disturbed me tremendously because I think this is a thoroughly vicious bill, not so much on account of what it would do at once, but because of its possibilities for the future. Accordingly, I asked Professor Frankfurter to come over, which he very courteously did. I showed him my letter to the President on the oil bill and he said it was a fine letter. I then showed him the President's memorandum to me and he was very much taken aback. He is inclined to think that I am right in my diagnosis of this bill, and he can't believe that the President could possibly be willing to see the bill become a law, although that is what his memorandum meant to me. I told Frankfurter, as I had previously told Burlew, Glavis, and Slattery, that if that bill did pass, I would be confronted with a very grave decision as to whether or not I could continue to go along with an Administration that had struck a vital blow not only at conservation but at my Department. Frankfurter said that he thought that I ought to say to the President that I didn't believe he meant that I wasn't to discuss the bill with friends on the Hill who might want to discuss it with me. I told Frankfurter that I had had a feeling lately that the President had gone a little sour on me. He insists that this isn't the fact but that the President has a very high regard for me and thinks that I am a man who gets things done. He has been spending the better part of every week at the White House for some time recently and he sees the President on occasions when the President can talk freely. I am quite certain that Frankfurter believes what he tells me and he ought to be in a position to know, although I have had somewhat of the feeling that I have described.

R. B. Brown, who was Executive Secretary of the Planning and Co-ordination Committee under the Petroleum Code, brought me in a list of oil men in Texas who had contributed money to the deficit of the Democratic National Committee. This list was supported by a statement prepared by certain people in Texas to the effect that these men had been induced to contribute on the representation that the Thomas bill would be defeated. I showed this to Frankfurter and later to Under Secretary West. It was my intention to show it to the President after the Cabinet meeting, or rather to leave it with him. Here would be the makings of a nice scandal if the Cole bill should pass and it should then appear in the newspapers that it was in return for political contributions made to the Democratic committee. Cabinet meeting kept right up until four o'clock, however, and I didn't get a chance to speak to the President. I sent him this statement with an accompanying note today.

I gave another dinner last night. The guests were Senators Johnson, Costigan, Shipstead, Bone, Wheeler, and La Follette, Dr. Frankfurter, Harry Slattery, Edgar Puryear, Under Secretary West, Tom Corcoran, and Ben Cohen. Senator McNary had accepted and so had Mayor La Guardia, of New York, but both declined at the last minute. I substituted Corcoran and Cohen for these two men. This was decidedly a Progressive crowd and we had a very good time. Fortunately, Tom Corcoran had brought his accordion along and after dinner he played and sang. All of us enjoyed it. In fact, the last guest did not leave until eleven o'clock.

Tuesday, August 13, 1935

I spent practically all day Sunday at home, except for an hour that I devoted to a watermelon party at Secretary Roper's. And I thoroughly enjoyed my separation from the office. I dictated for a while in the morning, getting onto paper another section of the running political biography that I have been trying to write at odd intervals. Then before dinner and just after, I finished hanging a lot of framed stamps. It was tiring work climbing a stepladder and adjusting and readjusting these stamps to make them form some sort of harmonious alignment. Then I gave up a couple of hours to working on my stamps, following which I went in the late afternoon to the Ropers'.

There was a mob at the Ropers'. He had had fifty-four huge watermelons shipped in from South Carolina. These are that special variety that I was privileged to enjoy the first summer I was here. These are really the most delicious watermelons that I have ever tasted. They are very fragile, with thin skins, so that they have to be carefully packed in wrappings before they can be safely shipped.

There was quite a crowd at the Ropers', but it was a stag party except for Mrs. Roper and one or two female friends who were helping her act as hostess. The Vice President was there as were a large number of Senators, Representatives, and Government officials. Other members of the Cabinet besides Roper and myself were Wallace and Cummings. Newspaper photographers bothered me about posing with these other Cabinet officers until I finally parted reluctantly from my watermelon and yielded to their importunities. I really don't see why photographers are permitted at a social affair, but I suppose that publicity is more to be desired than the observance of any social amenities.

At eleven forty-five I had an appointment with the President. First I discussed with him the matter of some United States Federal judges who are to be named for California. Hiram Johnson is very much interested in this matter and came up to my office to see me this morning. I think the President is inclined to appoint at least one man for Johnson. While I was in his office, he called Homer Cummings and it was plain from the conversation that Cummings had little enthusiasm for the man suggested by Johnson.

I also brought up the matter of a judge for the Virgin Islands. The President said there were a number of applicants and I presented to him for consideration Assistant Solicitor Hastie of this Department. Hastie is a light-colored Negro, a graduate of Harvard Law School, where he was a member of the *Harvard Law Review* staff. Subsequent to his graduation he received an honorary law degree from Harvard. He was practicing law in Washington and serving as instructor in law at Howard University when I heard of him and offered him a place on my staff. He has more than made good. He is not only an excellent lawyer but a man of fine character and sensibilities, who, in my judgment, is qualified to be judge of any United States District Court anywhere. Over here we are all for him for this judgeship and I have recommended him to Cummings, but so far I have not heard anything from that gentleman on the subject. The President listened sympathetically to what I had to say and seemed to think that Hastie's appointment might be a good thing.

Then I discussed the oil bill. I told the President about the revised Thomas bill. I urged that instead of turning over to the Federal Trade Commission authority to supervise trade agreements, that function ought to be left to the Interior Department. The President agreed and indicated that he would say so to Senator Thomas. I told the President that the Administration would be avoiding some very grave pitfalls if this bill should be passed as amended by Senator Thomas. I hope by this means that we can defeat the Cole bill and the palpable effort behind it to take all the oil administration, if possible, away from this Department. Before I started to talk to the President about the Thomas bill, I asked him whether his memorandum of last Friday to me telling me that the Interior Department must not interfere in the matter of this proposed legislation meant that I couldn't even discuss the bill with friends on the Hill who might want to discuss it with me. He said not at all and that, of course, I was free to discuss the bill as it affected the Interior Department.

The House Committee on Expenditures in the Executive Departments in executive session today defeated my Department bill by a vote of ten to five. This was not only a disappointment to me, it was a shock. I know perfectly well that if this bill had been brought to a vote after the hearings had been concluded, it would have been passed upon favorably by a very decisive vote. But Congressman Whittington moved for the appointment of a subcommittee and subsequently he was appointed chairman of a subcommittee of five. Whittington has been against this legislation, and he adopted the usual policy of refraining from calling a meeting of the subcommittee while in the meantime criticizing the bill and lining up opposition to it. We forced his hand on that, but the result was as I have stated.

The cold fact is that I don't think the President has put any pressure behind this bill at all. I wouldn't have introduced it without his consent and his assurance that he would send word up that he was in favor of the bill. Administration leaders on the Hill haven't turned a hand for the bill, and, on the contrary, the Department of Agriculture has actively lobbied against it. The War Department has also been against it, but has done most of its work on the side. The Navy Department opposed it at one hearing and Admiral Peoples has moved secretly against it. It is little wonder that Members of Congress are in doubt whether the President wants this legislation. In his heart I think the President does want it, but apparently he doesn't want it enough to help me get it. I have made my fight single-handed and while I have been very fortunate in getting results on the Senate side, I have so far had an uphill fight in the House of Representatives.

Jay Darling, Chief of the Biological Survey, came in to see me this afternoon. There isn't any doubt that he believes as I do that all conservation activities should be concentrated in one department. He said that if this wasn't done, conservation would go to hell. I pointed out that conservation organizations themselves were divided into small groups and that they seemed to think that the best way to serve the cause of conservation was in so continuing. Darling told me that he said to Secretary Wallace recently that I was right in theory and that all conservation activities ought to be together.

Saturday, August 17, 1935

Thursday I had a short conference with the President. Under Secretary West was at McIntyre's office when I went over and I took him in with me. The President told West that he could work for the Department bill and say up on the Hill that he was in favor of it. We also discussed Congressman Cole's oil bill and it was agreed that West would try to prevent that bill from passing the House. The Connally bill, which was substituted for the Thomas oil bill in the Senate, has passed that body but this bill has no provision for an independent commission. Neither does it take away from this Department any of its oil activities. Accordingly, I am not concerned about it, since it does not do any particular harm but on essentials leaves matters *in statu quo*.

My Department bill was called on the calendar in the Senate yesterday afternoon. Senator Smith, of South Carolina, threatens to filibuster against the bill. Senator Bankhead and Senator Borah also expressed opposition. Finally, Majority Leader Robinson promised Senator Lewis that he would permit him to call it up on motion on Monday. I think we have enough votes to pass the bill by a comfortable margin if we can only get a vote. However, if a filibuster develops, we won't get the bill through this session because Congress is too anxious to adjourn. From every source I hear of a terrific propaganda carried on against this bill by the Department of Agriculture and the interests that are allied with that Department. Senators tell me that they have been deluged with letters and telegrams from land-grant colleges, from forestry associations, from county agents, and from agricultural extension sources. West thinks that we can get a reconsideration and a favorable vote out of the House Committee on Expenditures in the Executive Departments if he can only get a line from the President to show to the members of the committee indicating his desire that the bill be reported favorably. This committee voted against the bill ten to five last Monday, but two or three of those in favor of the bill were absent and one or two are ready to reverse themselves. Definite word from the President would do the trick.

Last night I gave another dinner, this time to Senators. Those present were Norbeck, Nye, Capper, Bailey, Steiwer, Vandenberg, Carey, Reynolds, Black, Minton, Townsend, Thomas, White and Bulow. Here again there had to be some shifts at the last minute. Frazier couldn't come because he had developed laryngitis, and Bailey, who had had to decline an earlier dinner at the last minute, substituted for him. Senator Bulow came at the last minute in place of Senator Duffy, who substituted for Senator McNary, who declined in the morning. But the worst case was Senator Bachman. He had accepted and it wasn't until I got home at a quarter to seven that I got a telephone message from him that he couldn't come. I called up Harry Slattery and fortunately he was able to fill in.

It is curious how these Senators and Congressmen wait until the last minute to accept an invitation for dinner and sometimes wait until the last second before changing their minds about coming. Some of them distinctly are not housebroken when it comes to social affairs, even such an informal affair as a stag dinner. Some of the men from the South and West seem to be especially disregardful of ordinary social amenities. However, the dinner was good and the affair went off very successfully.

Thursday, August 22, 1935

I gave the last of my Congressional dinners Monday evening. The following Congressmen were present: Maverick, Disney, DeRouen, McKeough, Rankin, Murdock, Griswold, Faddis, Ayers, Robinson, Warren, Johnson, Lee, Scrugham and Will Rogers. I am glad I have given these dinners but I am equally glad that they are over with, at least for the time being. They have taken a lot out of me and I find myself very tired indeed this summer.

I took with me to the meeting of the Allotment Advisory Committee Tuesday afternoon a resolution of the sort I had discussed with the President on Monday. There were two provisions in it. The first was to the effect that an application for a PWA project might not be withdrawn and submitted to another Government agency without the approval of the Public Works Administrator. The second provided that no applicant would be entitled to money from the Government from any other source than PWA if it was able to finance its project as a PWA project even though it was unwilling to do so.

I handed this resolution to the President when I went in. He read it and put it aside on the little stand that he has at the left of his chair at these meetings. I don't think I have said so, but at these meetings I sit at the head of the Cabinet table where the President sits at the Cabinet meetings, while he sits back and to the right. Toward the end of the meeting I went quietly over to him and asked him whether the resolution was all right. He said it was and that he was going to introduce it himself. This, of course, not only surprised me, it delighted me because he hadn't seemed very enthusiastic about it when I discussed it with him on Monday. So he offered it and it went through without a word of discussion, although it created quite a lot of interest afterward, especially among Walker's and Hopkins' people. However, it is undoubtedly a sound policy to adopt, and it now remains to be seen whether we will adhere to it or whether Hopkins will find a means of chiseling in as he usually does.

Hopkins showed a disposition on Monday to oppose all of the requests made by Tugwell, but Tugwell's two main propositions went through anyhow. Then Mayor La Guardia, I think by prearrangement, brought up the question of the delay in PWA projects. This gave us a chance to point out that over a thousand applications for PWA projects are now backed up in Hopkins' office. The President indicated that word should be sent out that no application will be received after September 15, but we made it clear that so long as they are backed up here in Washington, we can't get them under way anyhow.

Tuesday night I had dinner with Senator Shipstead. We were alone in his little house down on East Capitol Street. He served two enormous steaks and a few vegetables. As a matter of fact, he served no vegetables aside from potato chips and a vegetable salad, but the food was good and I enjoyed the occasion.

I think Shipstead is a very fine man and undoubtedly he is a conscientious legislator. He is a tall, upstanding, well-built man, who speaks with a slight Norwegian accent. His father emigrated to Minnesota from Norway, but I don't know whether the Senator was born in that state or before he came here. He is a liberal, the only representative in the Senate of the Farmer-Labor party. He manages to hold on term after term in spite of opposition. The Democrats made the mistake of trying to defeat him last year but he came through without any trouble. I deplored the opposition to Shipstead, just as I did the effort that the Democrats made to defeat Senator Cutting in New Mexico.

Shipstead was very kind in what he said about my work as a member of the Cabinet. He said he had some friends to dinner the night before and all were in agreement that I was the strongest man in the Cabinet. Of course it is nice to hear this sort of thing.

Friday, August 23, 1935

I had a ten-thirty appointment with the President this morning. There were a great many people at the White House proper and I had to go in through the east gate because of the additions and repairs that are being built underground at the main entrance, resulting in the discontinuance of the use of the main driveway for the time. When I got up to his study, his valet ushered me into his bedroom, telling me that the President was shaving. He waved toward the bathroom and the President called out to me to come in. There he was, sitting before a mirror in front of the washstand, shaving. He invited me to sit on the toilet seat while we talked. When he was through shaving he was wheeled back to his room where he reclined on his bed again while his valet proceeded to help him dress. He was partly dressed when Mrs. Roosevelt came in to say good-by, as she was off again somewhere in her car. He had his braces put on because he had to go downstairs to greet a group of men and boys who had come all the way across the continent pony express fashion. He invited me to go along. After he was photographed and went through the usual ceremonies, he went back up to his room to take his braces off so that he might be more comfortable.

I was struck all over again with the unaffected simplicity and personal charm of the man. He was the President of the United States but he was also a plain human being, talking over with a friend matters of mutual interest while he shaved and dressed with the help of his valet. His disability didn't seem to concern him in the slightest degree or to disturb his urbanity.

I told the President I was expected to make a speech at Ann Arbor, Michigan, about the middle of September and asked him what he thought I ought to discuss. He at once referred to the tax question and said it ought to be treated humorously. This interested me because I have had it in mind to touch on the tax question, among others, in a lighter vein in this speech.

Under a plan suggested by the President, when Hopkins and I cannot agree whether a project is PWA or WPA, Frank Walker is to act as umpire. This arrangement was perfectly satisfactory to me. I know that in his heart Walker is afraid of Hopkins' program and does not believe in it. I know he thinks PWA has done a good job and that I have a fine staff. Today he sent me his decisions on two cases. Members of my staff who have been in close contact with him have had the feeling that he lacked courage and these decisions confirm that opinion.

I had had a secure feeling that Walker would be fair as between Hopkins and me. I have no such assurance now, and so far as I am concerned, if he can decide that the Atlanta project belongs to Hopkins, there is no use arguing any proposition before him. Of course, I could appeal to the President but I am not inclined to do that. I am more disposed, where we can't agree with Hopkins that a project does belong to PWA, simply to let him have it. I am tired squabbling with Hopkins over projects. After all, all I want is to build substantial projects and make money go as far as it can with as much coming back into the Federal Treasury as possible. If the Administration is willing to scatter this money in every direction with a free hand, there is nothing I can do about it. There are those in the Administration who will give lip service to PWA but nothing more than that.

Tuesday, August 27, 1935

Some interest is being shown at Cabinet meetings these days in the Italian-Ethiopian situation. The President said recently that the Italian army of occupation places most of its orders for supplies in the British colony of Kenya and that recently the first item on a large order that went to the suppliers in Kenya was for five hundred women of easy virtue. War is certainly a great civilizing influence.

Friday night Rex Tugwell gave a small stag dinner at the Mayflower Hotel in honor of Governor Cramer of the Virgin Islands. As a matter of fact, the dinner was smaller than he had intended it to be because Senators La Follette and Costigan and a Congressman didn't show up at all because of a late session of Congress that lasted until midnight. Congressman Maverick was there, Assistant Secretary Chapman, Dr. Gruening, and two or three others.

Saturday I worked steadily at the office and managed to clear my desk before going home to dinner. After dinner I went to the Senate Chamber. The expectation was that Congress would adjourn not later than midnight. As a matter of fact, a joint resolution to adjourn had been adopted, but the two chambers got all tied up because the Senate had amended the Deficiency Appropriation Bill by adding a big bonus on cotton and wheat. The bill was then sent back for conference, but Congressman Buchanan, chairman of the Appropriations Committee of the House, refused even to appoint conferees. The result was a deadlock. Finally Senator Byrnes moved to reconsider the motion to adjourn and to ask the House to send back the joint resolution to adjourn. This the House agreed to just before twelve o'clock, when Congress would have adjourned without more ado under the joint resolution.

While the motion was being debated in the Senate and the House, Huey Long took advantage of the situation to deliver one of his typical speeches. I had never really seen him at his best, and he was at his best Saturday night. He waved his arms, he contorted, he swayed, and at all times he talked in a very loud voice. I must admit, however, that he was clever. Any Senator who ventured to cross swords with him was usually discomfited. He has a sharp, quick wit, even though he is a blatant and unconscionable demagogue.

The Vice President had apparently had enough whisky to pep him up because he presided in a very sprightly manner. I do not mean to imply that he was under the influence of liquor because he didn't appear to be. But he was on his toes. Senator Clark also evidently had had one or two drinks too many because he tried to engage in a physical brawl with Senator Tydings when Tydings referred to a statement by Clark as not being the truth. Tydings is very sure of himself and he has a sharp tongue and a domineering manner. From all I hear, he is very far from being popular. I didn't get home until half past twelve.

Monday at noon I had an appointment with the President. Late in the afternoon a letter from him, dated August 22, was placed on my desk. This letter contained the following opening paragraph:

I am writing to inform you that, with respect to public works funds available for carrying out the purposes of the National Industrial Recovery Act, as amended, I desire that all future applications for allocations and all cancellations, rescissions, and modifications of previous allocations be submitted to the Advisory Committee on Allotments, to be acted upon in the same manner and to the same extent as that committee acts with respect to allocations made under the Emergency Relief Appropriation Act of 1935.

When I read this I went right up into the air, and I didn't feel any better when I discovered later that the noon edition of the *Washington Star* had carried a news release on this letter, the headline of which was: ICKES IS SHORN OF PWA POWER. This headline was sustained by the story itself and the story was a perfectly justified interpretation of the President's letter as practically doing away with the PWA.

I must admit that I was very angry. I resented PWA being put out of business in this manner, and I particularly took exception to my being advised of such an important action affecting me personally appearing in the newspapers before I had any knowledge of it. Slattery and Burlew went home to dinner with me and the more I considered the matter and the more we discussed it, the madder I got. I made up my mind that there was nothing left for me to do except to resign as Public Works Administrator and member and Chairman of the Advisory Committee on Allotments of the work-relief fund. Accordingly, right after dinner, the three of us came back to my office, I in the meantime having called Mike Straus to join me here.

I called Hiram Johnson to the telephone from the floor of the Senate. The Senate at that time was in its final session but was thoroughly tied up by a filibuster by Senator Long. I told Hiram about the President's letter, the newspaper publicity, and my purpose to resign. He agreed with me that this way of handling it constituted an affront which I was justified in resenting. He sympathized fully with my attitude and said he would feel himself just as I expressed myself as feeling if he were in my place. He told me, however, that he thought I ought to go and face the President and have it out with him before resigning. He said there might be some explanation after all, although he said he didn't see what explanation there could be. He was kind enough to say that he would regret my resigning because the President needed me and the country needed me. He said there were too few men of my kind in the Administration. He commented on the cunning way in which the President had done this, and I remarked that it was customary for him to deal with men on the basis of a *fait accompli.*

I was reluctant to do so, but I called the President after my talk with Hiram shortly before nine o'clock. I told him I hoped he would let me come over to see him and he asked me what it was all about. Of course, I had no option except to discuss it with him over the telephone. He told me that the newspaper story was not justified. I told him it was, that it was the only inference that could legitimately be drawn from that paragraph of his letter. He said he had had no intention of changing my status as PWA Administrator. I replied that he had in effect put PWA out of business. He said the newspapers were cockeyed and that I mustn't be childish. I told him I wasn't being childish and that I had good reason to take exception to learning first from a newspaper about a matter vitally affecting my administration.

I was pretty angry and I showed it. I never thought I would talk to a President of the United States the way I talked to President Roosevelt last night. I think I made it pretty clear that I wasn't going to stand for much more of the same kind of medicine. I reminded him that I had had occasion to complain before that Executive Orders affecting my Department had been issued without my being advised of them, and that more than once the first information of important news affecting myself I had gotten from the newspapers. He kept insisting that the interpretation of the *Star* was not justified, and I was equally obstinate in saying that it was and that no other interpretation was justified. Then he said that Steve Early was with him and he would have Steve give out a statement saying that his letter had been misinterpreted and that there was no change intended in my status as PWA Administrator. Finally we ended the conversation but with very poor grace on my part.

Subsequently Steve called me up to read a statement which he said the President had dictated. The statement was as good as was possible in the circumstances. It did categorically deny that there was any intention to change my status as Administrator of Public Works. The statement sounded fishy to me, but I couldn't suggest any improvement.

I talked again with Steve over the telephone this morning. He said he hoped that I had noticed that his press release was not interpretive but merely narrative. I told him he need never have any fear that I would misunderstand his attitude, and that I did notice that his release was just as he stated. He asked me who I thought had written the letter of the President. I told him I believed it had come from the Treasury. He said he suspected that also, although he had no facts on which to base his suspicion. He told me he had taken it on the chin last night because he took exception to the President's saying that the newspapers were a thousand per cent wrong and that their interpretation of his letter was not justified. He volunteered with me that I was exactly right when I said it was justified. I said to Steve that I wasn't going to stand very much more of this sort of thing and he said he understood and sympathized with me in many things.

The reason I wanted to send in my resignation right away was because I was afraid the President would do just what he did do. He sidetracked me. It is almost impossible to come to grips with him. I could have done that if I had sent him my resignation, but now I will have to go along, at least for the time being.

I did draft a resignation last night after I had talked with the President and it was couched in pretty stiff terms. If I do have to get out of the Administration for any reason, I am not going to take it lying down. My mind is made up on that. Mike Straus strongly argued last night that I mustn't resign at the moment, although I might have to later. He said that if I did resign, it must be on principle; it must not be an expression of pique or envy. I suspect he is right, although all day I have been pretty sore inside because of the humiliation that the President has deliberately put upon me and my apparent inability at the moment to do what in my heart I want to do. And this sort of thing does destroy one's morale.

One thing I am determined on, and that is that I am going to make a record of this PWA matter. I sent to the President today a letter, supported by explanatory statistics, showing how the PWA program is, in effect, being sabotaged by Hopkins. Then, at the instance of Frank Walker, I went to the President's office just before two o'clock, where I joined Walker and Corrington Gill, who is substituting for Hopkins during his illness. The three of us discussed the Louisiana situation, where I have stopped our entire PWA program. I told the President I thought we oughtn't to go into Louisiana at all, but he said we couldn't let the people there starve. I pointed out that WPA was subject to the new Long laws just as much as is PWA and that it seemed to me to be inconsistent for Hopkins to be in and for me to be out. I then took the position that, in any event, Hopkins should not be permitted to put in as a WPA project any project which we would be doing as a PWA project if we were operating in that state. With this the President agreed and he gave Gill instructions accordingly.

Then Walker brought up the question of the Atlanta sewer project. I told the President very concisely what my views were. He agreed with me that it would be bad policy to give any better terms to Atlanta than we were willing to give to other cities in like circumstances. Walker told him that he had suggested dividing the project, part of it to be PWA and the balance WPA but that I had declined to go ahead on that basis. I told the President the project was one thing or the other; it was not separable. Then the President suggested that we tell Atlanta that we would match dollar for dollar whatever it was willing to put into this project, assuring them that next year, if we were still doing projects, we would be willing to do the same thing. He also stipulated that if we went ahead on this basis, the project was to be a PWA project.

I am afraid I was a little unbending in the President's office. He must have felt that I was feeling at outs with him and I went at Gill pretty sharply on two or three occasions in discussing the Atlanta project. Subsequently we went into the Cabinet room for the meeting of the Advisory Committee on Allotments. We voted millions upon millions of dollars for Hopkins, all of it, absolutely blind. PWA projects are subjected to the closest possible scrutiny, with Hopkins exercising what amounts to a veto power. On the other hand, no one even looks at his projects except to the extent that we go over his list to see whether there are any PWA projects on it. We vote him money by the carload and he spends it at his own sweet pleasure. It is apparent now that instead of allocating for specific projects from here he will give lump sums of money to his local administrators to spend as they see fit. I can see all sorts of scandals ahead.

Rex Tugwell is preparing to go ahead with a lot of big housing projects in metropolitan areas. I blocked him this afternoon when he asked for a big allocation of money and appointed a subcommittee to consider the relationship of his low-cost housing program to our similar program. It is extraordinary how duplicating agencies intending to do precisely the same sort of thing keep bobbing up here like mushrooms after a rain.

Monday night James W. Fawcett, an editorial writer of the *Evening Star*, who has been very friendly to me, called me up to say that he had information that there were in this country two stenographic reports of the proceedings of the recent Communist International convention held at Moscow. One of these it appears, although an incomplete one, is in the hands of the State Department and the other, which is complete, the Hearst people have. He told me that the Hearst organization was having a man prepare a series of articles based on this record. The report is that a resolution was adopted to the effect that the Communist party should support President Roosevelt for re-election if a more radical candidate did not appear in this country. The inference is, of course, that the Hearst people will open up a tremendous barrage on Roosevelt as a communist on the basis of this record. I called Steve Early this morning and passed this information on to him. The breach between Hearst and the Administration is complete and, of course, there is no hope of bringing any pressure to bear to withhold these articles.

Significantly enough, on Monday morning there appeared a big story indicating the possibility of the severance of diplomatic relations between the United States and the Union of Soviet Socialist Republics. A sharp note has gone to the Soviet government through our Ambassador Bullitt, based upon supposed encouragement by the U.S.S.R. of communistic activities in this country in spite of the assurance of that country at the time that we resumed diplomatic relations that nothing of this sort would be done. Our State Department, of course, with the full encouragement of the President, is apparently pressing this matter vigorously. This movement to sever diplomatic relations is a very sudden one. At least there was no intimation of anything of the sort at the last Cabinet meeting or at any preceding one. My suspicion is that this is a shrewd counterattack to destroy the effect of the anticipated Hearst blast against the President.

Saturday, August 31, 1935

Wednesday was a very hard day. I started in with my conferences at ten o'clock and I ran as hard as I could right through until one, with interviews and conferences. Now that Congress has adjourned, Senators and Representatives pile in on me for some last word on something before they go home for their vacations. I have been literally besieged.

Unfortunately, too, on Wednesday, and in fact for most of the week since Monday night, I have been in very bad nervous condition. I felt that I couldn't hold out much longer. The President's action certainly had a bad effect on my morale. I have proved that I can work like a dray horse day after day, with nights and Sundays and holidays thrown in for extra measure, when I feel that I am producing results that are satisfactory to the Administration. But I don't take naturally to fighting such underhand efforts as Morgenthau and Hopkins have been putting in to undermine me and aggrandize themselves. The President certainly has a blind side so far as Morgenthau is concerned, and Hopkins seems to sing a siren song for him.

Friday, September 6, 1935

(I had reached this point in this dictation about eight forty-five at night, Saturday, August 31, when word came to me that Anna had been killed in an automobile accident on the Taos road, about forty miles north of Santa Fe.)

To resume, Morgenthau and Hopkins are, of course, fighting me on different fronts. Hopkins, on several occasions, has left no doubt in my mind that he wants to run the entire work-relief program, except for the specialized efforts of Tugwell and Cooke, and if he has made that clear to me, he has doubtless made it even clearer to others. I confess that I agree with him that one man ought to be in charge of this program, but whether or not that man should be I, it clearly, in my judgment, should not be Hopkins. Moreover, if the program is to be carried out along the lines laid down by Hopkins, then I would not be the man to place in charge, because I do not believe in that program. This I have also made clear on more than one occasion. So far as Morgenthau is concerned, he seems to be reaching out in all directions. He wants to build himself up, gathering to himself more and more power, and he is perfectly willing to do this at the expense of anyone else in the Administration.

On Friday at a Cabinet meeting there was some discussion of the notes that had passed between the United States and Russia. I did not hear anything very illuminating or very convincing on the matter. If Russia, officially or semiofficially, is encouraging communistic propaganda in this country, nothing was offered to prove it beyond a general statement that this was the fact. The President did say that we could not go on exchanging notes indefinitely and indicated that instead of sending another note a statement would probably be given to the press telling Russia to be good or suffer the consequences. Later, however, another note was sent, and there the episode seems to rest.

As I have indicated, I was dictating in my office on Saturday night about a quarter to nine when Fred Marx came to the main door of my office. I had never seen him here before at night and naturally I was surprised. He said that a newspaper man had called him to say that Anna had been in a bad automobile accident just outside of Santa Fe and was seriously injured. He told me that the other members of the party were only slightly hurt. I called Santa Fe by long distance at once and got the hospital that Fred told me Anna had been taken to. It was St. Vincent's. I asked the sister who answered the telephone whether they had an accident case there and she said to wait a minute, that the ambulance was just coming in. Then the driver of the ambulance took the telephone and told me that Anna had been killed.

With Frank Allen driving, Anna had taken Genevieve Forbes Herrick, who has been with her in New Mexico for several weeks, and Ibrahim Seyfullah, of the Turkish Embassy, whose car had broken down and to whom Anna was being courteous, to Taos to visit the Pueblo. On the return trip, about forty miles north of Santa Fe, with Allen apparently driving at a high rate of speed, estimated by some to be sixty miles per hour, the car struck some loose gravel on the shoulder of the road, turned over three or four times, and landed upright in the ditch. Anna and Frank Allen had broken through the top of the car with their heads. Anna must have suffered a severe concussion. She never regained consciousness and within a short time she was dead. Frank Allen was taken to the hospital in Santa Fe, where he remained unconscious until the following Tuesday, when he died. Genevieve Forbes Herrick and Ibrahim Seyfullah both suffered pelvic fractures, with the possibility of internal injuries for the man. This is a very serious and painful accident and they will both be in the hospital for several weeks, but according to reports, both will recover.

Tom Corcoran, who had had dinner with me Saturday night and who had gone over then to the White House, was sent over by the President when he learned of the accident. Later the President called me up himself to express his concern and sympathy. He offered to give up his trip to Hyde Park that night if he could be of the slightest service. Then he wrote me a very nice letter and later he sent Felix Frankfurter over.

I continued to work in the office until pretty late, making arrangements for the care of the body and the funeral. I called Congressman Dempsey of Santa Fe. He had not heard of the accident but, at my request, he generously offered to take charge of all arrangements there. Mike Igoe and Mrs. Igoe were house guests of his and they said they would come on to Chicago with the body, but I vetoed that. Congressman Dempsey expressed a wish to come, but I told him that I wished he would not do so. I got Mary Tyler at Evanston and discussed funeral arrangements with her. Raymond was at Peoria taking part with his team in the state skeet shoot. He heard of his mother's death through one of the news agencies and called me from there. I told him to go ahead and finish his contest since he was part of a team and so could not let his teammates down. He told me afterward that the captain of his team had offered to drop out of the match and return with him to Chicago.

Frances was out but she reached me by telephone later Saturday night. Wilmarth was at Mackinac with Betty and the children and I could not get through to him by long distance, but finally he called me. Arrangements were pretty well set in motion by the time I went home about midnight.

On Sunday I perfected the plans and took the 4:30 train to Chicago. Ruth Hampton had come out to the house at my request and selected one of Anna's dresses for her, and this, and a complete outfit of clothing, I took with me. In Chicago I went directly to my home. Bill McCrillis, Anna's cousin, felt that he wanted to go to the funeral, so he went on with me. Eric and Ruth had worked wonders and had put the house in shape to take care of the several people who were expected. We found both beds and meals furnished by the staff that Ruth had put together. Monday afternoon I went out to the Memorial Park Cemetery with Wilmarth and selected a lot. The Wilmarth family has a lot at Graceland, but it is pretty well filled and, besides, I wanted my own.

The funeral was Tuesday afternoon at three o'clock. Mrs. Roosevelt came on for it as did also Secretary and Mrs. Dern, Postmaster General Farley, Secretary and Mrs. Roper, Mrs. Wallace, and several officials of lesser rank, including Harry Hopkins, Assistant Secretary of Labor McGrady, and Turner Battle, also of the Department of Labor. Governor Horner and Senator Dieterich came up from down state, and Mayor Kelly also attended. Mr. Gerhard, of Christ Church of Winnetka, of which Anna was a member, read the service. I have never been enthusiastic about Mr. Gerhard, but I do not see how anyone could have done better than he did on this occasion. We had practically all the furniture taken out of the main floor and had camp chairs put in the living room, the hall, the sun porch, and the dining room. The coffin stood in the bay window of the living room. Back of it we opened the windows and there were some three or four hundred chairs placed on the lawn. Even at that, we did not have enough seats for the people who attended.

I have never seen so many or such beautiful flowers as were sent by people and organizations from everywhere. There were almost two hundred different pieces and they made a wonderful showing against the paneled walls of the living room and the stone walls of the hall. For the coffin I had ordered a simple blanket of asparagus fern. The President and Mrs. Roosevelt sent a beautiful wreath of white asters and white gladioli, and this wreath was placed on the coffin as the only flowers.

Everything was handled perfectly and I think that everything was in good taste. My object was to keep the ceremony as simple and dignified as possible, and in that we succeeded. After practically everyone had gone except the curious-minded who continued to hang around the front door and the driveway, we took the body to the cemetery for private interment. The pallbearers were Wilmarth, Raymond, Robert, ReQua Bryant, Bill McCrillis, and my old classmate and roommate who has been our friend for so many years, Stacy Mosser. The ceremony at the grave was very short and simple. Anna's face had been injured in the accident, so that the coffin was not opened. I would have preferred this in any event and so would the children.

The early afternoon of Wednesday Raymond and I started to Washington in my official car which I had sent on from Washington with Carl early Sunday. I was at the end of my nervous endurance and felt that I had to get away from Chicago, even if it should be necessary for me to go back in a few days, as it probably will be, in connection with Anna's estate. We made Delphos, Ohio, the first night, and by dint of hard, persistent driving, the latter part of it from Hagerstown into Washington through a drenching rain, we got home about half past nine last night. I went to bed promptly and had the first normal night's sleep I have had for nearly a week.

Monday, September 9, 1935

I came down to the office Saturday a little late, expecting to go back home in an hour or two, but I found so many things that needed attention that I didn't get away until about six o'clock. I spent the evening at home.

One thing that kept me at the office was a call from Under Secretary West. He has been called up to Hyde Park. He has received many complaints, some of a particularized nature, from different parts of the country with reference to the apparent scrapping of the public works program and the turning of the whole work-relief proposition over to Hopkins. Some illuminating facts and figures have been prepared by members of the PWA staff, but he wanted to talk with me before going to Hyde Park. I am glad he is going, since Hopkins is up there for the week end.

Later Tom Corcoran came in to see me. He is as much concerned about PWA as is West. We all agree that the way things are headed may mean political disaster for the President next year. Everyone seems to agree that Hopkins is deliberately planning to discredit and undermine PWA so that he will have the expenditure of all of the $4 billion. Aubrey Taylor, of our press staff, brought in a transcript of what happened at Hopkins' last press conference and this showed direct and unjustified slurs against PWA.

According to members of my staff, there is an increasing sentiment in the country both against Hopkins in connection with PWA and his own program. Worth-while projects are being turned down on specious allegations, while Hopkins himself is planning to spend billions of dollars on more or less trivial and ephemeral projects. He will turn down a PWA project on the ground that the labor cost per man is too high and then undertake a similar project in the same community on the basis of a one hundred per cent Federal grant. Big projects that under the classification of PWA and WPA projects approved by the President are distinctly PWA, he will have broken down into projects costing less than $25,000 and then claim them as WPA projects. In making up state lists a lot of phony projects are put on, we vote blanket sums of money, and then he rearranges projects to suit himself, discarding those approved and putting on new ones. No one checks or supervises what he is doing. I am thoroughly convinced that he is a lawless individual bent on building up a reputation for himself as a great builder, even at the expense of the President and the country. I think he is the greatest threat today to the President's re-election.

After talking with West and Corcoran, I wrote a letter to the President in which I temperately and courteously, but firmly, pointed out the political implications involved in Hopkins' methods. I told him that things were being done that could not be defended in the campaign next year and that the political repercussions might be serious to him and disastrous to the country.

Friday, September 13, 1935

Telegrams and letters have been pouring in on the White House to protest the scuttling of the PWA program. I had a press conference on Tuesday, the first I had had for a week, and of course a number of questions were asked me based upon Hopkins' ill-natured comments upon PWA at his last press conference. I tried to be very careful about reflecting in any way upon Hopkins or his program, but I did answer questions without comment. I said, for instance, in reply to a question, that under the Executive Order of the President setting up the tripartite work-relief program, no one was given veto power over anyone else. I also said that the projects turned down by Hopkins were good projects. I was asked when I was going to Hyde Park and I said that I was going on Wednesday, since the President had called me up on Monday night and asked me to go up on that day.

Apparently the PWA-WPA story has been smoldering in the newspaper offices because Wednesday morning all the papers that I saw broke out with big stories on the front page. There wasn't anything I said at my press conference that would lead to this sensational result and the only explanation is that the story has been smoldering. There was much said about my going to Hyde Park to have a showdown with the President over the program. The newspapers, generally speaking, are taking my side in this controversy and they are making the issue perfectly clear. As they put it, I am for substantial, worth-while, and socially desirable public works, while Hopkins is for what has come to be known as boondoggling, that is, trivial, and, in many instances, make-believe, work that will not stimulate business, help infuse life into the heavy industries, or add to the permanent assets of the country.

On Wednesday morning Under Secretary West and I left Washington at ten o'clock for Hyde Park, where we arrived late that same afternoon. We didn't get a chance to talk with the President at all at any time on Wednesday. Shortly after our arrival, all of us, including Mrs. Roosevelt and the President's mother, as well as the President, went over to the cottage where Miss Nancy Cook lives and where Mrs. Roosevelt carries on her furniture activities. Miss Le Hand was to have a birthday in a couple of days and as there was a full moon and she was going to Boston on Saturday, it was decided to celebrate her birthday on Wednesday. We had a very pleasant dinner, with movies and some talk afterward, and then we went back to Hyde Park. Frank Walker had reached Hyde Park Wednesday morning and he and I roomed together. He confided to me that his wife said he was a terrible snorer and he warned me that I ought to go to sleep before he went to bed. I wasn't able to do that and I don't think it would have done me any good anyhow. All I can say about Frank is that he fully lived up to the advance notices of his prowess in that direction. I have never heard anyone snore worse but there were intermissions and when he was going it the strongest, I would turn promptly over onto my good ear.

It seemed strange to room with a man that I know as slightly as I know Frank. I confess that it seemed even stranger to see him sink to his knees for a long prayer. I had hardly realized how far in the past that sort of thing was with me, and it all goes to show that religion has a much firmer grip on a Catholic than it has on a Protestant. At any rate, I admired his sincerity.

About half past ten Thursday morning the President sent for me to come to his study. I went over some departmental matters that I had taken up with me and then he broached the question of the work-relief program. I told him that the program as at present outlined had me scared. I tried to make it very clear that I had no faith in the program and that I believed it might jeopardize his re-election next year. He was in a friendly mood, but it was clear that he had made up his mind to some sort of a compromise which wouldn't mean anything at all. There was no use in the few minutes that I had, and single-handed as I was, to try to argue the matter very fully, but there can be no doubt at all that I left him with no illusions as to the way I felt.

In the meantime, Colonel Hackett, of my staff, Harry Hopkins and Corrington Gill and Lee Pressman, of his staff, Ironsides, of Walker's staff, Rex Tugwell, and Daniel W. Bell, Acting Director of the Budget, arrived and we all went into the lovely big library at the south end of the house. The President started in forthwith to discuss previous allocations and to attempt a readjustment. It was plainly his intention to pare here and prune there in an effort to find some extra money with which he might possibly satisfy the demands of Hopkins and myself for more. The bitterest loss I suffered was in Housing. Out of $249 million that had been earmarked for us, and most of which had been specifically allocated for definite projects, he gave $100 million. I argued and protested all I knew how but to no avail. He also cut $15 million from the Puerto Rico allocation, and $20 million from Reclamation. He justified these two by saying that there was still left all the money that could reasonably be expended by July 1 and that before that date Congress would make up these deficiencies. He cut quite a lot from Public Roads and here and there he managed to prune a bit. However, various sums had to be added to the budgets of various agencies. Finally he came down to an apportionment of what he had saved. First, he took care of Rex Tugwell, quite generously, as it seemed to me, in comparison with PWA, and then he gave Harry what Harry figured he had to have as a minimum. The rest, which amounted to about $200 million, he gave to PWA.

I argued very strenuously that this was not nearly enough. I pointed out that we had received applications for projects totaling more than $2 billion. I said that these projects were on a loan-and-grant basis and that by refusing to develop a considerable PWA program, we would be depriving the recovery fund of several hundred million dollars that would go in as the contributions of the bodies making the applications. There was no doubt, however, that the President had made up his mind to go ahead with the Hopkins program and no argument availed to prevent that.

Governor Curley, of Boston, and some other guests arrived, and so we all went down to Poughkeepsie, where we had dinner. The President said that he wanted Hopkins, Walker, and me back at half past nine and so we went back, taking West with us. We met in the President's study and he went over the figures that he had worked out in the afternoon and dictated brief memoranda to give effect to the changes that he had decided upon. When he announced that PWA would be allocated $200 million, I remarked sarcastically that that sum was made up of $149 million taken from PWA Housing, $15 million taken from Puerto Rico, and $20 million taken from Reclamation, the latter two of which enterprises are in the Interior Department. The President got a little sore at this and said that I shouldn't look a gift horse in the mouth. I was pretty angry, however, and didn't yield any. Later he said that he believed things would work out better than we anticipated and that it might be possible to give more money to public works. In reply to this I said that whenever there was a meeting to discuss public works, money was taken away from us instead of more being given to us and that I was a realist.

I told him that a terrific howl would go up from all parts of the country and that he was wise in planning to leave the country for two or three weeks as that would make it possible for him to escape the storm of protests. According to the President's plan, Hopkins will no longer have the veto power over PWA projects. He will furnish us with figures on unemployment in a given community, and we will then decide ourselves whether to submit a project to the President for final approval on the basis of the rules that he has laid down for PWA projects. At least this is the President's intention, whether Hopkins will consent to follow his regulations or not. Certainly he has not distinguished himself by the manner in which he has carried out previous orders of the President.

I was pretty sore and discouraged, but I have no option except to accept the President's decision. He brought up the matter of newspaper publicity and told us that we were not to say anything on the subject at all to any correspondent. He referred to the deluge of telegrams that had been coming in and said that wouldn't have happened if someone hadn't put a burr in the right place. He said that there had been a leak down the line in my Department and that there had been a leak also in Hopkins' office. I know there has been a leak in mine and I know where the leak has been, but I am not likely to discipline anyone who has been trying to protect PWA from the onslaughts of Harry Hopkins by starting a counterassault. I told the President that communities anxious about their projects had been begging for information. I told him also that Congressmen and Senators had been camping on our trail and making life miserable for us.

I didn't leave Hyde Park in a very pleasant state of mind. We caught a late train out, although the President had asked us to stay all night. While I was there he also asked me to take the trip to Boulder Dam and San Diego the latter part of the month and said he would be glad to have me take the sea voyage with him through the Panama Canal also.

I have no confidence myself in Hopkins' program. I think it is the greatest present threat to the President's re-election. It looks to me as if the WPA will be perhaps the major issue in the campaign next year. Its absurdities, its inefficiencies, its insufficiencies, its bunglings and its graftings will all be aired in the press and from the platform and I don't see how we can defend it. The whole program seems to me to be based upon an economic and social fallacy. The more I think of it, the more convinced am I that the only sound procedure is a program of worth-while public works. I happen to believe that secondary employment is more important than employment at the site, because secondary employment means employment in the factories, in the mills, and on the railroads, fabricating and transporting the materials to be used at the site to build the project. However, no one has been able to mention indirect employment to the President for a long time. He simply has no patience with the thought. Hopkins has finally convinced him that the goal ought to be to put men to work, regardless of what they were being put to work at, and if there is no legitimate work, to put them to work notwithstanding.

I really don't feel like going on that trip with the President. I am desperately tired and my morale is not any too good these days. I am worried over his program and I am also worried over Anna's estate. Her will was filed for probate on Thursday. In her will she left everything to me, but what I don't see is where in heaven's name I am going to get enough money to pay the state and Federal inheritance taxes. It looks as if these taxes would run well over $100,000, and the only way I can get that money is by mortgages or sale of real estate, both of which are exceedingly difficult in these times. This has been worrying me a lot because naturally I don't want to sacrifice the property and I don't see how I can make the grade without sacrificing it.

Wednesday, September 18, 1935

When I was at Hyde Park last week I brought up with the President the question of the plan of Mayor Kelly, of Chicago, to build an airport in the lake and to devote a large section of the lake front to a Coney Island. The reason I brought this up was because when I was in Chicago the papers carried a report that the President had assured Kelly that he could have these projects. Kelly has been carefully avoiding me in the matter and so I thought I would talk directly to the President, as I have on other occasions.

The President seemed to me to be distinctly evasive. I told him that the airport would be a job that would take two years to complete and that I didn't see how it could possibly qualify either as a PWA or a WPA project. I told him it would be nothing short of a crime to permit the lake front to be desecrated. The President said that he was in favor of permanent exhibition buildings in cities. I told him that was all right but that such buildings should not be put up on the lake front and that recreation and other buildings were proposed. I said to him that my family income largely depended on downtown real estate which would be benefited by this project, but that, notwithstanding this, I was opposed to it. He said that we might wait and see what kind of plans Mayor Kelly submitted. I suspect that the President made some commitments to Kelly. I also told the President that any funds given Kelly would be subject to twenty per cent for graft and he said he was afraid that was true.

The question of Mr. Delano's attitude toward these projects was also raised. The President told me that he understood that Mr. Delano was in favor of the airport, but I told him that my advice was to the contrary. Later Harry Hopkins told Colonel Hackett that I had been making an actual record on him with respect to these projects. He said that he had had orders from the President to give them to Kelly.

Last night I had dinner with Cissy Patterson at Dower House. She is very friendly and understanding. I have liked her ever since I came to know her in Washington and my liking for her has not grown less as I have known her better.

I continue to sleep very badly and I am thoroughly tired out. Last night I went to bed about twelve o'clock and was awake at four, from which time on I only dozed fitfully.

Anna had been sitting for her portrait for Mr. Hubbell. Today he brought in to me for my inspection two studies. They are terrible and I had to tell him frankly that I didn't like them at all. Naturally he was disappointed. I would like to have a portrait of Anna, but I wouldn't hang either of these where I would have to look at it. I can hardly believe that Hubbell did this work because it seems so unlike him. I had Ruth Hampton down to look at them and she had the same feeling about them that I did.

James Waldo Fawcett, an editorial writer on the *Evening Star,* who has me very much on his mind, came in to see me today and we had quite a long talk. Fawcett is one of the most serious men I have ever known, but he is thoroughly in earnest and I think has a sincere desire to see a rational progressive trend politically in the country.

He is very much disappointed in the President and says that the group with which he is in touch feels the same way. He agrees with my point of view that if Roosevelt should be defeated by a reactionary, the next movement to the left will be a radical movement of an extreme sort. This he would avoid as I would. He has come to feel that Roosevelt cannot be re-elected. He has no sympathy with Hopkins' program, which he regards as both bad politics and bad economics. He says there is no outstanding leader on the Republican side in whom the people have confidence.

Finally he got around to what he really had in mind. While he did not directly say so, he very strongly indicated that he hoped the occasion would arise when I would resign as a member of the Cabinet on a question of principle. He said that if I should do so, I would be surprised at the popular support that I would have. He told me that Andrew W. Mellon, former Secretary of the Treasury, in his hearing, had expressed great confidence in me and approval of the way I had conducted public affairs under my jurisdiction. He said that while a good many questionable things had been done in Mellon's name, Mellon himself was really fairly progressive in his outlook. He insisted that Mellon never oppressed his own labor and that he was kindhearted and desired to do the right thing. Of course, what he was driving at was that I might resign and become a candidate for President with the support of the liberal-minded element in this country, which would endeavor to capture the Republican organization for purposes of nomination.

I simply cannot conceive of a situation arising where I would be acceptable to the Republican party as its candidate. I think I can honestly say that I have no illusions in this matter at all. Even if I might have a chance of being elected, I could not conceivably be nominated. As I told him, the big business interests and the money power would have a great deal to say about the next Republican nominee. Their hold on the Republican organization is still very strong. Then there are the southern delegates, always bought and paid for to be used when they are needed. Added to this would be the natural Republican resentment against me because I deserted the party in 1928, to say nothing of other occasions. It simply isn't in the cards.

Moreover, I told Fawcett that I desired to see the re-election of President Roosevelt, conditioned, of course, upon his adhering to progressive ideas. I do feel that his re-election is not assured. I have been saying for some time now that his determination to go forward with the Hopkins program is likely to cause his defeat. I am realist enough to know that the best chance of defeating Roosevelt would lie in the candidacy of a man who is nationally known and who has made a reputation for careful and painstaking administration along moderately progressive lines. Some person like me might fit into the picture but I am not the man. The weakness of the Republican cause is that there is no outstanding Republican who looms big enough on the national stage to hope to contest successfully against Roosevelt. The President is vulnerable, but I see no Republican in sight so far with strength and dexterity enough to drive the weapon home. Notwithstanding all of this, Roosevelt may be beaten, but if he is, it will be as the result of the political trend; it will not be by any candidate.

One of the members of the engineering staff came to me today to show me a letter from Mrs. Roosevelt direct to him, in which she had urged favorable consideration of a grade-crossing elimination project in a New Jersey city because a woman there who was "a good Democrat" was interested and had written to her about it.

The engineer in question is only an examiner and has no authority to pass finally upon any project. He merely forwards his findings to his superior officer. He had examined this project, however, and apparently that was the reason his name reached Mrs. Roosevelt.

This annoyed me exceedingly. It is bad enough to have the President give orders or suggestions down the line without reference to the head of the department, and I regard it as little short of an impertinence for Mrs. Roosevelt to do it. The engineer was so taken aback that he came directly to me, and little wonder. However, this episode is typical of some of the things that have happened right along under this Administration. Soon I will expect Sistie and Buzzy to be issuing orders to members of my staff. Fortunately they can't write yet.

Monday, September 30, 1935

I presented our PWA program to the President last Wednesday. The staff had literally been working day and night under extreme pressure to get it in shape for approval before the President left Washington, and they had done a fine job of it. I took Colonel Hackett with me when I went to the President's office, and we presented him with a big book containing considerably more than three thousand projects scattered throughout the United States. There is at least one project in every county, excepting only in those where Hopkins said there was no one on relief.

The President was in good spirits and didn't dally long over our main program. He approved it without making any changes and he also approved a secondary list, at the same time signing an order giving me authority to substitute projects from the second list for those on the first that, for any reason, could not be put through in proper order and within the time limited by him. Then we took up some lists of special projects, each one of which involved the expenditure of a considerable sum of money. Some of these were cut out altogether and the amounts of others were sharply reduced so as to bring them within the total sum available. Among other projects, the President approved the Tri-County of Nebraska, in which Senator Norris is so much interested. However, he did not allocate the entire $20 million asked for this project, but he did allow enough to carry on the work for a year, leaving it to Congress to appropriate further sums next year. He allowed only $500,000 for the Santee-Cooper project, on the theory that only preliminary exploratory work could be done at this time, which would be covered by this sum of money.

He also approved a housing program, after eliminating certain projects in the South and substituting some in the North. This was in accord with my own theory. I have been urging for some time that the North ought to have the decided preference on this class of project. I was glad to see that the President agreed with me, although I had never raised the issue with him. Of course, it was too bad to have our housing program curtailed as has been the case. I think housing is one of the most worth-while things that we are doing, and I would like to see more money spent on it rather than less.

After the President had approved the amended housing program, he turned on Clas and scolded him roundly for "passing the buck" to him, as he expressed it. The President had brought this matter up at the last Cabinet meeting. It seems that certain people have gone to Clas about their projects and he has not been altogether discreet about what he has told them. They have gone back to the President and quoted Clas as saying that the President had cut out their pet projects. The President was really quite cross, for him.

I asked the others to excuse me, because I wanted to talk privately with the President about some other matters. One thing I had most at heart was a number of projects for the Indians totaling some $4 or $5 million. On Wednesday I had persuaded him, with difficulty, to approve $2 million worth of projects for the Indians and I hesitated to tackle him again. However, I suspected that after he had blown off steam in his talk with Clas, it would be a good opening for me. So I told him that after his spanking of Clas I hesitated to submit my proposition to him, but that I was going to run the risk just the same. My approach touched his sense of humor and before I was through I had him laughing. He remarked to Under Secretary West, who was with me, that I had been working him right along for the Indians, but finally he put his OK on the project book, and I went back to my office in high good humor.

Thursday was a hectic day, trying to get ready to leave. A number of people felt they just had to see me, and some of the Department personnel I felt I had to talk to. The result was that my nerves were just about shot to pieces before the close of the day.

I left my packing until after dinner and then I was so tired that it was all I could do to do the job. Going away, as I was, for a long trip involving a sea voyage through the Panama Canal, I had to take all kinds of clothes, with the result that I finally left for the station with four bags, a hatbox, a topcoat, and my brief case. Raymond and I got to the station about a quarter to eleven just ahead of the President and Mrs. Roosevelt. At the station Amon Carter and one or two others were waiting for me, to insist on a shift of projects. By that time I was so tired and my nerves were so shot that I was positively ill-natured, and showed it.

On the whole, the trip has been pretty good. It would have been exceptional if it had not been for the number of politicians who have crowded on board at every station wanting to see the President and, incidentally, to besiege me about PWA projects, or jobs, or both. Raymond and I have been quite comfortable in a drawing room in the car next to the President's private car. I have had two sessions with the President, talking over PWA and Interior Department matters. I lunched with him on Friday and he very kindly asked Raymond to have dinner with him last night.

We played a little poker en route, with more fortunate results than usual, so far as I was concerned. I managed to win just a little more than Raymond lost, but I have never counted myself much of a poker player, while Raymond is quite proud of his game. There have been two or three jolly people on board, so that the trip has not been altogether dull and profitless. On this trip I have gotten to know Colonel Watson, the President's military aide, and I find him a most amusing traveling companion. He exudes good nature. Captain Brown, the President's naval aide, is also aboard. He is quiet and seems to be a typical Yankee seafaring man. Mrs. Roosevelt, of course, is with the party, with her secretary, Mrs. Schneider, in addition to Steve Early, Colonel McIntyre, Miss Le Hand, and Grace Tully, who are on the President's staff. I think the number of persons on the train has averaged between seventy and eighty.

When I got aboard, I was told that the President wanted me to preside at the dedication ceremony at Boulder Dam. Under most trying circumstances, I dictated a speech Saturday. This turned out pretty well in spite of constant interruptions. I whipped it into final shape on Sunday. Steve Early thought it was unusually good and when I was in with the President Sunday morning, he came in with a copy I had given to him and the President read it. He was very complimentary in what he said about it. The President himself had a great deal of trouble in getting out a satisfactory speech. Late Sunday afternoon he sent a draft back by Steve Early for me to see, but Early, Marriner Eccles, and I all thought it was below par and did not do the President justice. The result was that he had to do it all over again that night. Meanwhile, at Early's suggestion, my speech was mimeographed and given out to the press.

We got to Boulder City early this morning. We started for the dam a little after half past nine. It certainly was a sight well worth seeing. It is a marvel of engineering skill in its picturesque and rugged beauty of setting. Over four hundred feet of water in depth have already been impounded just above the dam and the beautiful lake in process of formation already extends some eighty miles upstream. The Colorado River normally is of reddish color from the silt that it carries, but the lake is a beautiful blue after the silt has settled. We were all struck with the wonder and the marvel of the thing.

The dedication was held at eleven o'clock, Pacific Standard Time, and we had a national broadcast over both of the major circuits. By dint of exhorting and pushing, we were in the grandstand in ample time to start promptly at eleven. My speech took about twelve minutes, all told, and it seemed to go over well. I received many compliments upon it which seemed to be sincere. The President's speech was much improved over what I had seen in draft form yesterday afternoon. One thing I did in my speech was to try to nail down for good and all the name Boulder Dam.

A Boulder Dam memorial stamp was on sale here today for the first time. I have been anxious to have such a stamp issued because it seemed to me that it would also have the effect of fixing the name.

I forgot to say that we had a Cabinet meeting last Tuesday afternoon. It was unusually long, although there was not much of vital importance that was discussed. Secretary Hull reported on the Italian-Ethiopian situation. It is evident that he has in mind to classify, and then prohibit the export thereof as articles of war, certain raw materials the withholding of which would seriously impair the ability of Italy to fight to a successful conclusion. I have not met anyone whose sympathy in this situation is not with Ethiopia, and I suspect that, pretty generally speaking, the whole civilized world has the same point of view.

Wednesday, October 2, 1935

After leaving Boulder City, our train got well over the California line, where we stood on a siding for some five hours, which brought us into Los Angeles at eight o'clock Tuesday morning, October 1. I did not go to the meeting in the Coliseum or on the fifty-mile trip that the President took through the Los Angeles area, but he met with a great reception. Apparently, there were upward of seventy-five thousand people in the Coliseum, and he made a short but worth-while speech. It was estimated that in the Coliseum and en route he was greeted by pretty close to a million people. It was a great demonstration and proof of the President's personal popularity. All of the leading newspapers of the country played it up as an outstanding event.

Raymond and I had a chance to drive from Los Angeles to San Diego yesterday afternoon in the open Lincoln car that had been loaned to the President, so we came down that way instead of by train. It was a pleasant relief from the train. We had lots of fresh air and a good view of the Pacific Ocean most of the way down. The road was perfect. The Pacific looked calm enough, even for me. If it is as quiet on the trip that I am to take on it as it looked yesterday, I do not think that even I can get seasick.

The President's special train got into San Diego just before eight o'clock and I was at the station to meet it. Raymond pulled out of the station on the Chief at the same time, headed for Chicago. The trip on the President's train has been interesting, but Raymond was pretty tired of train travel. I was sorry that he had three nights and two days more of it ahead of him. I was very glad to have had him with me and I saw him depart with much personal regret. It has been an unusual pleasure for me to have him with me on his brief vacation. We seem to grow closer together as we grow older. There is undoubtedly a great bond between us.

Sunday, October 27, 1935

I nearly missed the *Houston* after all. I spent the morning of October 2 at the hotel dictating and getting off final letters and memoranda. Mr. Cubberley had called up the navy yard to find out when the *Houston* was to sail and was told vaguely about three-thirty. The President and all the rest of his party had gone to the Exposition, but I supposed that at least some of them would return to the hotel before going to the boat. Just before three o'clock the feeling came over me that I had better go over to the President's quarters myself to find out what the plans were. When I got there I could not find anyone. Fortunately, I was packed. As a matter of fact, all my baggage except my brief case had been sent to the *Houston* hours earlier. I ordered a taxicab and hurried over to the Municipal Pier, from which the *Houston* was to sail.

I managed to get through the Marine guard that was keeping the crowd back. I was directed up a certain ramp and was halfway up when a Marine officer hurried after me to tell me that was not the way to the ship. I dashed down again and had to go some way down the pier to the gangplank. I learned that the President was aboard and apparently the ship was ready to sail. I pushed my way through the crowd and was part way over the gangplank when I heard a voice call out "good-by" and, looking around, I saw Mrs. Roosevelt. I stepped back to shake hands with her and then went aboard, where Captain Baker and the officers were lined up anxiously wondering where I was. I learned afterward that at first it was supposed that I was on the ship but later inquiry developed that I was not. A call was made to the hotel and it was disclosed that I was on my way. A good deal of fun was poked at me, both then and later, for delaying the departure of the President, but when afterward I spoke to him about it jokingly, I found that he had not known anything about it. Considering my reluctance to go on this trip, it would have looked funny if I had missed the ship altogether. Of course, in that event they would have sent me out in a tender and I would have had the pleasure of climbing a swinging rope ladder to get aboard.

We sailed with due ceremony as soon as I got aboard. Certain naval maneuvers had been planned. The President and his party were on the bridge and Admiral Reeves, the Commander of the Fleet, was there also, explaining the maneuvers. These maneuvers constituted a mock naval battle. As the President explained afterward, under modern conditions a battle fleet can be annihilated before any of the ships are actually seen. So on this occasion, while we could see the turrets of the battleships miles away, we could not see the ships themselves. The cruisers, destroyers, and the torpedo boats were closer in and so was the airplane carrier. Smoke screens, however, were laid down to protect the ships, so that they were completely hidden except when the smoke had dissolved into the air. Instead of firing blank shots at each other, lights were flashed simulating the firing of cannon. I do not know who won the battle and I did not understand what it was all about, but it was an interesting experience. Practically the only ships that we really saw were a lot of old ones that, according to the naval officers, ought to have been scrapped long ago. They are old-timers that cannot make more than nine or ten knots an hour.

I was given very comfortable quarters on the *Houston,* consisting of a bedroom with a real bed in it, a private bath, and a large office. I had crossdrafts through the portholes and electric fans. It was really quite luxurious. The *Houston* is a flagship, and the President had the admiral's quarters, comprising a large bedroom, private bath, and a large room containing bookcases, easy chairs, a desk, and a dining table. It was in this room that his party messed during the entire trip. My quarters were only a short distance from the President's. During the trip we had our breakfasts in our rooms, but we lunched and dined together. On two or three occasions the President had guests outside of his immediate party but, as a general rule, those at his table were Harry Hopkins, Dr. Ross McIntire, Lieutenant Colonel Watson, his military aide, Captain Wilson Brown, his naval aide, and myself.

The first day out, we stopped to fish off Cerros Island. That was the third of October. Cerros Island is off the coast of Lower California. The island is mountainous, barren, and apparently uninhabited. The President asked me to fish with him on this first occasion. I caught a yellowtail weighing about 12 pounds, which turned out to be the biggest fish caught by any member of the party that day. However, many bigger fish were caught during the balance of the trip. We also caught some groupers. The yellowtail puts up a great fight and is a fine food fish. We had this particular one baked for dinner that night.

On October 4 we fished in Magdalena Bay, which is also just off Lower California. I was fishing with Colonel Watson and others on the fourth, and he landed a 65-pound tuna. It was worth the trip to be Watson's fishing companion. He is one of the best fellows I have ever known, bubbling over with genuine good humor and full of spontaneous fun. The way he talks to a fish after he has hooked it and is trying to land it beats the soliloquy of any intense crap player in the world. I landed a couple of yellowtails. There were three or four boats fishing that day and after a couple of hours they came back to the ship with many yellowtail and mackerel. I suppose we caught one hundred fish altogether in that time. The mackerel is a great fighter too. Even a little mackerel on the line can give the impression of a very large fish.

The sea was choppy on this occasion, but I found that I could stand pretty rough water in a small boat, whereas I was susceptible to a steady roll or plunge on the big ship. On only one occasion, and that was when I was trying to catch a sailfish off Cocos Island, did I have to ask to be taken back to the ship. Then we got five or six miles out to sea and it was very rough indeed.

It was a marvel to me to see the way the President was gotten into and out of his fishing boat. He had a special launch with two chairs in the stern. He always asked one of the party to go with him, but Captain Brown also went with him constantly. Captain Brown and a sailor who had been especially detailed to the *Houston* because he had had a lot of experience in deep-sea fishing stood on the top of the roof that sheltered the stern of the launch. When the *Houston* anchored, a companionway was lowered from the lee side of the ship and the President's fishing launch was brought alongside the little platform at the foot of the companionway. Then two men would carry him sideways down the companionway. They would hand him over to Captain Brown and the other man I have referred to, who would swing him around into his armchair. There he would sit and fish. Especially when the water was rough, as it was sometimes, I was a good deal worried about this transshipment of the President to and from his fishing launch. Any misstep or any sudden lurch of the launch might have caused an accident resulting in serious injury to him. But he never seemed to mind.

On this whole trip I marveled again and again at his high cheer and at his disposition. Never once did he act self-conscious; on no occasion did he seem to be nervous or irritated. Cheerfully he submitted to being wheeled up and down the special ramps that had been installed on the *Houston* for his use, or to being carried up and down like a helpless child when he went fishing. He was an avid fisherman and, with his strong arms and shoulders, he was able to give a good account of himself if he once got a fish on his hook. Fortunately, he was a lucky fisherman also. I think he caught more fish than any other member of the party, and I was glad, because he has so few resources that it would have been altogether too bad if he had not been lucky in the number and size of the fish that he caught.

All of Lower California is practically a desert land consisting of high, barren mountains. It did not appear that there was any water anywhere except in the ocean. On two or three occasions we saw signs of an attempt of people to establish themselves, but they looked like pretty dreary attempts. On one or two occasions also we saw solitary Indian huts.

At dinner on October 5, we talked a lot about the Italian-Ethiopian war. The sympathies of everyone were with Ethiopia. The President had left a neutrality proclamation with Secretary Hull to be issued, and he expressed regret that Hull had not already issued it. Although war had not been formally declared by either Italy or Ethiopia, the President's view was—and it seemed to me to be a sensible one—that a state of war actually existed, since hostilities had opened by various attacks on the part of Italy. The President had word from Hull that he was withholding the issuance of the proclamation at the instance of Hugh R. Wilson, Minister to Switzerland, who seemed to have some vague notion that some advantage would accrue if we were not too precipitate in the matter. The proclamation, however, was issued within a day or two, and I think had a very good effect generally.

There was some informal discussion between Captain Brown and me as to whether the President was justified in continuing on this vacation trip, in view of the Italian-Ethiopian war. Captain Brown thought the President ought to be back in Washington, and I thoroughly agreed. I believe Harry Hopkins was of the same opinion. I think also that Captain Brown intimated as much to the President. Harry Hopkins brought to me a statement that he thought the President ought to issue, and I suggested one or two changes. This statement did come out and was to the effect that the President was keeping in constant touch with Washington by radio on the war situation, which was a fact. I suggested the incorporation of a sentence saying that he was prepared to return to Washington at any time, but this sentence the President did not approve.

On October 6, which was Sunday, it was still hot and the ground swell was worse. The *Houston* tossed and pitched all day long. A chaplain had been assigned to the *Houston* and there were Episcopal services at ten forty-five on the well deck. I suppose this chaplain, who had the rank of lieutenant commander, was doing his best, but it seemed to me and to Harry Hopkins that his sermon was not only trite but shabby. He tried to talk down to the sailors, and it was easy to see that he was making no impression at all on the men, in spite of strenuous efforts. I talked with Captain Baker some days later about chaplains on warships and he did not have much of an opinion of them. Other officers seemed to have the same feeling and I confess that I agree with them. Chaplains are given the status and pay of officers under a bill that was passed at the instance of Secretary Daniels during the Wilson administration, and it would probably be impossible to change this status now, if it should seem to be advisable. The testimony of the officers was that the men did not consult the chaplains and that they had few personal problems that their own regular officers could not help them solve as well as, if not better than, the chaplains.

We reached Cocos Island on October 9 and anchored on the lee side of the island at about ten-fifteen in the morning. This is the island that figures in the story of Robinson Crusoe. It belongs to Costa Rica and was a favorite resort of pirates in the old days. It seems to rain more or less every day at Cocos Island, with the result that there is an abundance of fresh water, and this is probably one of the things that attracted the pirates. On account of the tropical climate and the heavy rains, the island itself is a mass of vegetation. So densely is it overgrown that it is impossible to get inland except by cutting one's way through the undergrowth. It is uninhabited and has no animal life except wild pigs, although recently the Costa Rican Government has sent over a buck and two does which were turned loose in the hope that they would propagate.

At this time there is a British trawler anchored off the island. Some four months ago it brought a group of people who are hunting for buried pirate treasure, but so far they have found no trace of this treasure. The legend is that there is an especially rich store of treasure here consisting of loot from Peru, but if there is, no one so far has been able to find it. A few Costa Rican soldiers are camped on the island, sent there by their country to make sure that if any pirate treasure is recovered, Costa Rica will get its share.

I went fishing again with the President on the ninth and he caught a 109-pound sailfish. This was the first sailfish he had ever caught. We discovered this day that there was apparently a school of sailfish, and several more were caught before we shipped anchor. It was fine to see the way the President handled that fish. He had a light rod and no shoulder straps. When he finally brought it in and it was securely gaffed, it was discovered that not only had he hooked it but that his line had become wound around the fish two or three times.

The President caught several other fish on this trip and had a wonderful strike by what seemed to be a pompano of very large size. This fish put up a great fight. It ran out a lot of line two or three times. On one occasion it looked as if the President was going to get it up to the boat, but once again it ran a lot of line. Then a shark struck the fish, broke it loose from the line, and we could see a fight between the shark and the fish a hundred yards away. The fish broke water once or twice so we could see that it was of very large size, and the fight that it put up with the shark proved it.

On the eleventh I did not go fishing. I was beginning to feel a little tired and I had been burned more or less. The rest of the President's party went. I stayed aboard all day reading and writing and having a very quiet, restful time. I finished reading Zweig's *Mary, Queen of Scotland and the Isles,* which I had found very absorbing and which I passed on to the President. Following that, I took to *Anthony Adverse,* which I had bought in Los Angeles.

Gus Gennerich, the President's bodyguard, came in with a 148-pound sailfish, which was the record catch on the trip, and later the President himself triumphantly brought in his 134-pounder, which was the handsomest sailfish caught by anyone. This fish had taken the President several miles out to sea and it took the President two hours and twenty minutes to land it. He came in tired but happy. We pulled up anchor shortly after six o'clock and headed toward Panama. The weather was cool at Cocos because it was cloudy most of the time and there were many light showers. The fishing was generally in rough waters. Harry Hopkins, who was out with the President when he caught his big sailfish, was actually seasick and had to stand a lot of twitting about it afterward.

We had a smooth trip to Bahia Honda, where we dropped anchor about noon on the twelfth. We were now in Panamanian waters. The landscape was lovely. There were several heavily wooded islands. The woods came down to the shores, and the mountain ranges were also heavily wooded. Everything was green and beautiful. I remarked to the President that in all that country I had not seen any dead trees or burnt-over areas such as we see so much of in American forests. This, of course, is due to the fact that they have such heavy and constant rainfalls, although it is true that even in those sections where they have long dry seasons we saw no evidence of forest fires. This would point to an absence of incendiarism, of which we have had so much in the United States, and also to greater care on the part of campers. Bahia Honda is a spot that worries the Navy. It belongs to the Republic of Panama, but is not fortified or even guarded. Hostile ships could slip in here without exciting much attention and within an hour could have bombing planes out over the Panama Canal. Under our treaty with Panama we have a right to use Panamanian waters to defend the canal, but we have no fortifications except on Panama itself. In case of war we would have to send some ships down to Bahia Honda to stand on guard.

There was a bit of a village on one of the bays and some isolated thatched huts. We did not go on shore and were anchored fairly well out, because Captain McIntire said that this was country of the malarial mosquito, and we were not looking for any visits from him. He said that this region was full of malaria. I went fishing again with the President in one of the whaleboats. We tried both trolling and bottom fishing, but neither of us caught anything. Some of the other boats brought in a few. There are plenty of sharks in these waters and Colonel Watson reported that he had seen a lot of red-and-yellow-striped snakes in the water. Others too spoke of snakes in these waters, but we kidded Watson about his snakes from that time until the end of the trip, all of which he took very good-naturedly. These snakes are said to be poisonous, but if they really are, I do not know. Some natives came over in small dugouts to inspect the ship. They are almost black in color with thick bushy hair, and they probably are descendants of aborigines. They looked rather miserable and were dirty and unkempt and dressed in ragged clothes. I think it may be said of Bahia Honda that it is beautiful to look at but unhealthy. The country here also is said to abound in poisonous snakes. It is said that boa constrictors and jaguars are also found.

October 13 was Sunday and we remained at anchor all day in Bahia Honda. Church services again, and the text of the parson was "A Deck of Cards." To my amazement, he produced a deck of cards to illustrate his sermon. I thought it was a tawdry exhibition and certainly unconvincing to one of any intelligence. It was very hot on deck during the services and I kept my straw hat on most of the time. Some of the others put on their hats intermittently. In the afternoon we had some poker in my cabin. Hopkins, Watson, McIntire, and Commander Robottom of the *Houston* played. Commander Robottom was the heavy winner and I lost about four dollars. That night after supper we played poker again in the President's cabin. Robottom did not play in that game, but the President and Captain Brown did. We played until nearly midnight and I lost $12.50. The President, Hopkins, and Brown were winners.

We pulled out of Bahia Honda late Sunday afternoon and anchored off the Perlas Islands the following morning. The Perlas Islands are off the west coast of Balboa, and in season this is good fishing grounds. However, we were not in season. Governor Schley of the Canal Zone came aboard early. We had very heavy rains in the morning, this being the rainy season in that section, and the weather was threatening most of the afternoon. The air was hot and enervating. I quite decidedly felt the change in climate. I would not care to live in climate of that kind. Once again I went fishing with the President that afternoon but the fishing was not good. We were out three or four hours, during which time he caught one small mackerel. I shared my rod with Gus Gennerich and we caught five fish each, mine being three mackerel, one bonita, and one garfish. The President started fishing with a feather, but I chose a spoon and I let out more line than the President. I think that is the reason I caught fish when he did not. It was necessary to go pretty deep for them.

At the Perlas Islands mail came to us by airplane—the first since leaving San Diego. I got a good deal of mail matter from the Department and two letters from Raymond, which he had sent on to Washington to catch the White House pouch. On account of the unsatisfactory fishing in these waters, the President decided to transit the canal on Wednesday instead of Thursday, as originally planned.

Early the morning of the sixteenth we tied up to the dock at Balboa to refuel, and just before eight o'clock Dr. McIntire, Harry Hopkins, and I went over to Panama in a government Ford to do some shopping. I bought three beautiful unblocked Panama hats of fine quality. I paid $10 for one and $15 for each of two. The $15 hats I am confident would cost from $75 to $100 in this country, and the $10 hat is of better quality than the one I paid $30 for last spring in Chicago. I also bought a kimono, a Chinese shawl that interested me, and some pongee wrappers.

Panama is a clean and attractive city. I wish I had had more time to spend there. However, we had only this one brief time for shopping and we had to be back early because the President and his party were due to leave the *Houston* at ten o'clock. At ten, with due ceremony, we all disembarked and were driven out to see Madden Dam. Then we had a review of the American troops on the west side of the Isthmus and lunch at the Army Club. After that we went back to the *Houston* to transit the canal, taking with us Governor and Mrs. Schley, Major General and Mrs. Lytle Brown, and other ranking officials, including several generals and admirals.

The trip through the canal was very interesting indeed. I forgot to say that President Arias of the Republic of Panama and his wife were with the party all day long. During the transit of the canal I was out on deck all the time and I was very much interested not only in the canal and its locks but in the scenery as well. When we went through the last lock and were off Cristobal, our Canal Zone and Panamanian guests left us in small boats. We anchored inside of the breakwater and stayed there all night. At dinner that night we had a very hilarious time over an extra issue of *The Blue Bonnet,* a weekly publication gotten out on board ship. This extra edition, I think, had been written by Harry Hopkins. At any rate, we promptly accused him of it. It was full of clever shafts at most of the members of the party, especially Colonel Watson and myself.

We left Cristobal about eight o'clock on the morning of the seventeenth bound for Porto Bello, where we anchored in the bay. This is an old town. It goes back to the early Spanish days on the

American continents. In those days it was the chief Spanish port on the Atlantic Coast and was strongly fortified. Spanish galleons used to foregather here to receive their loads of gold and silver looted from Central and South America. Even loot from the Pacific Coast was sent across the Isthmus at this point by mule-trains to be transshipped to Spain. Porto Bello was captured by Morgan, the English pirate, in sixteen hundred and something. He destroyed the forts. According to legend, he captured the forts in this way: there was a big Spanish nunnery at Porto Bello in those days and his pirates forced the nuns to march ahead of them up to the walls of the fort. It is also related that the nuns were all stripped naked and forced to march through the town in that fashion. They were then given to the pirates for their enjoyment for several days, after which Morgan sent word around that every man had to report on board his ship by a certain morning, failing which they would be summarily shot. A number of the crew were having too good a time to comply with this order, and Morgan sent out a searching squad that ruthlessly carried out his orders to shoot all who had failed to report. For the verity of this lurid tale, I do not vouch.

There are remains of the forts and of the old church. The President said he had suggested on two or three occasions to President Arias of Panama that this historic spot be preserved and made a tourist attraction. It is only a short distance from Cristobal and I think the President's suggestion is a very good one. If something is not done pretty soon, more of the walls of the old fort will be undermined by the water. Even if preserved in its present condition, it could be made a great attraction for tourists.

After we had inspected Porto Bello, we weighed anchor again and started for San Blas Bay, which we reached about five-thirty. I had been told about the San Blas Indians by Mrs. Schley and Madame Arias, both of whom said they were most interesting. The President too had heard about them and that is the reason we went down there. We had an extra day that we had saved as the result of transiting the canal one day earlier than we had originally planned. Late as it was, we at once took to our boats because we wanted to get some idea about where the Indians actually were. The islands on which the Indians live are coral islands that are only a foot or two above the surface of the water. Even our whale-boats drew too much water for us to land. However, we circled one or two of the islands and made plans to return the next day.

Then we returned to the *Houston*. It was well after dark when we got there. In the meantime, the President decided to stay another night so that we could have a chance to explore some of the islands the following day. After dinner that night we played poker again in the President's cabin, but we played only until ten o'clock.

On the eighteenth we spent several hours visiting the islands on which the San Blas Indians live. We managed to land on three or four of them. There are said to be about thirty thousand of these Indians living on the islands in San Blas Bay. Probably the Indians went there originally to escape from their enemies. The islands are free from insects, and the Indians and their surroundings appear to be very clean. They live in big thatched houses with apparently several families to a house. They are practically independent of the Panamanian Government, being ruled by three chiefs of their own. They occupy a number of islands, and still other islands are planted to coconut trees, the crops of which belong to the Indians as a community. They have farms on the mainland but they do not live on the mainland, going over there merely to attend to their farms during the day. On these farms they raise sugar cane, bananas, etc. The Indians are probably almost as primitive as in the days of Columbus.

The women are fully clothed. They wear bright waists, two of which I bought, and beads. Their beadwork is not notable. Generally speaking, the beads are made of cheap and uninteresting glass, usually black, which they get from the one or two boats that trade with the islands. I did manage to pick up one or two rather interesting coral necklaces. The women and even the little girls have gold rings in their noses and some of the women wear large gold disk earrings. I was very anxious to get a pair of these earrings but was not successful. The boys go stark naked until the age of puberty and the men wear trousers and shirts which apparently they pick up from traders. The houses are built closely together on the island, and there seem to be a great many children. To the casual observer, there appeared to be many more boys than girls.

The women are not allowed to marry outside of the tribe, so that it is kept pure. Both men and women are rather short and squatty and the men are muscular. They seem to be as much at home on the water as on the land. We could see them all over the bay in their dugout canoes, which were graceful and serviceable. They were apparently made out of coconut trees. On some of these canoes they rigged sails, and it was surprising to see how seaworthy those little cockleshells were. The boys would dive into the water and clamber back into their dugouts again with all the agility of monkeys. The attitude of the people was friendly. They had practically nothing to trade, except coconuts, fish spears, bows and arrows, women's waists, and necklaces. It would be interesting to spend some time among these islands making a study of these people. I suspect that there are few native Indian tribes anywhere in North or South America, at least of this size, that have preserved not only their strain but their religion and customs to the degree that these people have. Unfortunately, the missionaries are trying to "civilize" them, although I doubt whether they have made much of an impression so far.

The weather was very hot while we were in San Blas Bay and, for the first time, before going into the small boat I greased my face and hands to prevent excessive sunburn. While I had been burned, I had not been burned unduly and I did not want to get into trouble. Harry Hopkins has had a terrible lip from burn for practically the entire trip. More mail reached us by aiplane in San Blas Bay but nothing of official importance came to me. I had another letter from Raymond. We continued at anchorage here the night of October 18, but at seven o'clock the morning of the nineteenth we moved down the bay for some fifteen or twenty miles and again dropped anchor. We went out to fish and to see some more of the San Blas Indian islands.

Harry Hopkins, Colonel Watson, and I went in one of the whaleboats but we were not particularly interested in fishing that day. After some desultory fishing, during which Harry Hopkins landed one, we decided to land on one of the uninhabited islands for lunch. During the morning we had two or three heavy showers. We could not get close enough to the shore of the island that we picked out for our visit to land dryshod, so I went overboard right in my clothes in water up to my waist. We had hardly started eating our lunch when the heaviest rain that I think I have ever been in descended on us. I put my raincoat over the lunch to protect it. Harry Hopkins and Colonel Watson had bathing suits on under their clothes, so that they were ready for any kind of weather. I sought the protection of a coconut tree, but I was simply drenched to the skin. However, we loved it; we all had a good time. It looked as if the rain would never cease, so we decided that it might be the part of wisdom to go back to the *Houston*, especially since we were all wet to the skin and felt a little cool, although we could keep warm by lying in the ocean. So we got aboard our whaleboat again and went back to the *Houston*. It felt good to get out of my wet clothes and under a shower bath and into dry clothes again. The President did not return for a couple of hours later and as soon as he got aboard, we weighed anchor and headed for Charleston, S. C., intending to stop for half a day at Crooked Island to fish.

The weather was a little rough and when we got beyond the coast of Haiti, which I had a glimpse of quite late one afternoon, we got a radiogram from Washington that a hurricane was brewing in the Caribbean. We did not know at first whether or not the President would insist on carrying out his plans to fish off Crooked Island, but he decided to take the advice of Captain Brown and Captain Baker and head straight for Charleston. The navigators figured that we could beat the hurricane, although we might feel some disturbances due to it. On the twentieth the sea was choppy all day and it was cloudy and rainy. However, I managed to keep my sea legs. There were no services, although it was Sunday, on account of the weather. We kept bowling along at about twenty-one knots an hour. In the afternoon we had some more poker in my cabin and that night we played blackjack with the President in his cabin. I was luckier at blackjack than I was at poker, especially when I was banker. I was going along pretty well when we reached our time limit. At this time we were about twenty-four hours ahead of the hurricane. The weather all day was stuffy and murky and depressing.

On October 23 the weather was considerably rougher. I made an effort to keep going, but about ten o'clock I went to bed and stayed there for the balance of the day. I was not missing much by not being up, because the weather was hot and muggy and threatening. It was more comfortable in my cabin under an electric fan. That night the weather was really very rough. We tossed and pitched all night long. It seemed at times as if the *Houston* would simply lie over on its side, but I was not worried. The President remarked the next day that he was worried at times about being able to stay in his bed. The rest of the party felt the same way about it. The beds had no sides, so that it would have been perfectly easy to be pitched out.

Colonel Watson had been boasting about how he had stood the trip, although at the outset he had had some qualms about whether or not he would be seasick. After I had gone to bed I learned to my delight that Watson had betaken himself to his bunk also. Harry Hopkins followed our example, so that that night at dinner the President had with him only Captain Brown and Captain Ross McIntire. It was pretty rough the morning of the twenty-third but we were keeping well ahead of the hurricane and by noon the weather had quieted noticeably. The President wanted some pictures taken on the upper deck, so I got up at twelve-thirty. The sea kept getting quieter, so I stayed up. That afternoon we had some more poker in my cabin. That night about ten o'clock we anchored in Charleston Harbor.

Charleston Harbor was the deadest harbor I have ever seen. There seemed to be no commerce to speak of. This was the first time I had ever been at Charleston and so it was my first glimpse of Fort Sumter. It was easy to see how Sumter fell before the Confederate guns, because the island itself is nothing but a little mud flat. The fort that still exists there seemed from the *Houston* to have two eight-inch guns, but one or two shells would demolish it much more easily than the Confederates destroyed it in 1861.

I am glad I took this trip. I did not want to go and finally did go only under pressure from the President. I really was not seasick at any stage, although I would have been if I had not taken the precaution of going to bed when I felt seasickness coming on. While I am not much of a fisherman and have no real passion for the sport, it was good for me to be out in the open air and sun holding a rod in my hands, even if I did not catch many fish. I had a complete change and rest and there is no doubt at all that I badly needed them. I slept better than I have slept for many, many months. We had a congenial crowd and everything went off beautifully. I marveled at the smooth-running efficiency of the Navy. Captain Baker is a fine man and he and the other officers and members of the crew spared no pains to make our trip comfortable. My quarters really were luxurious. The food was excellent and varied. The only thing I did not like was the water and the coffee. The drinking water was distilled from sea water and was flat and had a taste that I did not relish. The coffee was simply badly made, but I switched to tea and got along all right. As a general thing, we went to bed very early and we got up when we pleased. I saw parts of the world that I have never seen before and will probably never see again.

Colonel Watson, the military aide of the President, is one of the best fellows I have ever known. He simply bubbles with good humor and one cannot feel grouchy or dispirited when he is about. He can take a joke on himself as well as he can on someone else. He was really the life of the party without being in any sense a sparkling wit. I have never known anyone just like him. He was great fun fishing and he was equally great fun playing poker. At the table he could be relied upon to keep us all in a mellow humor, and this without any effort on his part, but simply by being himself. Captain Brown, the naval aide of the President, is a Yankee from Connecticut, but he has a quiet humor and a capacity for good fellowship. Captain McIntire, the President's personal physician, was pleasant, and Harry Hopkins fitted in well with his easy manners and keen wit. The President is always a delightful host, ready to laugh at a joke or tell a good story.

I found things in quite good shape when I got back to the Department. Apparently, everything had moved along smoothly, although I found a feeling on the part of two or three of my staff that Colonel Hackett has been playing politics to some extent on public works. I have not yet had an opportunity to look into this for myself, but I shall do so. One can always talk frankly with Hackett, and I am confident that if he has departed from the path that I have tried to follow, it has been unwittingly and without any ulterior purpose.

Wednesday, October 30, 1935

One night at dinner on the *Houston* trip, the question of Lewis Douglas came up and the President told how he had asked Douglas to defer the offering of his resignation as Director of the Budget. The 1934 election was not far ahead and the President was worried about the effect of the resignation on election day. He asked Douglas to withhold it for that reason, but Douglas insisted that it had to be presented then. In quoting Douglas, the President imitated him and made the remark that the election was overwhelmingly Democratic, notwithstanding the resignation. Just as the President rarely expresses approval or approbation of anyone except in a very unconvincing and matter-of-fact way, so he does not often express disapproval except in the same manner.

Jim Farley met the President on his return to Charleston. He seemed friendlier to me than he had for a long time. As we were approaching Washington the morning of the twenty-fourth he sat down with me at breakfast. I referred to Huey Long's assassination and the situation in Louisiana. He told me that he was keeping hands off in Louisiana, because whichever faction won would be friendly to the Administration. He has no apprehensions now over that state. Then he made the significant statement that if Huey Long had lived, as a candidate for President he would have polled six million votes, although he thinks Roosevelt would have carried Louisiana. He said, "I always laughed Huey off, but I did not feel that way about him. He was good for that many votes," and then he named a number of states that Roosevelt would have lost if Long had lived and had been a candidate.

We had a meeting of the Cabinet Friday afternoon. Every member was there except George Dern, who is on a trip to the Philippine Islands. Secretary of State Hull gave a report of the Italian-Ethiopian situation. He does not seem to know just what moves are likely to be made there at any time. Apparently there is a lot of international politics being played. The President brought up the question of the possibility of publishing the names of all Americans who insist on sailing on Italian ships in spite of the warning that he gave in his neutrality message, and the names of American firms that continue to do business with Italy. He merely threw out these ideas as suggestions for consideration.

Saturday, November 9, 1935

Sunday morning I tried to dictate a speech that I have promised to make before the Detroit Town Hall on the fourth of December, but it didn't go very well. The fact is that I haven't been working hard enough lately to get the best results. To be sure, I am at the office the usual long hours in the day but during the last week I was only down twice at night. I can do more work and better work if I am under great pressure.

In the afternoon I left for Chicago, where I arrived on Monday morning. My main reason for this trip was to see Fred Marx about matters connected with the estate. I would have done this earlier except for my vacation trip with the President, although I confess that I would willingly have put it off longer. The will has been proved and heirship as well. Letters testamentary have issued to me as executor. My principal concern has been the question of the inheritance taxes.

Tuesday morning I cleaned up some further matters in connection with the estate and then attended to some PWA and housing business. Tom Courtney, the State's attorney, came over to see me in the morning. He complained that Farley never talks with anyone in Chicago except Mayor Kelly. He said that Mayor Kelly was disposed to shut him out of politics so far as possible and that there has been some talk of his becoming the organization candidate for governor. Governor Horner has, in effect, announced his candidacy for renomination but the organization is not very strong for him. As a matter of fact, Democratic leaders have been weakening Horner by criticizing him and minimizing his record as governor. Courtney says that he does not know whether the organization will be for him for renomination as State's attorney but that he intends to run anyhow. He doesn't get along well with Kelly or Pat Nash, the national committeeman.

Then Mabel Reinecke came in by appointment. She told me that Frank Knox had sent for her and other women who had been active in organizing for Hoover in 1932 and had asked them to organize for him. He told her very frankly that he wanted to be President. Mrs. Reinecke was utterly taken by surprise and so far has not given a definite reply. Knox also sent for General Nathan William MacChesney, a classmate of Hoover's at Stanford University who organized certain nonpolitical groups for Hoover in 1932, and asked him to repeat for Knox. MacChesney had a talk with Hoover, who told him that it would be all right for him to work for Knox on the understanding, however, that Knox was not to deliver any strength accruing from MacChesney's efforts to anyone else in the event of his failure to secure the nomination for himself. When this was repeated by MacChesney to Knox, the latter was distinctly noncommittal.

It seems to be the general opinion that Senator Borah is undoubtedly a candidate for the Republican nomination and that he is in a position to make all kinds of trouble for the regular organization. If he files in the primary states, and if he makes the fight on the control of the party that he has been threatening to make, there may be a regular cat-and-dog-fight result.

I left Chicago Tuesday afternoon and got back to Washington Wednesday morning. On Wednesday morning an Englishman by the name of Christopher Chancellor came in to see me. Elizabeth Robins, Raymond's sister, who has lived in England for many years, wrote me a letter about Chancellor the other day. He is at the head of the Reuter's news agency at Shanghai and was returning to his post after a vacation in England. He had never been in the United States, so he was going across the country to sail from San Francisco.

I found him very keen and interesting. He thinks that Great Britain is definitely on the road to recovery. He spoke of the heavy taxes that the Englishmen pay without complaint and said that the Englishmen believed, as a matter of course, that no one in the British Isles should be allowed to starve. He spoke of the obligation to the state that an Englishman always feels, and I agreed with him that the situation there is much different from what it is in this country. He thinks that Japan has definitely made up its mind to control the Far East economically, and he feels that the interests of both the United States and Great Britain will be crowded out of China. The British interests, of course, are much greater than ours.

As to Italy, he says that it is the belief in Government circles in London that the purpose of Mussolini is to take over all the British colonies in Africa. The occupation of Ethiopia will be only the first step, with Egypt as the next point of attack. Mr. Chancellor said that while there is a strong pacifist sentiment in Great Britain now, he does not believe that in the end Great Britain will consent to the loss of these colonies. I remarked that if this was Mussolini's objective, it would be far easier for Great Britain to stop her now than later after she had conquered and established herself in Ethiopia. With this Chancellor agreed but he does not think that Italy will be able to conquer Ethiopia. He thinks that when the economic sanctions voted against Italy begin to have their effect, Italy will crack up economically. In the meantime, the Ethiopians are not losing any of their men, largely because they are not offering mass resistance to the Italian armies. I said I hoped that Ethiopia would continue its guerrilla warfare and not come to real grips with Italy.

Chancellor confirmed the stories that have been coming to Washington to the effect that the casualty lists of the Italians are very heavy indeed. He said that the Italians are not fighters and he doesn't believe they will be able to stand the gaff in that climate and in the terrain in which they are called upon to fight. He told about one train full of Italian soldiers leaving an Italian city to embark for Ethiopia. The wives and the mothers of the soldiers clung to their men and threw themselves on the track in front of the train, from which they had to be removed by force. The offi-cers and men were openly weeping. In order to keep up the mo-rale of the Italian people, invalided soldiers are not returned to Italy but to islands in the Mediterranean where hospitalization is provided. He thinks that when Italy really finds out at what phys-ical cost the war is being carried on, Mussolini will have his hands full.

The election on Tuesday seemed to me to be very encouraging from the President's point of view. While the Republicans gained a few seats in the Assembly in New York State, the total Demo-cratic vote of the state as a whole exceeded the Republican vote by about 450,000. It is reasonable to suppose that if the President had been running, the aggregate would have been larger still. The Republicans elected a mayor of Philadelphia but by a smaller vote than for twenty or twenty-five years. The most significant result was in Kentucky. There a real fight was made to elect the Re-publican candidate for governor. He not only had his own party behind him, but Lafoon, the Democratic Governor, and his or-ganization, were openly supporting him. Notwithstanding this, the Democrat won by a bigger plurality than any since Reconstruction days. This would seem clearly to indicate that the border states are safe for the President next year. Senator Logan, of Kentucky, told me some time ago that he was fearful of the result this fall in his state and that if the Republicans carried it this year, they were almost sure to carry it next year in the presidential election.

At Cabinet meeting on Friday the President remarked: "We will win easily next year but we are going to make it a crusade." He seemed quite confident, and there appears to be a sound basis for his confidence.

He also discussed a reciprocity treaty with Canada that is in the making. Canada had a general election a short time ago that re-sulted in the overwhelming victory of Mackenzie King, the former Premier. King is in Washington now and spent a good deal of time yesterday with the President. This reciprocity treaty as outlined by the President at Cabinet meeting is distinctly to the advantage of the United States, and the President is anxious to have it set down in formal language and signed by Mackenzie King while he is in a mood to do it.

Glavis' key men were in Washington yesterday and I had them brought in for a talk. I told them that they ought to be very careful of their facts and not draw conclusions based upon incomplete or ex parte facts. I deprecated the disposition that has been shown on a good many occasions to try to "get" some member of the Interior Department or of the Public Works staff. I pointed out that we are all interested in maintaining the reputation and prestige of this Department. I made it clear that if any member of my staff strayed from the straight and narrow path I wanted to know it, but that I wanted every man to be given the benefit of the doubt and not to be prejudged on imperfect facts without being given a chance to defend himself.

Wednesday, November 13, 1935

The newspapers, particularly the Hearst press, the American Federation of Labor, and the steel interests are kicking up a row because on two PWA projects German steel piling has been bid on and the bids accepted. Under our present PWA rules, we allow a differential of fifteen per cent in favor of American materials, in addition to whatever tariff protection there may be. The German steel on one of the projects, at Morehead City, North Carolina, was fifty-two per cent lower than the bid for American steel, and the difference on the Triborough Bridge contract in New York was forty-seven per cent. There were three bids on American steel at Morehead City and all three were identical. Under the law and under the regulations I did not see what we could do except to allow these contracts. In any event, so far as the Triborough Bridge contract is concerned, the Federal Government had no right to reject the bid or interfere in any way. That Authority is required to accept the lowest responsible bid, but we do not draw the specifications and we do not have the right to dictate whether American or foreign-made materials are used. The contracts in both instances are for small amounts, but it gives occasion for criticism of the Government and agitation for a protection which, in my judgment, the steel interests are not entitled to. Of course, Germany is not popular in this country. The present government there is certainly unpopular with me but, nevertheless, I do not see why we should pay excessive rates for building materials when the American manufacturers insist on keeping their prices unduly high through collusive bidding.

I had lunch with the President yesterday and was with him for all of an hour and a half. He was very friendly and we had a good talk on many subjects. We discussed the coming campaign. He said, as he has said before, that he hoped the Republicans would nominate Hoover, but I told him that, in my judgment, there was no chance of that. I told him that it seemed to me the weakness of the Republicans was that they had no candidate. We discussed the probability of the Republicans raising a tremendous campaign fund, which I believe they will do unless they realize that they have no chance to win. Moreover, in my judgment, this campaign fund will find its way into the campaign through county and state organizations so that it will be hard to trace or locate.

We fell to discussing the attitude of the Supreme Court on New Deal legislation, and I asked the President whether any one of the present Justices was going to retire and give him a chance to appoint some liberals. He said he did not think so, and he went on to say that Justice Brandeis, as he got older, was losing sight of fundamentals. I asked him what Felix Frankfurter thought of Brandeis' changed attitude, and he said that he was heartbroken over it and did not like to discuss it. Then he said that while the matter could not be talked about now, he believed that the way to mend the situation was to adopt a constitutional amendment which would give the Attorney General the right, if he has any doubt of the constitutionality of a legislative act, to apply to the Supreme Court for a ruling, that ruling to state specifically in which respects the act is unconstitutional. Then, if the next succeeding Congress, with this opinion of the Supreme Court before it, should re-enact that statute, it would, by that fact, be purged of its unconstitutionality and become the law of the land. The amendment would also recognize the right of the Supreme Court to pass upon the constitutionality of laws, a right which is not granted in the Constitution as it stands, which was defeated on three or four occasions when it was discussed in the Constitutional

Convention, and which represents, in my judgment, a plain usurpation of power by the Court.

The President's mind went back to the difficulty in England, where the House of Lords repeatedly refused to adopt legislation sent up from the House of Commons. He recalled that when Lloyd George came into power some years ago under Edward VII, he went to the King and asked his consent to announce that if the Lords refused again to accept the bill for Irish autonomy, which had been pressed upon them several times since the days of Gladstone, he would create several hundred new peers, enough to outvote the existing House of Lords. With this threat confronting them, the bill passed the Lords.

There seems to me to be a great deal of merit in the President's suggestion of a constitutional amendment. Under this plan, the Supreme Court could be required to give a speedy and a specific ruling on a legislative act, and that ruling, if adverse to the act, would lie over until the election of a new Congress. This would give people a chance to study and discuss the act during the campaign, and Congress would have a mandate from the people when it again voted upon the question. I am firmly of the opinion that we cannot work out an adequate and modern social system in this country so long as we are held in the present strait jacket of the Supreme Court. Yet the bars should probably not be let down entirely, at least until we have educated ourselves to greater care and thoughtfulness in the passage of legislation than we sometimes show. But under this plan suggested by the President there would be plenty of time for deliberation and opportunity for hot heads to cool off and a further chance for the people to decide whether or not they wanted the particular legislation in spite of the finding of the Court. If they do, under these very reasonable and moderate safeguards, then, in my view, their will ought to prevail, if we are in fact a government by the people.

I had dinner with Cissy Patterson last evening. She had been in California visiting William Randolph Hearst and she brought him to New York in her private car. I did not ask her specifically whom Mr. Hearst had in mind for President in opposition to Roosevelt, but from what she said I got the impression that he is for Governor Landon, of Kansas. As a matter of fact, he has been building Landon up in his papers for some time now. She said that Hearst felt very friendly toward me personally.

Friday, November 15, 1935

The Hearst press has been screaming until it is red in the face about the contracts for German steel in connection with the Triborough Bridge and the Morehead City projects. Yesterday morning the *Washington Herald,* which is the local Hearst paper, devoted at least two full pages to this subject, with an impassioned editorial on the front page raking me fore and aft. Meanwhile telegrams and letters have been coming in to me from labor sources demanding that we cease to buy German steel. I had one letter of protest from William Green, president of the American Federation of Labor, and a long telegram from Matthew Woll, one of the vice presidents of the A.F. of L., who is the professional patriot of that organization.

I had to recognize the force of the public opinion that was being stimulated and brought to bear, but the problem was how to handle the matter without being in the position of beating a hasty retreat. As a matter of fact, the particular piling purchased under these two contracts is not manufactured in the United States. I am informed that for ten years the Army engineers have been trying to persuade the American steel interests to make this piling but they have refused to do so. The German piling when put in place is waterproof. The American piling has to be welded under water after it has been set, and the only company that can do this is the Raymond Concrete Pile Company, which has a patent on the process. It is this that makes the purchase of American piling so expensive. Moreover, both of these contracts were entered into with due regard to our rules and regulations and the statutes of the United States so far as I have been advised.

In answering the letter from William Green, I was offered an opportunity to present our side of the case, and accordingly I drafted a letter late Wednesday afternoon. I called the President by telephone to discuss with him what position we should take and I sent him a draft of my letter to Green just before leaving for dinner Wednesday night. On Thursday morning Mike Straus got in touch with Steve Early, who said that the President was not quite satisfied with my draft and suggested that I call the President myself. This I did and he asked me to come to the White House at ten minutes before two. He redictated my letter to Green and I am glad to say that he stood up in his letter better than I had in my draft. His letter refused to admit that in certain circumstances we would not buy foreign building supplies, and it more than hinted that there had been collusive bidding on the part of American manufacturers. I hurried back with this draft just before my press conference at three o'clock so that it would be mimeographed for release to the press. I had a big press conference and many questions were asked me about the steel situation. I discussed the whole matter fully and frankly and in general I satisfied the correspondents who were present. Of course the Hearst representative was eager to find a basis for continuing its unjust attack. I may say that the Hearst presentation of this question in the *Herald* on Wednesday was a gross misrepresentation of the facts. This I was in a position to prove in more than one instance.

As the result of my letter to Green and my press conference the newspaper accounts this morning, even in the Hearst press, were considerably toned down. It is only fair to say that, aside from the Hearst press, the newspapers have handled this matter quite decently. Raymond Clapper, in his column in the *Washington Post,* has been especially fair in presenting both sides. I think this particular storm has blown over. The substance of my final letter to Green was that no contracts for foreign materials in the future would be let for any PWA project without my personal approval. It went on to say that if it appeared that there was collusive bidding or any violation of the law by American suppliers, the matter would be referred to the Federal Trade Commission for investigation. I also indicated at my press conference that I would raise the differential against foreign materials from fifteen per cent to probably twenty-five per cent, which will bring it in line with the policy of the Procurement Division of the Treasury Department.

Yesterday while the President's dictation of my letter to William Green was being typed we had a chance to talk, as no one was waiting for him. He called up Secretary Roper, who has been grossly misquoted in the *Washington Herald,* to tell him he thought that he ought to send to the *Herald* a very categorical denial of the accuracy of that paper's quotation of him. The President remarked to me that "Dan was much more cautious than either of us." The interview the President outlined over the telephone to Roper was a savage one, and he told Roper he thought that was the kind of a statement he ought to send to the *Herald,* with a demand that it be printed on the front page this morning.

Roper indicated enthusiastic accord but the President was not fooled. He said: "I will bet that Dan will call me up about that statement later before he issues it." Dan didn't call the President up but he sent a greatly modified statement over to me late in the afternoon for my approval. I sent word back that it was a matter between Roper and the President and that I had no suggestion to make.

The American Bankers Association has been holding its annual convention in New Orleans and it has treated the Administration pretty roughly. The man who in ordinary course would have been elected second vice president was defeated because it was charged that he was a friend of the Administration. As a matter of fact, while he is a vice president of Marriner Eccles' bank in Ogden, Utah, he is a Republican. The man who made the charge and who elaborated it into a vicious attack against the Administration was elected second vice president. The President told me that customarily the newly elected officers of the American Bankers Association call on him after their election. He said that Fleming, the retiring president, who is a Washington banker, would in due course call him up and ask for an opportunity to present the new officers. He declared that he would arrange in advance to talk to Fleming himself and that he would tell Fleming that he would be very glad to receive all of the officers except the second vice president. The new second vice president in his speech actually declared that the bankers should place an embargo against the Government bonds. He talked like the ruler of an independent kingdom.

At Cabinet today there was a good deal of discussion about the German steel situation and about the trade agreement with Canada which has been negotiated with Mackenzie King, the newly elected Premier of Canada. The President told us that this trade agreement would be signed in his office at three-thirty and he asked us all to attend the ceremony. We did so and were introduced to Premier King. He made a very good impression on me. To the accompaniment of numerous flashlights, the agreement was signed by Premier King and Secretary Hull while sitting at the right of the President at his desk. From what little I know of it, I am heartily in favor of this agreement. To some extent, at any rate, it takes down the trade barriers that have existed between us and Canada and I hope that it will be mutually beneficial to both countries and restimulate trade between us. Miss Perkins, who stood by my side during the ceremony and kept up a constant chatter, much to my annoyance, deprecated the agreement. She seems to think that it had in it the germ of a new world war. I could not agree with her and I was annoyed by her garrulity.

While we were drafting the Green letter, the President also told me that Joe Kennedy had been at the White House the night before to talk about Hearst. It seems that Joe is always trying to reconcile the President with Hearst and Father Coughlin. He told the President that the trouble with Hearst was taxes, and the President asked him whether Hearst had told him, some time prior to his announcement in favor of higher taxes on incomes and estates, that the President had told Hearst, on the occasion of a visit to the White House, that he intended to advocate such higher taxes. Kennedy admitted that Hearst had told him of this interview.

The President told me that he said to Kennedy that in his opinion there was no man in the whole United States who was as vicious an influence as Hearst. Kennedy remarked that it didn't look as if there was much chance to get the two together in view of the President's opinion, and the President said that there wasn't; that he had never had very much of an opinion of Hearst.

Saturday, November 23, 1935

At my press conference on Thursday I was asked to comment upon the fact that our exports to Italy of petroleum and petroleum products had increased very rapidly, and in reply to a question I remarked that everyone should comply both in letter and in spirit with the efforts of the Government to prevent shipments of munitions to belligerents. The *Washington Post* and doubtless many other newspapers throughout the world the following day carried the news that I had asked oil producers not to ship to belligerents. This created quite a furor in Italy and in international circles generally. Secretary Hull called me up Friday morning to say that the Italian Ambassador had asked for an interview. He asked me to send to him a transcript of what I had actually said. This I gladly did. He made no comment or criticism about what I had said either before or after receiving a copy of this transcript and what transpired at the conference between him and Ambassador Rosso I do not know. The papers have continued to comment upon the incident since I made this original statement, but so far as I know the comments have been favorable.

[During the first Administration of President Roosevelt, Congress passed a series of laws on neutrality which in effect set up a new United States policy in respect to foreign hostilities. The legislation was an outgrowth of the Nye Committee hearings which stressed the heavy profits made by armament makers and financiers during the First World War, and of the default on war debts by all foreign governments except Finland. These defaults led first to the Johnson Act, passed on April 13, 1934, prohibiting loans to any foreign government in default on its war debts. The Neutrality Act of 1935, signed reluctantly by President Roosevelt on August 31, was extended by the Neutrality Act of 1936, passed on February 29, 1936. They called for an embargo on all shipments of arms whenever the President should proclaim "a state of war," certain restraints on other trade, and denial to American citizens of the right to travel on vessels of belligerent nations or to make loans to governments engaged in war.–ED.]

Thursday, November 28, 1935

The pressure for money for PWA projects still continues. Delegations come in to see me, apparently in the belief that by force of numbers they can make me produce money that I do not have. To the force of numbers they add the weight of insistence. They say the same thing over and over again, as if repeated reiterations of the desirability of and the necessity for a given project will prove an alchemy that will make gold out of thin air. I am finding it very difficult to keep even moderately patient. I say over and over again that although doubtless the suggested project is a good one, unfortunately we have no money. I keep saying this in tones that become increasingly acid. The actual fact is that I usually have to become quite sharp before I can get the members of the delegations out of the chairs in which they have every appearance of having comfortably settled themselves for the rest of the day.

These delegations go down to Public Works, where they are told exactly what I have to tell them, but they insist on coming in to see me. Yesterday a delegation from Cincinnati got in by what amounted to a subterfuge. These men wanted $2 million for a Negro slum clearance project. I asked them if they had seen Clas and they admitted that they had. They also admitted that Clas had told them that we had no money. I told them that in view of that fact there really was no occasion for their coming to see me. Their reply was that they wanted to go right to headquarters. I remarked that if we had to operate on that basis, it would not be necessary for me to have anyone on my staff at all. It is obvious that if everyone has to see me, there is no use of employing others to interview them.

This whole PWA program has been a good deal of a mess because the President made the mistake of announcing that he was going to administer the new fund himself. I have never seen so much buck-passing. Important men necessarily get in to see the President and he makes them promises or what are taken to be promises. Then they come to me for the fulfillment of those promises and I have to tell them that there is no money. Worse still, as in the case of Congressman Sam Rayburn, of Texas, recently with his Red River project, they give out statements to the press that the President has smiled upon their application and that the money will be forthcoming. Now Rayburn is wiring me frantically telling me what an embarrassing position he is in because he made an announcement, as he supposed with authority, and then could not produce. They keep running from the President to me and back again. They tell me that the President has made certain promises and when I check with him I find that he is not prepared to do what the promisees think that he has obligated himself to do.

Under the original PWA program we did not have any of these difficulties. We either approved a project or we did not, and, with rare exceptions, our verdict was accepted as final. There was practically no appeal to the President. At the outset of this program when he announced that he was going to be the administrator, I told him that in that direction lay a great deal of trouble. I pointed out to him that if he accepted such responsibility he would necessarily be blamed by every disappointed applicant. My prediction has come true and I also find that the President, in some instances at least, does not relish any too keenly having to take responsibility.

There seems to be a pretty general feeling that Rex Tugwell will soon be out of the Government. He has been under terrific attack lately on account of a speech he made in Los Angeles, excerpts of which did look as if he had not been altogether wise. As a matter of fact, I agree pretty generally with Tugwell in his social outlook, but I do think that he might guard himself more carefully in what he says and writes. I have no doubt, however, that one of these days I will find myself the subject of sharp attacks because of some statement taken out of the context of a speech and distorted by Hearstian editorial writers. I will be sorry to see Tugwell go, because I think he is a man of real vision and ability. I do feel, however, that he never should have undertaken the administrative job that he has in Rural Resettlement. I do not think that he is a competent executive, and word that comes to me from various sources is to the effect that his organization is a shambles. Louis Brownlow confirmed this recently. Brownlow is an expert along these lines, he is a Democrat, and he has social vision. I am sure he was not speaking out of prejudice. Harry Hopkins told me on the *Houston* that Tugwell has a life job at Columbia at $9,000 a year and that he would have to decide pretty soon whether to go back to Columbia or to resign. He cannot get much leave of absence. Hopkins thought that he would go back to Columbia.

Hopkins himself is away a good deal now. Frank Walker remarked on Tuesday that "Harry's dauber was down" and that the light seemed to have left his eyes. I have felt for some time that in his heart Harry realizes that he cannot make a real success of his program, and from what he said to me on the *Houston,* I would not be surprised if he would resign one of these days. It might well be the part of wisdom for him to resign while his reputation is still an asset to him so that he can get a good job in private life.

I had planned to leave for Puerto Rico and the Virgin Islands for a short official trip on the fifth of December, but yesterday I got an invitation for the official dinner to the Cabinet on December 11, so I will have to postpone my trip. I hope to get away a week later.

Sunday, December 1, 1935

There has been nothing of particular interest or importance to record during the last two or three days since I last dictated for this record. Thursday was Thanksgiving Day. I had for dinner Jane Dahlman, Bill McCrillis, Fred Marx and his bride, and a girl guest of the latter. It rained hard from noon on. I took Jane to the movies at night to see Arliss.

Genevieve Forbes Herrick has come home from Santa Fe. It was just three months ago that she was so severely injured in the accident in which Anna was killed, and all that time she has been in the hospital. John Herrick came in to see me on Friday and I talked to Genevieve over the telephone later. It seems that she will be in bed for probably two months longer, although she can hobble around a little on crutches.

Tuesday, December 3, 1935

I went over to the Herricks' Sunday evening for supper. Geno was in bed, and, according to the doctor, she will have to spend most of her time in bed for probably two months longer. Her face shows the suffering that she has been through, but she says that now she has no pain. One leg is decidedly shorter than the other and the problem is to bring it down to the proper length. She seemed cheerful and brave, but I suspect that there must be times when it is difficult for her not to be depressed. It is dreadful to think that the accident happened three months ago and she is still far from recovered.

Today at my press conference the Associated Press correspondent started to ask me questions about prohibiting the shipment of oil to Italy. I told them that I had never called upon the oil producers not to ship oil. I sent for the stenographic report of the former press conference at which I was first questioned about oil. I read what I had said there, which was to the effect that I had no jurisdiction in the matter but that I thought that everyone ought, both in letter and in spirit, to comply with the request of the Government not to ship munitions of war to belligerents.

A lot of questions were thrown at me, but I refused to add to or substract from what I had said at the previous conference. Then some of the correspondents tried to make it appear that I was retracting something that I had said or correcting a previous statement. I denied this very earnestly. I pointed out that I had not brought up the subject myself and had volunteered no statement and was merely replying, to the best of my ability, to questions that had been asked. Kluckhohn of *The New York Times*, was especially persistent and he waited after the conference to badger me some more on the subject. I went at him in considerable heat. I told him that even a newspaper man might make a mistake once in a while and that if I had been misquoted, as I was, on what I had said previously with respect to the shipment of oil to belligerents, it was up to the newspaper that misquoted me to get out of the difficulty; that I did not intend to be put in a position of making a correction or a retraction when I was doing nothing of the sort.

Saturday, December 7, 1935

I arrived in Detroit a little after eight Wednesday morning, after a very bad night on the sleeper. Dean Cooley, our Acting State Engineer for Michigan, a fine old chap, and Abner Larned, State Director for the National Emergency Council, met us at the train and took us up to the Detroit-Leland Hotel. Ed Foley, our General Counsel of PWA, was on the train because he was to make a speech in Detroit also on Wednesday, and Mr. Cubberley went along with me.

The forum was held in a big moving-picture theater in the palatial and ornate Fisher Brothers Building, and the meeting opened at eleven o'clock. Mr. Larned introduced me. For some reason the lights were not turned on in the theater proper and it was a curious experience talking into a dark cave. I was told afterward that there were from two thousand to twenty-five hundred people there and that it was the biggest crowd that had ever attended one of the forum meetings. A great many of the audience consisted of women. It was a well-fed, well-dressed, prosperous crowd, mainly Republican, I should judge.

I talked a little over an hour. It was the longest speech I have ever made, but they asked for about an hour and so I had added to my original draft in order to bring it up to the time that they wanted. It was a very vigorous speech, discussing what I regarded as fundamental political conditions in this country. Against the background of a ruthless, exploiting past and present, my speech was a plea for a return to the America of the Founding Fathers, where the great majority of the people would actually own some property and would have the means of sustaining themselves and their families in reasonable comfort and of living in economic security. It hit out pretty vigorously in several directions. Following the speech, I submitted to questions for fifteen or twenty minutes. The questions came mostly from women and they were contentious both in substance and in tone. Apparently I had gotten under some soft skins. I didn't do much temporizing in my answers.

I didn't expect this speech of mine to attract much attention because it was not on the air. To my surprise, it has attracted a great deal of attention. The newspapers, even those of the opposition, carried a good deal of my speech and there has been quite a good deal of editorial comment, some of it quite flattering. I have had a number of letters, too, commending my speech, and a number of people have spoken to me about it. There seems to be a feeling that it was the kind of a fighting speech that has been needed for some time. Some of the commendation has come from people whose opinions I particularly value.

It seems to me that my speech went to the fundamental issue that will be fought out in the coming campaign. In drafting this speech I was merely trying to do myself credit and say something worth while. As I see it now, I have put it up to the Administration pretty hard to follow along the same lines or to repudiate me, and I don't think they will want to do the latter. I find that I struck a real note. As I say, I was not trying to do this and I didn't know I was doing it; I was merely being myself the best I knew how. If anything should happen to me politically at the moment as the result of any action on the part of the Administration, it would be regarded at once as a repudiation of a pronounced progressive stand on my part. I haven't heard from the President or anyone near him, but, as I say, I have had some very flattering comments made by people whose opinions I value.

It is still doubtful whether I will be able to get away next week for Puerto Rico and the Virgin Islands. My lawyers want to take my testimony in a power case in South Carolina. If it can be arranged to do that by deposition, I can get away; otherwise, I won't be able to go, and if I don't go now, there is no telling when I will be able to go. A good deal of pressure is being brought to bear also to have me speak at the University of Louisville next Saturday. An appeal has even been made to the President to use his influence with me.

Under Secretary West is away most of the time. When he is here, he won't take any responsibility and is practically useless as an executive. The Under Secretaryship is merely a convenient berth into which the President could place him while using him as his liaison officer with Congress and on confidential political work in Ohio and elsewhere. He is a pleasant person and I think he wants to go along and do what is right, but as an Under Secretary, he isn't worth a damn.

Monday, December 9, 1935

Mike Straus came in the other day to tell me that Harry Hopkins is being billed for speeches through an agency which retains a fee of twenty-five per cent and that he is insisting on being paid $400 for each speech. In Highland Park, Illinois, the League of Women Voters made a special effort to raise the $400 and when he stood up in front of the audience, he remarked that he had no idea what he was going to talk about. This agency had him billed for seven speeches, and the report that came to Mike Straus was that all of the meetings were poorly attended and showed lack of interest. This surprised him, as it did me, because I would have thought that Harry Hopkins would be a real drawing card.

Wednesday, December 11, 1935

I had lunch with the President on Tuesday. He had returned from Warm Springs via Chicago and Notre Dame late in the morning. We lunched in the Oval Room on the second floor of the White House. He seemed quite well and fit and in a cheerful state of mind. I was with him for almost two hours.

He surprised me by saying that he wouldn't be surprised if there were a war in 1936. I asked him whether he meant in Europe or in the Pacific, and he said it might be either.

We discussed politics a good deal. More and more his mind is working on the campaign next year and the chances of re-election. Here is clear enough illustration of the effect on public affairs of our national elections at intervals of four years. It has always been said that when first elected a President has three years to devote to the public business, but the last year of his term he gives up to an effort to be re-elected.

I think the President is pretty well satisfied with the political situation generally and yet I don't think he is at all overconfident. He seems to be very much interested in any information bearing on the situation. He was enthusiastic about his reception in Chicago, where he spoke at the stockyard pavilion on the farm question, and he was equally pleased with the reception accorded him at South Bend, Indiana, where he went to receive an honorary degree at a special convocation of Notre Dame. Cardinal Mundelein, of Chicago, introduced him at Notre Dame and his introduction seemed to me to carry a pretty complete endorsement of the President. I was also much struck by what the Cardinal said about the necessity of reducing swollen fortunes.

I told the President again what I have told him on other occasions, namely, that I believed the general sentiment of the country to be much more radical than that of the Administration. He said he agreed. We discussed some of the Republican candidates. He said that he was going to have some matters that he wanted to turn over to Glavis for investigation because he would rather that he handle them than the Department of Justice. Whether or not he had read anything about my Detroit speech, he did not indicate. I have had no reactions on that speech from the White House one way or the other, but I have had a good many letters approving the position I took, and Mike Straus tells me that there has been a greater general demand for copies of this speech than for any I have made.

The President is holding back on some housing projects that I am very much interested in and hope he will go ahead with. He says he wants to find out just what his balance is on December 15 before he makes any more commitments. What I am afraid of is that, as usual, he will find himself under the necessity of taking money from PWA to take care of relief. In fact, I will be very much surprised if he doesn't take away from us practically all the balance that we have.

Coming back to my Detroit speech again, a New York paper published a statement the other day that Congressman Hamilton Fish had challenged me to a joint debate, but no challenge has come in. Some bureau in New York is trying to arrange a debate between me and Ogden Mills or someone of that class.

I sent for Glavis yesterday morning and told him that I had heard that he was proposing to resign. He said that some time ago he had had an offer from some other Federal agency at a higher salary but had declined. He indicated that he had not been happy with us recently and that he thought he would look into that prior offer and see whether it was still open. I didn't try to dissuade him from resigning but I did tell him that I wanted to talk to him very frankly as a friend. He told me that if he should resign, there would be no reflection on me in any way, that he was strong for me and loyal to me, and that even if he left and I wanted him to come back and do any particular work, he would do it.

The position I took with him was that from his own point of view he could not afford to resign. I told him that he was cordially hated by nearly everyone in the Department and that the minute he stepped out everyone would be yapping at his heels. He said that if both he and I denied that there was any break between us, that would settle any such question, and my reply to that was that it wouldn't do anything of the sort. There would be all kinds of stories afloat. My view, as I expressed it to him, is that there are only two positions that he could afford to leave us to take. One would be as successor to Hoover in the Department of Justice, and the other would be a commanding position in the Secret Service under Chief Moran. I told him that any other move would be to his distinct disadvantage and would discredit him.

I told him again that we simply couldn't keep hounding members of the staff with investigations. I pointed out that with all of the new contracts that we were entering into he would have his hands full protecting the Government from being gypped by people on the outside. I said that, of course, if there was any occasion at any time to investigate any member of the staff, I would authorize such an investigation and that I had no intention of protecting anyone who was doing wrong.

I feel sure that Glavis left in a much happier state of mind, and information that has come to me since then has confirmed that impression. I told him about the President's reference to him and indicated that the President would probably have matters to turn over to him that would engage all his interest and call for all his ingenuity.

For some reason that I couldn't understand, for the last ten days or two weeks I have been sleeping very badly indeed. Even soporifics haven't done me much good. A few days ago Harry Slattery said to me that he thought it was the pile drivers' working on the new Interior Department Building just across Rawlins Park. I know now that Harry is right. Last night, for instance, I felt the rhythm and throbbing of those pile drivers—there have been seven of them working in the corner right opposite my office—all night long. They have gotten my goat in very truth. I think another day or two and I would go to pieces nervously.

Tonight is the annual dinner of the President and Mrs. Roosevelt to the members of the Cabinet. I am going but frankly I dread it. And then the musicale afterward in the East Room, sitting in one of those uncomfortable chairs with an overhanging ridge that reaches right into the small of the back!

I am taking a late train tonight to Spartanburg, South Carolina, to testify in an injunction proceeding that has been brought to restrain PWA from assisting in the financing of a county power project. This case was badly tried once before, before an antagonistic judge, but at our request it was remanded by the United States Circuit Court of Appeals last week. One of our witnesses at the former hearing undertook to state what the PWA policy was with respect to power plants and he got into the mire up to his neck. It is now proposed for me to try to get the record into better shape to go back to the United States Circuit Court of Appeals and then possibly to the Supreme Court. I hate to take this trip because I will be going down one night and back the next, but I have no option. This means that I will change my clothes in the office after the White House affair and go on from there to the train.

Sunday, December 15, 1935

I took Miss Perkins in to dinner at the White House Wednesday night and that meant that I sat with her on my left and Mrs. Farley on my right. This certainly was an improvement over previous Cabinet dinners at the White House. Miss Perkins talks a lot and she was on my deaf side but, at any rate, she is interesting and has ideas.

After I had escorted her into the East Room, I excused myself to her and to Mrs. Roosevelt. Then I went back to the office, changed my clothes, signed the mail and other matters that I had dictated to Mr. Mack in the afternoon, and went down to take the Southern Railway to Spartanburg, S.C.

Our train was an hour late, so that we did not get in until shortly after noon. The hearing of our case had been continued by Judge Watkins pending my arrival, and he sent word to me that he would like to meet me in chambers before I went on the stand. I found him to be a courteous gentleman, and he has the reputation of being a very good judge, although ultraconservative. I was on the stand for about two hours and a half. On direct examination, I put in evidence what our lawyers thought would put the record in better shape. The chief thing I had to overcome was testimony given at the prior hearing by one of our electrical engineers, who took it upon himself to explain what the policy of PWA was with respect to power grants. I repudiated his authority to testify as to policy and remarked that he apparently had been suffering from delusions of grandeur when he was on the stand.

On cross-examination, Robinson, chief counsel for the Duke power interests, started after me hammer and tongs. I had been told that he was looking forward with real anticipation to cross-examining me, and it was evidently his intention to put me on the defensive and break me down. This he failed to do. He read a good many passages from my book, *Back to Work,* and questioned me as to my personal and official attitude with respect to loans and grants for power projects. I went back at him good and strong and my counterattacks evoked laughter from the well-filled courtroom on several occasions. Finally, Robinson apparently gave me up as a bad job and concluded in a more or less perfunctory manner. He had become much friendlier. I think that in the tug of wits between us he came to have at least some measure of respect for me. Jerome Frank, who represented PWA, questioned me on direct examination and told me afterward that I was the best witness he had ever seen on the stand. If I satisfied our lawyers, I did all that was to be expected of me.

It rained all day. After adjournment, U.S. District Attorney Wyche took Mr. Cubberley and me over to his house for old-fashioned cocktails. He used to be the law partner of Senator James F. Byrnes and lives next door to the Senator. Then we took the 6:12 p.m. train back to Washington, where we arrived Friday morning, an hour and a half late.

At Cabinet meeting Friday afternoon there was a good deal of discussion, particularly between the President and Secretary of State Hull, about enlarged powers to maintain neutrality. Specific terms of a proposed bill were not discussed, but evidently the President wants wider discretion, probably making it possible for him to decide in given cases whether particular commodities, even if they are not munitions of war, should be denied shipment to belligerents if they have the effect of maintaining or prolonging war.

The President spoke of having the Archbishop of York and Sir Ronald Lindsay at the White House to tea Thursday afternoon. He told the Archbishop that he had been very much interested in a newspaper quotation to the effect that we could help greatly in international matters if we joined the League of Nations. The Archbishop said that this was his belief, and the President told him that America might have felt more strongly disposed to do that a few days before than it did then. The Archbishop asked what had brought about the change in feeling, and the President said that it was the attempt on the part of Great Britain and France to dismember Ethiopia in order to bring about peace with Italy. The President thinks this is an outrageous proceeding and, of course, it is. Secretary Hull had a map showing just how serious this proposed dismemberment would be.

The price of silver has broken badly in the world markets recently, especially in London. The President informed us that we had been pegging the price of silver, but that the policy of purchasing it, pursuant to the statute passed by Congress, had been changed. Instead of paying the full price for it in the London market, the Treasury now asks for bids from any part of the world. The President said that this change in policy was made necessary by the fact that practically all of the countries that had been using silver as the base for their currency for many years were rapidly demonetizing silver and going on a regulated paper-currency base. The result was that practically all of the available silver in the world was being offered to the United States at prices that were out of line with the real value of the commodity.

Secretary Perkins gave a very enthusiastic report about the manner in which the Social Security Administration is being set up. Morgenthau contentiously interjected the remark that officials of his Department thought the organization was terrible. This quite took Miss Perkins aback, and it was evident that she was not altogether sure of her ground because she did not stand up to Morgenthau a bit.

There is more and more campaign talk at Cabinet meetings in anticipation of the fight next year.

I went to the Gridiron dinner last night and stopped at Ciss Patterson's for a drink afterward. There were several men there after the Gridiron affair. I got there shortly after twelve. I think Cissy must have been at the White House party and when she did not show up at one o'clock, I came on home. I am glad I went, however, because I had a little time to talk with her brother, Joe Patterson, who is editor and publisher of the *New York News*. I have never really known him, but I have always felt that I wanted to know him. He is not afraid to do some independent thinking, despite his wealth and social position, and he is a forthright, hard-hitting individual, with a social outlook. In his early days he was a socialist. Then he became fairly conservative, but I would rank him now as a real Progressive.

The Gridiron show was along conventional lines, but it seemed to me that it was not so savagely critical of the New Deal as it has been heretofore. The Republicans came in for a lot of fun poked in their direction, and there was a skit on the Supreme Court that I enjoyed very much indeed. I hope it helped to give a proper sense of balance to the six Justices, headed by Chief Justice Hughes, who were there. Norman Thomas was to have made the speech to which the President was to have replied, but Thomas did not show up and apparently no word came from him. So the President had to talk against a putative antagonist. He did very well indeed.

Monday, December 16, 1935

Miss Le Hand called me up Sunday afternoon to tell me the President would see me at a quarter after five. I stopped at my office because I wanted to take over a model to show the President where the Pan American Union proposes to put its new building. It is to be south of the new Interior Building and it will stick out like a sore thumb because it ignores the building line of all the other buildings in the two blocks of which it will be a part. I have objected very strenuously to the erection of this building on that precise site, but so far I haven't been able to make any real progress. I sent for Dr. Rowe, of the Pan American Union, a couple of weeks ago, and repeated the representations that I had previously put to him in opposition to this site. A day or two ago he wrote me a letter turning down my plea that this little block of land be left free.

The President agreed with me and told Miss Grace Tully, to whom he was dictating, to have Dr. Rowe come in and see him Monday morning. He told me he didn't know what he could do about it, and I doubt whether he has any powers, but perhaps the Pan American Union people will give heed to his objections. He said he would suggest to Rowe that that space be kept for a colonnade for statues of South and Central American heroes. Such a use would not be objectionable.

The matters I had up for discussion with the President were mostly routine, principally public works projects, all of which he approved. We talked some politics and we talked about the Gridiron Club dinner Saturday night. I told him that I hoped he understood that I would be willing to do anything I could for him next year, and he replied that there would be plenty of work for all of us to do. I think I believe that more firmly than he does. I can't get away from the notion that it is likely to be a hard fight, full of many surprises, although I still think that his chances of re-election are good.

I woke up Sunday morning with a fully developed and most annoying head cold which got worse during the day, and today is causing me a lot of genuine distress. I had the mail sent out from the office this morning and worked at home until ten o'clock, when I went to the White House to have Dr. McIntire treat my nasal passages, my right ear, of which the Eustachian tube seemed to be filled up, and my uvula, which is red and swollen. At any rate, he gave me temporary relief.

It was my intention to come home again, bringing with me all the work that was on my desk, but a message came that the President had called a conference for two o'clock to consider the financial situation with respect to PWA, WPA, etc. That lasted until four o'clock, following which I did come home.

This conference was attended by Secretary Morgenthau, Acting Director of the Budget Bell, Rex Tugwell, Harry Hopkins, and his principal assistant, Aubrey Williams, with Colonel Hackett, Clas, Schnepfe, and myself, of my staff.

I have been perfectly certain ever since the Hyde Park conference that we had not heard the last of the distribution of the $4 billion fund, and this conference proved the accuracy of my belief in the matter. The President is on the hunt for a few hundred millions in order to tide Harry Hopkins' WPA program over until the first of July. It is going to be hard to find any large sum of money. What he is proposing to do is to draw on the various agencies for unexpended funds on the theory that these funds will be repaid after July 1, next, out of a new appropriation by Congress. I can't see the philosophy of the thing myself. It will either mean a larger appropriation for the next fiscal year than he had intended to ask for, or, if several hundred thousand borrowed dollars are to be paid back to the various agencies, it will mean that the sums thus returned will have been expended in anticipation of an appropriation. In either event, it seems to me he is going to run into political difficulties.

I have felt from the beginning that the President is likely to find himself short of money just at the critical time before election, with the result of throwing men out of jobs and even of denying them relief, which may be serious enough to return the Republicans to power. I have no confidence in the situation and I hate to see more money go down the Hopkins rat hole. I pretty well satisfied the President that all of our money was obligated. At the end of the conference he turned to me with a laugh and remarked that he hadn't taken any money away from us, to which I replied that it was the first occasion that I had gone into his office to discuss finances without losing money. One thing I must say about the President and that is that his disposition is buoyant. At the conclusion he remarked that he thought things looked much more cheerful than he had anticipated, but I didn't see smiles on the faces of anyone else. I think that he is in a tight corner and that he will discover this to be the fact before he is through with it.

At Cabinet meeting last Friday the President remarked that it was absolutely necessary for farm prices to be kept at least at their present levels next year. Henry Wallace remarked that with average weather the crops next year would be larger and that the prices would be lower as the result. The President said that in that case we would have to see to it that the weather was not normal. There are a good many gambles in the Presidential situation now and unforeseen ones doubtless lie ahead of us.

At our Sunday conference the President told me that Phil and Bob La Follette had made a suggestion, which he believed originated with Phil because Bob did not seem to be very enthusiastic about it. The suggestion was that the President forthwith suspend all relief, PWA, WPA, and other Recovery Program projects, with the announcement that this was what the businessmen of the country were demanding and that he was giving them what they wanted. The President did not seem to think much of the idea himself, and I expressed distinct and utter disapproval. I said that it would give the appearance of a lack of leadership and of yielding to pressure. I told him that the strong thing to do was to follow through on the program that he had approved.

The President said that he was turning over in his mind another proposition and that was to send two budgets to Congress. One budget would be a balanced budget. It would have nothing for relief or PWA or even for the ECW camps that are so popular. The other budget would carry on for ECW and provide something for relief and public works. With these alternative budgets would be a message calling attention to the fact that there is a good deal of demand, especially in business circles, for a balanced budget, and that if the Congress wanted to adopt a balanced budget, here was one. The message would also indicate clearly, however, the President's preference for the second budget. I told him I thought there was some merit in that suggestion. It would have the effect of bringing sharply home to the country just what this budget issue is.

Thursday, December 19, 1935

I had a short appointment with the President this morning. He is holding up approvals of further PWA and Housing projects, with a few exceptions, until the fifteenth of January. I haven't much confidence that he will allow us any more money for PWA except where we have already obligated our funds. Harry Hopkins will need all the loose change that the President can scrape together, and I think the President is really somewhat concerned as to what he can work out. He hasn't had a chance yet to talk to the congressional leaders, with the exception of Buchanan. He doesn't talk nearly so confidently as he did about a further large appropriation. He says he hopes that Congress will give an additional appropriation and authority to spend that appropriation. I think what he has in mind is something like $1 billion to be spent by Harry Hopkins on a continuation of WPA. The President said that, of course, Congress couldn't name a great many small projects in a bill. That is true but I think he is going to run into trouble in asking Congress to appropriate any more money for the Hopkins program.

I told the President that I didn't think we had had an adequate report on the effect of the Santee-Cooper project on wildlife, especially migratory water fowls. He seems to think that the migratory water fowls will adjust themselves to changed conditions. I told him that even if it cost a little more, the engineers in building Santee-Cooper ought to provide new marshes for those destroyed.

Then I told him that the project that gave me the greatest concern was the Trans-Florida Canal. He really listened for the first time, which indicated to me that perhaps he is beginning to have some doubts himself about the practicability of that canal. I told him that geologists were of the opinion that a canal at sea level would mean the impregnation of salt water into the underground water courses and the drainage of important surface water areas upon which Florida depends for its domestic water supply. He seems to think that because some of the West Indian islands, which are small and totally surrounded by salt water, are able to get domestic water from wells, the canal would not have the effect that some geologists predict that it would have. I don't pretend to know, since I am no geologist, but I don't think that one can logically argue from one widely separated terrain to another. Moreover, there has been no interference with natural processes in Bermuda, for instance, such as there will be if this Trans-Florida Canal is finished. The President said that he was going to put the whole thing up to Congress and let Congress take the responsibility. I anticipate a rather lively fight on the floor of Congress.

At the instance of Colonel McIntyre, he, Homer Cummings, Harry Hopkins, two of Cummings' assistants, and myself sat down and discussed some way of working out the St. Louis-Jefferson Memorial project. This project was going along all right until Cummings rendered an adverse opinion. One thing for Homer, however, is that he is agile. He found against it on one ground and now he discovers that he can qualify it under the Historic Sites Act which was passed last session. I rather hooted at this, but since we are all committed up to our eyes on this project, I think we ought to go through with it under whatever guise. We worked out what appeared to be a solution and Homer Cummings will draft a new Executive Order. Under the order, Harry Hopkins will make a certain contribution to the Interior Department, so will St. Louis, and Public Works will furnish the balance up to $9 million to do what can be done on the project until July 1, next.

I drove Harry Hopkins back to his office. He told me that his wife Barbara has been having a very tough time indeed. She had a bad cancer on the right breast, and according to Harry, some of the chest tissues were also involved, requiring a radical operation. Harry is plainly worried and it is hard to blame him. He said that he had told Barbara that it was beneficent growth, but he rather suspects that she knows it was cancerous. It will take five years to assure immunity against a resumption of the growth. Not a pleasant thing to have hanging over one's head.

Senator Byrnes was in my office this afternoon. He has a pleasant habit of coming in at whatever time happens to suit him and announcing to Fred Marx that he is going to stay until he sees me. Fred is utterly unable to handle him, and mad as it makes me, I haven't much recourse except to see him. Of course it was Santee-Cooper again. He said he had told the President that I had advised him that the whole matter was up to the President and that the President hadn't been very much pleased that I had said this. After all, I don't know what else to do. He insisted on being the administrator of this new fund and yet he doesn't like to have to make final decisions when they are negative. Byrnes showed me a memorandum from the President in which he indicated that he thought that Harry Hopkins ought to supply $4.5 million worth of labor, and PWA cash amounting to $5.5 million out of our revolving fund. He told me that Jesse Jones had been called into the conference and that he had said that RFC would buy these bonds. I told him that on that basis we would go ahead and do what we could, but that I would not pay excessive prices for the property and rights of the old company down there.

Sunday, December 22, 1935

There was a full Cabinet meeting Friday afternoon for the first time for several months; Secretary Dern was back from his visit to the Philippine Islands and the Orient, and the Vice President was also in attendance. The President referred to the speech reported in the morning papers as having been made in Las Vegas, Nevada, by Senator Pittman, chairman of the Committee on Foreign Relations, in which he was most indiscreet in what he said about Japan and the ambitions of that country to dominate not only Asia but the rest of the world. He compared Japan to Germany prior to the world war and predicted an armed conflict with the United States. The President deprecated this talk and said that he could not understand why Pittman should have said what he did, considering the position that he occupies in the Senate. Of course, the explanation may be that Pittman had been drinking too much. This would not be an unusual situation with him.

The Vice President commented on the fact that while the members of the congressional delegation that went to Manila as guests of the Philippine Government to take part in the installation of the first President of the Islands had been very discreet in what they had said about foreign affairs while out of the country, some of them were beginning to talk now. He referred particularly to Senator Nye, from whom he anticipated more or less inflammatory remarks while on the lecture platform.

The Cabinet meeting held longer than usual, but, as usual, Miss Perkins held forth at great length on the subject of the number of the unemployed. The trouble with Miss Perkins is not that she is not an able woman; she is that, but she cannot make a simple statement to a group or to an individual without making a speech about it.

More complications with reference to the Red River project in Congressman Sam Rayburn's district in Texas! I think I have related that the President promised several million dollars for this and then after Rayburn had announced that fact, he was unable to find where the money was to come from. Finally, Rayburn came to me in his distress, although he has pretty much opposed everything I have ever wanted on the Hill. I told him that I would do what I could. He wanted at least $500,000 for a preliminary survey.

I took this up with the President and he said to refer it to the National Resources Committee. That I did, and an adverse report came back, which I sent to the President. Recently, Rayburn has been up here again begging for this project. He has become quite jittery on the subject. The utilities will undoubtedly make a tremendous effort to defeat him for Congress next year. The Vice President thinks they cannot do that, but he also thinks that something ought to be done about the Red River project on Rayburn's account. Generally speaking, I have always opposed grants of money for preliminary surveys unless we have definitely decided to go ahead with the projects. To give money for surveys creates a moral commitment in the event of a favorable finding, and I do not believe in making commitments of that sort. For this reason, I have turned down a number of similar requests, several of them lately, notably one from Congressman Disney, of Oklahoma, and another from Governor Tingley, of New Mexico.

But to get back to Sam Rayburn. He has been besieging the White House. Colonel McIntyre talked it over with Hopkins and me the other day and we decided to recommend $150,000. This did not go at all well with Rayburn, and at Cabinet meeting the President brought up the matter again. The Vice President expressed sympathy with Rayburn, and the President told me to call in Mr. Delano and General Markham and, in effect, tell them that he wanted them to recommend an allocation of $500,000 for the survey. Both men are out of town and I won't be able to get them in until after Christmas. In the meantime, the Vice President called me up to say that Rayburn was in his office and asked me whether I would see Rayburn. I told him I was willing to see him but there would not be anything I could say to him until I had gotten Delano and Markham together. This is just one example of many of what seems to me a very bad way of handling public business under the work-relief appropriation.

Cissy Patterson called me up Saturday morning. She told me that the first edition of the *Washington Herald* had carried a column editorial bitterly attacking me as a communist on the basis of my Detroit speech. When she got her first edition, she ordered this editorial pulled out. She said the editorial was not only mean; it was stupid. I told her that I appreciated her doing what she had but that she should not have done it. She said, in a facetious vein, that both of us might lose our jobs. It was one of those editorials that is printed in all of the Hearst press. She told me who wrote it, but I did not get the name. I asked Harry Slattery to get the editorial for me so that I could see it. This was certainly a fine thing for her to do just on the basis of friendship, but it really served no good purpose. The editorial undoubtedly has appeared in all the other Hearst newspapers, and I fully expected an attack by the Hearst press following my Detroit speech. The only thing that surprised me is that it has been so long delayed.

Naturally, the social and political philosophy that I gave expression to in my Detroit speech would not please Mr. Hearst and his editorial prostitutes. But to attack me as a communist reflects on their intelligence. It seems that the *New York Daily Worker,* which is a radical publication, commented editorially on that part of my speech in which I pointed out the fascist threat that exists in America today. Then the Hearst editorial writer took the quotation from the *Daily Worker* and, on the basis of favorable editorial comment in that newspaper, declared me to be a dangerous communist who ought to be given a ticket along with "Comrade" Tugwell and dismissed from the Government.

The whole theory underlying my Detroit speech was that the future happiness and welfare of America depend upon the ownership of property, and it is difficult for me to understand how one can be charged with being a communist if he advocates the very antithesis of communism. Moreover, in that speech I attacked communism as well as fascism. It was a case of either the editorial writer in question not having read my speech, or of his trickily using the editorial in the *Daily Worker* as the authority for charging me with being a communist.

Monday, December 23, 1935

Governor Horner, of Illinois, came in to see me early this afternoon. He had come to Washington to complain to the President personally that Harry Hopkins is utterly ignoring him in his state. He says that he is the only governor, Democratic or Republican, anywhere in the country who is being passed over completely by Harry Hopkins. He cannot even get Hopkins on the telephone. Hopkins is working closely with Mayor Kelly, of Chicago. Horner tells me that when Hopkins goes to Chicago, Kelly and his friends lay themselves out to entertain him and play him up.

Horner talked about the gubernatorial situation and insisted that he was going to be a candidate for the Democratic nomination at the primaries whether he won or not. Kelly is plainly against him. I wonder if Horner will make the race if the Cook County organization opposes him, and also, if he wins the nomination, whether he can be elected. Both propositions seem a little doubtful to me— the first, because Horner is not notable for his courage, and second, because Illinois will be a hard state for him to win next November. Horner is an honorable man and an able man, but he is a poor politician and he certainly lacks guts.

I had a short conference with the President following Horner's visit to my office. The President told me that he had told Horner that he did not think he would win the nomination, with Kelly against him. He said that if he were in Horner's place, he would be satisfied with a judgeship or a Federal position. I told him that this bait had been dangled in front of Horner. He advised Horner to get hold of Kelly and sit down and talk the whole matter through from beginning to end. I told the President that Kelly was fundamentally Colonel McCormick's man and that, in spite of whatever lip service he might give, in the end he would do, if possible, whatever McCormick wanted him to do. The President said that it was the intention to tell Horner before the next election just how big a vote he was to bring from Cook County for the national ticket, but I told him not to expect any such vote as Kelly had gotten for himself. The President seemed surprised at this, but I explained to him that that was a phony vote and that Kelly would not be permitted to get away with it in a hotly contested election with the Republicans really fighting. I do not think Horner has many illusions about Kelly and Pat Nash and the rest of the Chicago crowd. The trouble is, he has played with that gang right along and it is going to be difficult for him now to stand up against it.

It started to snow shortly after noon yesterday and since then the ground has been covered with a light covering of white. It is very beautiful out here in the country.

Friday, December 27, 1935

The President has a very bad cold, so the Cabinet met in the Oval Room in the White House. Secretaries Hull and Morgenthau were not present. Under Secretary Coolidge reported for Morgenthau but the President, for some reason, did not have him sit with the Cabinet. He told the rest of us that he wanted only the fathers and mothers present and not any of the children.

The President told of a letter recently received from Ambassador Dodd at Berlin. He said it was the most pessimistic letter he has ever read. Dodd sees European civilization on the brink of the precipice. He thinks that nothing can restrain Hitler. The President remarked that, of course, some allowance should be made for Dodd's intense prejudice against Hitler, but there seems to be no question that the international situation is very grave indeed.

Information in possession of the President is to the effect that there is an understanding between Germany and Japan which may result in a squeeze play against Russia. Great Britain, concerned as usual for the Empire, and anticipating what a threat this combination would be against the British colonies, especially in Asia, decided to come to some sort of an understanding with Hitler. The feeling is that Great Britain has done so. One member of the Cabinet remarked that England had always been able to get along better with Germany than with France.

The President had a good deal to say about what the Supreme Court is likely to do on New Deal legislation. As once before in talking with me, he went back to the period when Gladstone was Prime Minister of Great Britain and succeeded in passing the Irish Home Rule Bill through the House of Commons on two or three occasions, only to have it vetoed by the House of Lords.

Later, when Lloyd George's social security act was similarly blocked, Lloyd George went to the King, who was in favor of the bill, and he asked Lloyd George whether he wanted him to create three hundred new peers. Lloyd George said that he did not but that he was going to pass through Commons a bill providing that in the future any bill vetoed by the House of Lords should, notwithstanding that, become the law of Great Britain if passed again by the Commons. He told the King that when that bill was ready to go to the Lords he would like the King to send word that if it didn't pass, he would create three hundred new Lords. This the King did, with the result that the bill was accepted by the House of Lords.

Clearly, it is running in the President's mind that substantially all of the New Deal bills will be declared unconstitutional by the Supreme Court. This will mean that everything that this Administration has done of any moment will be nullified. The President pointed out that there were three ways of meeting such a situation: (1) by packing the Supreme Court, which was a distasteful idea; (2) by trying to put through a number of amendments to the Constitution to meet the various situations; and (3) by a method that he asked us to consider very carefully.

The third method is, in substance, this: an amendment to the Constitution conferring explicit power on the Supreme Court to declare acts of Congress unconstitutional, a power which is not given anywhere in the Constitution as it stands. The amendment would also give the Supreme Court original jurisdiction on constitutional questions affecting statutes. If the Supreme Court should declare an act of Congress to be unconstitutional, then—a congressional election having intervened—if Congress should repass the law so declared to be unconstitutional, the taint of unconstitutionality would be removed and the law would be a valid one. By this method there would be in effect a referendum to the country, although an indirect one. At the intervening congressional election the question of the constitutionality or unconstitutionality of the law would undoubtedly be an issue.

Homer Cummings suggested that the Supreme Court would have an undue burden cast upon it if it had to hear the evidence in every constitutional case that was taken before it. He suggested that the U.S. District Courts be given the power to hear evidence and certify the record to the Supreme Court without themselves giving judgment.

There wasn't much discussion of this proposition of the President because he didn't ask for any expression of opinion. I may say that, for my part, I think there is much to commend this idea. I have long believed that the Supreme Court should at the very least have the power that it has usurped to declare laws unconstitutional seriously curtailed. As the President remarked, if all the New Deal legislation is thrown out, there will be marching farmers and marching miners and marching workingmen throughout the land.

Someone, I think it was Miss Perkins, remarked that in some parts of the country the Supreme Court is now coming to be regarded as a third branch of Congress. Formerly, laws passed by Congress and signed by the President were recognized as laws until they were declared unconstitutional. Now they are nullified at once by some district judge in some corner of the land on the basis of a bill for an injunction filed by some interested party.

Toward the close of the session, Miss Perkins raised the question about a continuance of some sort of a public works program. The President had indicated that in his budget message he was going to say that the budget offered would be a balanced budget except for relief, thus leaving the question of relief up to Congress for later consideration when the President would have more facts upon which to base a recommendation. Miss Perkins made a good argument for public works as against work relief and made some very pointed criticisms of the Hopkins program. The President didn't hear her with very much patience. There isn't any doubt that he is deeply committed to the Hopkins theory and has taken his advice that public works are an ineffective means of recovery and not the proper way to deal with unemployment.

Harry Hopkins certainly did a good job as a salesman when he put his work-relief program over with the President. Apparently the President expects to ask for a sum of money, not less than $1 billion and not more than $2 billion, for a continuation of Hopkins' work-relief program during the next fiscal year. I suspect that there will be some explosive language on the Hill when he sends up such a program. However, I am also persuaded that the President's mind is closed to what seem to me to be the obvious merits of a public works program, if money is to be spent at all to relieve the unemployment situation and to stimulate business. The President thinks of the whole thing in terms of the men actually employed at the site of the job and these men have to be taken from the relief rolls.

The Vice President said that five Senators, two of them Republicans, were in his office recently and he made the statement to them that never in history had such large sums of money been spent by any Administration as has been spent by this one without any suspicion of crookedness or graft. He said that some of the money might have been better spent or spent to better advantage in other places than where it was spent but that it was being honestly spent. He said all of the Senators agreed with him.

Monday, December 30, 1935

The *New Republic* last week had a long editorial criticizing WPA and urging that it be liquidated. What struck me particularly about the editorial was that the writer was in ignorance of some very important facts. The tone adopted was that the President had conceived of the work-relief idea and that poor Harry Hopkins was doing his best in an impossible situation to carry out the stubbornly supported wishes of the President.

Of course, this is just as far from the truth as it can be. I was in on this whole last relief program from the very beginning. At the outset, the program was to be distinctly one of public works, with an appropriation of $5 billion. Everything was to be self-liquidating. There were not even to be grants, as under the original program, until he finally won the President completely to his side. From that point on, it was difficult to save anything for self-liquidating PWA projects. That is the situation today. It is foolish to try to make Hopkins appear to be a martyr in carrying out a program that he himself is responsible for. It is not only foolish; it is misinforming and unfair to the President. Not that I can exonerate the President in my own mind for adopting such a program, but at any rate, the man responsible for it ought at least to share whatever blame attaches.

That the President is absolutely committed to the WPA theory of Hopkins was made abundantly clear at the last Cabinet meeting, as I have already related, when Miss Perkins was listened to with distinct impatience on the part of the President when she advocated a continuance of the PWA program, as distinguished from the Hopkins theory. I haven't the slightest doubt but that what the President has in mind now is to ask Congress for a considerable sum of money to continue Hopkins and his program. But I also have a sneaking notion that after Hopkins gets the money, he will veer around to a PWA program, but probably on the basis of one hundred per cent Federal grants instead of on a loan-and-grant basis which I have advocated. As a matter of fact, Hopkins is doing his best now to build more substantial projects, but of course he is doing it with practically no contributions from the local communities. I think that when the next relief bill goes to Congress there will be some fireworks, but unless Congress stops it, Hopkins will emerge in control not only of what has been his program but what has been mine to date.

Tuesday, December 31, 1935

I saw the President today to clear up a number of matters before I start on my travels on Thursday. He was in his office again and apparently he had overcome his cold. He approved all the PWA projects I presented to him, much to my surprise, because I thought he would hold up some of them, as he has been doing lately. Among his approvals was Santee-Cooper. I did not present this to him in the form of a recommendation from me, as I have done in practically all other instances. I merely transmitted it to him without recommendation. He said that one thing that had made him stubborn about the Santee-Cooper project was the fact that so many of his rich friends had urged him not to go ahead with it. He spoke scornfully of rich men of the North buying fine old plantations in South Carolina and turning them into "hunting lodges."

One thing he did approve that I am strongly in favor of was a loan and grant of $58,365,000 for the Queens Midtown Tunnel at Thirty-eighth Street, New York City. The reason I was so strongly in favor of this is because Senator Wagner wants it badly and he is such a fine, forward-looking Senator that I like to do for him what I can. Something over $11 million of this will be a grant, but the Midtown Tunnel has just repaid something over $10 million to us, so that I felt warranted in recommending the new project to the President, especially since Jesse Jones will at once buy from us all the bonds covered by the loan.

When we were through discussing Government business, I told the President that some day I wanted to talk politics with him. As I stood up to go, I bluntly asked him how much further we were going to retreat before standing to face the enemy. I told him that I believed in fighting and that I thought we ought to fight. He said that he believed it too and that his message to Congress would be a fighting message. I remarked that I hoped so.

Sunday, January 5, 1936

Jane Dahlman and I had dinner New Year's Eve with Ruth Hampton and Bess Beach in their apartment, and the four of us had a very good time. Ruth is enthusiastic about Jane. I did not feel much like working on New Year's Day and I largely yielded to my inclination. In the afternoon I made a final revision of my Rochester speech and Jane and I went to the movies at night. We saw *Captain Blood,* and both of us thought it was very poorly done.

Thursday morning there was a light rain falling which froze as it fell on the ice and snow that already covered the streets. It made the going very difficult indeed. I worked at the house until about twelve o'clock. By that time there was a heavy rain, but it was warm enough so that it made the streets passable. At the office I worked right through until two-thirty, when Mike Straus, Mr. Cubberley, and I left to catch the three o'clock train to New York.

In New York we were met by Commissioner of Licenses Moss and a captain of police in a police car. We went to the Fifth Avenue Hotel. This was the first time I had ever been at this hotel. Congressman Sirovich lives there and Burlew had arranged through him for a rate for the party. I get rather tired paying the high prices at the Hotel Roosevelt. Congressman Sirovich was on hand to greet us when we were shown to our rooms. They had reserved very satisfactory quarters; indeed, the quarters were much more extensive than we needed. On a table in my sitting room was a large array of whisky and brandy bottles, together with White Rock, soda water, ginger ale, etc. We had had our dinner on the train, but Congressman Sirovich ordered up something for himself and after he was through we went to the theater to see *First Lady*.

The tickets ordered for Burlew and Slattery had not been given up, so Sirovich and a friend of his went along, although the Congressman had already seen the play. It really was lots of fun. The lines were clever and the plot engaging. It was a contest on the stage between a character representing Alice Longworth and one representing Cissy Patterson as to who was to be the next First Lady, with Alice Longworth triumphant in the end. Kaufman was one of the authors of the play, and I always like his work.

I forgot to say that Congressman Sirovich greeted me with a New Year's present, consisting of a dozen neckties which he had had made to order by his haberdasher. This man really overwhelms me and I do not know what to do about it, although, as I reflected on the matter afterward, I need not have gone to his hotel. When we got back from the theater, he brought in the owner of the hotel, whom he described as his closest friend, and proceeded to tell us that at one time he had been worth $20 million and was earning a salary out of the leather goods business alone of $900,000 a year. Midnight lunch was served and I had to eat it whether I wanted it or not. I never eat at night and I did not want anything on this occasion. However, there was no resisting Sirovich. He insisted that he was going to send me a case of sauterne, after he had asked me what wine I particularly liked.

When I stepped into the elevator at the hotel upon my arrival, I ran into my old friend Judge Julian S. Mack, who has been on the Federal bench since his appointment by President Taft. He lives in the penthouse of the hotel, and he asked me to have breakfast with him. This I did Friday morning. Judge Mack will reach the retiring age on his next birthday, which will be his seventieth. He was one of my law school teachers at the University of Chicago, and, aside from law school, I had a very close relationship with him while he lived in Chicago.

Mayor La Guardia and Langdon Post, chairman of the New York City Housing Commission, called for us at ten o'clock and we drove over to Brooklyn, where work was to be started on the Williamsburg housing project. It rained hard all day Thursday and all that night and it was still hard at it on Friday. The ceremonies were held in the assembly hall of the school right at the edge of the site. I was on the air on a national hookup for half an hour. Mayor La Guardia and others spoke, with Post presiding. Later I was the luncheon guest of our State Director of PWA, Arthur Tuttle, at the Engineers Club. He had the heads of his various departments present.

I got into Rochester tired, because Mayor La Guardia gave us a dinner at his favorite Italian restaurant, Little Venice, Thursday night and then took us to the theater. The dinner was good, but I did not care for the show nearly as well as I had for the play the night before. Beatrice Lillie was the star, and she is a very good actress. The show was not dull but, except for Beatrice Lillie, it was not particularly interesting either.

The speech went off as well as, if not better than, any I have made. It was an intelligent audience and my points were appreciated and well received. I talked for all of an hour, and perhaps a little longer, but they had wanted a long speech. At the end I was very well satisfied with my effort. Mike Straus was pleased with the result and the audience seemed to enjoy it, although undoubtedly many did not agree with much that I said.

After my speech, which followed a luncheon, I went out to see my old teacher, Miss Agnes A. Rogers. She taught me Latin and Greek in the Englewood High School many years ago. Not only was she one of the two best teachers I ever had in my life, but I think there is no doubt that I would not have gone to college if she had not stirred my ambitions in that direction. In high school she was a great help to me. In order to prepare me for my college examinations she gave me the *Anabasis* in Greek outside of regular hours. I always felt that I owed her a great deal.

I had not seen her for all of forty years. I doubt if I would have known her if I had met her on the street, but as we talked, I could see some of the old characteristics. She travels a good deal and apparently is as keen mentally as she ever was. She is really a cultured woman and I enjoyed the few hours that I spent with her. The newspapers in Rochester had learned that an old teacher of mine was there whom I proposed to visit and they tried to interview me about her and wanted to send photographers out to the house. However, Miss Rogers had written me a note pleading with me not to permit any publicity, and so I frowned on every proposal and succeeded in keeping the reporters and photographers from going to the house. Miss Rogers did not even come to my meeting, although I had had a special invitation sent to her.

We caught an early train out of Rochester and got into Washington this morning. I went to the office, where I arrived at eight o'clock. There was plenty of work waiting for me—in fact, more than I could well attend to. I worked at top speed until I simply had to leave for home in order to pack for my trip to Puerto Rico and the Virgin Islands. By utilizing every minute at home, except for a hasty dinner, I had just completed my packing when Carl drove up for me. With Mr. Cubberley and Mike Straus, I took the Atlantic Coast Line train at three o'clock for Miami. We will pick Raymond up at Richmond.

Monday, January 13, 1936

At Miami there were a number of people at the train to meet us, including the mayor, various public officials, newspaper reporters, photographers, members of the PWA and Housing staffs, etc. Glavis was also at the station. We went to the McAllister Hotel and all of the members of the party except myself went swimming. After doing some dictating I went to work on the manuscript of my Washington Town Hall speech, which is due to be delivered on January 26.

Colonel Shutts, one of the leading lawyers of Miami and the owner of the *Miami Herald,* called on me about seven o'clock. I had met him before, but only casually. We had quite a long, friendly talk. He brought up the question of the Florida canal and told me that he was leaving for Washington in a day or two to fight the canal. He said that Senator Vandenberg had written to him for facts and that while he was a Democrat and New Dealer and hated to fight the Administration through a Republican Senator, he felt that he had to do so in this instance. His view is that if the Administration goes along with this canal, Roosevelt will lose Florida next year. He says that that part of Florida which lies south of the canal line is bitterly opposed to the canal, and that this section contains more people than north Florida. He is fearful of the effect the canal will have upon the fresh-water resources of Florida. I told him that, while as a member of the Administration I could not say anything publicly in opposition to the canal, I was in full sympathy with the position he had expressed. I told him also that I had done everything in my power to prevent the building of this canal.

I got into San Juan pretty tired. We had sent one or two messages en route by wireless to Governor Winship. The Pan American World Airways people had promised to send word from Miami but apparently did not do so. Accordingly, he had gone ahead with his dinner but he fed us when we arrived at the Governor's Mansion.

A number of the leading officials of Puerto Rico were at the Governor's Mansion that night, including the Chief Justice of the Supreme Court, the Attorney General, and others. I, of course, met them all and we sat about smoking and drinking until fairly late, when Governor Winship finally saw to it that I went off to bed. I was terribly tired and slept like a log.

The Governor's Mansion is an old Spanish building and very lovely. It is big and spacious and stands right on the water's edge, where it gets all the cool breezes. Governor Winship says that one can catch fish right in the bay. Governor Winship is a retired major general of the Regular Army. He was in the Judge Advocate General's office and has been in all parts of the world. His native state is Georgia, and he is a fine-looking, courteous man, but highly conservative.

Dr. Gruening had been in Puerto Rico for some time getting his rehabilitation work going. The Puerto Rican head of this rehabilitation work is Dr. Chardon, president of the University of Puerto Rico, and a liberal. Puerto Rico is very political. Just at present the Puerto Rican Legislature is in the control of a coalition group which is conservative. The expectation is that the liberals will win the next election, but in the meantime there is a strong contention between the two elements. The liberals are strongly opposed to Winship and want him recalled. One of the chief items of contention has been the failure of the Puerto Rican Government to break up the big sugar estates into five-acre holdings, as provided by the law of Congress. This is one reason why, a short time ago, Dr. Gruening and I, after much hard work, succeeded in forcing the retirement of Attorney General Horton and the appointment in his place of a native Puerto Rican by the name of Benigno Fernandez-Garcia. This attorney general is now preparing to try to enforce the five-acre law, but two or three weeks ago Cummings served notice on me that he was opposed to having Fernandez-Garcia appointed permanently as attorney general. However, this issue is still to be fought out before the President, and I shall oppose strongly the replacing of Fernandez-Garcia by another of Cummings' political lawyers.

Wednesday morning we set out in automobiles on a tour of inspection. We first went over the old Spanish fort which occupies the heights along the water front. Colonel Cole, the American commander, apparently is very much interested in this old fort as well as in other historic buildings. However, he is strongly resisting our desire to have the whole water front, including this old fort, made into a national monument. His troops still occupy this old fort and naturally he is averse to giving it up. However, I am convinced that this should be done.

We visited several points of interest in San Juan, including a hospital where research into the causes and cures of tropical diseases is being carried on under the auspices of Columbia University. We inspected two or three slum areas, and they are the worst slums that I have ever seen. The dwellings looked as if a breath would blow them over. They are thoroughly disreputable and disagreeable. Open sewage runs through the streets and around the buildings and there are no sanitary facilities at all. The children play in this sewage, which in many cases is covered with a thick, green scum. The houses appear to be dirty and unkempt. The cooking is done on little charcoal stoves, and the furniture is of the simplest and scantiest. Notwithstanding these terrible conditions, generally speaking, the people in the slums, and especially the younger women, had the appearance of being neat and clean, although I cannot see how they can possibly be clean, considering the surroundings in which they live. Such slums are a reflection not only upon the Puerto Rican Government but upon that of the United States. It is unbelievable that human beings can be permitted to live in such noisome cesspools.

The economic problem in Puerto Rico is a very serious one. There is not enough work to go around, with the result that unemployment is at a high rate. Moreover, the people breed like rabbits and any talk of contraception is frowned upon by the Catholic Church and clergy. The Catholic religion strongly predominates in Puerto Rico.

We drove up into the national forest for luncheon. This forest is a very interesting one and the area covered by it should be a national park. A good deal of work in reforestation is being done, not only in the national forest but in other places in the island, and the Department of Agriculture has in operation several experimental stations. After luncheon we covered a good deal of additional territory, and late in the afternoon arrived at the Governor's summer camp well up in the mountains. The mountains here look high and are rugged. They have the appearance of being six or seven thousand feet in altitude, but, as a matter of fact, the highest mountain is only about twenty-three hundred feet. The Governor's camp is stationed well up overlooking a mountain range, with a magnificent view off across the Caribbean. It was very cool up there. We had dinner and spent the night.

Early Thursday morning, the ninth, we started down the mountains. Most of our party had spent the night at Coama Springs Hotel. From there we traveled hither and yon, seeing various points of interest. We passed through great fields of sugar cane, practically all of them owned by the big sugar companies. It looked like an abundant crop. We also passed numerous tobacco fields. The coffee crop has not recovered from the hurricane of a year or two ago. It seems that coffee bushes are rather brittle and are prone to be blown to pieces by a strong wind. When this happens the results are serious, as it takes six years for a coffee bush to mature a crop. Much to my surprise, I found that coffee is grown under the protective covering of other bushes and trees. I had visualized it as a cultivated crop grown in rows in an open field. They are experimenting in Puerto Rico with a new kind of long staple cotton. The island also produces coconuts, pineapples, oranges, and grapefruit. In the woods large quantities of wild oranges grow. Most of these go to waste, although Governor Winship told me that the wild oranges are an especially sweet fruit, very juicy, and well adapted for conversion into canned orange juice.

In various parts of the island subsistence homestead developments are already in progress or have been protected. I noticed as we drove about the island that the overwhelming mass of the people seemed to be very poor, if their living conditions are any indication. Their dwellings are distinctly substandard, and in not a single one of these dwellings where the people, outside of the small prosperous class, live, did I see a single carpet or rug. Pigs, chickens, and burros live in close fellowship with the members of the family. Dr. Chardon told me that school facilities for one hundred and forty thousand children were lacking. The rate of illiteracy is high, and there doesn't seem to be a very keen desire on the part of Puerto Ricans to learn English. Meanwhile, the political pot is always boiling. It was the period of registration when we were in Puerto Rico, and everywhere we could see cars (although there are few automobiles in the island) and animal-drawn vehicles, decorated with the colorful bunting of the various political parties. The Puerto Rican is said to be an inveterate politician, and I saw many evidences of this.

I expect that I had always thought of Puerto Rico as a rather flat country. As a matter of fact, it is very hilly. The roads have not been laid out any too well, with the result that there are steep grades and sharp turns. A drive to Mayagüez was one of the most uncomfortable and most dangerous that I have ever taken. We were trying to make Mayagüez by three o'clock and we were behind schedule. The result was that we drove at a really reckless rate of speed, considering the road conditions. I was all but carsick from the swaying and twisting of the automobile. There was a constant blowing of horns, grinding of brakes, and swishing of tires. Most of the bridges were old and not any too secure and, generally, they were placed at a sharp angle in the road, so that if anything had gone wrong we would have been over the road, into a gulley, or down a declivity in no time at all. Raymond remarked afterward that our average speed was only twelve miles an hour. Even so, this was a dangerous rate, considering the roads, and I who say this am perfectly willing, as I frequently do in my own car with Carl at the wheel, to go from eighty to ninety miles an hour.

We reached Mayagüez shortly after three o'clock, hot and tired and very dirty, because many of the roads we traveled over did not have hard surfaces. Here we found waiting for us a Marine airplane, with Lieutenant Colonel James T. Moore in charge as pilot. This had come over from the Marine air base at St. Thomas. Our baggage had been taken over earlier. We filled the airplane, and had a smooth ride to St. Thomas.

We got to St. Thomas in about an hour and a quarter. Governor Cramer and other officials were waiting for me on the pier, and I was taken at once to a meeting of the St. Thomas Municipal Council. Here I received an official welcome and I made a short informal talk. Then we went to Government House, which was next door, where I had a chance to have a bath and change into fresh clothes for dinner. Governor Cramer had a number of people in for a buffet dinner. They included the principal members of his staff and some of the leading citizens of the island. For the occasion, we put on dinner coats.

St. Thomas is a small, mountainous island. The city is clustered around the bay at the foot of the mountains and presents a very picturesque appearance. Whereas in Puerto Rico the language generally spoken is Spanish, the universal language in the Virgin Islands is English. The great portion of the population is Negro, but they are intelligent and there is a high degree of literacy on the Islands.

Friday morning, the tenth, Governor Cramer took me out to see what the island had to show. This was not much except scenery, but there were some beautiful specimens of that. I was especially interested in the home that a Mr. Fairchild has built well up in the mountains. He bought an old house and made it over and added to it until he has a very beautiful home with a magnificent view. On one side one can see across the Caribbean. On this side the island of St. John, which is one of the Virgin Islands group, and the island of British Tortola seemed to be almost within a stone's throw. On the other side one can see on a clear day across the Atlantic as far as Puerto Rico. On this side too there are some small islands which belong to the Virgin Islands group.

Late in the morning there was an official reception at Government House, with two or three hundred people in attendance. After greeting all of these people I was called on for a short talk. In all of my talks while in the Virgin Islands I emphasized the necessity for co-operation between the people of the Islands and the Federal Government if we were to work out our plans for the economic rehabilitation of the Islands. I said that the Islands were especially adapted for winter tourist business and that permanent winter residents might be attracted. I pointed out, however, that if the newspapers continued to carry stories to the effect that there was bad feeling on the Islands that might develop at any time into physical disorder, there would be little chance of attracting outside people.

Friday night Governor Cramer took us up to the Bluebeard Castle Hotel for dinner. On the hillside stands an old tower known as Bluebeard Tower, evidently part of an old Danish fortification. The Hoover administration authorized the building of a hotel for tourists and appropriated $30,000. This sum was increased to about $120,000 by PWA, largely at the solicitation of Governor Pearson. The hotel is attractive and well built. I did not inspect the hotel carefully, but I did notice that the bedrooms all contain parquet floors. I criticized this as an unjustified expense in connection with such an enterprise. Later the manager pled with me to give them another $5,000 for a hot-water supply. I was perfectly astounded that a new hotel should be built in these days without a supply of hot water. I am afraid that there has been a good deal of waste and extravagance in building this hotel, for which, sooner or later, we will be called to account. I found the floors of the gallery and the shutters to be splattered with plaster. The manager said that the money had run out before these defacements could be removed. I was critical of this, too, and suggested to Governor Cramer that he might get men from the CCC camp to remove them.

Saturday Colonel Moore took us to St. Croix, which is the largest of the Islands and contains most of the tillable land. It is here that we have been buying land and planting it to sugar cane in order to supply ourselves with raw material for the manufacture of the rum that is being made by the Virgin Islands Company—a Government corporation of which I am chairman of the board. I was told by several people that the contrast between the St. Croix of today and that of a few years ago is nothing short of remarkable. Certainly, the island had the appearance of being a fairly prosperous place. I saw a number of fine fields of sugar cane, most of which were the property of the Virgin Islands Company. We have one or two grinding mills in operation, and we expect soon to buy the Bethlehem plant, which is the largest on the island but in a rundown condition. This we will rehabilitate. We already own about 1,500 acres of cane land and with the additional $1 million of capital which the President approved recently, after buying and rehabilitating the Bethlehem plant, we will buy and put into cultivation additional lands of 2,000 acres.

I visited the rum distillery, where we have now maturing in barrels about 250,000 gallons of rum. We have already contracted for the sale of some 60,000 gallons to a Haitian rum company, to be blended with Haitian rum. Of this total, some 1,500 gallons have already been delivered at a profit of sixty or sixty-five cents a gallon. Within two or three months our oldest rum will be two years old and we will then begin to market it, although rum ought to mature for five years to be the best quality.

We reached Miami just before seven o'clock on Sunday. It had been planned for me to turn the first spadeful of earth in connection with our Miami housing project at five o'clock, but due to the fact that we started from St. Thomas, this had to be given up. The customs officer put my party through in fast order. He was satisfied with our declarations and we did not have to open any of our very numerous bags.

William C. Edens, whom I have known for a good many years and who was formerly a vice president of the Central Trust Company of Illinois, met us at the dock with a big touring car and a station wagon to take us to the Boca Raton Club, forty miles north of Miami on the road to West Palm Beach. We had to stop at the McAllister Hotel to pick up some baggage that we had checked there. It was a particularly long, tiresome ride to Boca Raton because I was very tired and the chauffeur was a slow driver. We did not get there until nearly ten o'clock and we had had nothing to eat since a very early breakfast, except a light sandwich lunch at Port au Prince. The man who owns the club, C. H. Geist, was waiting to have dinner with us, and after dinner I went promptly to bed. I was so tired that I dropped to sleep almost before my head touched the pillow.

A luncheon had been given to me at this club last April when I was in Florida in connection with the Seminole Indian celebration, and I described it then as the most luxurious club that I had ever seen or heard of. It continues to live up to its reputation. Geist had impressed me last April as an exceedingly rough diamond, but he had been seated some distance from me at the luncheon table, so that I did not get any real appreciation of him. But I did on this trip.

Geist is the son of a German farmer and was born near LaPorte, Indiana. According to his own story, he refused to go to college when his father wanted him to because, in his opinion, all college men were "saps." Not only that, but he had dropped out of school altogether even before he was ready for college. He says he started trading horses at the age of thirteen. He has been in the utility game most of his life, and apparently has been able to compete on equal terms with that gang of buccaneers. He told me this morning that if he had sold everything he owned before the crash, he would have been worth between $50 and $60 million.

Apparently he succeeded in saving quite a lot. He bought control of the Boca Raton Club and seems to be running it as a fad. He bought it very cheaply but has put in $6 million of his own money, and apparently is prepared to put in a lot more. He has bought 2,000 acres of beach property, which he is laying out in a subdivision. He says this is going to be one of the best paying investments he has ever made. Apparently Florida real estate is coming back very rapidly. Colonel Shutts told me that when I saw him in Miami on my way south. Geist is one of those rough individuals with a lot of native power. He has a rugged face and a projecting lower jaw. His English is terrible and his manners are worse. He certainly does not suffer from any inferiority complex. Apparently he likes to make money to satisfy his sense of power. He orders everyone about in a loud, peremptory manner, but I think that with it all he is a big-hearted fellow, as that type is very likely to be. At that, I would not expect him to be big-hearted or show much mercy to a business rival.

Just now he is very much interested in an invention which, if perfected, will enable every automobile to run on its own power. This invention involves a process of generating electricity as the car goes along, and if it works out for automobiles, it will work out for engines, airplanes, and steamships. He seems to have control of the basic patents, but the thing has not yet been thoroughly developed. He says that it will be worth $1 billion a year and that Ford and Rockefeller will look like pikers.

This morning he took me out in his car to see his subdivision and swimming pools and golf links. I must say that he seems to be lavish in his expenditure of money on his properties. The subdivision is just being laid out, but the appurtenances to the club are in perfect condition. It costs $5,000 to join the club, in addition to which there are annual dues. On top of this, everything anyone buys at the club is very expensive. He says that he has applications for seven hundred memberships that he has turned down. He chooses to suit himself, and while the thing is called a club, it is not a club at all because the members have no voting power except as they own the stock which, however, he controls. He says he will not admit any Jew to the club and never will, because Jews and Gentiles will not mix in that sort of an enterprise. I have never seen better putting greens, and his beach cabanas and everything else seem to be perfect.

No one else went with us on the drive because he said he wanted me alone. It did not take him long to tell me what he had on his mind, and what he told me was in confidence. He has great hopes of this invention that he talked about and when he is ready to go ahead with it, he says he is going to send for me and take me out of politics. He says that he has always had a habit of picking the right men and that his judgment has rarely gone astray. He has decided that I am the man he wants, and his idea (inchoate, of course, because the whole thing is highly speculative and tentative) is to put me in control of Great Britain and France. He said that he thought I was diplomatic and a good mixer. I told him I was not either and that I had a reputation of being a slave driver. He said he was himself and that was the kind of man he liked. He also said that he had heard a lot of people talk about me, both for and against me, but that no one had ever criticized me.

Geist is very sure of himself. He is a loud and assertive talker. I merely listened. The only comment I made was in reply to his remark that I was diplomatic and a good mixer. I just let him talk on since it seemed to interest him and did not do me any harm. He became more friendly toward the end of the drive and said he would like to call me by my first name and have me call him by his. It was all very amusing, and yet there is a rough sincerity about the big grizzly bear that one has to give him credit for. The management of the club absolutely refused to give us a bill for our entertainment or to accept any compensation.

A little before eleven this morning we took the train at Boca Raton station and headed back to Washington.

Thursday, January 16, 1936

I got into Washington Tuesday morning at nine o'clock. While a good deal of work was waiting for me, it wasn't so bad on the whole and I was able to clear my desk before going home for dinner. Raymond went out to the house to repack and pick up some things he left there and took the 4:30 train on the Pennsylvania to Chicago. I think he had a good time on the trip and at any rate he did find relief from the cold that seems to bother him rather persistently.

In my Rochester, New York, speech, I made the statement that during the Hoover administration three laws had been passed which later were declared to be unconstitutional. While I was in the Virgin Islands, Mr. Hoover sent a telegram to me at the Department denying this statement and calling on me for an apology. He referred to this statement as an "untruth" and as being "false." He gave his telegram to the newspapers, and the Associated Press correspondent at St. Thomas attempted to interview me. I declined to make any comment because I wanted to get back to Washington and see the precise statement that Hoover had made. In the meantime I kept in touch with my office by radio, and Harry Slattery sent me the complete text of the telegram.

On the train back to Washington I dictated a reply to Mr. Hoover. I worked this over again on Tuesday and conferred with several members of my staff with reference to it. As a matter of fact, I worked it over three or four times and finally got it into shape which was quite satisfactory to me and to the others in my Department with whom I had consulted. In the meantime Tom Corcoran and Ben Cohen came in with a suggestion and they were both delighted with my final draft. When I sent it over to Steve Early, however, he made some drastic corrections. It seemed to me that he cut out the best part of the letter, but of course I redrafted it finally along the lines of his suggestion and mailed it to Mr. Hoover Wednesday afternoon. Today I gave copies to the Washington correspondents for publication.

Much to my surprise, I found when I got back that I was almost completely exhausted. I didn't realize how tired I was until late Tuesday afternoon when I was discussing the Hoover letter with members of the staff. As usual, Mike Straus took sharp issue with me and I went back at him pretty savagely. That night when I got home to dinner I was very tired indeed. The paces they put me through both in Puerto Rico and the Virgin Islands had taken a heavier toll that I had realized. I went to bed fairly early and slept like a log right through the night, but I awoke Wednesday morning so tired that I didn't see how I could get out of bed. However, as always, I did get up and went to my office for a full day's work.

I talked with Grace Tully by telephone yesterday and she told me she thought my Rochester speech was fine. I hadn't supposed that she had read it and, of course, I expressed proper gratification. She told me that I said things worth while in my speeches and that I made "better speeches than any of them." I don't know just what she meant by "them" and I didn't inquire. She went on to say that she thought that I would be sent out to make some speeches, and I told her that I believed that we ought to make fighting speeches. She agreed. As Grace Tully is one of the personal secretaries of the President and takes most of his confidential dictation, I feel that I have a right to assume that she was reflecting the President's views in some degree.

Then Mike Straus came in this morning to tell me about a talk he had had yesterday with Steve Early. He said Steve had said some very nice things about me and that he had also commented favorably upon my speeches and had made the remark that they would be sending me out to make more of them. Taking the two incidents together, I believe that their expressions must be a reflection of the President's point of view.

Fertich was in to see me again today. He is a busy man and covers a lot of ground. He told me that he had talked with Secretary of War Dern and that Dern had said that Farley never consulted him about political matters. Attorney General Cummings made the same statement to Fertich and asked him whether Farley ever consulted me. Apparently Farley is running a one-man show. I knew he never consulted me, but I didn't suppose that he had the same attitude toward other members of the Cabinet. According to Fertich, Secretary Hull is never consulted either, and yet both Secretary Hull and the Attorney General are former chairmen of the Democratic National Committee.

Late this afternoon the President called me and he frankly told me that he was in a good deal of a jam. The estimated cost for building the Passamaquoddy project was originally about $35 million, and it was on this basis that the President decided to go ahead with it. Recently the Army engineers brought in a supplemental report showing a final cost of about $65 million. The President said that, of course, that made it an entirely different proposition. He sent for George Dern and Dern said that he didn't know anything about it, but that the estimate of $35 million was accepted as the estimate of Dexter Cooper, the engineer who pioneered the project, and had not been checked until recently. The President told George Dern that he ought to fire all of his Army engineers. He went on to tell me that General Markham had made a very labored written report to him, and he has had General Markham and Major Fleming in. The $35 million originally estimated as the cost will take care of only one pool and the power produced from that will cost more than if it were produced from coal. The President said that, of course, this would never do. He also said that word is quietly going around Boston that the Passamaquoddy project will never be built. I told the President that I always had my fingers crossed with respect to the Army engineers when it came to power projects, and he said "That's right." I also told him that

I thought their figures on the cost of the Florida canal were "cockeyed."

The President told me that Dexter Cooper is in Washington and that Cooper said he will stake his reputation as an engineer that the whole project can be built within his original estimate. He told me to send for Cooper tomorrow and have him tell me his story. Then he wants me to send two or three of our best reclamation engineers up to Passamaquoddy to study the project. He told me that I could justify this by saying that since PWA money was being used, I want to check back and see just what the actual cost will be. He said that he would tell Dern that I was doing this on his instructions.

Friday, January 17, 1936

There was a full attendance at Cabinet meeting today with no substitutes present. There was considerable discussion about the Neutrality Bill which is being worked out in Congress. The President said he believed that after the European countries had carved up Africa and Asia to satisfy themselves, their eyes in time would turn toward South America. He doesn't expect this to happen for ten or fifteen, or perhaps even twenty, years but he predicted that some future American President will be called upon to face the problem of possible invasion of the sovereignty of South American countries by European nations. For this reason he wants the Neutrality Bill to give the President the right to extend the protection of the Monroe Doctrine to all American countries that do not now belong to any European nation. He pointed out that in the past both President Cleveland and President Theodore Roosevelt were called upon to act on pretty short notice with respect to South American affairs when Congress was not in session. Moreover, if the Neutrality Bill should apply equally to all the countries in the world, and if the President were not given some freedom of action with respect to this hemisphere, it might be necessary during a crisis to urge Congress, in special session if necessary, to repeal the act so far as it might inhibit applying the protection of the Monroe Doctrine to a threatened American country. Such a repeal proposal might be difficult of passage and would elicit bitter debate and opposition on the part of the professional pacifists.

While we were still in session, Steve Early brought in a considerable section from the ticker quoting Senator Glass's attack on Senator Nye and his investigating committee for the recent slur upon the memory of President Wilson. It was hot stuff all right. Secretary Hull remarked that the Nye committee had gone to the State Department for certain information and had been shown the Balfour memoranda in confidence, notwithstanding which this information went into the record. He also told us, in confidence, that many important and valuable memoranda had been taken from the State Department by Secretary Lansing when he retired as Secretary of State and had not been returned until after Mr. Lansing's death. He remarked that other countries would refuse to submit confidential information to us if that information could not be protected from divulgence through an investigating committee.

Henry Morgenthau complained because when he appeared before the Appropriations Committee of the Senate at an executive session, Senator Couzens, of Michigan, refused to regard it as executive and then, according to Morgenthau, gave out a garbled report of what Morgenthau had said. At this juncture, Vice President Garner remarked that there ought not to be any executive sessions of any congressional committee. He made the point that it was all public business and that reporters should be permitted to attend any committee meeting. I think he is right. Several instances were cited of confidential information leaking out of committee executive sessions.

The Attorney General discussed the recent decision of the Supreme Court in the AAA case. Henry Wallace thinks that we ought to join issue on the Supreme Court and I agree with him. As we left the Cabinet meeting, Cummings said that we were rapidly approaching a state of judicial autocracy in this country, and I told him that we had already arrived there and that we ought to fight it out on those lines.

Until Cabinet meeting today I had not seen the President since January 2. I was rather struck with the change in his appearance that has taken place, not only recently but particularly as compared with the way he looked when he was sworn in on March 4, 1933. He looks many years older and his face looked drawn and tired. Moreover, he seems to be much more nervous than formerly. Henry Wallace looks fifteen years older than when he entered the Cabinet. Today his face was really haggard. It was drawn and full of lines. This Washington job is certainly taking a heavy toll in many directions.

The President referred to a report that Sir Ronald Lindsay, Ambassador from Great Britain, is to be recalled to London to become permanent Under Secretary of State. He saw Sir Ronald at the White House recently and asked him about this report. Sir Ronald said that he hoped it was not so and that he did not want to be Under Secretary of State because Great Britain did not seem to have any established foreign policy these days.

One interesting incident took place at the Cabinet meeting. At one point the Vice President spoke up and said, in effect: "Mr. President, you know that I have never asked you any questions on any subject, although I have always been willing to respond to any suggestion from you. I don't know what your attitude is going to be on the bonus bill, but it is sure to pass the Senate tomorrow and, in my judgment, will be passed even over your veto. You haven't told me your attitude and I haven't asked, but a number of the Senators urged me to ask you a certain question about it and if you are willing that I should do so, I am prepared to ask the question." The President did not ask him what the question was and the matter was dropped.

Saturday, January 18, 1936

I am worried about the political situation and I decided to go over and have a talk with Steve Early about it this morning. It was a good opportunity because the President went up to New York last night. I told Steve that I thought that we were losing ground. He said he had thought so until two or three weeks ago but that he thought the turn came then. His judgment is based upon what comes to him from the newspaper correspondents. I replied that the turn might have come but that we weren't going to be able to kiss our way through this next election and that we were in grave danger of being put on the run. I had quite a long talk with him and in general we were in agreement.

Here is the situation. Al Smith is to speak in Washington at a big dinner next Saturday night under the auspices of the Liberty League. He has been getting a wonderful build-up for this meeting. Harry Slattery tells me that his information is that it will be the biggest banquet ever held at the Mayflower Hotel. Demands are coming in at such a rate that tables will be placed in the main corridor of the hotel. Smith is to have up to an hour on a national hookup. He has already declined to be a guest at the White House on the occasion of this visit, and every indication is that he is going after the Administration with a savage attack. The whole country will be listening in and the newspapers will give wide publicity to the speech. Now we have done absolutely nothing to discount this speech or to counteract it. Steve told me that he and Charley Michelson were discussing with the President the selection of someone to reply to Al Smith. The President suggested Governor McNutt, of Indiana, but Early said he wasn't big enough or well enough known. Early said Senator Robinson, the Democratic Leader of the Senate, who is a forceful speaker and who ran as a candidate for Vice President on the ticket with Al Smith, was the man. The President at once agreed but Michelson said that the selection of Robinson would be dignifying Smith unduly. At this Steve scoffed, but Michelson has done absolutely nothing to get Robinson. Neither has Jim Farley. The result is that with Smith scheduled to speak a week from now, nothing has been done.

I told Steve that the situation generally called for a fighting attitude on our part. I pointed out that the President's message to Congress was a fighting message but that there has been no follow-up. I criticized Jim Farley and told Steve that if I were the President, I would forbid him to make any speeches anywhere. I think his speeches are doing harm. Steve agreed with me so far as the country outside of New York is concerned. Steve said that the President would have to run his own campaign and I said that this was too much of a load for him to carry but that somebody ought to be running it. I spoke of how Farley does not consult anyone on political matters, so far as I know. I related what has come to my ears lately with reference to his plan not to discuss politics even with men like George Dern, Cordell Hull, and Homer Cummings, the latter two of whom have been chairmen of the Democratic National Committee.

I reminded Steve that many a big politician has been spoiled by making himself believe that he is an orator. I think Farley has succumbed to this malady. Speeches are written for him and he travels about the country delivering them, only to be ridiculed by the newspapers and by people generally. He carries no conviction because people know he hasn't any settled views on any subject and no background against which to set up any views if he did have them. In the meantime details are not being attended to. Steve said that Farley's chief value was as a man out in front and I agreed that this was his forte. He told me of two or three instances where Farley had pressing engagements elsewhere when meetings were being held here in Washington on important political matters involving strategy and procedure.

He talked to me about Charley Michelson, and it was clear that he is far from satisfied with what Michelson is doing. Steve says that all the stuff that Michelson is turning out is purely critical. He thinks Michelson ought to be permitted to fill out his three years' contract, but he remarked that Claude Bowers would soon be in the country and indicated that Bowers will take over a large part of Michelson's work. Steve expressed the hope that this could be done without unduly hurting Michelson's feelings because Michelson would be dangerous if he went over to the enemy. He made the statement that Michelson was really with Shouse and Al Smith and that crowd, with whom he was associated before Roosevelt's nomination. He said that Michelson was really opposed to Roosevelt and did not like him. He said that he had information that occasionally Shouse and Michelson lunched together in an obscure corner of the Mayflower dining room with their heads almost touching over a small table as they conferred. He tried to reach Michelson a day or two ago to see what has been done about getting Robinson to answer Smith and found that he had done nothing and was in Philadelphia looking over the arrangements for the Democratic National Convention next June.

My own view of this situation is that unless it is taken hold of pretty quickly, it may well spell disaster to the Democratic ticket next November. Steve agreed with me that there is no head to anything and no direction from any quarter and that the fight that ought to be put up is entirely lacking. I tried to make it clear to him that my own view is that we ought to be fighting all along the line. I think that instead of allowing Smith to start the offensive by his speech here next Saturday, he should have been put on the defensive by a savage attack prior to that date.

The newspapers this morning carried a story of the resignation of Under Secretary of the Treasury Coolidge, who is a direct descendant of Thomas Jefferson, and of L. W. Robert, Jr., an Assistant Secretary of the Treasury. Steve told me that there had been a row between Coolidge and Morgenthau and that Morgenthau had asked for this resignation. He remarked that nobody seemed to be able to get along with Morgenthau. This resignation was asked for and given two or three weeks ago but its announcement was withheld at Steve's instance because he did not want it to appear at a time when the Budget message was going into Congress. It was at Steve's suggestion that the resignation of Robert was asked for. As he remarked to me, and as I agreed, that resignation should have been forthcoming a long time ago. It was Steve's idea to tie these two resignations in together and announce them at a time that would do least damage to the President's cause. They were to have been announced next Monday, but the *Baltimore Sun* had a tip yesterday that Coolidge was about to resign, so Steve let them go this morning.

I brought up with Steve Early, as I have with the President, the question of William Randolph Hearst, who has been attacking the Administration viciously now for months. I think that there should be a counterattack. I thoroughly believe that all that it will be necessary to do in order to discredit him will be to show him to the American people for what he is and what he represents.

Steve told me that a friend of his who was close to Marion Davies was convinced that Hearst's attitude toward the Administration was mellowing. He went on to say that Marion Davies was strong for the President and the Administration and that she was working persistently on Hearst. Steve said that none of the Hearst newspapers any more were carrying the expression "raw deal" instead of "new deal." I left Steve's office far from being convinced that there is any basis for the belief that Hearst is mellowing in his attitude toward the Administration and I told Steve that I was skeptical. I recalled that the President had made the same statement to me recently. I think the President and Steve are just fooling themselves about Hearst. He is against the Administration and the Administration might just as well face the fact. I believe a real offensive ought to be opened up against Hearst with the determination to show him to the country for what he really is.

Thursday, January 23, 1936

Monday morning I had a short session with the President. I hadn't seen him since before I went on my recent trip so that I had an accumulation of matters. We cleared up a large number but I wasn't able to get through and McIntyre put me down for luncheon with the President on Wednesday. I did have an opportunity to talk just a little politics with the President. I find him much more ready to talk politics than he has been and he seems quite friendly. I have a feeling that he is overconfident as a result of the optimistic reports that Jim Farley keeps pouring in to him.

On Wednesday I went back to the White House to lunch. Norman Hapgood had the appointment just ahead of me. When I went in, the President told me that Hapgood had recently seen Al Smith and had discussed with him the scope of the speech that he is to make here Saturday night. According to Hapgood, Al is going to advocate the return of the United States to what he regards as fundamental constitutional principles, which means a larger exercise of states' rights.

Before Otto Kahn died recently, Hapgood had a talk with him, and he asked Kahn whether the bankers had learned anything as the result of this depression. Kahn admitted that they hadn't learned a thing and predicted that in ten or fifteen years we would have another terrific crash. That one, according to Kahn, will be the last one, meaning that our social and political structure will not stand the shock. Hapgood related this incident to Al Smith in his talk with him, but Smith scouted the suggestion that there might be such a crash. Hapgood asked him whether, if he thought Kahn was right, it would alter his views about having state control of banking, etc. Al replied that it would not, that he would rather go through another crash on the constitutional principles that he advocates.

Among other questions, I discussed with the President the Democratic political situation in Illinois. I showed him an editorial from the *Chicago Tribune* to the effect that the refusal of the Democratic organization to endorse Governor Horner for renomination was a just penalty that Horner had to pay for putting through in Illinois legislation in support of the national recovery program. I pointed out to the President that Horner was being penalized for his support of the Administration. I told him also that late reports were to the effect that the Kelly-Nash machine would refuse an endorsement to State's Attorney Courtney and to John Sonsteby, chief justice of the Municipal Court. The President knows Courtney but he didn't know who Sonsteby was. I explained that Sonsteby was one of the leaders among the Scandinavians in Chicago, and in addition had always been strong with labor. I remarked that here was a Democratic organization offending at one and the same time a Jewish governor, a Scandinavian chief jus-

tice of the Municipal Court, and a young Irish-Catholic state's attorney. I told the President that my information was that Governor
Horner, who has announced his intention to make a primary fight
for the Democratic nomination for governor, has already endorsed
both Courtney and Sonsteby, and that if the three made common
cause, they would probably smash the machine.

The President asked me about Dr. Herman Bundesen, who has
been selected as the organization candidate for governor. I have a
very poor opinion of Bundesen and told the President so. Then I
talked about "Curley" Brooks who is being strongly supported by
the *Tribune* for the Republican nomination for governor, telling
the President that some people thought that Kelly was putting up
Bundesen as a pushover for Brooks.

The whole trouble with the Illinois situation from the Democratic point of view is that Farley has every faith in Kelly and is
going along with him to the limit. The Kelly organization has also
contributed generously toward the payment of the debt of the
Democratic National Committee. I still think that the President
has illusions about the size of the vote that Kelly will be able to
deliver to him in Cook County as a result of the tremendous vote
that Kelly himself got for mayor last year, although on a previous
occasion I tried to make it clear that this was a phony vote and that
the President could not possibly expect to receive anything like it.

Mike Igoe, United States Attorney, came in to see me today. I
have known Mike for a good many years and he talked freely to
me. He is one of the smartest politicians I know and I talked
frankly to him. I find that he is not being consulted at all on the
Illinois situation, although when he was appointed he was told
that he would be. Although he is a loyal Catholic, he knows that
Cardinal Mundelein is mixing up in local politics in support of
Kelly, and he resents it. I remember that years ago George Brennan
told me that while many Continental Catholics will take orders
from their priests as to how to vote, if a priest should tell an Irish-
man how to vote, his parishioner would tell him to go to hell. I related this to Mike today and he said that was right.

Mike sizes the situation up as I do. He says that Horner is going
to make a fight and that the Jews, even those who until recently
have been criticizing Horner, are now out for him. He pointed
out that Dr. Bundesen was born in Berlin, which is further fuel
to the Jewish flame on account of Hitler's attitude toward that race.

He said that the plan originally was to squeeze Horner out, in which event Kelly would have been the candidate for governor. When Horner refused to make way, Kelly inspired a lot of candidacies. At first he said it had to be a downstate man, but in the end he and his machine swung to Bundesen. Igoe also agrees that Senator Lewis can probably be re-elected and will be a tower of strength to the Democratic ticket. I told him that it looked to me as if Illinois would go Republican next November and he believes it will.

Igoe says that Kelly is in absolute control of the machine and that he is a vindictive and unforgiving man, although he carefully and skillfully conceals his real feelings. He remarked on the closeness of Kelly with Frank Hague, of Jersey City, and said he believed that both of them wanted to occupy prominent positions in the national scene. I told him that I had been told that Kelly had bargained for my place as his price for delivery for the ticket next fall, but I also expressed the opinion that he wouldn't be able to deliver and wouldn't have anything to cash in on. Igoe agreed with the latter part of this although he had not heard any reports about Kelly's possible Cabinet aspirations. Mike thinks the fight is going to be a hard one all over the country. He spoke of the high repute in which I stand with everyone, even with those who do not like me personally. He said that Tom Courtney had not solicited the support of the Kelly machine but, on the contrary, had announced that he was going to be a candidate whether he had the organization endorsement or not. He said that if Courtney had to fight, he would fight with him without asking Washington what it wanted him to do, but that on the governorship he would bide his time for the present.

Last night was the annual dinner of the American Planning and Civic Association at the Mayflower Hotel. I have attended these meetings the last three years and I went again last night at the especial request of Mr. Delano. After some preliminary talks, Henry Wallace read a prepared speech on the topic of co-operation with the Department of the Interior. I followed as the last speaker and I spoke extemporaneously but without any bitterness or harshness of expression or manner.

I twitted Henry rather unmercifully about the co-operation which he had been boasting about. Of course the crowd was friendly to this Department, since one of its fundamental objects is to support the national parks. The crowd was with me all along the line and seemed to enjoy my slams. Although I had had a wretched night the night before, not having slept after half past two in the morning, with the result that all day yesterday I was almost ill, and despite the fact that I had a raging headache last night and was unutterably bored at the dinner, since I had to sit between two impossible dowagers, I did quite well. I felt this myself, and it seemed to be the general opinion of my friends and others who spoke to me afterward.

Unfortunately, the newspapers this morning printed a garbled report of the meeting and conveyed the impression that I had been caustic and sarcastic. Naturally, they want to try to make it appear that there is a row on if two Cabinet officers kid each other. At the conclusion of my speech Henry and I shook hands and he said to me that he appreciated the fine spirit in which I took the thing. I certainly never for once gave the appearance of bitterness. My remarks were kept in a humorous vein and were never caustic or sarcastic. As a matter of fact, as I have said on other occasions, I am personally very fond of Henry Wallace, although I don't like some things about his Department or the way in which some of its bureaus, especially the Forest Service, tries to undermine this Department.

Friday, January 24, 1936

At Cabinet meeting this afternoon Henry Morgenthau went out, as he usually does, about three o'clock. Apparently he calls up his Department to find out what late news there may be. When he came back a little later, he spoke in a whisper to the President and then the President, with his eyes on the clock, said that he wanted us to remember that just before half past three on this particular date General Motors was selling the American dollar short. The pound sterling is over the five-dollar mark today. The President made some caustic reference to the patriotism of this particular corporation in selling short the currency of its own country. The Vice President raised some question as to the accuracy of the information, but Morgenthau vouched for it and said that he knew it absolutely. He explained that while General Motors bought British exchange from time to time in fairly large quantities, this particular transaction was a very unusual and heavy one. The surmise is that this depreciation of the dollar by selling it short has some connection with a speech that Al Smith is to make here at the Mayflower Hotel tomorrow night. The du Pont interests have very heavy investments in General Motors and largely control its policies. Alfred Sloan, Jr., the president of General Motors, used to be a du Pont employee.

There was a good deal of general discussion of the constitutional issue which may be interjected in this campaign before we are through with it. The President said that word is coming to him from widely separated parts of the country that people are beginning to show a great deal of interest in the constitutional questions that have been raised by recent Supreme Court decisions. Attorney General Cummings said that his Department looked through the files recently to see who had endorsed Justice Roberts for appointment to the Supreme Court bench but that this information was missing from the files. The President made the point, based upon some statement by Harold J. Laski, that the Supreme Court, in its decisions on New Deal legislation, was dictating what it believed should be the social philosophy of the nation, without reference either to the law or the Constitution. Miss Perkins is fearful that the general run of citizens will be against the Administration on this issue and that they will feel that the New Deal has proved a failure, as the result of the opinions of the Supreme Court on New Deal legislation. It is plain to see, from what the President said today and has said on other occasions, that he is not at all averse to the Supreme Court declaring one New Deal statute after another unconstitutional. I think he believes that the Court will find itself pretty far out on a limb before it is through with it and that a real issue will be joined on which we can go to the country.

For my part, I hope so. Here is an issue that must be faced by the country sooner or later, unless we are prepared to submit to the arbitrary and final dictates of a group of men who are not elected by the people and who are not responsible to the people: in short, a judicial tyranny imposed by men appointed for life and who cannot be reached except by the slow and cumbersome process of impeachment.

Henry Wallace remarked that some sort of a background ought to be built up against which this issue could be presented to the people, and at this point I said that if any members of the Administration were to make speeches on Lincoln's Birthday they could not have a better opportunity to make a strong point of

Lincoln's attitude toward the Constitution. In this connection, I spoke of the fact that Lincoln himself had amended the Constitution by issuing his Emancipation Proclamation.

The President referred to his veto of the bonus bill. He said he had written it out in longhand and had worked on it until one o'clock Thursday morning. He had told neither McIntyre nor Early what he proposed to do on the bill, but he had instructed Early to prepare two press releases, one on the basis of a veto and the other on that of an approval. Henry Wallace was in to see him at ten-thirty this morning and he gave Wallace the first knowledge of what he intended to do.

Now this struck me as being a curious attitude on the part of the President of the United States on such an important measure. He chuckled as he spoke of how he had "put it over" on McIntyre and Early. When I saw Early last Saturday, he brought up the question of the bonus and said that he did not know what the President intended to do, but that he very much hoped that he would be consistent and veto it.

Here was a very important measure and the President permitted the country to wonder whether he would be for it or against it until his veto message was dispatched to Congress. The veto message itself merely referred to the one on the previous bill and was totally lacking in vigor or argument of any sort. Even Administration members of Congress were left in the dark as to the Administration attitude. I cannot see either the politics or the statesmanship in a course of this sort. The bill would throw a further heavy strain on the Treasury. If the President was against it, he ought to have fought it and he should have allowed the congressional leaders to know what his position was. I do not like this playful attitude on such an important measure. As I have already set down, at last Cabinet meeting he would not even give the Vice President the opportunity that he requested to ask him a question about the bonus.

Monday, January 27, 1936

Last Saturday was the lightest day I ever have had in this office. I was actually through by half past ten and I ran out for the rest of the day. Saturday night I worked on my Lincoln speech until ten o'clock, when I turned on the radio to listen to Al Smith, who was speaking at a dinner under the auspices of the American Liberty League. This dinner had been widely commented upon in all the newspapers of the country for the last couple of weeks and there was a big crowd in attendance on the assurance that Smith would go after the Administration without gloves.

It was a good political speech but not startling. Al was all for up-holding the Constitution, and he charged the President, without mentioning him by name, with direct violation of the planks in the last Democratic national platform. The hits he scored were pal-pable ones but, of course, there is an answer to most of his charges. The only thing he said of particular significance was something which indicated that he and his friends might bolt the next Democratic convention if Roosevelt is renominated on a platform endorsing his Administration. Toward the end of the speech he labeled the Administration policies as being communistic and pleaded for a return to constitutional government.

I was struck with Al Smith's bad radio voice. His utterance is so thick that at times it is difficult to understand. As a matter of fact, with the closest attention on my part there were words and phrases that were unintelligible to me.

Shortly after seven o'clock, while I was dressing, Mike Straus called me on the telephone to tell me about the discovery of a de-fense made by Al Smith, when he was a candidate for President in 1928, to a charge by Hoover that he was advocating a social-istic state. Hoover had made this charge in a speech in Madison Square Garden and Smith, two or three days later, had replied to it in Boston. In his reply Smith said that the cry of socialism had always been raised by powerful interests that desired to put a damper upon progressive legislation. It was raised, according to him, by reactionary elements in the Republican party and he had fought it for twenty-five years.

I told Mike to write the thing out and when I got to the Shore-ham Hotel, where the Washington Town Hall has its meetings, he handed it to me. Senator Barkley, of Kentucky, was on my panel, and I told Mike to ask Senator Barkley to put to me a question that would give me a chance to quote the colloquy between Hoover and Smith. This Barkley did, and the way the thing was handled and what was said brought down the house. The audience just loved it and the newspapers grabbed it off. I understand that usually the newspapers pay little attention to the Washington Town Hall, but there was a full gallery of correspondents present last night in anticipation of a possible reply to Al Smith on my part. I gave them what they wanted and I gave it in a form that from our point of view was very useful.

The President called me up this afternoon to pat me on the back for what I had said about Al Smith last night. Naturally, this pleased me very much indeed, as nothing like it has ever happened before. He said he was perfectly delighted with it and went on to tell me how it had been played in *The New York Times* and the *Baltimore Sun*.

There was a meeting in the office of Secretary Dern this afternoon, attended by Dern, Henry Wallace, Dr. Kneipp, a member of his Forestry staff, Burlew, and myself. The occasion was to discuss whether certain scattered parcels of public land in Utah should be turned over to the Forest Service. I made the direct charge that there was no local demand for this to be done and that the whole thing had been fomented and encouraged and kept going by the Forest Service. I was pretty savage in my onslaught and deliberately so. At one stage Henry Wallace got pretty much worked up, but I didn't back down at all, although after the session adjourned I put my arm through Henry's and told him I wasn't going to get into any personal row with him.

Kneipp fought very strenuously for a favorable report, but I fought so savagely that I beat him back. On the facts, neither Henry Wallace nor George Dern was convinced that the land should be transferred to the Forest Service, so that Burlew and I left with the flag of victory perched upon our banners, at least temporarily, although we had gone into the meeting expecting that we would have to make a modified report.

Wednesday, January 29, 1936

Monday was Jane Dahlman's birthday and I gave a small dinner party for her. The guests were Miss Marguerite Le Hand, Miss Grace Tully, Mr. and Mrs. Rollin Larrabee, Tom Corcoran, and Edward J. Foley, Jr. It was a cold day with a high wind and the wind certainly did whistle through the house. We just managed to keep it comfortable with the fire going full tilt all day and with the door leading to the sun porch firmly closed. We had a very good time. Practically everyone knew everyone else and it was a jolly party. Tom Corcoran brought his accordion and guitar and kept things going after dinner.

Jane had been invited to the musicale at the White House, following the official dinner to the Supreme Court Justices, on Tuesday night. I had asked Mrs. Helm, Mrs. Roosevelt's social secretary, to put her on the list for one or more of the musicales and she had done so. While Jane has a very minor position in the Park Service, she ranks this sort of thing as the niece of John Cudahy, our Ambassador to Poland, and by reason of her close connection with my own family. She loves music and I wanted her to have a chance to go to a party at the White House, although I always shun them myself whenever I can.

Jane was happy to get the invitation but said that she wouldn't go unless I went with her. That I was glad to do. She had bought a new evening gown for the occasion and, unlike most red-headed women, she has a real sense of color in clothes. I don't think I am exaggerating at all when I say that she was the most striking-looking woman at the White House last night. She has the freshness of youth and her coloring is superb. Her hair is really beautiful. She was happy and it was evident that many people found her interesting. I took malicious pleasure in introducing her to Mrs. Homer Cummings, Mrs. J. Fred Essary, and one or two other women who I knew would be burning up with curiosity as to who she was and why I happened to have her at the White House. Before we left, two or three young officers who had not even been introduced to her found means of entering into conversation with her, and if it had been a general party with people moving around, I think she would have been the center of a very interested group. Captain Brown, the naval aide of the President, whom I ran across at the White House today, commented upon Jane's appearance, and so did the President when I was in with him. Both of them thought that she was not only very good looking but that she was sweet and attractive. They were right on all of these propositions. She is with me a good deal and I have never had anyone in the house, man or woman, who creates such a genuinely happy atmosphere, who is so companionly and so pleasant to get along with.

Dr. Elwood Mead, Commissioner of Reclamation, died Sunday night and I went to his funeral this morning. Dr. Mead was a fine type of public servant, zealous, incorruptible, and intelligent. He has done a fine job for his country. Generally speaking, he had no enemies. He always seemed to be able to get along with Senators and Congressmen and others in the West where his work lay, and yet he wasn't a yes man by any means. He was seventy-nine or eighty years old. He had a sudden stroke and died within a few days.

I had a session with the President this afternoon, following Senator Norris, who had luncheon with him. He and Senator Norris had been discussing the constitutional situation and he continued that discussion with me. He went over the same ground that he covered in a recent talk which I have set down in these memoranda. On that other occasion his proposal was for an amendment to change the Constitution so as to limit drastically the power of the courts to pass upon the constitutionality of legislative acts. What he said to me today by way of background was precisely what he said then, except that he has come to the conclusion that he can accomplish his purpose by congressional act which would be preferable to a constitutional amendment. He discussed this with Senator Norris and he told me he had not mentioned it to anyone else. I gathered that Norris, who has been rather despairing of what would happen to the country in view of the recent decisions by the Supreme Court, was considering offering a bill or joint resolution.

The plan suggested is for Congress to pass an act taking away from all lower courts the right to pass upon the constitutionality of statutes. This right would be given to the Supreme Court as a matter of original jurisdiction. The Court would be required to give advisory opinions. It would be expected to say in advance of the passing of a law whether it was constitutional. If in its opinion the law was unconstitutional, then it would have to specify in what respects it was unconstitutional and point out what language, if substituted, would make it constitutional. With this advice, the act would go back to Congress and Congress could either modify the language as suggested by the Supreme Court, or it could pass the act again in its original form, in which event it would be the law of the land, whatever the Supreme Court might say.

I made the obvious remark that the Supreme Court would declare unconstitutional such an act as the President had in mind and he said that of course it would. To meet that situation his plan would be somewhat as follows: Congress would pass a law, the Supreme Court would declare it unconstitutional, the President would then go to Congress and ask it to instruct him whether he was to follow the mandate of Congress or the mandate of the Court. If the Congress should declare that its own mandate was to be followed, the President would carry out the will of Congress through the offices of the United States Marshals and ignore the Court.

I told him that this would be taking a leaf out of the book of Andrew Jackson, who, on the occasion when the Supreme Court declared a banking act in which he was interested unconstitutional, declared: "Well, let the Court enforce its decree."

There isn't any doubt at all that the President is really hoping that the Supreme Court will continue to make a clean sweep of all New Deal legislation, throwing out the TVA Act, the Securities Act, the Railroad Retirement Act, the Social Security Act, the Guffey Coal Act, and others. He thinks the country is beginning to sense this issue but that enough people have not yet been affected by adverse decisions so as to make a sufficient feeling on a Supreme Court issue.

I told the President that I hoped this would be the issue in the next campaign. I believe it will have to be fought out sooner or later, and I remarked to him that the President who faced this issue and drastically curbed the usurped power of the Supreme Court would go down through all the ages of history as one of the great Presidents.

Henry Wallace has made two or three very caustic criticisms recently of the Supreme Court. I mentioned this to the President with approval and he said that he had told Henry that he could go as far as he liked. This ought to make the way clear for what I want to say about the Supreme Court in my speech on Lincoln at Springfield on February 11.

Friday, January 31, 1936

At the Cabinet meeting this afternoon Homer Cummings brought up for discussion the question of whether we should prosecute our appeal in the Supreme Court of the decision in the Louisville case, which denied the Government the right to condemn property for a low-cost housing project. Nathan R. Margold, Solicitor for the Interior Department, has been working on this case. When I was in the Virgin Islands, he sent me a radio telling me that on further consideration and in line with the opinions expressed by Tom Corcoran and Ben Cohen, he was of the opinion that this case should be dismissed on the motion of the Government because he was afraid that we would lose it and that the decision might affect the whole PWA program. My reply to him was to the effect that a matter of Administration policy was involved. I was of the opinion that it was the desire of the President to go ahead with all of these New Deal cases and let the Supreme Court knock them all out if that is what it wants to do. I advised him to talk with the Attorney General and be guided by Administration policy.

Yesterday Tom Corcoran and Ben Cohen came in to renew their representations that we ought not to go ahead with this case. Their fear is that the Court may declare the case unconstitutional because of a defect in the powers under which the President has delegated his authority to me. They think that if the case should be decided on this point, public opinion would be adverse to the Administration. The opinion would be that if all that was the matter with the law was due to imperfect drafting of the power to delegate authority, the Administration would come in for criticism. In other words, an adverse decision in this case would not help to build up the body of opinion that we are hoping is being built up in the country against the Supreme Court as a result of its adverse decisions on New Deal legislation. They also thought that the whole PWA program might be knocked out by a possible adverse opinion.

At their suggestion I talked yesterday over the telephone with Homer Cummings about this matter, and today he brought it up at the Cabinet meeting. The President was firmly of the opinion that we ought to go ahead with the case. He scouted the idea that anyone could draw an act that would pass the scrutiny of the Supreme Court in its present outlook on New Deal legislation. He thought that if all PWA projects should be suspended as the result of an adverse decision by the Supreme Court, it would be all to the good.

The only member of the Cabinet who expressed a contrary view on this matter was Miss Perkins, but I suppose that that was to be expected of a woman. Apparently she thinks that we ought to pussyfoot on the Supreme Court issue and not present anything, if possible, that is likely to elicit an adverse opinion. The President seems quite firmly set the other way. There doesn't seem to me to be any doubt that he is entirely willing to have the Supreme Court knock out every New Deal law. It is clear that he is willing to go to the country on this issue but he wants the issue to be as strong and clear as possible, which means that he hopes the Supreme Court will declare unconstitutional every New Deal case that comes before it.

It happens that I am fully in accord with the President's view on this matter. I believe that this issue will have to be fought out sooner or later and no more important issue has arisen since the Civil War. Naturally, I would like to be in this fight and be a member of the Administration that is carrying it on.

Governor Talmadge, of Georgia, at a convention of anti-Roosevelt Democrats held in Macon, Georgia, two days ago, made an attack on me. He said that, contrary to law, I had bought certain Georgia road certificates in connection with some PWA projects and that I had tried to drag him in with me in my unlawful course. Yesterday at my press conference I gave out a statement covering the real facts. The truth is that Talmadge deliberately lied when he made this statement. He came to Washington begging me to take these certificates, and when I told him that they were not legally saleable to us, he promised that at the next session of the legislature he would support a law which would legalize them. He made this promise in a letter over his own signature and he annexed to his letter a draft of a bill which had been agreed to by his own attorney general and by the legal staff of PWA. The man is beneath contempt. He not only lies but, like most poor liars, he follows up his original lies with additional prevarications.

Tuesday, February 4, 1936

I had an appointment with the President at twelve-thirty, and while I was waiting for him, Steve Early came in. He had not known that I was there, but it happened that he had the copy of my Lincoln speech which Mike Straus had sent over to him for clearance. Steve told me that it was a great speech. He insisted on reading some passages of it to McIntyre and told him about others. When I went into the President's office, Steve followed me in and he told the President it was a great speech and that I wanted it cleared. He pointed out one or two passages for the President to read, and the President passed it over to me with a smile and said to go ahead.

The President asked me at our conference if I would call in Senators Norris, Johnson, and others and go ahead with the revamping of the Progressive League that supported him in 1932. I told him I would do this after my return from Chicago.

It sounded today as if the President is about ready to turn someone loose on William Randolph Hearst. He has dug up a letter written by Theodore Roosevelt to Hearst in which he flays Hearst unmercifully, and he also has what Elihu Root said about Hearst when Root attacked him. He said he was going to have a speech written for Dan Roper and turn Dan loose on one of the occasions when he speaks to a business group. I couldn't help joking a little about this. I can't quite see Dan Roper launching any such thunderbolt as the President has in mind.

Sunday, February 9, 1936

The President told me on Friday that he would be re-elected all right, but that the next four years would be very tough ones, with a crisis in 1941. I told him I hoped that something would be done during the next four years to build up a leader who could carry on the work of this Administration. He said that he believed there would be a realignment of parties, and he pointed to the defection of Al Smith and Governor Talmadge as indicating a trend of that sort.

The President said that by a combination of good luck and good judgment some things had been accomplished in this Administration. He told me that this was the longest period since Arthur was President in 1882 that Federal troops had not been called out in some part of the country on account of labor troubles. He also said that it was the longest period since 1892 that Marines or soldiers had not been landed by the United States on foreign soil. I had not known either of these two facts and they certainly speak well for this Administration. Personally, I am especially pleased that this Administration has not landed soldiers or Marines in any foreign country. I think there is a real disposition to keep hands off, although I do not like the situation in Cuba. I think that this Government is interfering altogether too much in the internal affairs of Cuba, but it is being done through diplomatic channels.

At the Cabinet meeting we spent almost an hour discussing the Neutrality Bill. There does not seem to be much possibility of the passage of the bill that the President wants and which would give him rather wide powers. The conclusion was that it would perhaps be better to re-enact the present "bob-tailed" neutrality law, leaving a more complete bill for consideration after election. The Vice President insisted that Congress had never made war in this country but it had always been made by the Executive. There seemed to be no disagreement on this point. The Vice President went on to say that the President ought to give definite and specific assurance to the country that we are not going to be dragged into war. There has never been any doubt in my mind that the President has not the slightest desire or intention of getting us into war; quite the contrary.

Friday, February 14, 1936

At Cabinet meeting today the Vice President said that he had heard that the Federal Reserve Board Advisory Committee of twelve had been sending out word that Government bonds should not be bought or held, with the view to unsettling the bond market and casting doubt upon the Government credit. The President said that one way to handle that situation, if it arose, would be to print enough greenbacks in order to buy every Government bond when it got below par. The bonds thus retired would mean a great saving in interest and the greenbacks themselves could be retired from year to year until we were again on a normal currency base. Morgenthau said that the bond market recently had been strong and entirely satisfactory. The President remarked further that to put greenbacks into circulation instead of bonds would be good financial policy, provided, of course, Congress would set up a sufficient sinking fund every year to retire the greenbacks in an orderly manner.

Mr. Delano came in to see me today to talk about my hope that this can be made the Conservation Department of the Government. He said he had been talking to John Gray, formerly of the faculty of Northwestern University, who had told him that I was the strongest and most outstanding member of the Cabinet but that I was not a good negotiator. Mr. Delano expressed this as his own opinion and I told him that he was exactly right. I recognized this fault in myself. I went on to say that there was a background to the bill that I have in Congress to change the name of the Department that I thought he didn't know.

Then I told him about my negotiations with Wallace and Tugwell, their agreement to an interchange of bureaus which would bring Forestry over here among other agencies, our going to the President and telling him that we had made this agreement, and Wallace's subsequent reneging on the whole thing. I told him that

Wallace was the last man in the Cabinet that I wanted to get into a controversy with because I liked him better than any other member of the Cabinet. Then I told him that the bill was introduced as the result of a talk over the telephone with the President just before he went on his spring vacation last year. I showed how the creation of the office of Under Secretary fitted in with Wallace's and my understanding about an interchange of bureaus between our two Departments. I explained that with this background and with the President's approval of the bill changing the name of the Department, I went ahead in all good faith only to find that Wallace and others in his Department were fighting this bill and were appearing at hearings in opposition to it. I told him that at this point I had to fight since I had no other option, making it clear, however, that I had not started the fight and would have avoided it if I could.

Mr. Delano said that he was in full sympathy with my position on conservation and my desire to build up a Conservation Department. With reference to Forestry, he said specifically and categorically that Forestry had no right to establish recreation areas, that all such areas ought, as a matter of course, to come to Interior, and that we also ought to have all forests that are not to be lumbered for commercial purposes, leaving it to Agriculture to administer lands where new tree crops are to be grown. I did not discuss this at length with him, but for my part I would be willing to work out something on that basis. I believe that in the end all of the forest activities would come to this Department if we once got them headed this way, and even if they didn't, we would have in this Department the established forests and the recreational facilities which are now being set up in the forest areas.

At the end I remarked casually to Mr. Delano that the question was perhaps an academic one with me, since there was a feeling in a number of quarters that even if the President should be re-elected he would not keep me on as Secretary of the Interior. He said he didn't believe this at all and indicated that he thought the President would feel that he would want me to continue as a member of his Administration. Mr. Delano has always been very considerate and gracious to me, giving me to understand that he believes in me. Today he told me how much he admired my ability, integrity, and intellectual honesty.

Homer Cummings repeated some interesting gossip about the

Supreme Court at the last Cabinet meeting. He said there was a report to the effect that Chief Justice Hughes was willing to go either way in the AAA case. The Chief Justice does not like five-to-four opinions and if Justice Roberts had been in favor of sustaining AAA, the Chief Justice would have cast his vote that way also. Attorney General Cummings also said that the general opinion now seems to be that a majority of the Court cannot agree on an opinion in the TVA case, which explains the delay in handing it down.

Tuesday, February 18, 1936

I had a session with the President on Monday. He asked me whether I had heard Father Coughlin on the radio Sunday afternoon and I told him that I had never heard him. He said he was worth listening to. On Sunday afternoon Coughlin made a violent attack on Congressman O'Connor, chairman of the Rules Committee directly, and on President Roosevelt also, indirectly. He charged that O'Connor was Roosevelt's man and that Roosevelt could either cause him to resign or have him removed as chairman of the Rules Committee. He demanded such action unless O'Connor should report out a rule which would bring up the Frazier-Lemke Farm Mortgage Bill. From what the President quoted to me, Father Coughlin must have made a very violent attack. It sounded outrageous to me—arrogant and blustering and altogether presuming. In the Monday morning papers Congressman O'Connor invited Coughlin to come to Washington and give him the pleasure of kicking him all the way from the Capitol to the White House. He said that he was a disgrace to the Catholic Church, of which Congressman O'Connor is a member. Father Coughlin also accused O'Connor of putting through a questionable bill involving payment for damages claimed on account of the world war. This bill the President vetoed and Coughlin said that he had vetoed it because he was afraid of the exposure that would follow if he should sign it.

According to the President, Father Coughlin's Washington representative went in to see Colonel McIntyre recently. He told McIntyre that he had never blackmailed the Administration but that there was something that Father Coughlin wanted. As I recall it, the demand was that the President put on pressure to get the Frazier-Lemke bill through, failing which Father Coughlin would attack the President. McIntyre told the man that this savored very strongly of blackmail and that he wouldn't even put up such a proposition to the President.

While I was with the President, the TVA decision was being read by Chief Justice Hughes, but the first reports that came over the ticker left us in utter confusion as to what the decision really was. I left before learning that the right to buy transmission lines from the Alabama Power Company had been sustained by a vote of eight to one, while the right of stockholders to file suit, thus giving the court jurisdiction, was upheld by a vote of five to four. Mr. Justice McReynolds was the sole dissenter on the main opinion.

It was mostly public works projects that I had to take up with the President. He is approving very few, although necessarily we have to take care of some rescissions and amendments. He told me that it would be necessary to give Pat Harrison $5 million more for Mississippi roads, making a total of $15 million in all.

Just as I was leaving, Miss Le Hand came in and said that some time she wished I would drop into her office as there was something that she wanted to speak to me about. The President inquired: "The thing we were discussing the other day?" and "Missy" answered yes. I went into her office with her and then she told me that the President had said recently that he wished there were some quiet place in the country where he could go occasionally without anyone knowing it, and "Missy" told him that she knew just the place. She then went on to describe my home and apparently painted it in glowing terms.

She pointed out that absolute secrecy would be necessary because, of course, to visit the home of one Cabinet officer and not that of others would arouse jealousies. I told her that I was sure the thing could be kept absolutely quiet and that he would not be disturbed there by anyone. She said when the weather got a little better she thought the President would want to come out with just a few friends to sit on the sun porch or the lawn and have a drink. She thinks that the President would like to bring Tom Corcoran along with his accordion and guitar because the President and his group like to sing together. I told her that, of course, I would be delighted to have the President come at any time and that if he ever wanted the house, I would be very glad to turn it over to him and his friends to use as they pleased.

I learned yesterday that apparently the President has turned thumbs down on my Department bill. Congressman Dempsey told me that he had told Congressman Cochran that he did not want anything done with this bill at this session. I must say that if he has done this, I do not like it. The bill was introduced originally at his suggestion and with his knowledge and consent. At the opening of this session of Congress I asked him whether he had any objection to my pressing my bill and he said he had not, provided only that it would not prolong the session of Congress. It could not possibly do that. I also feel that it is due to me that he should tell me if he does not want the bill pressed rather than kill it indirectly. We have struck some serious snags in the House lately and probably his opposition is the explanation for them. I shall talk to him about this at my first opportunity.

Mrs. Hiram Johnson called me up Wednesday evening to say that she had heard I was ill. I was out but I called her back later. She seemed like her old self. She really sounded friendly and cordial. I do not know what was the matter with her for the last year or so, but all of her old friends think that she has been unusually temperamental. She said that Hiram is laid up with some trouble with his foot and she suggested that if I were ill I had better come down and let her take care of both of us.

Late yesterday afternoon I had a call from Congressman Sweeney, of Ohio. He just had to see me on a matter that was important politically and otherwise! When he came in, he brought with him a man by the name of Ward, who is Father Coughlin's representative here. Ben Cohen also came along. Ward entered into a voluble statement which, when I unraveled it, disclosed to me that apparently there is a disposition on the part of one of the investigating committees on the Hill to find out whether he has had any interest in PWA contracts. He was a frothy talker, the kind that uses language to conceal thoughts as much as to express them. He did not make a very good impression on me. I told him that he would be given every chance to explain any circumstance that might seem to connect him with an interest in PWA contracts if an investigation should disclose such an interest. He kept referring to Ben Cohen for a certificate of character, but Cohen said nothing, and when he came in to see me today on another matter, all he said about Ward was that Ward had helped on the holding company bill at the last session.

Ward left, protesting innocence of any improper conduct in connection with PWA contracts and telling me what a fine job I was doing as Administrator of Public Works. He made very far from a good impression on me. Congressman Sweeney said practically nothing, but he did not look any too good either. Ward is the man who had the "blackmail" talk with Colonel McIntyre that the President told me about. McIntyre was at Secretary Hull's dinner last night and I told him about Ward and Sweeney having been in. He said they were both birds of a feather and both would bear close watching.

Tuesday, February 25, 1936

During my appointment with the President on Friday I told him that word had come to me that he was opposed to my Department bill and had told Congressman Cochran, of Missouri, or Senator Byrd, that he was not in favor of it passing at this session. He promptly denied this, saying that he had not talked with anyone about the bill for three or four weeks and that he had not told anyone that he was opposed to it. He said, however, that he did not think the bill would pass at this session. Then I asked him whether he would have any objection to our trying to pass that portion of the bill which provides for a change in name and he said he would not. I asked him further whether he would call off the dogs of war in the Administration who had been lobbying against the bill and he agreed to do this.

He brought up a matter that seemed at least slightly significant to me. He spoke of an estate in Maryland owned by Gordon Strong, of Chicago. This estate lies at the top of a mountain about an hour's drive from Washington. The President has in mind acquiring that property and developing it so that members of the Cabinet during the summer could have some restful, cool place within easy distance of Washington. He said that he wanted Henry Wallace and me to go out and look at it, but that, of course, nothing could be done on the proposition until after election. While this is not very significant, it did indicate that, at least for the moment, he has no thought in mind as to any change in the Cabinet so far as I am concerned. I realize, of course, that the incident is trivial.

I found myself in pretty good shape this morning. The final revised draft of my Union League speech was on my desk when I got to the office and it read all right as I went through it. At eleven-fifteen I went to the funeral of Colonel Henry L. Roosevelt, Assistant Secretary of the Navy, who died suddenly of heart disease on Saturday. Colonel Roosevelt was a distant cousin of the President's, and his career had been in the Marine Corps. He looked more like the late Theodore Roosevelt than any member of the family I have ever seen, and he was one of the two or three of the family to support Franklin D. Roosevelt. So far as I know, everyone liked him and respected him. I know I did. The funeral was at Saint John's Episcopal Church. The President, who had gone to Cambridge, Massachusetts, on Saturday and then on to Hyde Park, and who had not expected to return to Washington until Thursday, came down last night for the funeral. I think that all of the members of the Cabinet were there, although I did not see Secretary Hull.

Just to show that I am not immune to the meannesses that occasionally spring out in human nature, I must relate the following incident: The Cabinet and practically everyone else who could get into the church were in and seated, with the exception of the Presidential party and those who made up the immediate family of Colonel Roosevelt. Then the Presidential party came in, and looming large among it was Henry Morgenthau. For some reason, he did not go and seat himself with the President and Mrs. Roosevelt but turned up the first aisle. Here the pews were all marked off by ribbons, since they were being held in reserve for the immediate funeral cortege. Without waiting for an usher, Henry lifted the ribbon and came into the other section of the pew where I was sitting. In a couple of minutes a young naval officer came and told him he would find a place for him elsewhere. So Henry found himself ushered into a pew two or three back of where he had injected himself.

Tuesday, March 3, 1936

Monday was Charter Day at Howard University and I made the address. When I was in Chicago I had ordered a new cap and gown so that I was properly clad. At these college functions I have been borrowing caps and gowns and sometimes they have fitted me and sometimes they haven't. The gowns have been of poor quality and usually merely bachelors' gowns, whereas I am entitled to wear a doctor's gown. I selected from my doctors' hoods the one that seemed to have the best color effect and I believe it was the University of Alabama one. I talked for only about twenty-two minutes and my address was an amalgam of that part of my speech before the Chicago Urban League which dealt with Negro education and part of my University of Alabama commencement address on academic freedom. The two had pieced together very well and it was most cordially received by the audience. The Charter Day exercises were held in the chapel of the university. It is not a large auditorium and it was packed. Dr. Mordecai Johnson, president of the university, presented me in remarks that were very complimentary and eloquent. I was the only speaker.

I had about an hour with the President this morning going over an accumulation of Department matters. He told me that he had had a brain storm last night and that he had worked out a way to "let go of the bear's tail" on the Trans-Florida Ship Canal project. I remarked that I was glad that he realized it was a bear's tail and that he was willing to let go of it. His plan is to build a barge canal with locks over the highest section of land where otherwise a deep cut would have to be made with possible disturbances of the underground water supply. I told him that I hoped he wouldn't bind himself even to this but simply would suggest the possibility of a barge canal based upon a careful study of its geologic and economic effects. This is certainly one bad mess that the President rushed into over my protests.

Last night was the annual dinner of the Cabinet to the President and Mrs. Roosevelt. There are always a few others in addition to the ones mentioned, but who invites them or just why, I do not know. For instance, Mr. and Mrs. Morgenthau, Sr., are always there. The members of the President's secretariat I do not object to. The dinner itself was well cooked and well served and generous. I suspect that there will be a pretty stiff bill coming in for my share of the cost. The ten Cabinet members pay for the dinner. A baritone sang after the dinner and the whole affair passed off very well.

Colonel McIntyre called me to say that the President wanted General Markham and me to lunch with him and that I was to bring what data I had on the Passamaquoddy and Florida canal projects. However, General Markham didn't show up. I think he was at some hearing before a congressional committee. John Roosevelt, who is down from Harvard, lunched with us, and I found him a very attractive young chap. He is twenty-one and will graduate in June. He is well set up now. He is over six feet tall and weighs 190 pounds but he carries his weight well.

The President is trying to let go the tail of the Passamaquoddy bear, too. I told him that there was a good deal of local dissatisfaction with the way the project was being run. The Army engineers have bought a $17,000 yacht, and, according to what Dexter Cooper says, they have built seven houses costing $30,000 each. These are in addition to many less expensive houses. The natives of Eastport and that part of Maine seem to think that the Army engineers are spending money with a lavish hand and, of course, that goes against the Yankee grain. I told the President that the special board of engineers that I appointed some time ago to investigate the cost of this project had not yet reported. We commented again on the fact that the Army engineers had accepted Dexter Cooper's figures on cost without ever checking them until after the Government was committed and work was actually started. I remarked that this was like accepting a promoter's estimate of costs and that Dexter Cooper, with all due respect, was a promoter so far as this project is concerned.

We really didn't talk Government business to any extent. The President got to reminiscing about some of his political experiences in connection with the Boston police strike, which allegedly was settled by Coolidge but wasn't at all, and the Democratic National Conventions that nominated Cox and John W. Davis and Smith. He was most interesting and we had a very good time together. John followed the talk closely and intelligently. I didn't get away until almost half past two, with practically not a lick of work done.

In the House of Representatives today there was introduced a bill merely changing the name of the Department to the Department of Conservation. We think we can get this bill through this session, whereas the bill that was introduced last year seems to have no chance. I decided to take the best I could get and let it go at that. That, at least, will give us a substantial start toward what I want to accomplish.

At the Cabinet dinner Miss Le Hand told me that the other day the President said to her that no members of his Cabinet had been influenced by the social lobby but that Dan Roper had succumbed to big business influences. Her comment was that this seemed strange since Roper was such an old-timer both in politics and in Washington.

Monday, March 9, 1936

General Markham and I were called to the White House last Friday on the Quoddy project and the President again frankly expressed his wish to get out of this project as quickly and as gracefully as possible. He said that he thought it would be unconstitutional to go ahead with it in view of the TVA decision. He brought up the question of the cost of the current as compared with current produced by steam. General Markham said that unless the whole project was developed, which would mean an international agreement with Canada, the per kilowatt cost would be higher than for current produced by steam. Then the President started to do some figuring. He suggested that if a generous allowance of WPA money was put in, the cost on the basis of other than WPA money would be lower than for current produced by · steam. I told him that the country would consider the total cost, regardless of how it was divided or what it was called, and that, in my judgment, the best position to take was that the project would not be justified unless it went forward as a whole in co-operation with Canada. He agreed with this.

He asked General Markham about some alleged high costs in building of houses, etc., but the General seemed to have a satisfactory explanation. He told of having made a personal investigation.

I decided to play hooky for a day or two and went to New York on the two o'clock train Friday afternoon. I asked the President at the conclusion of the conference on Quoddy Friday whether I might run away and he said it would be all right. Friday night I went to see Helen Hayes in *Victoria Regina* and enjoyed it very much. It was well acted and well staged and was well worth seeing. I went to the opera Saturday afternoon, and Saturday night I again saw *First Lady*. I think I really enjoyed it more than I did the first time. I took the midnight train back to Washington.

Wednesday, March 11, 1936

During an interview with the President yesterday, I asked him whether in his opinion I would be of greater help in the coming campaign by openly affiliating with the Democratic party or by maintaining my political independence. He said that if I meant going to the convention as a delegate, he didn't see why I would want to go and that he thought it would be better for me to line up with Senator Norris and other Progressive Republicans. This decision is quite satisfactory to me because I would much rather do that than become a party Democrat.

McIntyre called me early in the afternoon and said that Ambassador Bingham was giving a cocktail party in his rooms at the Carlton and wanted me to come. I dropped in about half past five and partook of some excellent bourbon whisky. I had a talk with the Ambassador. He believes it is true that King Edward has a friendly feeling toward Germany and is anxious to bring about a better understanding between that country and his own. He spoke with some bitterness of a certain type of American who goes to London full of criticism of the American Government, requiring him to give out statements and make speeches correcting wrong impressions created.

Friday, March 13, 1936

I went to the Japanese Embassy for dinner last night. Miss Perkins was the ranking woman guest and I was ranking man guest. Senator King, Senator Burke, and Minority Leader Snell of the House were also guests. Among those at the dinner were several members of the Japanese Embassy staff. After the dinner, when the men were sitting together smoking, Senator King, in a very definite but very courteous manner, sparred with the Ambassador about Japan's attitude toward peace. I must say that the Japanese Ambassador handled himself with skill and tact, but he was altogether too clever not to notice the implied criticism. The Embassy itself is one of the most interesting and beautiful in Washington, according to my way of thinking. I especially love the table china. The dishes are handmade and hand-painted and they are very attractive.

At Cabinet meeting today Under Secretary Phillips of the Department of State, who was present in the absence of Secretary Hull, read from some dispatches from Europe. According to his information, the determination of Hitler to send troops into the neutralized Rhine region was made suddenly, although apparently preparations for this occupation have been under way for some time. It appears also that the conservatives in Germany were against this move. He also reported that there was a difference of opinion in France as to whether to negotiate with Germany or stand by the demand of the French Premier that there would be no negotiations until all of the German soldiers had been withdrawn from the occupied territory. He said that the French army wanted to move across the line at once, and the President remarked that probably it was only the lack of a popular leader in France who could rally the nation that held back the army.

It also developed that Great Britain proposes to lay down two battleships to match the two that Japan is building and that France also intends to lay down in the near future. Admiral Standley, from London, has sent word to the President that the British would like us to lay down two battleships, but the President is unwilling to ask Congress for money for this purpose at this time. It seems that a battleship costs $52 million. Admiral Andrews, who represented the Navy Department in the continued absence of the Secretary of the Navy on account of illness, said that plans for the battleships could be put in course of preparation without any additional funds, and this is what will be done. Then if it seems necessary at the next session of Congress, an appropriation for the ships will be asked for.

The Vice President believes that the relief situation will not be solved until the Federal Government takes the position that it will share the cost of relief with the local communities only on a fifty-fifty basis. He says that so long as the Federal Government will stand all the cost, there will be plenty of people to go on relief and an indisposition on the part of the local communities to see that only those go on the rolls who ought to be there.

Saturday, March 21, 1936

Sunday began as a nice day and I started off with Jane Dahlman early in the morning for a trip into Pennsylvania. We left her apartment building at nine-twenty and drove first to Gettysburg. She had never been there and we drove about just enough to give her an idea of the place. Then we went on to Harrisburg, where we had lunch, and after lunch we started for Ickesburg. The roads from Harrisburg to Ickesburg were not in very good shape. Although there had been no snow in Washington for some time, I was surprised to see the drifts that still remained in Pennsylvania north of Harrisburg. The winter has done a great deal of damage to the hard surface of the roads. The frost has heaved them in a number of places so that we could not make very good time. However, we managed to get to Ickesburg. This was the second time in my life that I have ever been there. I hoped to get out to the old church and the graveyard where my grandfather and great-grandmother are buried, but I missed the road somehow after I had gone through the village and as it was getting late and we were a long way from Washington, I decided not to tarry. Returning to Washington we went through Carlisle and Gettysburg, thus avoiding Harrisburg, and we reached home at seven-fifteen. This was extraordinarily good running, considering the fact that it was Sunday and that the roads were not in very good shape in many instances.

I had lunch with the President on Tuesday. I reminded him that a year ago on two occasions I had offered to resign as Public Works Administrator and asked him whether he did not want my resignation at this time. He said that he did not, and then he took a pad of paper and a pencil and proceeded to put down a lot of figures from which he tried to demonstrate to me that there would be a very large public works program during the coming year. He also said that in two or three years he wanted to discontinue the Works Progress program and turn it all into Public Works. I told the President that one reason I made the remark that I had was because Senator Hayden had introduced a bill for an appropriation for public works with which I had nothing to do and that I did not want to get caught between two millstones. The President said that we could not have a public works program, because that would throw his financial program out of gear.

I told him that another reason I had brought up the matter was on account of the housing situation. I pointed out that he had been holding conferences on housing to which I had not been invited, although the housing program was under my jurisdiction as Public Works Administrator, and whatever information there was in the Government on this subject was in the possession of my Housing Division. I told him that I hoped we would have a chance to present our case before a final decision was reached. The President was a little evasive on this matter. He said that at each conference a different plan had been proposed and that none had been satisfactory. I remarked that Peter Grimm, who has been acting as special adviser to the Secretary of the Treasury on housing, had proposed a program under which housing would not be possible. The President spoke of participation by municipalities, and I told him that in my speech at the dedication of the Williamsburg project in New York early in January, I had taken the position that the Federal Government could not carry this load longer alone but must have the co-operation of the local bodies, both financial and otherwise.

The Cabinet met on Wednesday instead of yesterday because the President planned to leave Washington Thursday afternoon on his spring fishing trip. One of the matters to be brought up was that of compulsory finger printing of the enrollees in the CCC camps. There has been a system of voluntary finger printing, but apparently the great body of the boys in the camps have not submitted to finger printing of their own free will. Robert Fechner, who is in charge of the CCC camps, wants compulsory finger printing and so does the Secretary of War and the Department of Justice. All the rest of us were against it and the President was of that opinion too.

Another matter that we considered which was of especial interest was whether a bill should be introduced in Congress providing for a plebiscite in Puerto Rico on the question of independence. Since Puerto Rico is in this Department, the President first asked me for my opinion. I expressed myself as being strongly in favor of such a bill. I pointed out that if Puerto Rico wanted its independence, it ought to be granted it, but if it should vote against independence, then such agitation as has been going on in Puerto Rico recently would be put an end to for probably twenty years.

There is a bad situation in Puerto Rico. The chief of police was assassinated recently and two or three local officials were also killed. There is reason to believe that there is a general plot to assassinate other island officials, including the Governor. The other members of the Cabinet, at least those whose opinion the President particularly sought, were also in favor of this legislation. Then the question arose whether such a bill should be introduced at this session or should wait until the next Congress. I strongly urged its immediate introduction, although it might not pass at this session of the Congress, because of the quieting effect that I anticipated it might have on Puerto Rican public opinion. I told the President that we had drafted such a bill in my Department and he authorized me to send it to Senator Tydings, with the suggestion that he introduce it, although not as an Administration bill.

Wednesday, March 25, 1936

The President got away on Sunday on his vacation trip which had been delayed. He had expected to start on Thursday but first the flood and then a change for the worse in Secretary Swanson's condition kept him here.

There seems to be growing opinion that Governor Landon has been stopped for the Republican nomination for President. Apparently Herbert Hoover is definitely opposed to him. I have been told that Senator Dickinson, of Iowa, went to New York last week to see Hoover and that Hoover pledged him his support. On the other hand, Hilles and the Old Guard interests that he represents are supposed to have made up their minds to try to nominate Senator Steiwer, of Oregon. To help bring this about, Steiwer, according to the tale, is to be the temporary chairman of the convention. That will make him the keynoter, following which an effort will be made to stampede the convention for him.

Raymond Tucker came in to see me on Monday. He, too, has heard the story that Harry F. Sinclair, the oil man, is contributing heavily to the finances of the Landon campaign. He said he got the story from a group of Republicans and he is trying to have it verified from some source that will make it possible for him to print it. The President also has heard this story. It certainly looks as if Hoover is strongly opposed to Landon. In addition to this, there is more than a hint abroad in the land that Borah will not stand for Landon. It looks as if Landon would be cracked between Hoover and Borah. I don't think that either of these two men can stage a winning fight for himself and that will mean a dark horse —either Vandenberg, of Michigan, Dickinson, of Iowa, Steiwer, of Oregon, or someone else. It looks like a hard fight and perhaps a split in the Republican convention, which, of course, will redound to the advantage of President Roosevelt.

Fawcett was in again to see me yesterday. He told me that he was with a group of prominent Republicans on Sunday. I don't know who was there, except that he mentioned Senator Dickinson. He said that there was some talk about me for Secretary of the Interior in the next Cabinet if the Republicans should win. The feeling was expressed that this office ought not to be a football of politics and it was recognized that I had made a good record. Fawcett expressed the hope that in the campaign, in which, of course, it is expected that I will take part, I will confine my attacks to the Republican party and not go after individuals. I told Fawcett that when I went into a fight, I went into it pretty hard.

This suggestion is interesting and highly complimentary, but I know that nothing would come of it even in the remote possibility of the Republicans' winning in November. There would be too many Republican claimants for important positions, and I would have stirred up new animosities by that time if I had taken an active part in the campaign. I told Fawcett that if Dickinson were elected, he would not consider me for such an appointment and he asked me why. I said that I didn't think Dickinson liked me and he told me that he thought I was mistaken about that. He added that Dickinson would appoint a strong Cabinet and that Dickinson had taken part in the discussion that he had reported to me. I have set this down merely as an item of interesting gossip.

Saturday, April 4, 1936

With the President away on his fishing trip, there isn't much of importance to set down in these notes at this time except the Glavis situation. It is now exactly three weeks since a blowup in the Division of Investigations resulting in the resignation of McLaughlin, who was Glavis' first assistant. Following interviews with various members of Glavis' staff, I inquired each day whether Glavis was in the office, but the report came back to me, without variation, that he was very ill in his apartment at the Wardman Park Hotel. I was told that his throat was in such bad condition that he couldn't even talk to people.

Then word came to me that Glavis had gone to New York. This without any word from him, although both McLaughlin and Smith had told me that they had passed word on to Glavis that I wanted to see him. Glavis is a Christian Scientist so that he has not had any medical attention for his laryngitis, or whatever it is that is the matter with him. I learned indirectly that he had gone to New York "for a rest," and later Puryear told me that he had gone there to put himself in the hands of a well-known Christian Science practitioner.

Later still, in fact only a few days ago, word reached me that Glavis was trying to line up a job for himself in New York. It seems that Mayor La Guardia had had a telegram from Senator Wagner suggesting that Glavis be employed as a project expediter in Washington in connection with the Midtown Tunnel PWA project. This was later verified by Tuttle, our State Director, who was asked by the Midtown Tunnel Authority whether he would permit the setting up in its budget of a salary of $3,000 for Glavis as the expediter of the project in Washington. This was to be part-time work, the understanding being that Glavis was to be free to seek part-time employment of the same sort in connection with other projects.

This has created a very serious situation. I cannot see how I could permit anyone connected with the PWA staff to resign and at once become the Washington representative of a PWA project. The situation would be aggravated so far as Glavis is concerned because he has had a free hand here to investigate all records and files in connection with any project.

Last Saturday the Associated Press carried a report that Glavis was about to resign or had resigned. This report I denied personally at once. On Monday or Tuesday of this week I received a letter from Glavis from his New York hotel telling me that he hadn't been able to get in to see me and that he had been advised to take a long rest until he could recover from his illness.

I am not only discouraged, I am disappointed with Glavis. There is no member of my staff who is under deeper obligation to me. I did not know him when I came to Washington. As a matter of fact, I didn't know whether he was still alive. I had read about him in connection with the Ballinger-Pinchot blowup and I have had a great admiration for the distinct public service that he performed on that occasion. When the President instructed me to make an investigation of the way power was being handled at Muscle Shoals and I asked two or three of my advisers to suggest an investigator, Margold recommended Glavis. He was practicing law and investigating in New York. I sent for him, gave him the assignment, and he did a good job. Thereafter I appointed him Director of the Division of Investigations and this has become a very large division on account of Public Works and the Oil Administration. I have given him a free hand in selecting his own personnel and I permitted him really to run wild in his investigations of members of my own staff until I began to lose faith in some of his methods. Then, in the interest of the morale of the service, some time ago I gave orders that no member of the staff was to be investigated without written authorization from me. He has been one of the closest men to me of all the members of my staff. I have felt free to talk with him frankly and confidentially.

When the story was printed in all the newspapers that Glavis and Burlew were *personae non gratae* at the White House—which was in large measure true—and that the President was going to demand their resignations, I went to the front in vigorous style. I defended both Glavis and Burlew all along the line and if the issue had been forced, as the papers indicated, I would have resigned my office rather than see them punished because, in my opinion, they had done good work for the Government. Glavis knew that I was prepared to walk out of this Department at that time on his account and that of Burlew. In spite of this record, he apparently now runs out on me at a critical time. I feel that if he would come in and talk matters over frankly I could make him see very soon that he could not afford to make a false step. I forgot to say that, at my instance, President Roosevelt signed an order in 1933 restoring to him the civil-service status that he had lost when he had been discharged from the service by President Taft in connection with the Ballinger investigation.

So far as Glavis' doing me any harm is concerned, I am not worried. Even if I knew that he had both the power and the disposition to revenge himself on me, I, nevertheless, could not do anything other than I am doing. I am willing to continue him as Director of Investigations but only under clearly defined and restricted powers. I will no longer put up with his highhanded methods. He has raised up a veritable Frankenstein's monster. These investigators have become persecutors, man hunters, and they are just as eager to hunt and drag down members of my staff as they are lobbyists and crooked contractors against whom we are trying to protect the Department and PWA.

Saturday, April 11, 1936

On Wednesday I received a telephone call asking me to call at the Naval Hospital and see Colonel Howe at four-thirty and so I went. I had not seen him for over a year, just prior to his sudden turn for the worse, when the doctors didn't give him a chance to live. Since that time he has been bedridden, first at the White House and for several months now at the hospital.

He presented a strange figure. The President said on one occasion recently that Louis looked like a goat and this was an accurate description. He has let both his hair and his beard grow and his beard has never been trimmed. It is as ragged and unkempt as that of a goat, only more luxurious. Louis is one of the homeliest men I have ever known. The condition of his heart makes it more comfortable for him to spend his time on his elbows and knees atop of his bed and this was the posture that he maintained throughout my call. He commented on the fact that he had always wanted to see how he would appear in a beard and that the result satisfied him that he was better off smooth-shaven.

He wanted to discuss certain campaign plans. Mrs. Howe was with him and shortly after I arrived, Henry Wallace came in. It seemed to me that Louie's plans were not very practical in most instances. His mind has always been active and he has had a shrewd mind, but he spoke of one or two ideas that, for my part, I could not approve as being sound and wise. He presented me with a long list of questions and asked me for my answers to such of them as come within my purview. I don't know what he expects to do after he gets these answers. He also wanted me to send him pictures of the principal PWA projects in Michigan, and this I promised to do.

The President got back to Washington early yesterday afternoon and we had a Cabinet meeting at half past two. The President looks fine and as if the fishing trip had done him good.

The Vice President said at Cabinet meeting that there were two men in the Senate, namely, Senator Smith, of South Carolina, and Senator King, of Utah, both Democrats, who, he believed in his heart, would like to see the Democratic party beaten next November. He thinks that neither of these men has any sympathy with or interest in any of the things that the President has been trying to accomplish.

On Thursday, at my press conference, I was asked to explain the basis upon which Campbell, the big wheat grower of Montana, was leasing Indian lands. It appears that Campbell has received a very large check from AAA for reduction of acreage, and from the story it would seem that the Indians received the same percentage from the check that they would have received from the price paid for grain grown on their lands. There was a little exchange, principally as the result of questions asked by Paul W. Ward, of the *Baltimore Sun,* about crop sharers, and in the *Sun* of yesterday morning there was quite a long story by Ward covering this phase of my press conference.

Henry Wallace had the *Baltimore Sun* at the Cabinet meeting and brought up the question of my statement. He was quite critical of it and said that he had been irritated by what I had said. I explained what had transpired at my press conference and remarked that Ward was merely trying to bolster up opinions of his own. The incident was not at all an important one, but I was surprised that Henry should make such a point of it at a Cabinet meeting. If he had wanted to take an exception to anything that I was supposed to have said, that was well within his rights, but it seemed to me that he was looking for a chance to criticize me before others. I have always liked Henry Wallace. As a matter of fact, I have felt closer to him than any other member of the Cabinet, but perhaps the jealousy of this Department that exists more or less all along the line among members of his Department is beginning to affect his attitude.

I took Jane to the National Theater Wednesday night to see *Tobacco Road.* This play is written around the poor-white sharecroppers in Georgia. The play was strong, excellently staged, and well acted, but it gave one a depressed feeling about the economic and social status of a considerable section of American citizens of old lineage.

Assistant Secretary Chapman, who has been in Colorado for several months engaged in Senator Costigan's campaign for renomination, came in today. Two or three days ago I saw an item in the paper to the effect that Costigan had withdrawn as a candidate. What Chapman told me today shocked me greatly. It seems that Costigan has broken both physically and mentally and is in Johns Hopkins Hospital in Baltimore. The doctors say that he could not possibly go through a campaign. There are intervals when he does not recognize his closest friends and he seems to have lost track of what is transpiring. This is really dreadful news, because Costigan is one of the outstanding men in the Senate, both from the point of view of ability and of single-minded devotion to the public interest. I am quite sure that no one can come out of Colorado as his successor who is at all comparable to him.

Tuesday, April 14, 1936

Last night I went over to Baltimore at the invitation of Senator Radcliffe. He gave a dinner at the Maryland Club to eighty people —members of the Cabinet, Democratic Senators, a few members of the lower House, and some others, including heads of independent agencies in the Federal Government. The terrapin was unusually good. In fact, the whole dinner was excellent and abundant, with the result that I ate too much.

After the dinner we all went to the armory, where Woodrow Wilson was nominated for President in 1911, and where there was a big meeting under the auspices of the Young Democratic Club, at which President Roosevelt spoke. He went on the air at ten thirty-five. I really didn't get much of the speech, although I had a seat in the front row to his right. The acoustics were very bad on the platform but apparently they were better in the body of the armory because of the loud-speakers that were located there. According to the newspapers, the audience numbered about four thousand and I imagine that that was not far from the fact. It was a big meeting and an enthusiastic one.

I drove over and back alone. Carl didn't take me on the main road, so that we made very good time, but I was very tired when I got home at half past twelve this morning.

This sort of affair takes a lot out of me. I have about come to the conclusion never to drink champagne again at dinner. I had only one glass last night, and that not a large one, but I do not sleep well after drinking champagne and I feel it all the next day. I got awake this morning at half past five feeling terribly tired and I have not been able to shake it off all day long.

At the dinner last night Jim Farley was one place removed from me. He seemed to have a lot to say to me and was more friendly, I think, than he has ever been. He asked me what I thought about the Illinois situation, and then he went on to tell me that he had told Mayor Kelly that he was making a mistake in not getting behind Horner for governor again. He said that it would be better for Roosevelt if Horner should win. I was rather surprised at this because I had supposed that Farley was supporting Kelly in his opposition to Horner, not necessarily because he was against Horner, but just to be in line with Kelly.

Jim also told me that I had made a fine speech in Pittsburgh.

Senator Guffey was there and he also mentioned my speech, which seemed to please him very much. He was kind enough to say, although it isn't the fact, that as a result of that speech the final registration in Pittsburgh showed a Democratic majority over the Republicans. One thing about Guffey, however, is that he does appreciate what is done for him. He showed this after I had spoken for him in his election campaign in the fall of 1934.

Jim brought up the subject of public works. He said that he had heard no complaint of public works anywhere and I told him that that was the way I found it. I remarked that it had been pretty hard sledding for me and I reminded him that a year or two ago there was general dissatisfaction expressed with respect to public works on the Hill. I said that I believed that the course I was following was the right one and that I had simply dug in, taken my punishment, and tried to make the best of it. Farley frankly said that he had been one of those who believed that I was on the wrong track but that he was convinced now that he was wrong.

The President sent for me a little after two this afternoon. He told me that the Senate was going to set up its usual Campaign Fund Investigating Committee and he said that two plans were under consideration. One is to name a perfectly respectable Senator as chairman, one who stood pretty well in public opinion, and then to name as chief investigator a man of the same type. He said the other plan was to make Senator Black chairman of the committee and give him a vigorous, aggressive chief investigator. In this connection he has Glavis in mind, and that is the reason he wanted to talk to me.

I told him that I always believed in going after a thing if I was going after it. He said he agreed with me and that he would send for Senator Robinson tomorrow and suggest Black. Then, if that went through, he would try to "sell" Glavis to Black. He asked me whether I could spare Glavis until November, and I told him that the Division of Investigations was well organized and that I could spare him. The President told me that he had not discussed this plan with anyone except me.

As a matter of fact, if it works out this way it might relieve me of an embarrassing situation over here with respect to Glavis. I think Glavis wants to make a change and this would give him a change which would be to his advantage and credit without thought of any disagreement or misunderstanding over here. Harry

Slattery told me this morning that Glavis was not in Washington but had sailed on his boat several days ago. Where he is or when he will return, I have no means of knowing. He did not send me word that he was planning to leave on his boat, and I think he is acting in a very peculiar manner.

After this talk, the President reached over to the right of his desk and produced a section of ticker tape conveying a lot of misinformation about my press conference this morning. He asked me laughingly, but seriously nevertheless because he handles personal matters in that manner, when I was going to stop criticizing other departments. I was very much surprised and I told him I hadn't been criticizing any other department. He then handed me the ticker tape and from it I learned, to my astonishment, that I had given out a release criticizing Hopkins' figures on the man-year cost under his WPA program. I told the President that I had done nothing of the sort. The release I had given out referred to the man-year cost under the first PWA program based solely upon the thirty per cent grant of the Government. It showed that the cost to the Government was $741 a year per man based upon the grant alone. I pointed out that this wasn't even intended to show a basis of comparison with WPA because under our second program our grants are forty-five per cent, which admittedly makes the man-year cost higher than under the first program. He caught the point and when I offered to send him a copy of the release, he said he wished I would do so and that he would have a question planted at his press conference tomorrow which would give him an opportunity to comment upon the misinformation that had come over the ticker today. After I got back to the office I sent him a copy of the release.

Thursday, April 16, 1936

I was very much pleased with the result in Illinois on primary day last Tuesday so far as Governor Horner was concerned. He trimmed the Kelly-Nash machine handsomely by a majority of approximately one hundred and twenty thousand. The attempt to turn him down was not only bad politics, it was unpardonable from every point of view. It was to be expected that the organization would carry Cook County for Bundesen, but it did it by about only one hundred and twenty thousand to one hundred and twenty-five thousand votes. If Bundesen had been a strong candidate, or if Horner had made a less aggressive campaign, Bundesen might well have come out of Cook County with 300,000 plurality. The vote he got there in excess of Horner's was overcome by the downstate vote. I haven't seen the full returns, but I have been told that Horner carried every county downstate, and some communities he carried by five or six or seven to one over Bundesen, and in one or two instances, by as much as ten to one.

I have thought all along that the Administration made a mistake in not forcing Kelly and Nash to support Horner. Former Congressman James T. Igoe, who was Horner's manager in Cook County, called me up about the middle of the day to tell me about the results. He claimed that Horner had elected his list of delegates to the national convention and would control the state convention. I hope both items are true. I called the President and I opened the conversation by telling him that God had certainly been good to him in Illinois in that Horner had won. There isn't much doubt in my mind that Horner's victory will help Roosevelt. Bundesen would have been a load on the ticket. The President expressed himself as being entirely satisfied with the result and remarked that he had not heard a word from Kelly. He also said that since Kelly wanted to elect his county ticket, he would have to go along and be good so far as Horner is concerned. I didn't recall to the President that on two or three occasions I had volunteered my views with respect to the Illinois situation, but the President was so sure that Kelly would swamp Horner in Cook County that he was willing to permit Horner to be defeated so far as any help from him was concerned. Notwithstanding this, and in spite of the fact that Harry Hopkins apparently has played very open and flagrant politics with WPA in Illinois for the benefit of the Kelly-Nash machine, Horner went through like a good soldier and through his primary fight supported the national Administration all along the line.

I called Horner about the middle of the afternoon to congratulate him and he seemed glad to hear from me. I told him that if there was any help I could give him in Illinois, all he had to do was to call upon me. I would be perfectly willing to make one or more speeches for Horner. If I do, I want to pay my respects to the *Chicago Tribune,* which succeeded in nominating "Curley"

Brooks, as its own hand-picked candidate for governor on the Republican ticket. I certainly would like to go after the *Chicago Tribune* and this "Curley" fellow.

I told Horner that I hoped he would finish the job that he had started against the Kelly-Nash machine. He remarked: "I certainly was pretty soft for two years and a half," and at that point I remarked that that was the only criticism that I had ever felt against him even in my own mind. He declared that he didn't intend to be soft any longer and I told him that I hoped he would not be. I also told him that, in my judgment, he ought to come to Washington and demand what he is entitled to. When I called the President again after Cabinet meeting to give him some final figures that I had had from Paul Leach, the Washington correspondent of the *Chicago Daily News,* I said that I thought it would be a good thing for him to send for Horner and he agreed that it was a good idea.

Borah apparently didn't make as strong a showing on delegates against Colonel Knox in the Presidential preference primaries in Illinois as I had expected. Knox carried Cook County by a large vote, thanks to the support given him by the Republican machine. Borah had a plurality downstate, but Knox won on the total vote throughout the state by over seventy thousand votes. Borah apparently carried the primaries in thirteen districts, but he elected only one declared Borah delegate, according to what Leach reported to me late this afternoon. The other delegates elected in the districts where Borah had a plurality were Knox men. This creates a delicate situation. Here are Knox delegates elected in districts where it was made clear that the majority of the Republicans voting at the primary preferred Borah. If I were Knox, I would instruct these delegates to vote for Borah so long as he has a chance to be nominated.

The Cabinet met this afternoon instead of tomorrow, its usual day. The other day I received a letter from the President suggesting that with warm weather coming members of the Cabinet might want to spend occasional week ends away from Washington and so for that reason, for the time being, Cabinet meetings would be held on Thursday afternoons. There was little of importance that was discussed at the Cabinet meeting.

Tuesday, April 21, 1936

I had dinner with Cissy Patterson at her home Thursday night. I hadn't seen her for some time, as our dates had conflicted on several occasions. She seemed to think that President Roosevelt's election is inevitable. She isn't for Roosevelt, although she isn't strongly against him. She said that she was pulled both ways as between Hearst and her brother Joe. Hearst is bitterly fighting Roosevelt, and she is publisher of his *Washington Herald*. Naturally she is loyal to him, but she adores Joe. Her state of mind seemed to me to be significant of what the Hearst organization really believes.

Saturday night I went to the Gridiron Club dinner. As usual, it was long drawn out, with cocktail parties before and drinking parties afterward. The dinner was set for seven o'clock but of course we didn't sit down until some time after that. My coffee was served at eleven twenty-five and I got home about twelve-thirty. I dropped in at two of the cocktail parties before the meeting, but I didn't accept Cissy Patterson's invitation to her home for supper afterward. It was simply too late.

Some of the skits were clever. I think on the average they were better than they have been on most occasions, but the thing is just too long drawn out. There was a skit on Hoover and the Republican candidates for President that was amusing, although it hit Hoover pretty hard, and one on Landon was good too.

The custom is to have two speeches, the last by the President and the earlier by a leader of the opposing party. This time, instead of a Republican, the "anti" speaker was Frank R. Kent, the political columnist of the *Baltimore Sun*. He was pretty savage in his onslaught on the New Deal. It was the most outspoken attack I have listened to yet in the presence of the President. He was like a little bantam cock fighting a big rooster. He said he knew that the President's extensive research staff had looked up everything which he had ever said or done and intimated that he was prepared for the worst. He plainly thought that he was offering himself as a martyr to a cause. In somewhat plaintive terms he referred to the fact that the President would speak last and that he would have no chance to reply. He took some terrific slaps at the Republican party, but he devoted his main efforts to an attack on the New Deal—all that it had done and stood for. He also expressed his personal disapproval of the leaders of the New Deal.

I kept wondering how the President would answer Kent because to have answered him would have been to descend to personalities. Shortly after he began to speak, I came to the conclusion that he wasn't even going to mention Kent or refer to what he had said. About halfway through, the President began to pay sarcastic respects to certain columnists and Washington correspondents and then I wondered whether he would include Kent. However, he did not. There was no slightest intimation that he had ever heard of Kent or that Kent had made a speech preceding his own. It must have been a sore trial to Kent to mount the funeral pyre, prepared bravely to suffer martyrdom, and then find that his posturing had escaped the attention of the man who was to apply the match to the faggots.

The President's speech was well done but very sarcastic. What he said about some of the political commentators must have made them writhe. He had a lot of fun with the Republican candidates for President, as well as with the newspaper correspondents. I think the President acquitted himself pretty well, although his sarcasm in some places was so subtle that I do not doubt that it was over the heads of a good many of his auditors.

Jim Farley sat on my right at the dinner and on my left was Senator Dickinson, of Iowa, one of the candidates for the Republican nomination, and next to him was Frank Knox. Jim Farley was very friendly. It seems to me that he feels differently about me than he used to. He commented on the Illinois situation and seemed to be satisfied with Horner's nomination. I believe he is genuine about this, although I also think that Kelly had him fooled about the situation until almost the end. Frank Knox seemed to be chipper. Senator Vandenberg told me before we went in to dinner that Frank believed that he was not only nominated but elected. On the contrary, I don't see how he has a chance, especially in view of the big vote that Borah got in Illinois.

Morgenthau's name came up during my desultory talk with Jim Farley during the evening. He remarked that Morgenthau kept worrying because the next offering of bonds might not sell at par. He seemed to think that Morgenthau did a good deal of worrying about everything, especially small matters that were of little concern. I told him that if he was doing that sort of thing he would not last long, and Jim thought he wouldn't. I said that a Jewish friend had told me that Morgenthau did not stand well with his fellow Jews and that they do not feel that they are under any obligation to the President for his appointment. Jim said this was true; that the President got no credit from the Jews for Morgenthau's appointment, while he was criticized by certain classes of non-Jews for making the appointment. I referred to the fact that I was being called upon to make speeches at Jewish meetings and wondered why they didn't ask Morgenthau instead. Jim said again that he didn't have much standing with his own people and added that he couldn't make a speech anyhow.

Senator Dickinson, who has been one of the consistent and severe critics of the New Deal from the beginning, was friendly. James Waldo Fawcett told me some time ago that Dickinson felt friendly to me personally, although I had always had a contrary opinion. Of course, in any event, he wouldn't show any adverse feeling to a fellow dinner guest with whom he was rubbing elbows. Late in the evening Jim Farley leaned over to tell Dickinson that unless Landon was stopped, he would be nominated on the second or third ballot at Cleveland. Then it became clear to see that Dickinson does not relish the thought of Landon's nomination. He made the remark that a candidate for President ought to know something about the affairs of Government and commented on the fact that Landon knew absolutely nothing. I said that if he didn't know how to run the Government, in the event of his election someone would have to tell him and I asked who that someone would be.

I saw William Allen White on my way in to dinner but only to shake hands with him. I had hoped that I could have a little time with him while he was here, but he had not come in and he went to New York late Saturday night.

Betty, Jane, and I had luncheon at the White House on Sunday. Mrs. Roosevelt had learned that Betty was here and very kindly asked us and I was glad to go because it was a real opportunity for both of the girls. Some of the teachers and a bunch of the students from Todhunter girls' school, in which Mrs. Roosevelt has been interested for a number of years, were there. We had a very pleasant luncheon and afterward Mrs. Roosevelt took the two girls to see the upstairs rooms. I went along because I never had seen all of the upstairs. We left immediately thereafter.

The President asked me what I thought of his speech and I complimented him upon it. I told him that I didn't know he had such a mean disposition as he had shown in not even referring to Kent.

The President said that Mr. Justice McReynolds had turned his back so that he wouldn't have to speak to him when he left the table. He said that McReynolds had done this at the last Gridiron Club dinner. Mr. Justice Butler sat at the right of Jim Farley and McReynolds next.

The President continued to appear to be very friendly toward me. It seems to me that there has been a change in his attitude from several months ago. He agreed to give me three more housing projects in which I am very much interested, the money to come out of the $20 million that we are to get back as a result of a reduction of the size and cost of the Allegheny County, Pennsylvania, Authority project. Other matters that I had for consideration and decision he handled in a friendly and sympathetic manner.

At one point he interrupted to ask my opinion about a campaign plan that he has in mind. He said that he dreaded going to the Pacific Coast again because it is such a long trip and he has been there twice since election. The plan he suggested to me was going down the Mississippi River in one of the War Department boats from the beginning of navigation. I told him that I thought that plan showed imagination and that I believed that it would make a great hit. I think this would appeal to the people of the country, especially the section through which the main stem of the Mississippi flows. He could stop at various points to make speeches and he might even take short automobile trips to certain points. I asked him whether the report that he was going to visit the Governor General of Canada at the time of the Republican National Convention was true, and with a grin he said that he was thinking of it. I remarked that the Republicans wouldn't relish sharing the front pages of the newspapers with him during the time that they are nominating their candidate for President.

Colonel Louis McHenry Howe died suddenly in his sleep shortly after eleven o'clock Saturday night while the President was at the Gridiron Club dinner. The President was not told of this until after the adjournment of the dinner. After all, it was better that Louie should go now. It would have broken his heart not to have been able to take an active part in the campaign and that would have been obviously impossible. As a matter of fact, he has been failing for some time and for over a year he has been bedridden in the Naval Hospital.

Saturday, April 25, 1936

Ray Tucker was in to see me on Wednesday. He told me that in a talk recently with Jim Farley he asked Farley who would be the principal Democratic campaign speakers and Farley replied, "Homer Cummings and Harold Ickes." I remarked to Tucker that there had been a great change in Farley's attitude toward me, and he said that my standing was entirely different than it had been. He thinks everything is shaping up well for the President.

In the afternoon of the same day I had a long talk with Raymond G. Carroll, the Washington correspondent of the *Saturday Evening Post*. He is more liberal than the journal that he represents. He has just been pretty much all over the country, and in the absence of something now unforeseen he does not see how Roosevelt can be defeated. He has been in Washington a long time and knows many interesting back-of-the-stage facts. He thinks PWA has done a good job and stands well in the country, but that WPA doesn't stand so well.

On Thursday Tom Corcoran and Ben Cohen came in to see me. Tom is still on crutches, giving a broken ankle a chance to heal. They told me that A. Mitchell Palmer, who had a large hand in drafting the Democratic platform in 1932, has been entrusted with the same responsibilities this year. Palmer told them that the President had said to him that I would be a member of the Resolutions Committee and Palmer was very much distressed because in his own mind he ranked me with Tugwell and Hopkins. Corcoran tried to assure him that I was a different breed of cat. Corcoran and Cohen are preparing the preliminary draft for Palmer and they wanted me to know that any so-called Palmer draft would probably be their draft.

I have signed and promulgated an opinion written for me in the Solicitor's office, but carefully revised by me, passing upon the several plans submitted to me some time ago by the city and county of San Francisco in response to my earlier opinion that San Francisco was violating the Raker Act in selling the power generated at Hetch Hetchy to the Pacific Gas & Electric Company. I held that one plan informally presented as an alternative to more formal and perfected plans would comply with the statute. This plan will involve the expenditure of a considerable sum on the part of San Francisco and will put it in the distributing business.

Yesterday Mike Igoe came in to see me. He told me that Governor Horner and his friends would control the Democratic State Convention in Illinois and a majority of the delegates to the national convention, which will give them the power to name the next national committeeman. He said that the Governor was in favor of me as a delegate-at-large. I told him that while I wasn't a candidate for the place, I would be glad to accept it if it were tendered to me, on the understanding, however, that there was no opposition to me at the state convention on May 1, at which the delegates will be selected. He said he didn't think there would be any opposition.

He went on to say that Tom Courtney, State's attorney of Cook County, was even more insistent than was Governor Horner that Kelly be eliminated from Democratic politics in that city. He remarked that while I knew a good deal about Chicago politics and kept in touch with it, he didn't believe I had any idea of the degree of unpopularity into which Kelly has fallen. He said that Governor Horner was in Chicago and would have a talk with Pat Nash. Apparently Horner is willing to come to terms with nearly everyone except Kelly. Igoe asked me to speak to the President and ask him to tell Farley to pass word on to Kelly and Nash that they must fade out of the picture.

I was out of the office for half an hour just before my receiving hour and when I came back, I found a message to call Judge John J. Sullivan, of Chicago. Sullivan is a member of the Appellate Court and has been on the superior court bench for many years. All his life he has been active and influential in Chicago politics. He and his three brothers have grown up in the "back-of-the-yards" section and they know the give-and-take of rough-and-tumble Democratic politics. Jack is one of the close inside members of the Kelly organization.

I guessed at once what he wanted to talk to me about, but I didn't call him until I had gone through my receiving list and had had my talk with Igoe. Then I called him and just as I had supposed, he wanted to assure me that if I cared to go to the Democratic National Convention as a delegate-at-large, the Kelly organization would be for me. I repeated to him what I had told Igoe, and he concluded with the remark that if he didn't see me in the meantime, he would see me in Philadelphia.

This gesture on the part of the Kelly machine is rather significant but not unexpected by me. If Kelly had won a smashing victory, as he had expected to, I have no doubt at all that one of the prices he would have asked the President to pay would have been my head. Now that he is hanging over the ropes he doesn't want to make unnecessary enemies; on the contrary, he is willing to curry favor even with a man whose scalp he was after. I had a great laugh over it and called in Harry Slattery to enjoy the talk with me. It is really amusing that both factions in Illinois should be currying my favor when I am not a party Democrat. To be sure, I have always had friends among the Democratic leaders, but also I have had bitter and numerous enemies. Now they all seem to be lined up. There isn't any doubt that the whole situation helps me very much and I am willing to let it. Not only am I being openly recognized and honored (or will be unless something goes wrong) by the Democratic party of Illinois, regardless of faction, but there isn't any doubt that I am very strong on the Hill.

Speaking of the Hill reminds me to set down that I was given a list of members of the House of Representatives who have signed a petition for the earmarking for PWA of $700 million of the proposed relief fund of $1.5 billion for WPA. This list contains one hundred and thirty-seven names and I am told that fifty more representatives have given oral promises that they would support such a proposition. This means that they are taking a position against the expressed wishes of the President. Of course, few of the actual leaders of the House have signed but that is to be expected. I don't expect anything to come of this movement, but the fact that so many Congressmen should go on record is strong corroboration of my belief that if Congress were left free, it would vote overwhelmingly for PWA. I doubt whether ten per cent of the Congressmen would vote for Hopkins' program as opposed to mine. However, in the end, the Administration will be strong enough to hold the lines for its own program.

James Waldo Fawcett, of the *Star,* came in to see me at my invitation a couple of days ago. He confirmed the fact that Farley is saying that I am to be one of the principal Democratic speakers in the campaign. He told me that the story is going around that the President has received AAA benefit checks and that the money that was raised at the first President's birthday dance for the Warm Springs Foundation was used to lift a mortgage on the Warm Springs Foundation that was held by the President. I repeated these rumors today to the President when I had lunch with him at the White House. He said that the Warm Springs Foundation actually hadn't paid the interest due him; that he had refused to accept the interest because it would have had to be paid out of the fund that was raised in his name in celebration of his birthday. He also told me that he had denied the superintendent of his Georgia farm permission to grow cotton because that would have entitled him to AAA benefits.

Elliott Roosevelt lunched with his father today, I being the other guest. I don't much care for Elliott.

Thursday, April 30, 1936

Arthur E. Morgan, Chairman of the Tennessee Valley Authority, came in to see me on Wednesday. He was seeking information from me about David E. Lilienthal, a co-member of the Board, on the theory that Lilienthal was at one time a law partner of mine. I explained to him that Lilienthal worked for Don Richberg after Richberg had separated from the firm, and that I had never met him but once and then only casually before coming to Washington. I have seen him on a few official occasions here, but I do not really feel that I know the man.

Morgan said that Lilienthal's term expires this year and that if he were reappointed it would be for a nine-year term. He said that he was under the necessity of telling the President that if Lilienthal were reappointed, he himself would have to resign. He is very much interested in the Tennessee Valley experiment, but he says Lilienthal has hampered him at all stages. He seems to be under the distinct impression that Lilienthal is trying to build himself up. He betrays confidences to the newspapers, carries on negotiations for power contracts without contacting Morgan, and gives out figures as to costs and consumption of power that, according to Morgan, will not stand close scrutiny. Morgan fears a bad explosion sooner or later if Lilienthal remains on the Board, and he does not care to be involved.

Under the division of authority Morgan has been in charge of building the dams because he is an engineer. When I first met Morgan here in Washington, he gave me the impression of being a dreamer of an impracticable sort, but my opinion of him has changed as time has passed. In fact, I have felt very differently about him since I visited the Tennessee Valley development with the President in the fall of 1934. I now regard him as a very fine person and as a high type of citizen. Apparently he is a capable engineer and executive as well. Another difference he has had with Lilienthal has been over appointments. Morgan absolutely refuses to make a political appointment, but according to him, Lilienthal doesn't make any other kind.

The report is current in Washington that Morgenthau is going to resign as Secretary of the Treasury and go as Ambassador either to Great Britain or to France. It seems that Bingham, who is at present at the Court of St. James's, wants to return to the United States on account of the health of his wife. For my part, I would almost be willing to go down and wave a handkerchief at Henry as his ship leaves the dock. I do not like him any better as time goes on.

A real fight is being made in the House of Representatives to earmark some $700 million of the proposed relief fund of $1.5 billion for the PWA program, as I mentioned recently. Today, as I was waiting in the President's outside office, a committee of five, headed by Congressman Beiter, of New York, came out from an interview with the President on this matter. Congressman Beiter told me that the President had suggested that they have a session with Hopkins and me to see what could be worked out, and I told them that I would be willing to meet with them at any time that was satisfactory to them and Hopkins.

Congressman Zioncheck, who has been cutting quite a swath lately, mainly by playboy pranks and being arrested and fined for traveling through the streets of Washington at a high rate of speed, called me up yesterday to say that he wanted to see me with someone. I made the desired appointment and about half past eleven he appeared with a blonde vision all dressed in white. He announced to me that he and Miss Nix, the blonde in question, were about to be married and he wanted me to perform the ceremony. In the back of my mind I saw visions of my name appearing in the headlines of the papers, because Zioncheck has been getting in bad with the newspapers generally on account of his irrational conduct. I told him that I had no authority to marry anyone and fortunately Harry Slattery, whom I summoned, confirmed that, although Harry told me afterward that I did have such authority. Fortunately, I did not know this at the time that the request was made.

Zioncheck had a marriage license, in which the name of the officiating clergyman, a man by the name of Aaron, was inserted. It seems that under the local law a license runs to a named clergyman or magistrate, and Zioncheck selected the first name on the list. Zioncheck then conceived the brilliant notion of having Aaron brought here to perform the ceremony in my office so that I could be a witness. When he found that Aaron could not be located, he called the marriage license bureau to have the license changed, but when he was told that he would have to go to the bureau to have the change effected, he told the clerk to go to hell. Then, at Burlew's suggestion, he decided to go to Annapolis for the ceremony and he and Miss Nix departed with the object in view, much to my relief.

Just as I had expected, the whole story appeared in all the local newspapers in a sensational manner, in which, fortunately for me, I was not involved. I could not very well have refused to have been a witness, but that would have been difficult, and I was glad of a turn of affairs which made it necessary for me either to refuse or to accept.

I had lunch with the President today, but although the Beiter committee had just left him, he said not one word to me about relief or PWA or the meeting he had suggested with the committee and Hopkins.

I told the President that I was now going to press for passage of my Department bill and I asked him if he would notify Agriculture, and particularly the Forest Service, that they were not to lobby against the bill. This is the bill to change the name of this Department to that of Department of Conservation. He said he would do this.

This reminds me that yesterday I went up to the Senate, where I had talks with Senators Robinson, Byrd, and Wagner about this bill. Senator Robinson seemed to be very friendly when I appealed to him for help. He said that while Senator Lewis was a fine person, he did not know much about procedure, but that he would help him. He proposed to give Lewis a chance to bring the bill up on the unanimous consent calendar and if there should be objection, then to set a day when he could bring it up for a roll call. He said he could see no objection to the bill and he asked me to send him a memorandum so that he could explain it when it was called up.

I also took up with the President the question of the Wagner-Ellenbogen Housing Bill. I told him that the administrative setup-was bad since it provided for a separate board instead of giving the responsibility to some department. He agreed and then I told him that I hoped the administration of Housing would come to Interior. He said he didn't know about that and I pressed the matter. He said it would depend on what the bill proposed. His idea is that, under the bill, the interest in housing on the part of the Government would be largely financial and in that case it would be a Treasury function. I said that it would be more than financial: there would be both supervisory and management functions similar to those now exercised by the Housing Division of the Public Works Administration. He said that, in that event, it ought to be in Interior and I told him I would send him a short statement covering the functions of the bill.

At my press conference this morning one of the correspondents said that Senator Lewis had said that if I declared myself to be a Democrat, I would be nominated tomorrow as a delegate-at-large from Illinois to the Democratic National Convention. I was asked what my party was and I replied that I was an Independent—the same reply that I made at the press conference a week ago. Senator Lewis has said nothing to me of this sort and neither has anyone else. I told the President at luncheon about this matter and he said that I had taken exactly the right position and that I could be much more effective as an Independent than as a member of the Democratic party. He told me that he was trying to impress on some of the Democratic Congressmen from normally Republican districts that they could not hope to be elected without independent Republican support. I am glad he sees this matter as I do. I could not declare myself to be a member of the Democratic party as an inducement to the state convention tomorrow selecting me as a delegate-at-large.

Cabinet meeting this afternoon was a little longer than usual. One reason was that Miss Perkins got started in a general discussion at the beginning and she went strong for almost half an hour. Then we got into a discussion of the tariff and that kept us a long time. Assistant Secretary of War Woodring, who was there in the absence of George Dern, reported that he had just come back from the Democratic State Convention in Kansas. He expressed absolute confidence that Roosevelt would carry Kansas in November by fifty thousand votes.

Saturday, May 2, 1936

The committee of Congressmen, headed by Congressman Beiter, of New York, which called on the President yesterday to urge the earmarking, for PWA, of $700 million of the proposed relief funds, intended originally to have a joint meeting with Hopkins and me. Later the plan was changed. Yesterday morning the committee called on Hopkins and he told it that he could get along until next February with $450 million less than the $1½ billion provided for in the bill. He said that if the President were willing to earmark this amount for PWA, he would not oppose it, but apparently he indicated that he would try to prevent the President from so doing. He said that if any sum were allocated to PWA, we should have complete jurisdiction over it without having anything to say about it.

In the afternoon the committee came over to see me to report what Hopkins had said. I told them that they couldn't rely on Hopkins' apparent willingness that some of this money should come to PWA. I believe, and I expressed that belief to the committee, that he will run at once to the President and try to persuade him to stand firm for all of this money going to WPA. I may say that I learned later that the committee had barely left Hopkins' office before he called Congressman Buchanan, chairman of the House Appropriations Committee, to insist that all of this money be reserved for WPA.

The following Congressmen were present in my office: Beiter, Kramer, of California, Dobbins, of Illinois, and Lambeth, of North Carolina. Dempsey, of New Mexico, and Dies, of Texas, were not here but they are in full sympathy with the efforts that are being made. We had a very friendly talk and there is no doubt of the interest in PWA on the part of these Congressmen. It is rather remarkable to me that Congressman Beiter should undertake a movement of this kind. When he came into my office I didn't know him by sight. As a matter of fact, I thought that Congressman Kramer was he, although I should have known better because I have seen Kramer on a number of occasions. They all have a pretty wide knowledge of what PWA has done and they have no respect at all for the Hopkins program. Congressman Kramer said that in southern California WPA was an actual drag on the Democratic ticket, and Congressman Dobbins remarked that WPA as a political force hadn't amounted to much in Illinois, as was demonstrated at the recent primaries when Governor Horner was overwhelmingly renominated in spite of the fact that WPA was actively opposed to him.

Congressman Beiter told me that Congressman Buchanan had called him to his office and told him that if all of this money was not voted for WPA, it would mean the loss of 15,000 jobs in his own district. The Hopkins organization has also sent publicity throughout his district to the effect that 15,000 people would starve to death if this money were not all given to WPA. Beiter said that this statement when published in the newspapers made him pretty nervous and he anticipated an uprising in his district. He has received just one letter, which persuades him that the people know that the Government will not let them starve. There has been other evidence recently of an active campaign of propaganda undertaken by the WPA forces in all parts of the country to bring pressure to bear on Congressmen in support of this bill. Meanwhile, my hands are tied because I cannot oppose an announced policy of the President's.

The Congressmen realize that WPA is under fire and will be increasingly under fire during the campaign. They say that PWA and the CCC camps are the two outstanding accomplishments of the Administration along relief lines and yet they are asked to repudiate PWA and vote $1.5 billion to WPA, in spite of its mismanagement, its scandals, and its inefficiency. They realize that the brunt of the fight will have to be borne by the Congressmen in the districts and they don't care to face that fight. Their purpose is to try to line up as many of the Democratic Members of Congress as possible for their program. They take it for granted that the Republicans will support the PWA program anyhow as against WPA, even though they may vote against the relief bill on the final poll.

In connection with this controversy an interesting fact has come to my knowledge. Congressman Sirovich told Puryear that two or three days ago Under Secretary West called together a group of some twenty Democratic Congressmen and told them that they ought to support the President in his plan to turn all this money over to WPA, that it was an Administration measure and that loyalty required them to be for it. According to Sirovich, he announced that he would be damned before he would do this.

Today West was in my office at a conference on pending Interior

Department bills. He came to my desk early and told me about Hopkins' telephone call to Buchanan. He said that a group of Pennsylvania Congressmen had learned of this from Buchanan and that they were furious at Hopkins and were calling him a double-crosser. After the conference, West enlarged upon the situation. He told me that there was a tremendous sentiment on the Hill in favor of earmarking some of this money for PWA. He had told the President of this sentiment and he had also told him that he ought to see the Beiter committee. Then, with a little leading from me, he went on to say how popular PWA was and that he thought it would be a mistake to abandon the PWA program.

Now West either did not make the statement that he is alleged to have made to the twenty Congressmen, or he is a damned hypocrite. Moreover, if he made that statement he has put himself in a very equivocal position. As Under Secretary of this Department he was lobbying against the Department. This, in self-respect, he could not do, even at the behest of the President.

West has been a distinct disappointment as Under Secretary. I welcomed him here and thought he might be of great use along certain lines. I didn't know whether he was an executive or not, but it did not take me long to find out that as an executive he is a total failure. At the very least I thought he could help on the bills in which the Department is interested. Here, too, he has been a failure. Word comes to me from a number of sources that he has no standing at all on the Hill, where he is regarded merely as an office boy of the President's. The report came to me two or three days ago that Jim Farley, when West was mentioned recently, exclaimed: "Charley West! I have never heard him say no. No one has ever heard him say no. He isn't capable of saying no." That about sums up West. I recall the occasion when he sat at my desk and told me that one thing he envied in me was my ability to say no. He explained that he wasn't able to say no himself and that Mrs. West had often told him that he ought to cultivate that ability.

Yesterday I was selected by the Democratic State Convention at Springfield, Illinois, as one of the delegates-at-large to the Democratic National Convention. This establishes a unique record for me—one that I do not believe is equaled in American history. In 1912 I was an alternate delegate-at-large to the Progressive National Convention, and now I have been selected as a delegate-at-large to the Democratic National Convention. According to newspaper reports, it was declared at the Democratic State Convention that I have become a member of the Democratic party. I don't know whether this declaration was made on my behalf or not but certainly it was without my knowledge or consent.

On the whole, while it may be that the President will not want me to continue in the Cabinet, I think that would not necessarily be a foregone conclusion even if it is his present disposition. He cannot fail to be influenced somewhat in his decision by the result of the campaign and the contribution toward that result that I and others may have made.

I do not find that I am very much disturbed over these reports. I haven't any doubt that I would leave this position with great reluctance because I would like to have a few more years in which to devote myself more strictly to Interior Department matters. However, there are reasons why I would like to quit. As I look ahead, we are likely to have some turbulent times during the next four years. The country is much more radical than many people realize, and much more radical than the Administration. The people have seen in President Roosevelt the one leader who is trying to do something for them. They see no one in sight of the same sort who is in a position to give them national leadership. That is the reason they are for him now and that is the reason he will be re-elected. If, however, after two more years there has not been a greater improvement in the economic status of the people than there has been during the last four years, trouble may be looked for, in my judgment. The President is likely to lose Congress and in all probability a very fierce battle will be waged at the polls in 1940 with a much more radical and much more determined electorate trying to get control of the Government as against concentrated wealth. If such a movement comes, I would have my usefulness. Moreover, an opportunity as an independent citizen once more to criticize whatever I believe to call for criticism would not be unwelcome. As a former member of the Administration I would not lack such opportunities.

I recall that the President said to me not very long ago that he was looking to 1940 as the time when there would be a real fight which might determine the destinies of the Government for many years to come. He may be right.

It would be a curious thing if the President, relying upon the progressive sentiment of the country and re-elected by that sentiment, should as one of his first acts accept the resignation of that member of his Cabinet who, in a good many quarters at least, is regarded as the most progressive of the Cabinet. But then such things have happened.

Wednesday, May 6, 1936

Yesterday I appeared before the Public Lands Committee of the House in support of a bill under consideration for enlarging the boundaries of the Mount Olympus National Monument and making it a national park. The Forest Service has been fighting this bill vigorously and a number of witnesses have appeared before the committee both pro and con, although the sentiment seems to be rather strongly in favor of the bill. This is an outstanding park area but, as usual, the Forest Service is fighting it with all its might. At a former hearing Horace Albright, former Director of the National Park Service, made a vicious onslaught on the Forest Service. At the opening today Mr. Kneipp, of the Forest Service, asked for an opportunity to reply and offered for insertion into the record a great mass of documents. The committee on a vote declined to hear him because he admitted that what he wanted to say was in reply to Albright and did not go to the merits of the bill. It gave him permission, however, to prepare a statement for insertion in the record.

I made a very vigorous prepared statement in which I paid my respects, humorously and otherwise, to the Forest Service for its opposition to this bill. When I was through, Kneipp avoided looking at me and it was evident that he was very angry. I understand that later he said to the committee that Secretary Wallace might want to answer me, when the announcement was made that no further hearings would be held. The committee said of course that it would be willing to hear from Secretary Wallace. I doubt very much whether Henry appears because he hasn't shown up very well so far in controversies with me at the Senate or House committee hearings. The report that came back to me afterward was that I had made a very good impression, although some of the Republicans thought that I had gone a little far in kidding the Forest Service.

Saturday, May 9, 1936

At my press conference on Tuesday I was asked to explain the delay in getting certain PWA projects under construction and one reason I assigned was the holding up by Harry Hopkins of our projects. I reminded the correspondents that most of them had printed that story two or three times. The record will certainly prove this charge.

The President made some statements at his press conference which followed mine on Tuesday which were of great importance to PWA and to me personally but which I did not know about until Wednesday morning because I left the office Tuesday earlier than usual.

In commenting on the fight to earmark some of the new relief funds for PWA, in response to questions from correspondents, the President made it perfectly clear that he would not permit any earmarking. He also made it perfectly clear that he was prepared to help Harry Hopkins carry out the desire that he has had at heart for the last two years to scuttle PWA and salvage from it whatever he can for the benefit of his own administration. The President said that such PWA projects as might qualify under the program could be carried on by WPA. He also said that there might be an arrangement by which loans from RFC could be used to help finance projects which heretofore have been within the jurisdiction of PWA.

There was also another article in the morning papers of Wednesday which was of great interest to me. It related to housing and from it, it appears that the President has been continuing his conferences on housing without any notice to me or any indication that he is interested in our Housing Division or in my views. It was reported that after a conference with Senators Wagner and Walsh, at which Morgenthau was present, a housing program had been agreed upon. In his interview the President said one or two things that were critical of our housing program, as, for instance, that while we are building fine, substantial projects, they do not provide quarters at a low enough rate. He seemed by this remark to imply that, without a Government subsidy, it is impossible to provide decent living quarters for those in the lowest income groups, thus ignoring the experience in those European countries where public housing programs have been under way for several years.

I was not in a pleasant state of mind when I realized that the President had apparently repudiated his whole PWA program and had expressed what seemed to me to be a lack of confidence in me. On Tuesday afternoon I had applied to Colonel McIntyre for an appointment with the President and as soon as he could be reached on Wednesday, I got in touch with him again to tell him that it was important for me to see the President that day. At least three times on Wednesday I called McIntyre, but on each occasion he told me that it was doubtful whether the President would be able to see me. As a matter of fact, I wasn't able to see him on Wednesday, and on Thursday morning I came to the office and proceeded at once to draft a letter to send to the President in the event that I could not get to him on that day. My draft was objected to by Slattery, Burlew, and Straus on the ground that it was too personal and too strong in tone. I told them I would like them to work it over for me, which they did.

Later in the morning, McIntyre called to say that the President would see me at twelve-thirty. This period is always a poor one because by twelve-thirty the President is behind on his schedule and he lunches at one. I went over determined not to discuss with him the issues that I had in mind because the time would be too short and I wanted to go into them rather fully. I took with me the letter referred to, intending to leave it with him if I had no opportunity of bringing to his attention the grave issues involved in his apparent willingness to scrap PWA. When I got in to the President, which was about ten minutes to one, just as I had expected, I told him that there were certain important matters that I wanted to discuss with him but that there wouldn't be time enough to take them up in the short time left of my period. He told me that he was going down the river on Saturday and that he would give me an appointment Saturday morning. I told him I would like an hour. Later Mac came in and the appointment was confirmed to him at which time the President said that he hadn't given an hour to anyone since January. We then took up some routine departmental matters upon which I desired Presidential action.

One significant statement was made by the President during this interview. He said that next year if Governor Lehman was re-elected in New York, as he would be if he consented to run, he and I would take up with him a proposition to bring the Saratoga Battlefield into the national park system.

Tuesday morning before going to the White House I was told that Under Secretary West, the day before, had appeared before a group of Democratic Congressmen to urge support of the WPA program. After he had started to talk, Congressman McKeough, of Chicago, asked him whether he had talked with me. This seemed to embarrass him. He explained that he hadn't had time to talk to me after the President had told him to go up to the Hill to deliver his message, which was to the effect that Democratic Congressmen ought to be loyal to the Administration and support the relief bill without attempting to earmark any funds for PWA. McKeough then told him to go back and tell the White House that they were for Ickes and PWA and that he didn't give a damn what orders were sent up. He demanded that $300 million or $400 million be earmarked for PWA.

Thursday morning when I went in to see the President I found West also waiting to see him. He at once hurried up to me to tell me how much he was trying to help me on the Hill. He said that there was a great deal of sentiment for PWA and he thought that with the Democratic insurgents plus the Republican votes, we would get enough to earmark money for PWA.

He had gotten out on a limb, he assured me, by telling the President that Congressman Beiter had been unable to secure an appointment with him through McIntyre, although the President had told Beiter that he might come back again to see him after conferring with Hopkins and me. West said that this was his interest in the matter. He said that McIntyre was helping to play Hopkins' hand and was keeping Beiter and his group away from the President. He told the President that he ought to see Beiter and he also told him how strong the sentiment was for PWA. The President authorized him to go to Beiter and talk it over with him. He was to tell the Beiter group that there would be hope for PWA if the bill as it stood were adopted, but the report he was to carry back was so vague and indefinite that I blurted out that it didn't mean anything. West agreed. He deprecated the President's attitude on PWA, told me how unpopular Hopkins and his program were in every part of the country, and both by express language and even stronger inference, condemned WPA and questioned the President's judgment in supporting that program.

Later the same afternoon West called to say that he was going up again on the Hill at the request of the President on the same matter. He held another meeting in which he tried to calm the insurgency of the Beiter group. Once again word came back to me that he was lobbying for the relief bill. West almost convinced me by his assurances when I met him in the President's offices that he was more or less an innocent bystander and was really laboring hard in the vineyard for PWA. However, reports that came to me directly after his conferences with groups of Congressmen persuaded me that he was trying to carry water on both shoulders.

Friday morning I sent for West. I told him that he had placed both himself and me in an embarrassing position. I confronted him with the statement that I understood he had been up on the Hill working for the WPA bill. He was clearly embarrassed. I pointed out that he had placed himself in an equivocal position and that Congressmen felt justified in believing that he was representing me. I said that it was not fair to me for him to go up there as he had, considering his position in the Department. He admitted that the President had placed him in a very embarrassing position and I told him that he had given ground to Congressmen to question his good faith. He protested his loyalty and hoped that I didn't doubt his sincerity. At this point I kept silent. He went on again to deprecate the WPA program and to tell what a fine job PWA had done. He was plainly on the anxious seat and I let him stew in his own juice. I didn't give him any reassurances. On the contrary, I told him that he was distinctly on the spot.

Thursday night there was a meeting of the Democratic caucus called on a petition that was circulated by the Beiter group. There was not a very large attendance and the PWA champions were defeated by some twenty-two or twenty-three votes. Altogether this was a very good showing, considering that the Administration was putting pressure on in favor of the WPA bill. Speaker Byrns, Chairman Buchanan of the Appropriations Committee, Congressman Woodrum, and others urged support of the President's program. I think there was a good deal of fervid debate but PWA was licked.

It was a mistake for the Beiter group to insist upon a caucus because they were bound by the result. I never believed that his group would win, but if they had not gone into a caucus they could, with Republican support, have earmarked a considerable fund for PWA when the bill was under consideration in the House. Most of the Beiter group are young and less experienced men and they had arrayed against them the old and experienced leadership on the Democratic side of the House. I feel grateful to them for what they voluntarily tried to do. Chairman Buchanan made a statement which, while on its surface fair to me, contained implications and inferences that were not fair. I still believe, and my belief is supported by the testimony of many Congressmen, that if the Democratic Congressmen had been left to vote their own free will, WPA would not have gotten ten per cent of the votes.

I asked Congressman McKeough to come in to see me Friday morning because I wanted his report on the caucus. He told me that he had come to the conclusion that the President was worried about me because he regarded me as a possibility for the Presidency. I asked McKeough whether he meant 1940 and told him that I would be too old by 1940 and that, besides, I had no Presidential ambitions. McKeough said: "Well, either 1940 or 1936," which of course was ridiculous. Then he added that if I were a candidate for President, he would support me against all comers.

Farley called me early Friday morning to ask how things were going on the Hill, and since he opened up the matter I told him I would like to have a talk with him. Accordingly, I went over. I found Jim very friendly and somewhat disturbed over the relief situation. He told me that he hadn't made the suggestion to anyone else except one person, but that he believed Hopkins was a candidate for President in 1940 and was working toward that end. I told him that by a strange coincidence I had made the same statement to Slattery and Burlew that very morning. Jim said that it was perfectly clear to him. According to him, Hopkins is playing with Frank Hague, of Jersey City, Mayor Ed Kelly, of Chicago, and other Democratic leaders who might be able to control delegates at national conventions. He said, of course, it was absurd for Harry to think of himself as a candidate for President, but he added that it was a dangerous thing for a man with an ambition like that, although it was a legitimate one, to have so much money to spend with so little check and supervision. Naturally, I agreed.

Jim told me what he had already told me at the Gridiron dinner, namely, that he had never heard any criticism of PWA anywhere. He thinks it is one of the best things that the President has ever done. I told him that it seemed to me bad politics for the President on the eve of a campaign to repudiate one of the best acts of his Administration and to announce what amounts to an expression of a lack of confidence with respect to the man who has been responsible for that job and has made it a success. I told him that I didn't know to what extent I was expected to make speeches during the campaign but that I had hoped to contribute whatever I could. I went on to say, however, that I could not defend WPA and that, PWA having been repudiated, I would not be in a position to say anything about that. I also told him that if I were called before the Senate Finance Committee on this program, I would give my honest opinion and he said that I ought to.

Jim's feeling is that the two points of greatest attack of the Republicans will be WPA and Tugwell. He said that as Relief Administrator, Hopkins had made some very injudicious wisecracks. Jim said that while he was in no sense a reformer, he hated to see money wasted. He believes in the PWA program because the money goes for substantial public works. He thinks the Hopkins administration is wasteful and inefficient. And, too, I may also say that he must regard it as being political in view of what he said about Hopkins lining up with such men as Hague and Kelly.

He told me he had not had a talk with the President about this program and asked me about my talks with him. He was astonished when I told him that the subject had never been mentioned between us. He couldn't understand it. He remarked that Hopkins seemed to have "put the thing over on the Boss" and we speculated as to how Hopkins had attained his position of influence with the President. I said that word had come to me that it was through cultivation by Hopkins of Mrs. Roosevelt and the President's mother. Jim said that he didn't know about the President's mother but that Hopkins was very close to Mrs. Roosevelt.

Then in confidence, he told me about a talk he had had with the President during which they had discussed campaign plans. The President, in speaking of talks over the radio, made the suggestion that he would make a speech and then Hopkins would go on the air for half an hour to explain WPA. According to Jim, he looked the President squarely in the eye and said: "Mr. President, if I were you I wouldn't let Harry Hopkins talk about WPA anywhere. You are the only one who can explain WPA to the country."

I had an hour with the President today in his study in the White House proper. I lost no time in coming to grips with him on his relief program. I told him that I hadn't been consulted or given an opportunity to express my views but that considering certain statements printed in the newspapers and made on the Hill I felt that it was important to tell him how I felt even if he totally disagreed with me.

I may say that during the last two or three days my choler has been gradually rising. It has been pretty well under control, however. My anger has taken the form of determination and when I am in that state of mind, there is not likely to be an outburst of temper such as often happens when it is more on the surface. I told the President that I didn't think that he understood PWA or what it had done for the recovery program or in enhancement of the reputation of his Administration. He protested that he had followed it closely and that we had done a fine job. He said he had even seen a number of PWA projects. Then I said that while it was apparent that nothing could defeat him for re-election, it didn't seem to me to be the part of political wisdom at the outset of a campaign to repudiate one of the best things he had done. I told him that what he had said about PWA was in effect a declaration on his part of a lack of confidence in me as Administrator.

Then I went on to demonstrate to him along one or two general lines just what PWA had done and was doing. I told him that on the basis of figures prepared by the Department of Labor, an independent agency, as between Hopkins and me the cost to the Federal Government per man-hour was about four and one-half cents more for WPA than for PWA. I pointed out that the figures quoted by Hopkins of men at work under PWA were as of March 15, at the end of a hard winter. I gave him the figures as of May 5, and these figures show a very sharp increase in employment over the earlier ones. Then I argued that regardless of how many men it might be possible to put to work under PWA projects, it seemed to me to be sound sense to put as many men to work as possible in view of the low per-hour cost and the permanency of the projects.

I made no vicious attack on Hopkins, but I did tell the President that our program under the relief bill last year had been sabotaged from the beginning. I told him how Hopkins had failed to clear our projects. I reminded him that I had had to go to him on two or three occasions to ask him to order Hopkins to clear our projects and then Hopkins would bring them in in great armfuls. The President said, "That's right." Then I said that while Hopkins was holding up our projects on the one hand, he was criticizing us for failure to put men to work. I pointed out how during the winter months we could not secure skilled labor on our projects because men could work only two or three days a week which would net them less pay than the wages given them by Hopkins, who paid them whether they worked or not. I told him that Hopkins had competed with us for projects. If we could be assured that this competition would cease, we could find plenty of projects to finance on the old 30-70 basis. I said, however, that we could not do any projects on any basis requiring a contribution from the borrower if Hopkins offered to do those same projects on the basis of an expenditure of one hundred per cent of Federal funds. I recalled to him the instance of the Atlanta, Georgia, sewer project, where Hopkins' people had put both him and me in a position where we could not move, with the result that while Atlanta was amply able to finance the building of its own sewerage system, a substantial part of it was built as a WPA project at the expense of the Federal Government.

The President agreed with me on all these points and on some others that I made. Then he tried to explain that it was not his intention to do away with PWA. It was clear to me that he had been doing some muddled thinking and in fact had committed himself to Hopkins' program. I told him that not only he at his newspaper conference on Tuesday but Hopkins, when he appeared before the House Appropriations Committee, had said that what PWA program was continued would be done under WPA. After more or less sparring, the President said that he expected us to do the engineering and the finance work. It was his idea that we would use up all that was left in the RFC revolving fund and that after that Jones would lend money on PWA projects. I pointed out that Jones had no power under the law to do this and that possibly Jones would want to set up his own machinery. He said that he must get authority for Jones to make such loans and that Jones had no intention of setting up a rival organization. His idea was that grants could be made out of Hopkins' funds and loans out of RFC funds, but I said that these funds ought to come to PWA and allow us to handle that part of the program because we not only were equipped to do it but had had the necessary experience. He said that would be all right—that Jones could check the money to us for loans and Hopkins for grants and we could handle it. He said, however, that he would want a weekly report on employment. I told him that there would be no difficulty about that. Then I suggested that Hopkins and I get together to see whether we could agree upon a program and then submit it to him. This was satisfactory to him.

I had gone to see the President with my mind fully made up that if there was no yielding on his part, my resignation would shortly follow. I think I made some progress with him, but whether anything can be worked out is still a matter of grave doubt. I know that Hopkins will fight like a tiger to hold on to the power that this bill gives him. As a matter of fact, the bill gives him unlimited power—all that the President had under the relief bill last year. Tugwell can't get any money under this bill. If he continues with his resettlement program, it will be merely as an agent of Hopkins. The same is true of every agency that can even hope to get money under the bill. As for me, I am determined that I will not work in any such capacity under Hopkins.

If the President is willing that certain sums of money should be allocated to PWA for use in our discretion, then it will be satisfactory and I will do the best I can. But I will not work under the orders of Hopkins or be subject to his direction. I am willing that we should make the weekly reports on employment and that on our projects we should employ people from relief rolls. That is only fair, since it is the object of the President to give employment to men on relief rolls. I do not agree with this as a policy, but he has the right to determine policy and it is the duty of his subordinates either to conform or to resign. However, there is no obligation running to me to subordinate myself as Public Works Administrator to Harry Hopkins, and this I will not do. What will be the outcome is anyone's guess. The danger is that the President has already committed himself so deeply to the Hopkins program that he will not yield. My resignation in the near future is still a distinct possibility, but I will make every effort to work out a policy which will make it possible for me to continue to do the work that I have been doing.

I told the President about the Forest Service violation of his order in connection with the Mount Olympus National Park Bill. I pointed out that the Forest Service would not give us an inch of land anywhere if it could avoid it. I reminded him that at a Cabinet meeting, just about the time Congress met for this session, he had told us that no department was to oppose legislation offered by any other department. He said that was true. It was as clear as day that he did not know of the National Forest Service's opposition to our park bill. He said that this area ought to be a national park and he asked me whether he couldn't give us the land by Executive Order. I told him I didn't know but would look it up and advise him. He said there were three areas out there now, one the Mt. Olympus National Monument, which he had transferred to us by Executive Order in 1933, a surrounding tract of timber which the National Forest Service says ought not to be cut, and still another stretch which the Forest Service thinks ought to be cut. He said he didn't think any of the three should be cut. I told him that if it shouldn't be cut, the only way to insure against that was to set up a national park. Then we would be certain that there would be no cutting of timber except for necessary cleaning out. The President made a note to write to the Forest Service and ask how it happened that it had opposed this bill without consulting him.

I also referred to our Department bill and told him that with his little finger he could get that bill through. He made a note to talk to Senator Robinson. Then he told me that he had discussed a Department of Conservation with Louis Brownlow, who is heading up the committee appointed by him some time ago to make a study of a reorganization of Federal agencies and that he and Brownlow were both agreed that there should be such a Department and that National Forests should be in it. I told him that this was fine but that there would be no need of both a Department of the Interior and a Department of Conservation. There wouldn't be enough agencies to go around. I urged this as another reason for changing the name of this Department.

I also brought up the housing situation. I urged again that the administrative agency be set up in the Interior Department. He said that Senator Wagner had suggested Colonel Hackett as a competent man to head it up. I told the President that it was all right for him to name the head of the Housing Administration but that it ought to be here under one man. I urged him again against setting up an administrative function under a commission of five. He said he was opposed to any more commissions. I pointed out that he named the Commissioner of Reclamation and that it was one of the best run and most efficient agencies in the whole Government.

Henry Wallace read a very interesting letter from a member of his staff who is in Europe with Chester Davis in which he related a talk he had had with John Maynard Keynes, the English economist. Keynes seems to think that Great Britain is some fifteen months ahead of the United States on the road to recovery. He also seems to think that we will have a temporary upturn to be followed by another depression, the upturn to be of short duration.

Wednesday, May 13, 1936

After thinking the matter over carefully, I have come to the conclusion that I cannot talk to Hopkins as I suggested to the President I would do at our conference on Saturday. I know full well that he would not yield any of the authority granted him under the pending bill and I do not propose to put myself in the position of a suppliant to him. I shall tell the President the next time I see him—and I have asked for an appointment—that there is no use of my talking to Hopkins and that only he can settle the issues involved.

Until I came back from my talk with the President on Saturday I really did not realize the extraordinary powers granted to Hopkins under this bill. The huge sum of almost $1.5 billion is granted outright to the Works Progress Administrator, which means Hopkins. The only power originally reserved to the President was the right to determine wage scales and that was the hot end of the program. Even that has been cut out by an amendment. While the bill purports to break down the appropriation into several classes of permissible expenditures, in effect it gives Hopkins blanket authority to spend this huge sum of money as, when, and where he pleases, without check or hindrance from anyone, not even from the President himself. Having granted the money, Congress will have no control nor will the courts have any power to interfere. Of course, Hopkins could be removed by the President for cause and he could be impeached by the Congress. To all effects and purposes, however, here is a man who is given the largest sum of money in the history of this country, except to the President himself under previous bills, to administer in his uncontrolled discretion. I doubt whether in all history any comparable man has been given such power. It is an extraordinary situation.

Last session Hopkins was afraid to appear before the Appropriations Committee of the Senate and hid out in Florida. I saved the bill for the President in the form in which he wanted it. In order to get the bill through Congress the President had to have the appropriation run to himself and give the assurance that he would be the Administrator. At that time Hopkins was poison to both branches of Congress. While I had a good many enemies up there, the tide was beginning to run heavily in my favor. I think Congress would not have objected to me as Administrator, but it would not have listened to the suggestion of Hopkins as Administrator. Even now the overwhelming sentiment, both in the House and the Senate, is against Hopkins and his program, notwithstanding which the House has voted him this extraordinary sum of money without any restraint worth mentioning. Under the bill as it stands and as explained by Chairman Buchanan of the Appropriations Committee, neither the President nor Hopkins could grant money to PWA, to Resettlement, or to any other Federal agency even if he wanted to. All the money had to be expended under the personal direction of WPA.

Senator Guffey came in to see me Thursday morning at his own instance. He announced that he had nothing to ask of me but merely wanted to say that he thought I had been given pretty rough treatment in connection with this relief bill. He said that Hopkins was clearly a candidate for President in 1940 and he referred to his close connection with Frank Hague, of Jersey City, and Mayor Kelly, of Chicago. He asked me where Hopkins got his influence with the President and I told him that I had been told that it was through Mrs. Roosevelt and the President's mother. It was in connection with this statement that he made the comment he did about Hague and Kelly.

He criticized Hopkins' program and Hopkins' administration of that program. On the contrary, he said I had done a fine job and an honest job. He went on to say that his leaders in Pennsylvania thought that I was the man for President in 1940. I told him this was flattering but that I was not a candidate for anything. His reply was a repetition of what he had already said and he added that his people were for me, not because I was a Pennsylvanian, but because I had done a fine and honest job as PWA Administrator and for the further reason that I was the only man in the Administration who could stand up on the platform and make a forthright speech on the issues. He added that I was the only member of the Cabinet who could make a decent speech. As he left he told me to call on him for any service that he could perform. This interview not only surprised me, it touched me. I had never met Guffey until I came to Washington and certainly I have never regarded him as much of an idealist. He is close to Farley and a loyal supporter of the President. That he should have made the statement to me that he did was highly gratifying and, of course, his references to 1940 were more than complimentary.

Tom Corcoran also came in to see me on Tuesday. The reason for his call was to find out whether I would have any objection to Foley's being urged for appointment as a United States judge in New York. I told him that I was committed to Margold, but neither he nor I think that Margold has a chance of being appointed. I assured him that I would not stand in the way of any man on my staff advancing himself. Jocularly I asked Corcoran whether he couldn't find a nice, soft berth for me. Then, to my surprise, he said that there was one place in the Administration that he thought I was pretty well fitted for, although he imagined that it would not particularly appeal to me. He referred to the Comptroller Generalship. McCarl's term expires next month. This is a fifteen-year appointment at $10,000 a year.

I asked Corcoran whether he was responsible for the story that appeared in a Washington paper the other day to the effect that Senator Harrison and I were the leading candidates for this place. I told him that it had given me a good laugh, and that the Comptrollership had never occurred to me and did not appeal to me. He said that I was in the unfortunate position of being the only real conservationist in the Administration and at the same time the best qualified man for this office. He added that I am that rare combination, an honest administrator, adding that there were many honest men but few good administrators. He pointed out that the Comptroller Generalship was the most powerful office in the Government barring only the Presidency, and with this view I agreed, as I have had ample opportunity to learn from personal experience with McCarl just how powerful this office is. I ventured the guess that Henry Morgenthau would be able to secure the selection of one of his hand-picked men for this place.

He told me of a talk with Felix Frankfurter during which Frankfurter had said that, after canvassing the situation pretty generally in the country, he had come to the conclusion that only two men in the Administration had enhanced their reputations during their connection with it. The two men he mentioned were Secretary Hull and myself. Corcoran and I touched very lightly on the Hopkins situation. I told him that if I had wanted to make trouble,

I could have stirred up a lot of it but that I had kept hands off. Corcoran said that that was the difference between a fair fighter and a man who would use any implement to fight with.

Meanwhile lines of battle are forming in the Senate. Senator Hayden yesterday introduced an amendment to the bill providing for a separate appropriation of $700 million for PWA. I don't expect for a minute that he will be able to pass this amendment, but the bill itself represents sound tactics at this stage. Senator Vandenberg offered a substitute bill. I understand that Senator Norris went to the President on Monday and strongly supported PWA as against WPA. Word came to me this morning that not only Norris but Johnson and La Follette had sent word to Hayden that they would support him in his efforts to get money for PWA. In the meanwhile, members of the PWA staff are hard at work preparing a statement of what we have done and are capable of doing in anticipation of my being called before the Senate Appropriations Committee, as it appears that I will be either on Friday or Monday. I understand that other outside pressure is being brought to bear on the President. It is being pointed out to him that he is not only making a grave mistake from the point of view of relief administration but one equally as grave from the political point of view. It seems quite clear to me that if this bill goes through substantially as it is and no further appropriation is made for PWA, I shall have no other course than to resign.

Saturday, May 16, 1936

The last two days have been eventful and busy ones. I started in on Wednesday afternoon to try to get an appointment with the President without success. I wanted to follow up my interview of last Saturday with the President, but McIntyre seems to be playing Hopkins' game now and I haven't been able to get through him. Of course, I could get through Miss Le Hand but I hate to do that, except in extreme cases. I had been asked to appear before the subcommittee of the Appropriations Committee of the Senate to give a review of the work of PWA, and members of my staff have been working desperately to get a statement in shape for me. First, I was scheduled to appear Thursday afternoon but as this conflicted with the regular Cabinet meeting, I called up Senator Adams and told him I would come Friday morning at ten o'clock.

At Cabinet meeting Thursday afternoon, after the President had gone the usual rounds, he began to talk about the work-relief program. There was no doubt that he was addressing his remarks to me. I don't know who had told him that I was expecting to go before the subcommittee as a witness, although I had intended to do that at the conclusion of the Cabinet meeting. That he knew, there was no doubt, for he told me that he didn't want me to give any figures that he had not seen in advance. In this connection he told me that the figures I had submitted to him last Saturday were all wrong, but how he could say that I cannot understand because I believed then, and I believe now, that they were accurate. Probably Hopkins and his minions had been given a chance to knock them down.

I told the President that perhaps it would be better for me not to go before the committee at all, since I did not care to make a statement that was not full and free and frank. Then he talked about indirect employment, taking the line that he usually takes in that regard. He didn't want me to give any figures on indirect employment, and my reply was that since one of the objects of the PWA program was to stimulate indirect employment, no picture of PWA would be accurate without figures on indirect employment. We hammered back and forth at each other on this subject and it was plain to see that the President was not in the best of temper. Neither was I, if the truth be told, although I kept good control of myself without, however, weakening at any point. The President said that I must not criticize the program of WPA and that it would be a criticism of that program if I should show to the subcommittee what PWA had done. He added that if the Congress should earmark for PWA any of the money proposed to be appropriated for the Works Progress Administration, he would veto the bill.

I was pretty angry by this time. It was as clear as day that the President was spanking me hard before the full Cabinet and I resented that too. All the other members appeared to be embarrassed, but I could see Henry Morgenthau stealing a covert glance at me from time to time. Doubtless he enjoyed the spanking very much.

When the President had gone down the line of the Cabinet, I had told him that I wanted to speak to him for a minute after the Cabinet meeting. As a matter of fact, what I had in mind was to say that I had been called before the Adams subcommittee. However, before I could get to the President at the conclusion of the meeting, George Dern had crowded in ahead of me to show the President some figures in a book dealing with the Florida canal project. Then Miss Perkins, as usual, shifted in ahead on the other side and began to chatter about some legislation, although the President had said that he could not be delayed because he was going out on the south lawn to meet a delegation of Navajo and Pueblo Indians. I caught Miss Perkins' eye and indicated that I wished she would withdraw, but although she understood what I was driving at, she went on. Then I stalked out of the Cabinet room in no very good temper. I had wanted an opportunity then and there to tell the President that he had put me in an untenable position, having in mind to follow promptly with my written resignation.

After I got back to my office, Miss Perkins called me up to explain that she had purposely not responded to my signal to betake herself off because she knew the President so very well and knew that it was a mistake when he was in that sort of humor to allow things to crystallize, this being her precise expression. She begged me not to let things crystallize until he had had two or three days to come to himself. She said that plainly he was under some great personal pressure. I told her that so far as I was concerned, matters had crystallized and that even the President couldn't spank me publicly.

Before Miss Perkins called me, I had already called for one of my personal secretaries, as well as for Slattery and Burlew. Then I proceeded to dictate a resignation both as Secretary of the Interior and as Public Works Administrator. I didn't call Mike Straus in on this because my mind was made up and I knew that he would hang around my neck like a heavy weight trying to dissuade me from a course of action that I was determined upon. Wishing an outside newspaperman's point of view, I called up James Waldo Fawcett at the *Evening Star* office and asked him to come over. We worked on the letter until almost seven o'clock, when I suggested that we go home for dinner and return afterward. At that time it was then in the minds of all of us that my resignation ought to go to the White House Thursday night.

In the meantime, Tom Corcoran came in to see me. I told him what had happened at Cabinet meeting, but I did not tell him that I was working on my resignation because I knew, first, that he would attempt to dissuade me and, second, that he might let the matter drop at the White House in advance of my resignation reaching the President's hand. I did indicate to him, however, that I had come pretty nearly to the end of my rope and he said he hoped that I wouldn't do anything for at least a day or two. He, too, told me, with some specifications, that the President had been under great personal pressure. He said that he was having trouble with Morgenthau because Morgenthau had made such an ass of himself in connection with the pending revenue bill. Corcoran deprecated what the President has been doing with respect to PWA and he also thinks it is a great mistake to give $1.5 billion to Hopkins to spend in his uncontrolled discretion. He wanted to go to Hiram Johnson and talk the matter over with him to see if he would espouse the cause of PWA. I told him that whatever he wanted to do would be all right with me, but that, personally, I was not particularly interested in the matter.

Thursday night Burlew, Slattery, Fawcett, and I again met in my office and we whipped into shape a rather long letter in which I presented my resignation and gave reasons supporting my action. My original idea had been to write a very short resignation, covering less than a page of letter paper. However, my three advisers thought I ought to give my reasons, in fact, prepare a document which would state my case to the public. We also decided, however, that there was no imperative necessity of sending the resignation to the White House that night. When we finally left my office after eleven o'clock, the resignation along the line that we were working was practically in final shape.

I got to the office early Friday morning and made certain corrections in the letter. These corrections were merely matters of form and not of substance. But all the way to my office and while I was working over this first draft for the last time, I could not rid myself of the notion that it would be a mistake to send that particular letter to the President. It was simply a knockout and left him no recourse. It was a fighting letter and while I was prepared to fight and was really looking forward to a separation from a service which has been so distasteful to me in many particulars, I did not think it was quite fair to kick the President in the face before closing the door. So I called my three advisers together again and after discussing the matter they agreed with me, whereupon I dictated a further draft as follows:

The Secretary of the Interior
Washington, May 14, 1936

My dear Mr. President:

I find myself differing fundamentally with your work-relief program as extended and modified under the bill now pending before the Senate. As I see it, the passage of this bill as written will destroy the Public Works Administration, a purpose which was indicated in statements made by you at recent press conferences by which, in effect, you repudiated PWA and indicated a lack of confidence in me as Administrator. Little doubt of your attitude in this matter remains in my mind in view of your statement at the Cabinet meeting today when your orders made it impossible for me to respond to the request of the Senate Appropriations Committee to present a statement of what PWA has accomplished to date.

In the circumstances I have no option except to tender my resignation, both as Secretary of the Interior and as Administrator of Public Works. This I hereby do with my thanks to you for the opportunity that you have given me to serve the country and with profound regret that the situation makes this action necessary. I hope that you will accept this resignation, to take effect at your earliest convenience.

Sincerely yours,

(Signed) Harold L. Ickes
Secretary of the Interior

The President
The White House

Wishing to get this letter into the President's hands without going through McIntyre, I called Miss Le Hand to tell her I was sending her a letter to the President. She said she would give it to him. I sent it over between ten and eleven o'clock. In the meantime, McIntyre had called me to ask me whether I could lunch with the President at one. This was the appointment that I had been trying to get for the previous couple of days, but I think it also meant that the President was feeling a little sorry for his actions at Cabinet meeting. While I was working on my resignation, Tom Corcoran came in to see me again. I think he was worried as to what I might do. He brought Ben Cohen with him and they both urged me to stick it out at least for a few months longer. I reminded them that they have been coming to me periodically begging me to "stick it out" for a few months longer but that matters had reached the point where I couldn't stand it much longer. All this without telling them that I was actually on the point of sending in my resignation. They both admitted that I had had a rough deal and they deprecated the action of the President both at Cabinet meeting and in his support of the Hopkins program. Corcoran wanted to know whether I had any objection to his going to the White House to suggest that there might be a way out all around, with a general saving of face, if the bill could be amended so as to give certain enlarged powers to RFC under which a considerable PWA program could be financed. I told Tom he could do as he pleased, but I did not want the President to think that he was representing me or that I had sent him.

Naturally, I didn't want McIntyre to know what was doing, so I told him I would lunch with the President at one. After Miss Le Hand had had a chance to give my letter to the President, I called her, told of my engagement with the President for luncheon, and said that perhaps in the circumstances the President would not want me to come. She said that she was sure he did because she had just come from his office and that he had told her I was lunching with him. I asked her whether he had read my letter and she said he had. I asked her nevertheless to find out discreetly whether he really wanted me. She called me back shortly and told me the President was expecting me.

When I went into his office shortly after one o'clock, Jesse Jones was about to leave. As Jesse left, the President looked at me with an expression of mock reproach and then, without saying a word, he handed to me a memorandum in his own handwriting as follows:

The White House
Washington

Dear Harold—

1. P.W.A. is not "repudiated."
2. P.W.A. is not "ended."
3. I did not "make it impossible for you to go before the committee."
4. I have not indicated lack of confidence.
5. I have *full* confidence in you.

6. You and I have the same big objectives.

7. You are needed, to carry on a big common task.

8. Resignation *not* accepted!

Your affectionate friend,
(Signed) Franklin D. Roosevelt

I read this communication and was quite touched by its undoubted generosity and its evident sincerity of tone. I had gone expecting that he might say that he did not want me to resign, although my resignation was in no sense a bluff. I also had in mind, if he wanted me to continue with his Administration, to discuss with him quite frankly certain matters that I have objected to. This I proceeded to do. I told him that on various occasions I had learned from the newspapers of the issuance of important Executive Orders vitally affecting matters within my jurisdiction. He asked me to give him an example and offhand I gave him three. One example was the Executive Order issued last summer which in effect wiped out PWA. At that time, after talking the matter over with Hiram Johnson, I called the President by telephone to ask for an immediate appointment that evening. Failing to get that, I told him very frankly over the telephone what I thought about the matter and he issued a modifying and explanatory statement in which, in effect, the Executive Order was recalled, but there never was any doubt what the intention was.

Another example that I gave him was the Executive Order making Dr. Gruening Reconstruction Administrator for Puerto Rico without consulting me. The President said he thought that I had recommended Gruening, but I told him that I had written him a letter telling him that I would make a suggestion if he desired one but that no request for a suggestion had ever come. I told him that the Department of the Interior should have been made the agency in this case, in which event Gruening would have been the person to run the show. I pointed out to him that there was no check on Gruening unless the President was checking on him, a suggestion that he promptly negatived, and that there might be a first-class blowout one of these days in Puerto Rico for which he and I would be held responsible, when I had no authority in the matter. He suggested an amendment to this order which would give me immediate supervisory authority. The third instance I cited was with reference to the youth movement.

I recalled to the President that at no time had I been consulted with respect to the continuance of the relief program and that no information had been given to me except through the newspapers. Then I brought up the question of housing and there were one or two other matters that I frankly took up with him.

I must say that the President took everything in the best possible spirit. He told me that he was not going to discontinue PWA and that there were two or three plans that he had in mind for working matters out. It seems that someone had already said to him that instead of the $1.5 billion going to Hopkins as WPA Administrator it should go to the President. I urged him very strongly to have the bill amended in the Senate in this respect. I pointed out that WPA could be the biggest joint in our armor during the coming campaign. I said that, whether justly or unjustly, Hopkins was being criticized in all parts of the country, and that while I had no opinion to express as to the justice of any of these criticisms, I did think that it was not a good time for him to be thumbing his nose at the country as he would be doing if he allowed a bill to go through that would give Hopkins greater power and authority than had ever been given to anyone in history.

The President said that Hopkins, of course, would take any suggestions from him. I told him that undoubtedly he would but that under the bill he wouldn't have to. In that event the only recourse of the President would be to discharge him, and I said that a good deal of damage might be done before the President would be able to get around to that even if he wanted to. Even then, if Hopkins should be let out as Administrator, his successor would have the same powers.

The President has in mind that through widening the powers of RFC and by some contributions from the WPA fund to us as grants, it would be possible to go ahead with a considerable PWA program. As a matter of fact, I know this can be done because we have been working on an amendment to the law here which, however, I have not disclosed to the President, although at this session with him I told him that we had an amendment which I would like to send him for his consideration. He said that he would call in Jones and Hopkins and me and work out a plan of action. At this point I jocularly remarked that a simple person like me would be at a disadvantage sitting down with three candidates for the Presidency. The President had a good laugh at this and remarked,

"Well, two anyhow," meaning, I think, Jones and himself. I did not follow up the matter, although more and more people are coming to believe that Hopkins is an active candidate.

Wednesday afternoon my bill changing the name of this Department to that of Conservation passed the Senate, thanks to the clever generalship of Senator Robinson. I at once called the President and asked him if he would let me get a rule in the House. I told him if we got the rule we would pass the bill through the House easily. He said he would. During our talk on Friday he told me that he had sent word to Speaker Byrns that he wanted a rule on this bill and that he believed we had a good chance of getting the legislation through.

This led him to discuss the reorganization of the executive branch of the Government, which I think he really has very much at heart. Among other things he is developing in his own mind a theory of having two or three executive assistants each of whom would coordinate certain departments, take care of routine matters, and bring to him others for consideration. I told him I thought this would be a good plan, as it would save him a lot of time and trouble. As a matter of fact, as I have said on other occasions, I marvel at his ability to handle the mass of detail that he finds in his lap from day to day.

As an example of the matters that were brought to him, the President made a statement which came nearer to being a criticism of Morgenthau than any I have ever heard. He said that Henry had to get in to see him at least four times a week to tell him what francs were selling at or how he believed the next bond issue would go, and that on the other days of the week he had to call him by telephone to give him the same information. He said that with an executive assistant it wouldn't be necessary for him to have to take care of such small details. I made no comment.

Among other things that I have been objecting to, as I said to the President, was the disposition on the part of several men on my staff to short-cut me to the White House. I mentioned this to the President.

Along toward the end of our interview the President said: "My dear fellow, you mustn't get any idea that I am working at cross purposes with you," to which I replied: "Mr. President, I have a real affection for you and I hope you know that at all times I have been loyal. It will always be my purpose to work out things as you want them worked out, but I would like to know what is going on with respect to matters under me before they get too far along."

While I was about it, I brought up the question of housing. The President said he hoped that the Wagner-Ellenbogen bill would pass at this session, and that he had told Wagner that he did not want another independent agency set up. He said he wants the administration in the Department of Interior and he suggested a committee of three, of which I should be the chairman. I told him I did not think we should have any such setup as that. I pointed out that the Bureau of Reclamation was one of the best administrative agencies in the Government and that housing could be set up that way, with the head of the bureau appointed by him, just as the Commissioner of Reclamation is appointed by him. I think he is more than half inclined to this view.

This talk with the President undoubtedly cleared the sky. I don't know what he has in mind for the future so far as I am concerned, nor could I ask him. However, I must say this: even if he wanted to keep me for selfish political reasons of his own until after election, it was not necessary for him to express himself in the written communication that he handed to me. It was not necessary for him to commit himself in writing at all. It is my own thought that the President has no present purpose of not continuing me as a member of the Administration in the event of his re-election. I don't mean by this to say that he will keep me on. He may change his mind and he may have a good reason for changing his mind. All that I mean is that he has no present plan, if indications go for anything. During our talk he referred on two or three occasions to certain things that we both would be interested in working out next year. I have already pointed out on one or two previous occasions references by him to future events on the basis of his re-election.

The Eustachian tube of my right ear, which is the only one I have for hearing purposes, filled up before I went to the White House, so that the President had to talk quite loudly to me all during lunch. However, I had no difficulty in hearing him. Following the luncheon I went over to the White House proper to have Dr. McIntire give me a treatment. As I came out and started out in my car, Mrs. Roosevelt and a companion came out. I could easily have driven off without seeing her because I did not notice her until one of the guards called my attention to her. Then when I looked up I saw Mrs. Roosevelt waving most cordially to me. No one could have had a friendlier attitude than she seemed to have. Again this morning, when I came out of the White House after seeing Dr. McIntire, I met her with a group of Congressional ladies. She was even more cordial than she was yesterday. She not only greeted me in the most friendly manner, but she stopped to shake hands with me and to make one or two remarks.

Tom Corcoran says that all is not well between the President and Henry Morgenthau. He thinks that Hopkins will blow up in a few weeks and that is all the more reason for my hanging on. He says that the President has knowledge of the criticism of the Hopkins program from all parts of the country. Corcoran went over to see Emil Hurja at Democratic headquarters yesterday afternoon and Hurja showed him press clippings on WPA and PWA. Hurja is keeping careful track of editorial expressions in newspapers in all parts of the country and he finds only six per cent of the newspapers supporting WPA while there is very widespread approval of PWA. Jim Farley called me up from New York on Friday to ask how things were going. This was before I saw the President. I told him that things were in bad shape and that he had better get down here and see what he could do to help straighten them out. He said he would be down on Monday. In the meantime, some of the newspaper articles are openly saying that Farley is sympathetic to the PWA as against WPA, and these articles are being printed by men who, according to Corcoran, have talked to Farley and so speak with authority.

I forgot to say that yesterday Senator Clark, of Missouri, called me up to warn me that Kneipp and others of the Forest Service had been trying to get a reconsideration in the Senate of the vote carrying my Conservation Department Bill. He also told me that they have been sending telegrams through the country trying to build up a backfire. I at once called the President, who said that he would get hold of Chief Forester Silcox and tell him to instruct the members of his staff that this bill was none of their business and that they were to lay off. Here is another example of bureaucracy running wild even to the extent of defying the express orders of the President and opposing a bill which was introduced with his knowledge and consent and which he is supporting. I fervently hope that some day someone will curb this lawless organization. Certainly Henry Wallace isn't able to, even if he has that inclination.

Tuesday, May 19, 1936

The *Washington News* had quite a circumstantial story last night about my threatening to resign if the President continued to refuse to support a PWA program. Of course, there have been various rumors to the effect that I have resigned or was considering doing so, and all of this I have had no recourse except to deny. After all, one can't rush into print with an affirmation that he either has resigned or is planning to do so. I dislike exceedingly not to be entirely frank and truthful in such matters, but, after all, it wouldn't be fair to the President for me to do this. There is also something to be said for the proposition that if a lie is ever permissible, it is when someone tries to pry into your own private affairs.

While this story came pretty close to the truth, it after all missed the mark. I did not threaten to resign; that I would never do. When I make up my mind that my situation has become intolerable, I will either go along with it or resign, just as I did in this instance. My resignation was there for the President to accept if he wished to do so, but he was so friendly and kind and apparently so sincerely desirous that I continue in my present job that I had no option except to drop the matter. I am sorry that these stories are appearing now because they may be embarrassing to him.

This story also set out in some detail that there was a stormy Cabinet session last Thursday at which Secretaries Hull, Farley, Wallace, and Perkins supported my position in favor of a public works program. Farley was not at the Cabinet meeting, and, as I have already set down, no other member of the Cabinet had a word to say during the colloquy between the President and myself.

On Saturday I sent a radiogram through Naval Communications to the President, who was on his boat down the Potomac, telling him that I thought it would create a very bad impression if I did not appear on Monday before the Senate Committee on Appropriations. I had left with him a copy of the statement that had been prepared for me to make at this hearing and he had said he would take it on the trip with him. He radioed back that he saw no reason why I should not go and that he would go over the statement with me at the White House at nine o'clock Monday morning, since he had not taken it with him. Accordingly, I went up before the Senate committee and made my statement. Following it some questions were asked by various Senators.

I came away with the feeling that, after all, this had been lost motion on my part. The truth was that I was not free to make such a statement as I wanted to make. I really would have liked to point out the advantages of PWA or WPA, which would have involved some pretty sharp criticisms of the Hopkins organization. This I could not do. My statement was a factual one of what PWA has already done under its program, but there was nothing very exciting or interesting in it and little that was new. The Senators received me courteously and considerately, as they always do, and Senator Glass was kind enough to say that he thought that PWA was better administered and had a better program than the other relief agencies.

Senator Hayden is working on an amendment which was drafted for him by Foley of the PWA legal staff which would make it possible to finance a considerable PWA program up to $1 billion by enlarging the powers of RFC. This would not involve any additional appropriation. Later in the day Senator Byrnes called me up. He seems anxious to work out something that will give us additional funds to go along on, and I think that is the general disposition of the Senators.

Senator Dickinson, of Iowa, was present during my testimony for part of the time and later in the day, on the floor of the Senate, he made a speech vigorously attacking Hopkins and his program but saying some complimentary things about my administration of PWA. Dickinson has been one of the most consistent and vigorous critics of the New Deal since 1933. I think his attitude toward PWA expresses the general attitude of individual Senators.

I spent four hours on the witness stand in the courtroom of Chief Justice Wheat of the Supreme Court of the District of Columbia as a witness for the Government in some municipal power litigation involving the right of PWA to make loans and grants for municipal power plants. Five cases have been consolidated with the idea that they can all be presented as one case to the Supreme Court. I went over somewhat the same ground that I covered when I took the stand at Spartanburg, South Carolina, some months ago, and lawyers representing the Government seemed to think that I acquitted myself creditably.

Friday, May 22, 1936

After everything seemed to be in good shape in the House on my Department bill, rumors began to come to me that things were not so well. The President had promised to call off the Forest Service from further lobbying, but I do not know whether he really did anything about it. Even if he did, the damage had already been done because the opposition had been stirred up. Moreover, the lobbying continued as before.

I had been told on several occasions that word was sent to Speaker Byrns that the President wanted this bill put through and a rule to put it through. Puryear had word from Speaker Byrns' secretary that the thing was all set for a rule. Then word came to me that John O'Connor, chairman of the Rules Committee, had never heard from the White House and that his impression was that the White House did not want the bill passed. I had an appointment with the President on Wednesday and I spoke to him again about my very deep personal interest in this bill. He said that Henry Wallace had told him that there was a big political issue involved and that a number of members of the House had called up to say that the bill would precipitate a fight. I told him that Henry Wallace and his people had gone out to stir up trouble and then had come back to say that there was trouble. I said to the President that he would not lose a single farmer's vote in the whole country if this bill should go through. I referred to the fact that his orders had been violated by the Department of Agriculture when members of that Department had lobbied against this bill and that the opposition was purely local, being centered here in Washington. He kept repeating that he did not want a fight and when I asked him if he would help me get a rule, he said the same thing all over again.

It was perfectly clear to me that he had reneged on the whole proposition. I told him how much this bill meant to me personally, but he was not moved. I had talked to McIntyre about it before I went in to see the President and he had told me that the President was still back of the bill and that he (McIntyre) had asked for a rule in the President's name. Later in the afternoon he called me up to say that he had talked with the President and that the President had told him what he had told me, namely, that he did not want a fight. McIntyre pretended that they were still going through the motions of trying to get a rule. I do not believe it.

Hearing that Felix Frankfurter was in Washington, I asked him to come in to see me Wednesday afternoon. I told him about the status of the bill. I did not ask him to help and he did not really say that he would, but I think that he was sympathetic, and I wanted him to know the situation. He asked me what I thought about the campaign and I told him I thought it was going to be a hard fight. He thinks so too. He said that recently when he was at the White House he made the remark that he did not like the air of optimism that prevailed there then any better than two or three months earlier he had liked the air of defeatism that he had found.

We also discussed the constitutional question, in view of the opinion of the Supreme Court declaring the Guffey Coal Act unconstitutional and that of the United States Circuit Court of Appeals for the District in upholding an injunction against one of Tugwell's resettlement projects. He asked me if I agreed with him that the Constitution should not be brought into this campaign as an issue, and I told him that I did agree, because the groundwork had not been laid. I told him, however, that I believed the issue should be built up during the next few years. It is perfectly obvious that the Supreme Court is going to do everything in its power to give the big business interests what they want. Beginning with John Marshall, the Court built up a system of extreme nationalism because that was what the business interests wanted in those days. Now that business is in the saddle and only the Federal Government can hope to cope with it, the Supreme Court has swung away from the theory of nationalism and is trying to divide up the United States into forty-eight states of different ideals and background and with different laws. We are no longer one nation. The big corporations operate as entities in the whole country, but the United States, according to Chief Justice Hughes and his four reactionary associates, is not to be allowed to exercise powers commensurate with the social and economic needs of the people.

Emil Hurja came in to see me on Wednesday. He talked to me very confidentially, giving me some information and figures that he had not yet submitted even to Farley. He is really concerned to have someone get across to the President the idea that this campaign is going to be the toughest kind of a fight. Hurja thinks that Landon will be a formidable candidate and he believes that when test polls are taken, with Landon running against Roosevelt, the showing will not be any too good for Roosevelt. As he put it, he thinks the *Literary Digest* poll will be "terrible." He goes so far as to say that, on the basis of present indications, the result of the election may hinge on the vote in a very few states, and he believes that the Democratic strategy ought to be to concentrate every effort on the states that must be carried in order to assure a victory for Roosevelt.

He showed me some confidential polls that he has had taken. These have been taken in circumstances that precluded any possibility of being doctored. These polls were taken in states where Roosevelt is supposed to be well in the lead, and while the voters tested were small in numbers, the results were really alarming. I asked Hurja what was the main issue that he thought we would have to meet and he said extravagant use of money. He thinks Hopkins will be the main issue and that we are in a bad way on that issue.

Thursday night Farley made a speech before the Democratic State Convention in Grand Rapids, Michigan, and he attacked Landon, of Kansas, although not by name. He referred to him as an inexperienced Governor of a "typical prairie state." This has already stirred up quite a storm and the end is not yet. Republican members of the House from the Middle West replied to Farley yesterday, and I would not be surprised if this grew into a major political issue.

As soon as I read this report of Farley's speech, I felt that he had made a grave political mistake. I have heard through Fawcett that a real effort is being made among Republicans to prevent Landon's nomination. Apparently Hoover is definitely opposed to him. Fawcett has told me this. Senator Dickinson quite openly criticized Landon to Farley and me at the Gridiron Club dinner. According to Fawcett, there is a feeling among the anti-Landon Republican leaders that if they can prevent him from being nominated for four ballots, they can beat him, and Senators Vandenberg and Dickinson are talked of as very likely dark-horse candidates.

It is my opinion that Farley, by this remark, greatly strengthened Landon's chances of nomination and that he gave him quite a boost toward the White House. In the first place, Farley was the last man in the Administration who should have opened fire on Landon.

That would have come with better grace from any other member of the Cabinet. My own opinion is that either Henry Wallace or I should have opened the attack on Landon, for two reasons. In the first place, we have both been Republicans. But for Jim Farley, a more or less typical Irish-Catholic politician from New York, to go into the Middle West and make such a remark was a grave error. I predict that we will hear more of this incident before the campaign is over, especially if Landon is nominated, as seems now to be the probability.

Congressman Dempsey, of New Mexico, came in to see me this morning. He has been a great friend of this Department and of me personally since coming to Congress, and while he has had only one term here, he has proved himself to be a very adroit and clever member of the House. He has been especially interested in my Department bill and he came back from New Mexico, where he was attending the Democratic convention, in response to a telegram from Puryear to help with the bill. He told me that he had talked to John O'Connor this morning. O'Connor is an old friend of his and he told Dempsey very frankly that the White House was against this bill and for that reason he could not bring in a rule.

Here is a plain case of being "sold down the river" by the President. When this bill was introduced at the last session, it was with the knowledge and consent of the President. He said that he would not make it a "must" bill but he would let it be known that he was in favor of the legislation. He said further that he would give orders to the other departments, particularly Agriculture, not to lobby against it. There was an open, active, and persistent lobby against the bill in that session. Wallace himself appeared before both the Senate and House committees in opposition. So did Silcox, the Chief Forester. Not only did they fight it directly, they fought it indirectly through the farm organizations and through their field forces. On three different occasions I called this to the President's attention and on each occasion he told me that he would put a stop to it. However, the lobbying persisted in spite of the fact that the President told me that he had told Wallace to put a stop to it. I felt that I had to believe the President, although it seemed to me to be an impossible situation that a member of the Cabinet was openly disobeying specific orders from the President.

At the beginning of this session I again asked the President whether I could go ahead with the bill and he said that I might. He told me again that he would not make it a "must" bill. Again I asked him whether he would call off the dogs of war of the Department of Agriculture and he said he would. Without any aid from the White House, largely through the friendly interest of Senator Robinson, the bill passed the Senate about two weeks ago. At once the Department of Agriculture got busy. Its lobbyists tried to get a motion of reconsideration in the Senate, and, failing that, they moved over in full force to the House. Lobbying against the bill was open and flagrant, and last Saturday I called the President on the telephone about it and he said he would get in touch with Silcox, the Chief Forester, and tell him that it was none of the business of Forestry and that they were to lay off.

He may have done this, but if he did, once again he was openly flouted, because the lobbying has continued without interruption. So successful has the lobbying been that it has succeeded in blocking the bill by raising fears in the President of a fight that might have serious political repercussions. I do not know whether the President really believes that the result would be serious or whether he is just rationalizing. I do know that once again he has broken faith with me. He did it with respect to soil erosion; he has done it on other occasions; and now he has done it in a manner that affects me very deeply.

Unfortunately, there isn't anything that I can do about it. We cannot pass the bill without a rule and we cannot get a rule unless the President gives the word. I cannot go to the White House again with my resignation in my hands. That would make me appear ridiculous. I can only regret that my resignation was not accepted last week. I would like to be in a position to let off a little steam at the expense of the Department of Agriculture, and I would not be averse to telling how I have been double-crossed at the White House. Dempsey talked quite frankly to me. He said that the feeling is growing among Members of Congress that the President cannot be relied upon even after he has given his word. He told me that Congressman Greever and a few other Congressmen were in his office talking the other day. Greever made the remark that he had not known me until I came here as Secretary of the Interior, but that there was no doubt that I was the strongest member of the Cabinet. He said that if it was left to the House, I could have nearly anything I wanted. There are a few disgruntled members there, according to Greever, but when he puts it up to them whether I have ever double-crossed them or acted otherwise than as a square shooter, they all admit that I have not. He concluded his remarks by expressing wonder that in spite of what I have done for the Administration and what I mean in the way of strength to the Administration, I am the one man who seems to get nothing at the hands of the Administration.

Dempsey related this incident to me, which is interesting: after Huey Long had made one of his speeches on the floor of the Senate in which he had practically accused the President of being a liar, a fellow Congressman remarked to him that Long ought to be impeached. Dempsey cautioned him that an impeachment meant a trial and that at a trial it might not be possible to prove the case against Long.

It is pretty tough when things like this can be said about the President of the United States and when members of his own official family and of his own party in Congress feel that his word cannot be relied upon. It hurts me to set down such a fact, but it is the fact, as I have had occasion to know more than once. For a long time I refused to admit even to myself that it was the fact, but there is no use fooling myself any longer.

I had an appointment with the President this afternoon. I did not bring up again the question of this Department, although I have sent him two written memoranda on the subject recently—one a general one and another, which went over today, telling him what O'Connor had told Dempsey and quoting Dempsey also to the effect that with a rule the bill would go through easily. I told the President today that I was sticking my neck out, but that there were two or three things I wanted to say to him.

I told him, first, that, in my opinion, Landon would make a very formidable candidate. I know that the President has been of the opinion that he would be an easy man to beat. The President said that he thought Landon would be formidable but that he would defeat him. He did not say this with his usual overconfident air. I told him that he would beat Landon, but that it would be a hard, bitter fight to the very end.

Then I told him that, in my judgment, Jim Farley had made a great mistake in his Grand Rapids speech. The President said, "It was terrible, and I had told Jim not to talk about Landon." I said that it would require a good deal of effort on our part to overcome the damage that Jim had done.

Then I told him that while I had changed my opinion entirely about John Garner and felt that the country would be safe in his hands as Vice President, it was only fair to say that he would not bring to the President a single vote where he needed votes. The President agreed in general, but did say that Garner might be helpful in Colorado, Montana, and Washington.

I haven't agreed with the President that Landon should not be mentioned in any of our speeches. As a matter of fact, I told him some time ago that we ought to begin to open up on him, not with a savage attack, but with some gentle kidding. I think it would have done a lot of good if we had taken advantage of an obvious situation to poke some fun at Landon, his supporters, and his pretensions. If this was to be done, it should have been started some time ago. After all, if he is nominated he will have to be taken rather seriously and the greater the build-up, the more difficult to pierce the armor with ridicule. But not only was Jim Farley's onslaught a mistake in method, it was a mistake in the personality of the man making the attack.

Monday, May 25, 1936

Saturday morning I worked hard in order to catch the one o'clock train to New York. I had a talk with Senator Hayden about the relief bill. He told me that Jones had submitted an amendment, the looks of which he did not like. I told him that I did not see why Jones was sitting in when we were not, and expressed the hope that no amendment would be decided upon without conference with members of my staff. I told him that Hackett, Foley, and Burlew would be available at any time during my absence from Washington. I told him also that PWA did not care to be subordinate to RFC any more than it did to Hopkins and WPA.

I got into New York shortly after six o'clock. Ann Dahlman, who had driven on from Washington on Thursday to visit some friends, came to the Roosevelt to take me to dinner. Then I took her to the theater. We saw *Call It a Day*. It was very bright and clever, but I must confess that I was too dead tired to enjoy it. I simply could not keep my mind on it, but Ann liked it and had a good time.

Sunday was very hot. For the twenty-fourth of May it broke all records for well over twenty years. I went out for a short walk in the morning and at one o'clock Ann came in again and we lunched in my rooms. Then Merriam, who happened to be in New York attending some meetings, came down and the three of us chatted for a couple of hours. In the meantime, I managed to do a little work, although not very much. For the last time, I went over the speech I was to make at night and, as usual, found some corrections that I wanted to make.

At eight o'clock I went to the Hotel Astor, where I was the guest of honor and principal speaker at a meeting held under the auspices of the United Palestine Appeal. Although it was a hot night, there were over a thousand people present, among them many of the prominent Jews of the city. Rabbi Wise was there and so was my old friend Judge Julian W. Mack, of the United States Circuit Court of Appeals. Nathan Straus presided.

These people and others were so gracious that they almost embarrassed me. Rabbi Wise, before we went in to dinner, told me, as he had told Judge Mack previously, that he had read my speech, a draft of which had been sent to him, and that it was the best speech that had ever been made before this group. He characterized it as "eloquent." They both spoke in warm terms of the speech that I made before the same group in Washington in January of 1935.

Rabbi Wise and several other speakers preceded me and they were all very kind in what they said about me and my liberal attitude toward minority groups. Rabbi Wise assured those present that they were about to hear the most eloquent and touching address they had ever listened to, or words almost as fulsome. I knew this could not be so, and it really embarrassed me. In a preliminary extemporaneous sentence I assured my audience that while I appreciated Rabbi Wise's generous statements, I knew I could not live up to the expectations that he had aroused in them.

I was on the air for approximately half an hour. It was a national hookup over the National Broadcasting Company's network. I must say that my audience treated me most generously. Judge Mack drove me back to the Roosevelt after the conclusion of the ceremonies.

This morning Burlew called me up from Washington to tell me that Jones and a subcommittee of the Appropriations Committee of the Senate had worked out an amendment, which he and others of my staff regard as highly unsatisfactory. I concurred in their judgment. I told Burlew, as I later told Slattery, to serve notice all around that I was not satisfied with the amendment and that I would not go along on it. Then Foley took the telephone and read to me a draft of a telegram that he offered for my consideration to send to the President. I told him to send the telegram as drafted. In it I told the President that I was not satisfied with the Jones amendment. Then I called Senator Hayden and asked him what he thought of the amendment. He said he did not like it. It seems that Jones has told the members of the subcommittee that the amendment was satisfactory to the President. Hayden told them that they ought not to take that for granted, and he proposed that he see the President tomorrow when the latter returns to Washington from Hyde Park, where he went over the week end on account of the injury suffered by his mother when she fell two or three days ago. Hayden said they had no writing from the President, and he did not feel like taking any oral assurances from anyone. Subsequently the President denied that Jones spoke with authority.

I told Hayden what I had already told Burlew and Slattery, only in more forcible language. He had said that Congress either ought to give me a program to go ahead on or ought not to. With this sentiment I heartily agreed. I told him that if Congress wanted to take PWA away from me and thus give me a kick in the pants, that was one thing, but that I would be "God-damned" before I would be a tail to either Jones's kite or to Hopkins' kite. He said that he did not blame me. If this is the kind of a deal that the President is going to stand for, after assuring me at the time he declined to accept my resignation that something would be worked out that would keep PWA going on a basis that I had a right to assume would be satisfactory to me, then all I can say is that I am more sorry than ever that I did not insist upon the acceptance of my resignation.

I wrote to the President yesterday telling him that I had gone through all of the editorial clippings that had come to me through the clipping bureau whose service I take, with respect to the Department bill. As I advised him, while some of these clippings expressed a neutral attitude on the change in name, some were favorable and not a single one was in opposition. This certainly does not comport with Henry Wallace's statement to the President that a big political issue is involved and that a terrific fight impends in Congress unless this bill is put in the cooler.

I had breakfast with Merriam this morning, or rather he came back and sat with me while I had mine, he having had his first. Then we lunched together. I told him the latest development in

Washington and he told me that he did not think I ought to resign. He is going to Chicago this afternoon but will be back on Friday, when he sails for Germany. He cautioned me two or three times not to do anything rash, but I confess that I do not feel very cheerful in my mind.

At lunch he commented on the fact that men like Moley, Tugwell, and Frankfurter had kept away from the President older and more experienced men whose disposition it was to be with the President but who are now critical of the Administration. He said that neither Wesley C. Mitchell nor himself would have been in the Administration at all if it had not been for me, referring to the fact that I put them on the National Resources Executive Committee. He said that Harold Moulton, of the Brookings Institution, had been friendly to the President but had never been called in, and that the same was true of Professor Dodds, head of the Department of Political Science of Princeton, and others.

Tuesday, June 2, 1936

I left New York the afternoon of Monday, May 25, and reached Chicago the following morning. Tuesday afternoon I took Mr. Inman, who is in charge of our Housing office in Chicago, in my car to inspect the Jane Addams and the Julia Lathrop housing projects. From what I saw and heard I was very much disappointed with the progress that has been made. There isn't any doubt that something is wrong in the Housing Division, in fact, has been wrong for a long time. We are not getting results. There is a failure to accept responsibility and an inability to decide questions as they come up, with too much of a disposition to build alibis to be invoked in case of future criticism and a general lack of an effective, aggressive organization. Moreover, we are still overstaffed, and there seems to be a flock of high-priced executives attached to the Washington office, who, in order to give an appearance of being busy, spend their time riding on Pullman cars around the country. I found, too, that the Housing Division has not even had intelligence enough and pride of organization enough to put proper signs on our projects. I cannot see how anyone reading any of these project signs could fail to believe that they were being constructed by WPA.

During the time that I was in New York and Chicago I kept in constant touch with Washington. Naturally, I was very much interested in what was to happen to PWA in the relief bill that had already passed the House and was pending in the Senate. For a while we had some pretty rough going, but the President kept faith with me and came to our rescue with an endorsement of the Hayden amendment, which had been drafted by Foley. Even so, there was some trouble in ironing things out, both with the Appropriations Committee and in the Senate after the bill had been reported. The men who really did the work on this matter during my absence were Burlew and Foley, and they both did a thoroughly good job. After many ups and downs and not a few vicissitudes the Senate finally passed the bill yesterday, after adopting in open session two or three amendments which we wanted and the incorporation of which strengthened our position very much indeed. On the face of the bill, as it left the Senate for the House, there will be available for both loans and grants out of our revolving fund the sum of $300 million, which, of course, will mean quite a respectable PWA program. Moreover, the Senate amended the bill in another important particular. Instead of appropriating approximately $1.5 billion to be used by Hopkins in his uncontrolled discretion, the appropriation runs to the President. Thus not only has my face been saved by a considerable margin, but Hopkins will not be occupying the seat of high power upon which he had envisaged himself as sitting.

On Saturday, which was Memorial Day, Jane and I got an early start, with Carl driving, and went up to Altoona. On our way through Hollidaysburg I decided to take another look at what was left of my Grandfather McCune's farmhouse and grist mill on the banks of the Juniata River, about three miles outside of Hollidaysburg, where I was born.

Some years ago the Pennsylvania Railroad made a freight yard out of the land just across the river from my grandfather's farm, an area which theretofore had not contained a single railroad track. When I tried to find the old road and the historic covered bridge that used to span the Juniata River just opposite the old farmhouse, I found, to my surprise, that there wasn't any road left. So we had to turn back to Hollidaysburg to the court house, where we turned and finally found a bridge across the river. Then we drove up the right bank of the river along a road in very bad repair until we came to what was left of the grist mill. Only the stonework that had comprised the lower part of the mill was left, and the covered bridge had entirely disappeared. The old farmhouse looked quite run down and disreputable. The farmhouse had been cut in half years ago by the then owner, so that it had long ceased to be the capacious, comfortable, and respectable farmhouse of my boyhood's recollection. The old apple orchard that used to lie between the farmhouse and the little schoolhouse where my mother and her brothers and sisters went to school had also disappeared, although the schoolhouse itself still stood. It, too, was thoroughly disreputable. There have been radical changes, and none of them for the better, with respect to these properties since I last saw them when Anna and Raymond and I drove through that section of Pennsylvania shortly after the world war.

I thought I would like to push on into what we used to know as the "loop," where my Uncle "Adie" (Andrew) Moore, who was married to my mother's sister Mary, used to farm on shares one of my grandfather's farms. I had visited this farm many times as a boy, but my recollection is that if I ever saw it after going to Chicago in 1890, it was on only one occasion, and that about 1893 or 1894. I found the farm all right. We drove along the edge of it and came to a place inside the fence where there was a pleasant spot where we could eat the picnic lunch that we had taken with us. This part of the country has run down too. I could not help but reflect that when I was a boy this whole countryside was covered by farms which yielded a comfortable, although not a luxurious, living to native American stock of a fine sort. Now I doubt whether anyone is able to eke out of these farms more than a mere existence.

Then we drove back through Hollidaysburg and over to Altoona. There we did not pause, although we passed our old homestead at 1518 Fifth Avenue, the house that my father and mother had built and in which we were living at the time of my mother's death in 1890. When father died, eleven or twelve years later, we sold the place, and either that owner or a subsequent one had turned the house into two apartments. This whole neighborhood looked badly run down. We drove by the old Second Presbyterian Church, where as a boy I attended church and Sunday school, and paused to take a look at what used to be known as "the green corner" at Ninth Avenue and Twelfth Street, which my Grandfather Ickes had owned and where my own immediate family had lived as well as my Grandfather and Grandmother Ickes. It was here that all of the older children of my father and mother were born, except myself.

This ramshackle old wooden building may have been green once, but it did not look as if it had had a coat of paint for forty years. Then down Seventh Avenue to the Sixth Street bridge, over to Eleventh Avenue and so on out to the Horseshoe Bend Road. We drove up into the bend, but the view from there is not nearly so impressive as it is from the Pennsylvania Railroad. Then we started back to Washington, where we arrived after eight o'clock. It was a long, hard day's drive, but I was glad for many reasons to see again some of these familiar old landmarks, although it was sad to see them in such a rundown condition.

Yesterday morning I had an appointment with the President. I told him that the amendment to the relief bill, giving continued life to PWA, was, in general, satisfactory to us. I told him also that Congressman Buchanan, chairman of the Appropriations Committee of the House, had been to see me Friday. He said to me that he had not heard from the President about the Hayden amendment but indicated that if the President told him that he wanted the amendment adopted, he would do whatever the President wanted. The President promised to get in touch with Congressman Buchanan and tell him that the amendment was all right.

The President asked me whether I was willing to make a speech over the air on Sunday night for the purpose of somewhat taking the wind out of the sails of the Republican National Convention with respect to its platform. This convention will meet in Cleveland next week. He outlined one or two things that he thought I might develop in my speech. I told him that I was willing to do anything that he wanted me to do. The plan appeals to me as being a good one, provided I can deliver on my end of it. The subject can be handled in such a way as to deflate the platform pomposities and insincerities of the Republicans to a considerable extent. It seems that Stanley High, who is now very close to the President in a confidential capacity and who appears to be a highly intelligent and certainly a progressive individual, first conceived the idea. He approached Senators Norris and La Follette to see whether either of them would make such a speech, but they did not get the point. They both said that they would rather wait until after the convention and then criticize the platform. Then thoughts turned to me, with the result that the President made the proposal to me and I accepted.

In the afternoon Stanley High came over to see me, at the

President's instance, and we discussed further the plan for the speech. High, I believe, used to be a minister, but he doesn't act ministerial nor look it. He is a young man whose background I know very little about and whom I had never met previously except on one occasion when he introduced himself to me in Colonel McIntyre's office. He makes a good impression. My belief is that he was a very vigorous supporter of President Hoover in 1932.

The Supreme Court yesterday handed down a five-to-four decision which, in effect, held that neither the nation nor a state may pass any law interfering in any respect with the right of an employer to come to such terms as may please him with any employees as to wages and hours of employment. The sacred right of liberty of contract again—the right of an immature child or a helpless woman to drive a bargain with a great corporation. If this decision does not outrage the moral sense of the country, then nothing will. Even the highly conservative Republican *Washington Post* this morning contained a critical editorial on it, and a vigorous one at that. Such a decision is not even as modern as the horse-and-buggy age. This is positively medieval, and I am frank to say that if this decision is constitutional, we need either an entirely new or a radically amended Constitution. If it isn't constitutional, then we need a different Supreme Court. The dissenting opinion was a vigorous one written by Mr. Justice Stone. It seems to me that his reasoning is unanswerable. Chief Justice Hughes joined on this occasion the enlightened minority that, generally speaking, consists of Justices Brandeis, Stone, and Cardozo. I doubt whether even the Republican party and William Randolph Hearst, who are so sure of the infallibility of the present Supreme Court majority, can stand up for such a terrible opinion as this, an opinion that affects the life and welfare of every individual who has to work for wages.

Sunday, June 7, 1936

Speaker Joseph W. Byrns of the House of Representatives died suddenly Tuesday night of heart disease. I did not know him at all well but he seemed to me to be a very interesting character. A product of the Tennessee mountains, he was tall and angular. His face was full of character, and altogether he presented a striking appearance. I believe that he stood high in the regard of practically all members of the House, including both Democrats and Republicans. Congressman Bankhead, of Alabama, has been selected as Speaker to succeed Byrns.

I got to work promptly on the speech that the President told me on Monday he would like to have me deliver. Stanley High came in to see me early Thursday morning. He was most enthusiastic about the speech and had only two or three suggestions of verbal changes to make. He said it was perfect in every way and struck just the right note. He asked me whether I dictated a speech like that and when I told him that I did, he expressed surprise. The members of my staff also like the speech, and on Thursday afternoon the President called me to say that it was a "peach." He said that "Missy" Le Hand was sitting by him as he was reading the speech and she asked him what he was chuckling about.

I have not taken a heavy hitting attitude in this speech. I gently kid the Republican leadership, the platform makers, and Governor Landon, who, from every indication, will be the Republican nominee, perhaps on the first ballot. I even poke fun at my old friends William Allen White, Gifford Pinchot, and Frank Knox. I do discuss possible Republican party planks in a serious vein, but I go no further than to point out the dilemma in which the Republicans will find themselves at Cleveland. I comment on the fact that William Randolph Hearst was the discoverer of Governor Landon, and I picture him as the dictator of the Republican platform and the absentee boss who will determine the deliberations at Cleveland as successor to former Republican bosses, such as Tom Platt, Murray Crane, Mark Hanna, Matt Quay, and Boise Penrose. I point out that an effort apparently has been made to select as the candidate of the Republican party the man who is the least troubled by views on any subject and who is least qualified, on the basis of experience, to be President of the United States. On Friday I cut the speech to get it within my radio time and on Saturday morning I sent the final revised draft out to be typed.

Wednesday, June 10, 1936

I have had a number of complimentary references to this speech. It seemed to make quite a hit. Not only did Dr. High express himself most enthusiastically on reading the original draft and after hearing me on the air Sunday night, but he called me up Monday afternoon to congratulate me all over again. Everyone seemed to think that my delivery was good, except Cissy Patterson. She said I talked so fast that I was hard to follow, but this was contrary to the expressions from others with whom I have talked. They all seemed to think that my delivery was unusually good. Cissy admitted that her radio was not in very good shape.

I had a short conference with the President on Monday. When I went in, he remarked about my being the cat that had swallowed the canary. He left Monday night for the Texas Centennial.

I played hookey from the office yesterday. This is the first time I have done this since I came to Washington and I am going to try to do it again during the next few days. Jane and I drove down to the Blue Ridge Mountains, not far from the Hoover Camp on the Rapidan, where we had a picnic lunch, and then home again.

I have given Robert a job on a housing project at Boston, at a salary of $1,260 a year. I want to try him out. My plan is for him to study stenography and typewriting. I expect him to live on his salary, or approximately that, although I will pay the cost of the business college. One reason for sending him to Boston was the hope that his employment there would escape the attention of the *Chicago Tribune*. However, much to my disgust, the *Evening Star* of today carries an AP story out of Boston telling about his job there. I called Boston promptly and found that newspaper correspondents had been photographing Robert and interviewing him. I only hope that he showed proper circumspection.

There isn't any doubt now that much will be made of this incident. I will be hearing it from all parts of the country. In my heart I hate nepotism and I really have been very careful not to lay myself open to the charge. I really can see little harm in giving a minor clerkship to Robert. However, I cannot forget that the *Tribune* made much of the fact that he was a temporary ranger at Yellowstone last summer.

Wednesday, June 17, 1936

The Republican convention has come and gone. In the end, it turned out to be a runaway nomination for Governor Landon, of Kansas, for President. My old friend Frank Knox, of Chicago, was nominated by acclamation for Vice President, after Senator Vandenberg had refused to run. The platform is not a remarkable document. Characteristically, it looks both ways in many respects. At the last minute Governor Landon sent a long telegram to the convention explaining his personal position as to three of the planks on which he did not agree with the convention draft. So the Republican party is going into the campaign with two platforms, one a personal platform of Governor Landon's and the other the official platform of the party.

All told, it seems to me that the Republicans put a pretty strong foot forward. They have as good a ticket as might be expected, considering all the circumstances, and the platform is at least something that they can vigorously argue about. Both candidates are from the Middle West, and a terrific fight will be waged in that territory. For some time I have been of the opinion that Governor Landon would by no means be a pushover candidate. I haven't shared the views of the President and others that he would be the easiest candidate to beat. I think there is going to be a bitter fight, with a close result. In fact, I can see the possibility of a Republican victory, although I regard the Democratic chances as superior to those of the Republicans.

Farley gave out a statement which was published in the newspapers of Monday in which he attacked Landon as a "synthetic" candidate. In other respects also, what he said was not calculated either to hurt or to help Roosevelt. I asked Dr. High to come over to see me on Monday. I wanted to tell him that, in my opinion, Farley's continued presence in the newspapers on main issues was very damaging to our cause. It happened that he had come to the same conclusion. He believes that Landon will rally to his support the Protestant vote in the Bible belt. Farley is the worst possible spokesman for the Administration, so far as the great Middle West is concerned. Not only is he an ardent Catholic, in addition to being Irish, but he connotes to the western country Tammany and all of its works. I do not think that Farley is capable of comprehending the attitude of mind of the people of the great Middle West toward a man of his type. If I were Landon, I would pray that there might be two Farleys attacking me, because then I would feel reasonably sure of my success in November.

High was expecting to see the President and said that he would put this point of view up to him. Later, Congressman Cummings, of Colorado, came in and he told me that that state was a very doubtful one from the President's point of view. Then Mayor La Guardia, of New York, called, and he was outspoken in criticism of what Farley has been doing. He considers him a distinct handicap. He told me that he understands that Farley is already making promises of jobs in New York for 1937, and that he was going to have a showdown with the President. He doesn't propose to get out on a limb, but wants a distinct understanding. *The New York Times* on Tuesday had a strong anti-Farley editorial.

Today I lunched with the President. I asked him whether one could speak freely about political matters and after he had given his consent, I told him how I felt about the coming fight. He doesn't talk nearly so confidently of the result as he did a short time ago. He admitted that it would be a hard fight, and he made the further statement that we were losing ground heavily in the Middle West but that we were gaining ground in New England, and New York and New Jersey. As to the latter, I have no knowledge, but I agree in the President's statement about the Middle West. Then I told him that in my judgment, while I hated to criticize Farley, it was my view that if he continued to make the kind of statements that he has been making about Landon, it might result in his (the President's) defeat. He told me that Jim was not altogether to blame but that Michelson was. It seems that Michelson dashes off a snappy statement of the type I have referred to as having been given out by Farley last Monday, hands it to Jim, who doesn't take time to consider it but, relying on Michelson's judgment, gives it to the press. The President said that he had both Farley and Michelson in and had given them strict orders that no more statements attacking Landon were to be issued unless they had first been submitted to him. He said that he had told Farley that he must stay off the platform and stop giving interviews, and Farley had promised to do this.

I outlined to the President, as I had previously outlined to High, a speech that I think could be made with effect before the Democratic convention meets. It seems to me that an effective attack could be made on the two platforms, Landon's and that of the Republican convention. The speech should be not too serious but should point out the absurdity and inconsistency of having two platforms. They could be referred to as a "now you see it, now you don't see it" proposition, and Landon could be represented as having repudiated the Republican platform in advance without even waiting until after election to violate it. Personally, I do not believe that we ought to wait too long before opening up on the

Republicans. It is my thought that, having rushed Landon around the end for a touchdown at Cleveland, it will be the Republican strategy to rush him around the other end for a touchdown in November. I still think that the idea I suggested some time ago, that we open up on Landon in a satirical vein, was a good one. Now that he has been built up to the extent that he has, it will be difficult to make the country believe that he is not the political messiah that he is being represented as being.

An amazing story came to my ears the other day to the effect that Dr. High was claiming the authorship of the speech that I made the Sunday night before the opening of the Republican convention. It seems that he was at a little party where some friends of ours were also guests. High told them that he had written my speech and when he saw that there seemed to be some doubt in the minds of his hearers, he said that he had not written all of it but had written a good deal of it.

All of which amazes me and at the same time makes me a little mad. The President sent High to my office to talk over with me the matter of making this speech. At that time I asked High if he had any suggestions to make, but he had none. Then I dictated the speech and sent a revised draft to High for him to look over. He made three unimportant suggestions. This was precisely all that he had to do with my speech. As a matter of fact, two or three men on my own staff were responsible for more amendments than was High. After I have dictated a speech and revised it the first time, I send copies to several members of my staff for corrections and suggestions. They go over the draft very carefully and then I go over the speech again, giving considerations to their suggestions. Some of them I adopt and some of them I do not adopt. And yet I had never felt that any of these men were writing my speeches. I adopt this method merely because I think that everyone in my position, speaking to a national audience, needs some checks not only as to his facts but as to his expressions. It is curious that a man who would not steal property will commit grand larceny of an idea or of a reputation. This is precisely what High did when he tried to take credit for writing a speech with respect to which his influence was almost practically nil.

I have a telegram from George Horace Lorimer, editor of the *Saturday Evening Post,* asking me if I will write a five-thousand-word article on President Roosevelt, to follow an article which William Allen White is preparing on Landon for publication in July. I wired my acceptance.

Friday, June 19, 1936

The Cabinet meeting on Thursday was more interesting than usual. It really got down to business, although the business was political. The President read us a draft of a platform that he had written. He had already read this to me when I lunched with him on Wednesday. At that time I told him that I thought the idea was an inspiration and as I listened to him again at Cabinet, I was more than ever impressed with his idea and the way he presented it. His idea is that instead of having the conventional platform containing planks on every subject under the sun, a short declaration of principles, not to exceed two thousand words, be adopted. There is a swing to his draft which, it seems to me, would assure its being read by many thousands of people who would not think of reading a formal, dry-as-dust platform. It seemed to make a very good impression upon all of those present.

Secretary Dern has not been at the last two or three Cabinet meetings. I understand that he is ill of some heart trouble. Secretary Swanson hasn't been there for months, and I am wondering whether he will ever attend another Cabinet meeting.

The Deficiency Appropriation Bill, carrying appropriations for work relief and PWA, has passed the House and Senate and was signed this afternoon by the President. While PWA doesn't get a great deal of money, what we do get is ours without any interference by Hopkins. We ought to be able to put through a program of about $600 million, which isn't so bad. The important thing is that PWA is recognized as a going concern. The original bill started out to appropriate $1.5 billion to Hopkins, but in the law as finally passed Hopkins is not even mentioned. The money goes to the President. All told, I am quite satisfied with the way this matter has worked out. Instead of being kicked out of bed, PWA has been formally recognized, and the fight developed the fact that PWA has a good many friends on the Hill.

Wednesday, June 24, 1936

Monday morning at nine o'clock I started for Philadelphia in my car, with Carl driving. I had thought that we would make it in about three and one half hours, this being Carl's estimate, and he usually estimates conservatively. However, it was half past one before we reached the Benjamin Franklin Hotel, where I was due to attend a caucus of the Illinois delegation at that hour.

This caucus never did come off on Monday. Governor Horner and Mayor Kelly were bitterly fighting, as they have been fighting ever since Kelly undertook to defeat Horner for renomination as governor. A postponement was had until ten o'clock Tuesday, with the convention to meet for its opening session at noon. Even on Tuesday the caucus did not get together until after twelve o'clock.

In the meantime, an agreement had been reached on all points except as to who was to be the woman member of the national committee. I did not feel that I ought to be involved in this factional fight because it might be embarrassing to the Administration, and besides I had no personal interest. I discussed the matter with Senator Lewis and he was strongly of the same opinion. It was then nearly one o'clock and he advised me to slip away from the hotel and go over to the Convention Hall. He told me afterward that when my name was called on the roll to vote on this question, he announced that I had been called away to an important conference.

The first session of the convention was no more interesting than I had expected it to be. The Convention Hall itself is attractively arranged, but the acoustics are not particularly good. The Illinois delegation sat in the middle aisle about halfway of the delegations, but, even so, it was almost impossible to hear distinctly, even with the use of the amplifiers. It was Farley's duty, as chairman of the national committee, to call the convention to order. Usually, the national chairman makes a short, perfunctory speech, but Jim launched out in what, in effect, was a keynote speech. I sat next to Senator Lewis, and both he and I felt that Jim was rather blanketing Senator Barkley, who was to make the keynote speech, and Senator Robinson, who was to make a speech as permanent chairman. Lewis confided to me that Farley said both too much and too little. He said that he was making too many speeches and giving too many interviews and saying too little in what he did give out. He also is critical of the fact that a Catholic bishop, arrayed in scarlet with a scarlet cap, delivered the opening invocation. Lewis remarked that this was not helpful, considering the prominence of the religion of Farley himself and of some others.

Farley's speech came to a conclusion and ended with the name of the President. Thereupon, one of those stereotyped "demonstrations" broke out. It all seemed forced to me. It lasted for half an hour. Lewis and I kept our seats and so did Governor Horner, who was sitting just back of us. I was on the aisle and Lewis sat next to me. It was interesting to see the number of people who stopped to shake hands with Lewis. The women particularly seemed to be very much interested in him. I suspect that if a man gets a reputation of being a lady-killer, he appeals to the women even if he is too old to be other than perfectly safe even in his most deadly attacks. But they certainly did paw over him and he always handed back as good as he received. I told him that he had the whole thing reduced to a fine art and he said that I ought to substitute the word "bunk" for art. I replied that it might be bunk with anybody else, but that he had made an art of it. And he certainly has. He is always courteous and he gives everyone, man or woman, the impression that he or she was the one particular person that he had been looking forward to seeing.

There was an early adjournment and as I was looking for Carl, I ran across Ruth McCormick Simms. I think this is the first time that I have spoken to her since Medill died; certainly it was the first occasion that I have seen her to talk to since she married former Congressman Simms. She was at Cissy Patterson's home at a party when I was presented a couple of years ago. I saw her on that occasion and I thought that she saw me, although she did not speak. Cissy told me afterward that Mrs. Simms had not seen me.

We stopped for a few minutes and had a very pleasant talk. I have never approved very much of her political morals or of her outlook on life, but I have always enjoyed talking to her because she has a keen mind and knows how to take care of herself.

One reason that I wanted to get into this part of the country was because this is the section where my Ickes ancestors first settled in Pennsylvania. I used to think that the original American Ickes settled here, but there is recent evidence to the effect that the first one settled up in New York State and that the family came down to this section later. In any event, my great-grandfather lived on Perkiomen Creek. I crossed this creek east of Pottstown, and if I had had time I would have liked to turn north at that point, which I think, from what I have heard, would have brought me into the country where my great-grandfather had lived. My grandfather, as I remember it, enlisted in the Revolutionary Army from Limerick Township, and I went through Limerick on my way to Pottstown.

I haven't gone to the convention today, but I may go tonight. I went down to see Jim Farley this morning to tell him that I thought it was very important for the President to accept the invitation to take part in the opening of the Triborough Bridge in New York. I wrote the President to the same effect yesterday. Jim also thinks that it is important and said that he would talk to the President over the telephone. I haven't been invited to this affair except as a general spectator. That is the doing of Robert Moses. I think it is important for the President to go because it will give him nation-wide publicity, and he will have an opportunity to get over to the people just how beneficial the PWA program has been. It is very small indeed on the part of the Triborough Bridge Authority not to invite me to take part in the proceedings. Naturally, I ought to have a place on the program because this is a PWA project. Moreover, it is the first non-Federal project for which I signed a contract and it is one of the biggest ones in the whole country.

Saturday, June 27, 1936

I went to the convention Wednesday night and so did Ann Dahlman and Mike Straus after the three of us had had dinner together. Senator Joseph T. Robinson made his speech as permanent chairman of the convention. I must say that it seemed to me that his speech fell far short of the opportunity that he had. It was almost purely defensive, and in politics a defensive speech is a weak speech. It seems to me that Senator Barkley did a much better job than did Robinson. I did not stay until the end of the speech. Ann did not come out of the Convention Hall as early as I did, so that I had to wait almost an hour for her. Joseph Medill Patterson, editor and publisher of the *New York News,* happened to come along and I greeted him. He told me that he wanted to have a talk with me and that he was strong for what I was doing. Then Ambassador Daniels came along. He had no car and asked me if I would give him a lift. I said that I would be glad to do so if he would wait for my guest. So the three of us drove into town together.

I did not attend the day session of the convention on Thursday because I wanted to finish this article, but I did go Thursday night. The Committee on Rules reported. This report was significant in that it provided for the abolishment of the two-thirds rule which has been in force in Democratic National Conventions for over a hundred years. There was not a real fight against this, although there was some opposition and it had been predicted in advance that it would be seriously objected to. Following this came the report of the Committee on Resolutions. Senator Wagner read this report and I listened carefully because of my interest. It seems to me that, generally speaking, the Democratic platform is a fine document. It is forthright, progressive, and, by all odds, the least ambiguously phrased production of the sort that I have read for a long time. I cannot see how any intelligent, forward-looking citizen, on the basis of the platforms alone, could fail to accept the Democratic platform as being far superior to the Republican. Following this, Farley, Roper, and I said a few words over the radio commenting on the platform in very general and very sketchy terms.

Yesterday was the day for nominating President Roosevelt as the candidate of the party, and this duty was performed by Judge John E. Mack, of Poughkeepsie, New York. It was he who nominated Roosevelt four years ago at the Chicago convention. I went out to the Convention Hall but stayed only a very short time. I listened to the opening of Judge Mack's speech, but it did not seem to me to be very vigorous or inspiring or eloquent, and so I came back to the hotel, where, fortunately, I had work that I could do to keep me busy. The whole day, clear through the evening session, was taken up with the nominating and seconding speeches. Every state seconded the nomination, and the oratory must have been interminable. I did not go back again.

My lovely black Chow dog, Wu, died yesterday. He had been to the veterinary for eczema but had come home. Then his skin broke out in another place and he went back to the hospital. David reported that he had been down to see him and that he was getting along but would not be home for some time. Yesterday I had a telegram from the veterinary telling me that he was in a serious condition from some intestinal infection. I called up Ruth Hampton and she and Bill McCrillis went over to see about Wu, but he was dead before they got there. He was a young dog to whom I was very much attached. He was in fine physical condition when I brought him from Hubbard Woods last September, and I suspect that I should not have brought him on. I do not think the Washington climate is any too good for Chows. Like his grandfather, to whom I was devoted for fourteen or fifteen years, Wu had a lovely disposition and was one of the nicest and most companionable dogs I have ever known.

Tuesday, June 30, 1936

I did not attend the convention on Saturday but worked in my hotel room in the morning. In the afternoon Ann and I drove out to hunt for the old German Lutheran church in the graveyard of which my great-grandfather in my father's line and his father are supposed to be buried. We found this near New Hanover.

This is claimed to be the oldest German Lutheran church in America. The original church was built of logs but the present one is of stone. It has been remodeled. Preparations were being made to celebrate on Sunday the fiftieth anniversary of the present pastor. The church itself is a simple, quaint old thing, but substantial. The graveyard is very large, and practically all of the headstone inscriptions are in German. There are no headstones containing the name Ickes, but there are a number the lettering on which has become obliterated, and the theory is that among these graves are two or more occupied by my ancestors. This was my first visit to this place and, of course, it was interesting to me.

Saturday night was the occasion for the President's acceptance speech at Franklin Field. The weather had been threatening all day and in the afternoon there had been one or two heavy showers. I had a ticket for the speakers' platform and, in addition, several tickets which called for reserved seats. These latter were supposed to be held until eight o'clock. I reached the field before seven with Ann and found these reserved seats already occupied. Even private boxes had been overrun, as I learned a little later when Ambassador Bullitt told me that his daughter had not been able to get into his box. This was before seven o'clock and the President was not due to go on the air until ten. At this hour, in spite of the threatening weather and occasional light showers, the field was completely filled except the topmost bleachers at the far end. Even these were filled before the President spoke. It was estimated that there were from one hundred thousand to one hundred and ten thousand people present, and I certainly never saw such a crowd in my life. There were no showers after the President arrived.

That part of the crowd which was not enthusiastic seemed to be sympathetic. When the President appeared, he got a great reception. First, Vice President Garner was notified of his nomination and he accepted in an unimpressive, fumbling speech. He makes a terrible impression on the platform. He could not even read with any degree of credit the short speech that he had prepared. During his speech I remarked to Bullitt, who sat on my right, that there were not many votes to be hoped for from any appearance by Garner on the platform.

The President was notified of his nomination by Senator Robinson, and he then proceeded to make what I think was the greatest political speech I have ever heard. It was really a strong and moving statement of the fundamental principles underlying our politics today, and he put the issues so clearly and so strongly that I do not see how anyone can fail to understand them. He visualized our present struggle as one in the long battle for liberty, but this time liberty against the royalty of economic power. The speech went over in a big way, and even the opposition papers have had to do him the credit of admitting its greatness. I came away from the meeting feeling that, as matters stand, I would have no option except to support the President, no matter what my personal differences might be with him over policies affecting my Department. I simply would have no other choice in view of what I have believed in and stood for all my life.

I had quite a chance to talk to Bullitt while we were waiting for the main ceremonies to begin. I find Bullitt a very interesting person. I asked him about the chances of any serious disturbance in Europe this summer and he told me that he had had some confidential talks which led him to believe that things will probably be kept quiet. He says that Germany does not want any disturbance in Austria until she is prepared to push matters to a conclusion, which means the completion of her fortifications, especially on the French frontier. Germany does not want a Hapsburg dynasty to come back in Austria. It believes that Austria will fall into its lap sooner or later and that it is only a question of time and patience. On the other hand, Mussolini does want a Hapsburg restoration and he may precipitate some trouble.

On the whole, Bullitt thinks that things will be maintained *in statu quo,* at least for some time, but he did make the definite statement that the chances were better than sixty-five out of a hundred that during the term of the next President there would be a war in Europe. He thinks that, for this reason, it is all the more important to re-elect Roosevelt, who knows something about international relationships, and whose mind is so firmly set on peace. He believes that there is a real chance, with proper handling, of keeping this country out of the next war. He doesn't feel that Landon has either the competency, the experience, or the ability to bring the country through such a crisis, should it arise. Bullitt is returning to his post in Moscow about the first of August. In the meantime, the President has told him he wants him to represent him (the President) at the Patrick Henry celebration in Virginia. It seems that Bullitt is a direct descendant of Patrick Henry's sister and, although a Philadelphian, is related to practically all of the Virginia families of note.

Thursday, July 2, 1936

I lunched with the President yesterday. I sent him a telegram on Sunday telling him that I thought his speech of acceptance was really great, but I had not seen him until yesterday. I took the occasion again to tell him what I so deeply felt, namely, that it was the greatest political speech that I have ever heard. I told him that, as the result of that speech, I would have to support him even if he should fire me.

There is no doubt in my mind that he stated the fundamental issue that must be decided in this country sooner or later, and that is whether we are to have real freedom for the mass of people, not only political but economic, or whether we are to be governed by a small group of economic overlords. It is clear that the President's speech created a profound impression in the country.

I asked the President what part he expected me to play in the campaign and he said he wanted me to attack. Later, just as I was leaving after luncheon, I told him that I hoped he would feel free to call upon me for anything that I could do at any time and he said again that I made such a grand attack that that was what he wanted. He discussed with me several sections of the country where he thought I ought to go, particularly New England and the Middle West. He said that there would be little doing until after Landon had made his speech of acceptance, and he advised me to close up my office and go away for a vacation.

I took over with me a list of more than a thousand public works projects, aggregating over $70 million, together with an Executive Order for the President to sign, because, under the law, it will be necessary for him to sign an order permitting me to go ahead with the program. It seems that he hasn't gotten out of his head the notion that we have to have relief labor on the public works projects. I reminded him that none of the money available for public works could be used by Hopkins and that it won't be spent unless we spend it. However, apparently, he wants some statement from Hopkins that relief labor is available for these projects and I told him that I would have Hackett check it back with WPA, although I reminded him that in a good many instances now it was impossible to get building-trades men from relief rolls because they were not there to be had. I think it is simply a question of going through a certain form in order to clear this program and get it under way. In the meantime, two or three Senators have been in to see me or have talked with me about getting under way. With the campaign on, it seems to me rather important to get the program started for the public effect it will have.

I had a very pleasant luncheon with the President. He seems to be in good health and in good spirits, and his attitude was very friendly.

John Collier and I went to see the President this morning about eleven o'clock. He had vetoed a bill that we wanted for the benefit of the landless California Indians. He did this on the advice of the Department of Justice and of the Budget, neither of which consulted us before sending in adverse reports. I had asked the President yesterday whether he would give Collier and me a chance to present our cause. Collier made a very clear and convincing statement of the situation, but the President suggested that we set up a committee to bring in a finding of fact and a recommendation. He indicated that he would be willing to support an appropriation at the next session that would give the Indians all that they could probably hope to win through the Court of Claims if they could have proceeded under the vetoed bill. If he will do this, it will mean that the Indians will get all that they would get in any event, and they will get it several years sooner than they would if the bill had been signed and they had availed themselves of the remedy offered by that bill.

Tuesday, July 7, 1936

I was at the office last Friday morning just short of two hours. Shortly before ten I went to the White House to join the President's party for the Shenandoah National Park dedication. It was a threatening day, with the chances apparently ninety out of one hundred that we would have lots of rain. I was in one of the White House cars with Jim Farley and Judge Moore, an Assistant Secretary of State. He is an old Virginian who served several terms in Congress. We started down over the Lee Highway at a respectable pace and got up into the park about one o'clock. By that time the weather had cleared, with a beautiful day in prospect. We stopped to eat the lunch that we had brought with us and then we went up to Big Meadows for the ceremonies.

July 4 opened hot and clear but always with a possibility of rain. We drove up to Monticello, where the President made a speech on Jefferson after being introduced by Senator Glass in a most appropriate speech. Governor Peery also spoke. The ceremonies were brief, and there was a national hookup. After this event we embarked again and drove to Richmond, from which point some of the party went back to Washington. Judge Moore, Miss Le Hand, and I boarded the *Potomac* with the President and Mrs. Roosevelt and started down the James River.

At Upper Brandon Mr. and Mrs. Harry Byrd came aboard, and lower down, Mr. and Mrs. Robert Daniels. The four of them were guests at dinner. Both are Harvard graduates and apparently have known the President for some time. The ride down the river was interesting and pleasant. We saw a number of the old colonial residences sitting back among the trees. Some of these places are very famous and many of them have passed out of the hands of the families that originally owned them. Both Mr. Byrd and Mr. Daniels are farmers, by which I mean that they live on their land. They certainly are not farmers in the sense of husbandmen as I have known them. There isn't any doubt that there is a distinct culture in Virginia probably going back to the early colonial days when land holdings were large and slave labor cheap. However, even the abolition of slavery has not served to destroy this distinctive flavor of Virginia culture. I doubt whether there are many sections of the country where the men who live on the land are college graduates, know how to talk, take frequent trips abroad, and dress well, as do some of these Virginians that I have met.

We anchored about twelve miles up the river from Jamestown and in the morning dropped down so that we docked about ten o'clock. All the countryside was out to see the President and Mrs. Roosevelt. With Superintendent Flickinger, of the Colonial National Historical Park, in our car we saw some of the excavations that are being made and some of the pottery, silverware, etc., that is being dug up. Then we drove to Bruton Parish Church for the morning services. Dr. Goodwin, who looked much frailer than when I saw him last, met us at the entrance to the church and preached the sermon. He is the man who interested John D. Rockefeller, Jr., in the restoration of Williamsburg. He is full of early colonial history and his sermon was more nearly a dissertation on early history than anything else. It was interesting to attend services in this old church, where we sat in stiff, formal boxes that formerly were occupied by Presidents and Governors and those in high places generally, both in national and in early Virginian history.

We dropped down the York River into Chesapeake Bay, where we stopped to still-fish for a while. The President got a little shark but no one else got a bite. Before we fished, the President read the draft of the article that I have written for the *Saturday Evening Post*. I am quite sure he liked it from what he said, and today Dr. McIntire told me that he had heard the President say this morning that he liked it. Word also came over from Steve Early's office to the same effect. We had supper at eight o'clock and shortly thereafter the President went to his cabin. I followed his example and had a pretty good night's sleep, as the weather was cool, in striking contrast to the great heat that I tried to sleep through all the preceding night. At nine o'clock this morning we docked in the Navy Yard in Washington.

This trip gave me the best chance, and really the only chance, I have ever had to have a heart-to-heart talk with Jim Farley. He left us at Richmond to drive back to Washington but before he left, we had a good deal of time together. Part of the time Judge Moore was in the car with us, but all the way from Charlottesville to Richmond Jim and I were alone.

Among other things we talked about were possible shifts in the Cabinet in the event of Roosevelt's re-election. Jim had told me on a former occasion that he would not continue in the Cabinet because he felt he had to go into business to make money for his family. He told me that he had recently told the President this. Obviously, Jim is going to ask for a leave of absence for the balance of the campaign, which would mean that Howes would be made Acting Postmaster General. Jim thinks that this will take him out of the campaign as an issue, since he will not attend Cabinet meetings nor go to the Post Office Department. Apparently he feels that he is too much of an issue and that this is to the disadvantage of the President. In talking later with Miss Le Hand, she said that it was too bad that Jim didn't resign. I am absolutely certain that she reflects the opinion of the President in that remark. She thinks that he will continue to be an issue even if he takes a leave of absence, but that the President cannot suggest a resignation for personal reasons.

As to the other members of the Cabinet, Jim thought that Hull could stay on if he wanted to. So far as Morgenthau is concerned, he said that he couldn't be blasted out with a cannon. We talked quite some while about Morgenthau. I knew that Jim didn't like him and he made it abundantly clear how much he really does dislike him. He said that he never got along with him when he was Commissioner of Conservation at Albany, and that the President knows he doesn't like him.

Secretary Dern's health is said to be bad and, according to Jim, he has it on reliable information that Dern hasn't any idea of what really goes on in his Department. He said that this was a personal appointment of the President's, made because he liked Dern, after Jim had pointed out to the President that Dern would satisfy neither the Utah Democrats nor the western Democrats as being representative of his section. He told me that in August before election in 1932 the President had told him that he had settled in his own mind on only three appointments, two of whom were Jim Farley himself for Postmaster General and Dern for Secretary of the Interior. This confirmed reports that were current at the time the new Administration went in to the effect that Dern had been selected for Secretary of the Interior but that he was switched to War on account of the protests of western conservationists. Jim does not know whether Dern will want to continue in the Cabinet or whether the President will want to retain him.

As to Cummings, Jim said that he wants to go onto the Supreme Court bench and that he supposes he would like to stay in the Cabinet until that possibility is explored. Cummings, however, has told Jim that he is thinking of resuming private business in order to make money. Jim says that Cummings is lazy. He can't get him to make speeches. He even refused to make a speech before the state convention of Vermont and Jim had to go up there himself, although, as he said, as a New Englander Cummings was much better qualified to handle that meeting than he was. Jim commented on the fact that while Homer is too lazy to make the speeches that are asked of him, he insisted on making a seconding speech of the President's nomination at the Philadelphia convention, although he was the only member of the Administration to make such a speech, and despite the fact that the President had given orders that the members of the Administration were not to do that. However, Cummings got the President to waive this rule in his case.

As to the Secretary of the Navy, Jim thinks that the state of Swanson's health is such that he may drop off at any time. He thinks Henry Wallace will be continued in the Cabinet if he wants the job. He doesn't think Roper will want to stay on, and he thinks that Miss Perkins will probably go out to be president of some woman's college. I tried to draw him out with respect to myself by saying that there were a good many rumors to the effect that the President wouldn't retain me, but Jim said that he had never heard any such suggestion from the President.

In talking of the campaign that is ahead of us, Farley commented on the lack of speaking ability in the Cabinet. He said that Hull could be used probably to some extent over the radio, although he hasn't a good radio voice and he makes a dull speech. However, his standing in the country will be helpful. He said that Morgenthau couldn't be used at all, and that nothing could be expected from Dern. He thinks that Cummings is an effective speaker but that the President will have to give him orders to get him on the platform. He believes that Miss Perkins can be of a lot of value in New York State but that she ought to be kept there. She had a high standing in that state as Labor Commissioner. He believes Wallace can be of real use in the farming areas, and he thinks I can be effective on attack. He believes that I can be particularly useful in Pennsylvania and in the Middle Western states. He did me the compliment of saying that I had a general reputation of being honest and that anything that I might say would carry added conviction for that reason.

Jim told me that a few days ago Elliott Roosevelt, the second son of the President, and Amon Carter had come to him to ask him to use his influence to get a certain wave length for interests that either were Hearst interests or closely allied therewith. Elliott told him that there would be a commission of $40,000 in it for himself. Farley refused to have a thing to do with it and said that he not only wouldn't help but that he was opposed to the proposition. He told Elliott to go to Steve Early and have Steve put it up to his father.

Jim and I discussed the advisability of making Hearst one of the main issues in the campaign. He is apparently as strongly in favor of doing this as I am. He thought that I could handle that issue and he also thought of the possibility of using General Hugh Johnson. He said that Johnson wanted to do what he could for the Administration, and he believes that his ability to turn phrases and use picturesque language would be helpful. I told him that, in my judgment, it would be good tactics to open up on Hearst three or four days before Landon's speech of acceptance. If this is done and the Hearst brand put on Landon, it will create a background that may be difficult for Landon to take care of with any credit to himself in his speech of acceptance. Jim agreed with me and said that such a speech would be worth what it would cost to the national committee. He suggested that I discuss it with the President when I got a chance on the *Potomac* and that I did.

The President took to the idea but we didn't discuss it much. Later, however, when I saw him at the White House today the subject was brought up again. The President had apparently been thinking of it and discussing who might make such a speech with the greatest effect. He had me in mind but he doubted the propriety of a member of the Cabinet making an attack on Hearst. I reminded him that Theodore Roosevelt had delegated Elihu Root on one occasion to attack Hearst and that seemed to change his mind considerably. I told him that I was not anxious for the job because I realized that Hearst would smear anyone who went after him, but that the job ought to be done and that I was willing to do whatever he wanted me to do. I told him to let me know if he wished me to make this speech.

Friday, July 10, 1936

After dinner Tuesday I had a call from Miss Le Hand, who said that the President would like to come out to my house for dinner on Wednesday night. Several months ago the President had remarked to Miss Le Hand that he wished he knew some place in the country where he could go and have a quiet and undisturbed evening and she told him that my place was just right for that sort of thing, she just having been there for dinner. Ever since that time there has been some probability of the President's coming but it did not materialize. Since the President has not been in the home of any member of the Cabinet, the White House wanted the thing kept as quiet as possible.

I got in some extra help on Wednesday and invited the following persons at the suggestion of Miss Le Hand: Miss Grace Tully, Mr. and Mrs. C. R. Larrabee, Tom Corcoran, Alfred T. Hobson, Assistant Secretary of RFC, and Miss Le Hand herself.

The President got out about a quarter to seven. The dining table was set on the lawn, since it was a warm, clear day with no wind. Fortunately, the President's car could bring him within a very few feet of the place where the table was by coming around the house and the garage. From the car he was carried to my own favorite chair which I had had taken out on the lawn for him. After cocktails and cocktail sandwiches, we moved him over to the table where the eight of us sat down. We started with honeydew melon, then had cold salmon with mayonnaise dressing, as well as cucumbers and tomatoes, bread and butter, then squab with peas and potatoes. Then followed a green salad with a choice of cream, Swiss, or Roquefort cheese. For dessert there was my own special ice cream, black raspberry, with cookies and coffee to finish with. For wines, I served Château Yquem, a good claret, and a good vintage champagne. We had liqueurs afterward and when the dining table had been removed, the butlers brought out and put on a table, with a supply of cracked ice, Scotch, rye and bourbon whisky, gin and Bacardi rum. To go with these we had White Rock and ginger ale.

The party was a great success, although personally I did not contribute anything to it. I have been very much out of sorts lately. I have been sleeping worse than I have been sleeping for years, with the result that I have been taking soporifics practically every night. I have been very tired and depressed and even the honor of this occasion, graced as it was by the President, was not sufficient to shift the load that I have been carrying.

Tom Corcoran had brought his accordion with him and he played and sang practically the whole evening. Hobson sang two or three times and a few stories were told. The President seemed to enjoy himself hugely and he entered into the fun very naturally and spontaneously. I kept them all supplied with their favorite highballs. The President certainly carries his liquor well. He must have had five highballs after dinner. He drank gin and ginger ale but he never showed the slightest effect. I am glad to say that nobody showed any signs of having had too much to drink although everyone had all that he wanted. He must have had a good time because he didn't leave until half past twelve and then only after Miss Le Hand prodded him two or three times and insisted that he must go home and to bed. It really was a lovely party and, of course, I felt very much set up that the President should have been my guest. Toward the end he started in again to tell me, as he had done on the *Potomac,* that I must go away. He thinks I ought to take a boat and go to Europe for three weeks and he almost made me promise to do that. When I bade him goodnight and told him that I hoped he realized that I would be delighted to have him as my guest at any time, he said that he would come again if I would go away on a real vacation.

The weather could not have been better. It was lovely out on the lawn with almost an entire absence of insect life. Just before dessert we had candles lighted on the table and we kept them burning throughout the rest of the evening. This was all the light that we had, except what came from the house, until the late moon came up. Although the weather was warm, it was quite tolerable and no one suffered from the heat, while at the same time no one had to put on anything extra to keep warm. It was difficult to realize that this man who was so friendly and delightful and who entered into the affair so wholeheartedly was the President of the United States. We heard no sound and had no disturbance. Secret Service men, of course, were patrolling on the outskirts, but their presence was more felt than seen.

There was a Cabinet meeting yesterday afternoon, but there was no one there representing Treasury, Navy, or Agriculture. Practically the entire discussion related to the campaign and the President didn't want any substitutes. The President has had advance information that the first poll as between himself and Landon taken by "America Speaks," which is published in the *Washington Post* every Sunday, shows Landon ahead on electoral votes but himself ahead on popular votes, with fifty-one per cent of the total. He thinks that this is doctored, the desire being to indicate a tight race with an even start for both candidates.

There was a good deal of discussion about the location of headquarters in Chicago. Of those present, Hull, Cummings, Dern, Roper, and myself were strongly in favor of Chicago headquarters. There was a good deal of sentiment for Chicago as the location of the principal headquarters, and certainly all of us thought that there should be branch headquarters there. Jim has already announced that headquarters are to be in New York. I myself think that it will be a mistake to have the main headquarters in New York, since the fight will be mainly in the central and western states.

Sunday, July 12, 1936

It was very hot yesterday in New York, just as it has been during the last two or three days in Washington. As a matter of fact, I don't believe I ever felt the heat so much. It had been well over 100 degrees here. According to the paper, it was 117 on the street on Friday and I can readily believe that. It was very hot in New York also, but on the Triborough Bridge where the speakers' stand had been erected there was a cool breeze so that it was quite tolerable. The program was a long one with a number of supposedly three-minute speeches, except that of the President. He was given six minutes. Robert Moses, whom I tried to force off the Triborough Bridge Authority some time ago at the instance of the President, presided and his introductions for each were as long or longer than the subsequent speeches. The result was that the program ran twenty or twenty-five minutes beyond schedule time. In addition to the President and myself, the three borough presidents spoke, the chief engineer of the bridge, Governor Lehman, and Mayor La Guardia.

I was introduced to Moses before the proceedings began. We both greeted each other pleasantly and courteously with a slight passing reference to our late unpleasantness. When he introduced me, he touched on the same subject matter but in a manner that would not offend anyone. He remarked that we had met each other for the first time and that we had mutually discovered that neither had a hoof, horn, or tail. He expressed the desire to forget old differences and wished that we might know each other better, etc., etc., etc. Before opening my three-minute speech I assured him and the audience that his courteous references and pleasant wishes were fully appreciated and reciprocated. Mayor La Guardia introduced the President, he having insisted that he would not be introduced by Moses. But I noticed that, as usual, the President made one or two pleasant references to Moses in his speech. There certainly isn't much bitterness in the President's nature, although there is a streak of real stubbornness.

Jim Farley was at the Triborough Bridge ceremonies in New York. He told me that he had read a statement in the *New Republic* telling how bitterly he felt toward me. He passed it off as a joke and so did I. Jim said he was going to write a letter to the *New Republic* kidding it about the statement. He said he must be a terrible man indeed if he were guilty of all the things with which he is charged.

The Triborough Bridge is a wonderful affair. From the engineering point of view, it is one of the greatest in the world as it is one of the biggest.

Tuesday, July 14, 1936

Frank B. Noyes called me up on Sunday to ask me to have dinner with him, as he was in Washington for a few days. He had asked me to meet him at the Chevy Chase Country Club, but he got mixed himself and thought he had said the Metropolitan Club. After I had waited for him half an hour, I called him up at the Metropolitan Club and he had to find a taxi and drive up to Chevy Chase. This lost me practically an hour, which I regretted very much with all the work I had waiting for me at home. What Noyes wanted to talk to me about was the case that is in the courts between the Associated Press, of which he is president, and one of its writers, who is a prominent officer in the Newspaper Guild, involving the right of the Associated Press to discharge him. Noyes said that he wanted some member of the Administration to understand the position of the Associated Press.

He feels that writers who are sent out to get the news and interview people are really agents of the publisher or editor and that they therefore occupy a different status from that of the mechanical workers on the newspaper. He said that so far as the *Washington Star*, of which he is one of the owners and editors, is concerned, he has always recognized the right of the men in the mechanical department to join a union. As a matter of fact, in some instances he has advised such men to join the union. But he is strongly of the opinion that a writer is in a different category; that he occupies a peculiar relationship of trust and confidence with his employer. He thinks that a newspaper editor ought to have the right to discharge a reporter for a trivial reason, as, for instance, not liking the color of his hair.

I confess that I think there is a good deal to the point he made. If newspaper reporters, by virtue of their membership in unions, may not be discharged, it might be that a newspaper in course of time would find itself represented by men who could not even write, who distorted the news, or put on a coloration obnoxious to the owners. It seems to me that the answer for the newspaper reporters is not so much joining the union as fair hours, decent wages, and proper treatment by the publishers.

Noyes also went on to tell me about the pension system that has been in effect on the *Star* for a good many years. He says that it is much more generous than that set up under the Security Act of the Administration and that he does not want to see the pensions of his own men whittled down to the lower level that would obtain under the Security Act. As he gave me the figures, the system did seem to be generous. He spoke quite feelingly about its being assumed that employers have no sense of social justice but have to have their hands forced by the Government. I pointed out that while undoubtedly there are some employers such as himself who are fair and just, this is not true of the majority and that therefore legislation is necessary to make them do their duty.

Saturday, July 18, 1936

I had a talk with Tom Courtney after my speech on Tuesday in Chicago. I had also had from Mrs. Reinecke a confidential letter before going to Chicago. The situation in Illinois does not look any too good to me, nor am I happy over the national situation generally. The more I think of the inaction of the Democratic high command, the more puzzled and concerned I am. I do not blame Jim Farley for this, because I think that it is the President himself who is responsible.

One of the first things I did Wednesday morning after I reached my desk was to get Jim Farley on the long-distance telephone in New York. I made my visit to Chicago the occasion for telling him that I think that we are in grave danger of losing the election. I told him that the Landon situation has been badly handled from the beginning. We should never have permitted him to be built up as he has been. I reminded him that I had suggested to the President the making of a speech two or three months before the Republican convention—not a frontal attack but a kidding speech which would expose Landon's lack of qualifications and do something to put the American voters on notice. The President had not favored this when I suggested it to him and later I suggested it to Jim himself at a Cabinet meeting. Jim thought well of the idea, too well perhaps, because it was subsequent to my talk with him that he attacked Landon himself and referred to him as an inexperienced Governor of a "typical prairie state."

I went on to say to Jim that the President had forbidden the members of the Cabinet to say anything about Landon. This was well before the Republican convention. The President had the absurd idea that Landon was the weakest candidate who could be nominated by the Republicans and he did not want anything said or done that might make it difficult to nominate him. So we have sat by and allowed him to be built up. Even since the nomination we have continued to sit by. Landon's supporters are taking full advantage of a wonderful opportunity to continue to build him up while we do absolutely nothing. Day after day the newspapers headline the defection of some prominent Democrat to the Landon camp. Meanwhile, the President smiles and sails and fishes and the rest of us worry and fume.

I told Jim again that I thought the Hearst speech that I had been urging for some time should be made. He said that Governor McNutt had agreed to make the speech but that the President did not want it made until after Landon's acceptance speech. He is afraid that Landon will disavow Hearst in his acceptance speech if Hearst is tied around his neck before that occasion. I think that this is downright silly. Landon cannot repudiate Hearst now, and the whole point of the speech is to have the Hearst background for Landon when Landon makes his speech. His failure to mention Hearst—and he will not dare to do that—would make a lot of people suspicious and create a good effect for us. The whole strategy in making this speech is one of timing.

I explained all of this to Jim and I did not have to argue with him. He agreed with me fully on every point that I made. I told him that if we continued for a short time as we were, it would not be any use in attacking Landon or Hearst or anyone else because the fight would be over and we would be licked.

Then I called up Stanley High, who is also in New York. I went over the same ground with him and I found that he was worried.

He told me that Mrs. Roosevelt was of the opinion that the Hearst speech ought to be made before the Landon notification ceremonies. He said that he would talk to Mrs. Roosevelt and suggest that a radio message be sent to the President, who is off in a sailboat along the Maine coast with his sons. Later he called me back and said that Mrs. Roosevelt had agreed with my point of view and that a radio would be sent to the President.

Thursday morning Steve Early called me from the White House. Stanley High had called him on behalf of himself and Mrs. Roosevelt and myself and suggested that he radio the President. Later on Friday Steve called me again to say that Charley Michelson had called from New York and wanted me to send up some suggestions for the speech on Hearst. From this I gathered that the plan has finally been adopted. This morning I called High again to discuss with him the speech that I am to make over the radio following Landon's acceptance and once more I brought up the question of the Hearst speech. He said that it was to be made, probably next Tuesday night, and I suggested that there ought to be a build-up so that people would be looking forward to it and would listen in that night. He had talked with Michelson and Michelson had suggested that McNutt might get cold feet on the speech because it was such a hot one. High said that the speech started with the Spanish-American War and brought Hearst down to date. He said also that there had been some changes in campaign plans along the lines of my suggestions. What these are, I do not know.

With even our own private polls showing an alarming falling off in the President's vote, the whole situation is incomprehensible to me. It was loudly proclaimed that Louie Howe had supplied most of the political strategy that resulted in the nomination and election of President Roosevelt and I am beginning to believe that this must have been true. I do know that Howe was the only one who dared to talk to him frankly and fearlessly. He not only could tell him what he believed to be the truth, but he could hang on like a pup to a root until he got results. He could reach him not only directly but through Mrs. Roosevelt. Jim Farley tries to please the President. He will state a point of view and if the President takes issue with him, Jim will drop the subject. He won't fight even for what he profoundly believes in. Of course, I have never been close to the President politically. I do not think that he takes advice from anybody and the few times when I have given advice, I have done it as a volunteer. He listens courteously, but I do not think that he ever does anything about it.

Hurja came in to see me late Thursday afternoon. He had taken a sample poll before the publication in the Sunday *Post* last week of the "America Speaks" poll, and his results were exactly the same. They showed a drop in popular vote, with the President receiving slightly more than fifty per cent, but with Landon leading on electoral votes. Hurja thinks the situation is very serious. Giving the President all the states that look sure and which include the solid South and border states and, in addition, Nevada, Arizona, Utah, Montana, Wisconsin, California, Oregon, and Washington, the President would still lack thirty-six votes of having half of those in the electoral college. Even some of the states mentioned require special attention in order to make them absolutely safe for the President. Hurja thinks there is a good chance of carrying Pennsylvania, which has thirty-six electoral votes. He thinks we ought to make a special drive for that state and, in addition, for the following: Michigan, South Dakota, North Dakota, Idaho, New Mexico, and Wyoming. These states have a total of thirty-seven electoral votes and would take the place of Pennsylvania should we not carry that. Besides, the carrying of any one of them in addition to Pennsylvania, admitting that we can hold all of the states that now look safe, would give Roosevelt the election. Hurja doesn't think much of the chances of carrying New York or Illinois. He thinks there is an outside chance in Ohio, Indiana, and Minnesota.

Glavis finally resigned on Thursday and is now out of the Department, to my profound satisfaction and, I believe, to the equally keen delight of practically everyone in the Department and in Public Works. Things have been going from bad to worse so far as he is concerned and I had reached the point where something drastic had to be done. Ever since I started to assert the right to exercise some personal jurisdiction over his division, he has been surly and recalcitrant, although not on the surface. He has been feeding out stories to the newspapers favorable to himself and critical of me. This I know and I have accused him to his face of doing it. However, he has always strenuously denied it.

Tuesday, July 21, 1936

Before the President went away it was decided that, following the acceptance speech of Governor Landon, I was to go on the air on a national hookup with a speech discussing the rejuvenation of the Republican party. According to my idea, this was to be somewhat facetious but, in the main, I would discuss seriously the question whether or not the Republican party is now progressive. On Saturday afternoon I dictated my first draft of this speech.

Monday morning Charley Michelson called me from New York and told me that arrangements had been made for me to go on the air for half an hour Friday night, which would be the night following Landon's acceptance speech. He told me that Jim Farley had said that I wanted only twenty minutes and he asked about having someone introduce me. I told him that there was no object in having anyone use good time in introducing me and that I needed more than twenty minutes. So he assigned the whole half hour. He said that he hoped that I would listen to Landon's speech and leave enough time so that I could make some sort of a reply to him. I told him that if my speech was to be a reply to Landon it would be pretty close work having anything in shape for Friday night. I suggested that there ought to be a longer interval. He thought the psychological effect of a prompt reply would be good. I said that I would do the best I could.

I raised with Michelson the question of mentioning Landon by name, reminding him that the President had issued orders that none of us was to do that. He said that he understood that the prohibition still held and I said that it seemed to me to be damn foolishness to comment on a man's speech without mentioning him. I said I did not see how it could be done. Then I called Stanley High and told him the same thing. He said he agreed with me. After that, I talked with Steve Early at quite some length, as the result of which he agreed to send a radiogram to the President and put the question up to him again, the President still being at sea up near Nova Scotia. Steve also was in accord with me that it was pretty hard to comment on a man or his speech without mentioning his name. He, too, thinks the policy laid down by the President is a mistake.

Then Jim Farley called me from New York. He said that he understood that the prohibition was to run only until the speech of acceptance. I told him that I did not agree with the policy and that Steve Early was of my point of view. He said that he thought it was foolish and that he would call Steve in the morning.

Meanwhile, I had gone ahead working on my speech. Last night I

went over my first draft and early this morning I dictated some in-
serts and additions. Then Steve Early called me to tell me that he
had received word from the President that he thought it would be a
mistake for a member of the Cabinet to comment on Landon's
speech of acceptance or to mention him by name. He thought that
someone outside of the Administration ought to do it. I thought
this was all hooey and so expressed myself to Steve, who again
agreed with me. However, I told him that it would not hurt my
feelings at all not to have to make the speech. Steve Early
telephoned to Michelson to tell him what the President had said,
and Michelson indicated that he would try to find some Progressive
Republican to answer Landon. I call that a pretty short order for
anyone.

During the day there have been various telephonings back
and forth between Early and Michelson, between Early and me,
between High and me, and so forth. When I talked to High early
in the afternoon, he said that he understood my speech was not to
be a reply to Landon but the speech that it has been understood
for some time that I was to make. I asked him where Mrs. Roosevelt
was and he said that she was on her way to Campobello but that he
hadn't been able to reach her there yet. He proposed to reach her
by telephone and try to get the President to clear my speech for
Friday night. Late in the afternoon a cryptic message came in
from his secretary and I do not know now whether it is the intention
to go ahead Friday night with my speech or not.

One thing I think I do know, however, and that is that if this
campaign is run much longer as it is being run, there will be little
chance of defeating Landon. I told this to Steve yesterday and
again today. In fact, I jokingly told him that I was glad I would
not have to make a speech on Friday because I could go to New
York then and look for a job. He asked me to hunt for one for him,
too.

The situation is really serious. After talking at length with Steve
yesterday I think that it is more serious than ever. He told me that
there were no campaign plans and no budget. The Republicans
have plenty of money and fully developed plans which they are
carrying out. They have contracted for literature, for advertising
space, and for radio time. We haven't done a thing and Michelson
doesn't know what he can do or with what he can do. I am quite
serious in my belief that we are in bad shape and in grave danger.

Moreover, everyone that I have come in contact with is coming to feel the same way about it. Apparently, Farley is not in a position to give any orders. The President is off on his sailing and fishing trip, blandly letting the situation take care of itself. Naturally he is not in touch with the situation, and yet he undertakes to issue orders which necessarily are binding until he modifies them.

Take the speech attacking Hearst as an example of the mess we are in. I first suggested this to Jim Farley on July 4 and talked it over with the President on July 5. Jim particularly thought well of the plan, but the President approved it also. Now, the whole point, as I see it, was to build up a nation-wide interest in this speech so that millions would be listening in. My suggestion was that the date be fixed about two weeks in advance and the contract for the radio time be made. This was to have been followed by a newspaper build-up so that people would be curious to turn on their radios for the speech. The President backed and filled. First he thought well of it and then he thought that the speech should follow Landon instead of preceding him. I fought pretty hard for my idea and then the President gave his consent to have the speech in advance. McNutt was to make it. Then McNutt got cold feet. He said that he had to have a lot of his teeth out and he might not be able to talk. He also told Steve Early that he wanted a showdown with Jim Farley first—political trading, I suppose. Then he agreed to make the speech, or at least Michelson so told me yesterday, and the time he gave me was Thursday night.

I remarked to Steve Early this morning that I had seen no notice in the newspapers about McNutt's speech. He said maybe Michelson was just putting it on quietly and was depending on newspaper publicity. I made the point that the newspapers would carry little, if anything, of a speech attacking Hearst, and that, of course, no one would be listening in except the few who happened to turn on to McNutt's speech by chance. I do not know at this moment whether McNutt is to make the speech or not. Steve Early told me that Michelson had written a fine speech, but it won't do any good unless people hear it. As I have said, my whole idea was to have this Hearst setting for Landon's acceptance speech. I wanted a big question mark in the minds of the voters of the country about the relationship between Hearst and Landon when Landon goes on the air Thursday night. Now the whole thing is a flop.

It all passes my comprehension. I have thought all along that the

President was really an able politician, but I have come to the conclusion that I would not want him to be managing my campaign if
this is the best he can do. I think that he is defeating himself. I do
not mean that we may not be able to pull it out, but we are losing ground every day, and the longer this goes on, the less chance
there will be of winning. There is even doubt expressed as to
whether or not Farley really has a good organization. It is known
that the Republicans are working feverishly to build up an organization and have been doing this for some time. They are full of
confidence and gaining more every day.

The build-up for Landon goes on. Columns about him every day
and nothing at all on our side! Father Coughlin one day in Cleveland last week denounced the President as a liar and not a word
in reply from anyone! The President is having too much fun sailing
and fishing to resent a gross insult or to designate somebody else to
resent it. Even Mark Sullivan in his column yesterday commented
on the fact that a man could call the President of the United States
a liar and have no one take any exception to it. He is being bitterly
attacked in other quarters and no one answers. Some of us are willing to do so, but if we are to fight a campaign while pretending
that we have no opponent or that we do not know who he is if we
have one, is too damn silly a proposition to engross the attention
of a grown-up man. I suspect that if Louie Howe were alive we
could get somewhere with the President, as apparently he was the
only one who could talk to him and make him listen.

From what High tells me, Mrs. Roosevelt is worried and so is
Farley, but the President himself seems to be up in the clouds with
his mind fixed on more spiritual things than that of his own re-
election. I am in an unsettled state of mind. I do not mind taking a
licking, because I have been through lots of those, but I do hate to
take a licking lying down.

I am really sorry now that I did not resign a year ago. I had a
good issue then. When I was approached with the proposition that if
I should resign there was a good chance that I might be nominated
for President on the Republican ticket, I did not take it seriously.
But one reason I did not consider it seriously was on account of
my loyalty to the President. I could not see myself resigning from
his Cabinet and then opposing him. I have never done that sort of
thing. At that time Landon had been barely mentioned. The
build-up for him had not started. In the end he was built up be-

cause those opposed to this Administration had no one outstanding with any real standing and reputation in the nation. I do not say that the thing would have come my way, but I think the probabilities are that Landon would not have been thought of as a candidate. At any rate, I would have had as good a chance as anyone for the nomination. Of course, I know in my heart that I would not have been nominated because I would not have made the terms necessary to secure the support that I would have needed to be nominated. But as I see the thing now, if I had been nominated, in all probability I could have won in November with the situation standing as it does today. I am not shedding any tears, because, as I have set down on other occasions, I have not now and I never have had any ambition to be President. It is a back-breaking job and I think that the next four years are going to be pretty much hell for whoever is elected.

As a citizen, I am very much worried about the four years to come. I regard Landon as a man of very mediocre ability. He has no background or training or education for the job for which he is running. I do not believe that you can take a man at his time of life and make him all over again. Someone will have to run him. In this respect, he will be another Harding, although he will have more character and higher ideals than Harding. On the other hand, he won't have Harding's experience. As I say, someone will run him, and if it isn't the big interests I will be very much surprised. An honest and scrupulous man in the oil business is so rare as to rank as a museum piece. And Landon has been in oil all his life. Moreover, I do not like the nickname of "Fox" that became attached to him in his college days. He and his advisers would have their hands more than full trying to run this country for the next four years, if he is elected, with all the unemployment, industrial unrest, and economic inequalities that exist. On the other hand, Roosevelt, too, would have his hands full. I am beginning to fear that he is too sure of himself, too certain of his own judgment, and less and less willing to seek or take advice from competent men. To a diminishing extent does he confer with men of standing and substance. He is surrounding himself with men like Morgenthau and Hopkins and Tugwell, plus a lot of even lesser lights. I rather shudder to think of what his Cabinet will be during his next term if he is re-elected. So, whichever wins, the country is

likely to have to pay through the nose, and then God knows what
will happen in 1940.

Thursday, July 23, 1936

I was working late at the office Tuesday evening and Steve Early
got me on the telephone shortly after seven o'clock. He had just
had a telegram from New York signed by Farley, Charley Michelson, and Stanley High, addressed to the President, which they
wanted forwarded by Steve through naval communications. In this
telegram they strongly urged the President to give me permission
to make a speech on Landon, not following his speech of acceptance, but going to the point that he is not entitled to pose as a Progressive. In the telegram they said that I was the only one who
could do it and that my only mention of Landon by name would
be in connection with his claim to be a Progressive.

Steve asked me what I thought about it. I told him I was perfectly willing to do whatever was wanted of me and I emphasized
the fact that I thought we were already past due in opening up on
Landon. I told him, however, that I wouldn't want the President
to be under the impression, as he might be from the language in the
joint telegram, that I was going to mention Landon only once. I already have a draft of a speech and I mention Landon a number of
times. In the first place, I tie him up with Hearst and then I say
that he isn't entitled to claim support on the basis of his being a
Progressive, running on a Progressive platform. At Steve's suggestion I dictated a memorandum to the President covering these two
points and then Steve sent the whole thing along to the President.

I dined with Cissy Patterson Tuesday evening at her home in
Dupont Circle. She has been spending some time in her summer
home at Port Washington, Long Island. She called me up at the
house on Sunday to say that she would be in town on Tuesday
and asked me to dine with her. I haven't seen her for some time.
She had been doing some touring in the South, in Alabama and
other places, looking into the sharecropper situation, and she found
conditions pretty terrible.

She asked me if I was going to attack her boss again, meaning
Hearst, and I told her that I was. She asked me what I had against
him and I replied that I thought he was unscrupulous. Then I
asked her what her brother, Joe Patterson, thought about him. She

said that he, too, thought he was unscrupulous. We talked back and forth about Hearst. I didn't become vitriolic because, after all, she is the publisher of his paper here and their personal relationship is friendly, although I did take occasion to express some of my opinions about him. She thinks that he has great ability and a wonderful intellect. He must have both of these to have done what he has done, but that makes him only the more dangerous, according to my view.

She surprised me by saying: "You know, don't you, that I don't take any salary from Mr. Hearst." I told her that I didn't know that but, on the contrary, I had understood that she took a salary and then used that to supplement the salaries of people on the staff. She said that at one time she got $15,000 a year and that Hearst had offered her a two years' contract at $30,000 a year with a bonus. She declined this and since then has been working for nothing. She said that she didn't want to be in a position to be charged with being on his payroll. I told her that after all she was entitled to a salary if she worked for him and I asked her why she did it, although I knew the reason, which is that she has an active mind and she wants something to interest her. She does like to work. Then I asked her why she didn't buy the paper and she said that she had tried to but that it was not for sale. I told her I wished she would buy a paper somewhere else.

Friday, July 24, 1936

I listened to Governor Landon deliver his acceptance speech at Topeka, Kansas, last night as it came over the radio. There was little real substance to the speech. It did not strike fire at any point, as it seemed to me. His delivery was that of a freshman or sophomore in college. A good speaker could have made an impression even with the poor material that composed Landon's speech, but in the hands of such an unimpressive speaker as Landon himself, the effect was very drab. There was no vigor or spirit or inspiration at any point. It was just like a boy speaking a piece that had been written for him, and, unfortunately for him, the piece itself had no life or spirit to it.

I have talked today with a number of people who heard Landon and they all seem to have the same impression. Burlew, who is a Republican, was almost shocked with the effort. If this is the best that Landon can do, the Democratic Campaign Committee ought to spend all the money it can raise to send him out to make speeches.

Over the radio it was, of course, difficult to judge the effect of Landon's speech on his audience. He met with a great ovation when he was introduced by Congressman Snell, who, by the way, made a much better speech than did Landon. Landon's speech was in short sentences, and he paused at the end of practically every sentence in order to give an opportunity for applause. There was more or less applause throughout and a good deal at one point. But it was a diminuendo and it listened like "claque" applause. By that, I mean that it seemed to be the same group applauding in the same way for the same length of time at stated intervals. On the whole, what enthusiasm there was seemed to me to be that which expressed itself before the speech was made and not during the delivery.

Landon, in my judgment, has laid himself wide open to a devastating attack and I am eager to make it. Particularly in what he said about the Oil Administration he played right into my hands. We have in our files in this Department quotations from Landon's letters, telegrams, as well as a speech that he made as chairman of the oil conference here in 1933, with which we could rake him fore and aft. Jim Farley came to Washington today and I told him that I wanted to change my speech and answer Landon. Later I had a conference with him. He told me to go ahead and write the speech. He said the President would be ashore before it would be delivered and then we would gang up on him and try to get his consent.

I feel very keenly that Landon has let down his guard and that this is the time for a smashing blow. We may be able to recover some ground if we go at him now, but the Lord knows what will happen if we overlook this opportunity and permit the build-up to be resumed. In the hope that the President will let me make the speech I want to make, I am going to start today to work on it.

Monday, July 27, 1936

Cissy Patterson has been spending the summer in her home on Long Island and she asked me to spend the week end with her. I accepted, but with this new development with regard to my speech and considering the way I was feeling, I decided that I did not want to go. I called her on the telephone Friday night to tell her that I had found I could not come, but she was so insistent that I said I would go. She told me that she had been counting on me and had made her plans accordingly and it didn't seem fair to let her down. Moreover, I decided that it would do me good if I went. I took the nine o'clock train Saturday morning to New York. My night's sleep had done me good. I dictated to Mr. Cubberley all the way to North Philadelphia and the dictation went pretty well, so that I was through with what I wanted to do when we reached that point. Cissy's car met me at the Pennsylvania Station in New York and I was driven out to her place, which is near Port Washington, Long Island.

The place was originally owned by the late Burke Cochran, a very eloquent Congressman for many years who had quite a checkered career. Then it was owned for a period by Cosden, the man who made such a big and sudden fortune in oil. He contrived to have the Prince of Wales (now King Edward VIII) as his guest. That was before Cosden went broke. I think there was an intervening ownership before it was bought by Mr. and Mrs. Elmer Schlesinger, Mrs. Patterson then being Mrs. Schlesinger.

The house is a big frame, rambling structure on the top of a hill. Not the kind of a house one would build now, but comfortable and roomy. It is surrounded by some very beautiful trees and there is a vista down to the harbor. J. Pierpont Morgan's yacht, *Corsair*, was anchored a short distance off the shore all the time I was at Cissy's. There are sixty-five acres of land, and some little distance away Cissy has a bungalow where she goes to be alone and work. There is a very lovely salt-water swimming pool on the place, a big lawn, and nice gardens.

Saturday night we went to the Herbert B. Swopes' for dinner. There were fourteen at the table, among them Henry Luce and his wife. Luce is editor of *Time*. There was also a young Vanderbilt. I can only say for him that I hope he is not as dumb as he looks and acts. He didn't open his face, except for food, during the entire evening. Another interesting couple were Mr. and Mrs. William Randolph Hearst, Jr.

After dinner the men went into the library and the discussion turned on politics at once, although I did not bring up the subject. Later two other men came, one of them a Warburg and the other a man by the name of Lewis, who writes songs. With the exception of Swope and myself, both of whom were for Roosevelt, and of Lewis, who seemed to be open-minded, all the others were strong Landon men. Notwithstanding this fact, it was interesting to note that no one there had a kind word to say about Landon's speech of acceptance. They all thought it was at least a poor effort, and Swope was especially scathing in what he said about it.

Yet, with the exceptions mentioned, they were all for Landon. Luce, who seems to be a very able man, was especially strong in his opposition to the President. He thinks that Roosevelt has offended and hampered business. Young Hearst opined that the unemployment problem would be taken care of by private industry if the President would only let business alone. I took issue with that by pointing out to him that there were a couple of million men out of work even during our most prosperous year in 1929, and I ventured the prediction that with business going full tilt there would be many more people than this out of work in the future. I said that business would not put a single extra man on that it could get along without, and I pointed to the fact that during the depression many industries, notably steel, had been improving their technological techniques so that it could turn out the same amount of product with fewer hands.

I had been introduced to Mrs. Hearst before dinner, but if I was introduced to Hearst I did not know it. Cissy says that Mrs. Hearst is a good wife, is ambitious, and keeps him at work. She is his second wife, his first one having been divorced.

When we were in the library talking, I did not know that Hearst was in the group, although, as I say, I had met Mrs. Hearst. Not having been introduced to him, I concluded that she had come alone, and she was in with the ladies. So at one point I commented on the fact that Landon would not have been nominated if it had not been for Hearst, meaning, of course, the old man. When one of the others demurred somewhat to this, I said that there had never been such a build-up for anyone as the Hearst build-up for Landon. This is all I said about William Randolph, Senior, and, of course, there was nothing offensive about it. However, it was just as well, probably, that it began to dawn on me that the young man who was sitting just one removed from me on the sofa might be a young Hearst. During the course of the evening we exchanged several remarks and expressed our opinions on various points raised. He seemed rather alert and intelligent. I have heard that he is the most promising of all of Hearst's six sons, but that is not extravagant praise. He is the publisher of the *Journal-American*.

Sunday morning Harry F. Guggenheim, former Minister to Cuba and son of Simon Guggenheim, came over to see Cissy. He had been out to the notification ceremonies at Topeka and was quite enthusiastic not only about Landon but about his acceptance speech. He is the only man I have yet met of either party who has had even faint praise for the acceptance speech. I asked him, as I had asked others the night before, what were the specifications to support the charge that Roosevelt was antagonistic to business. My discussion with Guggenheim clarified the whole thing in my mind. It became clear that, exactly as I had said in my speech at the University of Virginia, the fundamental political issue today is taxation. Roosevelt, according to these very rich people, is penalizing business and tearing it down because he has increased the income tax rates in the higher brackets and because he is taxing surpluses in corporation treasuries. This was the only reaction that I could get to my insistent questions asking what Roosevelt had done or proposed to do that was inimical to business.

As Guggenheim put it, under the Roosevelt policies, there will be no incentive, as of old, in the heart of any young man to make a great success in life. His initiative will be destroyed. He brought in the name of Henry Ford as an ideal for the youth of the future to emulate. I asked him what harm had been done to Henry Ford, as he is still a very rich man, to which he replied that when he dies his property will be broken up. I remarked that even so, Edsel Ford stood to inherit at least a couple of hundred millions and I thought that the ability to acquire and possess such a fortune as that might be enough incentive for any young man. It was this that gave me the answer and made it abundantly clear that it isn't anything that Roosevelt has done or proposes to do to hurt business directly but simply the fear of increased taxes that has made such a bitter enemy out of practically everyone in the class with which I was associated over the week end.

Swope, during the discussion at his house, gave it as his opinion that if Landon should be elected, there might be the very hell to pay in a few years. I followed up with the argument that I have made on other occasions that people won't indefinitely endure hunger and that if we do not give them an opportunity to earn enough to live on, sooner or later we will run the risk of revolution. I said that it might be a question of giving up a portion of our fortunes and saving the rest or having all of them taken away from us.

After I knew who young Hearst was, I took two or three occasions, without mentioning any names, to show how I felt about men being called communists who were simply trying to improve the social order and give the underdog a chance. I insisted that Roosevelt really had saved capitalism. However, there is no use trying to talk to men of that type. They do not know what has happened in the world, they haven't sense enough to appraise the social forces of this generation, and they cannot see ahead into the future any farther than the ends of their noses.

Saturday, August 1, 1936

Thursday night Colonel Knox formally accepted the nomination for Vice President on the Republican ticket in a hammer-and-tongs speech. He certainly put it all over Landon so far as personality and vigor of utterance are concerned. I thought the biographical statement he made at the outset was not quite in keeping with the occasion and with the dignity of the office that he is running for, and, of course, he did not admit anywhere along the line that there could be any good in the New Deal. It was a smashing attack all along the line by a forthright and highly conservative opponent. Yesterday I wrote him a semijocular note of congratulations.

Thursday morning I got word from McIntyre by telephone from Campobello that the President had passed favorably on the draft of my speech. Steve Early, at the White House, was also on the telephone when I talked with Mac. Mac said that he and others who had read the speech particularly liked what I had to say about civil service and oil with reference to Landon.

I got to work immediately to cut down the speech to thirty minutes, having first called Michelson in New York to find out whether I could get any additional time. He tried, but he couldn't do it. I had to cut the speech almost exactly in half. This meant that I had to sacrifice all of my discussion on the Republican platform and on Landon's reactions to that platform. What is left of my speech is a highly concentrated attack on Landon. I go back into his record with respect to civil service when governor of Kansas, and I also quote from letters, telegrams, and statements made by him with reference to the Oil Administration, which he now says is a failure. I show pretty conclusively that while he denounces Roosevelt for attempting to make himself a dictator, he was in favor himself of a dictatorship until he became a candidate for President.

The President is still at Campobello but I think that he is due in Hyde Park next week. So far he hasn't said anything on the campaign since his acceptance speech at Philadelphia. He has done one thing at Campobello which I think is not wise, and that is to revive the Passamaquoddy tide-harnessing project as a possibility. This project has already been made a good deal of by the opposition and for him to advocate it now, in view of the refusal of Congress to allow any more money to be spent on it, seems to me to be very unwise indeed.

Tuesday, August 4, 1936

Last night I gave my speech on Landon over a national hookup at nine forty-five. At dinner I was so desperately tired that I didn't see how I was going to make the speech. However, a cold shower, fifteen or twenty minutes stretched out on my bed, and an aspirin seemed to hold me together and I was quite all right by the time I got to the Columbia Broadcasting Company studio. My speech just went into the half hour allotted me without having to crowd it.

I have had a number of reactions to the speech today. I have had telephone calls and telegrams, and the newspapers gave it quite a play. The *Washington Post* had a front-page story in the first column and carried the complete text of the speech. *The New York Times* carried the complete text, and I understand that the *New York Herald Tribune* carried practically all of it. Of course it is too early to tell what other papers did. A number of people who have heard it have spoken in complimentary terms. The delivery seemed to be all right and the text was, to say the least, vigorous.

I have just had a telegram from the President in which he says: THAT WAS A GREAT PHILIPPIC LAST NIGHT, which, after all, is perhaps just a little noncommittal.

Thursday, August 6, 1936

I am having a good many letters commenting on my radio speech last Monday night, and very few indeed are critical. I note that the approving ones are more enthusiastic and complimentary than I have ever received on a speech. There are many requests for copies for personal use and for distribution, and I have written today to Charley Michelson to ask him whether it is the purpose of the Democratic National Committee to print this speech. Some of the newspaper men have commented on it too, and favorably. I always think that favorable comment from this hard-boiled bunch means a good deal.

The newspaper editorials, generally speaking, are critical, but that was to be expected. Not a single one of them has met the issue that I raised in my speech or has denied that, on the face of the record, Landon has completely reversed himself. Republican politicians and headquarters attachés have met the speech in a complaining tone of voice. As with the case of the newspapers, of which eighty-five per cent are with Landon anyhow, they do not meet me on the issues. All of which means to me that my speech really hurt.

The campaign still seems to falter. With the exception of my speech Monday night, nothing has been done, and reports from all over the place continue to be discouraging. The President had a council of war at Hyde Park last Monday which was attended by Farley, Walker, Forbes Morgan, Chip Robert, Henry Wallace, and one or two others. I do not know whether to laugh or cry when I think of Forbes Morgan as treasurer of the Democratic National Committee and playboy Chip Robert as secretary. I cannot imagine what the President thinks he is doing.

Meanwhile, the Progressive situation is being badly fumbled. The President, for some unknown reason, charged Frank P. Walsh with responsibility for setting up a Progressive organization and he selected Senator La Follette to be chairman. La Follette has done some work and, of course, he ought to be in it, but my own view is that Senator Nye would be a better chairman because he has never openly bolted his party ticket. He is a party Republican, which La Follette is not, and he is one of the outstanding leaders of peace sentiment in the country. Roscoe Fertich has been trying to get matters straightened out, but when Farley is appealed to, he says that "the boss," meaning the President, is handling the thing himself and that he can do nothing about it.

La Follette came in to see me yesterday afternoon and we had a long talk. I think his idea is all right but I also continue to think that Nye is the better man for chairman. Nye came in to see me this morning and I told him how I felt. I also told him that if I were the President, in view of the civil war now raging in Spain, I would give out a statement pointing to the peace record of my Administration and assuring the country that I could not conceive of any circumstances which would make me favor this country intervening in another war in Europe. I would then send for Nye and ask him to make a statement supporting this peace move on my part.

I think the overwhelming sentiment of this country is for peace. The Republicans have done nothing on this issue and are not in nearly so good a position to do anything as this Administration. If the President can impress the country with his sincerity on this issue, I think it would go a long way toward assuring his re-election. And Nye can help as well as, or better than, any other man in the country. But the President never consults me on political matters and I do not feel like intruding on him with unsolicited views. Significantly enough, he doesn't consult Secretary Hull or Attorney General Cummings, although both were formerly chairmen of the Democratic National Committee and both are level-headed and shrewd. Dan Roper is a shrewd politician, too, but he is never consulted. So far as I know, the President never consults anyone except Farley, and Farley frankly says that he doesn't try to oppose the President's view when the President has made up his mind, even if he thinks that the President has arrived at a wrong conclusion. The sum total of it all is that here we sit and twiddle our thumbs while Landon continues to make headway.

The President has not come to time on public works funds, but, frankly, I am doing nothing more about this. Everybody agrees that he is making a great mistake. La Follette was shocked yesterday when I told him that the President had practically put the program on a high shelf. The newspapers are beginning to criticize him on his public works program. He has laid down harder terms for us than he has ever laid down for Hopkins' outfit. The newspapers are also writing stories to the effect that the old feud between Hopkins and me has been fanned into new life. That is not true. There is no feud between Hopkins and me. The whole trouble is with the President, and with the President alone. Apparently, he doesn't want to go ahead with the public works program and no one can make him. Well, he is the candidate and I am not, but I do hate to see a man play such poor politics as he seems to me to be playing right now.

Saturday, August 8, 1936

I put a call in yesterday for Miss Le Hand, who is with the President at Hyde Park, and word came back that the President

himself wanted to talk to me. He asked me how I was and I told
him I was pretty tired. He remarked that I should have taken that
trip that he had urged me to take, meaning a trip to Europe. I told
him that he was probably right but that I was planning to go away
next Monday for a week. Since he is to reach Washington Monday
morning, I said that I would like to have a chance to take up some
matters with him and he told me to be at the White House at half
past nine.

He spoke of my speech. He said it was "grand." He said he had
heard that Hearst didn't like the attacks that were being made upon
him and that there were indications of a willingness on his part to
compromise. He added that it might be necessary to go after him
once more to bring him to time.

I don't see how Hearst could compromise, or along what line.
The President had been too much disposed to think that Hearst was
about to modify his attitude toward the Administration. I don't
happen to believe it. I believe that Hearst will have to go through
along the line that he has adopted.

I called up Secretary Hull about the European situation. I am
a little anxious on account of Jane's being over there. He told me
that while the situation is serious and may become more so, he
thought there were enough counterbalancing influences to hold it
in check, at least for the time being. Germany and Italy want to
see the rebels in Spain win because they are Fascists. The sympathy
of France is with the government. However, France can't lend any
support because Germany would be on her back. Russian sympathies are also with the government. It is a serious situation all
around. Hull told me that at the moment he was working out a plan
to be put into immediate operation in order to protect our people
and their interests in Europe in the event of a spread of hostilities.

Monday, August 10, 1936

Late Sunday afternoon I drove out to Dower House. Cissy Patterson had come down on Saturday from Long Island and Ambassador Bullitt and a young woman by the name of Martin, who
takes photographs for the *Washington Herald,* were the only other
two guests. I had a good chance to talk to Bullitt both before dinner and during our drive into Washington, as we came in together
in my car.

He tells me that he predicted the present outbreak in Spain and he now says that probably by October France will be going through precisely the same experience. He doesn't think there will be a general involvement in Europe in the immediate future. As I have said, I have been anxious about Jane and so I inquired rather closely. He says that he had intended to go back to his post in Moscow the first of this month but that he has been kept busy working out some matters in the State Department. Just now he is working on a plan to evacuate Americans from Europe and protect property interests there in case of hostilities. He says there are fifty thousand Americans today in France, to say nothing of the other countries.

He thinks it is a tossup between the loyalists and the insurgents in Spain. If the loyalists win, there will be a general purge of the Fascist leaders and Spain will then go frankly communistic. He sees nothing short of that. On the other hand, if the Fascists win, they will have a little purge of their own and will set up a dictatorship. It looks like dark days ahead for Spain.

We discussed the campaign. He thinks it will be a hard one, but he has felt a little encouraged during the last few days. I do also but perhaps that is because I got my speech off my chest last Monday night. He thinks that if we win in November, it will be a pushover for the Democratic party in 1940 and that it will be the majority party for some time to come. He thinks a great wave of prosperity is on its way. On the other hand, he says that if we are defeated it will be sixteen years before the Democratic party can come back.

He told me one interesting incident which I will set down. Shortly after the President took office in March and when he was being pressed to make important decisions in many matters, one night Bullitt was at the White House and found the President in the long corridor on the second floor. He was looking into the money question and certain new facts had just been brought to his attention. He asked Bullitt what he thought ought to be done and Bullitt said that we ought to go off gold. Then Senator Key Pittman came in and his opinion was asked. He said: "Go off gold." Raymond Moley was the third who came in and gave the same advice. There followed Secretary of the Treasury Woodin and the President waved cheerfully at him and said: "Hello Will, we have just gone off gold." Woodin, taken aback, said: "Have we?"

Bullitt thought this was a rare incident and so do I. Here was a momentous decision affecting the economic welfare of the country that was decided in such an offhand manner. Or appeared to be. The probabilities are that the President had been turning it over in his mind for some time and had already reached a conclusion for which he needed only certain supporting opinions. Admittedly it was a sound and wise decision from the point of view of the country and a timely one.

Then James P. Warburg and Lewis Douglas came in and the President told them what decision had just been arrived at. They fought and argued against it for a long time. When they left and stopped for a final word at the White House entrance, Douglas turned to Bullitt and said: "Bill, this means the end of Western civilization." Bullitt relates that he burst out laughing, and when Douglas asked him what he was laughing at, he said he had heard that statement made on many occasions and that it always made him laugh. At four o'clock that morning, Douglas and Warburg came to Bullitt's room in the Carlton. They told him that they had been walking the streets discussing the decision and that they had come to the conclusion that if Bullitt felt as he did about it, perhaps something might be said for it after all.

This morning I saw the President and had a long conference with him. He spoke again of my speech last Monday night. He said he was getting repercussions from it and that they were grand. He has never been in a more friendly mood with me. He said that the trouble with the campaign was that they needed four Harold Ickeses and I was only one. He said I couldn't be the spearhead all the time and that three others were needed to supplement me. This was very flattering. He began to run over names but there didn't seem to be anyone that he was quite sure of who could fill the bill adequately. He said that people listened to me over the radio and might not listen to others. He suggested Governor McNutt and Governor Earle as possibilities. I told him that I thought there ought to be a follow-up of my speech very soon and he agreed with me. What he would like would be to put someone else on the air this week, a second person next week, and then have me go on again the following week.

By the way, Hearst was dining with Cissy Patterson at her Long Island home last Monday night. She suggested to him that they tune in and hear my speech but Hearst didn't seem to be interested. He left before I went on the air, so that Cissy heard it and she said she liked it. She thought it was a fine speech and she liked the way I delivered it.

To go back to the President, he told me this story in the utmost confidence. A friend of Hearst's came to him the other day. He thinks he came with Hearst's knowledge and approval, although the man insisted that he hadn't talked with Hearst but was merely canvassing the situation himself. I will set this down in indirect quotations and not try to give the direct language back and forth as between the President and myself. Here was the President's story:

The man in question, whose name the President did not disclose, asked the President what he thought of Hearst, and the President asked him whether he meant personally or politically. The man said politically and the President said that he thought very well of him and that he believed that he was improving his chances in the campaign by his attacks. Then the man wanted to know whether the President intended to criticize Hearst, and the President said he didn't know yet but that he might later. It was admitted that Hearst doesn't like the attacks that are being made on him. Then the man asked the President whether Victor Watson, formerly managing editor of the *Chicago Herald-Examiner,* was a friend of his, and the President said that he had been when he was governor of New York and Watson had been running the *New York American.* Then it was proposed that the President send a prominent Jewish friend of his to Watson to see whether there might be some basis for a sort of truce. He pointed out that, of course, Hearst would have to go along with Landon, and when the President asked him what kind of a truce he had in mind, he said the giving of equal space to both the Republican and the Democratic campaigns in his newspapers. The President asked whether the Hearst papers were losing in circulation and the man said they were. "How about advertising?" asked the President, and the man said that, of course, advertising followed circulation. The President wanted to know why it was suggested that a Jew be sent and the intermediary said that Hearst had great respect for the business acumen of successful Jews. There was some talk of sending one of the Strauses who own Macy's in New York. Isidor Straus, Ambassador to France, is on his way home and will be here in a few days.

The President asked me what I thought about it and whether in my opinion it would be wise to send somebody to Watson as had been suggested. I told him I didn't think so. I said: "You are President of the United States and Hearst has been attacking you. The move should come from him. Suppose you should send one of the Strauses to Watson and he should handle the thing with the utmost diplomacy, still what would prevent the Hearst press from breaking out one of these days with a statement that you had sent someone to Hearst to plead for mercy? It would be one man's statement against another. The interview couldn't be denied and the inference could legitimately be drawn that you had sent a friend for that purpose." The President said that he thought I was right.

I told the President that I thought it would be an excellent thing if he would make a statement to the effect that so long as he is President he will leave nothing undone to keep us from becoming embroiled in another European war. I had developed my ideas on this subject to Bullitt last night and he thought well of them. In fact, apparently he had been thinking somewhat along the same lines. I told the President I had discussed the matter with Senator Nye and that he would be prepared to follow up with an open declaration for the President on the record of his Administration in the cause of peace. We went into the subject quite deeply and the President seemed very much taken with the idea. He is going to make a speech at Chautauqua, New York, the end of the week and he thought that that might be a good occasion to make such a statement. I think that if he should do this with the Nye follow-up, and Nye is willing to do it, it would have a profound effect on the country, especially if Bullitt's predictions about the trouble in France come true. There isn't any doubt that the President was very much impressed with this idea. He talked about it quite some time, developing the different lines of argument that could be given to the people.

He told me that Secretary Dern was very ill and might die during the next few days. He thinks that perhaps I ought to come back for the funeral if this should happen. It seems that he is all full of poison from some bladder and kidney trouble that he had had. Bullitt told me last night that Dern had nearly died last week. The President and I talked about Dern and we both have about the same opinion of him. I have liked him very much since I got to know him. He is a sound Progressive and has a quiet courage. The President said that this poison has been in his system for the last couple of years and had slowed him down considerably mentally.

The President has also come off his high horse on Public Works and relief, and we will be now able to go ahead with a satisfactory program. He will be satisfied with forty-five per cent, or even less, of relief labor on PWA projects. This is entirely satisfactory to me. My only regret is that he had to wait all this time to arrive at a conclusion that it seemed to me from the very beginning he would have to arrive at.

Sunday, August 16, 1936

Mrs. Patterson asked me out to Dower House for dinner last night. I was dreadfully tired but I thought it might be a good thing for me to go. There were only four other guests, one of them being White, the general manager of the Hearst newspapers. Cissy noticed that I was pretty tired and after dinner she took me down by the swimming pool, where we sat and talked for quite some time. She told me how foolish she thought I was to work so hard and allow things to worry me, and of course I had to admit the force of everything she said. I know that I looked tired and acted tired because I couldn't do otherwise considering the way I felt.

I was impressed again with Cissy's gentleness and friendly understanding. I have come to be very fond indeed of her. I have found in her the best friend I have made in Washington. She seems to me to be a very genuine person with broad sympathies. She doesn't see why I stay on in the Cabinet considering the difficulties under which I have had to work during the last year or more. I have wondered myself why I do it, but she agreed with me that at least until after election I have no alternative but to stick because otherwise I would be regarded as a quitter. I left before the rest of the guests and was at home by half past eleven. I was so tired that I got out of my clothes as quickly as possible and dropped onto the bed like a log. All things considered, I had a pretty good night, much better than I have had recently in that I didn't have to take anything to put me to sleep. I was somewhat restless and awakened at intervals but I managed to get through the night pretty well.

Wednesday, August 19, 1936

Last Thursday night the President at Chautauqua, New York, made a peace speech which has had wide acclaim from many groups and sections of the country. I think the President helped himself enormously in the campaign by this speech. Last Sunday I called him up at Hyde Park to find out whether he had talked to Senator Nye. He said he had sent him a telegram to say that he was going to make a speech at Chautauqua that he thought he (Senator Nye) would like. This, of course, was not what I had expected him to do at all. Apparently there would be no follow-up unless something more were done. Accordingly, I got Senator Nye, who was in Yellowstone National Park, on the telephone last Monday. He didn't seem to be so anxious to make the statement that we had discussed, but I did my best to persuade him. He finally indicated that he would welcome an invitation to Hyde Park to discuss the matter with the President. I called the President back to ask him to send a telegram inviting Nye to Hyde Park. He said he would but in view of his failure to call Senator Nye in North Dakota, I checked back on Tuesday and found out from Miss Le Hand that the invitation had gone forward and that Nye would be in Hyde Park Friday night.

I hope that Senator Nye will give out a statement endorsing the President for re-election on the basis of his peace record and his peace talk. I would like to have his statement show very clearly that those elements in this country who would profit from a war, namely, the international bankers and the munitions makers, are all on the side of Landon. I have been anxious to have Senator Nye come out for President Roosevelt in this campaign because, while he is a Progressive Republican, he has never gone over the party line. He is very influential with the peace people.

I am receiving a number of letters complimenting me on my *Saturday Evening Post* article on the President and most of them are very flattering indeed. This article seemed to make quite an impression, and the opinion is that it will do the President a great deal of good. There is not any doubt that I have been putting more licks into this campaign on the speaking and publicity side than any other member of the Administration. As a matter of fact, I have been doing more than all the other members of the Cabinet combined. The President himself may have surpassed me in the extent of the work done, as he certainly does in the value of that work, but he is the only one. Now I have word that the President wants me to go on the air with my speech on Hearst and Landon next Thursday night. Charley Michelson called me up from headquarters to talk to me about it.

On going back over the last few months I find that I was one of the very first members of the Administration, if not the first, to begin a smashing attack on the American Liberty League. It was the night following the banquet of the league in Washington at which Al Smith made his ill-fated speech that I spoke before the Washington Town Hall. I had a question planted following my address that night and this was one of the opening guns on Al Smith and the Liberty League. I followed that up by expressions in press conferences and in speeches that I made shortly thereafter.

I thought after my talk with the President a week ago Monday that we would be able to work out a PWA program but it looks almost hopeless now. Yesterday at my press conference I was closely pressed with questions. In fact, I have never been subjected to such a barrage. I tried to answer them truthfully with the result that the newspapers this morning carried front-page stories showing the exact situation, which is that not a single project has been approved by the President under the bill adopted at the last session of Congress and that under the rules and regulations laid down by him there is little prospect of any project being approved. This isn't going to help the President any, but I can't do anything about that. It would be useless for me to try to conceal or mitigate the real facts even if I should attempt to do so. We have lost two months' time now while the President has dillydallied, apparently trying to find a way to strangle the child as quietly as possible.

Assistant Secretary Chapman went up to Pennsylvania to make a speech on the Oil Administration one day last week. He tells me that he was introduced by David L. Lawrence, chairman of the State Democratic Committee, who, in his introduction of Chapman, made very flattering remarks about me. Chapman had a private talk with Lawrence, during which the latter told Chapman that I was the man that the leaders of the Democratic organization were looking forward to as the candidate for President in 1940. Senator Guffey had indicated this to me some time ago but that was before the Democratic National Convention, at which time it became clear that Governor Earle, of Pennsylvania, had his eye on the nomination the next time. In view of this, however, the statement of Lawrence to Chapman is all the more interesting.

Saturday, August 22, 1936

I called the President yesterday to make sure that his engagement with Senator Nye was going through. At the time I talked to him Nye was in an outside room waiting to get in. I told him that I believed he could get Nye to make a statement for him on the basis of his own speech on peace and that I hoped he would tell Nye, if he did make such a statement, to link up the international bankers and the munitions makers with Landon because they are supporting him in this campaign.

Reading between the lines in the *Washington Post* this morning, I got the distinct impression that Landon's trip east has not struck ten so far. If he flops on this trip, it won't do his cause any good.

I am going up to Long Island today to visit Cissy Patterson but I will be back tomorrow night.

Tuesday, August 25, 1936

I went to Long Island Saturday afternoon to the home of Cissy Patterson. It was hot when I left Washington, as it had been for several days, but it was cool on Long Island, with a rain Saturday night. Sunday morning there was a heavy fog and when that cleared about noon it began to get very hot.

Cissy and I listened to Landon's speech at West Middlesex, Pennsylvania, his birthplace, Saturday afternoon. Literally, he did not say a thing. His delivery was somewhat better, but it was still schoolboyish. Of course I am prejudiced, but he did not make a good impression on me. Cissy, who was in Hearst's party when he went out to see Landon and who has been, and probably still is, for Landon, in spite of the fact that her brother, Joe Patterson, is supporting the President, admitted that Landon had not said anything. During the evening she also admitted that Landon would not have been heard of if it had not been for the Hearst build-up. As the publisher of Hearst's Washington paper, the *Herald,* she is loyal to Hearst and admires him, but she laughingly says to me that she does not care what I say in my speeches.

Sunday morning while at Cissy's I again worked over my speech, "Hearst over Topeka," which I am to make Thursday night over a national hookup. I did not tell Cissy that I was doing this in her home, but I chuckled to myself that I should be there polishing up an attack on her boss.

Cissy decided that she ought to come to Washington Sunday on account of the *Herald*. I was coming in on the 3:30 train, anyhow, and so we came together. She had her private car attached to the train. She teased me about its being one of the private cars carrying the Hearst party that I had referred to as standing on the sidetrack at Topeka, and she told me that she had arranged for the newspaper photographers to meet us at Washington and take my picture as I got off the car. I told her that I had arranged for some photographers of my own and that she would lose her job when Hearst saw us together in the picture. She replied that she would not, that he would think that she was clever.

Washington was terribly hot when I arrived on Sunday and it has been very hot ever since. I have been sleeping even worse than usual, and that is saying a good deal, because this summer has been the toughest spell I can remember in that regard. I had a bad night at Long Island and felt like the devil all day Sunday. I thought I would have a good night Sunday night at home, but I did not and it was the same story last night.

The President got back to Washington from Hyde Park Monday morning. I called up for an appointment and was told to be at the White House at ten-thirty. When I got there McIntyre told me that the President wanted a longer period with me than he could give at ten-thirty and wished me to come back to luncheon at one o'clock.

I was with the President at luncheon for about an hour and a half. As he has been with me recently, he was very pleasant and cordial. He talks things over with me now in a friendlier manner than before. He told me that Charley Michelson had said to him that my speech for Thursday night was fine. I handed a copy of it to him and he read it. He liked it and did not suggest a single correction. He did suggest one or two things that might be added, and these I put in later in the day, to the improvement of the speech.

The President told me at lunch that he was sounding out the Government of France to see whether William C. Bullitt would be acceptable as Ambassador. This is still a confidential matter and I cite it only as an example of how friendly he was.

When I was with the President yesterday, I did not bring up the subject of public works at all. Nor did I intend to. As I was leaving, he brought it up. His plan now is to approve an average of

$5 million worth of public works a week, in the meantime keeping his eye on his budget for the year. He still laid down qualifications which on their surface look difficult but which I do not think will bother us very much. As instructed by him, I went back to the Department and called in the Public Works people to prepare a list of projects to submit to him today, this list to show among other things the availability of labor on the relief rolls in the various communities to put to work on the projects. At two o'clock today I went to the White House again, this time with Hackett. The President went over the list and while he more or less stuck to his formula, we left with approximately $5 million worth of projects approved. These we selected, generally speaking, in northern and western states. He said that I could announce this list after I had worked it out with Hackett and that he would approve a similar list next week and one the week after.

For the first time today I understood what all of this public works pulling and hauling is about. The President wants to be in a position to say until election day that his deficit last year was less than the year before and that it will be less this year than last year. He is running on a very slender margin and if he over-reaches himself on public works projects, he won't be able to maintain this position. If he had only explained this to me in the first instance, I would have been understanding and sympathetic. He left me no option except to think that he was just deliberately scuttling our PWA program.

Congressman Sabath, of Chicago, was in to see me on Monday. Sabath is a typical old-line politician who comes from a district in Chicago just west of the river. He has no illusions and no ideals that I ever could discover. He told me that he had liked my speech on Landon and Hearst but that he had not gone to the bother to write to me about it. Then, to my surprise, he said, "If you keep that up, anything could happen in 1940." I made no reply to this but continued on some other subject, when he interrupted me to ask me whether I had heard what he said. I told him that I had. This is one of the funniest things yet. I would expect myself to be one of the last men in the world that Sabath would be for for anything of his own motion.

I had Bill White and his wife out to dinner one night last week. This is the first time that I have ever had a chance to talk with them about Landon. Of course, Bill knows Landon intimately because

Landon has been in his father's home in Emporia on a good many occasions and while young Bill was a member of the Kansas Legislature, he worked with Landon and saw a good deal of him.

Neither Bill nor his wife has any use at all for Landon. They say that a groan used to go up in the Emporia home when it was announced that Landon was to be there for dinner or to spend the night. Conversation always had to center on Landon. He is still the spoiled, only child and is tremendously engrossed in his own affairs and his own interests. They say he is a slow thinker and that he has only about one good speech in him every three months. They don't think he is entitled to be called a Progressive and that he would always allow his selfish interests to control his final judgment. They agreed with me that he would conform his opinions on public affairs to suit those who have built him up in this campaign. They believe that he is mediocre in ability and on every account a poor man to put in charge of the affairs of the nation at this time.

The *Chicago Tribune* published this week a leading editorial of a column in length charging that the President and I are pursuing the dire determination of the Administration to abridge the freedom of the press. The basis for this editorial is rather slim, but anything will serve the purpose of the *Tribune* that will give it even a toe hold in an assault upon me.

Hearst opened up on me yesterday in a front-page story charging that my book, *Back to Work,* was written by members of the staff and, therefore, at the expense of the taxpayers. There was a long, detailed story full of moral indignation expressed against me. The fact is that material was gathered by members of the staff. Various chapters were outlined by various people best qualified to do the work and then a final manuscript was prepared by Jack Latimer to submit to me. I went over that manuscript, spending many days on it, revising, eliminating, adding, and changing. It wasn't my book in the sense that I did all my research work and wrote every word of it myself. It was my book in the sense that the thoughts were mine, the language was mine, and the final form was mine.

Of course, my speeches are entirely my own, except a negligible few purely formal ones or speeches which are repetitions and only then when there are original texts of other speeches on the same subject that are available for a rewrite to be submitted to me. I always do all the dictating and the revising. The second or third draft I send to a select list of members of my staff for criticisms. These criticisms I adopt or reject on final consideration. I occasionally call on members of my staff for factual matter that I want, but if my speeches are not my own, then no man ever wrote his own speeches. Notwithstanding this fact, in the case of every speech that I make I get letters wisecracking about my speeches being the product of Charley Michelson.

But to get back to the Hearst attack. This was to be expected, in view of the way I have been criticizing him and linking him up with Landon. Several questions were asked me about the incident at my press conference yesterday afternoon and I told them that I availed myself of the same service that was furnished to any citizen by this Department. I pointed out the fact that Mr. Hearst's correspondents have the free use of Government stationery, Government telephones, Government office space, Government typewriters as well as Government stenographers if they want them. I pointed out also that, on demand, my staff was prepared to furnish anything from a rough draft to a finished product. In other words, I was taking only the services that were freely rendered to anyone else who wanted to avail himself of those services.

I made my second speech on Hearst and Landon last night over a nation-wide hookup. In this speech I used the sworn testimony from the case of *Harding* v. *Harding* pending in the Superior Court of Cook County, Illinois, from which it appeared that George F. Harding, the national committeeman, in company with Wayland Brooks, the Republican candidate for Governor of Illinois, flew out to see Hearst at San Simeon. They carried with them letters of introduction from Colonel Knox. From a memorandum from Hearst to Harding read into the record, it appeared that Hearst had already advised Landon not to make any more speeches than he had to. The whole thing showed a very close tie-up between Knox and Landon and Hearst. From what I have heard, the speech went over very well and there are likely to be some reverberations for some time to come. Undoubtedly Hearst will keep up his attack on me now rather vigorously. As a matter of fact, there was an editorial in the *Washington Herald* this morning telling how much better a Secretary of the Interior George Dern, who died yesterday, would have made than I have. There was an insinuation that I have been a dismal failure as the head of this Department and have done everything wrong.

The Republicans did one clever thing last night. Although I had withheld all copies of my speech until one o'clock yesterday afternoon, except a few that were sent by mail that would not reach newspaper offices until about the same hour, the Republicans managed to get one for William Hard, who is on the radio every night. Usually he is on early in the evening, but last night, although it must have cost them a lot of money, they put him on following my speech and he replied to it. It was well done and cleverly done. I must admit that.

As I have said, George Dern died yesterday morning and in the afternoon I called on Mrs. Dern to express my sympathy. It has been known for some time that he could not last much longer. As I have said on other occasions, I think that Dern was an unusually fine type of man and citizen and I am sorry that he has gone. The funeral will be tomorrow afternoon and the members of the Cabinet have been asked to serve as honorary pallbearers. Interment will be in Salt Lake City. The President is on a western trip in the drought area and he has arranged to attend the funeral there. I do not expect to go unless it is absolutely obligatory. As a matter of fact, I do not see how I very well can go.

Sunday, August 30, 1936

I got a big newspaper play on my Thursday night speech. The *New York Daily News,* which has the largest daily circulation in the country, printed it in full, beginning on the front page, and carried some sections of the photostatic copy of the record in the *Harding* v. *Harding* case. It is very unusual for a tabloid newspaper to print so much of any one story. *The New York Times* carried it in full with a front-page story, while even such papers as the *Baltimore Sun* and the *New York Herald Tribune* gave it large space.

As was the case with my earlier speech on Landon and Hearst, except for the few Administration papers in the country, the editorial comment has been unfavorable. The editorials on this last speech that I have seen generally take the position that the Hearst issue is an old one that fills the editorial writers with ennui. This leads me to the conclusion either that the Hearst issue is not as important as I had thought it would be or that the newspapers are unwilling to cheer on an attack against the greatest publisher, in point of newspapers, in the country. Both may be true. However, I believe that there is more widespread anti-Hearst feeling among the people than there has been for a great many years, if ever. I am told that when his name appears on the screen in some movie theaters, he is hissed, and there are anti-Hearst clubs being organized in some parts of the country.

The National Teachers Federation in a recent convention adopted a resolution condemning him by almost a unanimous vote and with only a few dissenting votes declared against any candidate supported by him. On the other hand, there is a good deal to what the newspapers say, but not to the extent to which they would like to have it appear. So far as I know, in no other Presidential campaign has Hearst been made a major issue. I believe that this issue should be developed for the good of the country, but it is evident that, generally speaking, the newspapers will not give it any aid or comfort.

That the Hearst press will overlook no opportunity to smear me from this time on, there isn't any doubt. My attack on Hearst I have kept strictly within proper bounds. It has been purely a political assault based on the record without any personal insinuations. The Hearst papers gave a reasonable amount of space to my Thursday night speech. They all carried the Associated Press story, I am told. The *Washington Herald* yesterday morning had an editorial commenting on the life of Secretary Dern, in which it pointed out how much better a Secretary of the Interior Dern would have made than I, who have made such a poor record in that office. It is typically Hearstian to attack me over a dead man's shoulder.

I went to George Dern's funeral at four o'clock yesterday afternoon. Only four members of the Cabinet were there, the others being out of town. However, the other Departments were represented by the Acting Secretaries, and the Cabinet members and acting members served as honorary pallbearers. All of the members of the Cabinet available went on to Salt Lake City for the interment except Secretary Hull and myself. The President exempted us. He did not want Hull to leave Washington on account of the international situation and he thought that I had too much to do to leave. I was grateful for this consideration because the trip would have been very tiresome and it would have been difficult for me on account of my Nebraska speech.

Monday morning I reached the office a little before eight and had barely started on my work before H. L. Woolhiser, the village manager of Winnetka, called me to tell me that Wilmarth had been found dead. Mike Straus wanted to go to Chicago with me, so we took the twelve o'clock plane out of Washington.

The funeral was held this morning at the Memorial Park Cemetery. Father Corrigan, of Oconomowoc, Wisconsin, conducted the services. They were as simple as possible.

Tuesday, September 8, 1936

I listened to the President's speech on the radio Saturday night. He was reporting on his trip West to get a firsthand impression of drought conditions. He also talked about jobs for the unemployed. He certainly has a wonderful voice and manner on the radio. His speech went over very well indeed.

Landon made a speech at Wichita, Kansas, before the Kansas Legionnaires. I read it in the paper this morning and it was as flat as ditch water. He didn't say a single thing that was worth saying, and there was no life or sparkle to his speech at any point.

I lunched with the President today. He got into Washington yesterday and is leaving again tonight. I felt flattered that he should have given his one luncheon period to me.

He continues to be very friendly indeed. We talked over his recent trip and about the situation in Illinois. He had luncheon at Springfield on his way east at the Executive Mansion. He sat between Governor Horner and Mayor Kelly and later he had both of them to dinner in his private car. He said that Kelly assured him that he would carry Cook County for him by a very big vote but that he doubted whether he could do very much for Horner because Horner was running as a downstate candidate and had antagonized a number of his organization people. The President also reported a talk with Mike Igoe, who said that Horner had to run as a downstate candidate because of the treatment that he had received in Cook County. Igoe thinks that the President will run ahead of Horner but that there is a chance of Horner's election.

The President was very much pleased with the reception that he got on this trip, although, as he said, "Crowds don't mean anything." From all reports he drew enormous crowds, and the political commentators who were on the trip seem to agree that he improved his chances considerably while he was away.

The President approved a number of new PWA projects totaling something in excess of $7 million. He spoke with great enthusiasm of some PWA projects that he had seen in Indianapolis. I told him that I supposed that he had referred to them as WPA projects. He laughed and asked me why I said that. I replied that he seemed to claim the Hannibal Bridge over the Mississippi as a WPA project when he dedicated it, and once again he queried me. Then I told him that he had referred to it as boondoggling, and then he had a good laugh.

He spoke especially of a housing project for Negroes that we are building in Indianapolis. He said that this was fine. He remarked also that he had driven through several streets in the Negro section near the housing project and that his picture was in the window of every house. This gave me an opportunity to tell him how much I regretted that we had not been able to go ahead with our Negro housing project in the black belt in Chicago. I told him that we had bought the land, or nearly all of it, for this project. Then, "thinking out loud," he developed a plan by which we might be able to go ahead with this project. He thought it might be possible to organize a corporation not for profit, the corporation to give us its notes for fifty-five per cent of the total cost of the project and PWA to contribute forty-five per cent. I told him I would have my lawyers consider the possibilities of such a plan.

He also told me that, if possible, he would like to go ahead with the housing projects in Bridgeport, Connecticut, and Lackawanna, Pennsylvania. He thought these projects would be of great advantage politically, and I said, "Hard-boiled Harold understands."

It is rather late for the President to come to a realization of the political benefits that would flow from housing projects. This is quite aside from the social desirability of such projects. I have urged this on him for months and now we are practically without money and it is too late to start much of anything. However, I will not overlook any opportunity to start two or three more projects if we can do so.

As I was leaving, the President spoke about Wilmarth. He was most kind and understanding. For a long time I have felt that the President isn't personal, and I don't think that he is in the sense that he particularly feels for or through another. But no one can be more friendly or interested than he or give so strong an impression of real concern. He has a very real touch in his human relationships.

While I was with him he had a long-distance telephone talk with Bernard Baruch. At its conclusion I asked him whether Baruch was still with him and he said that he was.

Tuesday night I got my speech for the dinner of the Third World Power Conference in final form. This is only an eight-minute speech, but naturally I want to acquit myself with credit because of the international character of the audience. There will be a national hookup, with short-wave to Europe.

Thursday, September 10, 1936

Last night I had dinner with Cissy Patterson at her home in Dupont Circle. There were just the two of us. She had a temporary Polish chef and he served us a wonderful dinner. We went out to the kitchen afterward to tell him how good it was. It was hot at Dupont Circle and Cissy proposed that she would drive me home and then go out to Dower House where it would be cooler.

She told me that she had seen both Raymond Moley and William C. Bullitt lately. Each of them told her that he thought I was the outstanding man in the Cabinet, that I was not only honest but that I had ability. Naturally I like to get bouquets like these once in a while, and this sort of thing means more to me if said out of my presence.

Driving out to my home Cissy said that the *Herald* was now so well organized that there was nothing for her to do. Formerly she had had to make decisions and attend to this or that or the other thing. She wondered what she could do next and I suggested that she buy a paper of her own. Apparently she has in mind the possibility of getting out of the *Herald,* and yet she feels that time would hang heavy on her hands and that she would be lonely without a job to engage her interest.

J. David Stern, publisher of the *Philadelphia Record* and two or three other papers, has asked me to lunch with him today at the Mayflower. Stern's papers are out in front in the fight for Progressive principles and he has been doing great work for the Administration. The *Record* now has the largest circulation of any paper in Philadelphia and is becoming more and more influential. From what I know of him, Stern is himself a real Progressive.

Governor Talmadge, of Georgia, who was running for the nomination for Senator, was badly beaten. I think he is one of the most contemptible figures in public life. He looks more like a rat than any other human being that I know and he has all of the mean, poisonous, and treacherous characteristics of that rodent. He has been a bitter critic of the New Deal and his overwhelming defeat will mean much to us.

I asked Cissy last night to tell me confidentially what her political writers felt about the election and she told me that they all thought it would be Roosevelt. She thinks so herself. She was in the Hearst party that went out to Topeka to see Landon and she said that he made a very fine impression on her on that occasion. However, his speeches and his appearance in the newsreels have destroyed whatever enthusiasm she may have had for him. Mike Straus tells me that he lunched yesterday with the correspondents of the *Kansas City Star* and other papers that are supporting Landon. The *Star* men told him that Landon himself now believed that he couldn't be elected. In a surprise move he is rushing up to Maine to make a speech in Portland Saturday night. Apparently the Republican strategists think that they will carry Maine and they want him to be in the picture. It will be a severe blow to him if he has guessed wrong.

The President said when I lunched with him on Tuesday that he thought Maine would go Republican. This has been my opinion too, although one or two sound political observers think that Governor Brann at least will be elected to the Senate.

Saturday, September 12, 1936

I lunched last Thursday at the Mayflower with J. David Stern, publisher of the *Philadelphia Record*. Bob Allen, his Washington correspondent, was there too.

Stern told me that three years from now he expected to have to make a very difficult decision—that is, whether to be for Governor Earle or for me for President. I told him that he shouldn't have had even the one cocktail that he had had. But apparently he was serious because he went on to discuss the matter. He finally remarked that Earle was a younger man than I and that he ought to be content to run for Vice President in 1940.

He brought up the question of the municipal power plant for Camden, New Jersey. His paper in Camden was strongly in favor

of this project and fought for it vigorously. We had made the allocation and then rescinded it because we needed some enabling legislation which the New Jersey Legislature refused to pass. He and I
had some vigorous correspondence on this matter because he insisted editorially and in his letters to me that we ought to finance
the project even without legislation. I explained our position to
him at the luncheon and I think that finally he was satisfied.

He has also been impatient from time to time because of what he
regarded as my undue slowness of going forward with our public
works program, but he admitted at the luncheon that perhaps I
had been right after all. There was a good deal of discussion, led by
Bob Allen, about the absence of scandal in carrying out our public
works program and the fact that it has not been attacked by the
Republicans at any point, except as to the advisability of one or
two projects, such as Passamaquoddy. On the way out of the dining
room, Stern said that I was the outstanding man in the Administration and a tower of strength to the President.

It is very flattering to have anyone suggest to you that you are a
Presidential possibility. There have been a number of such suggestions lately. However, I don't see it at all. I do not regard myself as
a possibility. First and foremost, I have no ambition to be President. I don't say that I wouldn't take it if I could get it; any man
would. What I mean is that it is a killing job that would tax the
strength of a far younger man than I will be four years from now.
I doubt whether I would be a popular candidate. I never have
been popular and I can't see any possible political setup that would
result in my nomination. Even if I could be nominated, I would be
fought more bitterly by the big interests and the possessors of big
incomes than President Roosevelt himself. As I see it now, if I
had resigned from the Cabinet a year ago, as was suggested at that
time, there might have been a very real possibility of my being nominated on the Republican ticket this year. And in that event I think
I would have had a good chance to be elected. But I see no such
possibility for 1940 and I don't intend to allow my head to grow
too large for my hat. If President Roosevelt is re-elected and I continue in his Administration, I will continue to do my job the best
I know how and let the future take care of itself.

The banquet of the Third World Power Conference was held in
the waiting room of the Union Station because there was no banquet hall in Washington big enough for so large an affair. Places

were set for about seventeen hundred people. It cost a pretty penny to set up the waiting room for this purpose and then restore it to its original status. The program was a long one. I responded to the toast of "The Chiefs of the States Represented Here" and I had eight minutes. In addition to a national hookup, there was a short wave that carried the speeches to every part of the world.

It was a very difficult place to speak in. I have a voice that carries pretty well, but it wouldn't carry through that banquet hall. At that, Owen D. Young was the only other of the long list of speakers who seemed to be able to do any better than I could. I knew that my voice was not carrying because of the hum of conversation that soon came up to me from the outskirts of the hall in all directions and my voice reverberated so that it literally came back and hit me in the face all during my speech. However, I understand that it carried very well over the air.

There was a short Cabinet meeting yesterday, the first for a long time. Only Hull, Morgenthau, Cummings, Acting Postmaster General Howes, Swanson, Henry Wallace, and myself were there. Swanson hadn't attended a Cabinet meeting for many, many months and he looked like a very ill and frail man. I don't understand why he tries to hold on. He looks as if he might drop dead any minute.

What little time we had was spent discussing the campaign. The President had to leave at a quarter before three because he was due to speak before the World Power Conference in Constitution Hall at three o'clock. I went over to that meeting too. The President got a great reception. It was surprisingly enthusiastic considering the nature of the audience.

Grace Tully called me up Saturday and said that the President would like to have me go down the Potomac with him if I cared to go. As a matter of fact, I had planned a number of things that I wanted to do at home over the week end and I didn't want to go, but since I had declined his invitation to go on his trip last week with him into the Great Smoky Mountains National Park, I felt that I couldn't refuse again after such a short interval. So I went, leaving the White House about three-thirty.

In the party, besides the President, were the Attorney General and Mrs. Cummings and Grace Tully. It was terribly hot on the Potomac in the afternoon and well through the night. We tried to console ourselves with the thought that it was cooler than it would be in Washington, but I am not so sure that it was cooler than it would have been out where I live.

Anyhow, we had a pleasant time. Late Saturday afternoon we tried fishing for half an hour after we had anchored, but no one got a nibble and interest soon died out. While we were at dinner, the boat on which the National Press Club was taking an outing caught up with us and came close enough so that there was an exchange of badinage. After some singing and music from the "show boat" of the National Press Club, it dropped on down the river. Later we went down farther and anchored for the night.

We had plenty of time to talk after dinner as we sat on the afterdeck, and, of course, the conversation all centered on the campaign. We pursued the subject further on Sunday.

The President said that after the Progressive conference in Chicago the other day, Bob La Follette called him up and that he then talked in succession to several of the conferees. They were all of the opinion that he should make a smashing campaign. He asked Homer and me what we thought. I told him that the Republicans were a whole lot better off than we were when it came to campaign speakers. They have Frank Knox, Senator Vandenberg, Senator Dickinson, John Hamilton, Henry Allen, and others who can carry on an offensive campaign. Moreover, they have the press with them to give publicity to their attacks. On our side, hardly anyone can break into the newspapers except the President himself and we haven't enough speakers to scatter them broadcast over the country. I said that for this reason it seemed to me that it might be necessary for the President to open up on Landon. The President himself felt that it would be better for him to remain more or less aloof and not enter into any personal controversy with Landon or even to mention his name. Cummings thought that he ought to do that and that we ought to organize a swarm of speakers and send them out in the highways and byways. This would be all right if we had the speakers and if such a campaign could be organized.

Then the President began to speculate on what our attitude ought to be if Landon should be elected. Suppose, for instance, he should ask some of the members of the present Cabinet to become members of his Cabinet. Suppose, even, that he should ask the President to take an active part in his administration. I told him that he could not afford to do that because it was a foregone conclusion that Landon's policies would not be such that he or any of us could subscribe to, and if the President should allow himself to be put in a position of underwriting Landon's administration, he would forfeit his right to leadership of the other school of thought. This was clearly the President's own opinion. He thinks that if Landon is elected, we will find ourselves in a grave situation within two or three months. I do not subscribe to this. I think that Landon would find himself in deep water sooner or later but certainly not earlier than six months after he went into office and probably not for a longer period than that.

Just after Landon had finished his speech in Maine, I said that he was probably on the air. None of us particularly wanted to listen to him and so we felt relieved when Grace Tully looked up the time in the newspaper and said that we were just too late.

We discussed in considerable detail one or two of the main speeches that we thought the President ought to make. I think there is the possibility of some very effective speeches, especially if the President makes them, and he seemed to like the ideas that Homer and I developed with him. There ought to be one on taxation and the budget, one on the national debt as compared with the national income, and one ridiculing Landon's statement that we must return to the "American way of life."

I do not think that the President has any real doubt but that he will be re-elected, and I confess that I cannot now see how Landon can win unless there is a sudden and decided change in the situation.

Landon's dash all the way from Topeka to Portland, Maine, looks a little absurd to me. This wasn't done to save Maine for the Republican party. As a matter of fact, the trip would not have been undertaken if the Republicans had not been quite sure that Maine was safely in the bag. They wanted Landon to be striking an attitude on the deck of the ship with his rod in his hand as the fish was being hauled aboard, although he hadn't hooked the fish.

As we read the speech Sunday morning, we all came to the conclusion that Landon hadn't written it. Harry Slattery, who heard him over the radio, said that Landon read it as if he were unfamiliar with it. He stumbled over some of the phraseology and on occasion had to back up and get a fresh start. Harry thinks that it bore the imprimatur of Jimmy Williams, one of Hearst's principal writers. It happens that Williams took this trip with Landon. It didn't seem to me that the speech said anything anyhow but merely repeated what Landon has been saying so far about free competition, although he did have the impertinence to call upon the President to confess the error of his ways. I think that if Landon edges out a little further, we may be able to push him overboard. Meanwhile the President is holding his fire and shows no disposition to be stampeded. At that, I think we ought to show more life and vigor on our side than we have shown to date. From what the President said, the campaign funds are not coming in any too rapidly and we may feel the pinch of poverty before election day.

I took occasion to feel Grace Tully out a little about myself. I told her that in the new building I was arranging for a very attractive layout for my successor. I described my office, the kitchen, the dining room, the Frigidaire, and the bedroom. She said it all sounded very interesting but that if the President were re-elected, I would be my own successor if I wanted to be, or words to that effect.

We got back to Washington a little before six o'clock Sunday evening.

Today Dr. Stanley High called me up to say that headquarters was arranging a big meeting for Negroes next Monday night at Madison Square Garden, to be followed by other meetings across the country, in an effort to round up the Negro vote for the President. He is very anxious to fill Madison Square Garden and when he consulted the various Negro leaders about speakers, he discovered that I was the one man in the Administration who had a real standing with them. He was very anxious for me to speak on Monday night. I have had two talks with him but I finally sent a telegram declining to go. My reason is that this would be my first political speech since Wilmarth died. I think it might make a bad impression for me to make that first speech so soon after his death and at a meeting where there would be stage performances, jazz music, etc. I know that I would not feel very comfortable about it and I might be laying myself open to criticism that wouldn't do the cause of the President any good.

Saturday, September 19, 1936

The President got back to Washington Saturday, but I did not see him until Thursday. There was a meeting of the Cabinet on Thursday and I had a few minutes with him before the meeting and another short session afterward. He approved a lot of PWA projects. After the Cabinet meeting he told me that he understood from

Glavis that Burlew was making trouble for some of the men who had been on Glavis' staff in the Division of Investigations. He wondered whether I could send Burlew to Hawaii on some sort of an inspection trip. I told him that Burlew had been away about three weeks. I told him, further, that Burlew had not made any trouble for any of Glavis' people but that I had, and that if Glavis would do less talking about me, things would go along better. He said that Glavis had not said anything about me.

After the Cabinet meeting I ran across Tom Corcoran in Miss Le Hand's office. He followed me to the door and asked me whether I knew that some of Glavis' men were making the threat that they were going to get me. I told him that I was not surprised. I told him further that people had been trying to get me for three years now and that I wasn't losing any sleep over it.

At Cabinet meeting the discussion turned mainly on the campaign. We now have behind us the election in Maine and the primary elections in Michigan and Massachusetts. As I read the result in Maine, there is no guaranty that Landon will win in November. As a matter of fact, although the Republicans elected their United States Senator, their Governor, and all the Congressmen, the results seemed to me to indicate that, while we are in a fight, Roosevelt continues to have the edge.

In Michigan the result was not so clear. Senator Couzens, who had declared for Roosevelt while offering himself as a candidate for renomination for Senator on the Republican ticket, got a very large vote, but he was defeated by former Governor Brucker by a plurality of one hundred thousand. However, Couzens did not make a speech and refrained entirely from making any kind of a campaign. The total Republican vote cast in the primaries exceeded by far the Democratic vote, but even so, I do not think that it is a foregone conclusion that Roosevelt, with the help of Couzens, cannot carry Michigan in November.

In Massachusetts there was a hard fight in both parties, mainly revolving around the United States Senatorship. Governor Curley, that hardened, old political reprobate, won the Democratic nomination, and Henry Cabot Lodge, grandson of the late Senator Henry Cabot Lodge, won the Republican nomination. It looks like a tough fight between the two in Massachusetts, but, in my heart, I hope that Lodge will win, although I would like to see Roosevelt carry the state. However, I think the chances are against that.

One thing that interested me at Cabinet meeting was the statement by Acting Secretary of War Woodring that we ought to take an advanced stand on the peace issue. He said that sentiment for peace in the West was very strong. The reason that this interested me is because Woodring has been one of the most warlike officials in Washington. We discussed, in general terms, certain phases of the campaign, how we should meet certain issues, and so forth. The President very particularly said that when we answered any of the Republican arguments, he wanted the answer to be in the form of an attack.

I started in a couple of days ago to write another speech, although I have no certain date ahead of me. Curiously enough, national headquarters will send down to me requests for speeches, leaving it to me to decline or accept. They even recommend speeches that it would not be worth my time to make. It seems to me a curious way to run a campaign. I should think that if my services on the platform are of any value at all, they would want to utilize them to the fullest possible value. Anyhow, I am writing a speech in which I expose Governor Landon's applications to PWA for money to finance a state telephone system for Kansas and a state-owned natural gas pipeline. Now he is an individualist and opposed to Government participation in or interference with business.

Tom Corcoran and Ben Cohen came in to see me yesterday. They had some ideas that they thought ought to be incorporated in my speeches, and they sounded good. I asked them to submit them in the form of written memoranda.

Corcoran asked me when I was going out on my campaign tour. I told him that I did not know anything about a campaign tour, and he said that Congressman Rayburn has told him that I was going on one. I remarked that I wished that Rayburn would take me into his confidence, since I cannot prepare speeches overnight. He told me that Rayburn had said to him that there were more requests for me as a speaker than for anyone else. He also said that Jim Farley had remarked that I was the best asset the Democratic party had and that my speeches went over big.

I really get a kick out of this. A year ago I was distinctly under a cloud. I seemed to have lost favor, to a large degree, with the President, and the sappers were at work on all sides trying to undermine me. Now I appear to be in high favor, even with people who had little good to speak of me a year ago.

I get a great kick out of the situation in another respect. I certainly was in no demand as a speaker anywhere or at any time before I became a member of the Cabinet. And the reason is not far to seek. I was a perfectly rotten speaker. I was scared to death when I stood before an audience and it isn't any wonder that I was not in demand. If I ever did have a chance to speak, I avoided it if I possibly could. With this record and background, I find it difficult to realize that my speeches go over well and that I am more in demand than anyone on the Democratic list, excepting always, of course, the President himself.

Corcoran told me that Morgenthau and Harry Hopkins are at swords' points. He said that Henry has reached into WPA until nothing can be done there without his approval. Things reached such a pass that recently Hopkins threatened to resign and the President had to pour oil on the troubled waters. It is a funny thing about Morgenthau. No one thinks that he has any ability, and yet he is spreading himself further and further. Corcoran remarked that in the next Cabinet, from the way it looks, it will be every other Cabinet member against Morgenthau.

Senator Norris made a speech at Omaha last night severely criticizing Governor Landon. He had a national hookup. I did not know that he was going to make the speech or I would have tuned in on him. Everyone said that it was a very able and effective speech.

I ran across Colonel McIntyre this morning in the office of Dr. McIntire. He says that the Hearst papers are coming out tomorrow with a front-page broadside charging that orders have issued from Moscow to the Communists in this country to support Roosevelt. This, of course, is to be expected from the unspeakable Hearst. Steve Early has prepared an answering blast.

Wednesday, September 23, 1936

Governor Landon made a speech at Des Moines, Iowa, last night on his farm policies, and as I listened to him over the radio I got the impression that he was for anything that any farmer anywhere might conceivably want. He was against the AAA, but he promised that all of the benefits accruing to the farmers under the AAA would be forthcoming, in the event of his election. He went as far as anyone could possibly go in promising cash benefits to the farmers and, at the same time, he insisted that he was going to lower taxes and prevent governmental waste. He was for a land-conservation program, and he told what wonderful progress had been made in Kansas in building artificial ponds and lakes. Then he said that this had been done out of WPA money, which is Federal money. In other words, he took credit to himself for a Federal program that was being financed in Kansas by Federal funds, while at the same time he is against the WPA program. He also expressed himself as being in favor of crop insurance. The Administration beat him to it on that issue by two or three days, and the Republicans were plainly annoyed about this. As a matter of fact, Governor Landon released that portion of his speech which dealt with crop insurance two or three days in advance of the delivery of his speech in order that it might appear in the papers coincidentally with the crop-insurance plan of the Administration.

Henry Wallace has been trying for some time to get favorable consideration of his plan of crop insurance. I know that he has brought it up at the last two Cabinet meetings. As the time approached for the statement by Landon of his farm policy, Henry became more and more anxious about the matter. He thought that it was of great importance to "beat Landon to it." Finally, at the Cabinet meeting last Thursday it was decided that the Administration would commit itself to a crop-insurance plan.

A short time ago the Pope issued a statement calling upon all Christians to join hands in opposition to the spread of communism. I referred to this at the last Cabinet meeting, suggesting that I was afraid that this might be used to our prejudice in this campaign. I did not press the matter and there was no discussion.

On Sunday morning the Hearst newspapers carried the anticipated blast against the President on the basis that he is, in fact, the candidate of the Communists and that orders have issued from Moscow to Communists to support him. It was the knowledge that this blast was about due that caused the statement by Steve Early that I have already referred to. This charge by the Hearst papers was widely carried in other newspapers. It consisted of the usual claptrap, innuendoes, and insinuations, with no factual basis to support such a charge.

Following this, and in reply to the Early statement, the Hearst newspapers on Monday carried a front-page, signed editorial by Hearst himself, in which he went after the President very viciously.

Apparently he was enraged by a reference by Early to himself, although he was not named.

On Tuesday the President called me up on a departmental matter and I took occasion to tell him that, in my judgment, it was important for him to land with the full force of his right on Hearst's chin. I told him that no one else could do this for him and that the editorial just referred to offered him an opportunity for a knockout blow. In my judgment, as I outlined my thought to him, he could issue a statement quoting what Theodore Roosevelt had said about Hearst, quoting Elihu Root on the same subject, and Al Smith, and one or two others. Then he could express his own opinion and end with some such declaration as Woodrow Wilson used in the Jeremiah O'Leary incident when he repudiated O'Leary and declared that he did not want his support in any circumstances.

The President said that perhaps he ought to "take a shot at the old man," and I offered to have some material gathered together and sent to him. I do not know what he will do, but I think that the very boldness of such an assault would have a telling effect. I do not think that it was particularly strong for the President to attack Hearst through Steve Early without even mentioning Hearst's name, although everyone knew who the man was who was referred to.

Saturday, September 26, 1936

Congressman Hamilton Fish called me up this morning on a PWA project. He is the Republican Congressman from the President's district in New York. He indicated clearly that he thought the President would be re-elected. He asked me what I thought about Illinois, and when I told him that my best information was that the President would carry the state, he said that this corresponded with the information that he had received. He thinks that the President is much stronger in the cities than anyone gives him any credit for and that he is also strong in the western farming country but very weak in the eastern farming sections, because in the East the farmers have received few benefits from his farm program.

I told Fish that he really ought to be ashamed of himself for having such a candidate for President and he said that I need not try to crowd Landon down his throat, because he agreed with me. He supported Borah for the nomination. He remarked that perhaps I had noticed that he was not doing much for the Republican ticket.

He has not been on the air for months and he is merely preserving his party regularity. He said that he made a couple of speeches in Maine for that purpose.

France went off the gold standard yesterday and there is a gentleman's agreement between the United States, Great Britain, and France to stabilize the currencies of the three countries. Great Britain and the United States are prepared to support the franc at its present value in the world market, and all three countries have served notice that they are not going to permit their position to be undermined. My thought is that this agreement will strengthen the President in this campaign.

Friday, October 2, 1936

I took the 2 A.M. train Tuesday for New York after spending Monday evening working on a speech. From New York I went to Hyde Park to accompany the President on his special train to Syracuse for the laying of the cornerstone in the new medical building at Syracuse University. The money for this building was loaned by PWA.

The President seemed very well and looked well. Except for the members of his immediate staff there was no one on the train to Syracuse, and I spent a good deal of time with him. He read to me the speech that he was to deliver Tuesday night before the Democratic State Convention at Syracuse. He asked me if I thought that it was too strong, but I didn't and told him so. I asked him what he thought about New York and he said that he believed it was safely Democratic.

There was a large crowd at the cornerstone laying in spite of the rather raw weather. It rained a great part of the way from New York to Syracuse, but the rain had stopped before we got there. There were very large crowds in the streets to see the President, although Syracuse is a heavily Republican city. After the cornerstone laying the Presidential party returned to his private train by way of the business district. The streets were lined with people.

The Democratic State Convention had renominated the entire state ticket during the day and it was to close after the President spoke at night. The armory, where the convention was held, was packed and it was a highly enthusiastic crowd. It was easy to see that the enthusiasm was spontaneous, and the President's speech was just the kind to keep the crowd at the top pitch. It was the first real political speech that he had made during the campaign. It was a fighting speech and it went over big.

I asked both Ed Flynn, the Bronx leader, and Senator Wagner what they thought about New York. Flynn said that while the situation wasn't perfect, he had no doubt of the result, and Senator Wagner was equally certain. In a talk with Senator Wagner he said that he had worked side by side with Al Smith for over twenty years and that Al Smith had never had an idea of his own. He wasn't saying this for publication but, according to him, all of Smith's ideas have been furnished to him by others. During his earlier years he happened to fall into the right hands, although Wagner intimated that his record in some particulars would not stand very close scrutiny. He also said that he thought that he himself was a pretty good politician, but that the President was the best he had ever known.

Driving back to the special train after the convention in the car with me were Ed Flynn, Miss Le Hand, and Grace Tully, all of them Catholics. They fell to talking about Father Coughlin, Flynn having brought up the subject. He remarked that if Coughlin kept on, he (Flynn) would be leaving the Catholic church, and Miss Le Hand indicated that she felt that way too. I do not think that either of them meant it seriously, but it shows how deep the feeling is running, even among Catholics, over Coughlin's political activities. I found that neither Flynn nor Wagner believes that Al Smith can do the President's cause very much harm.

I asked the President whether he had had any investigation made of Hearst's loans at the Giannini and Crocker banks in California. He said that these loans were so large that the banks did not dare to call them. I suspect that he was merely relaying to me the information that came to me some time ago and which I had given him on a previous occasion. I remarked that I thought he would be doing a patriotic service if the Administration would force the banks to call these loans.

The *St. Louis Post-Dispatch*, the old Pulitzer paper, came out for Landon a couple of days ago. It even went further than the *Baltimore Sun*, which so far has declared against Roosevelt but not for Landon. There seems to be no doubt that a new political alignment is going on in the country. People and institutions that belong to the rich classes are more and more opposed to the President. It is really remarkable that a newspaper of the Democratic traditions of the *Post-Dispatch* should have gone overboard from the Democratic ship. Yesterday *The New York Times* in a long editorial declared for Roosevelt. This was helpful and will counterbalance to some extent the defections to Landon.

Last night I listened to a lot of political oratory over the air—first, Frank Knox for half an hour talking from Pittsburgh, then the President for the same period, also from Pittsburgh, and then Al Smith for three-quarters of an hour from New York.

It is literally true that I would not have recognized Frank Knox's voice. Even though I knew that it was he who was speaking, I could not put the voice and the man together. He talked very loudly and seemed to be trying for an oratorical effect. His delivery was that of the old-time spellbinder, and I could almost see him wave his arms and perspire profusely. He returned to his earlier charge that under this Administration no life insurance policy is secure and no savings bank account is safe. When he originally made this charge it was obviously a blunder, but he has been trying to bluff through on it, since it has attracted so much attention. Coming from a man who also praises the Hoover administration and insists that if Hoover had been re-elected prosperity would have returned earlier and in greater measure, it seems to me that the whole thing is absurd. I do not know how big an audience Knox had, but there seemed to be a lot of enthusiasm. His crowd appeared to like his type of perfervid oratory.

The President was on the air immediately following Knox. He spoke at the baseball park in Pittsburgh, and the announcer said that there were thirty thousand people in the grounds and many more thousands outside. He certainly received a great ovation. He talked about national finances, and it seemed to me that he handled his subject well and in a manner that would be understood by the average man. Al Smith followed the President immediately. His speech was bitter, personal, and sarcastic. It is astounding to what lengths of vindictiveness a man of long experience in politics and public affairs will allow himself to go when he has suffered a serious setback to his ambitions. One of his criticisms was that Roosevelt had surrounded himself with advisers who are not Democrats. When he was discussing this subject he inquired—"Who is Ickes?" and with me he linked Wallace, Hopkins, and Tugwell.

Until the very end of the speech I thought that Al Smith would confine his remarks to an attack on Roosevelt and the Administration, but finally he declared himself in favor of the election of Landon.

Sunday, October 4, 1936

An amusing incident occurred at the cornerstone laying of the medical building at Syracuse University. The invocation was by the Reverend William H. Powers. At the conclusion of the ceremonies Mr. Powers congratulated me upon my remarks. "What you said," he told me, "was *multum in parvum.*" Then he said that he understood that I was deeply religious like himself. I replied that that would depend upon his definition of religion, and he said "my kind." I let it go at that without divulging to him that I was as weak in religion as he seemed to be in Latin.

I reached the Biltmore Hotel about noon. The President had gone over to Jersey City in the morning to lay the cornerstone of a medical center, which is also a PWA project. I had not been invited to this ceremony, although when I saw the President at luncheon he asked me why I hadn't been there. Tremendous crowds turned out to meet the President in Jersey City and there was a great demonstration for him.

There was a luncheon of about forty people at the Biltmore Hotel before we started to the Polo Grounds to see the second World Series game between the New York Giants and the Yankees. I was in the third car until we reached the Polo Grounds. Our route took us up through the Bronx and there were large and enthusiastic crowds all along the line. It was especially interesting to see the turnout of Negroes. Senator Wagner remarked to me afterward that in former times Negroes would not turn out to see any Democratic candidate. There were thousands of them and they displayed great enthusiasm. The Polo Grounds held a large crowd and the President got a fine reception. After the game we started for the ground-breaking ceremonies. I rode in the President's car, along with Mayor La Guardia and Senator Wagner.

Tremendous crowds lined the streets all the way. I don't know how many miles we covered but it was a considerable distance. There was no mistaking the genuine enthusiasm of the people who greeted the President. I have never seen a greater or a more spontaneous demonstration. In some places the crowds had pushed into the streets so that out-riding policemen on motorcycles had to crowd them back in order to have plenty of clearance for the President's car. The President, hat in hand, kept waving and bowing right and left. At the site of the ceremonies there was also a big crowd gathered. After we had made our speeches we started for the Grand Central Station, where the President was to take his train back to Hyde Park. It was dusk by this time but the crowds persisted, especially in the poorer sections of the city. Even when we got to Park Avenue, however, there were still crowds of considerable size, and they seemed to be cordial even if they lacked the enthusiasm that we had met with earlier.

The President remarked that on his trip from Jersey City to the Biltmore Hotel he heard the first boo about a block from Fifth Avenue, and another as he passed the Yale Club. No boos were heard after we left the Biltmore Hotel until we reached Grand Central Station about six o'clock. There were only enthusiastic cheers and cordial greetings.

On the way to the ball game I was in a car with Gerard Swope. For years he was extremely close to Al Smith and apparently was consulted by Smith on occasions when he had an important political decision to make. According to Swope, Smith has never gotten anything from the printed page. His close friends have to feed him material through his ears, and Smith's method of getting his mental pabulum is to fight and argue and thus force his interlocutor to prove the soundness of his views. I had always heard that Mrs. Belle Moskowitz was the most influential of the Smith inner group. She was very able and a Progressive. According to Swope it was she who kept Smith on the liberal path until 1928, after which he began to grow more and more conservative and Mrs. Moskowitz lost her influence with him. She died a few years ago.

Swope said that she could have been very helpful to Roosevelt but that Louie Howe was jealous of her and would not let her get close. According to Swope, Smith used to submit his important speeches to Mrs. Moskowitz, Robert Moses, and himself. Swope had listened to Smith on Thursday night and felt about the speech just about as I have expressed myself. He said that he did not believe that Moses had been consulted about this speech. Apparently he talked it over only with Raskob, who is acquiring more and more influence over Smith. Swope also said that Carnegie Hall was not filled for the Smith meeting, although arrangements had been made for an overflow meeting.

Friday, October 9, 1936

The day that France went off the gold standard, it was announced that the United States, Great Britain, and France would support the franc, the pound, and the dollar. The following day Henry Morgenthau called a special press conference and excitedly stated that Russia had tried to raid the pound and that he had used the stabilization fund of the Treasury to support it. The Treasury bought approximately a million pounds.

It shortly appeared that Henry was unduly excited or that he was playing a little politics. Russia needed some dollars and was selling pounds to buy dollars with. The amount involved, considered as an international transaction, was quite insignificant. I don't know whether it was intimated to Morgenthau that, in view of the alleged interest of Moscow in President Roosevelt's candidacy, it might be a good thing to take advantage of this situation to make it appear to be a battle between the United States and Russia. The whole thing was a very silly tempest in a very small teapot.

When the Russian delegation, headed by Litvinov, came to Washington a couple of years ago at the time that we recognized Russia, there was in the delegation a man by the name of Constantin Oumansky, who at that time was in charge of press relations for the Russian Foreign Office. I met him at a luncheon at the White House and it developed that he was a stamp collector. He gave me some Russian stamps and I gave him quite a lot of new American issues. I sent him some after his return to Russia but never had any acknowledgment from him. He is back in Washington now as Chancellor of the Russian Embassy and he called on me on Monday. He brought me some nice blocks of canceled Russian stamps mounted in a book. He was quite indignant about the Morgenthau incident and insisted that it was only an ordinary commercial transaction. I believe him because what he told me seems to be generally accepted as the truth. He posed me this question: Why should Russia be trying to hurt France, her ally and the only friend that she has in Europe? I did not know the answer.

The President got back to Washington on Tuesday. Wednesday morning the papers carried a sensational story about a contract entered into about two years ago between Fokker and Elliott Roosevelt, by which the latter was made Fokker's agent for a consideration of $500,000 to sell Fokker airplanes in Russia. It appeared that Elliott Roosevelt had been paid a retainer of $5,000. However, the price asked for the planes was so high that none ever was sold, so that the contract was ineffectual. This information had all been divulged before the Munitions Investigating Committee of the Senate, of which Senator Nye is chairman, but the committee by a unanimous vote, including the Republican members, decided not to make the contract public, because it was in effect a *nullum pactum,* for the reason that it would be regarded as an attempt to smear President Roosevelt. Now, in the closing days of the campaign, the story broke from an outside source.

Personally, I haven't any use for Elliott Roosevelt. I would not put it beyond him to capitalize on his father's position for his own personal advantage. They say that James Roosevelt does the same thing in Massachusetts in his insurance business. Jim Farley intimated to me on our trip into Virginia over the Fourth of July that both of these boys skated on very thin ice. Of course, Elliott Roosevelt's services were not worth $500,000. At the time the contract was made he was only twenty-three years old, and any influence that he had was reflected influence of his father. The whole thing has a bad smell, aside from its political involvements.

I lunched with the President on Wednesday. He read a copy of the speech I am to make at Columbus, Ohio, tonight and he liked it. He asked me to send him a copy.

The President told me that there was not enough money in the campaign fund to pay this week's headquarters' salaries. I know that they have been very hard up for funds. Jim Farley apparently thinks that money will be coming in from the various state organizations and, according to the President, he is not worried.

The President got on the subject of "prima donnas." He said that Ray Moley, while saying favorable things about him, said them in such a way as to hurt. It appears that Moley has alienated Vincent Astor from the President. He also said that he had to send for Joe Kennedy every few days and hold his hand. Then he went on to talk about Rex Tugwell. He remarked that no one connected with him or the Administration had been subjected to such criticism as Rex had. Yet Rex has never whimpered or asked for sympathy or run to anyone for help. He has taken it on the chin like a man. The other day the President thanked him for the way he had stood up under fire.

There is no doubt that the President thinks he will be re-elected. He said that he is going to bring back Adolph Berle into the Administration shortly. Berle was in Washington, but Mayor La Guardia made him City Chamberlain and he has done a good job there. The President expects to make him a member of the United States delegation to the Argentine conference and then apparently plans to keep him on in some capacity.

The Senate committee investigating campaign expenditures has discovered that the du Ponts sent much more money into Maine than was at first reported. However, Senator Lonergan, who is chairman of that committee, voted with the two Republican members not to publish this fact. Of course, the President wants this to be made public and I do not blame him. Yesterday he sent Under Secretary West up to see Lonergan to try to persuade him to change his attitude, but apparently Lonergan is standing pat. I think the public is entitled to know facts of this sort as soon as the facts themselves have been ascertained, and I cannot understand why Lonergan is protecting the du Ponts to the disadvantage of his own party. After election it won't so much matter whether the total contribution of the du Ponts was of a greater or lesser amount.

When I lunched with the President on Wednesday, he asked me if I knew anything about Hiram Johnson. I told him that I did not and that I did not know anyone else who did. Then he said, "Surely, he cannot be too sick to make a statement." I didn't think he was and I told the President that he was the only one who could get through to him. Miss Le Hand came in in the meantime and turning to her he said, "I will try to talk to Hiram before I leave." I also told the President that Cissy Patterson had remarked to me some time ago that perhaps Hiram was lying low until after the election. I am beginning to suspect something of this sort and so is the President. I simply cannot understand Hiram. They say that he has been quite ill and yet I hear that he has been going to the Naval Hospital for treatments every day or two. He certainly cannot be too ill to make a statement and yet it isn't like him to hide himself away. Both he and the "Boss" (Mrs. Johnson) were devoted to the President and I never supposed for a minute that he would not do everything he could to help in this campaign.

The President and Al Smith were both on the air the night of October 1. I was surprised when the announcement came out that the President had contracted for half an hour's time on one circuit within the hour that Al Smith had contracted for on another circuit.

The President was in Hyde Park when this happened. I thought it looked like a pretty cheap trick for the President. The other day I learned the real facts from Dr. McIntire, who was with the President at the time.

The President's time was arranged for at Democratic National Headquarters and he did not know that there was a conflict in time with Al Smith until he saw it in the newspapers. However, this fact was known at Democratic Headquarters, where apparently they thought they were doing something smart. When the President found out the situation, he was, according to Dr. McIntire, "the maddest I have ever seen him." He did some pretty sharp talking to headquarters and ordered a rearrangement of the schedule. He had on his desk a letter to Al Smith telling him that he would rearrange his time so as not to interfere with Smith's, but Smith beat him to it by announcing a change in his time so as not to interfere with the President's speech.

Last Thursday night the Democratic National Committee had contracted for an hour on the radio, half of it to be used by Secretary Perkins in a speech from New York and the other half by Secretary Hull at Minneapolis, where he was to reply to the attack by Landon on the reciprocity treaties. I did not hear either speech, but Harry Slattery told me the next morning that Perkins had run over twenty minutes on Hull's time and then had had to be cut off. Mike Straus said she ran over but he did not know for how long. Perhaps it wasn't twenty minutes, but there seems to be no doubt that she did encroach seriously on Hull's time. Both men reported that her speech was extremely uninteresting and dull. On the other hand, Hull's speech was a very important one.

Saturday, October 17, 1936

Naturally, no one is thinking or talking anything except politics these days. The President has been campaigning in the Middle West and, from all reports, he has met with wonderful receptions. In Chicago at the stadium last Wednesday night there was the greatest political demonstration that that city has ever seen. All indications are that a decided swing has started in favor of the President that bids fair to give him all of the doubtful states. If this happens, he will win by a very large vote in the electoral college. He himself is perfectly confident of re-election and so are the immediate members of his staff as well as Jim Farley. My own view is that he will be re-elected. I cannot conceive of anything that will turn the tide between now and election day, although that is not impossible. His speeches are wonderful political efforts, and his charm over the radio is as potent as it ever was. Everything looks quite encouraging.

Wednesday, October 21, 1936

I made a speech Monday night in the Academy of Music in Philadelphia. Mike Straus went up with me, and we arrived shortly after eight o'clock. Returning right after my speech, by airplane from Camden, we got into Washington at twelve o'clock midnight. The meeting was a large one, although the third gallery had only a few people in it. It was enthusiastic, too. I had a good reception and my speech seemed to go over very well.

Tuesday I had a short time with the President. This was the first time I had seen him since he went on his western trip. He is looking fine and says that he is standing the campaign well. He remarked, however, that toward the end of a campaign he got all worked up so that he could not sleep for a week. This does not seem so bad to me, who am a very bad sleeper.

The President was plainly both pleased and encouraged by his trip. He said that there was something terrible about the crowds that lined the streets along which he passed. He went on to explain what he meant, which was exclamations from individuals in the crowd, such as "He saved my home," "He gave me a job," "God bless you, Mr. President," etc.

James P. Warburg, who originally was with Roosevelt but who then came out against him and wrote two bitter books attacking his Administration, found himself back in the Roosevelt camp the other day. Two days ago Dean Acheson, who was Under Secretary of the Treasury at the beginning of this Administration and who had been asked by the President to resign, announced that he would support him on account of Hull's international trade policies. The President said yesterday that some of the economic royalists were beginning to take out a little insurance on the probability of Landon's defeat. By this he meant that some of the contributors to the Republican campaign fund were now giving smaller amounts to the Democratic fund. This is customary in political campaigns and shows how deep are the convictions of this type of citizen.

Last night I went on the air from Washington on a national hookup with a speech entitled "Is Landon Sincere?" In this, I related for the first time his suggestion, contained in a letter to me in 1935, that PWA ought to have the power to finance state-owned telephone systems and his subsequent informal application for a loan and grant of $35 million from PWA to finance a state-owned natural gas pipeline system for Kansas.

Cissy Patterson called me up yesterday to tell me that unless Hearst changed some of his policies, she intended to resign as publisher of the *Washington Herald*. I greeted this with loud applause. She said that her decision was purely a business one. Apparently she cannot sit idly by and see circulation and advertising falling off because of the way Hearst plays politics. She reminded me that in attacking Roosevelt the *Herald* had not gone so far as the other Hearst papers, for which she was responsible. She also said that Hearst might sell the *Herald* to her and that she had talked the matter over with Joe Patterson, her brother. I gave her enthusiastic cheers from my end of the telephone.

Friday, October 30, 1936

I have been lax in keeping up these memoranda for the past week or more because I found myself in a terrific jam preparing the speeches that I had undertaken to make.

I got into Chicago about six o'clock Wednesday afternoon on the twenty-first and drove at once to the University Club, where I had dinner. Then, with a police escort, I went to the Patten Gymnasium at Northwestern University, Evanston. Senator Lewis was speaking when I arrived. I went on the air at nine-thirty on a hookup that gave me a radius of five hundred miles. As a matter of fact, I had a wider radius than that, because this station is a powerful one. Harry Slattery got me here in Washington.

This speech was devoted to an attack on the anti-Roosevelt press of Chicago, particularly the *Tribune* and the *Daily News,* with some wallops for the Hearst press. There was enough humor in the speech to soften it without weakening the hard blows that I struck. The speech went over big with my audience and from the reports that I have had it went well with the radio audience also.

When the President was in Chicago just a week previously, the great crowds along the line of march had demonstrated against the Chicago papers, especially the *Tribune*. The out-of-town correspondents were very much impressed with this demonstration. So violent have been the attacks on the Administration by these papers that there has been a decided reaction in the Chicago territory. This gave a setting for my speech that I was not slow to take advantage of.

There were about thirty-five hundred or four thousand people at Patten Gymnasium, which is doing very well for that overwhelmingly Republican territory.

I spent the night at home. Raymond and I had a good chance for the nicest talk that we have had in some time. He is interested in his law school work but is worrying about his course on contracts.

I flew back to Washington on Thursday, leaving Chicago about noon. The weather was cloudy and rainy most of the way until we were almost into Washington. I have never seen such wonderful cloud effects as I saw over the Allegheny Mountains from Pittsburgh on. They were simply glorious. The wind was from the northwest so that it was quite a smooth trip. I didn't get airsick this time, but neither did I enjoy the trip. I don't like air travel.

We had a Cabinet meeting on Friday, but the only members present were Hull, Woodring, Swanson, Perkins, and myself. Most of our talk centered on the campaign. Everyone seemed to be satisfied with the way things were going, especially the President. He hasn't lost any of his confidence. Miss Perkins, as usual, was able to keep up her end of the conversation.

I saw the President briefly Tuesday morning. He approved a lot of PWA projects. He continues to look very well indeed and seems to be standing the strain in fine shape.

I asked the President what Hiram Johnson was going to do. He told me that Hiram had been going to the Naval Hospital for treatments and he was anxious to have him make a statement. Finally, he wrote a letter himself, which he addressed: "Dear Boss and Hiram," in which he expressed interest in and concern for Johnson as well as Mrs. Johnson, and said that he hoped that Hiram would give out a statement. Then Mrs. Johnson called "Missy" Le Hand by telephone. She told "Missy" that the letter from the President had been received, but that she was terribly sorry, but Hiram was in such a highly nervous state that the doctors had forbidden him even to read letters, etc., etc. This, of course, means that Mrs. Johnson either did not permit the letter to go to Hiram or that Hiram is dodging. Hiram has rarely dodged, but this situation looks highly suspicious to me. I don't believe that the doctors ever gave any such orders. I am driven to the unwelcome conclusion that Hiram has never intended to do anything for the President in this campaign and that the reason given by Mrs. Johnson to Miss Le Hand over the telephone was nothing less than pure fiction.

The President apparently didn't believe the story either and he speculated some as to what was motivating Hiram. The only reason he could see was that Hiram knew that he was finishing his last term and he wanted to be absolutely independent during the next four years. I did not agree with this. I pointed out that even if Hiram had issued a statement in the President's behalf, he would not permit that to abridge his independence in any degree. I stated in support of this view that during the last four years Hiram has held to an independent course. The President could not gainsay this and we were both left with the feeling that Hiram just didn't want to issue any statement in support of the President. What his reason was I haven't the slightest notion.

From early in the campaign Senator Nye has been telling me and others that it was his purpose to announce openly his support of President Roosevelt. I have talked to him, I have wired to him, and I have telephoned to him. He has always been on the verge of doing this but he has never done it. I spoke to the President about Nye and I volunteered to wire him on my own authority. This I did today. In my telegram I said that in view of Landon's speech on international affairs it would be a fine time for him (Nye) to declare himself, and expressed the hope that he would do so. It will be interesting to see if Nye replies to this telegram.

The sentiment in New York last Wednesday seemed to be that there was no doubt of the President's carrying the state by a very large vote. For part of the day Kelly, the Democratic leader of Brooklyn, rode in the same automobile with Steve Early and me. When I asked him how he felt about the election, he reached into his pocket and brought out figures on a poll that he had made. According to this poll, Roosevelt will carry Brooklyn by five hundred thousand votes. I remarked that if those figures were correct Roosevelt would carry Greater New York by a million and a half votes. To this Kelly agreed. He told me that well over ninety per cent of the Italian vote was for the President and as heavy a proportion of the Jewish vote. He also said that the Catholic vote was overwhelmingly for Roosevelt.

While waiting for the President to come over from Staten Island, I talked with the Democratic candidate for Congress in that Brooklyn district. He has a very large district, mainly of Catholics, and he told me that Al Smith's attitude had not hurt the President at all. As he put it: "Al Smith used to be very strong over here but he wouldn't dare to come to a meeting now." He told me what Kelly confirmed afterward, that the sentiment in all that territory was overwhelmingly for the Democratic ticket.

Returning from the Statue of Liberty celebration, Pope, who is a very prominent Italian newspaper publisher, told me that ninety-eight per cent of the Italian vote would be for the President. He looks for an overwhelming Democratic victory. He said that the Republicans had offered him $50,000 if he would support Landon with his newspapers and that he had not only refused this but he would not accept paid advertising for Landon. I met Pope for the first time several months ago in my office when Congressman Sirovich brought him in to introduce him to me.

Steve Early and I drove together most of the day. He recalled the campaign trips that he had made with Roosevelt when the latter was a candidate for Vice President in 1920. He said that if it hadn't been for the President's affliction, he never would have been President of the United States. In those earlier years, as Steve put it, the President was just a playboy. When he was campaigning for Vice President, he couldn't be made to prepare his speeches in advance, preferring to play cards instead. During his long illness, according to Steve, the President began to read deeply and study public questions, with the result that he is now one of the best informed men in the United States along those lines. In this latter I heartily concur. From the very first I have remarked upon the President's grasp of public questions.

In Steve Early's opinion, the President, if re-elected, will be somewhat more conservative than he has been during this Administration. This I can hardly credit and I hope that it is not true. After all, if the President is re-elected it will be over the hateful and violent opposition of practically every conservative interest in the country.

There was a little talk about the Cabinet. Steve thinks that it is weak in some particulars and said that the President knows this. I gathered that he thinks that the President will try to strengthen his Cabinet for his next term. Steve himself does not think much of Miss Perkins and from what he said I gathered that Woodring does not stand high in the President's regard. I have long thought that in the Administration, especially in the early days, there has been a feeling of impatience at the White House so far as Woodring was concerned. Personally, I do not regard him as a strong appointment.

Wednesday night I spoke at Carnegie Hall in New York City. I went on the air at ten o'clock. Carnegie Hall was crowded to the last seat, with people standing even in the topmost gallery. There was an overflow meeting outside that was served by loud-speakers. I was told by one person that there were two thousand people outside and another one said that the policemen had estimated the crowd at ten thousand. As I did not see the crowd myself, I have no independent opinion, but I don't think that the crowd was nearly as large as I was told. Anyhow, it was a highly successful meeting from every point of view.

In my speech I went after Landon hot and heavy on the basis of his inconsistencies and insincerities. I developed further the theme that I had adopted in my first speech, namely, that, in the East, Landon is a conservative, while in the West he poses as a Progressive. It is interesting that this idea of mine has been followed by a good many of the Democratic speakers, including the President himself, who, on a number of occasions, without mentioning Landon's name, has referred to a certain old Roman god who had two faces and who was named Janus.

Saturday, November 7, 1936

The campaign continued in high gear until the very end. Landon made a speech in New York at Madison Square Garden Thursday night, October 29, in which he challenged the President bluntly to state his position on a number of national issues and tell what he would do as to these matters if he should be re-elected. Then Landon started back, via St. Louis, for Topeka, Kansas, making speeches all along the way, with one particularly big meeting in St. Louis.

The President meanwhile was not idle. He coursed back and forth in eastern Pennsylvania, including Philadelphia, drawing tremendous crowds wherever he went. Then he made his last big speech at Madison Square Garden on Saturday night. This was a fine climax to his speaking campaign. He completely ignored the questions that had been asked of him by Governor Landon from the same platform two evenings earlier. An immense throng turned out for this meeting. From New York he went to Hyde Park. Both Landon and the President, as well as others, were on the air for a few last gasps on Monday night.

I have felt perfectly confident of the result for the past two months or more. I went to bed Monday night believing that New York, Ohio, and Illinois would certainly be for the President. Despite the fact that the President himself was uncertain about Indiana, I believed that, lying as it does between Ohio and Illinois, it would go the same as these other two states. I also believed that Pennsylvania would be carried by the President. I had my doubts about all of New England, except Connecticut. There, during the last few days it appeared that the President would win. I did not know much about Michigan or Iowa, but I was confident of Wisconsin and Minnesota and all of the western states generally, except South Dakota. I thought that Nebraska was safe, and I had a sneaking hope that the President would carry Kansas. However, this was nothing more than a hope. I also felt reasonably confident of West Virginia.

But, even believing as I did that the President would carry many more states than he needed in order to win, I was not prepared for the surprising results that came over the radio Tuesday night. I had been suffering from a severe attack of lumbago since Sunday afternoon, so that I was content to stay at home and listen to my own radio. It was soon clear that the President had not only won but that he had gone over by a tremendous popular and electoral college vote.

It is all over now, but even in retrospect the result is astonishing. Landon carried only two states—Maine and Vermont, with eight electoral votes between them. Although there are still some precincts missing, the President's popular majority is well over ten million. There has been nothing like it in the history of American politics. The Democrats gained Governors and Senators and Congressmen where already they had too many Congressmen and Senators and, with respect to some states, too many Governors. The President pulled through to victory men whose defeat would have been better for the country. It was a complete rout of the Republican party and the big financial interests that had hoped through that party to regain control of the Federal Government.

The Republicans ran a perfectly atrocious campaign and Landon proved to be even a weaker candidate than I had ever supposed him capable of being. Landon, in my judgment, would have been a stronger candidate if he had sat on his front porch at Topeka throughout. As a barnstormer, he lost votes, and his loss became progressively greater as the campaign continued. Frank Knox lost votes, in my judgment. He talked too much and he talked too recklessly. I doubt if toward the end of the campaign the people listened much to him or gave heed to his explosive denunciations of everything that the New Deal had ever done. Hamilton, as a national chairman, seemed to be a washout.

Landon started off rather temperately, admitting that there were some good things that the New Deal had done, but he allowed himself to be swept along with the tide. Then, too, the people pretty generally got the impression that he had neither the character nor the ability that a President of the United States ought to have.

To my view, the outstanding thing about the campaign was the lack of influence of the newspapers. With over eighty per cent of the newspapers of the country fighting Roosevelt, it is remarkable that he should have swept everything as he did. Cook County was an outstanding example. There, only the tabloid *Times* supported the President, with the *Tribune,* the *News,* and the Hearst papers in bitter opposition. Nevertheless, the President carried Cook County by over six hundred thousand votes, and he carried downstate Illinois as well. Never have the newspapers, in my recollection, conducted a more mendacious and venomous campaign against a candidate for President, and never have they been of so little influence. Apparently the people saw through the whole tissue of deceit and lies and misrepresentation. They sensed that the great financial interests which were backing Landon and pouring money into his campaign fund had some sinister purpose. In my judgment, they voted for the President because they believed that he had some interest in and concern for the welfare of the common man. The very bitterness of the assault upon the President by the newspapers reacted in his favor.

Immediately following the election the newspapers began to speculate about the makeup of the next Cabinet. It seems to be the general opinion that quite a few changes will be made. The general view is that Hull, Morgenthau, and Wallace are sure of reappointment, and the guess seems to be that, whereas a few months ago my chances for reappointment did not appear to be so good, I probably will be reappointed. In this connection, reference is made to the hard campaign that I made for the President. Farley is going out of the Cabinet of his own free will.

What the President has in mind with respect to his Cabinet or with respect to me in particular, I haven't the least idea. Probably he won't say or do anything until well along in January. In the meantime, we can do the worrying, if we are disposed to worry. For my part, I do not propose to worry. Naturally I would like to stay in the Cabinet, because to go out now would mean that my services had not been of such an outstanding character as to merit reappointment, although in my own case the feeling would probably be that personalities entered into the decision not to reappoint me. I still am of the opinion that I do not stand in too well with Mrs. Roosevelt, and there are doubtless others who would like to see my head fall into the basket. However, if I am not reappointed I will manage to struggle along and I won't harbor any resentment. After all, the President has given me a wonderful chance and if he prefers to have someone else for Secretary of the Interior, he is entitled to his preference.

I went over to see Dr. McIntire this morning for a treatment. Of course, he sees a great deal of the President and is rather close to the White House situation. The question of the Cabinet came up because he made some remark which called for a statement from me that of course I hadn't any means of knowing whether I would continue in the Cabinet or not. He said that he hadn't heard the President make the slightest intimation, but his own guess was that he would keep Hull, Morgenthau, Wallace, and me, filling the other six places with new people. He seemed quite strongly of the opinion that Miss Perkins would go, and that seems to be the general opinion.

The President seemed very happy yesterday. He talked a lot about the election and its implications. He spoke of the fact that he has now an absolutely free hand without the danger of being charged with having broken campaign promises. As a matter of fact, the political situation, from his point of view, is quite fortunate. Reactionary Democrats, like Al Smith, Jim Reed,

John W. Davis, and Bainbridge Colby, have definitely gone off a deep end. They certainly are through as Democrats, and I do not see how they can hope to become leaders in the Republican party, notwithstanding the almost total lack of competent leadership in that party.

The President's manner was as friendly as it could be. He is leaving a week from Tuesday for a brief fishing trip, but he has also made up his mind to go in the USS *Indianapolis* to Buenos Aires for the first day of the Pan American Conference that is to be held there. I think that this will be a fine thing for him to do. If all goes well, it will go far to cement our relationship with Central and South American countries that has made such fine progress under this Administration.

Jim Farley was at the Cabinet meeting. He told the President that he hoped he would never have anything more to do with Hearst, remarking that some of the President's own friends would be trying to effect a reconciliation. At this point the President said that Hearst had already made approaches and then he told this story:

Last Tuesday night at Hyde Park some of his sons were helping answer telephone calls. John Boettiger, his son-in-law, was also lending a hand. Late at night a call came through for Boettiger from the switchboard in the White House Executive Offices at Poughkeepsie. Boettiger took the call and this is what he listened to:

"Hello, John, this is Marion Davies. I just wanted to tell you that I love you. We know that a steam roller has flattened us out, but there are no hard feelings at this end. I just wanted you to know that." Then, while John was still holding the wire at the request of Marion Davies, Hearst himself took the telephone at the other end and he said something like this: "Hello, is that you, Boettiger? Well, I just wanted to repeat what Marion said, that we have been run over by a steam roller, but that there are no hard feelings at this end."

In the Hearst papers a couple of days ago appeared a signed editorial by Hearst in which he slobbered all over the President. I join in the fervent hope expressed by Farley at the Cabinet meeting that the President, in no circumstances, will have anything more to do with Hearst and his outfit. The President said that he had been considering excluding from his trip the press representatives of the

Hearst wire services. If I were he, I would do this, but I do not believe that he will.

At Cabinet meeting there was a good deal of discussion about the Supreme Court. I think that the President is getting ready to move in on that issue and I hope that he will do so. Solicitor General Reed, who attended in the absence of the Attorney General, reported that Mr. Justice Stone is ill. The President made the remark that he expected Mr. Justice McReynolds still to be on the bench when he was a hundred and five years old. Reed replied laughingly that McReynolds seemed to be in the best possible health. The President instructed Reed to go ahead as rapidly as possible with the Government cases that are pending, involving the constitutionality of New Deal legislation. He expects this legislation to be declared unconstitutional and evidently looks to that as a background for an appeal to the people over the head of the Court. I am keen myself that this question should be raised and I hope to be able to take part in that fight, if and when it comes.

INDEX

ACHESON, DEAN GOODERHAM (*1893-*), *Under-Secretary of the Treasury from May to November, 1933. Later Assistant Secretary of State from August, 1945, to July, 1947, and Secretary of State from 1949 to 1952*—9, 106, 174, 695

ADAMOWSKI, BENJAMIN, 36

ADDAMS, JANE (*1860-1935*), *settlement worker; founder of Hull House in Chicago*—210, 212, 356, 367

Addams, Jane, housing project, 610

Addams, Jane, national park, 385

ADAMS, ALVA B., 290, 340, 588

agrarian revolt, Roosevelt's remedy for, 110

Agriculture, Department of, transfer of bureaus, 21, 23, 52, 250, 350, 364-365, 534-535; on Taylor Grazing Bill, 169-170; and subsistence homesteads, 288; trouble in, 292; Puerto Rico experimental stations, 504; lobbies against Interior Department, 417-419, 601, 604-605: *see also* Henry Wallace, National Forest Service

AAA, 276, 292, 302-303, 515, 536, 552, 565-566, 683: *see also* Chester Davis, Rexford Tugwell

air mail contracts, cancellation of, 146-147

airplanes, experiments in, supported by Public Works, 142-143

airplane patents, bought by Wall Street money, 353

Alabama, University of, 541

Alabama Power Company, 537

Alaska, banking situation in, 3; delegation from, 5; Advisory Committee for, 151

ALBRIGHT, HORACE MARDEN (*1890-*), *director of National Park Service from January, 1929, to August, 1933; also a member of National Capital Park and Planning Commission; now president, U.S. Potash Co.*—18, 27, 574

ALFARO, RICARDO J., 105

All-American Canal, 113-114

Allegheny County, Pa., Authority project, 562

ALLEN, HENRY, 678

ALLEN, ROBERT S., 391, 675

Allotment Advisory Committee, 351, 354, 357, 365, 378, 409-412, 420, 424, 427

Altoona, Pennsylvania, 376-377, 611-613

Altoona Mirror, 376

American Bankers Association, 471

American Federation of Labor, 466

American Liberty League, 516, 524-525, 664

American Planning and Civic Association, 522

AMES, CHARLES B., 158

ANDERSON, PAUL, 77

ANDREWS, ADOLPHUS, 545

Amtorg, 113

Apex Building, Washington, D.C., 283

Appalachian Coals Case, 21

Apples, PWA purchase of surplus, 109

Appropriations Committee, Senate, 168, 285-286, 314-315, 515, 588, 599-600, 608, 611

Archbishop of York, 483-484

ARIAS, ARNULFO (*1897-*), *Harvard-trained physician and diplomat; president of Panama 1940-1941; later exiled from Panama for alleged Fascist sympathies*—105, 455

ARIAS, MADAME ARNULFO, 456

Army, building projects for, 71, 111, 216-217: *see also* Douglas MacArthur

Army planes, mail carried by, 147

artists, supported by CWA, 162

Associated Press, 346, 349-350, 637

ASTOR, VINCENT, 86, 158, 692

Atlanta, Georgia, sewer project, 409, 422, 427, 582; slum clearance project, 200

ATTERBURY, WILLIAM W., 116

Attorney General: *see* Homer Cummings

aviation, Army and Navy allocations, 111

AYERS, ROY E., 419

B

BACHMANN, NATHAN L., 225, 419

Back to Work (Ickes), 317, 344, 483, 668

BAER, 397

Bahia Honda, 453-454

BAILEY, JOSIAH W., 302, 419

BAKER, captain of the *Houston*, 451, 460

BALDWIN, ROGER (*1884-*), *director of American Civil Liberties Union from 1917 to 1950, and since then its national chairman*—350
Baldwin Locomotive Works, 116
BALLINGER, RICHARD A. (*1858-1922*), *Secretary of the Interior under President Taft 1909-1911. Attacked as an enemy of conservation by Gifford Pinchot and others, he was exonerated by a Congressional investigating committee but resigned in March, 1911*—21
"baloney dollars," 128
Baltimore and Ohio Railroad, 283
Baltimore Sun, 129, 242, 519, 527, 553, 559, 670, 687
Bangor and Aroostock Railroad, 190
bankers, attitude of, toward Government program, 108-109
bankers, international, Landon and, 663, 665
bank holiday, Executive Order for, 3
bank situation, 1933, 3, 4, 5, 41
BANKHEAD, JOHN H. (*1872-1946*), *Senator (Dem.) from Alabama 1931-1946*—418
BANKHEAD, WILLIAM B., 615
banks, 183
BARBOUR, W. WARREN, 368
BARKLEY, ALBEN W. (*1877-*), *Senator (Dem.) from Kentucky 1927-1948; majority leader 1937-1948; Vice President 1948-1952*—225, 526, 621, 623
BARNES, JULIUS H., 31
BARUCH, BERNARD MANNES (*1870-*), *financier and "adviser to Presidents"; member of Supreme Economic Council after First World War and adviser to War Mobilization Director after 1943*—18, 148, 173
BATTLE, GEORGE GORDON (*1868-1949*), *lawyer and former assistant district attorney in New York*—60-61, 135
BATTLE, TURNER, 432
BEACH, BESS, 499
BEATY, AMOS L., 97
BECK, JAMES M., 116
BECK, THOMAS H., 108
beet sugar industry, 147
BEITER, ALFRED F. (*1893-*), *Representative (Dem.) from New York 1933-1939 and 1941-1943; assistant to Secretary Ickes from 1939 to 1940*—567-568, 570-571, 577-578

Belgian Embassy, dinner at, 363
BELL, DANIEL W. (*1891-*), *Acting Director of the Budget from 1934 to 1939; Under-Secretary of Treasury from 1940 to 1946; now in commercial banking*—200, 306, 327, 348, 351, 436, 486
BENEDUM, MICHAEL LATE (*1869-*), *oil man and Pennsylvania Democratic leader; representative on NRA Planning and Coordinating Committee under oil code in 1933; member of Business Advisory and Planning Council Department of Commerce in 1933*—26, 84, 97-98
BENNETT, H. H., 325
BENNETT, Prime Minister of Canada, 27
Berea College, 166-167
BERLE, ADOLF A., JR. (*1895-*), *lawyer and professor at Columbia Law School since 1927; one of the original FDR "brain trust"; Assistant Secretary of State 1938-1944; U.S. Ambassador to Brazil 1945-1946*—9, 693
BERNOU, WALTER N., 58, 66
BETTERS, PAUL V., 96-97
BEVERIDGE, SIR WILLIAM, 114
Bible belt, Protestant vote in, 617
BIDDLE, MRS. FRANCIS, 249
Big Bend National Park, 385
BINGHAM, ROBERT WORTH (*1871-1937*), *newspaper publisher and diplomat; publisher of* Louisville Courier-Journal *and* Louisville Times; *U.S. Ambassador to Great Britain 1933-1937*—544, 567
Biological Survey, Bureau of, 4, 250, 281
Birmingham, Alabama, 368-370
Bituminous Coal Commission, 25
Bituminous Coal Division, of Interior Department, 25
BLACK, HUGO L. (*1886-*), *Senator (Dem.) from Alabama 1927-1937; Associate Justice of the Supreme Court since 1937*—419, 555
Blackfeet Indians, 185-187
BLANTON, THOMAS L., 263
BLOOD, HENRY H., 114
"blue eagle": *see* National Industrial Recovery Act
Bluebeard Castle Hotel, St. Thomas, Virgin Islands, 507
Boca Raton Club, 323-324, 509-511
BOETTIGER, JOHN (*1900-1950*), *news-*

paperman; Washington correspondent Chicago Tribune *1933-1934; later publisher* Seattle Post-Intelligencer; *married Anna Roosevelt Dall on Jan. 18, 1935*—204, 275, 704

BOGAN, Supt. of Schools, Chicago, 367

Bohemian Club, 178-179, 214

Bohemian Grove, 178

BONE, HOMER T. *(1883-   ), Senator (Dem.) from Washington 1933-1945; now a judge of U.S. Circuit Court of Appeals*—115, 300, 379, 390, 415

Bonneville Dam, 182-183

bonus legislation, 103-104, 158, 356, 516, 525

bonds, German, in U.S., 33; Government, 159, 534; municipal, 156; railroad, 273-274

boondoggling, 435, 673

BORAH, WILLIAM E. *(1865-1940), Senator (Rep.) from Idaho 1903 until his death; known as a Progressive and as an isolationist*—33, 276, 285, 418, 463-464, 548, 558, 685

Boston and Maine Railroad, 190

Boulder Dam, 32, 37-38, 444-445

BOWERS, CLAUDE E., 518

BRANDEIS, LOUIS DEMBITZ *(1856-1941), Associate Justice of the Supreme Court from 1916 until his resignation in 1939. A close friend of Holmes, he joined often with him in dissents from the court and many of these dissents upheld the New Deal point of view*—5, 39, 246-247, 342, 372, 467, 614

BRANN, LOUIS J., 190, 675

BRENNAN, GEORGE, 521

BRISBANE, ARTHUR, 354

British Embassy, dinner at, 162

BRITTAIN, MARION L., 200

BROCKWAY, FENNER, 109

Brook, New York Club, 278

Brookings Institution, 610

BROOKS, C. WAYLAND *(1897-   ), Senator (Rep.) from Illinois since 1939; previously active in law and politics in Chicago*—521, 557-558, 669

BROUN, HEYWOOD, 77

BROWN, LYTLE, 455

BROWN, R. B., 414-415

BROWN, WILSON, 444, 448-450, 460-461, 528

BROWNLOW, LOUIS *(1879-   ), journalist*

and public administrator; director Public Administration Clearing House, Chicago, 1931-1945, and chairman Public Administration Committee of the Social Science Research Council 1933-1939; chairman of President's Committee on Administrative Management 1936-1937—75, 475, 584

BRUCKER, WILBUR M., 681

Bruton Parish Church, Williamsburg, 630

BRYANT, REQUA, 432

BUCHANAN, JAMES P. *(1867-1937), Representative (Dem.) from Texas from 1913 until his death*—166, 276, 327, 333, 335-337, 423, 488, 570-572, 578, 613

Budget, Director of: see Lewis Douglas

budget, plans to cut, 11, 14, 16, 41, 487-488; *see also* Lewis Douglas

BULKLEY, ROBERT J., 144

BULLITT, WILLIAM CHRISTIAN *(1891-   ), special assistant to Secretary of State 1933; delegate to World Economic Conference in London, 1933; Ambassador to U.S.S.R. 1933-1936 and to France 1936-1941*—113-114, 428, 626-627, 657-659, 661, 666, 674

BULOW, W. J., 419

BUNDESON, HERMAN N. *(1882-   ), Chicago physician and president of the Chicago Board of Health since 1931; Democratic candidate for Governor of Illinois in 1936*—521, 556-557

Bureaus: see Biological Survey, Erosion Control, Fisheries, Indian Affairs, Mines, Public Roads, Reclamation

BURKE, EDWARD R., 412, 544

BURLEW, EBERT KEISER *(1885-1945), administrative assistant in Department of Interior 1923-1938; Assistant Secretary of Interior 1938-1943*—34, 74-75, 193, 216, 237-238, 252-255, 260-262, 270-273, 277, 279, 286, 289, 304, 325, 339-341, 364, 380, 424, 527, 551, 590-591, 608, 611, 648

BUTLER, PIERCE, 562

butter, WPA purchase of surplus, 109

BYRD, HARRY F., 539, 568

BYRNES, JAMES F. *(1879-   ), Representative (Dem.) from South Carolina 1911-1925; Senator 1931-1941; Associate Justice of the Supreme Court 1941-1942; director of economic stabiliza-*

BYRNES, JAMES F. (*continued*)
tion and later of war mobilization
1942-1945; Secretary of State *1945-1947;* now Governor of South Carolina
—57, 281, 286, 302, 313-314, 333, 340,
379-380, 400, 423, 483, 489, 600
BYRNS, JOSEPH W. (*1869-1936*), Representative (*Dem.*) from Tennessee *1909*
until his death; majority leader of
73rd Congress; speaker of *74th* Congress—34, 263, 333, 335, 578, 596, 601,
614

C

Cabinet, first meeting, 3, 5; in campaigns, 202; role of, 308, 315, 402; dinner for Roosevelt, 541; in Roosevelt's second term, 630-631, 699-700, 702-703
Cabinet, inner, 201
Call It a Day, 607
Camden, N. J., power plant, 675-676
Camp Curry, Yosemite, 177
campaign, influence of newspapers in, 702
campaign issues, WPA, 477, 595; constitutional amendment, 467, 602; Hopkins, 603; Hearst, 633, 671; taxation, 652; peace, 656, 682: *see also* Democratic campaign, Republican campaign
Campaign Fund Investigating Committee, two plans for, 555
Campaign speeches, by Farley, 606; no mention of Landon, 607, 639, 642-643; by Ickes, 202, 613, 615-616, 618-619, 627, 632-633, 638,640, 642-643, 647, 649, 653-654, 665-666, 668-670, 682, 692, 695-696, 700; by Cabinet, 632; by McNutt, 640, 644; by Norris, 683; by Knox, 653, 688; by Al Smith, 688, 693-694; by Landon, 648-649, 665, 672, 679-680, 683, 700; by Perkins, 694; by Hull, 694; by William Hard, 670; by Roosevelt, 625-627, 661-663, 672, 679, 685, 686, 688, 689-690, 693-695, 700
CAMPBELL, THOMAS D., 190-191, 552-553
Campobello Island, 190
Canada, Ogdenburg Bridge and, 385; reciprocity treaty with, 465-466, 471-472; agreement on Passamaquoddy project, 543
Canal Zone, coast defenses in, 71
CANFIELD, DAVID H., 180
CAPPER, ARTHUR (*1865-1952*), Senator

(*Rep.*) from Kansas *1919-1949*—37, 40, 44, 115, 419
Capper bill, 26
Captain Blood, 499
CARDOZO, BENJAMIN NATHAN (*1870-1938*), Associate Justice of the Supreme Court from *1932* until his death—614
CAREY, ROBERT D., 419
CARPENTER, FARRINGTON R. (*1886-   *), director of the Grazing Division of the Department of Interior *1934-1938*—229-230
CARROLL, RAYMOND G., 563
CARTER, AMON, 179, 444, 632
Carter Coal Company case, 25
Casper-Alcova Dam, 72, 118
Cement manufacturers, identical bids of, 32
Century of Progress, Exposition, 96
CERMAK, ANTON JOSEPH (*1873-1933*), elected Mayor of Chicago in *1931;* died on March 6, *1933*, from bullet fired at President-elect Roosevelt on Feb. *15* in Miami by Giuseppe Zangara—8
Cerros Island, 448
Chamber of Commerce: *see* U.S. Chamber of Commerce
CHAMBERS, C. R., 286
CHANCELLOR, CHRISTOPHER, of Reuter's, 464
chaplains, in U.S. services, 451
CHAPMAN, OSCAR LITTLETON (*1896-   *), Assistant Secretary of Interior, May, *1933;* Under-Secretary, March, *1946;* Secretary of Interior, *1949-1952*—206, 254-255, 273, 292, 298, 309, 319, 339, 362, 553, 664
CHARDON, DR. CARLOS E., 503, 505
Charleston, S.C., 459-460
CHAVEZ, DENNIS, 359
CHENERY, WILLIAM, 277
Chesapeake and Ohio Canal, 283
Chicago, University of, 32, 113, 349, 368, 376: *see also* Robert Maynard Hutchins
Chicago airport, 167-168, 439
Chicago American, 153, 158, 168
Chicago Bar Association, 155
Chicago Daily News, 149, 212, 246, 558, 696, 702
Chicago Daily Times, 150-151
Chicago Herald-Examiner, 153, 155, 211-212, 246, 355, 368, 660

Chicago mayoralty situation, 272, 275: *see also* Kelly, Kelly-Nash machine

Chicago teachers, pay situation of, 22, 26

Chicago Tribune, 44, 167, 204, 211-212, 275, 368, 378, 520-521, 557-558, 616, 668, 696, 702: *see also* Robert McCormick

Chicago Urban League, 541

Children's Bureau, 265

Citizens' Civilian Conservation Corps, organization of, 78: *see also* CCC camps

civil conservation corps, bill for, 7

Civil Liberties Union, 350, 352

Civil Service Commission, 113, 136

Civil Works Administration, 29, 119-120, 162, 228, 256-257, 277, 293: *see also* Harry Hopkins

Civilian Conservation Corps, appropriation for, 36, 41, 52; camps, 21, 78-79, 83, 185, 306, 508, 547, 571

Civilian Conservation Corps Act, 48

CLAPPER, RAYMOND (*1892-1944*), *newspaperman; special writer for* Washington Post *1934-1935; political commentator for Scripps-Howard newspapers from 1936 until his death*—470

CLARK, BENNETT CHAMP (*1890-   ), *Senator (Dem.) from Missouri 1933-1939; son of Champ Clark who was speaker of the House from 1911 to 1919*—379-380, 390, 423, 598

CLARK, SHELDON, 82

CLAUSON, FRED H., 31

Cleveland Plain Dealer, 280

coal bill, draft of, 24, 30, 33

coal code, NRA, 25, 91-92

Coal Creek, Tennessee, 225

coal industry, in 1933, 21, 24-25; conferences on, 21, 24, 30-31, 33; wages in, 30, 35

Coal Operators of Illinois, coal bill of, 33

Coal Operators of Indiana, coal bill of, 33

COCHRAN, BURKE, 650

COCHRAN, JOHN J., 350, 539

Cocos Island, 451

codes: *see* NRA codes

COHEN, BENJAMIN V. (*1894-   ), *associate general counsel PWA, 1933-1934; general counsel National Power Policy Committee, 1934-1941; assisted in drafting securities control legislation of 1933 and 1934, public utility holding company act of 1935, and fair labor standards act of 1938; since 1941 member of many American delegations to U.N. and other foreign conferences*—333-334, 341, 344, 415, 512, 530-531, 538-539, 563, 592, 682

COLBY, BAINBRIDGE, 704

COLE, COLONEL, 503-504

Cole oil bill, 413-418

COLLIER, JOHN (*1884-   ), *Commissioner of Indian Affairs 1933-1945; director of National Indian Institute 1945-1950*—20, 40, 61, 321, 324, 628

Collier's Weekly, 108, 277

Colonial National Historical Park, 629-630

Colorado River project, 247

Columbia Institution for the Deaf, 4

Columbia River, 183

Columbia River project: *see* Coulee Dam

Columbia University, tropical disease research in San Juan by, 504

commentators, political, Roosevelt on, 560

Commerce, Department of: *see* Daniel Roper

Commerce Department Building, 24, 56

Communist, Hearst calls Roosevelt a, 684; Hearst calls Ickes a, 492

Communist International Convention, reports of, 428

Communist party, alleged support of Roosevelt, 428, 683

communistic activities, investigation of, in Illinois, 349: *see also* University of Chicago

Comptroller General, power of, 587: *see also* John McCarl

congressional committee, executive sessions of, Ickes on, 515

CONNALLY, TOM (*1874-   ), *Representative (Dem.) from Texas 1917-1929; Senator 1929 to the present*—47, 49-50, 142, 302

Connally oil bill, 13, 50, 418

conservation, of natural resources, 22, 37, 170, 214, 240, 250, 280, 300, 310-311, 325, 418, 683-684

Conservation Department, proposed by Ickes, 328, 330, 344, 347, 350, 364, 379, 384, 386, 403, 414, 417-419, 534-535, 538-539, 542, 568, 584, 596, 598, 601, 604-605, 609 constitutional amendment, suggested by Roosevelt, 467-468, 495-496, 529-530, 602

Continental-Illinois National Bank, 179

COOK, NANCY, 154, 435

COOKE, MORRIS L. (*1872-   *), engineer active in Federal power projects of PWA and National Resources Board; administrator REA 1935-1937—174, 429

COOLEY, DEAN, 477

COOLIDGE, THOMAS JEFFERSON (*1894-   *), Under-Secretary of the Treasury, 1934-1936; now in private banking and business—200, 203, 206, 518

COOPER, DEXTER, 189, 513-514, 542

COPELAND, ROYAL S. (*1868-1938*), Senator (*Dem.*) from New York 1923 to his death—334

CORCORAN, THOMAS G. (*1900-   *), lawyer; assistant to Secretary of Treasury 1933; counsel to RFC 1932 and 1934-1941; associated with Benjamin V. Cohen in drafting many New Deal legislative acts; now in private law practice—333, 341, 344, 378, 415, 431, 433, 512, 527, 530-531, 537, 563, 587-588, 590-593, 598, 634, 681-682, 683

Corcoran Gallery, Washington, D.C., 162

CORRIGAN, FATHER, 672

COSDEN, JOSHUA S., 650

Costa Rica, 451-452

COSTIGAN, EDWARD P. (*1874-1939*), Senator (*Rep.*) from Colorado 1931-1937; one of the founders of the Progressive Party in 1912—14, 313, 315, 363, 415, 553

COUGHLIN, FATHER CHARLES E., 285, 319, 352-353, 363, 472, 536, 538-539, 645, 687

Coulee Dam, 71-72, 183-184

COUNTY, ALBERT J., 282

Court of International Justice: see World Court

COURTNEY, TOM J. (*1894-   *), State's Attorney of Cook County, Illinois 1932-1945; judge of Circuit Court since 1945—124, 153, 155, 463, 520-522, 564, 638

COUZENS, JAMES (*1872-1936*), Senator (*Rep.*) from Michigan 1922 until his death; one of the founders of the Ford Motor Co.—77, 515, 681

COX, JAMES M. (*1870-   *), newspaper publisher and politician; Governor of Ohio 1913-1915 and 1917-1921; Democratic nominee for President in 1920; member U.S. delegation to World Economic Conference in London 1933 —77

CRAM, FRANKLIN W., 190

CRAMER, LAWRENCE W. (*1897-   *), Lieutenant-Governor Virgin Islands 1933-1935; Governor 1935-1941; Secretary-General Caribbean Commission 1946—405-406, 423, 506-508

Crater Lake National Park, 179

CRAWFORD, WADE, 180

Crocker bank, California, 687

Crop-insurance plan, 684

Cuba, U.S. intervention in, 87, 93; recognition of, 92-93

CUBBERLEY, Ickes' secretary, 447, 477, 483, 499, 502, 650

CUDAHY, JOHN (*1887-1943*), diplomat; Ambassador to Poland 1933-1937; Minister to Eire 1937-1939; Ambassador to Belgium 1939-1940—528

CUMMINGS, FRED, 617

CUMMINGS, HOMER S. (*1870-   *), Attorney General of U.S. 1933-1939; since then in private law practice—30, 45, 53, 58, 89, 91, 125, 136, 157, 243, 254, 273-274, 279, 306-307, 400, 405, 416, 489, 495, 513, 515, 517, 531, 535-536, 631-632, 656, 677-678

CUMMINGS, MRS. HOMER, 528

CUMMINGS, WALTER J. (*1879-   *), Chicago banker; executive assistant to Secretary of Treasury 1933-1934; treasurer Democratic National Committee 1934-1936—22

currency stabilization: see International Economic Conference, gold standard

CURLEY, JAMES MICHAEL (*1874-   *), Mayor of Boston 1914-1919, 1922-1926, 1930-1934, and 1946-1950; Governor of Massachusetts 1935-1937; Representative (*Dem.*) from Massachusetts 1943-1946—96, 681

CUTTING, BRONSON (*1888-1935*), Senator (*Rep.*) from New Mexico 1927 until his death; leader of Progressive Party of 1912—17, 20, 27, 217, 358-359

D

DAHLMAN, ANN, 159, 607, 623, 625

DAHLMAN, JANE: see Ickes, Jane D.

DALL, MRS. CURTIS, 176, 193, 202, 275
DANIELS, JOSEPHUS, 451, 623
DANIELS, ROBERT, 629
Danish Bank, in Virgin Islands, 273
Danish Embassy, dinner at, 273
DARLING, JAY ("Ding") (*1876-*), *cartoonist for New York Herald Tribune, Des Moines Register and other newspapers since 1917; chief biologist, Department of Agriculture, 1934-1935; a leading U.S. conservationist—*311, 376, 418
DA SILVA, H. GABRIEL, 125
DAVIES, MARION, 519, 704
DAVIS, ABEL, 112
DAVIS, CHESTER (*1887-*), *AAA Administrator 1933-1936; member Industrial Emergency Policy Committee of National Emergency Council 1934-1936; member Board of Governors, Federal Reserve System 1936-1941; now president Federal Reserve Bank of St. Louis—*198, 292, 303
DAVIS, JOHN W., 350, 704
DAVIS, MORRIS, 365
DAVIS, NORMAN (*1878-1944*), *diplomat; chairman U.S. delegation to Disarmament Conference at Geneva 1933; head of U.S. delegation to Naval Conference at London 1935; later chairman American Red Cross—*46
DAWES, CHARLES, 273
DAWES, HENRY M., 84
DAWES, RUFUS, 96
DEEDS, J. F., 230
Deficiency Appropriation Bill, 168; amendment of, 423; appropriations for PWA, 620: *see also* work-relief appropriation, Work Relief Bill
DE LABOULAYE, AMBASSADOR, 27
DELANO, FREDERIC A. (*1863-*), *chairman National Resources Planning Board 1934-1943; uncle of Franklin D. Roosevelt—*162, 171-172, 281, 341, 354, 366, 439, 491, 534-535
Democratic campaign; Bullitt on, 658; expenditures, 693; failure to plan, 643-646, 655-656; fund for, 25, 467, 680, 692, 695; Ickes' part in, 627; platform, 620, 624; Roosevelt's plan for, 562: *see also* campaign issues, campaign speeches
Democratic National Committee, 204,

414-415, 513, 521, 621, 654, 655-656
Democratic National Convention, arrangements for, 518; Ickes a delegate-at-large at, 564, 572; first session of, 621-622; Farley's introduction at, 621; Robinson at, 623; Committee on Rules reports, 623-624; Committee on Resolutions reports, 623-624; nomination of Roosevelt, 624; acceptance speech, 625-626
Democratic National Headquarters, 621, 635-636, 682, 694
Democratic State Convention, in Illinois, 564, 572-573; in Michigan, 603; in Missouri, 569; in New York, 686
DEMPSEY, JOHN J. (*1875-*), *Representative (Dem.) from New Mexico 1935-1941 and 1950-*); *Under-Secretary of Interior 1941-1943; Governor of New Mexico 1943-1947—*431, 538, 570, 604-606
DENVIR, JAMES, 153
department, organization of new, proposed by Ickes, 265
"Department of Things in General," 4
departmental reorganization; Roosevelt's plan for, 47
Depression, teachers' pay in, 23, 26; school conditions in, pressures of, 28; improvement of technology during, 651
Deputy Administrators, of NRA, 100: *see also* National Industrial Recovery Act
DERN, GEORGE H. (*1872-1936*), *Governor of Utah 1925-1932; Secretary of War 1933 until his death—*3-5, 7, 27-28, 34, 36, 54, 58, 67, 111, 114, 147, 182, 399, 400, 402, 432, 513-514, 517, 527, 547, 590, 620, 631-632, 661-662, 669-671
DEROUEN, RENE, 419
DETERDING, SIR HENRI W., 192
Diamond Lake, 180
DICKINSON, JOHN (*1894-*), *lawyer; Assistant Secretary of Commerce 1933-1935; Assistant U.S. Attorney General 1935-1937; now vice president and general counsel Pennsylvania Railroad—*34, 71, 168, 548-549, 560-561, 600, 603, 678
DIENHART, JOHN W., 211
DIES, MARTIN, 570
DIETERICH, WILLIAM H., 400, 432

dinners, given by Ickes, 193, 527, 415, 419, 527, 633-634
dinners, White House, 25, 27, 123, 163, 248, 301, 481-482, 541
Director of Budget, 11, 16: see also Lewis Douglas
DISNEY, WESLEY E., 419, 491
District of Columbia, boundaries of, 283
DOBBINS, D. C., 570-571
DODD, WILLIAM E., 494
DODDS, HAROLD W., 610
DOHENY, EDWARD L., 22
DOHERTY, HENRY L. (*1870-1939*), businessman active in oil and in public utilities—31
dollar, devaluation of, 23; stabilization of, 76, 99: see also International Economic Conference
DONOVAN, Lieutenant Governor, Illinois, 91
DOUGLAS, KINGMAN, 121
DOUGHTON, ROBERT L. (*1863-   *), Representative (Dem.) from North Carolina *1911-*   —42
DOUGLAS, LEWIS W. (*1894-   *), Representative (Dem.) from Arizona *1927-1933;* Director of the Budget *1933-1934;* deputy War Shipping Administrator, *1942-1944;* Ambassador to Great Britain *1947-1952*—9, 11, 14, 28, 60-61, 67, 106, 109, 112, 115, 134-136, 143, 166, 173-174, 194, 345, 375, 461, 659
DOUGLAS, PAUL (*1892-   *), professor at University of Chicago since *1925;* member Consumers' Advisory Board NRA *1933-1935;* Senator (Dem.) from Illinois *1948-*   —32
Dower House, 44, 60, 440, 657, 662, 674
DRESSER, 103
DUFFY, RYAN, 400, 419
DUNN, BEVERLY C., 322
Du Pont, General Motors and, 524; campaign contributions, 693
Dutch Treat Club, 277
DYKSTRA, CLARENCE A., 224, 362, 366

E

EARLE, GEORGE HOWARD (*1890-   *), Governor of Pennsylvania *1935-1939;* Minister to Bulgaria *1940-1941*—208, 339, 659, 664, 675
EARLY, STEPHEN T. (*1889-1951*), news-paperman from *1903* until *1933;* assistant secretary to President Roosevelt until *1937* and secretary *1937-1945;* Under-Secretary of Defense *1949-1950* —12, 128, 141, 160, 231-235, 238, 261, 303-304, 333, 335, 337-338, 342, 346, 381-382, 404-405, 411, 426, 444-445, 512-513, 516-519, 525, 532, 633, 640, 642-644, 647, 683-685, 698-699
Eastport, Maine, 190-191, 542
ECCLES, MARRINER, 445, 471
ECKENER, HUGO, 112
Economic Conference: see International Economic Conference
EDENS, WILLIAM C., 509
Education, Office of, 265
ELBERT, ROBERT E., 379
election results, 701
electrification, rural, 226
electrification project: see Pennsylvania Railroad
ELIOT, CHARLES WILLIAM II (*1899-   *), city planner; executive officer National Planning Board PWA *1933-1934;* National Resources Board *1934-1935;* National Resources Committee *1935-1939;* director National Resources Planning Board *1939-1943*—171-172, 354
Elk Hills oil case, 279
ELLIOTT, JOHN B. (*1878-   *), business executive; active in California political campaigns for Wilson, Roosevelt and Garner, and Sheridan Downey—10, 11
ELY, JOSEPH BUELL (*1881-   *), Democratic Governor of Massachusetts *1931-1935;* now in private law practice—73, 80, 123
Emergency Appropriation Bill, 173
Emergency Council, 348
Emergency Relief Appropriation Act of *1935*, 424
EPSTEIN, MAX, 112
ERNST, MORRIS L. (*1888-   *), lawyer; member New York State Banking Board *1933-1945;* friend of President Roosevelt and his representative on foreign missions, including one to Virgin Islands in *1945*—268
Erosion Control Bureau: see Soil Erosion Control
ESSARY, J. FRED (*1881-1942*), newspaper-man, head of Washington bureau of Baltimore Sun *1912-1942*—17, 60, 129

ESSARY, MRS. J. FRED, 43, 60, 528
ESSINGTON, THURLOW, 33
Ethiopia, war in: see Italian-Ethiopian situation
EVANS, SILLIMAN, 295
EWING, CHARLES H., 116
Executive Department, Roosevelt's reorganization plan for, 596

F

FADDIS, CHARLES, 419
FAHY, CHARLES (*1892-   ), first assistant solicitor, Department of Interior in May, 1933; member and later chairman of Petroleum Administrative Board 1933-1935; general counsel National Labor Relations Board 1935-1940; Solicitor General of U.S. 1941-1949; now judge on U.S. Court of Appeals—97, 158, 169*
FAIRCHILD, DAVID G., 325
FAIRMAN, 321, 323
FALL, ALBERT B. (*1861-1944), Senator (Rep.) from New Mexico 1912-1921; Secretary of Interior under President Warren G. Harding 1921-1923; indicted and convicted of bribery and conspiracy in connection with Teapot Dome oil cases and sentenced to one year in prison and $100,000 fine*—21-23, 82
FARISH, WILLIAM S., 81
FARLEY, JAMES A. (*1888-   ), chairman Democratic National Committee 1932-1940; Postmaster General 1933-1940; chairman of board of directors of Coca-Cola Export Corp. since 1940*—20, 39, 51, 54, 57, 67, 84, 118, 124, 155, 179, 238, 240, 246, 254, 258, 263, 268, 270, 272, 274-276, 278, 284, 294, 297-298, 302, 316, 319, 360, 395, 400, 432, 462-463, 513, 517-518, 521, 554-555, 560-561, 563, 572, 579-580, 586, 598, 603-604, 607, 617-618, 621-624, 629-633, 636, 638-640, 642, 644-645, 647, 655-656, 682, 692, 694, 703-704
FARLEY, MRS. JAMES A., 249
FARLEY, JAMES I., 187-188
farm bill: see Frazier-Lemke Farm Mortgage Bill
farm commodities, prices of, 94, 487
FAWCETT, JAMES WALDO (*1893-   ), editorial and feature writer on staff of Washington Star*—428, 440, 548-549, 565-566, 590-591, 603
FECHNER, ROBERT (*1876-1939), director of Civilian Conservation Corps camps from 1933 until his death*—306, 547
Federal Emergency Relief Administration, 29, 287, 330: see also Harry Hopkins
Federal Housing Corporation, 140, 195, 219, 584
Federal Industrial Control Board, 71-72: see also Hugh Johnson
Federal Power Commission, 174
Federal Relief Administrator: see Harry Hopkins
Federal Reserve Board Advisory Committee, 534
Federal Stock Exchange Commission, 174
Federal Surplus Relief Corporation, 108
Federal Trade Commission, 53, 374, 417, 470
FERNANDEZ-GARCIA, BENIGNO, 503
FERGUSON, JAMES E., 6, 32
FERTICH, ROSCOE, 513, 655
FINCH, JOHN W., 258, 275
FINNEGAN, RICHARD J. (*1884-   ), newspaperman, editor or publisher of Chicago Times 1927-1947; editor of Chicago Sun-Times 1947-1950; now consulting editor*—150-151
First Lady, 499, 543
FISH, HAMILTON (*1888-   ), Representative (Rep.) from New York 1919-1945; a leader of isolationists before 1941*—480, 685
FISHER, HARRY, 112
FISHER, WALTER T., 354
Fisheries, Bureau of, 4, 161, 184, 254, 281
FLEMING, MAJOR GENERAL PHILIP B. (*1887-   ), executive officer and deputy administrator PWA 1933-1935; in charge of Passamaquoddy project 1935-1936; Federal Works Administrator 1941-1949; became Ambassador to Costa Rica in 1951*—114, 189-190, 333, 513
FLEMING, ROBERT V., 471
FLEXNER, ABRAHAM, 47
FLICKINGER, B. FLOYD, 629-630
flood control, for Ohio River, 91; for U.S., 145

Florida agricultural lands, settlement of, by unemployed, 4
Florida canal: see Trans-Florida Canal
FLYNN, EDWARD J. (*1891-1953*), *chairman Democratic County (Bronx) Committee 1922-1953; Secretary of State of New York 1929-1939; national committeeman from New York 1930-1953; chairman Democratic National Committee 1940-1942*—687
FLYNN, JOHN T., 332
FLYNN, MAC, 205, 227: see also Reedsville Subsistence Homestead project
Fokker airplanes, 691-692
FOLEY, EDWARD H., JR. (*1905-), assistant general counsel and later general counsel PWA 1933-1937; assistant general counsel and later general counsel U.S. Treasury 1937-1942; Assistant Secretary of Treasury 1946-1948; Under-Secretary of Treasury 1948-1952*—84, 302, 312, 327, 333-334, 341, 477, 527, 587, 600, 608-609, 611
FORD, EDSEL, 652
FORD, HENRY, 52, 319, 652
FOREMAN, CLARK (*1902-), adviser to Secretary of Interior Ickes on economic status of Negroes; later special counsel to Ickes and director of power division PWA; now member of board of Southern Conference on Human Welfare*—197, 344
Forest Service: see National Forest Service
Fort Meyer, commandant of, 17
FRAZIER, LYNN, J., 419
France, Spanish civil war and, 657-658, 661; goes off gold standard, 686, 691
FRANK, JEROME N. (*1889-), judge; from May, 1933, to February, 1935, general counsel of AAA; later held various New Deal posts including membership on Securities Exchange Commission; since May, 1941, judge of the U.S. Court of Appeals*—276, 292, 483
FRANKFURTER, FELIX (*1882-), professor at Harvard Law School 1914-1939; since then an Associate Justice of the Supreme Court; personal friend and adviser to President Roosevelt*—5, 91, 247, 342, 363, 402-403, 411-412, 414-415, 467, 587, 602, 610

FRANKLIN, WIRT, 97, 107
FRAZIER, LYNN T. (*1874-1947), Governor of South Dakota 1916-1922; Senator (Prog. Rep.) from South Dakota 1922-1940*—536
Frazier-Lemke Farm Mortgage Bill, 536
free assemblage, 203, 255, 346, 350
free press, 203, 255, 346, 350
free speech, 203, 255, 346, 350
Freedmen's Hospital, 4, 265
freedom, academic, 368: see also University of Chicago
FRENCH, EDWARD S., 190
furniture-making industry, of Eleanor Roosevelt, 83

G

GARDNER, OLIVER MAX (*1882-1947), Governor (Dem.) of North Carolina 1929-1933; appointed Ambassador to Great Britain shortly before his death*—120-123, 138
GARDINER, WILLIAM T., 113
GARNER, JOHN NANCE (*1868-), Representative (Dem.) from Texas 1903-1933; Vice President of the United States 1933-1941*—3, 16, 32, 40, 45, 141, 162, 241, 263, 280, 284, 293, 308, 315-317, 330-331, 339, 346, 374, 385, 399-400, 423, 491, 497, 516, 545, 607, 625-626
gasoline, prices, 146; production of, 158
GEIST, C. H., 509-511
General Electric Company, 52, 356
General Industries Bill, 46: see also Industries Control Bill
General Land Office, 4
General Motors, Inc., 523-524
GENNERICH, GUS, 452, 454
Geological Survey, 4, 413
GERARD, JAMES, 244
GERHARD, THE REVEREND MR., 432
German bonds, in United States, 33
German Embassy, dinner at, 353
German propaganda, in U.S., 111-112
Germany, agreement with Japan, 494; conservatives in, 545-546; Bullitt on conditions in, 626; attitude toward war in Spain, 657: see also Hitler
Gettysburg Cemetery, 72
GIANNINI, A. P., 179, 687

GIBSON, GEORGE H., 390

GILKEY, CHARLES, 367

GILL, CORRINGTON (*1898-1946*), *Government official; director of research, statistics and finance 1933, and assistant administrator, 1934-1936, of FERA; assistant administrator CWA 1933-1934; assistant administrator WPA 1936-1941*—427, 436

GINGERY, DON, 377

Glacier National Park, 185

GLASS, CARTER (*1858-1946*), *Representative (Dem.) from Virginia 1902-1918; Secretary of Treasury under President Wilson 1918-1920; Senator from Virginia 1920 until his death. One of the founders of the Federal Reserve System*—285-286, 290, 313-315, 318, 320, 335-336, 340, 514-515, 600, 629

Glass bill, 41

GLAVIS, LOUIS R. (*1883-*), *lawyer and Government official; special agent of the Field Division of the Department of Interior active in the Pinchot-Ballinger controversy of 1910-11; director of investigations for the same department 1933-1936; now in private practice*—18, 22, 64, 201, 252-255, 260-262, 270-272, 277-279, 293-296, 299, 304, 480-481, 549-551, 555-556, 641

gold, stopping exportation of, 3; Government purchase of, 103, 110-111, 113; to stabilize currencies; Roosevelt's message on, 140

gold certificate cases, Supreme Court considers, 273, 294

gold standard, U.S. goes off, 23, 658, 686, 691

GOODWIN, WILLIAM, 630

Grazing bill: see Taylor Grazing Control Bill

GRAY, HOWARD A., 266

GRAY, JOHN, 534

Gravelly Point airport, 283

GRAVES, BIBB, 369

Grazing Control Service, 259: *see also* Taylor Grazing Control Bill

Grazing Districts, 311

Grazing Division, 170, 229

Great Britain, debt to U.S., 106-107; Japanese oil situation and, 192; Roosevelt on, 242; relations with Italy, 464; agreement with Germany, 494; battle-

ships built by, 545; Public Works Board in, 288-289; role in Ethiopian war, 484; foreign policy of, 516: *see also* Archishop of York, Christopher Chancellor, International Economic Conference, Ramsay MacDonald

GREEN, WILLIAM, 469-470

GREEVER, PAUL R., 605

Gridiron Club, 161, 242, 484-485, 559-560

GRIMES, of Subsistence Homesteads, 152

GRIMM, PETER, 546-547

GRISWOLD, GLENN, 419

GUCK, HOMER, 153, 211-212, 355

GRUENING, ERNEST (*1887-*), *editor and Government official; managing editor of New York Tribune 1918, and of The Nation 1920-1923; director of division of territories and island possessions in Department of Interior 1934-1939, with jurisdiction over Alaska, Hawaii, Puerto Rico, Virgin Islands, South Sea and Equatorial Islands; administrator of Puerto Rican Reconstruction Administration 1935-1937; Governor of Alaska 1939-1953*—298, 304, 503, 594

GUFFEY, JOSEPH F. (*1875-*), *Senator (Dem.) from Pennsylvania 1935-1947; member of Democratic National Committee from Pennsylvania since 1920*—91, 202, 207, 400, 586-587, 664

Guffey-Snyder Coal Act, 25, 602

Guffey-Vinson Bill, 25

GUGGENHEIM, HARRY F., 651-652

GUGLER, ERIC, 152, 154, 254

H

HACKETT, COLONEL HORATIO B. (*1880-1941*), *general manager PWA from February to June, 1934; director of housing 1934-1935; assistant administrator PWA 1935-1937*—195, 436, 442, 461, 486, 584, 667: *see also* Federal Housing Corporation

HAGUE, FRANK (*1876-*), *Democratic politician and builder of "the Hague machine" in New Jersey; Mayor of Jersey City 1917-1947; member of Democratic National Committee from New Jersey since 1922*—522, 579, 586

HALE, FREDERICK, 285-286

HALE, PIERSON, 307

HALSEY, COLONEL EDWARD A. (*1881-1945*), *Secretary of the U.S. Senate 1933-1945* —314
HAMILTON, ALICE, 356
HAMILTON, JOHN, 678, 702
HAMPTON, RUTH (*1883-*), *field representative of the Division of Territories and Island Possessions of the Department of Interior, June to September, 1934; assistant director of the division until March, 1946*—431, 440, 499, 624
Hannibal Bridge, WPA project, 673
HAPGOOD, NORMAN (*1868-1937*), *editor and author; editor Collier's Weekly 1903-1912, Harper's Weekly 1913-1916, Hearst's International Magazine 1923-1925; U.S. Minister to Denmark in 1919*—39, 520
HARD, WILLIAM, 670
HARDING, GEORGE F., 669
HARDING, WARREN G., 22, 646
Harding v. Harding, 669-670
HARING, CAPTAIN, 54
HARRISON, PAT (*1881-1941*), *Representative (Dem.) from Mississippi 1911-1919; Senator 1919-1941; chairman U.S. Senate Finance Committee 1933-1941*—47, 49, 301-302, 363, 537, 587
Harrisonburg, Virginia, 78
Harrodsburg, Ky., 225
Harvard Law School, 5, 8
HASSENAUR, LEO J., 153, 155
HASTIE, WILLIAM H. (*1904-*), *assistant solicitor of the Department of Interior 1933-1937; judge in Virgin Islands 1937-1939; dean of Harvard University School of Law 1939-1946; Governor of Virgin Islands 1946-1949; since then judge on U.S. Circuit Court of Appeals*—416
HAVENNER, FRANCK, 213, 357
Hawaii, banking situation in, 3; Governorship of, 14, 37; coast defenses in, 71; Advisory Committee for, 151
HAWES, MISS, 60
Hawes-Cutting Bill, 145
HAYDEN, BEAUFORD E., 181
HAYDEN, CARL (*1877-*), *Representative (Dem.) from Arizona 1912-1927; Senator 1926-* ; *specialist on legislation pertaining to irrigation of arid lands*—10, 310, 588, 600, 607, 609, 613

Hayden amendment: *see* Work Relief Bill amendment
HAYES, HELEN, 543
HEALY, ROBERT E., 174
HEARST, WILLIAM RANDOLPH (*1863-1951*), *newspaper publisher and editor; proprietor of Hearst chain of newspapers and magazines. He backed Franklin D. Roosevelt in 1932, having helped him to secure the Democratic nomination, but then quarreled violently with the New Deal and supported Landon in 1936*—153, 155, 354, 384, 428, 468, 472, 519, 533, 559, 614-615, 633, 639, 644, 647-648, 651, 657, 659-660, 665-666, 668-671, 683-685, 687, 696, 704
HEARST, WILLIAM RANDOLPH, JR., 650-651, 652-653
HEARST, MRS. WILLIAM RANDOLPH, JR., 651
Hearst newspapers, oppose World Court, 285; attack Roosevelt as a communist, 428, 683-684; oppose German steel in WPA projects, 466; attack Ickes, 492, 671; Ickes on, 696; election and, 660-661, 702, 704
Hermitage, The, 225-226
HERRICK, GENEVIEVE FORBES, 430-431, 475-476
HERRICK, JOHN, 475-476
Hetch Hetchy Valley, 177, 214, 315, 357, 563
HIGH, STANLEY (*1895-*), *editor and radio commentator; roving editor of Reader's Digest since 1940*—613-615, 617, 619, 639-640, 642-643, 647, 680
highway, scenic, 123-124, 283; transcontinental, 244
HILL, T. ARNOLD, 60
HILLMAN, SIDNEY, 356
historic monuments bill, 385
Historic Sites Act, 489
HITCHCOCK, ETHAN ALLEN (*1835-1909*), *Secretary of the Interior 1898-1907; one of the first leaders of conservation movement, having cleaned up frauds in administration of public lands and cooperated with President Theodore Roosevelt in enlarging national forests and withdrawing mineral lands from exploitation*—22
HITZ, WILLIAM (*1872-1935*), *judge on U.S. Court of Appeals in District of*

Columbia from *1931* until his death
—7
HITLER, ADOLPH, occupation of Rhineland by, 544, 626
HOBSON, ALFRED T., 634
HOGUE, RICHARD W., 20
HOIDALE, EINAR, 21
Holland, Japanese oil situation and, 192
HOLMES, OLIVER WENDELL, JR. (*1841-1935*), *distinguished American jurist; Associate Justice of the Supreme Court 1902-1932*—312, 342, 352
HOLMES, RALPH CLAYTON (*1874-1950*), *oil executive; president of the Texas Co.*
—11
HOOPINGARNER, DWIGHT L., 103
HOOVER, HERBERT, 24, 30, 38, 463, 511-512, 526, 548, 603, 688
HOOVER, IKE, 94
HOOVER, J. EDGAR, 90
Hoover Camp, 18, 87
Hoover Dam: *see* Boulder Dam
HOPKINS, HARRY L. (*1890-1946*), *welfare worker and Government official; administrator of Federal relief (FERA) 1933-1935; Works Progress Administrator 1935-1938; Secretary of Commerce 1938-1940; head of Lend Lease (1941) and confidential friend and agent of President Roosevelt throughout the Second World War*—70, 96, 108, 116, 119, 142, 171, 194-195, 198, 200, 206, 216, 221, 228, 240, 254-255, 264-266, 276, 281, 288-289, 292-293, 306, 311, 329, 335, 337-339, 348, 351-352, 358, 362, 366, 378-379, 383, 386-388, 409-414, 420, 422, 429-430, 432-434, 436-439, 448, 450-452, 454-455, 458-459, 461, 475, 479, 486, 489, 491, 493, 496, 570-571, 580-583, 585-588, 595-596, 598, 611, 620, 628, 646, 656, 683
HOPKINS, BARBARA, 489
HORNBECK, STANDLEY K., 192
HORNER, HENRY (*1878-1940*), *lawyer and politician; judge of Cook County Probate Court 1914-1933; Governor of Illinois 1933-1940*—8-9, 432, 463, 493-494, 520-522, 554, 556-558, 564, 621-622, 672
HORTON, BENJAMIN, 503
HOUSE, COLONEL EDWARD M. (*1858-1938*), *diplomat; close personal friend and representative of President Woodrow Wilson for many years; later an elder statesman in Democratic party affairs*—109-110
housing, Icke's article on, 344; speech on, 366-367
Housing Authority, New York, 276, 308, 317: *see also* Langdon Post
housing bill: *see* Wagner-Ellenbogen Housing Bill
Housing Corporation: *see* Federal Housing Corporation
Housing Division, 206, 230-232, 239, 436-437, 546, 569, 575, 610: *see also* James Moffett, Wagner-Ellenbogen Housing Bill
housing policy, of Administration, 243
housing program, low-cost, 152, 206, 230, 239, 243, 428, 443, 575: *see also* Subsistence Homesteads Division
housing program, rural, 227-228
housing projects, approved by Roosevelt, 480, 488, 562; in metropolitan areas, 428; in the North, 443; condemning property for, 530; in Bridgeport, Conn., and Lackawanna, Pa., 673; political benefits from, 673; for Negroes, 673
Houston, 182, 446-461
"hot" oil: *see* oil, "hot"
HOWARD, EDGAR, 51, 57
Howard University, 4, 47, 265, 319, 416, 540-541
HOWE, COLONEL LOUIS M. (*1871-1936*), *personal secretary and friend to Franklin D. Roosevelt from 1920 until his death*—14, 18, 37, 54-55, 58, 60, 78, 80, 82, 88, 129, 141, 159, 184, 190, 207, 218, 254, 271-273, 280-281, 319-320, 327, 329-330, 342, 551-552, 562, 640, 645, 690
HOWES, WILLIAM W., 295, 630, 677
Hubbard Woods, Ickes' home in, 96, 175, 208, 367
HUBBELL, HENRY S., 245, 440
HUGHES, CHARLES EVANS (*1862-1948*), *Associate Justice of the Supreme Court 1910-1916; Republican nominee for President 1916; Secretary of State 1921-1925; Chief Justice of the Supreme Court 1930-1941*—105, 294, 485, 536, 602, 614
HULL, CORDELL (*1871-   ), Representative (Dem.) from Tennessee 1907-1921,*

HULL, CORDELL *(continued)*
*1923-1931; Senator 1931-1933; Secretary of State 1933-1944; winner of Nobel Peace Prize 1945—*8, 33, 35, 58, 75-77, 107, 110, 118, 225, 360, 462, 472, 483, 513, 515, 517, 587, 631-632, 656-657, 671, 677, 694-695, 697, 703
HULL, MRS. CORDELL, 75
Hull House: *see* Jane Addams, Alice Hamilton
HUMPHREYS, 374: *see also* Federal Trade Commission
Hungry Club, Pittsburgh, 207
HUNT, HENRY, 91, 134, 247
HURJA, EMIL *(1892-   ), editor and politician; executive director of Democratic National Committee 1932-1937; active since then in financial analysis and magazine editing—*598, 602-603, 641
HUTCHINS, ROBERT MAYNARD *(1899-   ), dean of Yale Law School 1928-1929; president of University of Chicago 1929-1945; chancellor 1945-1951; associate director of Ford Foundation since then—*36, 167, 198, 200-201, 208-211, 219, 236, 349, 375
HUTCHINS, WILLIAM J., 167
Hyde Park, 83-84

I

ICKES, ANNA WILMARTH THOMPSON, *Mr. Ickes' first wife, whom he married in 1911 and who was killed in an automobile accident in 1935—*82, 91, 95, 134, 162, 187, 206, 301, 305, 312-313, 320-321, 324, 332, 349, 353, 363, 371, 376, 407, 429-433, 438-440
ICKES, BETTY, 431, 561
ICKES, JANE DAHLMAN, *Mr. Ickes' second wife, whom he married on May 24, 1938—*159, 475, 499, 527-528, 545, 553, 561, 657-658
ICKES, RAYMOND W. *(1912-   ), son of Harold L. and Anna Ickes—*92, 133, 159, 190, 321, 323, 367, 431-433, 444-446, 454, 502, 511, 697
ICKES, ROBERT *(1913-   ), ward of Harold and Anna Ickes—*133, 432, 616
ICKES, WILMARTH *(1899-1936), son of Anna Ickes and stepson of Harold L.* —431-432, 672-673, 680
Ickes family, 376-377, 545-546, 611-613, 622-623, 625
IGOE, JAMES T., 557
IGOE, MICHAEL LAMBERT *(1885-   ), Representative (Dem.) from Illinois 1935; resigned to become U.S. district attorney for northern district of Illinois 1935-1939; judge on U.S. district court since then—*431, 521, 564, 672
Illinois, Democratic political situation in, 520-521, 556-558, 564-565
Illinois tax, on schools, 32, 36
Independent Legislative Bureau, 20
Independent Offices Appropriation Bill, 158
Indian Affairs, Office of, 4, 16, 20, 51, 57, 61, 180, 251
Indian Affairs, Commissioner of, 15, 19-20: *see also* John Collier
Indian agencies, selling beer on, 29
Indian Boarding School, Genoa, Nebraska, 51
Indian chief, Marcellus Hawk, 5
Indian lands, oil on, 38; leasing of, 552-553
Indian projects, 443
Indian rights: *see* Wheeler-Howard Indian Rights Bill
Indian schools, policy for, 61
Indians, Sioux, 4; California landless, 628
Indianapolis, 58, 77
Industrial Recovery Act: *see* National Industrial Recovery Act
Industries Control, section of Public Works and Industrial Control Bill, 51-52
Industries Control Bill, oil amendment to, 47-49: *see also* Hugh Johnson, Public Works Bill
INMAN, of Housing Division, Chicago, 610
INSULL, SAMUEL, 150
Interior, Department of, bureaus in, 4; cuts in budget of, 16, 41; bureau interchange with Agriculture, 21-24, 250, 534-535; with War, 72; administers White House, 54-55; coal administration and, 92; Treasury and, 222; Tugwell on, 240; reorganization of, 265; reputation of, 265; Housing Division in, 597; co-operation with Agriculture, 522: *see also* Conservation Department, National Forest Service
Interior Department Building, 221-223,

249, 408, 485, 680
International Economic Conference, 33, 42, 44, 58, 75-77: *see also* Cordell Hull, Hiram Johnson, Raymond Moley
Ironsides, 436
isolationism, World Court and, 285
Italy, Chancellor on situation in, 464-465; attitude toward Spain, 657
insurance, social, views of President on, 163; handled in new department: *see also* Social Security Act
Italian-Ethiopian situation, 422-423, 445-446, 450, 462, 464-465, 484

J

JACKSON, GARDNER, 77
Japan, planes of, 353; Chancellor on, 464; agreement with Germany, 494
Japanese Embassy, dinner at, 320, 544
Jayhawker (Sinclair Lewis), 206
Jefferson Club, 399
Jefferson Memorial, Washington, D.C., 283; St. Louis, 489
Jersey City Medical Center, PWA project, 689
JOHNSON, HIRAM W. (*1866-1945*), *Governor of California 1911-1917; one of the founders of the Progressive Party in 1912 and candidate for Vice President on its ticket in that year; Senator (Rep.) from California from 1917 until his death. He was asked by President Roosevelt to be Secretary of the Interior in 1933 before the post was offered to Ickes*—3, 14, 20, 33, 42, 44, 213-214, 217, 264, 285, 313, 415-416, 424-425, 532, 588, 591, 594, 693, 697-698
JOHNSON, MRS. HIRAM, 27, 42-43, 125-126, 538, 693, 697-698
JOHNSON, GENERAL HUGH S. (*1882-1942*), *planned and supervised selective draft in 1917-1918; administrator of NRA 1933-1934; WPA administrator for New York City 1935; editorial columnist for Scripps-Howard newspapers from 1934 until his death*—34, 48, 51-56, 60, 65-66, 71-73, 77, 83, 88, 91, 94, 100-101, 108, 128, 144, 147, 173, 195, 197, 219, 287, 313-314, 319, 375, 633
JOHNSON, MORDECAI, 541
JOHNSON, CONGRESSMAN, 419
Johnson Act, 473
JOHNSTONE, BRUCE, 39

JONES, DOROTHY, 187
JONES, JESSE H. (*1874-   ), banker and Government official; director RFC 1932-1939; member National Emergency Council 1933-1939; Secretary of Commerce 1940-1945; member Economic Stabilization Board 1942-1945*—22, 156, 383, 489, 498, 582, 594-596, 607-609: *see also* Reconstruction Finance Corporation
JONES, W. FRANK, 41
Journal of Land and Public Utility Economics, 344
Justice, Department of, 151, 243, 245, 247, 279, 480, 547, 628: *see also* Homer Cummings

K

KAHN, OTTO, 520
KALININ, President of Russia, 111
KANNEE, Col. McIntyre's assistant, 256
Kansas City Star, 675
KAUFMAN, GEORGE, 500
KELLY, EDWARD JOSEPH (*1876-1950*), *Mayor of Chicago 1933-1947 and builder of "the Kelly machine" in that city; an engineer by training who became a powerful Democratic party politician; member of Democratic National Committee from Illinois 1940-1944*—104, 167, 215, 246, 272, 275, 432, 439, 463, 493-494, 520-522, 554, 557, 560, 564-565, 579, 586, 621, 672
Kelly-Nash machine, 520-521, 556-558, 564-565
KELLY, Democratic leader, Brooklyn, 698-699
KENDRICK, JOHN B. (*1857-1933*), *Governor of Wyoming 1915-1917; Senator (Dem.) from Wyoming from 1917 until his death*—39, 49, 118
KENNEDY, JOSEPH P. (*1888-   ), businessman and Government official; member of Securities Exchange Commission from 1934 and its chairman in 1935; chairman U.S. Maritime Commission 1937; U.S. Ambassador to Great Britain 1937-1941*—173, 203, 206, 351, 472, 692
KENT, FRANK R., 559-560
Kenya, British colony of, 423
KEYNES, JOHN MAYNARD, 584-585
KHALIL BEY, NICHOLAS, 125

KIES, PRESTON, 211

KING, JUDSON, 32

KING, WILLIAM H. (*1863-1949*), *Representative (Dem.) from Utah 1897-1901; Senator 1917-1941*—69, 114, 379, 392, 397, 544, 552

KING, MACKENZIE, 465-466, 471-472

KINGSBURY, KENNETH R. (*1876-1937*), *oil man: president Standard Oil Co. of California from 1919 until his death*—11, 97

Klamath Indian Agency, 180

KLUCKHOHN, FRANK, 261-262, 476-477

KNEIPP, L. F., 527, 574, 598

KNOX, COLONEL FRANK (*1874-1944*), *newspaperman and Government official; publisher of Chicago Daily News from 1931; Republican nominee for Vice President in 1936; Secretary of the Navy 1940-1944*—149, 212, 245-246, 463, 558, 560, 615-616, 653, 669, 678, 688, 702

KOHN, ROBERT, 195

KRAMER, CHARLES, 570

L

Labor, Department of: *see* Frances Perkins

LA FOLLETTE, PHILIP F. (*1897-   ), lawyer; Governor of Wisconsin 1931-1933 and 1935-1939; organized National Progressives of America in 1938; son of Senator Robert M. La Follette*—149-150, 355, 487

LA FOLLETTE, ROBERT M., JR. (*1895-1953*), *for six years secretary to his father; Senator (Rep.) from Wisconsin 1925-1947; retired to private life after defeat by Senator Joseph McCarthy*—217, 248, 342, 355, 363, 415, 487, 588, 613, 655-656, 678

Lafoon, Ky, 225, 465

LA GUARDIA, FIORELLO H. (*1882-1947*), *Representative (Rep.) from New York 1917-1921 and 1923-1933; Mayor of New York City 1934-1945; chief Office of Civilian Defense 1941-1942; director UNRRA 1946*—126, 148, 229, 267-268, 291, 308-309, 317, 410, 415, 420, 500-501, 550, 617-618, 636, 689, 693

LAMBERT, JOHN, 195

LAMBETH, J. WALTER, 570

land, submarginal, purchase of, 105, 293

Land Use Planning, 171

LANDON, ALFRED M. (*1887-   ), Governor of Kansas 1933-1937; Republican nominee for President 1936*—10, 11, 548, 559, 561, 602-604, 606-607, 615-618, 620, 627, 633, 638-639, 641, 642-643, 645-646, 647, 648-649, 651-652, 655, 663, 665, 667-668, 669, 672, 675, 680-682, 683-684, 685, 689, 694-696, 698, 700-702

LANSING, ROBERT, 515

LARNED, ABNER, 477

LARRABEE, CHARLES R. (*1898-   ), Government official; assistant general counsel PWA 1938-1939; chief trial examiner for Bituminous Coal Division of Department of Interior 1940-1941; since then with RFC*—250, 527, 634

LARSON, C. W., 167

LASKI, HAROLD J., 524

Lathrop, Julia, housing project, 610

LATIMER, JACK, 668

LAWRENCE, DAVID L., 377, 664

LEACH, PAUL, 558

League of Nations, 9, 33, 46

League of Women Voters, 149, 479

LEE, Ickes' secretary, 175, 179-181, 321

Lee House, Arlington, 72

legal staffs, plan to consolidate, 243, 245

LE HAND, MARGUERITE ("MISSY"), *personal secretary to President Roosevelt*—61, 66, 127, 193, 238, 245, 250, 255, 270, 342, 364, 397-398, 435, 444, 527, 537, 542-543, 592, 615, 629, 631, 633-634, 687, 693

LEHMAN, HERBERT H. (*1878-   ), banker and Government official; Lieutenant Governor of New York 1928-1932; Governor 1932-1942; director general UNRRA 1943-1946; Senator (Dem.) from New York 1949-   *—267, 309, 576, 636

LEWIS, JAMES HAMILTON (*-1939*), *Senator (Dem.) from Illinois 1913-1919 and 1931-1939*—10, 350, 364, 379-380, 418, 568-569, 621-622, 696

LEWIS, JOHN L. (*1880-   ), president of United Mine Workers of America since 1920; member Labor Advisory Board and National Labor Board of NRA; a powerful supporter of President Roosevelt in the 1936 campaign; he*

opposed him bitterly in 1940—10, 25, 91
LEWIS, SINCLAIR, 206
LEWIS, composer, 650
Liberty Bond case, Supreme Court considers, 273
LILIENTHAL, DAVID E. (*1899-*), *lawyer and Government official; director TVA 1933-1946; chairman Atomic Energy Commission 1946-1950; now engaged in private business*—174, 566-567
LILLIE, BEATRICE, 501
Lincolniana, 137
LINDLEY, ERNEST K. (*1899-*), *newspaperman; Washington correspondent New York Herald Tribune 1933-1937; since then chief of Washington bureau of Newsweek*—260-261, 269-270, 279, 362
LINDSAY, SIR RONALD (*1877-1945*), *British Ambassador to U.S. 1930-1939*—125, 202, 483, 516
LINDSAY, LADY, 162
liquor control, 118
LITVINOV, MAXIM (*1876-1951*), *U.S.S.R. diplomat; People's Commissar for Foreign Affairs 1930-1939; Soviet Ambassador to U.S. 1941-1943*—117-118, 120, 124-125, 691: *see also* Russia
LLOYD GEORGE, DAVID, 468, 494-495
lobby, social, 170
lobbying, investigation of, 403
LODGE, HENRY CABOT, 681
LOGAN, M. M., 465
London Economic Conference: *see* International Economic Conference
London *Times*, 313
LONERGAN, AUGUSTINE, 693
LONG, BRECKINRIDGE (*1881-*), *diplomat; special assistant to Attorney General 1933; U.S. Ambassador to Italy 1933-1936; on special mission to South America 1938; special assistant to Secretary of State 1939-1940; Assistant Secretary of State 1940-1944*—312
LONG, HUEY P. (*1893-1935; Governor of Louisiana 1928-1931; Senator (Dem.) from Louisiana 1931 until his assassination in 1935; builder of "the Long machine" in Louisiana*—284, 294-295, 298-299, 302, 313, 345-346, 348, 352-353, 363, 400, 423, 462, 606
LONGWORTH, ALICE, 499-500

LORIMER, GEORGE HORACE, 619-620
Louisville case, Supreme Court decision in, 530
LOWDEN, FRANK O. (*1861-1943*), *Governor of Illinois 1917-1921; later an influential elder statesman in the Republican party*—18
LUCE, HENRY, 650
LUTHER, HANS, 112, 125
Lutheran Church, oldest in U.S., 625
LYNDS, CORNELIUS, 8

M

MACARTHUR, GENERAL DOUGLAS (*1880-*), *Chief of Staff U.S. Army 1930-1935; retired 1937; Commander U.S. armed forces in the Fast East 1941-1945; Supreme Commander occupational forces in Japan 1945-1950; Supreme Commander U.N. forces in Korea 1950-1951; now in private business*—68-69, 71
MACCHESNEY, NATHAN WILLIAM, 463
MACDONALD, RAMSAY, 25, 33
MACDONALD, THOMAS H., 244
MACK, JOHN E., 624
MACK, JULIAN S. (*1866-1943*), *Federal judge from 1911 to 1941, and before that a law professor at the University of Chicago*—500, 608
MACK, Ickes' stenographer, 64, 482
MACWHITE, MRS., 353
Madden Dam, 455
Magdalena Bay, 448
Maine, and Passamaquoddy project, 189, 542; and election, 675, 679, 693
MALLON, PAUL, 77, 278
MALMIN, LUCIUS J. M. *Chicago lawyer against whom Ickes started disbarment proceedings described in his diary. Ickes won, and the disbarment was confirmed in 1936 by the Supreme Court of Illinois. Malmin died on January 3, 1941, shortly after a petition for reinstatement to the bar had been granted*—64-65, 88-90, 155, 167
MANLY, BASIL (*1886-1950*), *member of Federal Power Commission 1933-1945; director Southern National Gas Co. 1945-1950*—248
MANN, RABBI, 112
MARGOLD, NATHAN R. (*1899-1947*), *lawyer and Government official; solicitor*

MARGOLD, NATHAN R. *(continued)*
of Department of Interior 1933-1942; special assistant to the Attorney General 1933-1935; judge of the Washington, D.C., Municipal Court 1942-1947— 8, 12, 24, 37, 40, 44, 46, 97-99, 102, 106-107, 114, 158, 169, 172, 362, 365, 530-531, 550, 587

Mariposa Grove, 176

MARKHAM, MAJOR GENERAL EDWARD M. *(1877-), chief of army engineers, War Department 1933-1938; member of National Capital Park and Planning Commission in 1937—*175, 337, 384, 491, 513, 543

MARLAND, ERNEST W. *(1874-1941), Representative (Dem.) from Oklahoma 1933-1935; Governor of Oklahoma 1935-1939—*37, 40

MARSHALL, J. HOWARD II *(1905-), lawyer; assistant professor Yale Law School 1931-1933; member of Petroleum Administrative Board 1933-1935; special assistant to Attorney General and assistant solicitor of Department of Interior 1933-1935; counsel to Standard Oil Co. of California 1935-1937; now president Ashland Oil and Refining Co.—*97-99, 107

MARSHALL, ROBERT, 180

MARTIN, CHARLES H. *(1863-1946), Representative (Dem.) from Oregon 1931-1935; Governor of Oregon 1935-1939* —182

MARX, FRED L. *(1908-), private secretary to the Secretary of the Interior 1933-1937—*64, 83, 121-122, 138, 204, 361, 462, 475

MASON, JULIAN, 278

Materials General Builders Supply Corporation, 297

MAVERICK, MAURY *(1895-), Representative (Dem.) from Texas 1935-1939; Mayor of San Antonio 1939-1941; member of War Production Board 1941-1946—*419

Maverick Springs District, oil leases in, 38

Mayors' Conference, resolutions of, on public works program, 96, 100

McADOO, WILLIAM G. *(1863-1941), Secretary of the Treasury under President Wilson 1916-1918; Senator (Dem.) from California 1933-1939; President Wilson's son-in-law—*4, 35, 44, 47, 49-50

McALISTER, HILL, 225

McCARL, JOHN RAYMOND *(1879-1940), Comptroller General of the U.S. 1921-1936—*140-141, 222, 333, 335, 346, 587

McCARRAN, PAT *(1876-), Senator (Dem.) from Nevada since 1933—*21, 302, 313, 315

McCORMICK, COLONEL ROBERT R. *(1880-), editor and publisher of the* Chicago Tribune *and bitter critic of the New Deal; cousin of Joseph M. Patterson, late publisher of the New York Daily News, and of Mrs. Eleanor Patterson, late publisher of the Washington Times Herald—*212, 493: *see also* Chicago Tribune

McCRILLIS, WILLIAM, 206, 431-432, 475, 624

McDOWELL, CAPTAIN RALPH W., 134

McGRADY, EDWARD F., 432

McINTIRE, VICE ADMIRAL ROSS T. *(1889-), personal physician to President Roosevelt 1933-1945; Surgeon General of U.S. Navy 1938-1946; now national administrator of the American Red Cross blood program—*132, 371, 448, 453, 455, 460-461, 694, 703

McINTYRE, COLONEL MARVIN H. *(1878-1943), one of President Roosevelt's secretaries 1933-1942—*20, 42, 55, 58, 120, 135, 154-155, 160, 231, 245, 300, 314, 337, 364, 397-399, 489, 491, 525, 536-537, 539, 576-577, 593, 602, 683

McKEOUGH, R. S., 419, 579

McNARY, CHARLES L. *(1874-1944), Senator (Rep.) from Oregon 1917-1944; Republican nominee for Vice President in 1940; minority leader of Senate 1933-1934—*39, 61-62, 282, 320, 415, 419

McNINCH, FRANK R., 174

McNUTT, PAUL V. *(1891-), Governor of Indiana 1933-1937; member national advisory board of WPA; Federal Security Administrator 1939-1945; U.S. High Commissioner to Philippine Islands 1937-1939 and 1945-1946* —366, 517, 639-640, 644, 659

McREYNOLDS, JAMES C., 537, 562, 705

McREYNOLDS, S. D., 41, 295

MEAD, DR. ELWOOD *(1858-1936), Commis-*

sioner of Reclamation in the Department of the Interior *1926-1936*—37-38, 175, 337, 376, 528-529: *see also* Bureau of Reclamation

MEDILL, JOSEPH, 44

MEIGS, MERRILL C., 168

MELLON, ANDREW W., 440-441

MENCKEN, HENRY L., 242

MERITT, EDGAR B. (*1874-*   ), *Assistant Commissioner of Indian Affairs 1913-1929; assistant solicitor of the Department of Interior, June to October, 1933*—19

MERRIAM, CHARLES E. (*1874-1953*), *taught political science at University of Chicago from 1900 until his death; unsuccessful Republican candidate for Mayor of Chicago in 1911 with Ickes as his campaign manager; member of National Resources Board 1933-1943; leading member of President Roosevelt's committee on administrative management which drew up reorganization plans for the executive branch of the Government in 1937*—26, 97, 136, 171-172, 211, 220-221, 235-236, 246 281, 341, 349, 355, 366, 368, 376, 607-610

"Merry-Go-Round" column, 269, 391, 408

MEYER, EUGENE (*1875-*   ), *banker and newspaper publisher; first chairman of the board of RFC in 1932; publisher of the* Washington Post *1933-1946 and chairman of the board of directors since then*—144, 148, 179

MEYERS, NORMAN, 97, 107

Miami Herald, 502

MICHELSON, CHARLES (*1874-1947*), *chief Washington correspondent of the New York World 1917-1929; director of publicity for the Democratic National Committee 1929-1940; director of public relations for NRA 1933-1934*—517-518, 618, 640, 642-644, 647, 664, 666, 669

Midtown-Hudson Tunnel, New York City, 84, 550

Midtown Tunnel Authority, New York City, 550

Migratory Bird Conservation Commission, 4

MILLER, PIERCE, 128

MILLS, OGDEN, 480

Mines, Bureau of, 4, 92, 258, 274, 413: *see also* John W. Finch

MINTON, SHERMAN, 419

Mississippi River Channel project, 72

Mississippi Valley Committee, 174

MITCHELL, WESLEY C. (*1874-1948*), *professor of economics; member national planning board PWA 1933; member National Resources Board 1934-1935*—171-172, 281, 341, 610

MOFFETT, JAMES A. (*1886-1953*), *oil man; director Standard Oil Co. of N. J. 1919-1933; member industrial advisory board NRA 1933; vice-president Standard Oil Co. of Cal. 1934-1936; Federal Housing Administrator 1934-1935; board chairman California Texas Oil Co. 1936-1953*—82, 84, 97, 230-237, 243-244, 251, 254, 276, 398

MOFFETT, MRS. JAMES A., 232-233

MOLEY, RAYMOND (*1886-*   ), *professor of public law and government at Columbia since 1923; one of members of the first Roosevelt "brain trust" and assistant Secretary of State in 1933; editor of* Today *1933-1937; contributing editor of* Newsweek *since 1937*—9, 34, 58-59, 75-76, 83, 375, 610, 658, 674, 692

Monticello, Virginia, 629

MOORE, COLONEL JAMES T., 506, 508

MOORE, ROBERT W., 125, 629

MORAN, WILLIAM H., 155

Morehead City, North Carolina, project, 466, 469

MORGAN, DR. ARTHUR E. (*1878-*   ), *president Antioch College 1920-1931; chairman TVA 1933-1938; president Community Service, Inc. since 1941*—62, 70, 119, 566-567: *see also* Tennessee Valley Authority

MORGAN, FORBES, 144, 655

Morgan, house of, 46: *see also* Norman Davis

MORGAN, J. PIERPONT, 45, 650

MORGENTHAU, HENRY, JR. (*1891-*   ), *chairman Federal Farm Board 1933; Under Secretary of Treasury 1934; Secretary of Treasury 1934-1945*—18, 35, 77, 80, 108, 113, 120, 125, 128, 199-200, 216, 221-224, 238-240, 245, 270, 279, 295-298, 301-302, 304, 306, 331,

MORGENTHAU, HENRY, JR. (*continued*)
351, 355, 365, 370-371, 373, 379, 382,
404-405, 429-430, 484, 486, 515, 518,
523, 540, 560-561, 567, 587, 589, 591,
596, 598, 631-632, 646, 677, 683, 691,
703
MORGENTHAU, HENRY, SR., 541
MOSES, ROBERT (*1888-   *), *chairman
New York State Emergency Public
Works Commission 1933; Republican
nominee for Governor of New York
1934; member Triborough Bridge
Authority 1934-1946; outstanding leader in park and highway development
in New York City and Long Island—*
148, 229, 263, 267-269, 277, 291, 307-
309, 317, 623, 636-637, 690
MOSKOWITZ, MRS. BELLE, 690
MOSS, PAUL, 349, 499
MOSSER, STACY (*1872-   *), *classmate of
Ickes at University of Chicago; invest-
ment banker—*432
MOULTON, HAROLD, 610
Mount Olympus National Monument,
574, 583-584
Mount Rainier National Park, 181-182
MULLEN, ARTHUR, 159
MUNDELEIN, GEORGE WILLIAM, CARDINAL
(*1872-1939*), *Archbishop of Chicago
from 1915 and Cardinal from 1924—*
479-480, 521
MUNGER, CAPTAIN, 134
MUNIR, MADAME, 320
munitions factories, allocation of funds
to, 69, 302: *see also* public works fund
Munitions Investigating Committee, 692
munition workers, Landon and, 663, 665
MURDOCK, ABE (*1893-   *), *Representa-
tive (Dem.) from Utah 1933-1941; Sen-
ator 1941-1947—*419
MURRAY, WILLIAM H., 6
Muscle Shoals project, 17, 226, 550
MUSSOLINI, BENITO, 464-465, 626

N

NASH, PHILIP C., 208
NASH, PAT, 8, 36, 463, 494, 520, 564
The Nation, 356
National Compliance Board, 210
National Emergency Council, 197-198,
242
National Forest Reservation Commis-
sion, 36, 52, 574

National Forest Service, 21-24, 151, 254,
258-259, 281, 350, 386, 523, 527, 534-
535, 569, 583-584, 598, 601
national forests, 52; in Puerto Rico, 504
National Industrial Council, 201
National Industrial Recovery Act, 29;
signed by Roosevelt, 53; Deputy Administrators under, 100; constitutionality of, 94, 100; declared unconstitutional, 54, 372-374; as amended, 424:
see also Hugh Johnson, Supreme Court
decision
National Industrial Recovery Board, 61,
101, 208-209, 220, 289-290
NRA: *see* National Industrial Recovery
Act
NRA code authorities, 53
NRA codes, 53; coal code, 25, 91-92; oil
code, 13; textile code, 60; violations
of, 101, 141: *see also* oil code
NRA Policy Committee, 220
NRA propaganda, 93
NRA, reorganization of, 197
national parks, 123, 278, 522-523, 574, 576
National Park Service, 4, 16, 21-23, 123,
251
National Planning Board, 136, 171-172,
216, 281, 341; *see also* National Re-
sources Board
National Power Policy Committee, 174
National Press Club, 13, 14, 203, 678
National Resources Board, 172, 219, 354,
491
National Teachers Federation, 671
Navy, building projects for, 111, 216-217
Navy Department, 417: *see also* Admiral
Peoples, Claude Swanson
Negroes, activities for, 16; in Virgin
Islands, 60-61; slum clearance for, 211-
212, 473; housing projects for, 674;
campaign meeting for, 680, 689; turn-
out for Roosevelt, 689
Neutrality Bill, 473, 483, 514, 533-534
New Deal, changes in Interior Depart-
ment under, 4; men in initial legisla-
tion of, 9; gibes at, 212, 242; Wallace
and Ickes on, 218; Supreme Court
decision on, 274; appointment of men
loyal to, 360; Perkins on, 524; Frank
Kent on, 559; Dickinson on, 600; Frank
Knox on, 653, 702; Talmadge on, 675;
Landon on, 702
"New Dealers, The," 147

New Democracy (Harold Ickes), 196-197, 199, 218
New Leader, The, 109
New Mexico, Democrats in, 359
New Republic, 497, 637
Newspaper correspondents, Roosevelt on, 560
Newspaper Guild, 637-638
New York American, 651, 660
New York Daily Worker, 492-493
New York Herald Tribune, 260-261, 279, 362, 654, 670
New York Daily News, 484, 623, 670
New York Post Office, contract for, 294, 296-297
New York Times, The, 9, 32, 220, 230-231, 261, 350, 476, 527, 618, 654, 670, 688
NILES, DAVID, 363
NORBECK, PETER, 419
NORCROSS, T. W., 174
NORMAN, MONTAGU, 83
NORRIS, GEORGE W. *(1861-1944), Representative (Rep.) from Nebraska 1903-1913; Senator from 1913 to 1943; he was the leader for a generation of the movement for public power, and the first dam built by TVA, of which he was the legislative father, was named Norris Dam*—15, 32, 119, 247, 359, 363, 532, 588, 613, 683
Norris, Tennessee, 225
Norris Dam, 225
North Platte River, use of waters of, 98
NOYES, FRANK B. *(1863-1948), newspaper publisher; president of Washington Evening Star 1910-1947; director of executive committee, president and finally honorary president of the Associated Press from 1894 until his death* —637-638
NYE, GERALD P. *(1892-   ), Senator (Rep.) from North Dakota 1925-1945, a leader of Progressives within the Republican party, and chairman of committees investigating Teapot Dome and the munitions industry*—419, 490-491, 655-656, 661, 663, 665, 692, 698
Nye Investigating Committee, 473, 515

O

O'CONNOR, JOHN T. *(1885-   ), Representative (Dem.) from New York 1923-

1939 and chairman of the House Rules Committee; now publisher of the Washington News Digest—536, 601, 604
O'DAY, CAROLINE, 356
Of Thee I Sing, 105
Ogden, Utah, 213
Ogdenburg Bridge, 385
oil, East Texas, 31, 142, 159, 218; leases, in Wyoming, 38; price fixing of, 85-86, 95, 97-99, 101, 106-107; California, 157, 307; Japan, 192; Federal control of, 413; exports, to Italy, 472, 476-477
oil, "hot," 13, 94, 142, 159, 164, 218, 306-307
Oil Administration, 101, 170, 221, 233, 237, 309, 649, 653, 664
oil bill, 36-37, 39, 41-42, 44, 46-47, 158, 164, 169, 374, 383, 414: *see also* Cole oil bill, Connally oil bill, General Industries Bill, Thomas oil bill
oil case, Supreme Court decision on, 273
oil code, 13, 73, 81-82, 85, 94, 141
Oil Committee, 84-86, 95, 98, 102
oil conference, 9; recommendations of, 11-12; results of, 14; Roosevelt's action on recommendations, 15-16
Oil Conservation Board, 15
oil industry, Government controls in, 13, 26, 29, 31-32; powers of Secretary of Interior in, 40; interstate commerce in, 65; Planning and Coordination Committee in, 107
oil production, curtailing, 6; allocation of, 86; crude, 155, 164
Okeechobee, Lake, 321-322
O'LEARY, JEREMIAH, 685
OLIPHANT, HERMAN, 404
Olney Inn, 77
O'MAHONEY, JOSEPH C. *(1884-   ), Assistant Postmaster General 1933; Senator (Dem.) from Wyoming 1934-1952; now in private law practice*—54, 129, 286, 302, 318, 340, 379-380
ONSLOW, 344
Order No. 129, 307, 309, 317: *see also* Robert Moses
OSTHAGEN, 237
OUMANSKY, CONSTANTIN *(1902-1945), Soviet diplomat; Ambassador to U.S. 1939-1941; succeeded by Litvinov under whom he had served at time of recognition*—117, 691

OWEN, RUTH BRYAN (MRS. BORGE ROHDE) (*1885-*), *Representative (Dem.) from Florida 1929-1933; Minister to Denmark 1933-1936; alternate U.S. representative to U.N. 1949—*5, 6, 30, 245

P

Pacific Gas & Electric Company, 357, 563
ʼALMER, A. MITCHELL (*1872-1936*), *Representative (Rep.) from Pennsylvania 1909-1915; Alien Property Custodian 1917-1919; U.S. Attorney General 1919-1921—*35, 563
Panama, Republic of, 453
Panama Canal, 151, 453, 455
Panama City, 455
Pan American Building, 283
Pan American Conference, 704
Pan American Union, 7, 485
Parks, National: *see* National Park Service
Passamaquoddy power project, 189, 333, 513-514, 542-543, 654, 676
patents, pooling of, 353
PATMAN, WRIGHT, 356
PATTERSON, MRS. ELEANOR MEDILL ("CISSY") (*1884-1948*), *was the sister of Joseph M. Patterson, publisher of the* New York Daily News, *and the cousin of Colonel Robert R. McCormick, publisher of the* Chicago Tribune. *After having leased the* Washington Times *and the* Washington Herald *from Hearst, she bought them and merged them into a single paper. Its editorial policies were strongly anti-New Deal*—43-44, 60, 134, 195, 440, 468, 484, 492, 500, 559, 616, 622, 647-648, 649-651, 657, 659-660, 662, 665-666, 674-675, 693, 696
PATTERSON, JOSEPH MEDILL, 484-485, 559, 623, 647-648, 665, 696
patronage, 9, 20, 47, 75, 143
PEABODY, GEORGE FOSTER, 83
PEARSON, DREW (*1897-*), *newspaper correspondent and columnist and radio commentator since 1922; son of Paul M. Pearson and former son-in-law of Mrs. Eleanor M. Patterson*—61, 77, 269, 391, 408
PEARSON, PAUL M. (*1871-1938*), *Governor of Virgin Islands 1931-1935; then assistant director of the housing division*

of PWA—61, 77, 83, 156-157, 298, 384, 396, 401-403, 405-406, 407, 408, 507: *see also* Governor of Virgin Islands
PECORA, FERDINAND, 411
PEEK, GEORGE M. (*1873-1943*), *in agricultural implements business until his appointment as AAA administrator in 1933; adviser to Export-Import Bank 1934-1935*—18, 108, 360
PEERY, GEORGE C., 629
Pennsylvania Railroad, electrification of, 81,115-116, 282
PEOPLES, ADMIRAL CHRISTIAN JOY (*1876-1941*), *Paymaster General of U.S. Navy and chief of the bureau of supplies and accounts of the Navy Department 1933-1935; director of Procurement Division, U.S. Treasury, 1933-1939; general inspector of supply corps for Pacific Coast 1939-1941*—221, 244, 254, 264-265, 288-289, 292-293, 295, 299, 311, 327, 351, 365, 410, 417: *see also* Procurement Division
PERKINS, FRANCES (*1882-*), *Industrial Commissioner of New York State 1929-1933; Secretary of Labor 1933-1945; member of U.S. Civil Service Commission 1945-1953*—3, 7, 10, 27-28, 34, 37, 53-54, 80, 111, 135, 142, 152, 171, 194, 198, 248, 277, 289, 293, 407, 471-472, 482, 484, 491, 496, 524, 537, 544, 569, 632, 694, 697, 700, 703
Perlas Islands, 454
Peruvian Ambassador, 320-321
PETER, MADAME, 305
Petroleum Administrative Board, 309
Petroleum Code: *see* oil code, NRA codes
Petroleum Conservation Division, 13
PEW, J. HOWARD (*1882-*), *oil man; president of the Sun Oil Co. 1912-1947; active in Pennsylvania Republican politics*—81
Philadelphia and Reading Railroad, 116
Philadelphia Board of Trade, 115
Philadelphia Record, 674-675
philately: *see* stamp collectors
Philippine Islands, proposed independence for, 145
PHILLIPS, WILLIAM (*1878-*), *diplomat; chief of mission during 1920's to Belgium, the Netherlands, and Canada; Under-Secretary of State 1933; U.S.*

Ambassador to Italy 1936-1941—125, 544-545

PICKETT, CLARENCE E., 154

PINCHOT, GIFFORD *(1865-1945), first professional forester and Chief Forester of U.S. 1898-1910; Governor of Pennsylvania 1923-1927 and 1931-1935; a leader in the conservation movement, as well as in the Progressive faction within the Republican party*—17, 22, 63, 91, 163, 202-203, 207-208, 615

PINCHOT, MRS. GIFFORD, 160, 207-208

PITTMAN, KEY *(1872-1940), Senator (Dem.) from Nevada 1913-1940; president pro tem of Senate in 73rd to 76th Congresses; chairman of Senate Foreign Relations Committee 1933*—101-102, 105, 302, 399, 490, 658

Planning and Coordination Committee: *see* oil industry

Planning Board: *see* National Planning Board

Planning Boards, State, 341

Platt Amendment, 93: *see also* Cuba

polls, *Literary Digest*, 603; "America Speaks," 635, 641; private, 640

Poole, 169

Porto Bello, 455-456

POST, LANGDON, 276, 308, 317, 500

post office, new buildings, 103, 110, 114; appropriations for, 168: *see also* New York Post Office

Post Office Department, 103, 147, 199, 295

Postmaster General, 202

Potomac, 629

power, cheap, Roosevelt on, 226

power, electric, for San Francisco, 215

power projects, municipal, 247; Roosevelt's attitude toward, 248

POWERS, THE REVEREND WILLIAM H., 689

press conferences, Hopkins', 257, 433; Ickes', 13, 88, 119, 230, 235, 345-346, 470, 476, 664, 669; Moffett's, 231; Morgenthau's, 691; Roosevelt's, 9, 371.

PRESSMAN, LEE, 436

PRICE, RICHARD, 180

price fixing: *see* price fixing of oil

prices, commodity, 109

primary elections, in Illinois, 556; in Michigan, 681; in Massachusetts, 681

Procurement Division, of Treasury Department, 221-222, 249, 251, 254, 264, 295, 299, 302: *see also* Morgenthau, Admiral Peoples

Progress Committees, of work-relief organization, 311, 328

Progressive League, 532

Progressive Republicans, 129, 150, 214, 217, 300, 643, 647, 655, 663, 668, 678, 700

Progressives, 300, 342, 661, 674, 690

propaganda in U.S., NRA, 93; German, 111; communist, 430

Public Buildings and Public Parks, Office of, 72

Public Health Service, 265

Public Lands Committee, of House, 49, 326

public range, grazing on, 49, 66, 143, 148

Public Roads, Bureau of, 56, 250, 281, 436

Public Works Administration, 29, 96, 101, 130, 134-136, 168, 193, 228, 286-287; for 1935, 289, 312, 319, 330, 335-336, 424, 589, 600, 607, 620

Public Works Administrator, provided for in bill, 34, 37; temporary, 54-55; for states, 57, 59; regional, 59; Ickes as, 55, 60, 130, 265, 276, 286-287, 351; Ickes threatens to resign as, 290-291, 337-338, 424-426, 546; Ickes resigns as, 590, 592, 609

PWA amendment: *see* Work Relief Bill

public works appropriations, 166, 168, 173, 188-189, 200-201, 203, 252, 255, 257, 436, 488, 588, 620

Public Works Bill, discussion of, 5, 7, 14; first draft of, 28; appropriation for, 34; reclamation in, 40; new bills for 1935, 275-277, 290; McCarran amendment, 302: *see also* Public Works and Industrial Control Bill, Industries Control Bill, Public Works and Business Control Bill

Public Works Board, 56, 62-63, 66-69, 70-71, 74, 81; plan for new, 288; in England, 289

Public Works and Business Control Bill, 36: *see also* Public Works Bill

Public Works and Industrial Control Bill, 37; Johnson and, 51-52: *see also* Public Works Bill

public works fund, 85, 116, 156, 257; allocation to Aeronautics Bureau, 142-143; to Army and Navy, 302; applica-

public works fund (*continued*)
tions for, 424, 656, 600; administered by Roosevelt, 474; earmarking WPA fund for, 488, 490, 565, 567, 570-571, 575, 577-579; Senate appropriation for, 588; Roosevelt threatens to veto, 589

public works organization, Johnson's place in, 53; plan for, 56; Farley and, 67; in states, 54, 57, 74-75; mayors' resolutions for, 100; work relief and, 119-120; strengthening of, 129-130; end of State Advisory Boards, 146; McNary on, 282; Roosevelt's plan for, 311

public works policy, Ickes and, 73; change in, 257; power grants and, 482-483; in first program, 497

public works program, first suggested, 21; Cabinet committee on, 27; list of public works for, 28; headed by Ickes, 55, 60; work of Bureau of Public Roads in, 56; state administrators under, 57; administrator of, 59; regional administrators under, 59; setting up, 67; mayors' attitude toward, 96-100; end of state organizations under, 146; for 1935-1936, 203-206; J. P. Kennedy on, 206; non-self-liquidating projects under, 216; bad publicity for, 217; Army and Navy building under 216-217; Hopkins and, 223-224, 228; 1935 plans for, 239, 255-257, 264, 275-276, 281-282, 289-292, 310, 315, 318, 320, 383; wage scale in, 248, 287; Morgenthau and, 239; sabotaged by Hopkins, 426-427, 433-434, 436-438, 496-497; indirect employment in, 438, 589, 592, 595; presented to Roosevelt, 442; Roosevelt's plan for, 546; man-year costs under, 556; repudiated by Roosevelt, 575; cost of, 580-582; financing, 600; saved by Senate, 611, 620; benefits of, 623; criticism of Roosevelt on, 656; slowdown of, 664; Landon and, 684

public works projects, first list, 28; and relief projects, 28-29; approved by Roosevelt, 62-63, 66, 71-72, 83, 102-103, 188, 537, 673, 697; Army list, 71, 111, 216; security for, 148; Columbia River, 72; national plan for, 145; financing, 156; in New York City, 228; power plants, 247, unemployed on, 252; in new bill, 310-311; versus work-relief projects, 257, 386; non-Federal, 290-

291, 333, 371, 383, 622, 686, 689; in Louisiana, 401, 427; Hopkins and, 409-414; application for, 420; in Atlanta, 409, 422, 427; Hopkins veto of, 427-428, 433-434, 437; foreign material used in, 470; pressure for money for, 473, 537; surveys for, 491; delay in construction on, 574-575; relief labor on, 628, 662, 667; power plant in Camden, N.J., 675-676; Landon and, 684

Puerto Rico, 151, 157, 436-437, 502-508, 547, 594

PURYEAR, EDGAR, 359, 415, 601, 604

PYNCHON, CHARLES, *general manager of the Subsistence Homestead Division of the Department of the Interior in 1934*—205-206, 218-219, 272, 443, 473, 486

Q

Queens Midtown Tunnel, New York City, 498

R

RABINOWITZ, 103

RADCLIFFE, GEORGE L., 400, 554

Railroad Commission, 142

railroads, Government purchases of rails for, 115

RAINEY, HENRY T. (*1860-1934*), *Representative (Dem.) from Illinois 1903-1921 and 1923-1934; Democratic leader of House and speaker-elect in 1933*—3, 137

Raker Act, 315, 357, 563

Rangers Club, 177

RANKIN, JOHN, 419

Rapidan Camp: *see* Hoover Camp

RASKOB, JOHN J., 690

RAYBURN, SAM (*1882-   ), Representative (Dem.) from Texas since 1913; majority leader in 75th and 76th Congresses; speaker of House 1940-1952*—169, 263, 400, 474, 491-492, 682

Raymond Concrete Pile Company, 469

Reclamation Bureau, 4, 163, 250-251, 584, 497

reclamation projects, in Wyoming, 39-40; for Utah, 114; WPA funds for, 436-437

Reconstruction Finance Corporation, 22, 156, 166, 168, 342, 383, 582, 593, 595, 600: *see also* Jesse Jones

Red River project, 474, 491

REED, DAVID A., 161, 202-203, 207
REED, JIM, 703
REED, STANLEY, 705
Reedsville, West Virginia, subsistence homestead project, 129, 152, 154, 162-163, 205, 207, 218, 227, 260, 266-267
Regional Advisers, for public works, 146
REID, OGDEN, 144
REINECKE, MABEL, 463, 638
REISNER, CHRISTIAN F., 361
relief rolls, getting men off, 248, 358, 360-361, 366, 387-388, 628
relief work, plan for, 116-117; funds for, 188, 200, 256; investigation of, 277, 287
Republican campaign, candidates in, 467, 480, 617, 653; plans for, 643, 645; platform, 615-618; speakers for, 678
Republican National Convention, 613, 616
Republican party, 30, 294, 441, 614
revenue bill, amendment of, 160, 591
REYNOLDS, ARTHUR, 179
REYNOLDS, ROBERT, 362, 365-366, 419
RICHBERG, DONALD R. (*1881-*), lawyer; former partner of Ickes in Chicago; counsel to NRA 1933-1935 and chairman in 1935; special assistant to Attorney General 1935; executive director National Emergency Council 1934-1935; in private practice since 1936—6, 34, 84-85, 87, 91, 94, 198, 208-211, 219-221, 242, 245, 247-248, 254, 259, 264, 276, 289, 293, 313-314, 348, 374-376, 378, 566
RICHEY, LAWRENCE, 30
ROA, SEÑOR DR. DON FERNANDO GONZALEZ, 7, 35
ROBERT, LAWRENCE W., JR. (*1889-*), Assistant Secretary of Treasury in charge of public works 1933-1936; secretary of Democratic National Committee 1936-1941—54, 56-57, 60, 66, 71, 74, 81, 88, 179, 295, 314, 398, 518-519, 665
ROBERTS, OWEN, 273, 524, 536
ROBINS, ELIZABETH, 464
ROBINS, RAYMOND (*1873-*), social economist and businessman who was in charge of American Red Cross in Russia at time of Bolshevik revolution and traveled in U.S.S.R. in 1933 prior to recognition; active in Progressive party under Theodore Roosevelt and

its candidate for Senator from Illinois in 1914; deeded Chinsegut Hill Sanctuary in Florida to Department of Agriculture in 1932—62-63, 381
ROBINSON, JOSEPH T. (*1872-1937*), Representative (Dem.) from Arkansas 1903-1913; Governor of Arkansas, 1913; Senator from Arkansas 1913 until his death; Democratic majority leader 1933-1937—19, 39, 114, 294, 299, 302, 313-314, 333, 336, 363, 396, 400, 403, 418-419, 517-518, 568, 596, 605, 621, 623, 626
ROBINSON, 483
ROBOTTOM, commander of the *Houston*, 454
ROCHE, JOSEPHINE (*1882-*), Assistant Secretary of Treasury 1934-1937; member of Colorado advisory board PWA 1933-1934; director of Rocky Mountain Fuel Co. since 1927—248, 292
ROCKEFELLER, JOHN D., JR. (*1874-*), philanthropist; director or trustee of various Rockefeller foundations and philanthropies since 1901, and especially interested in conservation and the National Parks—176, 278, 630
ROGERS, AGNES A., 501
ROGERS, LINDSAY, 116
ROGERS, WILL, 419
ROLPH, JAMES A., JR. (*1869-1934*), Mayor of San Francisco 1911-1932; Governor of California 1931-1934—6
ROOSEVELT, ELLIOTT, 119, 160, 566, 632-633, 691-692
ROOSEVELT, FRANKLIN, **activities of,** at Hoover Camp, 18; at White House dinner, 26; on yacht, 50-51; on *Indianapolis*, 58; at breakfast, 61; on *Sequoia*, 65-66; at CCC camp, 78; driving his car, 78, 127; with his family, 80, 184; at Hyde Park, 83-84, 435; on vacation, 86; at Warm Springs, 126-127, 238-239; at hospital to see Ickes, 132; fishing, 158, 449, 452; on *Houston*, 182, 444-461; at a party, 240; at Gridiron Club dinners, 161, 242, 485, 559-560; at press conferences, 9, 371; at Ickes' home, 537, 633-635; at Democratic National Convention, 625; at Smoky Mountain National Park, 628-630; at Williamsburg, Va., 630; at Triborough Bridge dedication, 636; in

ROOSEVELT, FRANKLIN (*continued*)
Nova Scotia, 642; on the Potomac, 677-680; at Syracuse University, 689; at Polo Grounds, N.Y., 689; at Jersey City Medical School dedication, 689; at Chicago Stadium, 694; at Madison Square Garden, 701; **personality of**, tactful, 19, 144, 354; amenable, 49; good humor, 40, 72, 145, 156, 244, 250, 287, 593; urbanity, 50; intimacy with crowds, 78; human, 79, 155, 422; wide range of interests, 79; keen mind, 79, 394; companionable, 79, 240; friendliness, 90, 122, 138, 155, 166, 174, 236, 240, 309, 311, 346, 467, 520, 628; cheerful, 103, 156, 160, 394, 442, 449, 479, 628; leadership, 104; understanding, 122, 155, 394; kindness, 122, 138; sympathy, 131, 133, 144, 165, 174, 256, 431; social consciousness, 264; makes own decisions, 308, 326, 331; simplicity, 132, 421-422; unreliability, 605-606; vision, 166, 206; charm, 421-422; **acts and opinions of**, policy of interstate commerce on oil, 16; on stabilizing currency, 23; signs National Recovery Act, 53; on price situation, 90; opposes veterans' bonus, 104; land policy, 105; in recognition of Russia, 111, 113; economy program, 158; on cheap power and electrification, 226, 248; on holding companies, 244; proposes transcontinental highway, 244; social consciousness of, 264; *public works:* approves projects, 62-63, 66, 83, 102-103, 188, 537, 673, 697; administers funds, 474, 589; repudiates program, 565, 575; *work relief:* plans for organization, 255, 340-341, 345-346, 546, 589; committed to, 496-497; decline in popularity, 304-305, 316; on taxation, 383-384; *Supreme Court:* proposes new legislation, 273-274; suggests constitutional amendment, 467-468, 529-530; Neutrality Bill, 514; on his own Administration, 533; *Democratic campaign:* plans for, 562; on election fight, 618; acceptance speech, 625-627; attitude toward, 644-645; speeches in, 662-663, 672-673, 686, 689-690, 693-695, 700-701

ROOSEVELT, MRS. FRANKLIN D., 18, 27, 54-55, 83, 129, 154, 156, 162, 176-177, 182, 184, 201, 205, 207, 218-219, 227-228, 237-238, 249, 252-255, 261-262, 266-267, 270-271, 285, 356, 397-398, 402, 432, 441-442, 444, 561, 586, 597-598, 640, 645, 703

ROOSEVELT, FRANKLIN, JR., 174, 184
ROOSEVELT, HENRY L., 58, 540
ROOSEVELT, JAMES, 182, 184, 238, 359, 692
ROOSEVELT, MRS. JAMES, 238, 240
ROOSEVELT, JOHN, 18, 541-542
ROOSEVELT, THEODORE, 22, 78, 361, 363, 533, 633, 685
Roosevelt Administration, attacks on, 30, 82-83, 108, 212, 217, 219, 278-279, 471
ROOT, ELIHU, 533, 633, 685
ROPER, DANIEL C. (*1867-1943*), *Assistant Postmaster General 1913-1916; Commissioner of Internal Revenue 1917-1920; Secretary of Commerce 1933-1938; Minister to Canada 1939—3*, 24, 37, 41, 48, 51, 53-54, 58-60, 72, 75, 100, 110, 112, 125, 129, 147, 244, 284, 400, 415-416, 432, 470-471, 533, 542-543, 624, 632, 656
ROSENBERG, MOE, 150, 153
ROSENWALD, JULIUS, 47
ROSS, SIR CHARLES, 313
ROSS, MARGARET, 377-378
ROSSI, ANGELO JOSEPH (*1878-1948*), *Mayor of San Francisco 1931-1944—*178, 213
ROSSO, AMBASSADOR, 472
ROWE, DR. LEO S. (*1871-1946*), *director of the Pan American Union from 1920 until his death—*8, 485
ROWELL, CHESTER, 214
Royal Dutch Petroleum Company, 192
rum distillery, Virgin Islands, 508
rural electrification, 226
Rural Resettlement, 475
Russia, recognition of, 111, 113, 118; possible break with, 428, 430; propaganda in U.S., 430; U.S. Government sympathies for, 657
Russian Embassy, dinner at, 332

S

SABATH, ADOLPH J., 667
St. Croix, Virgin Islands, 508
St. Elizabeths Hospital, 4, 265
St. Lawrence Treaty, 8
St. Louis Post-Dispatch, 687-688
St. Thomas, Virgin Islands, 506-508
SAITO, HIROSI, 320

salmon, in Columbia River, 183-184
San Blas Bay, 456-458
San Blas Indians, 456-458
San Francisco Chronicle, 214
Sanitary District, Chicago, 124, 215
San Juan, Puerto Rico, 504
Santee-Cooper project, 443, 488-490, 498
Saratoga Battlefield, 576
Saturday Evening Post, 227, 563, 619, 630, 663
Saunders estate case, 64, 89-90
SAWYER, COLONEL DONALD H. *(1879-1941), director Federal Employment Stabilization Board 1931-1936; director Procurement Division of U.S. Treasury 1936-1939*—54-55, 59
Schecter case, 54
SCHLESINGER, ELMER, 650
SCHLEY, JULIAN L., 454-455
SCHLEY, MRS. JULIAN L., 456
SCHNEIDER, MRS., 444
SCHNEPFE, FRED E., 286, 410, 486
School conditions, in depression, 26, 142: *see also* Chicago teachers, unemployed teachers
SCOYEN, EIVIND T., 186
SCRUGHAM, JAMES G. *(1880-1945), Representative (Dem.) from Nevada 1933-1943; Senator 1942 until his death*—276, 419
Securities Exchange Commission, 173, 203
Seminole Indians, 321-324
Sequoia, 65
sequoias, 176
SEUBERT, EDWARD, 81
SEYFULLAH, IBRAHIM, 430-431
Shenandoah National Park, 78, 123, 629-630
SHERMAN, E. A., 364
SHIPSTEAD, HENRIK *(1881-   ), Senator (Rep.) from Minnesota 1923-1947*—300, 415, 420-521
SHOLTZ, DAVE, 4
SHOUSE, JOUETT, 518
SHUTTS, COLONEL FRANK B., 502, 509
SILCOX, FERDINAND A. *(1882-1939), Chief of the U.S. Forest Service from 1933 until his death*—169, 364, 598, 604
SILLS, KENNETH, 190
silver, price of, 484
SIMMS, ALBERT GALLATIN, 622
SIMMS, RUTH MCCORMICK, 622

SINCLAIR, HARRY F. *(1876-   ), oil man who leased Teapot Dome properties through Albert B. Fall; served three months in prison for contempt of U.S. Senate but was acquitted in 1928 of charges of conspiracy and fraud*—22, 82, 84, 548
SINCLAIR, UPTON, 217
SIROVICH, WILLIAM I. *(1882-1939), doctor and Representative (Dem.) from New York 1927-1939*—262-263, 353, 499-500, 571, 699
SKELLY, W. G., 81
Skelly Oil Company, 81
Skokie Valley property, 155
SKVIRSKY, BORIS E., *official of Amtorg, Soviet trading agency in the U.S. before diplomatic recognition of Soviet Union; later served in Soviet Commissariat of Foreign Affairs and disappeared in the 1936-7 purge in Moscow*—113-114
Skyline Drive, Blue Ridge Mountains, 78
SLATTERY, HARRY *(1887-1949), personal assistant to Ickes in Department of Interior 1933-1938; Under Secretary of Interior 1938-1939*—34, 64, 77, 207, 216, 246-247, 262, 279, 304, 314, 319, 325, 339-340, 369, 411, 415, 419, 424, 516, 565, 567, 590-591, 679, 694, 696
Slaughter, Anderson and Fox, 120-122, 137-138, 204
SLEP, DAN, 376
SLOAN, ALFRED D., JR., 524
slum clearance program, in Atlanta, 199-200; allocations for, 206, 383; in Chicago, 211-212; Morgenthau and, 239; in Cincinnati, 473
SMART, O. B., 266-267, 271
SMITH, ALFRED E. *(1873-1944), Governor of New York 1919-1920 and 1923-1928; Democratic candidate for President in 1928; later president of company owning Empire State Building and by 1936 a bitter opponent of President Roosevelt*—128, 148, 308, 317, 516-518, 525-527, 533, 664, 685, 687-689, 690, 693-694, 699, 703
SMITH, BLACKWELL, 378
SMITH, ELLISON D., 164, 418, 552
SMITH, JAMES G., 369
SMITH, JAMES MONROE, 400

Smoky Mountain National Park, 123, 677
SMOOT, REED, 21
SNELL, BERTRAND, 385, 544, 649
Social Security Act, 383, 638
Social Security Administration, 484
Soil Erosion Control, Division of, 250, 259, 325, 327, 339, 343, 398
Solicitor General, 66, 67, 71, 88
SONSTEBY, JOHN, 520-521
South American conference, Hull in, 118
Soviet Union: *see* Russia
Spain, civil war in, 655-656
Spartanburg, N.C., county power project, 482
Special Board for Public Works: *see* Public Works Board
Special Industrial Board: *see* National Industrial Recovery Board
Special Industrial Recovery Board: *see* National Industrial Recovery Board
stamp collectors, 16, 25, 117, 305, 415, 691
Standard Oil Company of Indiana, 39, 81; of New Jersey, 39, 52, 81, 141, 146, 158, 192, 234; of California, 97
STANDLEY, ADMIRAL WILLIAM H., 545
STANNARD, AMY, 405
STARLING, COLONEL, of Secret Service, 238
State Advisory Committees, for public works, 74, 146
State, Department of, 192, 428, 515: *see also* Cordell Hull
Steagall bill, 41
steel, German, in WPA projects, 466, 469-472
STEELE-MAITLAND, SIR ARTHUR, 114
STEWER, FREDERICK, 419, 548
STEPHENS, JUDGE, 307
STERN, J. DAVID (*1886-   ), newspaper publisher; publisher Philadelphia Record 1928-1947 and of New York Post 1933-1939—674-675*
Stewart and Company, James, 294, 297, 299
STONE, FRED, 206
STONE, HARLAN FISKE (*1872-1946), Associate Justice of the Supreme Court 1925-1941; Chief Justice 1941 until his death—273, 614, 705*
STONE, MRS. HARLAN F., 353
STONE, of Blackfeet Indian Agency, 186
STRACHEY, JOHN, 354-355
STRAUS, ISIDOR, 660
STRAUS, MICHAEL W. (*1897-   ), news-*

paperman; Washington correspondent Universal News Service 1932-1933; director of information PWA 1933-1938; director of information Department of Interior 1938-1941; U.S. Commissioner of Reclamation 1945-1952—56, 166, 190, 204, 231-233, 279, 283, 286, 304, 369, 426, 479, 499, 501-502, 512, 526, 590, 623, 672, 675, 694-695
STRAUS, MRS. MICHAEL, 56-57
STRAUS, NATHAN (*1889-   ), business executive; member of New York State Senate 1921-1926; administrator U.S. Housing Authority 1937-1942; president radio station WMCA—608*
STRAWN, SILAS, 369
STRONG, GORDON, 539
STUDEBAKER, JOHN W., 409
subsistence farm program, 62, 70
subsistence homesteads, methods of organization, 159; program, 162-163; executive of, 206; 218, 226, 228, 252, 265; in England, 288, 309-310; in Puerto Rico, 505
Subsistence Homesteads Corporation, 129, 288
Subsistence Homesteads Division, executive of, 206, 218, 227, 250, 265, 272-273
sugar cane, in Virgin Islands, 508
sugar pine grove, Yosemite National Park, 176-177
SULLIVAN, JOHN J., 564
SULLIVAN, MARK, 645
Sun Oil Company, 81
Supervising Architect's Office, 281
Supreme Court, increase of justices on, 274; political issue, 372-373; attitude on New Deal legislation, 467-468, 494-495, 524, 530-531; constitutional amendment to change, 468, 602; Ickes on, 524; Roosevelt's plan for, 529-532; philosophy of, 602; after election, 705
Supreme Court decisions, in Appalachian Coals case, 21; against Guffey-Snyder Coal Act, 25; in Schecter case, 54; in gold certificates case, 273, 294; on NRA, 54, 124; on Federal Trade Commission, 374; ways of preventing unfavorable, 495; in AAA case, 515
SWANSON, CLAUDE AUGUSTUS (*1862-1939), Representative (Dem.) from Virginia 1893-1905; Governor of Virginia 1906-1910; Senator from Virginia 1910-1933;*

Secretary of the Navy *1933 until his death*—58, 125, 132, 151, 158, 548, 620, 632, 677, 697

SWANSON, MRS. CLAUDE A., 27

SWEENEY, MARTIN L., 538-539

Swiss Legation, dinner at, 305

SWOPE, GERARD (*1872-*), *president of General Electric Co. 1922-1939 and now honorary president; advisory member of many New Deal agencies including NRA industrial advisory board, Coal Arbitration Board, National Labor Board and Advisory Council on Social Security*—52, 356, 690

SWOPE, HERBERT, 650, 652

Syracuse University, WPA loan to, 686

SZE, AMBASSADOR, 306

SZE, MADAME, 306, 320

T

TAFT, WILLIAM H., 22

TALMADGE, EUGENE (*1884-1946*), *Governor of Georgia 1933-1937 and 1940-1943*—200, 532-533, 675

Tamiami Trail, 323

TAPLIN, F. E., 24

TAUSSIG, CHARLES W., 9

taxation, Roosevelt on, 383-384; treatment of, by Ickes, 422; political issue, 652

TAYLOR, AUBREY, 433

TAYLOR, EDWARD T. (*1858-1941*), *Representative (Dem.) from Colorado 1909-1941; majority leader in 1935; author of Taylor Grazing Act*—259

TAYLOR, GRAHAM, 367

Taylor Grazing Act, 170: *see also* Taylor Grazing Control Bill

Taylor Grazing Control Bill, 49, 143, 148, 169, 172

teachers, pay of, in Chicago, 23, 26; unemployed, 142; political force, 409

TEAGLE, WALTER C. (*1878-*), *president Standard Oil Co. of New Jersey 1917-1937, chairman of the board 1937-1942*—11, 39, 52, 141, 146, 158, 192

Teapot Dome, 23

Tender Board, 218, 307: *see also* oil in East Texas

Tennessee Development Bill, 32

Tennessee Valley Authority, 62, 225-226, 536-537, 566-567: *see also* Arthur Morgan

Tennessee Valley project, 15, 119, 225, 566

Territories and Island Possessions, Division of, 4

Texas Company, 158

textile industry, code for, 60

Third World Power Conference, 676

THOMAS, ELBERT D. (*1883-*), *professor of political science at University of Utah since 1924; Senator (Dem.) from Utah 1933-1951*—20-21

THOMAS, ELMER 49-50

Thomas oil bill, 415-416, 418

THOMPSON, WILLIAM H., 51

THOMPSON, WILLIAM HALE (*1869-1944*), *Chicago real estate man and politician; Mayor of Chicago 1915-1923 and 1927-1931*—245-246

THOMPSON, COLONEL, 177

TINGLEY, CLYDE, 491

Tobacco Road, 553

Today, 375

TOMLINSON, OWEN A., 181-182

Tortola, Virgin Islands, 507

TOWNSEND, JOHN G., 286, 419

TOWNSEND, DR., 352

Trans-Florida Canal, 488-490, 502, 514, 541

Treasury Department, 76, 103, 140, 222, 265, 279, 331, 426, 484, 525, 691: *see also* Henry Morgenthau, Jr.

TRESIDDER, DONALD B., 177

Triborough Bridge, 84, 269, 309, 466, 636-637

Triborough Bridge Authority, 148, 229, 263, 267, 291, 466, 623, 636-637

Tri-County of Nebraska project, 442

TROUT family, 190

TROY, JOHN WEIR (*1868-1942*), *Governor of Alaska 1933-1939*—5

TROYANOVSKY, MADAME, 332

TUCKER, RAY, 108, 548

TUGWELL, REXFORD G. (*1891-*), *professor of economics at Columbia University; Assistant Secretary of Agriculture in 1933 and one of the original "brain trust"; Under-Secretary of Agriculture 1934-1937; Governor of Puerto Rico 1941-1946; since then professor at University of Chicago*—9, 34, 66, 77, 112, 164-165, 169, 194, 238, 240-241, 250, 292-293, 302-303, 310-311, 337, 351-352, 410, 420, 423, 428-429, 436,

TUGWELL, REXFORD G. (*continued*)
474-475, 486, 534-535, 580, 583, 602, 610, 646, 692

TULLY, GRACE, *assistant private secretary to President Roosevelt 1928-1945*—250, 444, 512, 527, 634, 677, 679-680, 687

Tupelo, Mississippi, subsistence homestead project in, 226

Turkish Embassy, dinner at, 125

TUTTLE, ARTHUR, 500

TYDINGS, MILLARD E. (*1890-   ), Representative (Dem.) from Maryland 1923-1927; Senator 1927-1951; now in private law practice*—91, 332, 345, 362, 389-397, 399, 400, 402-408, 411, 423-424: *see also* Virgin Islands

U

unemployed, on Florida agricultural lands, 4; Government purchase of butter for, 109; Public Works plan for, 117

unemployment, in Pennsylvania, 81; in New York and New Jersey, 85; public works and, 496; Hearst, Jr., on, 651

unemployment bill, 5, 7, 14: *see also* public works bill

Union Station, Washington, D.C., 676-677

United Mine Workers of America, coal bill of, 33, 91: *see also* John Lewis

United Palestine Appeal, Ickes speaks for, 608

U.S. Chamber of Commerce, 31, 363, 369-370

U.S. Federal judges, in California, 416

U.S. Land Office, 27

UPHAM, 215

V

VANDENBERG, ARTHUR H. (*1884-1951), Senator (Rep.) from Michigan 1928 until his death; originally an isolationist, he became one of the fathers of the bi-partisan foreign policy which led to the establishment of the United Nations*—332, 419, 502, 588, 603, 616, 678

VANDERBILT, 650

VAUCLAIN, SAMUEL, 116

veterans, bonus for, 104: *see also* bonus legislation

Victoria Regina, 543

VILLARD, OSWALD GARRISON, 356

VINCENT, President of Haiti, 161

VINER, JACOB (*1892-   ), professor of economics at Princeton since 1946; special assistant to Secretary of Treasury in 1934 and consultant to the Treasury until 1942; consultant to Department of State since 1942*—200, 224

Virgin Islands, banking situation in, 3; Negroes in Federal offices in, 61; Advisory Committee for, 151, 156; Danish bank in, 273; Pat Harrion and, 301; investigation in, 320, 332, 345, 362, 384, 389-397, 402, 404-408; conditions in, 365-366; language of, 506: *see also* St. Thomas, St. Croix

Virgin Islands, Governor of, 3, 61, 83, 88-89, 151, 298: *see also* Paul Pearson

Virgin Islands Company, 508

Virginia culture, 629

W

wage scale, in public works, 248, 257, 287, 290, 302

WAGNER, ROBERT F. (*1877-1953), Senator (Dem.) from New York 1927-1949; introduced NRA, housing and labor relations acts which formed the legislative core of the New Deal*—17, 34, 57, 379, 498, 550, 568, 597, 624, 687-689

Wagner bill, 39

Wagner-Ellenbogen Housing Bill, 568-569, 597

WAITE, COLONEL HENRY MATSON (*1869-1944), consulting engineer; deputy administrator PWA 1933-1934*—59, 61-62, 74-75, 84, 114, 130, 141, 193, 329, 333, 362: *see also* Deputy Administrators

WALGREEN, CHARLES, 349, 368, 376

WALKER, FRANK C. (*1886-   ), treasurer Democratic National Committee in 1932; executive secretary of President Roosevelt's Executive Council, 1933; director National Emergency Council to December, 1935; Postmaster General 1940-1945*—238, 240, 253, 256-258, 348, 351-352, 355, 358, 366, 386-387, 409, 422, 435, 437, 475, 655

WALKER, JAMES A., 396

Wall Street, 113, 128, 331

Wall Street Journal, 350

WALLACE, HENRY A. *(1888-), Secretary of Agriculture 1933-1940; Vice President of United States 1940-1944; Secretary of Commerce 1944-1946; Presidential nominee of Progressive party 1948*—4, 5, 7, 14-15, 27-28, 36, 40-41, 45, 49, 53-54, 58, 70, 78, 111-112, 114, 116, 125, 128-129, 144, 161, 169, 171, 194, 218, 250, 259, 292, 303, 337, 363, 365, 384, 386, 388, 416, 487, 515, 522-523, 527, 530, 534-535, 553, 599, 601, 604, 609, 632, 655, 677, 684, 703

WALLACE, MRS. HENRY A., 25, 27, 432

WALSH, FRANK P., 655

WALSH, THOMAS J. *(1859-1933), Senator (Dem.) from Montana 1913-1933. At the time of his death he was the prospective Attorney General in President Roosevelt's first Cabinet*—3, 22, 34, 293

WALTERS, THEODORE AUGUSTUS *(1876-1937), first Assistant Secretary of Interior under Ickes from 1933 until his death. He had formerly been chairman of the Idaho State Board of Education and of the Democratic State Committee of Idaho*—326

War Department, 69, 72, 151, 251, 383-385, 417: see also George Dern

WARBURG, JAMES P., 659, 695

WARBURG, 650

WARD, PAUL W., 553

WARD, 536, 538-539

Warm Springs, Georgia, 124-127, 238

Warm Springs Foundation, 565-566

WARREN, LINDSAY, 419

Washington Herald, 230, 469-471, 492, 665-666, 669, 671, 674, 696

Washington News, 599

Washington Post, 147, 179, 243-244, 280, 350, 470, 472, 614, 635, 641, 654, 665

Washington Star, 278, 280, 424, 428, 440, 590, 616, 637-638

WATERBURY, LARRY, 237

WATKINS, JUDGE HENRY H., 482

WATSON, COLONEL EDWIN MARTIN *(1883-1945), army officer and secretary to President Roosevelt; died on the voyage home from the Yalta Conference in 1945*—444, 448-449, 453-455, 458-459, 460-461

WATSON, VICTOR, 153, 155, 246, 355, 660-661

WEST, CHARLES *(1895-), Representative (Dem.) from Ohio 1931-1935; Under Secretary of Interior 1935-1938; member U.S. Processing Tax Board of Review until 1940; since then professor of political science at Akron University*—406-407, 415, 418-419, 433, 435, 478, 571-572, 576-578, 693

wheat, Government purchase of, 108-109

WHEAT, JUDGE ALFRED A., 600

WHEELER, BURTON K. *(1882-), Senator (Dem.) from Montana 1923-1947; since then in private law practice*—20-21, 184, 313, 363-364, 415

Wheeler Dam, 226

Wheeler-Howard Indian Rights Bill, 169

WHITE, LEONARD, 113, 136

WHITE, THOMAS J., 195, 662

WHITE, WALLACE H., 332, 419

WHITE, WILLIAM ALLEN *(1868-1944), newspaperman; proprietor and editor Emporia Daily and Weekly Gazette from 1895 until his death; delegate to Republican National Conventions in 1920, 1928 and 1936*—10, 167, 561, 615, 620

WHITE, WILLIAM L., 667-668

WHITTINGTON, 417

WIENER, FRITZ, 365

WILBUR, RAY LYMAN *(1875-1949), Secretary of the Interior under President Hoover 1929-1933; president and later chancellor of Stanford University*—13, 38

wildlife, refuges for, 41, 376; effect of Santee-Cooper on, 488

WILLIAMS, AUBREY, 486

WILLIAMS, CLAY, 209, 220, 289

WILLIAMS, JIMMY, 679

Williamsburg, Virginia, 630

Williamsburg housing project, 500-501

WILSON, MILBURN LINCOLN *(1885-), chief of wheat production section AAA, 1933; director, division of subsistence homesteads 1933-1934; Assistant Secretary of Agriculture 1934-1937; Under Secretary of Agriculture 1937-1940; director of extension work in the department 1940- *—152, 154, 163, 218, 272

WILSON, THOMAS WEBBER *(1893-1948), Representative (Dem.) from Mississippi 1923-1929; Federal judge in Virgin Islands 1933-1935; member Federal*

WILSON, THOMAS WEBBER (*continued*)
  Parole Board 1936-1942—298, 301, 345,
  362, 366, 392-394, 396, 403, 405
WILSON, WOODROW, 61, 515, 685
Wilson Dam, 226
WINSHIP, MAJOR GENERAL BLANTON (*1869-
  1947*), *Governor of Puerto Rico 1934-
  1939*—157, 502-503
wire tapping, 284
WIRT, WILLIAM, 160
WISE, RABBI, 608
WOLL, MATTHEW, 469
Women's Bureau, 265
Women's International League for Peace
  and Freedom, 356
WOOD, MAJOR GENERAL ROBERT E. (*1879-
  *), *president Sears Roebuck & Co.
  1928-1939, and since then chairman of
  its board of directors*—329, 345
WOOD, WADDY, 222-223, 249
WOODHULL, ROSS, 124, 215
WOODIN, WILLIAM H. (*1868-1934*), *businessman; Secretary of Treasury 1933-
  1934*—3, 22, 45, 91-92, 99, 118, 122, 124,
  164, 658
WOODRING, HARRY H. (*1890- *), *Governor of Kansas 1931-1933; Assistant
  Secretary of War 1933-1936; Secretary
  of War 1936-1940; now retired from
  politics*—39, 69, 93, 101, 569, 682, 697,
  700
WOODRUM, CLIFTON A. (*1887- *), *Representative (Dem.) from Virginia 1923-
  1945*—578
WOOLHISER, H. L., 672
work relief, organization of, 29; plans
  for, 116-117: *see also* Federal Emergency Relief Administration, Civil Works
  Administration
work-relief appropriation, 255, 306, 383,
  486, 492, 620: *see also* public works
  appropriations
Work Relief Bill, before the Senate, 285,
  312; rate of wages in, 290; PWA
  amendment to, 313-315, 318, 320, 327,
  333-334; Garner on, 330; draft of,
  337-340; Ickes' draft of, 341; administration of, 352; Hopkins' power under,
  585-586; Hayden amendment, 588, 607,
  611, 613; Jones amendment, 607-609
Work Relief Board, 330
work-relief fund, 488-489, 565, 567, 570-
  571, 575, 577-580, 588-589, 595

work-relief program, funds for, 188;
  CWA and, 277; direct labor in, 333-
  334, 335; organization, 340-341, 345-
  348, 351; administration of, 351-352;
  Walker and, 370; Hopkins and, 328-
  329, 429, 433-434; Ickes on, 436-437,
  496-497, 592; appropriation for, 486-
  487, 492; Roosevelt committed to, 496-
  497; Roosevelt's plan for, 546, 589;
  man-year costs under, 556-580; Hopkins' power in, 585-586
work-relief projects, filed with Walker,
  355; non-Federal, 370-371, 373, 383;
  public works and, 386; list of, 409-411;
  no scrutiny of, 427-428, 433-434; La
  Follette on, 487: *see also* relief rolls
Works Progress Administration (WPA),
  287; campaign issue, 438; newspaper
  support of, 598: *see also* work-relief
  program, Harry Hopkins
WPA fund: *see* work-relief fund
Works Progress program: *see* world-re-
  lief program
World Court, 284-285, 287, 290
World Power Conference: *see* Third
  World Power Conference
WRIGHT, FRANK, 282
WRIGHT, of National Park Service, 323
WYCHE, CHARLES C., 483
WYZANSKI, CHARLES E., JR. (*1906 *),
  *secretary to Judge Learned Hand in
  1932; held various positions in Labor
  and Justice Departments 1933 to 1938;
  solicitor of the Department of Labor
  1933 to 1935; in 1941 he was ap-
  pointed a Federal judge in Massachusetts*—198

Y

Yale Club, 690
YATES, PAUL C., 389, 391, 397, 408
Yellowstone National Park, 175
Yosemite National Park, 175
YOUNG, OWEN D., 677
Young Democratic Club, 554
youth movement, 409, 594

Z

ZIONCHECK, MARION A., 567
ZOOK, GEORGE F. (*1885- *), *U.S. Commissioner of Education 1933-1934;
  president American Council on Education 1934-1950*—142